09-BTJ-944

iostream Class Library Reference

Microsoft® Visual C++™

Version 4.0

Development System for Windows® 95 and Windows NT™

Microsoft Corporation

Contents

Introduction

Microsoft Visual C++™ contains the C++ iostream class library, which supports object-oriented input and output. This library follows the syntax that the authors of the C++ language originally established and thus represents a de facto standard for C++ input and output.

About This Book

Chapter 1, iostream Programming, provides information you need to get started using iostream classes. After reading this material, you will begin to understand how to write programs that process formatted text character streams and binary disk files and how to customize the library in limited ways. The chapter includes advanced information on how to derive iostream classes and create custom multiparameter "manipulators." These topics will get you started on extending the library and doing specialized formatting. You will also learn about the relationship between the iostream classes and their subsidiary buffer classes. You can then apply some of the iostream library design principles to your own class libraries.

Chapter 2, Alphabetic Microsoft iostream Class Library Reference, begins with a detailed class hierarchy diagram. The iostream class library reference follows, arranged by classes in alphabetic order. Each class description includes a summary of each member, arranged by category, followed by alphabetical listings of member functions (public and protected), overloaded operators, data members, and manipulators.

Public and protected class members are documented only when they are normally used in application programs or derived classes. See the class header files for a complete listing of class members.

Note For information on Microsoft product support, see "Microsoft Support Services" in the PSS.HLP file.

CHAPTER 1

iostream Programming

This chapter begins with a general description of the iostream classes and then describes output streams, input streams, and input/output streams. The end of the chapter provides information about advanced iostream programming.

What Is a Stream?

Like C, C++ does not have built-in input/output capability. All C++ compilers, however, come bundled with a systematic, object-oriented I/O package, known as the iostream classes. The "stream" is the central concept of the iostream classes. You can think of a stream object as a "smart file" that acts as a source and destination for bytes. A stream's characteristics are determined by its class and by customized insertion and extraction operators.

Through device drivers, the disk operating system deals with the keyboard, screen, printer, and communication ports as extended files. The iostream classes interact with these extended files. Built-in classes support reading from and writing to memory with syntax identical to that for disk I/O, which makes it easy to derive stream classes.

Input/Output Alternatives

This product provides several options for I/O programming:

- C run-time library direct, unbuffered I/O
- ANSI C run-time library stream I/O
- Console and port direct I/O
- The Microsoft Foundation Class Library
- The Microsoft iostream Class Library

The iostream classes are useful for buffered, formatted text I/O. They are also useful for unbuffered or binary I/O if you need a C++ programming interface and decide not to use the Microsoft Foundation classes. The iostream classes are an object-oriented I/O alternative to the C run-time functions.

You can use iostream classes with the Microsoft® Windows® operating system. String and file streams work without restrictions, but the character-mode stream objects **cin**, **cout**, **cerr**, and **clog** are inconsistent with the Windows graphical user interface. You can also derive custom stream classes that interact directly with the Windows environment. If you link with the QuickWin library, however, the **cin**, **cout**, **cerr**, and **clog** objects are assigned to special windows because they are connected to the predefined files **stdin**, **stdout**, and **stderr**.

You cannot use iostream classes in tiny-model programs because tiny-model programs cannot contain static objects such as **cin** and **cout**.

The iostream Class Hierarchy

The class hierarchy diagram at the beginning of Chapter 2 shows some relationships between iostream classes. There are additional "member" relationships between the **ios** and **streambuf** families. Use the diagram to locate base classes that provide inherited member functions for derived classes.

Output Streams

An output stream object is a destination for bytes. The three most important output stream classes are **ostream**, **ofstream**, and **ostrstream**.

The **ostream** class, through the derived class **ostream_withassign**, supports the predefined stream objects:

- **cout**   standard output
- **cerr**   standard error with limited buffering
- **clog**   similar to **cerr** but with full buffering

Objects are rarely constructed from **ostream** or **ostream_withassign**; predefined objects are generally used. In some cases, you can reassign predefined objects after program startup. The **ostream** class, which can be configured for buffered or unbuffered operation, is best suited to sequential text-mode output. All functionality of the base class, **ios**, is included in **ostream**. If you construct an object of class **ostream**, you must specify a **streambuf** object to the constructor.

The **ofstream** class supports disk file output. If you need an output-only disk, construct an object of class **ofstream**. You can specify whether **ofstream** objects accept binary or text-mode data before or after opening the file. Many formatting options and member functions apply to **ofstream** objects, and all functionality of the base classes **ios** and **ostream** is included.

If you specify a filename in the constructor, that file is automatically opened when the object is constructed. Otherwise, you can use the **open** member function after invoking the default constructor, or you can construct an **ofstream** object based on an open file that is identified by a file descriptor.

Like the run-time function **sprintf**, the **ostrstream** class supports output to in-memory strings. To create a string in memory using I/O stream formatting, construct an object of class **ostrstream**. Because **ostrstream** objects are write-only, your program must access the resulting string through a pointer to **char**.

Constructing Output Stream Objects

If you use only the predefined **cout**, **cerr**, or **clog** objects, you don't need to construct an output stream. You must use constructors for:

- File streams
- String streams

Output File Stream Constructors

You can construct an output file stream in one of three ways:

- Use the default constructor, then call the **open** member function.

```
ofstream myFile; // Static or on the stack
myFile.open( "filename", iosmode );

ofstream* pmyFile = new ofstream; // On the heap
pmyFile->open( "filename", iosmode );
```

- Specify a filename and mode flags in the constructor call.

```
ofstream myFile( "filename", iosmode );
```

- Specify an integer file descriptor for a file already open for output. You can specify unbuffered output or a pointer to your own buffer.

```
int fd = _open( "filename", dosmode );
ofstream myFile1( fd );  // Buffered mode (default)
ofstream myFile2( fd, NULL, 0 );  // Unbuffered mode ofstream
myFile3( fd, pch, buflen);  // User-supplied buffer
```

Output String Stream Constructors

To construct an output string stream, you can use one of two **ostrstream** constructors. One dynamically allocates its own storage, and the other requires the address and size of a preallocated buffer.

- The dynamic constructor is used like this:

```
char* sp;
ostrstream myString;
mystring << "this is a test" << ends;
sp = myString.str();  // Get a pointer to the string
```

The **ends** "manipulator" adds the necessary terminating null character to the string.

- The constructor that requires the preallocated buffer is used like this:

```
char s[32];
ostrstream myString( s, sizeof( s ) );
myString << "this is a test" << ends; // Text stored in s
```

Using Insertion Operators and Controlling Format

This section shows how to control format and how to create insertion operators for your own classes. The insertion (**<<**) operator, which is preprogrammed for all standard C++ data types, sends bytes to an output stream object. Insertion operators work with predefined "manipulators," which are elements that change the default format of integer arguments.

Output Width

To align output, you specify the output width for each item by placing the **setw** manipulator in the stream or by calling the **width** member function. This example right aligns the values in a column at least 10 characters wide:

```
#include <iostream.h>

void main()
{
   double values[] = { 1.23, 35.36, 653.7, 4358.24 };
   for( int i = 0; i < 4; i++ )
   {
      cout.width(10);
      cout << values[i] << '\n';
   }
}
```

The output looks like this:

```
      1.23
     35.36
     653.7
   4358.24
```

Leading blanks are added to any value fewer than 10 characters wide.

To pad a field, use the **fill** member function, which sets the value of the padding character for fields that have a specified width. The default is a blank. To pad the column of numbers with asterisks, modify the previous **for** loop as follows:

```
for( int i = 0; i < 4; i++ )
{
   cout.width( 10 );
   cout.fill( '*' );
   cout << values[i] << endl
}
```

The **endl** manipulator replaces the newline character ('\n'). The output looks like this:

```
******1.23
*****35.36
*****653.7
***4358.24
```

To specify widths for data elements in the same line, use the **setw** manipulator:

```
#include <iostream.h>
#include <iomanip.h>

void main()
{
   double values[] = { 1.23, 35.36, 653.7, 4358.24 };
   char *names[] = { "Zoot", "Jimmy", "Al", "Stan" };
   for( int i = 0; i < 4; i++ )
      cout << setw( 6 )  << names[i]
           << setw( 10 ) << values[i] << endl;
}
```

The **width** member function is declared in IOSTREAM.H. If you use **setw** or any other manipulator *with arguments*, you must include IOMANIP.H. In the output, strings are printed in a field of width 6 and integers in a field of width 10:

```
  Zoot      1.23
 Jimmy     35.36
    Al     653.7
  Stan   4358.24
```

Neither **setw** nor **width** truncates values. If formatted output exceeds the width, the entire value prints, subject to the stream's precision setting. Both **setw** and **width** affect the following field only. Field width reverts to its default behavior (the necessary width) after one field has been printed. However, the other stream format options remain in effect until changed.

Alignment

Output streams default to right-aligned text. To left align the names in the previous example and right align the numbers, replace the **for** loop as follows:

```
for ( int i = 0; i < 4; i++ )
   cout << setiosflags( ios::left )
        << setw( 6 )  << names[i]
        << resetiosflags( ios::left )
        << setw( 10 ) << values[i] << endl;
```

The output looks like this:

```
Zoot        1.23
Jimmy      35.36
Al         653.7
Stan     4358.24
```

The left-align flag is set by using the **setiosflags** manipulator with the **ios::left** enumerator. This enumerator is defined in the **ios** class, so its reference must include the **ios::** prefix. The **resetiosflags** manipulator turns off the left-align flag. Unlike **width** and **setw**, the effect of **setiosflags** and **resetiosflags** is permanent.

Precision

The default value for floating-point precision is six. For example, the number 3466.9768 prints as 3466.98. To change the way this value prints, use the **setprecision** manipulator. The manipulator has two flags, **ios::fixed** and **ios::scientific**. If **ios::fixed** is set, the number prints as 3466.976800. If **ios::scientific** is set, it prints as 3.4669773+003.

To display the floating-point numbers shown in Alignment with one significant digit, replace the **for** loop as follows:

```
for ( int i = 0; i < 4; i++ )
   cout << setiosflags( ios::left )
        << setw( 6 )
        << names[i]
        << resetiosflags( ios::left )
        << setw( 10 )
        << setprecision( 1 )
        << values[i]
        << endl;
```

The program prints this list:

```
Zoot         1
Jimmy   4e+001
Al      7e+002
Stan    4e+003
```

To eliminate scientific notation, insert this statement before the **for** loop:

```
cout << setiosflags( ios::fixed );
```

With fixed notation, the program prints with one digit after the decimal point.

```
Zoot       1.2
Jimmy     35.4
Al       653.7
Stan    4358.2
```

If you change the **ios::fixed** flag to **ios::scientific**, the program prints this:

```
Zoot    1.2e+000
Jimmy   3.5e+001
Al      6.5e+002
Stan    4.4e+003
```

Again, the program prints one digit after the decimal point. If *either* **ios::fixed** or **ios::scientific** is set, the precision value determines the number of digits after the decimal point. If neither flag is set, the precision value determines the total number of significant digits. The **resetiosflags** manipulator clears these flags.

Radix

The **dec**, **oct**, and **hex** manipulators set the default radix for input and output. For example, if you insert the **hex** manipulator into the output stream, the object correctly translates the internal data representation of integers into a hexadecimal output format. The numbers are displayed with digits a through f in lowercase if the **ios::uppercase** flag is clear (the default); otherwise, they are displayed in uppercase. The default radix is **dec** (decimal).

Output File Stream Member Functions

Output stream member functions have three types: those that are equivalent to manipulators, those that perform unformatted write operations, and those that otherwise modify the stream state and have no equivalent manipulator or insertion operator. For sequential, formatted output, you might use only insertion operators and manipulators. For random-access binary disk output, you use other member functions, with or without insertion operators.

The open Function for Output Streams

To use an output file stream (**ofstream**), you must associate that stream with a specific disk file in the constructor or the **open** function. If you use the **open** function, you can reuse the same stream object with a series of files. In either case, the arguments describing the file are the same.

When you open the file associated with an output stream, you generally specify an **open_mode** flag. You can combine these flags, which are defined as enumerators in the **ios** class, with the bitwise OR (|) operator.

Flag	Function
ios::app	Opens an output file for appending.
ios::ate	Opens an existing file (either input or output) and seeks the end.
ios::in	Opens an input file. Use **ios::in** as an **open_mode** for an **ofstream** file to prevent truncating an existing file.
ios::out	Opens an output file. When you use **ios::out** for an **ofstream** object without **ios::app**, **ios::ate**, or **ios::in**, **ios::trunc** is implied.
ios::nocreate	Opens a file only if it already exists; otherwise the operation fails.
ios::noreplace	Opens a file only if it does not exist; otherwise the operation fails.
ios::trunc	Opens a file and deletes the old file (if it already exists).
ios::binary	Opens a file in binary mode (default is text mode).

Three common output stream situations involve mode options:

- Creating a file. If the file already exists, the old version is deleted.

```
ostream ofile( "FILENAME" );  // Default is ios::out
ofstream ofile( "FILENAME", ios::out ); // Equivalent to above
```

- Appending records to an existing file or creating one if it does not exist.

  ```
  ofstream ofile( "FILENAME", ios::app );
  ```

- Opening two files, one at a time, on the same stream.

  ```
  ofstream ofile();
  ofile.open( "FILE1", ios::in );
  // Do some output
  ofile.close(); // FILE1 closed
  ofile.open( "FILE2", ios::in );
  // Do some more output
  ofile.close(); // FILE2 closed
  // When ofile goes out of scope it is destroyed.
  ```

The put Function

The **put** function writes one character to the output stream. The following two statements are the same by default, but the second is affected by the stream's format arguments:

```
cout.put( 'A' ); // Exactly one character written
cout << 'A'; // Format arguments 'width' and 'fill' apply
```

The write Function

The **write** function writes a block of memory to an output file stream. The length argument specifies the number of bytes written. This example creates an output file stream and writes the binary value of the `Date` structure to it:

```
#include <fstream.h>

struct Date
{
   int mo, da, yr;
};

void main()
{
   Date dt = { 6, 10, 92 };
   ofstream tfile( "date.dat" , ios::binary );
   tfile.write( (char *) &dt, sizeof dt );
}
```

The **write** function does not stop when it reaches a null character, so the complete class structure is written. The function takes two arguments: a **char** pointer and a count of characters to write. Note the required cast to **char*** before the address of the structure object.

The seekp and tellp Functions

An output file stream keeps an internal pointer that points to the position where data is to be written next. The **seekp** member function sets this pointer and thus provides random-access disk file output. The **tellp** member function returns the file position. For examples that use the input stream equivalants to **seekp** and **tellp**, see The seekg and tellg Functions.

The close Function for Output Streams

The **close** member function closes the disk file associated with an output file stream. The file must be closed to complete all disk output. If necessary, the **ofstream** destructor closes the file for you, but you can use the **close** function if you need to open another file for the same stream object.

The output stream destructor automatically closes a stream's file only if the constructor or the **open** member function opened the file. If you pass the constructor a file descriptor for an already-open file or use the **attach** member function, you must close the file explicitly.

Error Processing Functions

Use these member functions to test for errors while writing to a stream:

Function	Return value
bad	Returns **TRUE** if there is an unrecoverable error.
fail	Returns **TRUE** if there is an unrecoverable error or an "expected" condition, such as a conversion error, or if the file is not found. Processing can often resume after a call to **clear** with a zero argument.
good	Returns **TRUE** if there is no error condition (unrecoverable or otherwise) and the end-of-file flag is not set.
eof	Returns **TRUE** on the end-of-file condition.
clear	Sets the internal error state. If called with the default arguments, it clears all error bits.
rdstate	Returns the current error state. For a complete description of error bits, see the *Class Library Reference*.

The **!** operator is overloaded to perform the same function as the **fail** function. Thus the expression

```
if( !cout)...
```

is equivalent to

```
if( cout.fail() )...
```

The **void*()** operator is overloaded to be the opposite of the **!** operator; thus the expression

```
if( cout)...
```

is equal to

```
if( !cout.fail() )...
```

The **void*()** operator is not equivalent to **good** because it doesn't test for the end of file.

The Effects of Buffering

The following example shows the effects of buffering. You might expect the program to print `please wait`, wait 5 seconds, and then proceed. It won't necessarily work this way, however, because the output is buffered.

```
#include <iostream.h>
#include <time.h>

void main()
{
   time_t tm = time( NULL ) + 5;
   cout << "Please wait...";
   while ( time( NULL ) < tm )
      ;
   cout << "\nAll done" << endl;
}
```

To make the program work logically, the **cout** object must empty itself when the message is to appear. To flush an **ostream** object, send it the **flush** manipulator:

```
cout << "Please wait..." << flush;
```

This step flushes the buffer, ensuring the message prints before the wait. You can also use the **endl** manipulator, which flushes the buffer and outputs a carriage return–linefeed, or you can use the **cin** object. This object (with the **cerr** or **clog** objects) is usually tied to the **cout** object. Thus, any use of **cin** (or of the **cerr** or **clog** objects) flushes the **cout** object.

Binary Output Files

Streams were originally designed for text, so the default output mode is text. In text mode, the newline character (hexadecimal 10) expands to a carriage return–linefeed (16-bit only). The expansion can cause problems, as shown here:

```
#include <fstream.h>
int iarray[2] = { 99, 10 };
void main()
{
    ofstream os( "test.dat" );
    os.write( (char *) iarray, sizeof( iarray ) );
}
```

You might expect this program to output the byte sequence { 99, 0, 10, 0 }; instead, it outputs { 99, 0, 13, 10, 0 }, which causes problems for a program expecting binary input. If you need true binary output, in which characters are written untranslated, you have several choices:

- Construct a stream as usual, then use the **setmode** member function, which changes the mode after the file is opened:

  ```
  ofstream ofs ( "test.dat" );
  ```

```
ofs.setmode( filebuf::binary );
ofs.write( char*iarray, 4 ); // Exactly 4 bytes written
```

- Specify binary output by using the **ofstream** constuctor mode argument:

```
#include <fstream.h>
#include <fcntl.h>
#include <io.h>
int iarray[2] = { 99, 10 };
void main()
{
    ofstream os( "test.dat", ios::binary );
    ofs.write( iarray, 4 ); // Exactly 4 bytes written
}
```

- Use the **binary** manipulator instead of the **setmode** member function:

```
ofs << binary;
```

  Use the **text** manipulator to switch the stream to text translation mode.

- Open the file using the run-time **_open** function with a binary mode flag:

```
filedesc fd = _open( "test.dat",
              _O_BINARY | _O_CREAT | _O_WRONLY );
ofstream ofs( fd );
ofs.write( ( char* ) iarray, 4 ); // Exactly 4 bytes written
```

Overloading the << Operator for Your Own Classes

Output streams use the insertion (**<<**) operator for standard types. You can also overload the **<<** operator for your own classes.

The **write** function example showed the use of a `Date` structure. A date is an ideal candidate for a C++ class in which the data members (month, day, and year) are hidden from view. An output stream is the logical destination for displaying such a structure. This code displays a date using the **cout** object:

```
Date dt( 1, 2, 92 );
cout << dt;
```

To get **cout** to accept a `Date` object after the insertion operator, overload the insertion operator to recognize an **ostream** object on the left and a `Date` on the right. The overloaded **<<** operator function must then be declared as a friend of class `Date` so it can access the private data within a `Date` object.

```
#include <iostream.h>
class Date
{
   int mo, da, yr;
public:
   Date( int m, int d, int y )
   {
      mo = m; da = d; yr = y;
   }
```

```
   friend ostream& operator<< ( ostream& os, Date& dt );
};
ostream& operator<< ( ostream& os, Date& dt )
{
   os << dt.mo << '/' << dt.da << '/' << dt.yr;
   return os;
}

void main()
{
   Date dt( 5, 6, 92 );
   cout << dt;
}
```

When you run this program, it prints the date:

```
5/6/92
```

The overloaded operator returns a reference to the original **ostream** object, which means you can combine insertions:

```
cout << "The date is" << dt << flush;
```

Writing Your Own Manipulators Without Arguments

Writing manipulators that don't use arguments requires neither class derivation nor use of complex macros. Suppose your printer requires the pair `<ESC>[` to enter bold mode. You can insert this pair directly into the stream:

```
cout << "regular " << '\033' << '[' << "boldface" << endl;
```

Or you can define the `bold` manipulator, which inserts the characters:

```
ostream& bold( ostream& os ) {
    return os << '\033' << '[';
}
cout << "regular " << bold << "boldface" << endl;
```

The globally defined `bold` function takes an **ostream** reference argument and returns the **ostream** reference. It is not a member function or a friend because it doesn't need access to any private class elements. The `bold` function connects to the stream because the stream's **<<** operator is overloaded to accept that type of function, using a declaration that looks something like this:

```
ostream& ostream::operator<< ( ostream& (*_f)( ostream& ) ); {
    (*_f)( *this );
    return *this;
}
```

You can use this feature to extend other overloaded operators. In this case, it is incidental that `bold` inserts characters into the stream. The function is called when it is inserted into the stream, not necessarily when the adjacent characters are printed. Thus, printing could be delayed because of the stream's buffering.

Input Streams

An input stream object is a source of bytes. The three most important input stream classes are **istream**, **ifstream**, and **istrstream**.

The **istream** class is best used for sequential text-mode input. You can configure objects of class **istream** for buffered or unbuffered operation. All functionality of the base class, **ios**, is included in **istream**. You will rarely construct objects from class **istream**. Instead, you will generally use the predefined **cin** object, which is actually an object of class **istream_withassign**. In some cases, you can assign **cin** to other stream objects after program startup.

The **ifstream** class supports disk file input. If you need an input-only disk file, construct an object of class **ifstream**. You can specify binary or text-mode data. If you specify a filename in the constructor, the file is automatically opened when the object is constructed. Otherwise, you can use the **open** function after invoking the default constructor. Many formatting options and member functions apply to **ifstream** objects. All functionality of the base classes **ios** and **istream** is included in **ifstream**.

Like the library function **sscanf**, the **istrstream** class supports input from in-memory strings. To extract data from a character array that has a null terminator, allocate and initialize the string, then construct an object of class **istrstream**.

Constructing Input Stream Objects

If you use only the **cin** object, you don't need to construct an input stream. You must construct an input stream if you use:

- File stream
- String stream

Input File Stream Constructors

There are three ways to create an input file stream:

- Use the **void**-argument constructor, then call the **open** member function:

```
ifstream myFile; // On the stack
myFile.open( "filename", iosmode );

ifstream* pmyFile = new ifstream; // On the heap
pmyFile->open( "filename", iosmode );
```

- Specify a filename and mode flags in the constructor invocation, thereby opening the file during the construction process:

```
ifstream myFile( "filename", iosmode );
```

- Specify an integer file descriptor for a file already open for input. In this case you can specify unbuffered input or a pointer to your own buffer:

```
int fd = _open( "filename", dosmode );
ifstream myFile1( fd );  // Buffered mode (default)
ifstream myFile2( fd, NULL, 0 );  // Unbuffered mode
ifstream myFile3( fd, pch, buflen );  // User-supplied buffer
```

Input String Stream Constructors

Input string stream constructors require the address of preallocated, preinitialized storage:

```
char s[] = "123.45";
double amt;
istrstream myString( s );
myString >> amt; // Amt should contain 123.45
```

Using Extraction Operators

The extraction operator (>>), which is preprogrammed for all standard C++ data types, is the easiest way to get bytes from an input stream object.

Formatted text input extraction operators depend on white space to separate incoming data values. This is inconvenient when a text field contains multiple words or when commas separate numbers. In such a case, one alternative is to use the unformatted input member function **getline** to read a block of text with white space included, then parse the block with special functions. Another method is to derive an input stream class with a member function such as `GetNextToken`, which can call **istream** members to extract and format character data.

Testing for Extraction Errors

Output error processing functions, discussed on page 9 in "Error Processing Functions," apply to input streams. Testing for errors during extraction is important. Consider this statement:

```
cin >> n;
```

If `n` is a signed integer, a value greater than 32,767 (the maximum allowed value, or MAX_INT) sets the stream's **fail** bit, and the **cin** object becomes unusable. All subsequent extractions result in an immediate return with no value stored.

Input Stream Manipulators

Many manipulators, such as **setprecision**, are defined for the **ios** class and thus apply to input streams. Few manipulators, however, actually affect input stream objects. Of those that do, the most important are the radix manipulators, **dec**, **oct**, and **hex**, which determine the conversion base used with numbers from the input stream.

On extraction, the **hex** manipulator enables processing of various input formats. For example, c, C, 0xc, 0xC, 0Xc, and 0XC are all interpreted as the decimal integer 12.

Any character other than 0 through 9, A through F, a through f, x, and X terminates the numeric conversion. Thus the sequence `"124n5"` is converted to the number 124 with the **ios::fail** bit set.

Input Stream Member Functions

Input stream member functions are used for disk input.

The open Function for Input Streams

If you are using an input file stream (**ifstream**), you must associate that stream with a specific disk file. You can do this in the constructor, or you can use the **open** function. In either case, the arguments are the same.

You generally specify an **open_mode** flag when you open the file associated with an input stream (the default mode is **ios::in**). For a list of the **open_mode** flags, see The open Function. The flags can be combined with the bitwise OR (|) operator.

To read a file, first use the **fail** member function to determine whether it exists:

```
istream ifile( "FILENAME", ios::nocreate );
if ( ifile.fail() )
// The file does not exist ...
```

The get Function

The unformatted **get** member function works like the **>>** operator with two exceptions. First, the **get** function includes white-space characters, whereas the extractor excludes white space when the **ios::skipws** flag is set (the default). Second, the **get** function is less likely to cause a tied output stream (**cout**, for example) to be flushed.

A variation of the **get** function specifies a buffer address and the maximum number of characters to read. This is useful for limiting the number of characters sent to a specific variable, as this example shows:

```
#include <iostream.h>

void main()
{
   char line[25];
   cout << " Type a line terminated by carriage return\n>";
   cin.get( line, 25 );
   cout << ' ' << line;
}
```

In this example, you can type up to 24 characters and a terminating character. Any remaining characters can be extracted later.

The getline Function

The **getline** member function is similar to the **get** function. Both functions allow a third argument that specifies the terminating character for input. The default value is the newline character. Both functions reserve one character for the required terminating character. However, **get** leaves the terminating character in the stream and **getline** removes the terminating character.

The following example specifies a terminating character for the input stream:

```
#include <iostream.h>

void main()
{
   char line[100];
   cout << " Type a line terminated by 't'" << endl;
   cin.getline( line, 100, 't' );
   cout << line;
}
```

The read Function

The **read** member function reads bytes from a file to a specified area of memory. The length argument determines the number of bytes read. If you do not include that argument, reading stops when the physical end of file is reached or, in the case of a text-mode file, when an embedded **EOF** character is read.

This example reads a binary record from a payroll file into a structure:

```
#include <fstream.h>
#include <fcntl.h>
#include <io.h>

void main()
{
   struct
   {
      double salary;
      char name[23];
   } employee;

   ifstream is( "payroll", ios::binary | ios::nocreate );
   if( is ) {  // ios::operator void*()
      is.read( (char *) &employee, sizeof( employee ) );
      cout << employee.name << ' ' << employee.salary << endl;
   }
   else {
      cout << "ERROR: Cannot open file 'payroll'." << endl;
   }
}
```

The program assumes that the data records are formatted exactly as specified by the structure with no terminating carriage-return or linefeed characters.

The seekg and tellg Functions

Input file streams keep an internal pointer to the position in the file where data is to be read next. You set this pointer with the **seekg** function, as shown here:

```
#include <fstream.h>

void main()
{
   char ch;

   ifstream tfile( "payroll", ios::binary | ios::nocreate );
   if( tfile ) {
      tfile.seekg( 8 );      // Seek 8 bytes in (past salary)
      while ( tfile.good() ) { // EOF or failure stops the reading
         tfile.get( ch );
         if( !ch ) break; // quit on null
         cout << ch;
      }
   }
   else {
      cout << "ERROR: Cannot open file 'payroll'." << endl;
   }
}
```

To use **seekg** to implement record-oriented data management systems, multiply the fixed-length record size by the record number to obtain the byte position relative to the end of the file, then use the **get** object to read the record.

The **tellg** member function returns the current file position for reading. This value is of type **streampos**, a **typedef** defined in IOSTREAM.H. The following example reads a file and displays messages showing the positions of spaces.

```
#include <fstream.h>

void main()
{
   char ch;
ifstream tfile( "payroll", ios::binary | ios::nocreate );
   if( tfile ) {
       while ( tfile.good() ) {
          streampos here = tfile.tellg();
          tfile.get( ch );
          if ( ch == ' ' )
             cout << "\nPosition " << here << " is a space";
       }
   }
   else {
      cout << "ERROR: Cannot open file 'payroll'." << endl;
   }
}
```

The close Function for Input Streams

The **close** member function closes the disk file associated with an input file stream and frees the operating system file handle. The **ifstream** destructor closes the file for you (unless you called the **attach** function or passed your own file descriptor to the constructor), but you can use the **close** function if you need to open another file for the same stream object.

Overloading the >> Operator for Your Own Classes

Input streams use the extraction (>>) operator for the standard types. You can write similar extraction operators for your own types; your success depends on using white space precisely.

Here is an example of an extraction operator for the `Date` class presented earlier:

```
istream& operator>> ( istream& is, Date& dt )
{
   is >> dt.mo >> dt.da >> dt.yr;
   return is;
}
```

Input/Output Streams

An **iostream** object is a source and/or a destination for bytes. The two most important I/O stream classes, both derived from **iostream**, are **fstream** and **strstream**. These classes inherit the functionality of the **istream** and **ostream** classes described previously.

The **fstream** class supports disk file input and output. If you need to read from and write to a particular disk file in the same program, construct an **fstream** object. An **fstream** object is a single stream with two logical substreams, one for input and one for output. Although the underlying buffer contains separately designated positions for reading and writing, those positions are tied together.

The **strstream** class supports input and output of in-memory strings.

Custom Manipulators with Arguments

This section describes how to create output stream manipulators with one or more arguments, and how to use manipulators for non-output streams.

Output Stream Manipulators with One Argument (int or long)

The iostream class library provides a set of macros for creating parameterized manipulators. Manipulators with a single **int** or **long** argument are a special case.

To create an output stream manipulator that accepts a single **int** or **long** argument (like **setw**), you must use the **OMANIP** macro, which is defined in IOMANIP.H. This example defines a `fillblank` manipulator that inserts a specified number of blanks into the stream:

```
#include <iostream.h>
#include <iomanip.h>

ostream& fb( ostream& os, int l )
{
   for( int i=0; i < l; i++ )
        os << ' ';
   return os;
}

OMANIP(int) fillblank( int l )
{
   return OMANIP(int) ( fb, l );
}

void main()
{
    cout << "10 blanks follow" << fillblank( 10 ) << ".\n";
}
```

The IOMANIP.H header file contains a macro that expands **OMANIP(int)** into a class, **__OMANIP_int**, which includes a constructor and an overloaded **ostream** insertion operator for an object of the class. In the previous example, the `fillblank` function calls the **__OMANIP_int** constructor to return an object of class **__OMANIP_int**. Thus, `fillblank` can be used with an **ostream** insertion operator. The constructor calls the `fb` function. The expression **OMANIP(long)** expands to another built-in class, **__OMANIP_long**, which accommodates functions with a long integer argument.

Other One-Argument Output Stream Manipulators

To create manipulators that take arguments other than **int** and **long**, you must use the **IOMANIPdeclare** macro, which declares the classes for your new type, as well as the **OMANIP** macro.

The following example uses a class `money`, which is a **long** type. The `setpic` manipulator attaches a formatting "picture" string to the class that can be used by the overloaded stream insertion operator of the class `money`. The picture string is stored as a static variable in the `money` class rather than as data member of a stream class, so you do not have to derive a new output stream class.

```
#include <iostream.h>
#include <iomanip.h>
#include <string.h>
```

```
typedef char* charp;
IOMANIPdeclare( charp );

class money {
private:
    long value;
    static char *szCurrentPic;
public:
    money( long val ) { value = val; }
    friend ostream& operator << ( ostream& os, money m ) {
        // A more complete function would merge the picture
        // with the value rather than simply appending it
        os << m.value << '[' << money::szCurrentPic << ']';
        return os;
    }
    friend ostream& setpic( ostream& os, char* szPic ) {
        money::szCurrentPic = new char[strlen( szPic ) + 1];
        strcpy( money::szCurrentPic, szPic );
        return os;
    }
};
char *money::szCurrentPic;  // Static pointer to picture

OMANIP(charp) setpic(charp c)
{
    return OMANIP(charp) (setpic, c);
}

void main()
{
    money amt = 35235.22;
    cout << setiosflags( ios::fixed );
    cout << setpic( "###,###,###.##" ) << "amount = " << amt << endl;
}
```

Output Stream Manipulators with More Than One Argument

The following example shows how to write a manipulator, `fill`, to insert a specific number of a particular character. The manipulator, which takes two arguments, is similar to `setpic` in the previous example. The difference is that the character pointer type declaration is replaced by a structure declaration.

```
#include <iostream.h>
#include <iomanip.h>

struct fillpair {
         char ch;
        int  cch;
};
```

```
IOMANIPdeclare( fillpair );

ostream& fp( ostream& os, fillpair pair )
{
    for ( int c = 0; c < pair.cch; c++ ) {
        os << pair.ch;
    }
    return os;
}

OMANIP(fillpair) fill( char ch, int cch )
{
    fillpair pair;

    pair.cch = cch;
    pair.ch  = ch;
    return OMANIP (fillpair)( fp, pair );
}

void main()
{
    cout << "10 dots coming" << fill( '.', 10 ) << "done" << endl;
}
```

This example can be rewritten so that the manipulator definition is in a separate program file. In this case, the header file must contain these declarations:

```
struct fillpair {
       char ch;
       int  cch;
};
IOMANIPdeclare( fillpair );
ostream& fp( ostream& o, fillpair pair );
OMANIP(fillpair) fill( char ch, int cch );
```

Custom Manipulators for Input and Input/Output Streams

The **OMANIP** macro works with **ostream** and its derived classes. The **SMANIP**, **IMANIP**, and **IOMANIP** macros work with the classes **ios**, **istream**, and **iostream**, respectively.

Using Manipulators with Derived Stream Classes

Suppose you define a manipulator, `xstream`, that works with the **ostream** class. The manipulator will work with all classes derived from **ostream**. Further suppose you need manipulators that work only with `xstream`. In this case, you must add an overloaded insertion operator that is not a member of **ostream**:

```
xstream& operator<< ( xstream& xs, xstream& (*_f)( xstream& ) ) {
    (*_f)( xs );
    return xs;
}
```

The manipulator code looks like this:

```
xstream& bold( xstream& xs ) {
    return xs << '\033' << '[';
}
```

If the manipulator needs to access `xstream` protected data member functions, you can declare the `bold` function as a friend of the `xstream` class.

Deriving Your Own Stream Classes

Like any C++ class, a stream class can be derived to add new member functions, data members, or manipulators. If you need an input file stream that tokenizes its input data, for example, you can derive from the **ifstream** class. This derived class can include a member function that returns the next token by calling its base class's public member functions or extractors. You may need new data members to hold the stream object's state between operations, but you probably won't need to use the base class's protected member functions or data members.

For the straightforward stream class derivation, you need only write the necessary constructors and the new member functions.

The streambuf Class

Unless you plan to make major changes to the iostream library, you do not need to work much with the **streambuf** class, which does most of the work for the other stream classes. In most cases, you will create a modified output stream by deriving only a new **streambuf** class and connecting it to the **ostream** class.

Why Derive a Custom streambuf Class?

Existing output streams communicate to the file system and to in-memory strings. You can create streams that address a memory-mapped video screen, a window as defined by Microsoft Windows, a new physical device, and so on. A simpler method is to alter the byte stream as it goes to a file system device.

A streambuf Derivation Example

The following example modifies the **cout** object to print in two-column landscape (horizontal) mode on a printer that uses the PCL control language (for example, Hewlett-Packard LaserJet printer). As the test driver program shows, all member functions and manipulators that work with the original **cout** object work with the special version. The application programming interface is the same.

The example is divided into three source files:

- HSTREAM.H—the LaserJet class declaration that must be included in the implementation file and application file
- HSTREAM.CPP—the LaserJet class implementation that must be linked with the application
- EXIOS204.CPP—the test driver program that sends output to a LaserJet printer

HSTREAM.H contains only the class declaration for `hstreambuf`, which is derived from the **filebuf** class and overrides the appropriate **filebuf** virtual functions.

```
// hstream.h - HP LaserJet output stream header
#include <fstream.h> // Accesses filebuf class
#include <string.h>
#include <stdio.h> // for sprintf

class hstreambuf : public filebuf
{
public:
    hstreambuf( int filed );
    virtual int sync();
    virtual int overflow( int ch );
    ~hstreambuf();
private:
    int column, line, page;
    char* buffer;
    void convert( long cnt );
    void newline( char*& pd, int& jj );
    void heading( char*& pd, int& jj );
    void pstring( char* ph, char*& pd, int& jj );
};
ostream& und( ostream& os );
ostream& reg( ostream& os );
```

HSTREAM.CPP contains the `hstreambuf` class implementation.

```
// hstream.cpp  - HP LaserJet output stream
#include "hstream.h"

const int REG  = 0x01;   // Regular font code
const int UND  = 0x02;   // Underline font code
const int CR   = 0x0d;   // Carriage return character
const int NL   = 0x0a;   // Newline character
const int FF   = 0x0c;   // Formfeed character
const int TAB  = 0x09;   // Tab character
const int LPP  = 57;     // Lines per page
const int TABW = 5;      // Tab width
```

```
// Prolog defines printer initialization (font, orientation, etc.
char prolog[] =
{ 0x1B, 0x45,                          // Reset printer
  0x1B, 0x28, 0x31, 0x30, 0x55,               // IBM PC char set
  0x1B, 0x26, 0x6C, 0x31, 0x4F,               // Landscape
  0x1B, 0x26, 0x6C, 0x38, 0x44,        // 8 lines per inch
  0x1B, 0x26, 0x6B, 0x32, 0x53};      // Lineprinter font

// Epilog prints the final page and terminates the output
char epilog[] = { 0x0C, 0x1B, 0x45 };   // Formfeed, reset

char uon[] = { 0x1B, 0x26, 0x64, 0x44, 0 }; // Underline on
char uoff[] = { 0x1B, 0x26, 0x64, 0x40, 0 };// Underline off

hstreambuf::hstreambuf( int filed ) : filebuf( filed )
{
    column = line = page = 0;
    int size = sizeof( prolog );
    setp( prolog, prolog + size );
    pbump( size );   // Puts the prolog in the put area
    filebuf::sync(); // Sends the prolog to the output file
    buffer = new char[1024]; // Allocates destination buffer
}

hstreambuf::~hstreambuf()
{
    sync(); // Makes sure the current buffer is empty
    delete buffer; // Frees the memory
    int size = sizeof( epilog );
    setp( epilog, epilog + size );
    pbump( size );   // Puts the epilog in the put area
    filebuf::sync(); // Sends the epilog to the output file
}
int hstreambuf::sync()
{
    long count = out_waiting();
    if ( count ) {
        convert( count );
    }
    return filebuf::sync();
}

int hstreambuf::overflow( int ch )
{
    long count = out_waiting();
    if ( count ) {
        convert( count );
    }
    return filebuf::overflow( ch );
}
```

```
// The following code is specific to the HP LaserJet printer

// Converts a buffer to HP, then writes it
void hstreambuf::convert( long cnt )
{
    char *bufs, *bufd; // Source, destination pointers
    int j = 0;

    bufs = pbase();
    bufd = buffer;
    if( page == 0 ) {
        newline( bufd, j );
    }
    for( int i = 0; i < cnt; i++ ) {
        char c = *( bufs++ );  // Gets character from source buffer
        if( c >= ' ' ) {       // Character is printable
            * ( bufd++ ) = c;
            j++;
            column++;
        }
else if( c == NL ) {             // Moves down one line
            *( bufd++ ) = c;     // Passes character through
            j++;
            line++;
            newline( bufd, j ); // Checks for page break, etc.
        }
        else if( c == FF ) {     // Ejects paper on formfeed
            line = line - line % LPP + LPP;
            newline( bufd, j ); // Checks for page break, etc.
        }
        else if( c == TAB ) {    // Expands tabs
            do {
                *( bufd++ ) = ' ';
                j++;
                column++;
            } while ( column % TABW );
        }
        else if( c == UND ) { // Responds to und manipulator
            pstring( uon, bufd, j );
        }
        else if( c == REG ) { // Responds to reg manipulator
            pstring( uoff, bufd, j );
        }
    }
    setp( buffer, buffer + 1024 ); // Sets new put area
    pbump( j ); // Tells number of characters in the dest buffer
}
```

```
// simple manipulators - apply to all ostream classes
ostream& und( ostream& os ) // Turns on underscore mode
{
    os << (char) UND; return os;
}

ostream& reg( ostream& os ) // Turns off underscore mode
{
    os << (char) REG; return os;
}

void hstreambuf::newline( char*& pd, int& jj ) {
// Called for each newline character
    column = 0;
    if ( ( line % ( LPP*2 ) ) == 0 ) { // Even page
        page++;
        pstring( "\033&a+0L", pd, jj );  // Set left margin to zero
        heading( pd, jj );               // Print heading
        pstring( "\033*p0x77Y", pd, jj );// Cursor to (0,77) dots
    }
    if ( ( ( line % LPP ) == 0 ) && ( line % ( LPP*2 ) ) != 0 ) {
    //  Odd page; prepare to move to right column
        page++;
        pstring( "\033*p0x77Y", pd, jj ); // Cursor to (0,77) dots
        pstring( "\033&a+88L", pd, jj );  // Left margin to col 88
    }
}

void hstreambuf::heading( char*& pd, int& jj ) // Prints heading
{
    char hdg[20];
    int i;

    if( page > 1 ) {
        *( pd++ ) = FF;
        jj++;
    }
    pstring( "\033*p0x0Y", pd, jj ); // Top of page
    pstring( uon, pd, jj );          // Underline on
    sprintf( hdg, "Page %-3d", page );
    pstring( hdg, pd, jj );
    for( i=0; i < 80; i++ ) {        // Pads with blanks
        *( pd++ ) = ' ';
        jj++;
    }
    sprintf( hdg, "Page %-3d", page+1 ) ;
    pstring( hdg, pd, jj );
    for( i=0; i < 80; i++ ) {        // Pads with blanks
        *( pd++ ) = ' ';
        jj++;
    }
    pstring( uoff, pd, jj ); // Underline off
}
```

```
// Outputs a string to the buffer
void hstreambuf::pstring( char* ph, char*& pd, int& jj )
{
    int len = strlen( ph );
    strncpy( pd, ph, len );
    pd += len;
    jj += len;
}
```

EXIOS204.CPP reads text lines from the **cin** object and writes them to the modified **cout** object.

```
// exios204.cpp
// hstream Driver program copies cin to cout until end of file
#include "hstream.h"

hstreambuf hsb( 4 ); // 4=stdprn

void main()
{
    char line[200];
    cout = &hsb; // Associates the HP LaserJet streambuf to cout
    while( 1 ) {
       cin.getline( line, 200 );
       if( !cin.good() ) break;
       cout << line << endl;
    }
}
```

Here are the main points in the preceding code:

- The new class `hstreambuf` is derived from **filebuf**, which is the buffer class for disk file I/O. The **filebuf** class writes to disk in response to commands from its associated **ostream** class. The `hstreambuf` constructor takes an argument that corresponds to the operating system file number, in this case 1, for **stdout**. This constructor is invoked by this line:

  ```
  hstreambuf hsb( 1 );
  ```

- The **ostream_withassign** assignment operator associates the `hstreambuf` object with the **cout** object:

  ```
  ostream& operator =( streambuf* sbp );
  ```

  This statement in EXIOS204.CPP executes the assignment:

  ```
  cout = &hsb;
  ```

- The `hstreambuf` constructor prints the prolog that sets up the laser printer, then allocates a temporary print buffer.
- The destructor outputs the epilog text and frees the print buffer when the object goes out of scope, which happens after the exit from **main**.

- The **streambuf** virtual **overflow** and **sync** functions do the low-level output. The `hstreambuf` class overrides these functions to gain control of the byte stream. The functions call the private `convert` member function.
- The `convert` function processes the characters in the `hstreambuf` buffer and stores them in the object's temporary buffer. The **filebuf** functions process the temporary buffer.
- The details of `convert` relate more to the PCL language than to the iostream library. Private data members keep track of column, line, and page numbers.
- The `und` and `reg` manipulators control the underscore print attribute by inserting codes 0x02 and 0x03 into the stream. The `convert` function later translates these codes into printer-specific sequences.
- The program can be extended easily to embellish the heading, add more formatting features, and so forth.
- In a more general program, the `hstreambuf` class could be derived from the **streambuf** class rather than the **filebuf** class. The **filebuf** derivation shown gets the most leverage from existing iostream library code, but it makes assumptions about the implementation of **filebuf**, particularly the **overflow** and **sync** functions. Thus you cannot necessarily expect this example to work with other derived **streambuf** classes or with **filebuf** classes provided by other software publishers.

CHAPTER 2

Alphabetic Microsoft iostream Class Library Reference

iostream Class Hierarchy Diagram

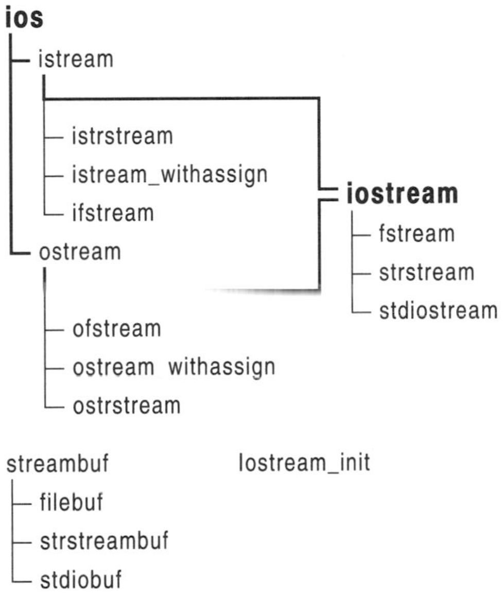

iostream Class List

Abstract Stream Base Class

ios	Stream base class.

Input Stream Classes

istream	General-purpose input stream class and base class for other input streams.
ifstream	Input file stream class.
istream_withassign	Input stream class for **cin**.
istrstream	Input string stream class.

Output Stream Classes

ostream	General-purpose output stream class and base class for other output streams.
ofstream	Output file stream class.
ostream_withassign	Output stream class for **cout**, **cerr**, and **clog**.
ostrstream	Output string stream class.

Input/Output Stream Classes

iostream	General-purpose input/output stream class and base class for other input/output streams.
fstream	Input/output file stream class.
strstream	Input/output string stream class.
stdiostream	Input/output class for standard I/O files.

Stream Buffer Classes

streambuf	Abstract stream buffer base class.
filebuf	Stream buffer class for disk files.
strstreambuf	Stream buffer class for strings.
stdiobuf	Stream buffer class for standard I/O files.

Predefined Stream Initializer Class

Iostream_init	Predefined stream initializer class.

class filebuf

#include <fstream.h>

The **filebuf** class is a derived class of **streambuf** that is specialized for buffered disk file I/O. The buffering is managed entirely within the Microsoft iostream Class Library. **filebuf** member functions call the run-time low-level I/O routines (the functions declared in IO.H) such as **_sopen**, **_read**, and **_write**.

The file stream classes, **ofstream**, **ifstream**, and **fstream**, use **filebuf** member functions to fetch and store characters. Some of these member functions are virtual functions of thc **streambuf** class.

The reserve area, put area, and get area are introduced in the **streambuf** class description. The put area and the get area are always the same for **filebuf** objects. Also, the get pointer and put pointers are tied; when one moves, so does the other.

Construction/Destruction — Public Members

filebuf Constructs a **filebuf** object.

~filebuf Destroys a **filebuf** object.

Operations — Public Members

open Opens a file and attaches it to the **filebuf** object.

close Flushes any waiting output and closes the attached file.

setmode Sets the file's mode to binary or text.

attach Attaches the **filebuf** object to an open file.

Status/Information — Public Members

fd Returns the stream's file descriptor.

is_open Tests whether the file is open.

See Also **ifstream**, **ofstream**, **streambuf**, **strstreambuf**, **stdiobuf**

Member Functions

filebuf::attach

filebuf* attach(filedesc *fd* **);**

Attaches this **filebuf** object to the open file specified by *fd*.

Return Value

The function returns **NULL** when the stream is already attached to a file; otherwise it returns the address of the **filebuf** object.

Parameter

fd A file descriptor as returned by a call to the run-time function **_open** or **_sopen**. **filedesc** is a **typedef** equivalent to **int**.

---

filebuf::close

filebuf* close();

Flushes any waiting output, closes the file, and disconnects the file from the **filebuf** object.

Return Value

If an error occurs, the function returns **NULL** and leaves the **filebuf** object in a closed state. If there is no error, the function returns the address of the **filebuf** object and clears its error state.

See Also **filebuf::open**

---

filebuf::fd

filedesc fd() const;

Returns the file descriptor associated with the **filebuf** object; **filedesc** is a **typedef** equivalent to **int**.

Return Value

The value is supplied by the underlying file system. The function returns **EOF** if the object is not attached to a file.

See Also **filebuf::attach**

---

filebuf::filebuf

filebuf();

filebuf(filedesc *fd* **);**

filebuf(filedesc *fd*, **char* pr, int** *nLength* **);**

Parameters

fd A file descriptor as returned by a call to the run-time function **_sopen**. **filedesc** is a **typedef** equivalent to **int**.

pr Pointer to a previously allocated reserve area of length *nLength*.

nLength The length (in bytes) of the reserve area.

Remarks

The three filebuf constructors are described as follows:

filebuf() Constructs a **filebuf** object without attaching it to a file.

filebuf(filedesc) Constructs a **filebuf** object and attaches it to an open file.

filebuf(filedesc, char*, int) Constructs a **filebuf** object, attaches it to an open file, and initializes it to use a specified reserve area.

---

filebuf::~filebuf

~filebuf();

Remarks

Closes the attached file only if that file was opened by the **open** member function.

---

filebuf::is_open

int is_open() const;

Return Value

Returns a nonzero value if this **filebuf** object is attached to an open disk file identified by a file descriptor; otherwise 0.

See Also **filebuf::open**

---

filebuf::open

filebuf* open(const char* *szName***, int** *nMode***, int** *nProt* **= filebuf::openprot);**

Opens a disk file and attaches it with this **filebuf** object.

Return Value

If the file is already open, or if there is an error while opening the file, the function returns **NULL**; otherwise it returns the **filebuf** address.

Parameters

szName The name of the file to be opened during construction.

nMode An integer containing mode bits defined as **ios** enumerators that can be combined with the OR (|) operator. See the **ofstream** constructor for a list of the enumerators.

nProt The file protection specification; defaults to the static integer **filebuf::openprot**, which is equivalent to the operating system default (**filebuf::sh_compat** for MS-DOS). The possible values of *nProt* are:

- **filebuf::sh_compat** Compatibility share mode (MS-DOS only).
- **filebuf::sh_none** Exclusive mode—no sharing.
- **filebuf::sh_read** Read sharing allowed.
- **filebuf::sh_write** Write sharing allowed.

You can combine the **filebuf::sh_read** and **filebuf::sh_write** modes with the logical OR (||) operator.

See Also **filebuf::is_open**, **filebuf::close**, **filebuf::~filebuf**

filebuf::setmode

int setmode(int *nMode* **= filebuf::text);**

Parameter

nMode An integer that must be one of the static **filebuf** constants. The *nMode* parameter must have one of the following values:

- **filebuf::text** Text mode (newline characters translated to and from carriage return-linefeed pairs under MS-DOS).
- **filebuf::binary** Binary mode (no translation).

Return Value

The previous mode if there is no error; otherwise 0.

Remarks

Sets the binary/text mode of the stream's **filebuf** object.

See Also **ios binary** manipulator, **ios text** manipulator

class fstream

#include <fstream.h>

The **fstream** class is an **iostream** derivative specialized for combined disk file input and output. Its constructors automatically create and attach a **filebuf** buffer object.

See **filebuf** class for information on the get and put areas and their associated pointers. Although the **filebuf** object's get and put pointers are theoretically independent, the get area and the put area are not active at the same time. When the stream's mode changes from input to output, the get area is emptied and the put area is reinitialized. When the mode changes from output to input, the put area is flushed and the get area is reinitialized. Thus, either the get pointer or the put pointer is null at all times.

Construction/Destruction — Public Members

fstream Constructs an **fstream** object.

~fstream Destroys an **fstream** object.

Operations — Public Members

open Opens a file and attaches it to the **filebuf** object and thus to the stream.

close Flushes any waiting output and closes the stream's file.

setbuf Attaches the specified reserve area to the stream's **filebuf** object.

setmode Sets the stream's mode to binary or text.

attach Attaches the stream (through the **filebuf** object) to an open file.

Status/Information — Public Members

rdbuf Gets the stream's **filebuf** object.

fd Returns the file descriptor associated with the stream.

is_open Tests whether the stream's file is open.

See Also **ifstream**, **ofstream**, **strstream**, **stdiostream**, **filebuf**

Member Functions

fstream::attach

void attach(filedesc *fd* **);**

Attaches this stream to the open file specified by *fd*.

Parameter

fd A file descriptor as returned by a call to the run-time function **_open** or **_sopen**; **filedesc** is a **typedef** equivalent to **int**.

Remarks

The function fails when the stream is already attached to a file. In that case, the function sets **ios::failbit** in the stream's error state.

See Also **filebuf::attach**, **fstream::fd**

---

fstream::close

void close();

Remarks

Calls the **close** member function for the associated **filebuf** object. This function, in turn, flushes any waiting output, closes the file, and disconnects the file from the **filebuf** object. The **filebuf** object is not destroyed.

The stream's error state is cleared unless the call to **filebuf::close** fails.

See Also **filebuf::close**, **fstream::open**, **fstream::is_open**

---

fstream::fd

filedesc fd() const;

Remarks

Returns the file descriptor associated with the stream. **filedesc** is a **typedef** equivalent to **int**. Its value is supplied by the underlying file system.

See Also **filebuf::fd**, **fstream::attach**

---

fstream::fstream

fstream();

fstream(const char* *szName*, **int** *nMode*, **int** *nProt* **= filebuf::openprot);**

fstream(filedesc *fd* **);**

fstream(filedesc *fd*, **char*** *pch*, **int** *nLength* **);**

Parameters

szName The name of the file to be opened during construction.

nMode An integer that contains mode bits defined as **ios** enumerators that can be combined with the bitwise OR (|) operator. The *nMode* parameter must have one of the following values:

- **ios::app** The function performs a seek to the end of file. When new bytes are written to the file, they are always appended to the end, even if the position is moved with the **ostream::seekp** function.
- **ios::ate** The function performs a seek to the end of file. When the first new byte is written to the file, it is appended to the end, but when subsequent bytes are written, they are written to the current position.
- **ios::in** The file is opened for input. The original file (if it exists) will not be truncated.
- **ios::out** The file is opened for output.
- **ios::trunc** If the file already exists, its contents are discarded. This mode is implied if **ios::out** is specified, and **ios::ate**, **ios::app**, and **ios:in** are not specified.
- **ios::nocreate** If the file does not already exist, the function fails.
- **ios::noreplace** If the file already exists, the function fails.
- **ios::binary** Opens the file in binary mode (the default is text mode).

Note that there is no **ios::in** or **ios::out** default mode for **fstream** objects. You must specify both modes if your **fstream** object must both read and write files.

nProt The file protection specification; defaults to the static integer **filebuf::openprot**, which is equivalent to the operating system default, **filebuf::sh_compat**, under MS-DOS. The possible *nProt* values are as follows:

- **filebuf::sh_compat** Compatibility share mode (MS-DOS only).
- **filebuf::sh_none** Exclusive mode—no sharing.
- **filebuf::sh_read** Read sharing allowed.
- **filebuf::sh_write** Write sharing allowed.

The **filebuf::sh_read** and **filebuf::sh_write** modes can be combined with the logical OR (||) operator.

fd A file descriptor as returned by a call to the run-time function **_open** or **_sopen**. **filedesc** is a **typedef** equivalent to **int**.

pch Pointer to a previously allocated reserve area of length *nLength*. A **NULL** value (or *nLength* = 0) indicates that the stream will be unbuffered.

nLength The length (in bytes) of the reserve area (0 = unbuffered).

Remarks

The four **fstream** constructors are:

- **fstream()** Constructs an **fstream** object without opening a file.
- **fstream(const char*, int, int)** Contructs an **fstream** object, opening the specified file.
- **fstream(filedesc)** Constructs an **fstream** object that is attached to an open file.
- **fstream(filedesc, char*, int)** Constructs an **fstream** object that is associated with a **filebuf** object. The **filebuf** object is attached to an open file and to a specified reserve area.

All **fstream** constructors construct a **filebuf** object. The first three use an internally allocated reserve area, but the fourth uses a user-allocated area. The user-allocated area is not automatically released during destruction.

fstream::~fstream

~fstream();

Remarks

Flushes the buffer, then destroys an **fstream** object, along with its associated **filebuf** object. The file is closed only if it was opened by the constructor or by the **open** member function.

The **filebuf** destructor releases the reserve buffer only if it was internally allocated.

fstream::is_open

int is_open() const;

Return Value

Returns a nonzero value if this stream is attached to an open disk file identified by a file descriptor; otherwise 0.

See Also **filebuf::is_open**, **fstream::open**, **fstream::close**

fstream::open

void open(const char* *szName*, **int** *nMode*, **int** *nProt* **= filebuf::openprot);**

Opens a disk file and attaches it to the stream's **filebuf** object.

Parameters

szName The name of the file to be opened during construction.

nMode An integer containing mode bits defined as **ios** enumerators that can be combined with the OR (|) operator. See the **fstream** constructor for a list of the enumerators. There is no default; a valid mode must be specified.

nProt The file protection specification; defaults to the static integer **filebuf::openprot**. See the **fstream** constructor for a list of the other allowed values.

Remarks

If the **filebuf** object is already attached to an open file, or if a **filebuf** call fails, the **ios::failbit** is set. If the file is not found, then the **ios::failbit** is set only if the **ios::nocreate** mode was used.

See Also **filebuf::open**, **fstream::fstream**, **fstream::close**, **fstream::is_open**

---

fstream::rdbuf

filebuf* rdbuf() const;

Remarks

Returns a pointer to the **filebuf** buffer object that is associated with this stream. (This is not the character buffer; the **filebuf** object contains a pointer to the character area.)

---

fstream::setbuf

streambuf* setbuf(char * *pch*, **int** *nLength* **);**

Attaches the specified reserve area to the stream's **filebuf** object.

Return Value

If the file is open and a buffer has already been allocated, the function returns **NULL**; otherwise it returns a pointer to the **filebuf** cast as a **streambuf**. The reserve area will not be released by the destructor.

Parameters

pch A pointer to a previously allocated reserve area of length *nLength*. A **NULL** value indicates an unbuffered stream.

nLength The length (in bytes) of the reserve area. A length of 0 indicates an unbuffered stream.

---

fstream::setmode

int setmode(int *nMode* **= filebuf::text);**

Sets the binary/text mode of the stream's **filebuf** object. It can be called only after the file is opened.

Return Value

The previous mode; –1 if the parameter is invalid, the file is not open, or the mode cannot be changed.

Parameter

nMode An integer that must be one of the following static **filebuf** constants:

- **filebuf::text** Text mode (newline characters translated to and from carriage-return–linefeed pairs).
- **filebuf::binary** Binary mode (no translation).

See Also **ios binary** manipulator, **ios text** manipulator

class ifstream

#include <fstream.h>

The **ifstream** class is an **istream** derivative specialized for disk file input. Its constructors automatically create and attach a **filebuf** buffer object.

The **filebuf** class documentation describes the get and put areas and their associated pointers. Only the get area and the get pointer are active for the **ifstream** class.

Construction/Destruction — Public Members

ifstream Constructs an **ifstream** object.

~ifstream Destroys an **ifstream** object.

Operations — Public Members

open Opens a file and attaches it to the **filebuf** object and thus to the stream.

close Closes the stream's file.

setbuf Associates the specified reserve area to the stream's **filebuf** object.

setmode Sets the stream's mode to binary or text.

attach Attaches the stream (through the **filebuf** object) to an open file.

Status/Information — Public Members

rdbuf Gets the stream's **filebuf** object.

fd Returns the file descriptor associated with the stream.

is_open Tests whether the stream's file is open.

See Also **filebuf**, **streambuf**, **ofstream**, **fstream**

Member Functions

ifstream::attach

void attach(filedesc *fd* **);**

Attaches this stream to the open file specified by *fd*.

Parameter

fd A file descriptor as returned by a call to the run-time function **_open** or **_sopen**; **filedesc** is a **typedef** equivalent to **int**.

Remarks

The function fails when the stream is already attached to a file. In that case, the function sets **ios::failbit** in the stream's error state.

See Also **filebuf::attach**, **ifstream::fd**

---

ifstream::close

void close();

Remarks

Calls the **close** member function for the associated **filebuf** object. This function, in turn, closes the file and disconnects the file from the **filebuf** object. The **filebuf** object is not destroyed.

The stream's error state is cleared unless the call to **filebuf::close** fails.

See Also **filebuf::close**, **ifstream::open**, **ifstream::is_open**

---

ifstream::fd

filedesc fd() const;

Return Value

Returns the file descriptor associated with the stream; **filedesc** is a **typedef** equivalent to **int**. Its value is supplied by the underlying file system.

See Also **filebuf::fd**, **ifstream::attach**

---

ifstream::ifstream

ifstream();

ifstream(const char* *szName*, **int** *nMode* **= ios::in, int** *nProt* **= filebuf::openprot);**

ifstream(filedesc *fd* **);**

ifstream(filedesc *fd*, **char*** *pch*, **int** *nLength* **);**

Parameters

szName The name of the file to be opened during construction.

nMode An integer that contains mode bits defined as **ios** enumerators that can be combined with the bitwise OR (|) operator. The *nMode* parameter must have one of the following values:

- **ios::in** The file is opened for input (default).
- **ios::nocreate** If the file does not already exist, the function fails.
- **ios::binary** Opens the file in binary mode (the default is text mode).

Note that the **ios::nocreate** flag is necessary if you intend to test for the file's existence (the usual case).

nProt The file protection specification; defaults to the static integer **filebuf::openprot** that is equivalent to **filebuf::sh_compat**. The possible *nProt* values are:

- **filebuf::sh_compat** Compatibility share mode.
- **filebuf::sh_none** Exclusive mode—no sharing.
- **filebuf::sh_read** Read sharing allowed.
- **filebuf::sh_write** Write sharing allowed.

To combine the **filebuf::sh_read** and **filebuf::sh_write** modes, use the logical OR (||) operator.

fd A file descriptor as returned by a call to the run-time function **_open** or **_sopen**; **filedesc** is a **typedef** equivalent to **int**.

pch Pointer to a previously allocated reserve area of length *nLength*. A **NULL** value (or *nLength* = 0) indicates that the stream will be unbuffered.

nLength The length (in bytes) of the reserve area (0 = unbuffered).

Remarks

The four **ifstream** constructors are:

- **ifstream()** Constructs an **ifstream** object without opening a file.
- **ifstream(const char*, int, int)** Contructs an **ifstream** object, opening the specified file.
- **ifstream(filedesc)** Constructs an **ifstream** object that is attached to an open file.
- **ifstream(filedesc, char*, int)** Constructs an **ifstream** object that is associated with a **filebuf** object. The **filebuf** object is attached to an open file and to a specified reserve area.

All **ifstream** constructors construct a **filebuf** object. The first three use an internally allocated reserve area, but the fourth uses a user-allocated area.

ifstream::~ifstream

~ifstream();

Remarks

Destroys an **ifstream** object along with its associated **filebuf** object. The file is closed only if it was opened by the constructor or by the **open** member function.

The **filebuf** destructor releases the reserve buffer only if it was internally allocated.

---

ifstream::is_open

int is_open() const;

Return Value

Returns a nonzero value if this stream is attached to an open disk file identified by a file descriptor; otherwise 0.

See Also **filebuf::is_open**, **ifstream::open**, **ifstream::close**

---

ifstream::open

void open(const char* *szName*, **int** *nMode* **= ios::in, int** *nProt* **= filebuf::openprot);**

Parameters

szName The name of the file to be opened during construction.

nMode An integer containing bits defined as **ios** enumerators that can be combined with the OR (|) operator. See the ifstream constructor for a list of the enumerators. The **ios::in** mode is implied.

nProt The file protection specification; defaults to the static integer **filebuf::openprot**. See the **ifstream** constructor for a list of the other allowed values.

Remarks

Opens a disk file and attaches it to the stream's **filebuf** object. If the **filebuf** object is already attached to an open file, or if a **filebuf** call fails, the **ios::failbit** is set. If the file is not found, then the **ios::failbit** is set only if the **ios::nocreate** mode was used.

See Also **filebuf::open**, **ifstream::ifstream**, **ifstream::close**, **ifstream::is_open**, **ios::flags**

ifstream::rdbuf

filebuf* rdbuf() const;

Return Value

Returns a pointer to the **filebuf** buffer object that is associated with this stream. (This is not the character buffer; the **filebuf** object contains a pointer to the character area.)

---

ifstream::setbuf

streambuf* setbuf(char* *pch*, **int** *nLength* **);**

Attaches the specified reserve area to the stream's **filebuf** object.

Return Value

If the file is open and a buffer has already been allocated, the function returns **NULL**; otherwise it returns a pointer to the **filebuf**, which is cast as a **streambuf**. The reserve area will not be released by the destructor.

Parameters

pch A pointer to a previously allocated reserve area of length *nLength*. A **NULL** value indicates an unbuffered stream.

nLength The length (in bytes) of the reserve area. A length of 0 indicates an unbuffered stream.

---

ifstream::setmode

int setmode(int *nMode* **= filebuf::text);**

Return Value

The previous mode; –1 if the parameter is invalid, the file is not open, or the mode cannnot be changed.

Parameters

nMode An integer that must be one of the following static **filebuf** constants:

- **filebuf::text** Text mode (newline characters translated to and from carriage return–linefeed pairs).
- **filebuf::binary** Binary mode (no translation).

Remarks

This function sets the binary/text mode of the stream's **filebuf** object. It may be called only after the file is opened.

class ios

#include <iostream.h>

As the iostream class hierarchy diagram (on page 29) shows, **ios** is the base class for all the input/output stream classes. While **ios** is not technically an abstract base class, you will not usually construct **ios** objects, nor will you derive classes directly from **ios**. Instead, you will use the derived classes **istream** and **ostream** or other derived classes.

Even though you will not use **ios** directly, you will be using many of the inherited member functions and data members described here. Remember that these inherited member function descriptions are not duplicated for derived classes.

Data Members (static) — Public Members

basefield Mask for obtaining the conversion base flags (**dec**, **oct**, or **hex**).

adjustfield Mask for obtaining the field padding flags (**left**, **right**, or **internal**).

floatfield Mask for obtaining the numeric format (**scientific** or **fixed**).

Construction/Destruction — Public Members

ios Constructor for use in derived classes.

~ios Virtual destructor.

Flag and Format Access Functions — Public Members

flags Sets or reads the stream's format flags.

setf Manipulates the stream's format flags.

unsetf Clears the stream's format flags.

fill Sets or reads the stream's fill character.

precision Sets or reads the stream's floating-point format display precision.

width Sets or reads the stream's output field width.

Status-Testing Functions — Public Members

good Indicates good stream status.

bad Indicates a serious I/O error.

eof Indicates end of file.

fail Indicates a serious I/O error or a possibly recoverable I/O formatting error.

rdstate Returns the stream's error flags.

clear Sets or clears the stream's error flags.

User-Defined Format Flags — Public Members

bitalloc Provides a mask for an unused format bit in the stream's private flags variable (static function).

xalloc Provides an index to an unused word in an array reserved for special-purpose stream state variables (static function).

iword Converts the index provided by **xalloc** to a reference (valid only until the next **xalloc**).

pword Converts the index provided by **xalloc** to a pointer (valid only until the next **xalloc**).

Other Functions — Public Members

delbuf Controls the connection of **streambuf** deletion with **ios** destruction.

rdbuf Gets the stream's **streambuf** object.

sync_with_stdio Synchronizes the predefined objects **cin**, **cout**, **cerr**, and **clog** with the standard I/O system.

tie Ties a specified **ostream** to this stream.

Operators — Public Members

operator void*() Converts a stream to a pointer that can be used only for error checking.

operator !() Returns a nonzero value if a stream I/O error occurs.

ios Manipulators

dec Causes the interpretation of subsequent fields in decimal format (the default mode).

hex Causes the interpretation of subsequent fields in hexadecimal format.

oct Causes the interpretation of subsequent fields in octal format.

binary Sets the stream's mode to binary (stream must have an associated **filebuf** buffer).

text Sets the stream's mode to text, the default mode (stream must have an associated **filebuf** buffer).

Parameterized Manipulators

(**#include <iomanip.h>** required)

setiosflags Sets the stream's format flags.

resetiosflags Resets the stream's format flags.

setfill Sets the stream's fill character.

setprecision Sets the stream's floating-point display precision.

setw Sets the stream's field width (for the next field only).

See Also **istream**, **ostream**

Member Functions

ios::bad

int bad() const;

Return Value

Returns a nonzero value to indicate a serious I/O error. This is the same as setting the **badbit** error state. Do not continue I/O operations on the stream in this situation.

See Also **ios::good**, **ios::fail**, **ios::rdstate**

---

ios::bitalloc

static long bitalloc();

Remarks

Provides a mask for an unused format bit in the stream's private flags variable (static function). The **ios** class currently defines 15 format flag bits accessible through **flags** and other member functions. These bits reside in a 32-bit private **ios** data member and are accessed through enumerators such as **ios::left** and **ios::hex**.

The **bitalloc** member function provides a mask for a previously unused bit in the data member. Once you obtain the mask, you can use it to set or test the corresponding custom flag bit in conjunction with the **ios** member functions and manipulators listed under "See Also."

See Also **ios::flags**, **ios::setf**, **ios::unsetf**, **ios setiosflags**, **ios resetiosflags manipulator**

---

ios::clear

void clear(int *nState* **= 0);**

Parameter

nState If 0, all error bits are cleared; otherwise bits are set according to the following masks (**ios** enumerators) that can be combined using the bitwise OR (|) operator. The *nState* parameter must have one of the following values:

- **ios::goodbit** No error condition (no bits set).
- **ios::eofbit** End of file reached.
- **ios::failbit** A possibly recoverable formatting or conversion error.
- **ios::badbit** A severe I/O error.

Remarks

Sets or clears the error-state flags. The **rdstate** function can be used to read the current error state.

See Also **ios::rdstate**, **ios::good**, **ios::bad**, **ios::eof**

---

ios::delbuf

void delbuf(int *nDelFlag* **);**

int delbuf() const;

Parameter

nDelFlag A nonzero value indicates that **~ios** should delete the stream's attached **streambuf** object. A 0 value prevents deletion.

Remarks

The first overloaded **delbuf** function assigns a value to the stream's buffer-deletion flag. The second function returns the current value of the flag.

This function is public only because it is accessed by the **Iostream_init** class. Treat it as protected.

See Also **ios::rdbuf**, **ios::~ios**

---

ios::eof

int eof() const;

Return Value

Returns a nonzero value if end of file has been reached. This is the same as setting the **eofbit** error flag.

---

ios::fail

int fail() const;

Return Value

Returns a nonzero value if any I/O error (not end of file) has occurred. This condition corresponds to either the **badbit** or **failbit** error flag being set. If a call to **bad** returns 0, you can assume that the error condition is nonfatal and that you can probably continue processing after you clear the flags.

See Also **ios::bad**, **ios::clear**

ios::fill

char fill(char *cFill* **);**

char fill() const;

Return Value

The first overloaded function sets the stream's internal fill character variable to *cFill* and returns the previous value. The default fill character is a space.

The second **fill** function returns the stream's fill character.

Parameter

cFill The new fill character to be used as padding between fields.

See Also **ios setfill** manipulator

---

ios::flags

long flags(long *lFlags* **);**

long flags() const;

Return Value

The first overloaded **flags** function sets the stream's internal flags variable to *lFlags* and returns the previous value.

The second function returns the stream's current flags.

Parameter

lFlags The new format flag values for the stream. The values are specified by the following bit masks (**ios** enumerators) that can be combined using the bitwise OR (|) operator. The *lFlags* parameter must have one of the following values:

- **ios::skipws** Skip white space on input.
- **ios::left** Left-align values; pad on the right with the fill character.
- **ios::right** Right-align values; pad on the left with the fill character (default alignment).
- **ios::internal** Add fill characters after any leading sign or base indication, but before the value.
- **ios::dec** Format numeric values as base 10 (decimal) (default radix).
- **ios::oct** Format numeric values as base 8 (octal).
- **ios::hex** Format numeric values as base 16 (hexadecimal).
- **ios::showbase** Display numeric constants in a format that can be read by the C++ compiler.

- **ios::showpoint** Show decimal point and trailing zeros for floating-point values.
- **ios::uppercase** Display uppercase A through F for hexadecimal values and E for scientific values.
- **ios::showpos** Show plus signs (+) for positive values.
- **ios::scientific** Display floating-point numbers in scientific format.
- **ios::fixed** Display floating-point numbers in fixed format.
- **ios::unitbuf** Cause **ostream::osfx** to flush the stream after each insertion. By default, **cerr** is unit buffered.
- **ios::stdio** Cause **ostream::osfx** to flush stdout and stderr after each insertion.

See Also **ios::setf**, **ios::unsetf**, **ios setiosflags** manipulator, **ios resetiosflags** manipulator, **ios::adjustfield**, **ios::basefield**, **ios::floatfield**

---

ios::good

int good() const;

Return Value

Returns a nonzero value if all error bits are clear. Note that the **good** member function is not simply the inverse of the **bad** function.

See Also **ios::bad**, **ios::fail**, **ios::rdstate**

---

ios::init

Protected →

void init(streambuf* *psb* **);**

END Protected

Parameter

psb A pointer to an existing streambuf object.

Remarks

Associates an object of a **streambuf**-derived class with this stream and, if necessary, deletes a dynamically created stream buffer object that was previously associated. The **init** function is useful in derived classes in conjunction with the protected default **istream**, **ostream**, and **iostream** constructors. Thus, an **ios**-derived class constructor can construct and attach its own predetermined stream buffer object.

See Also **istream::istream**, **ostream::ostream**, **iostream::iostream**

ios::ios

ios(streambuf* *psb* **);**

Parameter

psb A pointer to an existing streambuf object.

Remarks

Constructor for **ios**. You will seldom need to invoke this constructor except in derived classes. Generally, you will be deriving classes not from **ios** but from **istream**, **ostream**, and **iostream**.

---

ios::~ios

virtual ~ios();

Remarks

Virtual destructor for **ios**.

---

ios::iword

long& iword(int *nIndex* **) const;**

Parameters

nIndex An index to a table of words that are associated with the **ios** object.

Remarks

The **xalloc** member function provides the index to the table of special-purpose words. The **pword** function converts that index to a reference to a 32-bit word.

See Also **ios::xalloc**, **ios::pword**

---

ios::precision

int precision(int *np* **);**

int precision() const;

Return Value

The first overloaded **precision** function sets the stream's internal floating-point precision variable to *np* and returns the previous value. The default precision is six digits. If the display format is scientific or fixed, the precision indicates the number of digits after the decimal point. If the format is automatic (neither floating point nor fixed), the precision indicates the total number of significant digits.

The second function returns the stream's current precision value.

Parameter

np An integer that indicates the number of significant digits or significant decimal digits to be used for floating-point display.

See Also **ios setprecision** manipulator

ios::pword

void*& pword(int *nIndex* **) const;**

Parameter

nIndex An index to a table of words that are associated with the **ios** object.

Remarks

The **xalloc** member function provides the index to the table of special-purpose words. The **pword** function converts that index to a reference to a pointer to a 32-bit word.

See Also **ios::xalloc**, **ios::iword**

ios::rdbuf

streambuf* rdbuf() const;

Return Value

Returns a pointer to the **streambuf** object that is associated with this stream. The **rdbuf** function is useful when you need to call **streambuf** member functions.

ios::rdstate

int rdstate() const;

Return Value

Returns the current error state as specified by the following masks (**ios** enumerators):

- **ios::goodbit** No error condition.
- **ios::eofbit** End of file reached.
- **ios::failbit** A possibly recoverable formatting or conversion error.
- **ios::badbit** A severe I/O error or unknown state.

The returned value can be tested against a mask with the AND (**&**) operator.

See Also **ios::clear**

ios::setf

long setf(long *lFlags* **);**

long setf(long *lFlags*, **long** *lMask* **);**

Return Value

The first overloaded **setf** function turns on only those format bits that are specified by 1s in *lFlags*. It returns a **long** that contains the previous value of all the flags.

The second function alters those format bits specified by 1s in *lMask*. The new values of those format bits are determined by the corresponding bits in *lFlags*. It returns a **long** that contains the previous value of all the flags.

Parameters

lFlags Format flag bit values. See the **flags** member function for a list of format flags. To combine these flags, use the bitwise OR (|) operator.

lMask Format flag bit mask.

See Also **ios::flags**, **ios::unsetf**, **ios setiosflags** manipulator

---

ios::sync_with_stdio

static void sync_with_stdio();

Remarks

Synchronizes the C++ streams with the standard I/O system. The first time this function is called, it resets the predefined streams (**cin**, **cout**, **cerr**, **clog**) to use a **stdiobuf** object rather than a **filebuf** object. After that, you can mix I/O using these streams with I/O using **stdin**, **stdout**, and **stderr**. Expect some performance decrease because there is buffering both in the stream class and in the standard I/O file system.

After the call to **sync_with_stdio**, the **ios::stdio** bit is set for all affected predefined stream objects, and **cout** is set to unit buffered mode.

---

ios::tie

ostream* tie(ostream* *pos* **);**

ostream* tie() const;

Return Value

The first overloaded **tie** function ties this stream to the specified **ostream** and returns the value of the previous tie pointer or **NULL** if this stream was not previously tied. A stream tie enables automatic flushing of the **ostream** when more characters are needed, or there are characters to be consumed.

By default, **cin** is initially tied to **cout** so that attempts to get more characters from standard input may result in flushing standard output. In addition, **cerr** and **clog** are tied to **cout** by default.

The second function returns the value of the previous tie pointer or **NULL** if this stream was not previously tied.

Parameter

pos A pointer to an **ostream** object.

---

ios::unsetf

long unsetf(long *lFlags* **);**

Return Value

Clears the format flags specified by 1s in *lFlags*. It returns a **long** that contains the previous value of all the flags.

Parameter

lFlags Format flag bit values. See the **flags** member function for a list of format flags.

See Also **ios::flags**, **ios::setf**, **ios resetiosflags** manipulator

---

ios::width

int width(int *nw* **);**

int width() const;

Return Value

The first overloaded **width** function sets the stream's internal field width variable to *nw*. When the width is 0 (the default), inserters insert only the number of characters necessary to represent the inserted value. When the width is not 0, the inserters pad the field with the stream's fill character, up to *nw*. If the unpadded representation of the field is larger than *nw*, the field is not truncated. Thus, *nw* is a minimum field width.

The internal width value is reset to 0 after each insertion or extraction.

The second overloaded **width** function returns the current value of the stream's width variable.

Parameter

nw The minimum field width in characters.

See Also **ios setw** manipulator

ios::xalloc

static int xalloc();

Return Value

Provides extra **ios** object state variables without the need for class derivation. It does so by returning an index to an unused 32-bit word in an internal array. This index can subsequently be converted into a reference or pointer by using the **iword** or **pword** member functions.

Any call to **xalloc** invalidates values returned by previous calls to **iword** and **pword**.

See Also **ios::iword**, **ios::pword**

Operators

ios::operator void* ()

operator void* () const;

Remarks

An operator that converts a stream to a pointer that can be compared to 0.

Return Value

The conversion returns 0 if either **failbit** or **badbit** is set in the stream's error state. See **rdstate** for a description of the error state masks. A nonzero pointer is not meant to be dereferenced.

See Also **ios::good**, **ios::fail**

---

ios::operator ! ()

int operator !() const;

Return Value

Returns a nonzero value if either **failbit** or **badbit** is set in the stream's error state. See **rdstate** for a description of the error state masks.

See Also **ios::good**, **ios::fail**

---

ios::adjustfield

static const long adjustfield;

Remarks

A mask for obtaining the padding flag bits (**left, right,** or **internal**).

Example

```
extern ostream os;
if( ( os.flags() & ios::adjustfield ) == ios::left ) .....
```

See Also **ios::flags**

---

ios::basefield

static const long basefield;

Remarks

A mask for obtaining the current radix flag bits (**dec**, **oct**, or **hex**).

Example

```
extern ostream os;
if( ( os.flags() & ios::basefield ) == ios::hex ) .....
```

See Also **ios::flags**

---

ios::floatfield

static const long floatfield;

Remarks

A mask for obtaining floating-point format flag bits (**scientific** or **fixed**).

Example

```
extern ostream os;
if( ( os.flags() & ios::floatfield ) == ios::scientific ) .....
```

See Also **ios::flags**

Manipulators

ios& binary

binary

Remarks

Sets the stream's mode to binary. The default mode is text.

The stream must have an associated **filebuf** buffer.

See Also **ios text** manipulator, **ofstream::setmode**, **ifstream::setmode**, **filebuf::setmode**

ios& dec

dec

Remarks

Sets the format conversion base to 10 (decimal).

See Also **ios hex** manipulator, **ios oct** manipulator

---

ios& hex

hex

Remarks

Sets the format conversion base to 16 (hexadecimal).

See Also **ios dec** manipulator, **ios oct** manipulator

---

ios& oct

oct

Remarks

Sets the format conversion base to 8 (octal).

See Also **ios dec** manipulator, **ios hex** manipulator

---

resetiosflags

SMANIP(long) resetiosflags(long *lFlags* **);**

#include <iomanip.h>

Parameter

lFlags Format flag bit values. See the **flags** member function for a list of format flags. To combine these flags, use the OR (|) operator.

Remarks

This parameterized manipulator clears only the specified format flags. This setting remains in effect until you change it.

---

setfill

SMANIP(int) setfill(int *nFill* **);**

#include <iomanip.h>

Parameter

nFill The new fill character to be used as padding between fields.

Remarks

This parameterized manipulator sets the stream's fill character. The default is a space. This setting remains in effect until the next change.

---

setiosflags

SMANIP(long) setiosflags(long *lFlags* **);**

#include <iomanip.h>

Parameter

lFlags Format flag bit values. See the **flags** member function for a list of format flags. To combine these flags, use the OR (|) operator.

Remarks

This parameterized manipulator sets only the specified format flags. This setting remains in effect until the next change.

---

setprecision

SMANIP(int) setprecision(int *np* **);**

#include <iomanip.h>

Parameter

np An integer that indicates the number of significant digits or significant decimal digits to be used for floating-point display.

Remarks

This parameterized manipulator sets the stream's internal floating-point precision variable to *np*. The default precision is six digits. If the display format is scientific or fixed, then the precision indicates the number of digits after the decimal point. If the format is automatic (neither floating point nor fixed), then the precision indicates the total number of significant digits. This setting remains in effect until the next change.

---

setw

SMANIP(int) setw(int *nw* **);**

#include <iomanip.h>

Parameter

nw The field width in characters.

Remarks

This parameterized manipulator sets the stream's internal field width parameter. See the **width** member function for more information. This setting remains in effect only for the next insertion.

---

ios& text

text

Sets the stream's mode to text (the default mode).

Remarks

The stream must have an associated **filebuf** buffer.

See Also **ios binary** manipulator, **ofstream::setmode**, **ifstream::setmode**, **filebuf::setmode**

class iostream

#include <iostream.h>

The **iostream** class provides the basic capability for sequential and random-access I/O. It inherits functionality from the **istream** and **ostream** classes.

The **iostream** class works in conjunction with classes derived from **streambuf** (for example, **filebuf**). In fact, most of the **iostream** "personality" comes from its attached **streambuf** class. You can use **iostream** objects for sequential disk I/O if you first construct an appropriate **filebuf** object. More often, you will use objects of classes **fstream** and **strstream**.

Derivation

For derivation suggestions, see the **istream** and **ostream** classes.

Public Members

iostream Constructs an **iostream** object that is attached to an existing **streambuf** object.

~iostream Destroys an **iostream** object.

Protected Members

iostream Acts as a **void**-argument **iostream** constructor.

See Also **istream**, **ostream**, **fstream**, **strstream**, **stdiostream**

Member Functions

iostream::iostream

Public →

iostream(streambuf* *psb* **);**

END Public

Protected →

iostream( );

END Protected

Parameter

psb A pointer to an existing **streambuf** object (or an object of a derived class).

Remarks

Constructs an object of type **iostream**.

See Also **ios::init**

---

iostream::~iostream

virtual ~iostream();

Remarks

Virtual destructor for the **iostream** class.

class Iostream_init

#include <iostream.h>

The **Iostream_init** class is a static class that initializes the predefined stream objects **cin**, **cout**, **cerr**, and **clog**. A single object of this class is constructed "invisibly" in response to any reference to the predefined objects. The class is documented for completeness only. You will not normally construct objects of this class.

Public Members

Iostream_init A constructor that initializes **cin**, **cout**, **cerr**, and **clog**.

~Iostream_init The destructor for the **Iostream_init** class.

Member Functions

Iostream_init::Iostream_init

Iostream_init();

Remarks

Iostream_init constructor that initializes **cin**, **cout**, **cerr**, and **clog**. For internal use only.

Iostream_init::~Iostream_init

~Iostream_init();

Remarks

Iostream_init destructor. For internal use only.

class istream

#include <iostream.h>

The **istream** class provides the basic capability for sequential and random-access input. An **istream** object has a **streambuf**-derived object attached, and the two classes work together; the **istream** class does the formatting, and the **streambuf** class does the low-level buffered input.

You can use **istream** objects for sequential disk input if you first construct an appropriate **filebuf** object. More often, you will use the predefined stream object **cin** (which is actually an object of class **istream_withassign**), or you will use objects of classes **ifstream** (disk file streams) and **istrstream** (string streams).

Derivation

It is not always necessary to derive from **istream** to add functionality to a stream; consider deriving from **streambuf** instead, as illustrated on page 22 in “Deriving Your Own Stream Classes.” The **ifstream** and **istrstream** classes are examples of **istream**-derived classes that construct member objects of predetermined derived **streambuf** classes. You can add manipulators without deriving a new class.

If you add new extraction operators for a derived **istream** class, then the rules of C++ dictate that you must reimplement all the base class extraction operators. See the “Derivation” section of class **ostream** for an efficient reimplementation technique.

Construction/Destruction — Public Members

istream Constructs an **istream** object attached to an existing object of a **streambuf**-derived class.

~istream Destroys an **istream** object.

Prefix/Suffix Functions — Public Members

ipfx Check for error conditions prior to extraction operations (input prefix function).

isfx Called after extraction operations (input suffix function).

Input Functions — Public Members

get Extracts characters from the stream up to, but not including, delimiters.

getline Extracts characters from the stream (extracts and discards delimiters).

read Extracts data from the stream.

ignore Extracts and discards characters.

peek Returns a character without extracting it from the stream.

gcount Counts the characters extracted in the last unformatted operation.

eatwhite Extracts leading white space.

Other Functions — Public Members

putback Puts characters back to the stream.

sync Synchronizes the stream buffer with the external source of characters.

seekg Changes the stream's get pointer.

tellg Gets the value of the stream's get pointer.

Operators — Public Members

operator >> Extraction operator for various types.

Protected Members

istream Constructs an **istream** object.

Manipulators

ws Extracts leading white space.

See Also **streambuf**, **ifstream**, **istrstream**, **istream_withassign**

Member Functions

istream::eatwhite

void eatwhite();

Remarks

Extracts white space from the stream by advancing the get pointer past spaces and tabs.

See Also **istream ws** manipulator

---

istream::gcount

int gcount() const;

Remarks

Returns the number of characters extracted by the last unformatted input function. Formatted extraction operators may call unformatted input functions and thus reset this number.

See Also **istream::get**, **istream::getline**, **istream::ignore**, **istream::read**

---

istream::get

int get();&

istream& get(char* *pch*, **int** *nCount*, **char** *delim* = **'\n');**

istream& get(unsigned char* *puch*, **int** *nCount*, **char** *delim* = **'\n');**

istream& get(signed char* *psch*, **int** *nCount*, **char** *delim* = **'\n');**

istream& get(char& *rch* **);**

istream& get(unsigned char& *ruch* **);**

istream& get(signed char& *rsch* **);**

istream& get(streambuf& *rsb*, **char** *delim* = **'\n');**

Parameters

pch, puch, psch A pointer to a character array.

nCount The maximum number of characters to store, including the terminating **NULL**.

delim The delimiter character (defaults to newline).

rch, ruch, rsch A reference to a character.

rsb A reference to an object of a **streambuf**-derived class.

Remarks

These functions extract data from an input stream as follows:

Variation	Description
get();	Extracts a single character from the stream and returns it.
get(char*, int, char);	Extracts characters from the stream until either *delim* is found, the limit *nCount* is reached, or the end of file is reached. The characters are stored in the array followed by a null terminator.
get(char&);	Extracts a single character from the stream and stores it as specified by the reference argument.
get(streambuf&, char);	Gets characters from the stream and stores them in a **streambuf** object until the delimiter is found or the end of the file is reached. The **ios::failbit** flag is set if the **streambuf** output operation fails.

In all cases, the delimiter is neither extracted from the stream nor returned by the function. The **getline** function, in contrast, extracts but does not store the delimiter.

See Also **istream::getline**, **istream::read**, **istream::ignore**, **istream::gcount**

istream::getline

istream& getline(char* *pch*, **int** *nCount*, **char** *delim* = **'\n');**

istream& getline(unsigned char* *puch*, **int** *nCount*, **char** *delim* = **'\n');**

istream& getline(signed char* *psch*, **int** *nCount*, **char** *delim* **= '\n');**

Parameters

pch, puch, psch A pointer to a character array.

nCount The maximum number of characters to store, including the terminating **NULL**.

delim The delimiter character (defaults to newline).

Remarks

Extracts characters from the stream until either the delimiter *delim* is found, the limit *nCount*–1 is reached, or end of file is reached. The characters are stored in the specified array followed by a null terminator. If the delimiter is found, it is extracted but not stored.

The **get** function, in contrast, neither extracts nor stores the delimiter.

See Also **istream::get**, **istream::read**

---

istream::ignore

istream& ignore(int *nCount* **= 1, int** *delim* **= EOF);**

Parameters

nCount The maximum number of characters to extract.

delim The delimiter character (defaults to **EOF**).

Remarks

Extracts and discards up to *nCount* characters. Extraction stops if the delimiter *delim* is extracted or the end of file is reached. If *delim* = **EOF** (the default), then only the end of file condition causes termination. The delimiter character is extracted.

---

istream::ipfx

int ipfx(int *need* **= 0);**

Return Value

A nonzero return value if the operation was successful; 0 if the stream's error state is nonzero, in which case the function does nothing.

Parameter

need Zero if called from formatted input functions; otherwise the minimum number of characters needed.

Remarks

This input prefix function is called by input functions prior to extracting data from the stream. Formatted input functions call **ipfx(0)**, while unformatted input functions usually call **ipfx(1)**.

Any **ios** object tied to this stream is flushed if *need* = 0 or if there are fewer than *need* characters in the input buffer. Also, **ipfx** extracts leading white space if **ios::skipws** is set.

See Also **istream::isfx**

---

istream::isfx

void isfx();

Remarks

This input suffix function is called at the end of every extraction operation.

---

istream::istream

Public →

istream(streambuf* *psb* **);**

END Public

Protected →

istream( );

END Protected

Parameter

psb A pointer to an existing object of a **streambuf**-derived class.

Remarks

Constructs an object of type **istream**.

See Also **ios::init**

---

istream::~istream

virtual ~istream();

Remarks

Virtual destructor for the **istream** class.

istream::peek

int peek();

Return Value

Returns the next character without extracting it from the stream. Returns **EOF** if the stream is at end of file or if the **ipfx** function indicates an error.

istream::putback

istream& putback(char *ch* **);**

Parameter

ch The character to put back; must be the character previously extracted.

Remarks

Puts a character back into the input stream. The **putback** function may fail and set the error state. If *ch* does not match the character that was previously extracted, the result is undefined.

istream::read

istream& read(char* *pch*, **int** *nCount* **);**

istream& read(unsigned char* *puch*, **int** *nCount* **);**

istream& read(signed char* *psch*, **int** *nCount* **);**

Parameters

pch, puch, psch A pointer to a character array.

nCount The maximum number of characters to read.

Remarks

Extracts bytes from the stream until the limit *nCount* is reached or until the end of file is reached. The **read** function is useful for binary stream input.

See Also **istream::get**, **istream::getline**, **istream::gcount**, **istream::ignore**

istream::seekg

istream& seekg(streampos *pos* **);**

istream& seekg(streamoff *off*, **ios::seek_dir** *dir* **);**

Parameters

pos The new position value; **streampos** is a **typedef** equivalent to **long**.

off The new offset value; **streamoff** is a **typedef** equivalent to **long**.

dir The seek direction. Must be one of the following enumerators:

- **ios::beg** Seek from the beginning of the stream.
- **ios::cur** Seek from the current position in the stream.
- **ios::end** Seek from the end of the stream.

Remarks

Changes the get pointer for the stream. Not all derived classes of **istream** need support positioning; it is most often used with file-based streams.

See Also **istream::tellg**, **ostream::seekp**, **ostream::tellp**

---

istream::sync

int sync();

Synchronizes the stream's internal buffer with the external source of characters.

Return Value

EOF to indicate errors.

Remarks

Synchronizes the stream's internal buffer with the external source of characters. This function calls the virtual **streambuf::sync** function so you can customize its implementation by deriving a new class from **streambuf**.

See Also **streambuf::sync**

---

istream::tellg

streampos tellg();

Gets the value for the stream's **get** pointer.

Return Value

A **streampos** type, corresponding to a **long**.

See Also **istream::seekg**, **ostream::tellp**, **ostream::seekp**

Operators

istream::operator >>

istream& operator >>(char* *psz* **);**

istream& operator >>(unsigned char* *pusz* **);**

istream& operator >>(signed char* *pssz* **);**

istream& operator >>(char& *rch* **);**

istream& operator >>(unsigned char& *ruch* **);**

istream& operator >>(signed char& *rsch* **);**

istream& operator >>(short& *s* **);**

istream& operator >>(unsigned short& *us* **);**

istream& operator >>(int& *n* **);**

istream& operator >>(unsigned int& *un* **);**

istream& operator >>(long& *l* **);**

istream& operator >>(unsigned long& *ul* **);**

istream& operator >>(float& *f* **);**

istream& operator >>(double& *d* **);**

istream& operator >>(long double& *ld* **);** (16-bit only)

istream& operator >>(streambuf* *psb* **);**

istream& operator >>(istream& (***fcn***)(istream&));**

istream& operator >>(ios& (***fcn***)(ios&));**

Remarks

These overloaded operators extract their argument from the stream. With the last two variations, you can use manipulators that are defined for both **istream** and **ios**.

Manipulators

istream& ws

ws

Remarks

Extracts leading white space from the stream by calling the **eatwhite** function.

See Also **istream::eatwhite**

class istream_withassign

#include <iostream.h>

The **istream_withassign** class is a variant of **istream** that allows object assignment. The predefined object **cin** is an object of this class and thus may be reassigned at run time to a different **istream** object. For example, a program that normally expects input from **stdin** could be temporarily directed to accept its input from a disk file.

Predefined Objects

The **cin** object is a predefined object of class **ostream_withassign**. It is connected to **stdin** (standard input, file descriptor 0).

The objects **cin**, **cerr**, and **clog** are tied to **cout** so that use of any of these may cause **cout** to be flushed.

Construction/Destruction — Public Members

istream_withassign Constructs an **istream_withassign** object.

~istream_withassign Destroys an **istream_withassign** object.

Operators — Public Members

operator = Indicates an assignment operator.

See Also **ostream_withassign**

Member Functions

istream_withassign::istream_withassign

istream_withassign(streambuf* *psb* **);**

istream_withassign();

Parameter

psb A pointer to an existing object of a **streambuf**-derived class.

Remarks

The first constructor creates a ready-to-use object of type **istream_withassign**, complete with attached **streambuf** object.

The second constructor creates an object but does not initialize it. You must subsequently use the second variation of the **istream_withassign** assignment operator to attach the **streambuf** object, or use the first variation to initialize this object to match the specified **istream** object.

See Also **istream_withassign::operator =**

istream_withassign::~istream_withassign

~istream_withassign();

Remarks

Destructor for the **istream_withassign** class.

Operators

istream_withassign::operator =

istream& operator =(const istream& *ris* **);**

istream& operator =(streambuf* *psb* **);**

Remarks

The first overloaded assignment operator assigns the specified **istream** object to this **istream_withassign** object.

The second operator attaches a **streambuf** object to an existing **istream_withassign** object, and it initializes the state of the **istream_withassign** object. This operator is often used in conjunction with the **void**-argument constructor.

Example

```
char buffer[100];
class xistream; // A special-purpose class derived from istream
extern xistream xin; // An xistream object constructed elsewhere

cin = xin; // cin is reassigned to xin
cin >> buffer; // xin used instead of cin
```

Example

```
char buffer[100];
extern filedesc fd; // A file descriptor for an open file
filebuf fb( fd ); // Construct a filebuf attached to fd

cin = &fb;      // fb associated with cin
cin >> buffer; // cin now gets its intput from the fb file
```

See Also **istream_withassign::istream_withassign**

class istrstream

#include <strstrea.h>

The **istrstream** class supports input streams that have character arrays as a source. You must allocate a character array before constructing an **istrstream** object. You can use **istream** operators and functions on this character data. A get pointer, working in the attached **strstreambuf** class, advances as you extract fields from the stream's array. Use **istream::seekg** to go backwards. If the get pointer reaches the end of the string (and sets the **ios::eof** flag), you must call **clear** before **seekg**.

Construction/Destruction — Public Members

istrstream Constructs an **istrstream** object.

~istrstream Destroys an **istrstream** object.

Other Functions — Public Members

rdbuf Returns a pointer to the stream's associated **strstreambuf** object.

str Returns a character array pointer to the string stream's contents.

See Also **strstreambuf**, **streambuf**, **strstream**, **ostrstream**

Member Functions

istrstream::istrstream

istrstream(char* *psz* **);**

istrstream(char* *pch*, **int** *nLength* **);**

Parameters

psz A null-terminated character array (string).

pch A character array that is not necessarily null terminated.

nLength Size (in characters) of *pch*. If 0, then *pch* is assumed to point to a null-terminated array; if less than 0, then the array length is assumed to be unlimited.

Remarks

The first constructor uses the specified *psz* buffer to make an **istrstream** object with length corresponding to the string length.

The second constructor makes an **istrstream** object out of the first *nLength* characters of the *pch* buffer.

Both constructors automatically construct a **strstreambuf** object that manages the specified character buffer.

istrstream::~istrstream

~istrstream();

Remarks

Destroys an **istrstream** object and its associated **strstreambuf** object. The character buffer is not released because it was allocated by the user prior to **istrstream** construction.

---

istrstream::rdbuf

strstreambuf* rdbuf() const;

Return Value

Returns a pointer to the **strstreambuf** buffer object that is associated with this stream. Note that this is not the character buffer itself; the **strstreambuf** object contains a pointer to the character area.

See Also **istrstream::str**

---

istrstream::str

char* str();

Return Value

Returns a pointer to the string stream's character array. This pointer corresponds to the array used to construct the **istrstream** object.

See Also **istrstream::istrstream**

class ofstream

#include <fstream.h>

The **ofstream** class is an **ostream** derivative specialized for disk file output. All of its constructors automatically create and associate a **filebuf** buffer object.

The **filebuf** class documentation describes the get and put areas and their associated pointers. Only the put area and the put pointer are active for the **ofstream** class.

Construction/Destruction — Public Members

ofstream Constructs an **ofstream** object.

~ofstream Destroys an **ofstream** object.

Operations — Public Members

open Opens a file and attaches it to the **filebuf** object and thus to the stream.

close Flushes any waiting output and closes the stream's file.

setbuf Associates the specified reserve area to the stream's **filebuf** object.

setmode Sets the stream's mode to binary or text.

attach Attaches the stream (through the **filebuf** object) to an open file.

Status/Information — Public Members

rdbuf Gets the stream's **filebuf** object.

fd Returns the file descriptor associated with the stream.

is_open Tests whether the stream's file is open.

See Also **filebuf**, **streambuf**, **ifstream**, **fstream**

Member Functions

ofstream::attach

void attach(filedesc *fd*);

Parameter

fd A file descriptor as returned by a call to the run-time function **_open** or **_sopen**; **filedesc** is a **typedef** equivalent to **int**.

Remarks

Attaches this stream to the open file specified by *fd*. The function fails when the stream is already attached to a file. In that case, the function sets **ios::failbit** in the stream's error state.

See Also **filebuf::attach**, **ofstream::fd**

ofstream::close

void close();

Remarks

Calls the **close** member function for the associated **filebuf** object. This function, in turn, flushes any waiting output, closes the file, and disconnects the file from the **filebuf** object. The **filebuf** object is not destroyed.

The stream's error state is cleared unless the call to **filebuf::close** fails.

See Also **filebuf::close**, **ofstream::open**, **ofstream::is_open**

---

ofstream::fd

filedesc fd() const;

Return Value

Returns the file descriptor associated with the stream. **filedesc** is a **typedef** equivalent to **int**. Its value is supplied by the underlying file system.

See Also **filebuf::fd**, **ofstream::attach**

---

ofstream::is_open

int is_open() const;

Return Value

Returns a nonzero value if this stream is attached to an open disk file identified by a file descriptor; otherwise 0.

See Also **filebuf::is_open**, **ofstream::open**, **ofstream::close**

---

ofstream::ofstream

ofstream();

ofstream(const char* *szName*, **int** *nMode* **= ios::out, int** *nProt* **= filebuf::openprot);**

ofstream(filedesc *fd* **);**

ofstream(filedesc *fd*, **char*** *pch*, **int** *nLength* **);**

Parameters

szName The name of the file to be opened during construction.

nMode An integer that contains mode bits defined as **ios** enumerators that can be combined with the bitwise OR (|) operator. The *nMode* parameter must have one of the following values:

- **ios::app** The function performs a seek to the end of file. When new bytes are written to the file, they are always appended to the end, even if the position is moved with the **ostream::seekp** function.
- **ios::ate** The function performs a seek to the end of file. When the first new byte is written to the file, it is appended to the end, but when subsequent bytes are written, they are written to the current position.
- **ios::in** If this mode is specified, then the original file (if it exists) will not be truncated.
- **ios::out** The file is opened for output (implied for all **ofstream** objects).
- **ios::trunc** If the file already exists, its contents are discarded. This mode is implied if **ios::out** is specified and **ios::ate**, **ios::app**, and **ios:in** are not specified.
- **ios::nocreate** If the file does not already exist, the function fails.
- **ios::noreplace** If the file already exists, the function fails.
- **ios::binary** Opens the file in binary mode (the default is text mode).

nProt The file protection specification; defaults to the static integer **filebuf::openprot** that is equivalent to **filebuf::sh_compat**. The possible *nProt* values are:

- **filebuf::sh_compat** Compatibility share mode.
- **filebuf::sh_none** Exclusive mode; no sharing.
- **filebuf::sh_read** Read sharing allowed.
- **filebuf::sh_write** Write sharing allowed.

To combine the **filebuf::sh_read** and **filebuf::sh_write** modes, use the logical OR (||) operator.

fd A file descriptor as returned by a call to the run-time function **_open** or **_sopen**; **filedesc** is a **typedef** equivalent to **int**.

pch Pointer to a previously allocated reserve area of length *nLength*. A **NULL** value (or *nLength* = 0) indicates that the stream will be unbuffered.

nLength The length (in bytes) of the reserve area (0 = unbuffered).

Remarks

The four **ofstream** constructors are:

Constructor	Description
ofstream()	Constructs an **ofstream** object without opening a file.
ofstream(const char*, int, int)	Contructs an **ofstream** object, opening the specified file.
ofstream(filedesc)	Constructs an **ofstream** object that is attached to an open file.
ofstream(filedesc, char*, int)	Constructs an **ofstream** object that is associated with a **filebuf** object. The **filebuf** object is attached to an open file and to a specified reserve area.

All **ofstream** constructors construct a **filebuf** object. The first three use an internally allocated reserve area, but the fourth uses a user-allocated area. The user-allocated area is not automatically released during destruction.

ofstream::~ofstream

~ofstream();

Remarks

Flushes the buffer, then destroys an **ofstream** object along with its associated **filebuf** object. The file is closed only if was opened by the constructor or by the **open** member function.

The **filebuf** destructor releases the reserve buffer only if it was internally allocated.

ofstream::open

void open(const char* *szName*, **int** *nMode* **= ios::out, int** *nProt* **= filebuf::openprot);**

Parameters

szName The name of the file to be opened during construction.

nMode An integer containing mode bits defined as **ios** enumerators that can be combined with the OR (|) operator. See the **ofstream** constructor for a list of the enumerators. The **ios::out** mode is implied.

nProt The file protection specification; defaults to the static integer **filebuf::openprot**. See the **ofstream** constructor for a list of the other allowed values.

Remarks

Opens a disk file and attaches it to the stream's **filebuf** object. If the **filebuf** object is already attached to an open file, or if a **filebuf** call fails, the **ios::failbit** is set. If the file is not found, the **ios::failbit** is set only if the **ios::nocreate** mode was used.

See Also **filebuf::open**, **ofstream::ofstream**, **ofstream::close**, **ofstream::is_open**

ofstream::rdbuf

filebuf* rdbuf() const;

Return Value

Returns a pointer to the **filebuf** buffer object that is associated with this stream. (Note that this is not the character buffer; the **filebuf** object contains a pointer to the character area.)

Example

```
extern ofstream ofs;
int fd = ofs.rdbuf()->fd(); // Get the file descriptor for ofs
```

ofstream::setbuf

streambuf* setbuf(char* *pch*, **int** *nLength* **);**

Attaches the specified reserve area to the stream's **filebuf** object.

Return Value

If the file is open and a buffer has already been allocated, the function returns **NULL**; otherwise it returns a pointer to the **filebuf** cast as a **streambuf**. The reserve area will not be released by the destructor.

Parameters

pch A pointer to a previously allocated reserve area of length *nLength*. A **NULL** value indicates an unbuffered stream.

nLength The length (in bytes) of the reserve area. A length of 0 indicates an unbuffered stream.

ofstream::setmode

int setmode(int *nMode* **= filebuf::text);**

Return Value

The previous mode; –1 if the parameter is invalid, the file is not open, or the mode cannot be changed.

Parameter

nMode   An integer that must be one of the following static **filebuf** constants:

- **filebuf::text**   Text mode (newline characters translated to and from carriage return–linefeed pairs).
- **filebuf::binary**   Binary mode (no translation).

Remarks

This function sets the binary/text mode of the stream's **filebuf** object. It may be called only after the file is opened.

See Also   **ios binary** manipulator, **ios text** manipulator

class ostream

#include <iostream.h>

The **ostream** class provides the basic capability for sequential and random-access output. An **ostream** object has a **streambuf**-derived object attached, and the two classes work together; the **ostream** class does the formatting, and the **streambuf** class does the low-level buffered output.

You can use **ostream** objects for sequential disk output if you first construct an appropriate **filebuf** object. (The **filebuf** class is derived from **streambuf**.) More often, you will use the predefined stream objects **cout**, **cerr**, and **clog** (actually objects of class **ostream_withassign**), or you will use objects of classes **ofstream** (disk file streams) and **ostrstream** (string streams).

All of the **ostream** member functions write unformatted data; formatted output is handled by the insertion operators.

Derivation

It is not always necessary to derive from **ostream** to add functionality to a stream; consider deriving from **streambuf** instead, as illustrated on page 22 in "Deriving Your Own Stream Classes." The **ofstream** and **ostrstream** classes are examples of **ostream**-derived classes that construct member objects of predetermined derived **streambuf** classes. You can add manipulators without deriving a new class.

If you add new insertion operators for a derived **ostream** class, then the rules of C++ dictate that you must reimplement all the base class insertion operators. If, however, you reimplement the operators through inline equivalence, no extra code will be generated.

Construction/Destruction — Public Members

ostream Constructs an **ostream** object that is attached to an existing **streambuf** object.

~ostream Destroys an **ostream** object.

Prefix/Suffix Functions — Public Members

opfx Output prefix function, called prior to insertion operations to check for error conditions, and so forth.

osfx Output suffix function, called after insertion operations; flushes the stream's buffer if it is unit buffered.

Unformatted Output — Public Members

put Inserts a single byte into the stream.

write Inserts a series of bytes into the stream.

Other Functions — Public Members

flush Flushes the buffer associated with this stream.

seekp Changes the stream's put pointer.

tellp Gets the value of the stream's put pointer.

Operators — Public Members

operator << Insertion operator for various types.

Manipulators

endl Inserts a newline sequence and flushes the buffer.

ends Inserts a null character to terminate a string.

flush Flushes the stream's buffer.

See Also **streambuf**, **ofstream**, **ostrstream**, **cout**, **cerr**, **clog**

Example

```
class xstream : public ostream
{
public:
    // Constructors, etc.
    // ........
    inline xstream& operator << ( char ch ) // insertion for char
    {
          return (xstream&)ostream::operator << ( ch );
    }
    // ........
    // Insertions for other types
};
```

Member Functions

ostream::flush

ostream& flush();

Remarks

Flushes the buffer associated with this stream. The **flush** function calls the **sync** function of the associated **streambuf**.

See Also **ostream flush** manipulator, **streambuf::sync**

ostream::opfx

int opfx();

Return Value

If the **ostream** object's error state is not 0, **opfx** returns 0 immediately; otherwise it returns a nonzero value.

Remarks

This output prefix function is called before every insertion operation. If another **ostream** object is tied to this stream, the **opfx** function flushes that stream.

---

ostream::osfx

void osfx();

Remarks

This output suffix function is called after every insertion operation. It flushes the **ostream** object if **ios::unitbuf** is set, or **stdout** and **stderr** if **ios::stdio** is set.

---

ostream::ostream

Public →

ostream(streambuf* *psb* **);**

END Public

Protected →

ostream( );

END Protected

Parameter

psb   A pointer to an existing object of a **streambuf**-derived class.

Remarks

Constructs an object of type **ostream**.

See Also   **ios::init**

---

ostream::~ostream

virtual ~ostream();

Remarks

Destroys an **ostream** object. The output buffer is flushed as appropriate. The attached **streambuf** object is destroyed only if it was allocated internally within the **ostream** constructor.

---

ostream::put

ostream& put(char *ch* **);**

Parameter

ch The character to insert.

Remarks

This function inserts a single character into the output stream.

---

ostream::seekp

ostream& seekp(streampos *pos* **);**

ostream& seekp(streamoff *off*, **ios::seek_dir** *dir* **);**

Parameters

pos The new position value; **streampos** is a **typedef** equivalent to **long**.

off The new offset value; **streamoff** is a **typedef** equivalent to **long**.

dir The seek direction specified by the enumerated type **ios::seek_dir**, with values including:

- **ios::beg** Seek from the beginning of the stream.
- **ios::cur** Seek from the current position in the stream.
- **ios::end** Seek from the end of the stream.

Remarks

Changes the position value for the stream. Not all derived classes of **ostream** need support positioning. For file streams, the position is the byte offset from the beginning of the file; for string streams, it is the byte offset from the beginning of the string.

See Also **ostream::tellp**, **istream::seekg**, **istream::tellg**

---

ostream::tellp

streampos tellp();

Return Value

A **streampos** type that corresponds to a **long**.

Remarks

Gets the position value for the stream. Not all derived classes of **ostream** need support positioning. For file streams, the position is the byte offset from the beginning of the file; for string streams, it is the byte offset from the beginning of the string. Gets the value for the stream's put pointer.

See Also **ostream::seekp**, **istream::tellg**, **istream::seekg**

---

ostream::write

ostream& write(const char* *pch*, **int** *nCount* **);**

ostream& write(const unsigned char* *puch*, **int** *nCount* **);**

ostream& write(const signed char* *psch*, **int** *nCount* **);**

Parameters

pch, puch, psch A pointer to a character array.

nCount The number of characters to be written.

Remarks

Inserts a specified number of bytes from a buffer into the stream. If the underlying file was opened in text mode, additional carriage return characters may be inserted. The **write** function is useful for binary stream output.

Operators

ostream::operator <<

ostream& operator <<(char *ch* **);**

ostream& operator <<(unsigned char *uch* **);**

ostream& operator <<(signed char *sch* **);**

ostream& operator <<(const char* *psz* **);**

ostream& operator <<(const unsigned char* *pusz* **);**

ostream& operator <<(const signed char* *pssz* **);**

ostream& operator <<(short *s* **);**

ostream& operator <<(unsigned short *us* **);**

ostream& operator <<(int *n* **);**

ostream& operator <<(unsigned int *un* **);**

ostream& operator <<(long *l* **);**

ostream& operator <<(unsigned long *ul* **);**

ostream& operator <<(float *f* **);**

ostream& operator <<(double *d* **);**

ostream& operator <<(long double *ld* **);** (16-bit only)

ostream& operator <<(const void* *pv* **);**

ostream& operator <<(streambuf* *psb* **);**

ostream& operator <<(ostream& (*fcn***)(ostream&));**

ostream& operator <<(ios& (*fcn***)(ios&));**

Remarks

These overloaded operators insert their argument into the stream. With the last two variations, you can use manipulators that are defined for both **ostream** and **ios**.

Manipulators

ostream& endl

endl

Remarks

This manipulator, when inserted into an output stream, inserts a newline character and then flushes the buffer.

---

ostream& ends

ends

Remarks

This manipulator, when inserted into an output stream, inserts a null-terminator character. It is particularly useful for **ostrstream** objects.

ostream& flush

flush

Remarks

This manipulator, when inserted into an output stream, flushes the output buffer by calling the **streambuf::sync** member function.

See Also **ostream::flush**, **streambuf::sync**

class ostream_withassign

#include <iostream.h>

The **ostream_withassign** class is a variant of **ostream** that allows object assignment. The predefined objects **cout**, **cerr**, and **clog** are objects of this class and thus may be reassigned at run time to a different **ostream** object. For example, a program that normally sends output to **stdout** could be temporarily directed to send its output to a disk file.

Predefined Objects

The three predefined objects of class **ostream_withassign** are connected as follows:

cout Standard output (file descriptor 1).

cerr Unit buffered standard error (file descriptor 2).

clog Fully buffered standard error (file descriptor 2).

Unit buffering, as used by **cerr**, means that characters are flushed after each insertion operation. The objects **cin**, **cerr**, and **clog** are tied to **cout** so that use of any of these will cause **cout** to be flushed.

Construction/Destruction — Public Members

ostream_withassign Constructs an **ostream_withassign** object.

~ostream_withassign Destroys an **ostream_withassign** object.

Operators — Public Members

operator = Assignment operator.

See Also **istream_withassign**

Member Functions

ostream_withassign::ostream_withassign

ostream_withassign(streambuf* *psb* **);**

ostream_withassign();

Parameter

psb A pointer to an existing object of a **streambuf**-derived class.

Remarks

The first constructor makes a ready-to-use object of type **ostream_withassign**, with an attached **streambuf** object.

The second constructor makes an object but does not initialize it. You must subsequently use the **streambuf** assignment operator to attach the **streambuf** object, or use the **ostream** assignment operator to initialize this object to match the specified object.

See Also **ostream_withassign::operator =**

ostream_withassign::~ostream_withassign

~ostream_withassign();

Remarks

Destructor for the **ostream_withassign** class.

Operators

ostream_withassign::operator =

ostream& operator =(const ostream&_os);

ostream& operator =(streambuf* ***_sp*** **);**

Remarks

The first overloaded assignment operator assigns the specified **ostream** object to this **ostream_withassign** object.

The second operator attaches a **streambuf** object to an existing **ostream_withassign** object, and initializes the state of the **ostream_withassign** object. This operator is often used in conjunction with the **void**-argument constructor.

Example

```
filebuf fb( "test.dat" ); // Filebuf object attached to "test.dat"
cout = &fb;          // fb associated with cout
cout << "testing"; // Message goes to "test.dat" instead of stdout
```

See Also **ostream_withassign::ostream_withassign**, **cout**

class ostrstream

#include <strstrea.h>

The **ostrstream** class supports output streams that have character arrays as a destination. You can allocate a character array prior to construction, or the constructor can internally allocate an expandable array. You can then use all the **ostream** operators and functions to fill the array.

Be aware that there is a put pointer working behind the scenes in the attached **strstreambuf** class. This pointer advances as you insert fields into the stream's array. The only way you can make it go backward is to use the **ostream::seekp** function. If the put pointer reaches the end of user-allocated memory (and sets the **ios::eof** flag), you must call **clear** before **seekp**.

Construction/Destruction — Public Members

ostrstream Constructs an **ostrstream** object.

~ostrstream Destroys an **ostrstream** object.

Other Functions — Public Members

pcount Returns the number of bytes that have been stored in the stream's buffer.

rdbuf Returns a pointer to the stream's associated **strstreambuf** object.

str Returns a character array pointer to the string stream's contents and freezes the array.

See Also **strstreambuf**, **streambuf**, **strstream**, **istrstream**

Member Functions

ostrstream::ostrstream

ostrstream();

ostrstream(char* *pch*, **int** *nLength*, **int** *nMode* **= ios::out);**

Parameters

pch A character array that is large enough to accommodate future output stream activity.

nLength The size (in characters) of *pch*. If 0, then *pch* is assumed to point to a null-terminated array and **strlen(** *pch* **)** is used as the length; if less than 0, the array is assumed to have infinite length.

nMode The stream-creation mode, which must be one of the following enumerators as defined in class **ios**:

- **ios::out** Default; storing begins at *pch*.
- **ios::ate** The *pch* parameter is assumed to be a null-terminated array; storing begins at the **NULL** character.
- **ios::app** Same as **ios::ate**.

Remarks

The first constructor makes an **ostrstream** object that uses an internal, dynamic buffer.

The second constructor makes an **ostrstream** object out of the first *nLength* characters of the *pch* buffer. The stream will not accept characters once the length reaches *nLength*.

ostrstream::~ostrstream

~ostrstream();

Remarks

Destroys an **ostrstream** object and its associated **strstreambuf** object, thus releasing all internally allocated memory. If you used the **void**-argument constructor, the internally allocated character buffer is released; otherwise, you must release it.

An internally allocated character buffer will not be released if it was previously frozen by an **str** or **strstreambuf::freeze** function call.

See Also **ostrstream::str**, **strstreambuf::freeze**

ostrstream::pcount

int pcount() const;

Return Value

Returns the number of bytes stored in the buffer. This information is especially useful when you have stored binary data in the object.

ostrstream::rdbuf

strstreambuf* rdbuf() const;

Return Value

Returns a pointer to the **strstreambuf** buffer object that is associated with this stream. This is not the character buffer; the **strstreambuf** object contains a pointer to the character area.

See Also **ostrstream::str**

---

ostrstream::str

char* str();

Return Value

Returns a pointer to the internal character array. If the stream was built with the **void**-argument constructor, **str** freezes the array. You must not send characters to a frozen stream, and you are responsible for deleting the array. You can, however, subsequently unfreeze the array by calling **rdbuf->freeze(0)**.

If the stream was built with the constructor that specified the buffer, the pointer contains the same address as the array used to construct the **ostrstream** object.

See Also **ostrstream::ostrstream**, **ostrstream::rdbuf**, **strstreambuf::freeze**

class stdiobuf

#include <stdiostr.h>

The run-time library supports three conceptual sets of I/O functions: iostreams (C++ only), standard I/O (the functions declared in STDIO.H), and low-level I/O (the functions declared in IO.H). The **stdiobuf** class is a derived class of **streambuf** that is specialized for buffering to and from the standard I/O system.

Because the standard I/O system does its own internal buffering, the extra buffering level provided by **stdiobuf** may reduce overall input/output efficiency. The **stdiobuf** class is useful when you need to mix iostream I/O with standard I/O (**printf** and so forth).

You can avoid use of the **stdiobuf** class if you use the **filebuf** class. You must also use the stream class's **ios::flags** member function to set the **ios::stdio** format flag value.

Construction/Destruction — Public Members

stdiobuf Constructs a **stdiobuf** object from a **FILE** pointer.

~stdiobuf Destroys a **stdiobuf** object.

Other Functions — Public Members

stdiofile Gets the file that is attached to the **stdiofile** object.

See Also **stdiostream**, **filebuf**, **strstreambuf**, **ios::flags**

Member Functions

stdiobuf::stdiobuf

stdiobuf(FILE* *fp* **);**

Parameter

fp A standard I/O file pointer (can be obtained through an **fopen** or **_fsopen** call).

Remarks

Objects of class **stdiobuf** are constructed from open standard I/O files, including **stdin**, **stdout**, and **stderr**. The object is unbuffered by default.

stdiobuf::~stdiobuf

~stdiobuf();

Remarks

Destroys a **stdiobuf** object and, in the process, flushes the put area. The destructor does not close the attached file.

---

stdiobuf::stdiofile

FILE* stdiofile();

Remarks

Returns the standard I/O file pointer associated with a **stdiobuf** object.

class stdiostream

#include <stdiostr.h>

The **stdiostream** class makes I/O calls (through the **stdiobuf** class) to the standard I/O system, which does its own internal buffering. Calls to the functions declared in STDIO.H, such as **printf**, can be mixed with **stdiostream** I/O calls.

This class is included for compatibility with earlier stream libraries. You can avoid use of the **stdiostream** class if you use the **ostream** or **istream** class with an associated **filebuf** class. You must also use the stream class's **ios::flags** member function to set the **ios::stdio** format flag value.

The use of the **stdiobuf** class may reduce efficiency because it imposes an extra level of buffering. Do not use this feature unless you need to mix iostream library calls with standard I/O calls for the same file.

Construction/Destruction — Public Members

stdiostream Constructs a **stdiostream** object that is associated with a standard I/O **FILE** pointer.

~stdiostream Destroys a **stdiostream** object (virtual).

Other Functions — Public Members

rdbuf Gets the stream's **stdiobuf** object.

See Also **stdiobuf**, **ios::flags**

Member Functions

stdiostream::rdbuf

stdiobuf* rdbuf() const;

Return Value

Returns a pointer to the **stdiobuf** buffer object that is associated with this stream. The **rdbuf** function is useful when you need to call **stdiobuf** member functions.

stdiostream::stdiostream

stdiostream(FILE* ***fp*** **);**

Parameter

fp A standard I/O file pointer (can be obtained through an **fopen** or **_fsopen** call). Could be **stdin**, **stdout**, or **stderr**.

Remarks

Objects of class **stdiostream** are constructed from open standard I/O files. An unbuffered **stdiobuf** object is automatically associated, but the standard I/O system provides its own buffering.

Example

```
stdiostream myStream( stdout );
```

---

stdiostream::~stdiostream

~stdiostream();

Remarks

This destructor destroys the **stdiobuf** object associated with this stream; however, the attached file is not closed.

class streambuf

#include <iostream.h>

All the iostream classes in the **ios** hierarchy depend on an attached **streambuf** class for the actual I/O processing. This class is an abstract class, but the iostream class library contains the following derived buffer classes for use with streams:

- **filebuf** Buffered disk file I/O.
- **strstreambuf** Stream data held entirely within an in-memory byte array.
- **stdiobuf** Disk I/O with buffering done by the underlying standard I/O system.

All **streambuf** objects, when configured for buffered processing, maintain a fixed memory buffer, called a reserve area, that can be dynamically partitioned into a get area for input, and a put area for output. These areas may or may not overlap. With the protected member functions, you can access and manipulate a get pointer for character retrieval and a put pointer for character storage. The exact behavior of the buffers and pointers depends on the implementation of the derived class.

The capabilities of the iostream classes can be extended significantly through the derivation of new **streambuf** classes. The **ios** class tree supplies the programming interface and all formatting features, but the **streambuf** class does the real work. The **ios** classes call the **streambuf** public members, including a set of virtual functions.

The **streambuf** class provides a default implementation of certain virtual member functions. The "Default Implementation" section for each such function suggests function behavior for the derived class.

Character Input Functions — Public Members

in_avail Returns the number of characters in the get area.

sgetc Returns the character at the get pointer, but does not move the pointer.

snextc Advances the get pointer, then returns the next character.

sbumpc Returns the current character, and then advances the get pointer.

stossc Moves the get pointer forward one position, but does not return a character.

sputbackc Attempts to move the get pointer back one position.

sgetn Gets a sequence of characters from the **streambuf** object's buffer.

Character Output Functions — Public Members

out_waiting Returns the number of characters in the put area.

sputc Stores a character in the put area and advances the put pointer.

sputn Stores a sequence of characters in the **streambuf** object's buffer and advances the put pointer.

Construction/Destruction — Public Members

~streambuf Virtual destructor.

Diagnostic Functions — Public Members

dbp Prints buffer statistics and pointer values.

Virtual Functions — Public Members

sync Empties the get area and the put area.

setbuf Attempts to attach a reserve area to the **streambuf** object.

seekoff Seeks to a specified offset.

seekpos Seeks to a specified position.

overflow Empties the put area.

underflow Fills the get area if necessary.

pbackfail Augments the **sputbackc** function.

Construction/Destruction — Protected Members

streambuf Constructors for use in derived classes.

Other Protected Member Functions — Protected Members

base Returns a pointer to the start of the reserve area.

ebuf Returns a pointer to the end of the reserve area.

blen Returns the size of the reserve area.

pbase Returns a pointer to the start of the put area.

pptr Returns the put pointer.

epptr Returns a pointer to the end of the put area.

eback Returns the lower bound of the get area.

gptr Returns the get pointer.

egptr Returns a pointer to the end of the get area.

setp Sets all the put area pointers.

setg Sets all the get area pointers.

pbump Increments the put pointer.

gbump Increments the get pointer.

setb Sets up the reserve area.

unbuffered Tests or sets the **streambuf** buffer state variable.

allocate Allocates a buffer, if needed, by calling **doalloc**.

doallocate Allocates a reserve area (virtual function).

See Also **streambuf::doallocate**, **streambuf::unbuffered**

Member Functions

streambuf::allocate

Protected →

int allocate();

END Protected

Return Value

Calls the virtual function **doallocate** to set up a reserve area. If a reserve area already exists or if the **streambuf** object is unbuffered, **allocate** returns 0. If the space allocation fails, **allocate** returns **EOF**.

See Also **streambuf::doallocate**, **streambuf::unbuffered**

---

streambuf::base

Protected →

char* base() const

END Protected

Return Value

Returns a pointer to the first byte of the reserve area. The reserve area consists of space between the pointers returned by **base** and **ebuf**.

See Also **streambuf::ebuf**, **streambuf::setb**, **streambuf::blen**

---

streambuf::blen

Protected →

int blen() const;

END Protected

Return Value

Returns the size, in bytes, of the reserve area.

See Also **streambuf::base**, **streambuf::ebuf**, **streambuf::setb**

streambuf::dbp

void dbp();

Remarks

Writes ASCII debugging information directly on **stdout**. Treat this function as part of the protected interface.

Example

```
STREAMBUF DEBUG INFO: this = 00E7:09DC
base()=00E7:0A0C, ebuf()=00E7:0C0C,  blen()=512
eback()=0000:0000, gptr()=0000:0000, egptr()=0000:0000
pbase()=00E7:0A0C, pptr()=00E7:0A22, epptr()=00E7:0C0C
```

---

streambuf::doallocate

Protected →

virtual int doallocate();

END Protected

Return Value

Called by **allocate** when space is needed. The **doallocate** function must allocate a reserve area, then call **setb** to attach the reserve area to the **streambuf** object. If the reserve area allocation fails, **doallocate** returns **EOF**.

Remarks

By default, this function attempts to allocate a reserve area using operator **new**.

See Also **streambuf::allocate**, **streambuf::setb**

---

streambuf::eback

Protected →

char* eback() const;

END Protected

Return Value

Returns the lower bound of the get area. Space between the **eback** and **gptr** pointers is available for putting a character back into the stream.

See Also **streambuf::sputbackc**, **streambuf::gptr**

streambuf::ebuf

Protected →

char* ebuf() const;

END Protected

Return Value

Returns a pointer to the byte after the last byte of the reserve area. The reserve area consists of space between the pointers returned by **base** and **ebuf**.

See Also **streambuf::base**, **streambuf::setb**, **streambuf::blen**

---

streambuf::egptr

Protected →

char* egptr() const;

END Protected

Return Value

Returns a pointer to the byte after the last byte of the get area.

See Also **streambuf::setg**, **streambuf::eback**, **streambuf::gptr**

---

streambuf::epptr

Protected →

char* epptr() const;

END Protected

Return Value

Returns a pointer to the byte after the last byte of the put area.

See Also **streambuf::setp**, **streambuf::pbase**, **streambuf::pptr**

---

streambuf::gbump

Protected →

void gbump(int *nCount* **);**

END Protected

Parameter

Count The number of bytes to increment the get pointer. May be positive or negative.

Remarks

Increments the get pointer. No bounds checks are made on the result.

See Also **streambuf::pbump**

---

streambuf::gptr

Protected →

char* gptr() const;

END Protected

Return Value

Returns a pointer to the next character to be fetched from the **streambuf** buffer. This pointer is known as the get pointer.

See Also **streambuf::setg**, **streambuf::eback**, **streambuf::egptr**

---

streambuf::in_avail

int in_avail() const;

Return Value

Returns the number of characters in the get area that are available for fetching. These characters are between the **gptr** and **egptr** pointers and may be fetched with a guarantee of no errors.

---

streambuf::out_waiting

int out_waiting() const;

Return Value

Returns the number of characters in the put area that have not been sent to the final output destination. These characters are between the **pbase** and **pptr** pointers.

---

streambuf::overflow

virtual int overflow(int *nCh* **= EOF) = 0;**

Return Value

EOF to indicate an error.

Parameter

nCh **EOF** or the character to output.

Remarks

The virtual **overflow** function, together with the **sync** and **underflow** functions, defines the characteristics of the **streambuf**-derived class. Each derived class might implement **overflow** differently, but the interface with the calling stream class is the same.

The **overflow** function is most frequently called by public **streambuf** functions like **sputc** and **sputn** when the put area is full, but other classes, including the stream classes, can call **overflow** anytime.

The function "consumes" the characters in the put area between the **pbase** and **pptr** pointers and then reinitializes the put area. The **overflow** function must also consume *nCh* (if *nCh* is not **EOF**), or it might choose to put that character in the new put area so that it will be consumed on the next call.

The definition of "consume" varies among derived classes. For example, the **filebuf** class writes its characters to a file, while the **strsteambuf** class keeps them in its buffer and (if the buffer is designated as dynamic) expands the buffer in response to a call to **overflow**. This expansion is achieved by freeing the old buffer and replacing it with a new, larger one. The pointers are adjusted as necessary.

Default Implementation

No default implementation. Derived classes must define this function.

See Also **streambuf::pbase**, **streambuf::pptr**, **streambuf::setp**, **streambuf::sync**, **streambuf::underflow**

---

streambuf::pbackfail

virtual int pbackfail(int *nCh* **);**

Return Value

The *nCh* parameter if successful; otherwise **EOF**.

Parameter

nCh The character used in a previous **sputbackc** call.

Remarks

This function is called by **sputbackc** if it fails, usually because the **eback** pointer equals the **gptr** pointer. The **pbackfail** function should deal with the situation, if possible, by such means as repositioning the external file pointer.

Default implementation

Returns EOF.

See Also **streambuf::sputbackc**

streambuf::pbase

Protected →

char* pbase() const;

END Protected

Return Value

Returns a pointer to the start of the put area. Characters between the **pbase** pointer and the **pptr** pointer have been stored in the buffer but not flushed to the final output destination.

See Also **streambuf::pptr**, **streambuf::setp**, **streambuf::out_waiting**

---

streambuf::pbump

Protected →

void pbump(int *nCount* **);**

END Protected

Parameter

nCount The number of bytes to increment the put pointer. May be positive or negative.

Remarks

Increments the put pointer. No bounds checks are made on the result.

See Also **streambuf::gbump**, **streambuf::setp**

---

streambuf::pptr

Protected →

char* pptr() const;

END Protected

Return Value

Returns a pointer to the first byte of the put area. This pointer is known as the put pointer and is the destination for the next character(s) sent to the **streambuf** object.

See Also **streambuf::epptr**, **streambuf::pbase**, **streambuf::setp**

streambuf::sbumpc

int sbumpc();

Return Value

Returns the current character, then advances the get pointer. Returns **EOF** if the get pointer is currently at the end of the sequence (equal to the **egptr** pointer).

See Also **streambuf::epptr**, **streambuf::gbump**

---

streambuf::seekoff

virtual streampos seekoff(streamoff *off*, **ios::seek_dir** *dir*, **int** *nMode* **= ios::in | ios::out);**

Return Value

The new position value. This is the byte offset from the start of the file (or string). If both **ios::in** and **ios::out** are specified, the function returns the output position. If the derived class does not support positioning, the function returns **EOF**.

Parameters

off The new offset value; **streamoff** is a **typedef** equivalent to **long**.

dir One of the following seek directions specified by the enumerated type **seek_dir**:

- **ios::beg** Seek from the beginning of the stream.
- **ios::cur** Seek from the current position in the stream.
- **ios::end** Seek from the end of the stream.

nMode An integer that contains a bitwise OR (|) combination of the enumerators **ios::in** and **ios::out**.

Remarks

Changes the position for the **streambuf** object. Not all derived classes of **streambuf** need to support positioning; however, the **filebuf**, **strstreambuf**, and **stdiobuf** classes do support positioning.

Classes derived from **streambuf** often support independent input and output position values. The *nMode* parameter determines which value(s) is set.

Default Implementation

Returns EOF.

See Also **streambuf::seekpos**

streambuf::seekpos

virtual streampos seekpos(streampos *pos*, **int** *nMode* = **ios::in | ios::out);**

Return Value

The new position value. If both **ios::in** and **ios::out** are specified, the function returns the output position. If the derived class does not support positioning, the function returns **EOF**.

Parameters

pos The new position value; **streampos** is a **typedef** equivalent to **long**.

nMode An integer that contains mode bits defined as **ios** enumerators that can be combined with the OR (|) operator. See **ofstream::ofstream** for a listing of the enumerators.

Remarks

Changes the position, relative to the beginning of the stream, for the **streambuf** object. Not all derived classes of **streambuf** need to support positioning; however, the **filebuf**, **strstreambuf**, and **stdiobuf** classes do support positioning.

Classes derived from **streambuf** often support independent input and output position values. The *nMode* parameter determines which value(s) is set.

Default Implementation

Calls **seekoff((streamoff)** *pos*, **ios::beg,** *nMode*). Thus, to define seeking in a derived class, it is usually necessary to redefine only **seekoff**.

See Also **streambuf::seekoff**

---

streambuf::setb

Protected →

void setb(char* *pb*, **char*** *peb*, **int** *nDelete* **= 0);**

END Protected

Parameters

pb The new value for the base pointer.

peb The new value for the **ebuf** pointer.

nDelete Flag that controls automatic deletion. If *nDelete* is not 0, the reserve area will be deleted when: (1) the base pointer is changed by another **setb** call, or (2) the **streambuf** destructor is called.

Remarks

Sets the values of the reserve area pointers. If both *pb* and *peb* are **NULL**, there is no reserve area. If *pb* is not **NULL** and *peb* is **NULL**, the reserve area has a length of 0.

See Also **streambuf::base**, **streambuf::ebuf**

streambuf::setbuf

virtual streambuf* setbuf(char* *pr*, **int** *nLength* **);**

Return Value

A **streambuf** pointer if the buffer is accepted; otherwise **NULL**.

Parameters

pr A pointer to a previously allocated reserve area of length *nLength*. A **NULL** value indicates an unbuffered stream.

nLength The length (in bytes) of the reserve area. A length of 0 indicates an unbuffered stream.

Remarks

Attaches the specified reserve area to the **streambuf** object. Derived classes may or may not use this area.

Default Implementation

Accepts the request if there is not a reserved area already.

---

streambuf::setg

Protected →

void setg(char* *peb*, **char*** *pg*, **char*** *peg* **);**

END Protected

Parameters

peb The new value for the **eback** pointer.

pg The new value for the **gptr** pointer.

peg The new value for the **egptr** pointer.

Remarks

Sets the values for the get area pointers.

See Also **streambuf::eback**, **streambuf::gptr**, **streambuf::egptr**

---

streambuf::setp

Protected →

void setp(char* *pp*, **char*** *pep* **);**

END Protected

Parameters

pp The new value for the **pbase** and **pptr** pointers.

pep The new value for the **epptr** pointer.

Remarks

Sets the values for the put area pointers.

See Also **streambuf::pptr**, **streambuf::pbase**, **streambuf::epptr**

---

streambuf::sgetc

int sgetc();

Remarks

Returns the character at the get pointer. The **sgetc** function does not move the get pointer. Returns **EOF** if there is no character available.

See Also **streambuf::sbumpc**, **streambuf::sgetn**, **streambuf::snextc**, **streambuf::stossc**

---

streambuf::sgetn

int sgetn(char* *pch*, **int** *nCount* **);**

Return Value

The number of characters fetched.

Parameters

pch A pointer to a buffer that will receive characters from the **streambuf** object.

nCount The number of characters to get.

Remarks

Gets the *nCount* characters that follow the get pointer and stores them in the area starting at *pch*. When fewer than *nCount* characters remain in the **streambuf** object, **sgetn** fetches whatever characters remain. The function repositions the get pointer to follow the fetched characters.

See Also **streambuf::sbumpc**, **streambuf::sgetc**, **streambuf::snextc**, **streambuf::stossc**

---

streambuf::snextc

int snextc();

Return Value

First tests the get pointer, then returns **EOF** if it is already at the end of the get area. Otherwise, it moves the get pointer forward one character and returns the character that follows the new position. It returns **EOF** if the pointer has been moved to the end of the get area.

See Also **streambuf::sbumpc**, **streambuf::sgetc**, **streambuf::sgetn**, **streambuf::stossc**

---

streambuf::sputbackc

int sputbackc(char *ch* **);**

Return Value

EOF on failure.

Parameter

ch The character to be put back to the **streambuf** object.

Remarks

Moves the get pointer back one character. The *ch* character must match the character just before the get pointer.

See Also **streambuf::sbumpc**, **streambuf::pbackfail**

---

streambuf::sputc

int sputc(int *nCh* **);**

Return Value

The number of characters successfully stored; **EOF** on error.

Parameter

nCh The character to store in the **streambuf** object.

Remarks

Stores a character in the put area and advances the put pointer.

This public function is available to code outside the class, including the classes derived from **ios**. A derived **streambuf** class can gain access to its buffer directly by using protected member functions.

See Also **streambuf::sputn**

streambuf::sputn

int sputn(const char* *pch*, **int** *nCount* **);**

Return Value

The number of characters stored. This number is usually *nCount* but could be less if an error occurs.

Parameters

pch A pointer to a buffer that contains data to be copied to the **streambuf** object.

nCount The number of characters in the buffer.

Remarks

Copies *nCount* characters from *pch* to the **streambuf** buffer following the put pointer. The function repositions the put pointer to follow the stored characters.

See Also **streambuf::sputc**

---

streambuf::stossc

void stossc();

Remarks

Moves the get pointer forward one character. If the pointer is already at the end of the get area, the function has no effect.

See Also **streambuf::sbumpc**, **streambuf::sgetn**, **streambuf::snextc**, **streambuf::sgetc**

---

streambuf::streambuf

Protected →

streambuf();

streambuf(char* *pr*, **int** *nLength* **);**

END Protected

Parameters

pr A pointer to a previously allocated reserve area of length *nLength*. A **NULL** value indicates an unbuffered stream.

nLength The length (in bytes) of the reserve area. A length of 0 indicates an unbuffered stream.

Remarks

The first constructor makes an uninitialized **streambuf** object. This object is not suitable for use until a **setbuf** call is made. A derived class constructor usually calls **setbuf** or uses the second constructor.

The second constructor initializes the **streambuf** object with the specified reserve area or marks it as unbuffered.

See Also **streambuf::setbuf**

---

streambuf::~streambuf

Protected →

virtual ~streambuf();

END Protected

Remarks

The **streambuf** destructor flushes the buffer if the stream is being used for output.

---

streambuf::sync

virtual int sync();

Return Value

EOF if an error occurs.

Remarks

The virtual **sync** function, with the **overflow** and **underflow** functions, defines the characteristics of the **streambuf**-derived class. Each derived class might implement **sync** differently, but the interface with the calling stream class is the same.

The **sync** function flushes the put area. It also empties the get area and, in the process, sends any unprocessed characters back to the source, if necessary.

Default Implementation

Returns 0 if the get area is empty and there are no more characters to output; otherwise, it returns **EOF**.

See Also **streambuf::overflow**

---

streambuf::unbuffered

Protected →

void unbuffered(int *nState* **);**

int unbuffered() const;

END Protected

Parameter

nState The value of the buffering state variable; 0 = buffered, nonzero = unbuffered.

Remarks

The first overloaded **unbuffered** function sets the value of the **streambuf** object's buffering state. This variable's primary purpose is to control whether the **allocate** function automatically allocates a reserve area.

The second function returns the current buffering state variable.

See Also **streambuf::allocate**, **streambuf::doallocate**

---

streambuf::underflow

mfvirtual int underflow() = 0;

Remarks

The virtual **underflow** function, with the **sync** and **overflow** functions, defines the characteristics of the **streambuf**-derived class. Each derived class might implement **underflow** differently, but the interface with the calling stream class is the same.

The **underflow** function is most frequently called by public **streambuf** functions like **sgetc** and **sgetn** when the get area is empty, but other classes, including the stream classes, can call **underflow** anytime.

The **underflow** function supplies the get area with characters from the input source. If the get area contains characters, **underflow** returns the first character. If the get area is empty, it fills the get area and returns the next character (which it leaves in the get area). If there are no more characters available, then **underflow** returns **EOF** and leaves the get area empty.

In the **strstreambuf** class, **underflow** adjusts the **egptr** pointer to access storage that was dynamically allocated by a call to **overflow**.

Default Implementation

No default implementation. Derived classes must define this function.

class strstream

#include <strstrea.h>

The **strstream** class supports I/O streams that have character arrays as a source and destination. You can allocate a character array prior to construction, or the constructor can internally allocate a dynamic array. You can then use all the input and output stream operators and functions to fill the array.

Be aware that a put pointer and a get pointer are working independently behind the scenes in the attached **strstreambuf** class. The put pointer advances as you insert fields into the stream's array, and the get pointer advances as you extract fields. The **ostream::seekp** function moves the put pointer, and the **istream::seekg** function moves the get pointer. If either pointer reaches the end of the string (and sets the **ios::eof** flag), you must call **clear** before seeking.

Construction/Destruction — Public Members

strstream Constructs a **strstream** object.

~strstream Destroys a **strstream** object.

Other Functions — Public Members

pcount Returns the number of bytes that have been stored in the stream's buffer.

rdbuf Returns a pointer to the stream's associated **strstreambuf** object.

str Returns a pointer to the string stream's character buffer and freezes it.

See Also **strstreambuf**, **streambuf**, **istrstream**, **ostrstream**

Member Functions

strstream::pcount

int pcount() const;

Return Value

Returns the number of bytes stored in the buffer. This information is especially useful when you have stored binary data in the object.

strstream::rdbuf

strstreambuf* rdbuf() const;

Return Value

Returns a pointer to the **strstreambuf** buffer object that is associated with this stream. This is not the character buffer; the **strstreambuf** object contains a pointer to the character area.

See Also **strstream::str**

---

strstream::str

char* str();

Return Value

Returns a pointer to the internal character array. If the stream was built with the **void**-argument constructor, then **str** freezes the array. You must not send characters to a frozen stream, and you are responsible for deleting the array. You can unfreeze the the stream by calling **rdbuf->freeze(0)**.

If the stream was built with the constructor that specified the buffer, the pointer contains the same address as the array used to construct the **ostrstream** object.

See Also **strstreambuf::freeze**, **strstream::rdbuf**

---

strstream::strstream

strstream();

strstream(char* *pch*, **int** *nLength*, **int** *nMode* **);**

Parameters

pch A character array that is large enough to accommodate future output stream activity.

nLength The size (in characters) of *pch*. If 0, *pch* is assumed to point to a null-terminated array; if less than 0, the array is assumed to have infinite length.

nMode The stream creation mode, which must be one of the following enumerators as defined in class **ios**:

- **ios::in** Retrieval begins at the beginning of the array.
- **ios::out** By default, storing begins at *pch*.
- **ios::ate** The *pch* parameter is assumed to be a null-terminated array; storing begins at the **NULL** character.
- **ios::app** Same as **ios::ate**.

The use of the **ios::in** and **ios::out** flags is optional for this class; both input and output are implied.

Remarks

The first constructor makes an **strstream** object that uses an internal, dynamic buffer that is initially empty.

The second constructor makes an **strstream** object out of the first *nLength* characters of the *psc* buffer. The stream will not accept characters once the length reaches *nLength*.

strstream::~strstream

~strstream();

Remarks

Destroys a **strstream** object and its associated **strstreambuf** object, thus releasing all internally allocated memory. If you used the **void**-argument constructor, the internally allocated character buffer is released; otherwise, you must release it.

An internally allocated character buffer will not be released if it was previously frozen by calling **rdbuf->freeze(0)**.

See Also **strstream::rdbuf**

class strstreambuf

#include <strstrea.h>

The **strstreambuf** class is a derived class of **streambuf** that manages an in-memory character array.

The file stream classes, **ostrstream**, **istrstream**, and **strstream**, use **strstreambuf** member functions to fetch and store characters. Some of these member functions are virtual functions defined for the **streambuf** class.

The reserve area, put area, and get area were introduced in the **streambuf** class description. For **strsteambuf** objects, the put area is the same as the get area, but the **get** pointer and the **put** pointer move independently.

Construction/Destruction — Public Members

strstreambuf Constructs a **strstreambuf** object.

~strstreambuf Destroys a strstreambuf object.

Other Functions — Public Members

freeze Freezes a stream.

str Returns a pointer to the string.

See Also **istrstream**, **ostrstream**, **filebuf**, **stdiobuf**

Member Functions

strstreambuf::freeze

void freeze(int *n* **= 1);**

Parameter

n A 0 value permits automatic deletion of the current array and its automatic growth (if it is dynamic); a nonzero value prevents deletion.

Remarks

If a **strstreambuf** object has a dynamic array, memory is usually deleted on destruction and size adjustment. The **freeze** function provides a way to prevent that automatic deletion. Once an array is frozen, no further input or output is permitted. The results of such operations are undefined.

The **freeze** function can also unfreeze a frozen buffer.

See Also **strstreambuf::str**

strstreambuf::str

char* str();

Return Value

Returns a pointer to the object's internal character array. If the **strstreambuf** object was constructed with a user-supplied buffer, that buffer address is returned. If the object has a dynamic array, **str** freezes the array. You must not send characters to a frozen **strstreambuf** object, and you are responsible for deleting the array. If a dynamic array is empty, then **str** returns **NULL**.

Use the **freeze** function with a 0 parameter to unfreeze a **strstreambuf** object.

See Also **strstreambuf::freeze**

---

strstreambuf::strstreambuf

strstreambuf();

strstreambuf(int *nBytes* **);**

strstreambuf(char* *pch*, **int** *n*, **char*** *pstart* **= 0);**

strstreambuf(unsigned char* *puch*, **int n, unsigned char*** *pustart* **= 0);**

strstreambuf(signed char* *psch*, **int** *n*, **signed char*** *psstart* **= 0);**

strstreambuf(void* (**falloc***)(long), void (****ffree***)(void*));**

Parameters

nBytes The initial length of a dynamic stream buffer.

pch, puch, psch A pointer to a character buffer that will be attached to the object. The **get** pointer is initialized to this value.

n One of the following integer parameters:

- positive *n* bytes, starting at *pch*, is used as a fixed-length stream buffer.
- 0 The *pch* parameter points to the start of a null-terminated string that constitutes the stream buffer (terminator excluded).
- negative The *pch* parameter points to a stream buffer that continues indefinitely.
- *pstart, pustart, psstart* The initial value of the **put** pointer.

falloc A memory-allocation function with the prototype **void* falloc(long)**. The default is **new**.

ffree A function that frees allocated memory with the prototype **void ffree(void*)**. The default is **delete**.

Remarks

The four **streambuf** constructors are described as follows:

Constructor	Description
strstreambuf()	Constructs an empty **strstreambuf** object with dynamic buffering. The buffer is allocated internally by the class and grows as needed, unless it is frozen.
strstreambuf(int)	Constructs an empty **strstreambuf** object with a dynamic buffer *n* bytes long to start with. The buffer is allocated internally by the class and grows as needed, unless it is frozen.
strstreambuf(char*, int, char*)	Constructs a **strstreambuf** object from already-allocated memory as specified by the arguments. There are constructor variations for both unsigned and signed character arrays.
strstreambuf(void*(*), void(*))	Constructs an empty **strstreambuf** object with dynamic buffering. The *falloc* function is called for allocation. The **long** parameter specifies the buffer length and the function returns the buffer address. If the *falloc* pointer is **NULL**, operator **new** is used. The *ffree* function frees memory allocated by *falloc*. If the *ffree* pointer is **NULL**, the operator **delete** is used.

strstreambuf::~strstreambuf

~strstreambuf();

Remarks

Destroys a **strstreambuf** object and releases internally allocated dynamic memory unless the object is frozen. The destructor does not release user-allocated memory.

Index

A

B

C

D

E

F

G

H

I

L

M

N

O

P

R

S

T

U

V

W

X

Contributors to *iostream Class Library Reference*

Richard Carlson, Index Editor
Matt LaBelle, Production
Roger Haight, Editor
Marilyn Johnstone, Writer
Seth Manheim, Writer
David Adam Edelstein, Art Director

Your One-Stop Source for Creating Custom Business Applications Using Microsoft® Office for Windows® 95

ISBN 1-55615-898-X
600 pages, one 3.5" disk
$39.95 ($53.95 Canada)

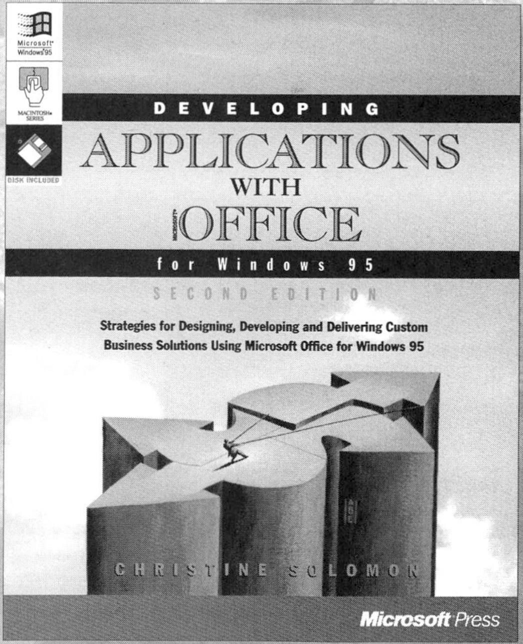

Here is all the information that corporate managers, developers, and consultants need to design, develop, and deliver custom business applications using the built-in programming languages in Microsoft Office Professional for Windows 95. Every phase of the process is explained, from choosing which tools to use, to designing a good user interface, to providing end-user support. Case studies from the author's extensive work with Fortune 500 companies, along with fully functional sample applications and sample code on disk, make this book both an interesting read and a valuable reference.

Available November 1995!

Microsoft Press® books are available wherever quality books are sold and through CompuServe's Electronic Mall—**GO MSP**.
Call **1-800-MSPRESS** for more information or to place a credit card order.*
Please refer to **BBK** when placing your order. Prices subject to change.
*In Canada, contact Macmillan Canada, Attn: Microsoft Press Dept., 164 Commander Blvd., Agincourt, Ontario, Canada M1S 3C7, or call 1-800-667-1115.
Outside the U.S. and Canada, write to International Coordinator, Microsoft Press, One Microsoft Way, Redmond, WA 98052-6399, or fax +1-206-936-7329.

Microsoft Press

Run-Time Library Reference

Microsoft® Visual C++™

Version 4.0

Development System for Windows® 95 and Windows NT™

Microsoft Corporation

PUBLISHED BY
Microsoft Press
A Division of Microsoft Corporation
One Microsoft Way
Redmond, Washington 98052-6399

Copyright © 1995 by Microsoft Corporation

All rights reserved. No part of the contents of this book may be reproduced or transmitted in any form or by any means without the written permission of the publisher.

Library of Congress Cataloging-in-Publication Data
Microsoft Visual C++ programmer's references / Microsoft Corporation.
-- 2nd ed.
p. cm.
Includes index.
v. 1. Microsoft Visual C++ user's guide -- v. 2. Programming with MFC -- v. 3. Microsoft foundation class library reference, part 1 -- v. 4. Microsoft foundation class library reference, part 2 -- v. 5. Microsoft Visual C++ run-time library reference -- v. 6. Microsoft Visual C/C++ language reference.
ISBN 1-55615-915-3 (v. 1). -- ISBN 1-55615-921-8 (v. 2). -- ISBN 1-55615-922-6 (v. 3). -- ISBN 1-55615-923-4 (v. 4). -- ISBN 1-55615-924-2 (v. 5). -- ISBN 1-55615-925-0 (v. 6)
1. C++ (Computer program language) 2. Microsoft Visual C++.
I. Microsoft Corporation.
QA76.73.C153M53 1995
005.13'3--dc20 95-35604
CIP

Printed and bound in the United States of America.

1 2 3 4 5 6 7 8 9 MLML 0 9 8 7 6 5

Distributed to the book trade in Canada by Macmillan of Canada, a division of Canada Publishing Corporation.

A CIP catalogue record for this book is available from the British Library.

Microsoft Press books are available through booksellers and distributors worldwide. For further information about international editions, contact your local Microsoft Corporation office. Or contact Microsoft Press International directly at fax (206) 936-7329.

For Run-Time Library Reference: Macintosh is a registered trademark and Power Macintosh is a trademark of Apple Computer, Inc. Intel is a registered trademark of Intel Corporation. OS/2 is a registered trademark of International Business Machines Corporation. Microsoft, MS, MS-DOS, Win32, Win32s, Windows, and XENIX are registered trademarks and Visual C++, and Windows NT are trademarks of Microsoft Corporation. MIPS is a registered trademark of MIPS Computer Systems, Inc. Motorola is a registered trademark of Motorola, Inc. Unicode is a trademark of Unicode, Incorporated. UNIX is a registered trademark in the United States and other countries, licensed exclusively through X/Open Company, Ltd.

For iostream Class Library Reference: Hewlett-Packard and LaserJet are registered trademarks of Hewlett-Packard Company. IBM is a registered trademark of International Business Machines Corporation. Microsoft, MS, MS-DOS, and Windows are registered trademarks and Visual C++, and Windows NT are trademarks of Microsoft Corporation.

Acquisitions Editor: Eric Stroo
Project Editor: Brenda L. Matteson

Contents

Appendixes

Tables

Introduction

The Microsoft® run-time library provides routines for programming for the Microsoft Windows NT™ and Windows 95™ operating systems. These routines automate many common programming tasks that are not provided by the C and C++ languages.

C Run-Time Libraries

The following table lists the release versions of the C run-time library files, along with their associated compiler options and environment variables. When a specific library compiler option is defined, that library is considered to be the default and its environment variables are automatically defined.

Library	Characteristics	Option	Defined
LIBC.LIB	Single threaded, static link	/ML	
LIBCMT.LIB	Multithreaded, static link	/MT	_MT
MSVCRT.LIB	Multithreaded, dynamic link (import library for MSVCRTx0.DLL)[1]	/MD	_MT, _DLL

[1] In place of the "x0" in the DLL name, substitute the major version numeral of Visual C++ that you are using. For example, if you are using Visual C++ version 4, then the library name would be MSVCRT40.DLL.

To build a debug version of your application, the **_DEBUG** flag must be defined and the application must be linked with a debug version of one of these libraries. For more information about the debug versions of the library files, see "C Run-Time Debug Libraries" in Chapter 4 on page 72.

Compatibility

The Microsoft run-time library supports American National Standards Institute (ANSI) C and UNIX® C. In this book, references to UNIX include XENIX®, other

UNIX-like systems, and the POSIX subsystem in Windows NT and Windows 95. The description of each run-time library routine in this book includes a compatibility section for these targets: ANSI, Windows 95 (listed as Win 95), Windows NT (Win NT), Win32s, Macintosh® (68K), and Power Macintosh™ (PMac). All run-time library routines included with this product are compatible with the Win32 API.

ANSI C Compliance

The naming convention for all Microsoft-specific identifiers in the run-time system (such as functions, macros, constants, variables, and type definitions) is ANSI-compliant. In this book, any run-time function that follows the ANSI/ISO C standards is noted as being ANSI compatible. ANSI-compliant applications should only use these ANSI compatible functions.

The names of Microsoft-specific functions and global variables begin with a single underscore. These names can be overridden only locally, within the scope of your code. For example, when you include Microsoft run-time header files, you can still locally override the Microsoft-specific function named **_open** by declaring a local variable of the same name. However, you cannot use this name for your own global function or global variable.

The names of Microsoft-specific macros and manifest constants begin with two underscores, or with a single leading underscore immediately followed by an uppercase letter. The scope of these identifiers is absolute. For example, you cannot use the Microsoft-specific identifier **_UPPER** for this reason.

Power Macintosh and 68K Macintosh

Many run-time library routines can be implemented for either or both of the Macintosh platforms. In this book, run-time routines that are compatible with Macintosh computers that use the Motorola® 68000-series processor list the 68K label in their compatibility section. Routines that are compatible with RISC-based Macintosh computers list the PMac label.

UNIX

If you plan to transport your programs to UNIX, follow these guidelines:

- Do not remove header files from the SYS subdirectory. You can place the SYS header files elsewhere only if you do not plan to transport your programs to UNIX.
- Use the UNIX-compatible path delimiter in routines that take strings representing paths and filenames as arguments. UNIX supports only the forward slash (/) for this purpose, whereas Win32 operating systems support both the backslash (\) and the forward slash (/). Thus this book uses UNIX-compatible forward slashes as

path delimiters in **#include** statements, for example. (However, the Windows NT and Windows 95 command shell, CMD.EXE, does not support the forward slash in commands entered at the command prompt.)

- Use paths and filenames that work correctly in UNIX, which is case sensitive. The file allocation table (FAT) file system in Win32 operating systems is not case sensitive; the installable Windows NT file system (NTFS) of Windows NT preserves case for directory listings but ignores case in file searches and other system operations.

Note In this version of Visual C++, UNIX compatibility information has been removed from the function descriptions.

Win32 Platforms

The C run-time libraries support all of the Win32-based platforms, including Windows 95, Windows NT, and Win32s. Although all these platforms support the Win32 Application Programming Interface (API), only Windows NT provides full Unicode support. In addition, any Win32 application can use a multibyte character set (MBCS). Win32s applications use a subset of the Win32 API, and can run on the Windows 3.1, Windows NT, and Windows 95 operating systems without being recompiled.

Backward Compatibility

The compiler views a structure that has both an old name and a new name as two different types. You cannot copy from an old structure type to a new structure type. Old prototypes that take **struct** pointers use the old **struct** names in the prototype.

For compatibility with Microsoft C professional development system version 6.0 and earlier Microsoft C versions, the library OLDNAMES.LIB maps old names to new names. For instance, **open** maps to **_open**. You must explicitly link with OLDNAMES.LIB only when you compile with the following combinations of command-line options:

- /Zl (omit default library name from object file) and /Ze (the default—use Microsoft extensions)
- /link (linker-control), /NOD (no default-library search), and /Ze

For more information about compiler command-line options, see “CL Reference” in the *Visual C++ Users Guide*.

Required and Optional Header Files

The description of each run-time routine in this book includes a list of the required and optional include, or header (.H), files for that routine. Required header files need to be included to obtain the function declaration for the routine or a definition used by another routine called internally. Optional header files are usually included to take advantage of predefined constants, type definitions, or inline macros. The following table lists some examples of optional header file contents:

Definition	Example
Macro definition	If a library routine is implemented as a macro, the macro definition may be in a header file other than the header file for the original routine. For instance, the **toupper** macro is defined in the header file CTYPE.H, while the function **toupper** is declared in STDLIB.H.
Manifest constant	Many library routines refer to constants that are defined in header files. For instance, the **_open** routine uses constants such as **_O_CREAT**, which is defined in the header file FCNTL.H.
Type definition	Some library routines return a structure or take a structure as an argument. For example, stream input/output routines use a structure of type **FILE**, which is defined in STDIO.H.

The run-time library header files provide function declarations in the ANSI/ISO C standard recommended style. The compiler performs "type checking" on any routine reference that occurs after its associated function declaration. Function declarations are especially important for routines that return a value of some type other than **int**, which is the default. Routines that do not specify their appropriate return value in their declaration will be considered by the compiler to return an **int**, which can cause unexpected results. See "Type Checking" on page xiii for more information.

Choosing Between Functions and Macros

Most Microsoft run-time library routines are compiled or assembled functions, but some routines are implemented as macros. When a header file declares both a function and a macro version of a routine, the macro definition takes precedence, because it always appears after the function declaration. When you invoke a routine that is implemented as both a function and a macro, you can force the compiler to use the function version in two ways:

- Enclose the routine name in parentheses.

```
#include <ctype.h>
a = toupper(a);    //use macro version of toupper
a = (toupper)(a);  //force compiler to use function version of toupper
```

- "Undefine" the macro definition with the **#undef** directive:

  ```
  #include <ctype.h>
  #undef toupper
  ```

If you need to choose between a function and a macro implementation of a library routine, consider the following trade-offs:

- Speed versus size. The main benefit of using macros is faster execution time. During preprocessing, a macro is expanded (replaced by its definition) inline each time it is used. A function definition occurs only once regardless of how many times it is called. Macros may increase code size but do not have the overhead associated with function calls.
- Function evaluation. A function evaluates to an address; a macro does not. Thus you cannot use a macro name in contexts requiring a pointer. For instance, you can declare a pointer to a function, but not a pointer to a macro.
- Macro side effects. A macro may treat arguments incorrectly when the macro evaluates its arguments more than once. For instance, the **toupper** macro is defined as:

  ```
  #define toupper(c) ( (islower(c)) ? _toupper(c) :  (c) )
  ```

  In the following example, the **toupper** macro produces a side effect:

  ```
  #include <ctype.h>

  int a = 'm';
  a = toupper(a++);
  ```

  The example code increments a when passing it to **toupper**. The macro evaluates the argument a++ twice, once to check case and again for the result, therefore increasing a by 2 instead of 1. As a result, the value operated on by **islower** differs from the value operated on by **toupper**.
- Type-checking. When you declare a function, the compiler can check the argument types. Because you cannot declare a macro, the compiler cannot check macro argument types, although it can check the number of arguments you pass to a macro.

Type Checking

The compiler performs limited type checking on functions that can take a variable number of arguments, as follows:

Function Call	Type-Checked Arguments
_cprintf, **_cscanf**, **printf**, **scanf**	First argument (format string)
fprintf, **fscanf**, **sprintf**, **sscanf**	First two arguments (file or buffer and format string)
_snprintf	First three arguments (file or buffer, count, and format string)
_open	First two arguments (path and **_open** flag)
_sopen	First three arguments (path, **_open** flag, and sharing mode)
_execl, **_execle**, **_execlp**, **_execlpe**	First two arguments (path and first argument pointer)
_spawnl, **_spawnle**, **_spawnlp**, **_spawnlpe**	First three arguments (mode flag, path, and first argument pointer)

The compiler performs the same limited type checking on the wide-character counterparts of these functions.

CHAPTER 1

Run-Time Routines by Category

This chapter lists and describes Microsoft run-time library routines by category. For reference convenience, some routines are listed in more than one category. Multibyte-character routines and wide-character routines are grouped with single-byte–character counterparts, where they exist.

The main categories of Microsoft run-time library routines are:

Argument access	Floating-point support
Buffer manipulation	Input and output
Byte classification	Internationalization
Character classification	Memory allocation
Data conversion	Process and environment control
Debug	Searching and sorting
Directory control	String manipulation
Error handling	System calls
Exception handling	Time management
File handling	

Argument Access

The **va_arg**, **va_end**, and **va_start** macros provide access to function arguments when the number of arguments is variable. These macros are defined in STDARG.H for ANSI C compatibility, and in VARARGS.H for compatibility with UNIX System V.

Argument-Access Macros

Macro	Use
va_arg	Retrieve argument from list
va_end	Reset pointer
va_start	Set pointer to beginning of argument list

Buffer Manipulation

Use these routines to work with areas of memory on a byte-by-byte basis.

Buffer-Manipulation Routines

Routine	Use
_memccpy	Copy characters from one buffer to another until given character or given number of characters has been copied
memchr	Return pointer to first occurrence, within specified number of characters, of given character in buffer
memcmp	Compare specified number of characters from two buffers
memcpy	Copy specified number of characters from one buffer to another
_memicmp	Compare specified number of characters from two buffers without regard to case
memmove	Copy specified number of characters from one buffer to another
memset	Use given character to initialize specified number of bytes in the buffer
_swab	Swap bytes of data and store them at specified location

When the source and target areas overlap, only **memmove** is guaranteed to copy the full source properly.

Byte Classification

Each of these routines tests a specified byte of a multibyte character for satisfaction of a condition. Except where specified otherwise, the test result depends on the multibyte code page currently in use.

Note By definition, the ASCII character set is a subset of all multibyte-character sets. For example, the Japanese katakana character set includes ASCII as well as non-ASCII characters.

The manifest constants in the following table are defined in CTYPE.H:

Multibyte-Character Byte-Classification Routines

<table>
<tr><th>Routine</th><th>Byte Test Condition</th></tr>
<tr><td>isleadbyte</td><td>Lead byte; test result depends on LC_CTYPE category setting of current locale</td></tr>
<tr><td>_ismbbalnum</td><td>isalnum || _ismbbkalnum</td></tr>
<tr><td>_ismbbalpha</td><td>isalpha || _ismbbkalnum</td></tr>
<tr><td>ismbbgraph</td><td>Same as _ismbbprint, but _ismbbgraph does not include the space character (0x20)</td></tr>
<tr><td>_ismbbkalnum</td><td>Non-ASCII text symbol other than punctuation. For example, in code page 932 only, _ismbbkalnum tests for katakana alphanumeric</td></tr>
<tr><td>_ismbbkana</td><td>Katakana (0xA1–0xDF), code page 932 only</td></tr>
<tr><td>_ismbbkprint</td><td>Non-ASCII text or non-ASCII punctuation symbol. For example, in code page 932 only, _ismbbkprint tests for katakana alphanumeric or katakana punctuation (range: 0xA1– 0xDF).</td></tr>
<tr><td>_ismbbkpunct</td><td>Non-ASCII punctuation. For example, in code page 932 only, _ismbbkpunct tests for katakana punctuation.</td></tr>
<tr><td>_ismbblead</td><td>First byte of multibyte character. For example, in code page 932 only, valid ranges are 0x81–0x9F, 0xE0–0xFC.</td></tr>
<tr><td>_ismbbprint</td><td>isprint || _ismbbkprint. ismbbprint includes the space character (0x20)</td></tr>
<tr><td>_ismbbpunct</td><td>ispunct || _ismbbkpunct</td></tr>
<tr><td>_ismbbtrail</td><td>Second byte of multibyte character. For example, in code page 932 only, valid ranges are 0x40–0x7E, 0x80–0xEC.</td></tr>
<tr><td>_ismbslead</td><td>Lead byte (in string context)</td></tr>
<tr><td>_ismbstrail</td><td>Trail byte (in string context)</td></tr>
<tr><td>_mbbtype</td><td>Return byte type based on previous byte</td></tr>
<tr><td>_mbsbtype</td><td>Return type of byte within string</td></tr>
</table>

The **MB_LEN_MAX** macro, defined in LIMITS.H, expands to the maximum length in bytes that any multibyte character can have. **MB_CUR_MAX**, defined in STDLIB.H, expands to the maximum length in bytes of any multibyte character in the current locale.

Character Classification

Each of these routines tests a specified single-byte character, wide character, or multibyte character for satisfaction of a condition. (By definition, the ASCII character set is a subset of all multibyte-character sets. For example, Japanese katakana includes ASCII as well as non-ASCII characters.) Generally these routines execute faster than tests you might write. For example, the following code executes slower than a call to **isalpha**(*c*):

```
if ((c >= 'A') && (c <= 'Z')) || ((c >= 'a') && (c <= 'z'))
    return TRUE;
```

Character-Classification Routines

Routine	Character Test Condition
isalnum, iswalnum, _ismbcalnum	Alphanumeric
isalpha, iswalpha, ismbcalpha	Alphabetic
__isascii, iswascii	ASCII
iscntrl, iswcntrl	Control
__iscsym	Letter, underscore, or digit
__iscsymf	Letter or underscore
isdigit, iswdigit, _ismbcdigit	Decimal digit
isgraph, iswgraph, _ismbcgraph	Printable other than space
islower, iswlower, _ismbclower	Lowercase
_ismbchira	Hiragana
_ismbckata	Katakana
_ismbclegal	Legal multibyte character
_ismbcl0	Japan-level 0 multibyte character
_ismbcl1	Japan-level 1 multibyte character
_ismbcl2	Japan-level 2 multibyte character
_ismbcsymbol	Non-alphanumeric multibyte character
isprint, iswprint, _ismbcprint	Printable
ispunct, iswpunct, _ismbcpunct	Punctuation
isspace, iswspace, _ismbcspace	White-space
isupper, iswupper, _ismbcupper	Uppercase
iswctype	Property specified by *desc* argument
isxdigit, iswxdigit	Hexadecimal digit
mblen	Return length of valid multibyte character; result depends on **LC_CTYPE** category setting of current locale

Data Conversion

These routines convert data from one form to another. Generally these routines execute faster than conversions you might write. Each routine that begins with a **to** prefix is implemented as a function and as a macro. See "Choosing Between Functions and Macros" on page xii for information about choosing an implementation.

Data-Conversion Routines

Routine	Use
abs	Find absolute value of integer
atof	Convert string to **float**
atoi	Convert string to **int**
atol	Convert string to **long**
_ecvt	Convert **double** to string of specified length
_fcvt	Convert **double** to string with specified number of digits following decimal point
_gcvt	Convert **double** number to string; store string in buffer
_itoa, _itow	Convert **int** to string
labs	Find absolute value of **long** integer
_ltoa, _ltow	Convert **long** to string
_mbbtombc	Convert 1-byte multibyte character to corresponding 2-byte multibyte character
_mbcjistojms	Convert Japan Industry Standard (JIS) character to Japan Microsoft (JMS) character
_mbcjmstojis	Convert JMS character to JIS character
_mbctohira	Convert multibyte character to 1-byte hiragana code
_mbctokata	Convert multibyte character to 1-byte katakana code
_mbctombb	Convert 2-byte multibyte character to corresponding 1-byte multibyte character
mbstowcs	Convert sequence of multibyte characters to corresponding sequence of wide characters
mbtowc	Convert multibyte character to corresponding wide character
strtod, wcstod	Convert string to **double**
strtol, wcstol	Convert string to **long** integer
strtoul, wcstoul	Convert string to **unsigned long** integer
strxfrm, wcsxfrm	Transform string into collated form based on locale-specific information
__toascii	Convert character to ASCII code
tolower, towlower, _mbctolower	Test character and convert to lowercase if currently uppercase
_tolower	Convert character to lowercase unconditionally
toupper, towupper, _mbctoupper	Test character and convert to uppercase if currently lowercase
_toupper	Convert character to uppercase unconditionally
_ultoa, _ultow	Convert **unsigned long** to string
wcstombs	Convert sequence of wide characters to corresponding sequence of multibyte characters

Data-Conversion Routines *(continued)*

Routine	Use
wctomb	Convert wide character to corresponding multibyte character
_wtoi	Convert wide-character string to **int**
_wtol	Convert wide-character string to **long**

Debug

With this version, Visual C++ introduces debug support for the C run-time library. The new debug version of the library supplies many diagnostic services that make debugging programs easier and allow developers to:

- Step directly into run-time functions during debugging
- Resolve assertions, errors, and exceptions
- Trace heap allocations and prevent memory leaks
- Report debug messages to the user

To use these routines, the **_DEBUG** flag must be defined. All of these routines do nothing in a retail build of an application. For more information on how to use the new debug routines, see Chapter 4, "Debug Version of the C Run-time Library."

Debug Versions of the C Run-time Library Routines

Routine	Use
_ASSERT	Evaluate an expression and generates a debug report when the result is FALSE
_ASSERTE	Similar to **_ASSERT**, but includes the failed expression in the generated report
_CrtCheckMemory	Confirm the integrity of the memory blocks allocated on the debug heap
_CrtDbgReport	Generate a debug report with a user message and send the report to three possible destinations
_CrtDoForAllClientObjects	Call an application-supplied function for all **_CLIENT_BLOCK** types on the heap
_CrtDumpMemoryLeaks	Dump all of the memory blocks on the debug heap when a significant memory leak has occurred
_CrtIsValidHeapPointer	Verify that a specified pointer is in the local heap
_CrtIsMemoryBlock	Verify that a specified memory block is located within the local heap and that it has a valid debug heap block type identifier

Debug Versions of the C Run-time Library Routines *(continued)*

Routine	Use
_CrtIsValidPointer	Verify that a specified memory range is valid for reading and writing
_CrtMemCheckpoint	Obtain the current state of the debug heap and store it in an application-supplied **_CrtMemState** structure
_CrtMemDifference	Compare two memory states for significant differences and return the results
_CrtMemDumpAllObjectsSince	Dump information about objects on the heap since a specified checkpoint was taken or from the start of program execution
_CrtMemDumpStatistics	Dump the debug header information for a specified memory state in a user-readable form
_CrtSetAllocHook	Install a client-defined allocation function by hooking it into the C run-time debug memory allocation process
_CrtSetBreakAlloc	Set a breakpoint on a specified object allocation order number
_CrtSetDbgFlag	Retrieve or modify the state of the **_crtDbgFlag** flag to control the allocation behavior of the debug heap manager
_CrtSetDumpClient	Install an application-defined function that is called every time a debug dump function is called to dump **_CLIENT_BLOCK** type memory blocks
_CrtSetReportFile	Identify the file or stream to be used as a destination for a specific report type by **_CrtDbgReport**
_CrtSetReportHook	Install a client-defined reporting function by hooking it into the C run-time debug reporting process
_CrtSetReportMode	Specify the general destination(s) for a specific report type generated by **_CrtDbgReport**
_RPT[0,1,2,3,4]	Track the application's progress by generating a debug report by calling **_CrtDbgReport** with a format string and a variable number of arguments. Provides no source file and line number information.
_RPTF[0,1,2,3,4]	Similar to the **_RPT*n*** macros, but provides the source file name and line number where the report request originated
_calloc_dbg	Allocate a specified number of memory blocks on the heap with additional space for a debugging header and overwrite buffers
_expand_dbg	Resize a specified block of memory on the heap by expanding or contracting the block
_free_dbg	Free a block of memory on the heap

Debug Versions of the C Run-time Library Routines *(continued)*

Routine	Use
_malloc_dbg	Allocate a block of memory on the heap with additional space for a debugging header and overwrite buffers
_msize_dbg	Calculate the size of a block of memory on the heap
_realloc_dbg	Reallocate a specified block of memory on the heap by moving and/or resizing the block

The debug routines can be used to step through the source code for most of the other C run-time routines during the debugging process. However, Microsoft considers some technology to be proprietary and, therefore, does not provide the source code for these routines. Most of these routines belong to either the exception handling or floating-point processing groups, but a few others are included as well. The following table lists these routines.

C Run-time Routines that are Not Available in Source Code Form

acos	**_fpclass**	**_nextafter**
asin	**_fpieee_flt**	**pow**
atan, atan2	**_fpreset**	**printf, wprintf**[1]
_cabs	**frexp**	**_scalb**
ceil	**_hypot**	**scanf, wscanf**[1]
_chgsign	**_isnan**	**setjmp**
_clear87, _clearfp	**_j0**	**sin**
_control87, _controlfp	**_j1**	**sinh**
_copysign	**_jn**	**sqrt**
cos	**ldexp**	**_status87, _statusfp**
cosh	**log**	**tan**
exp	**log10**	**tanh**
fabs	**_logb**	**_y0**
_finite	**longjmp**	**_y1**
floor	**_matherr**	**_yn**
fmod	**modf**	

1 Although source code is available for most of this routine, it makes an internal call to another routine for which source code is not provided.

Some C run-time functions and C++ operators behave differently when called from a debug build of an application. (Note that a debug build of an application can be achieved by either defining the **_DEBUG** flag or by linking with a debug version of the C run-time library.) The behavioral differences usually consist of extra features or information provided by the routine to support the debugging process. The following table lists these routines.

Routines that Behave Differently in a Debug Build of an Application

C **abort** routine	C++ **delete** operator
C **assert** routine	C++ **new** operator

For more information about using the debug versions of the C++ operators in the preceding table, see "Using the Debug Heap from C++" on page 86 in Chapter 4.

Directory Control

These routines access, modify, and obtain information about the directory structure.

Directory-Control Routines

Routine	Use
_chdir, _wchdir	Change current working directory
_chdrive	Change current drive
_getcwd, _wgetcwd	Get current working directory for default drive
_getdcwd, _wgetdcwd	Get current working directory for specified drive
_getdrive	Get current (default) drive
_mkdir, _wmkdir	Make new directory
_rmdir, _wrmdir	Remove directory
_searchenv, _wsearchenv	Search for given file on specified paths

Error Handling

Use these routines to handle program errors.

Error-Handling Routines

Routine	Use
assert macro	Test for programming logic errors; available in both the release and debug versions of the run-time library
_ASSERT, _ASSERTE macros	Similar to **assert**, but only available in the debug versions of the run-time library
clearerr	Reset error indicator. Calling **rewind** or closing a stream also resets the error indicator.
_eof	Check for end of file in low-level I/O
feof	Test for end of file. End of file is also indicated when **_read** returns 0.

Error-Handling Routines *(continued)*

Routine	Use
ferror	Test for stream I/O errors
_RPT, _RPTF macros	Generate a report similar to **printf**, but only available in the debug versions of the run-time library

Exception Handling

Use the C++ exception-handling functions to recover from unexpected events during program execution.

Exception-Handling Functions

Function	Use
_set_se_translator	Handle Win32 exceptions (C structured exceptions) as C++ typed exceptions
set_terminate	Install your own termination routine to be called by **terminate**
set_unexpected	Install your own termination function to be called by **unexpected**
terminate	Called automatically under certain circumstances after exception is thrown. **terminate** calls **abort** or a function you specify using **set_terminate**
unexpected	Calls **terminate** or a function you specify using **set_unexpected**. **unexpected** is not used in current Microsoft C++ exception-handling implementation

File Handling

Use these routines to create, delete, and manipulate files and to set and check file-access permissions.

The C run-time libraries have a preset limit for the number of files that can be open at any one time. The limit for applications that link with the single-thread static library (LIBC.LIB) is 64 file handles or 20 file streams. Applications that link with either the static or dynamic multithread library (LIBCMT.LIB or MSVCRT.LIB and MSVCRT1X.DLL), have a limit of 256 file handles or 40 file streams. Attempting to open more than the maximum number of file handles or file streams causes program failure.

The following routines operate on files designated by a file handle:

File-Handling Routines (File Handle)

Routine	Use
_chsize	Change file size
_filelength	Get file length
_fstat, _fstati64	Get file-status information on handle
_isatty	Check for character device
_locking	Lock areas of file
_setmode	Set file-translation mode

The following routines operate on files specified by a path or filename:

File-Handling Routines (Path or Filename)

Routine	Use
_access, _waccess	Check file-permission setting
_chmod, _wchmod	Change file-permission setting
_fullpath, _wfullpath	Expand a relative path to its absolute path name
_get_osfhandle	Return operating-system file handle associated with existing stream **FILE** pointer
_makepath, _wmakepath	Merge path components into single, full path
_mktemp, _wmktemp	Create unique filename
_open_osfhandle	Associate C run-time file handle with existing operating-system file handle
remove, _wremove	Delete file
rename, _wrename	Rename file
_splitpath, _wsplitpath	Parse path into components
_stat, _stati64, _wstat, _wstati64	Get file-status information on named file
_umask	Set default permission mask for new files created by program
_unlink, _wunlink	Delete file

Floating-Point Support

Many Microsoft run-time library functions require floating-point support from a math coprocessor or from the floating-point libraries that accompany the compiler. Floating-point support functions are loaded only if required.

When you use a floating-point type specifier in the format string of a call to a function in the **printf** or **scanf** family, you must specify a floating-point value or a pointer to a floating-point value in the argument list to tell the compiler that floating-point support is required. The math functions in the Microsoft run-time library handle exceptions in the same way as the UNIX V math functions.

The Microsoft run-time library sets the default internal precision of the math coprocessor (or emulator) to 64 bits. This default applies only to the internal precision at which all intermediate calculations are performed; it does not apply to the size of arguments, return values, or variables. You can override this default and set the chip (or emulator) back to 80-bit precision by linking your program with LIB/FP10.OBJ. On the linker command line, FP10.OBJ must appear before LIBC.LIB, LIBCMT.LIB, or MSVCRT.LIB.

Floating-Point Functions

Routine	Use
abs	Return absolute value of **int**
acos	Calculate arccosine
asin	Calculate arcsine
atan, atan2	Calculate arctangent
atof	Convert character string to double-precision floating-point value
Bessel functions	Calculate Bessel functions **_j0**, **_j1**, **_jn**, **_y0**, **_y1**, **_yn**
_cabs	Find absolute value of complex number
ceil	Find integer ceiling
_chgsign	Reverse sign of double-precision floating-point argument
_clear87, _clearfp	Get and clear floating-point status word
_control87, _controlfp	Get old floating-point control word and set new control-word value
_copysign	Return one value with sign of another
cos	Calculate cosine
cosh	Calculate hyperbolic cosine
difftime	Compute difference between two specified time values
div	Divide one integer by another, returning quotient and remainder
_ecvt	Convert **double** to character string of specified length
exp	Calculate exponential function
fabs	Find absolute value
_fcvt	Convert **double** to string with specified number of digits following decimal point
_finite	Determine whether given double-precision floating-point value is finite
floor	Find largest integer less than or equal to argument
fmod	Find floating-point remainder

Floating-Point Functions *(continued)*

Routine	Use
_fpclass	Return status word containing information on floating-point class
_fpieee_flt	Invoke user-defined trap handler for IEEE floating-point exceptions
_fpreset	Reinitialize floating-point math package
frexp	Calculate exponential value
_gcvt	Convert floating-point value to character string
_hypot	Calculate hypotenuse of right triangle
_isnan	Check given double-precision floating-point value for not a number (NaN)
labs	Return absolute value of **long**
ldexp	Calculate product of argument and 2 to specified power
ldiv	Divide one **long** integer by another, returning quotient and remainder
log	Calculate natural logarithm
log10	Calculate base-10 logarithm
_logb	Extract exponential value of double-precision floating-point argument
_lrotl, _lrotr	Shift **unsigned long int** left (**_lrotl**) or right (**_lrotr**)
_matherr	Handle math errors
__max	Return larger of two values
__min	Return smaller of two values
modf	Split argument into integer and fractional parts
_nextafter	Return next representable neighbor
pow	Calculate value raised to a power
printf, wprintf	Write data to **stdout** according to specified format
rand	Get pseudorandom number
_rotl, _rotr	Shift **unsigned int** left (**_rotl**) or right (**_rotr**)
_scalb	Scale argument by power of 2
scanf, wscanf	Read data from **stdin** according to specified format and write data to specified location
sin	Calculate sine
sinh	Calculate hyperbolic sine
sqrt	Find square root
srand	Initialize pseudorandom series
_status87, _statusfp	Get floating-point status word

Floating-Point Functions *(continued)*

Routine	Use
strtod	Convert character string to double-precision value
tan	Calculate tangent
tanh	Calculate hyperbolic tangent

Long Double

Previous 16-bit versions of Microsoft C/C++ and Microsoft Visual C++ supported the **long double**, 80-bit precision data type. In Win32 programming, however, the **long double** data type maps to the **double**, 64-bit precision data type. The Microsoft run-time library provides **long double** versions of the math functions only for backward compatibility. The **long double** function prototypes are identical to the prototypes for their **double** counterparts, except that the **long double** data type replaces the **double** data type. The **long double** versions of these functions should not be used in new code.

Double Functions and Their Long Double Counterparts

Function	Long Double Counterpart	Function	Long Double Counterpart
acos	**acosl**	**frexp**	**frexpl**
asin	**asinl**	**_hypot**	**_hypotl**
atan	**atanl**	**ldexp**	**ldexpl**
atan2	**atan2l**	**log**	**logl**
atof	**_atold**	**log10**	**log10l**
Bessel functions **j0, j1, jn**	Bessel functions **j0l, j1l, jnl**	**_matherr**	**_matherrl**
Bessel functions **y0, y1, yn**	Bessel functions **y0l, y1l, ynl**	**modf**	**modfl**
_cabs	**_cabsl**	**pow**	**powl**
ceil	**ceill**	**sin**	**sinl**
cos	**cosl**	**sinh**	**sinhl**
cosh	**coshl**	**sqrt**	**sqrtl**
exp	**expl**	**strtod**	**_strtold**
fabs	**fabsl**	**tan**	**tanl**
floor	**floorl**	**tanh**	**tanhl**
fmod	**fmodl**		

Input and Output

The I/O functions read and write data to and from files and devices. File I/O operations take place in text mode or binary mode. The Microsoft run-time library has three types of I/O functions:

- Stream I/O functions treat data as a stream of individual characters.
- Low-level I/O functions invoke the operating system directly for lower-level operation than that provided by stream I/O.
- Console and port I/O functions read or write directly to a console (keyboard and screen) or an I/O port (such as a printer port).

Warning Because stream functions are buffered and low-level functions are not, these two types of functions are generally incompatible. For processing a particular file, use either stream or low-level functions exclusively.

Text and Binary Mode File I/O

File I/O operations take place in one of two translation modes, text or binary, depending on the mode in which the file is open. Data files are usually processed in text mode. To control the file translation mode, you can:

- Retain the current default setting and specify the alternative mode only when you open selected files.
- Change the default translation mode directly by setting the global variable **_fmode** in your program. The initial default setting of **_fmode** is **_O_TEXT**, for text mode. For more information about **_fmode**, see page 44.

When you call a file-open function such as **_open**, **fopen**, **freopen**, or **_fsopen**, you can override the current default setting of **_fmode** by specifying the appropriate argument to the function. The **stdin**, **stdout**, and **stderr** streams are always opened in text mode by default; you can also override this default when opening any of these files. Use **_setmode** to change the translation mode using the file handle after the file is open.

Unicode™ Stream I/O in Text and Binary Modes

When a Unicode stream I/O routine (such as **fwprintf**, **fwscanf**, **fgetwc**, **fputwc**, **fgetws**, or **fputws**) operates on a file that is open in text mode (the default), two kinds of character conversions take place:

- Unicode-to-MBCS or MBCS-to-Unicode conversion. When a Unicode stream-I/O function operates in text mode, the source or destination stream is assumed to be a sequence of multibyte characters. Therefore, the Unicode stream-input functions convert multibyte characters to wide characters (as if by a call to the **mbtowc** function). For the same reason, the Unicode stream-output functions convert wide characters to multibyte characters (as if by a call to the **wctomb** function).
- Carriage return–linefeed (CR-LF) translation. This translation occurs before the MBCS–Unicode conversion (for Unicode stream input functions) and after the Unicode–MBCS conversion (for Unicode stream output functions). During input, each carriage return–linefeed combination is translated into a single linefeed character. During output, each linefeed character is translated into a carriage return–linefeed combination.

However, when a Unicode stream-I/O function operates in binary mode, the file is assumed to be Unicode, and no CR-LF translation or character conversion occurs during input or output.

Stream I/O

These functions process data in different sizes and formats, from single characters to large data structures. They also provide buffering, which can improve performance. The default size of a stream buffer is 4K. These routines affect only buffers created by the run-time library routines, and have no effect on buffers created by the operating system.

Stream I/O Routines

Routine	Use
clearerr	Clear error indicator for stream
fclose	Close stream
_fcloseall	Close all open streams except **stdin**, **stdout**, and **stderr**
_fdopen, wfdopen	Associate stream with handle to open file
feof	Test for end of file on stream
ferror	Test for error on stream
fflush	Flush stream to buffer or storage device
fgetc, fgetwc	Read character from stream (function versions of **getc** and **getwc**)
_fgetchar, _fgetwchar	Read character from **stdin** (function versions of **getchar** and **getwchar**)
fgetpos	Get position indicator of stream
fgets, fgetws	Read string from stream
_fileno	Get file handle associated with stream
_flushall	Flush all streams to buffer or storage device

Stream I/O Routines *(continued)*

Routine	Use
fopen, _wfopen	Open stream
fprintf, fwprintf	Write formatted data to stream
fputc, fputwc	Write a character to a stream (function versions of **putc** and **putwc**)
_fputchar, _fputwchar	Write character to **stdout** (function versions of **putchar** and **putwchar**)
fputs, fputws	Write string to stream
fread	Read unformatted data from stream
freopen, _wfreopen	Reassign **FILE** stream pointer to new file or device
fscanf, fwscanf	Read formatted data from stream
fseek	Move file position to given location
fsetpos	Set position indicator of stream
_fsopen, _wfsopen	Open stream with file sharing
ftell	Get current file position
fwrite	Write unformatted data items to stream
getc, getwc	Read character from stream (macro versions of **fgetc** and **fgetwc**)
getchar, getwchar	Read character from **stdin** (macro versions of **fgetchar** and **fgetwchar**)
gets, getws	Read line from **stdin**
_getw	Read binary **int** from stream
printf, wprintf	Write formatted data to **stdout**
putc, putwc	Write character to a stream (macro versions of **fputc** and **fputwc**)
putchar, putwchar	Write character to **stdout** (macro versions of **fputchar** and **fputwchar**)
puts, _putws	Write line to stream
_putw	Write binary **int** to stream
rewind	Move file position to beginning of stream
_rmtmp	Remove temporary files created by **tmpfile**
scanf, wscanf	Read formatted data from **stdin**
setbuf	Control stream buffering
setvbuf	Control stream buffering and buffer size
_snprintf, _snwprintf	Write formatted data of specified length to string
sprintf, swprintf	Write formatted data to string

Stream I/O Routines *(continued)*

Routine	Use
sscanf, swscanf	Read formatted data from string
_tempnam, _wtempnam	Generate temporary filename in given directory
tmpfile	Create temporary file
tmpnam, _wtmpnam	Generate temporary filename
ungetc, ungetwc	Push character back onto stream
vfprintf, vfwprintf	Write formatted data to stream
vprintf, vwprintf	Write formatted data to **stdout**
_vsnprintf, _vsnwprintf	Write formatted data of specified length to buffer
vsprintf, vswprintf	Write formatted data to buffer

When a program begins execution, the startup code automatically opens several streams: standard input (pointed to by **stdin**), standard output (pointed to by **stdout**), and standard error (pointed to by **stderr**). These streams are directed to the console (keyboard and screen) by default. Use **freopen** to redirect **stdin**, **stdout**, or **stderr** to a disk file or a device.

Files opened using the stream routines are buffered by default. **stdout** and **stderr** are flushed whenever they are full or, if you are writing to a character device, after each library call. If a program terminates abnormally, output buffers may not be flushed, resulting in loss of data. Use **fflush** or **_flushall** to ensure that the buffer associated with a specified file or all open buffers are flushed to the operating system, which can cache data before writing it to disk. The commit-to-disk feature ensures that the flushed buffer contents are not lost in the event of a system failure.

There are two ways to commit buffer contents to disk:

- Link with the file COMMODE.OBJ to set a global commit flag. The default setting of the global flag is **n**, for "no-commit."
- Set the mode flag to **c** with **fopen** or **_fdopen**.

Any file specifically opened with either the **c** or the **n** flag behaves according to the flag, regardless of the state of the global commit/no-commit flag.

If your program does not explicitly close a stream, the stream is automatically closed when the program terminates. However, you should close a stream when your program finishes with it, as the number of streams that can be open at one time is limited.

Input can follow output directly only with an intervening call to **fflush** or to a file-positioning function (**fseek**, **fsetpos**, or **rewind**). Output can follow input without an intervening call to a file-positioning function if the input operation encounters the end of the file.

Low-level I/O

These functions invoke the operating system directly for lower-level operation than that provided by stream I/O. Low-level input and output calls do not buffer or format data.

Low-level routines can access the standard streams opened at program startup using the following predefined handles:

Stream	Handle
stdin	0
stdout	1
stderr	2

Low-level I/O routines set the **errno** global variable when an error occurs. (For more information, see "**_doserrno, errno, _sys_errlist,** and **_sysnerr**" on page 41.) You must include STDIO.H when you use low-level functions only if your program requires a constant that is defined in STDIO.H, such as the end-of-file indicator (**EOF**).

Low-Level I/O Functions

Function	Use
_close	Close file
_commit	Flush file to disk
_creat, _wcreat	Create file
_dup	Return next available file handle for given file
_dup2	Create second handle for given file
_eof	Test for end of file
_lseek, _lseeki64	Reposition file pointer to given location
_open, _wopen	Open file
_read	Read data from file
_sopen, _wsopen	Open file for file sharing
_tell, _telli64	Get current file-pointer position
_umask	Set file-permission mask
_write	Write data to file

_dup and **_dup2** are typically used to associate the predefined file handles with different files.

Console and Port I/O

These routines read and write on your console or on the specified port. The console I/O routines are not compatible with stream I/O or low-level I/O library routines. The console or port does not have to be opened or closed before I/O is performed, so there are no open or close routines in this category. In Windows NT and Windows 95, the output from these functions is always directed to the console and cannot be redirected.

Console and Port I/O Routines

Routine	Use
_cgets	Read string from console
_cprintf	Write formatted data to console
_cputs	Write string to console
_cscanf	Read formatted data from console
_getch	Read character from console
_getche	Read character from console and echo it
_inp	Read one byte from specified I/O port
_inpd	Read double word from specified I/O port
_inpw	Read 2-byte word from specified I/O port
_kbhit	Check for keystroke at console; use before attempting to read from console
_outp	Write one byte to specified I/O port
_outpd	Write double word to specified I/O port
_outpw	Write word to specified I/O port
_putch	Write character to console
_ungetch	"Unget" last character read from console so it becomes next character read

Internationalization

The Microsoft run-time library provides many routines that are useful for creating different versions of a program for international markets. This includes locale-related routines, wide-character routines, multibyte-character routines, and generic-text routines. For convenience, most locale-related routines are also categorized in this reference according to the operations they perform. In this chapter and in this book's alphabetic reference, multibyte-character routines and wide-character routines are described with single-byte–character counterparts, where they exist.

Locale

Use the **setlocale** function to change or query some or all of the current program locale information. "Locale" refers to the locality (the country and language) for which you can customize certain aspects of your program. Some locale-dependent categories include the formatting of dates and the display format for monetary values.

Locale-Dependent Routines

Routine	Use	setlocale Category Setting Dependence
atof, atoi, atol	Convert character to floating-point, integer, or long integer value, respectively	**LC_NUMERIC**
is Routines	Test given integer for particular condition.	**LC_CTYPE**
isleadbyte	Test for lead byte ()	**LC_CTYPE**
localeconv	Read appropriate values for formatting numeric quantities	**LC_MONETARY, LC_NUMERIC**
MB_CUR_MAX	Maximum length in bytes of any multibyte character in current locale (macro defined in STDLIB.H)	**LC_CTYPE**
_mbccpy	Copy one multibyte character	**LC_CTYPE**
_mbclen	Return length, in bytes, of given multibyte character	**LC_CTYPE**
mblen	Validate and return number of bytes in multibyte character	**LC_CTYPE**
_mbstrlen	For multibyte-character strings: validate each character in string; return string length	**LC_CTYPE**
mbstowcs	Convert sequence of multibyte characters to corresponding sequence of wide characters	**LC_CTYPE**
mbtowc	Convert multibyte character to corresponding wide character	**LC_CTYPE**
printf family	Write formatted output	**LC_NUMERIC** (determines radix character output)
scanf family	Read formatted input	**LC_NUMERIC** (determines radix character recognition)
setlocale, _wsetlocale	Select locale for program	Not applicable
strcoll, wcscoll	Compare characters of two strings	**LC_COLLATE**

Locale-Dependent Routines *(continued)*

Routine	Use	setlocale Category Setting Dependence
_stricoll, _wcsicoll	Compare characters of two strings (case insensitive)	**LC_COLLATE**
_strncoll, _wcsncoll	Compare first *n* characters of two strings	**LC_COLLATE**
_strnicoll, _wcsnicoll	Compare first *n* characters of two strings (case insensitive)	**LC_COLLATE**
strftime, wcsftime	Format date and time value according to supplied *format* argument	**LC_TIME**
_strlwr	Convert, in place, each uppercase letter in given string to lowercase	**LC_CTYPE**
strtod, wcstod, strtol, wcstol, strtoul, wcstoul	Convert character string to double, long, or unsigned long value	**LC_NUMERIC** (determines radix character recognition)
_strupr	Convert, in place, each lowercase letter in string to uppercase	**LC_CTYPE**
strxfrm, wcsxfrm	Transform string into collated form according to locale	**LC_COLLATE**
tolower, towlower	Convert given character to corresponding lowercase character	**LC_CTYPE**
toupper, towupper	Convert given character to corresponding uppercase letter	**LC_CTYPE**
wcstombs	Convert sequence of wide characters to corresponding sequence of multibyte characters	**LC_CTYPE**
wctomb	Convert wide character to corresponding multibyte character	**LC_CTYPE**
_wtoi, _wtol	Convert wide-character string to **int** or **long**	**LC_NUMERIC**

Code Pages

A *code page* is a character set, which can include numbers, punctuation marks, and other glyphs. Different languages and locales may use different code pages. For example, ANSI code page 1252 is used for American English and most European languages; OEM code page 932 is used for Japanese Kanji.

A code page can be represented in a table as a mapping of characters to single-byte values or multibyte values. Many code pages share the ASCII character set for characters in the range 0x00–0x7F.

The Microsoft run-time library uses the following types of code pages:

- System-default ANSI code page. By default, at startup the run-time system automatically sets the multibyte code page to the system-default ANSI code page, which is obtained from the operating system. The call

  ```
  setlocale ( LC_ALL, "" );
  ```

  also sets the locale to the system-default ANSI code page.

- Locale code page. The behavior of a number of run-time routines is dependent on the current locale setting, which includes the locale code page. (For more information, see "Locale-Dependent Routines" on page 21.) By default, all locale-dependent routines in the Microsoft run-time library use the code page that corresponds to the "C" locale. At run-time you can change or query the locale code page in use with a call to **setlocale**.
- Multibyte code page. The behavior of most of the multibyte-character routines in the run-time library depends on the current multibyte code page setting. By default, these routines use the system-default ANSI code page. At run-time you can query and change the multibyte code page with **_getmbcp** and **_setmbcp**, respectively.
- The "C" locale is defined by ANSI to correspond to the locale in which C programs have traditionally executed. The code page for the "C" locale ("C" code page) corresponds to the ASCII character set. For example, in the "C" locale, **islower** returns true for the values 0x61–0x7A only. In another locale, **islower** may return true for these as well as other values, as defined by that locale.

Interpretation of Multibyte-Character Sequences

Most multibyte-character routines in the Microsoft run-time library recognize multibyte-character sequences according to the current multibyte code page setting. The following multibyte-character routines depend instead on the locale code page (specifically, on the **LC_CTYPE** category setting of the current locale):

Locale-Dependent Multibyte Routines

Routine	Use
mblen	Validate and return number of bytes in multibyte character
_mbstrlen	For multibyte-character strings: validate each character in string; return string length
mbstowcs	Convert sequence of multibyte characters to corresponding sequence of wide characters
mbtowc	Convert multibyte character to corresponding wide character
wcstombs	Convert sequence of wide characters to corresponding sequence of multibyte characters
wctomb	Convert wide character to corresponding multibyte character

Single-byte and Multibyte Character Sets

The ASCII character set defines characters in the range 0x00–0x7F. There are a number of other character sets, primarily European, that define the characters within the range 0x00–0x7F identically to the ASCII character set and also define an extended character set from 0x80–0xFF. Thus an 8-bit, single-byte–character set (SBCS) is sufficient to represent the ASCII character set as well as the character sets for many European languages. However, some non-European character sets, such as Japanese Kanji, include many more characters than can be represented in a single-byte coding scheme, and therefore require multibyte-character set (MBCS) encoding.

Note Many SBCS routines in the Microsoft run-time library handle multibyte bytes, characters, and strings as appropriate. Many multibyte-character sets define the ASCII character set as a subset. In many multibyte character sets, each character in the range 0x00–0x7F is identical to the character that has the same value in the ASCII character set. For example, in both ASCII and MBCS character strings, the one-byte **NULL** character ('\0') has value 0x00 and indicates the terminating null character.

A multibyte character set may consist of both one-byte and two-byte characters. Thus a multibyte-character string may contain a mixture of single-byte and double-byte characters. A two-byte multibyte character has a lead byte and a trail byte. In a particular multibyte-character set, the lead bytes fall within a certain range, as do the trail bytes. When these ranges overlap, it may be necessary to evaluate the context to determine whether a given byte is functioning as a lead byte or a trail byte.

SBCS and MBCS Data Types

Any Microsoft MBCS run-time library routine that handles only one multibyte character or one byte of a multibyte character expects an unsigned **int** argument (where 0x00 <= character value <= 0xFFFF and 0x00 <= byte value <= 0xFF). An MBCS routine that handles multibyte bytes or characters in a string context expects a multibyte-character string to be represented as an unsigned **char** pointer.

Caution Each byte of a multibyte character can be represented in an 8-bit **char**. However, an SBCS or MBCS single-byte character of type **char** with a value greater than 0x7F is negative. When such a character is converted directly to an **int** or a **long**, the result is sign-extended by the compiler and can therefore yield unexpected results.

Therefore it is best to represent a byte of a multibyte character as an 8-bit **unsigned char**. Or, to avoid a negative result, simply convert a single-byte character of type **char** to an **unsigned char** before converting it to an **int** or a **long**.

Because some SBCS string-handling functions take (signed) **char*** parameters, a type mismatch compiler warning will result when **_MBCS** is defined. There are three ways to avoid this warning, listed in order of efficiency:

1. Use the "type-safe" inline function thunks in TCHAR.H. This is the default behavior.
2. Use the "direct" macros in TCHAR.H by defining **_MB_MAP_DIRECT** on the command line. If you do this, you must manually match types. This is the fastest method, but is not type-safe.
3. Use the "type-safe" statically linked library function thunks in TCHAR.H. To do so, define the constant **_NO_INLINING** on the command line. This is the slowest method, but the most type-safe.

Unicode: The Wide-Character Set

A wide character is a 2-byte multilingual character code. Any character in use in modern computing worldwide, including technical symbols and special publishing characters, can be represented according to the Unicode specification as a wide character. Developed and maintained by a large consortium that includes Microsoft, the Unicode standard is now widely accepted. Because every wide character is always represented in a fixed size of 16 bits, using wide characters simplifies programming with international character sets.

A wide character is of type **wchar_t**. A wide-character string is represented as a **wchar_t[]** array and is pointed to by a **wchar_t*** pointer. You can represent any ASCII character as a wide character by prefixing the letter L to the character. For example, L'\0' is the terminating wide (16-bit) **NULL** character. Similarly, you can represent any ASCII string literal as a wide-character string literal simply by prefixing the letter L to the ASCII literal (L"Hello").

Generally, wide characters take up more space in memory than multibyte characters but are faster to process. In addition, only one locale can be represented at a time in multibyte encoding, whereas all character sets in the world are represented simultaneously by the Unicode representation.

Using Generic-Text Mappings

Microsoft Specific →

To simplify code development for various international markets, the Microsoft run-time library provides Microsoft-specific "generic-text" mappings for many data types, routines, and other objects. These mappings are defined in TCHAR.H. You can use these name mappings to write generic code that can be compiled for any of the three kinds of character sets: ASCII (SBCS), MBCS, or Unicode, depending on a manifest constant you define using a **#define** statement. Generic-text mappings are Microsoft extensions that are not ANSI compatible.

Preprocessor Directives for Generic-Text Mappings

#define	Compiled Version	Example
_UNICODE	Unicode (wide-character)	**_tcsrev** maps to **_wcsrev**
_MBCS	Multibyte-character	**_tcsrev** maps to **_mbsrev**
None (the default: neither **_UNICODE** nor **_MBCS** defined)	SBCS (ASCII)	**_tcsrev** maps to **strrev**

For example, the generic-text function **_tcsrev**, defined in TCHAR.H, maps to **mbsrev** if **MBCS** has been defined in your program, or to **_wcsrev** if **_UNICODE** has been defined. Otherwise **_tcsrev** maps to **strrev**.

The generic-text data type **_TCHAR**, also defined in TCHAR.H, maps to type **char** if **_MBCS** is defined, to type **wchar_t** if **_UNICODE** is defined, and to type **char** if neither constant is defined. Other data type mappings are provided in TCHAR.H for programming convenience, but **_TCHAR** is the type that is most useful.

Generic-Text Data Type Mappings

Generic-Text Data Type Name	SBCS (_UNICODE, _MBCS Not Defined)	_MBCS Defined	_UNICODE Defined
_TCHAR	**char**	**char**	**wchar_t**
_TINT	**int**	**int**	**wint_t**
_TSCHAR	**signed char**	**signed char**	**wchar_t**
_TUCHAR	**unsigned char**	**unsigned char**	**wchar_t**
_TXCHAR	**char**	**unsigned char**	**wchar_t**
_T or **_TEXT**	No effect (removed by preprocessor)	No effect (removed by preprocessor)	**L** (converts following character or string to its Unicode counterpart)

For a complete list of generic-text mappings of routines, variables, and other objects, see Appendix B, "Generic-Text Mappings."

The following code fragments illustrate the use of **_TCHAR** and **_tcsrev** for mapping to the MBCS, Unicode, and SBCS models.

```
_TCHAR *RetVal, *szString;
RetVal = _tcsrev(szString);
```

If **MBCS** has been defined, the preprocessor maps the preceding fragment to the following code:

```
char *RetVal, *szString;
RetVal = _mbsrev(szString);
```

If **_UNICODE** has been defined, the preprocessor maps the same fragment to the following code:

```
wchar_t *RetVal, *szString;
RetVal = _wcsrev(szString);
```

If neither **_MBCS** nor **_UNICODE** has been defined, the preprocessor maps the fragment to single-byte ASCII code, as follows:

```
char *RetVal, *szString;
RetVal = strrev(szString);
```

Thus you can write, maintain, and compile a single source code file to run with routines that are specific to any of the three kinds of character sets.

A Sample Generic-Text Program

The following program, GENTEXT.C, provides a more detailed illustration of the use of generic-text mappings defined in TCHAR.H:

```
/*
 * GENTEXT.C: use of generic-text mappings defined in TCHAR.H
 *            Generic-Text-Mapping example program
 */

#include <stdio.h>
#include <stdlib.h>
#include <string.h>
#include <direct.h>
#include <errno.h>
#include <tchar.h>

int __cdecl _tmain(int argc, _TCHAR **argv, _TCHAR **envp)
{
    _TCHAR buff[_MAX_PATH];
    _TCHAR *str = _T("Astring");
    char *amsg = "Reversed";
    wchar_t *wmsg = L"Is";

#ifdef _UNICODE
    printf("Unicode version\n");
#else /* _UNICODE */
#ifdef _MBCS
    printf("MBCS version\n");
#else
    printf("SBCS version\n");
#endif
#endif /* _UNICODE */

    if (_tgetcwd(buff, _MAX_PATH) == NULL)
        printf("Can't Get Current Directory - errno=%d\n", errno);
```

```
    else
        _tprintf(_T("Current Directory is '%s'\n"), buff);
    _tprintf(_T("'%s' %hs %ls:\n"), str, amsg, wmsg);
    _tprintf(_T("'%s'\n"), _tcsrev(str));
    return 0;
}
```

If **_MBCS** has been defined, GENTEXT.C maps to the following MBCS program:

```
/*
 * MBCSGTXT.C: use of generic-text mappings defined in TCHAR.H
 *             Generic-Text-Mapping example program
 *             MBCS version of GENTEXT.C
 */

int __cdecl main(int argc, char **argv, char **envp)
{
    char buff[_MAX_PATH];
    char *str = "Astring";
    char *amsg = "Reversed";
    wchar_t *wmsg = L"Is";

    printf("MBCS version\n");
    if (_getcwd(buff, _MAX_PATH) == NULL)
        printf("Can't Get Current Directory - errno=%d\n", errno);
    else
        printf("Current Directory is '%s'\n", buff);
    printf("'%s' %hs %ls:\n", str, amsg, wmsg);
    printf("'%s'\n", _mbsrev(str));
    return 0;
}
```

If **_UNICODE** has been defined, GENTEXT.C maps to the following Unicode version of the program. For more information about using **wmain** in Unicode programs as a replacement for **main**, see "Using wmain" in *C Language Reference*.

```
/*
 * UNICGTXT.C: use of generic-text mappings defined in TCHAR.H
 *             Generic-Text-Mapping example program
 *             Unicode version of GENTEXT.C
 */

int __cdecl wmain(int argc, wchar_t **argv, wchar_t **envp)
{
    wchar_t buff[_MAX_PATH];
    wchar_t *str = L"Astring";
    char *amsg = "Reversed";
    wchar_t *wmsg = L"Is";

    printf("Unicode version\n");
    if (_wgetcwd(buff, _MAX_PATH) == NULL)
        printf("Can't Get Current Directory - errno=%d\n", errno);
```

```
    else
        wprintf(L"Current Directory is '%s'\n", buff);
    wprintf(L"'%s' %hs %ls:\n", str, amsg, wmsg);
    wprintf(L"'%s'\n", wcsrev(str));
    return 0;
}
```

If neither **_MBCS** nor **_UNICODE** has been defined, GENTEXT.C maps to single-byte ASCII code, as follows:

```
/*
 * SBCSGTXT.C: use of generic-text mappings defined in TCHAR.H
 *             Generic-Text-Mapping example program
 *             Single-byte (SBCS) Ascii version of GENTEXT.C
 */

int __cdecl main(int argc, char **argv, char **envp)
{
    char buff[_MAX_PATH];
    char *str = "Astring";
    char *amsg = "Reversed";
    wchar_t *wmsg = L"Is";

    printf("SBCS version\n");
    if (_getcwd(buff, _MAX_PATH) == NULL)
        printf("Can't Get Current Directory - errno=%d\n", errno);
    else
        printf("Current Directory is '%s'\n", buff);
    printf("'%s' %hs %ls:\n", str, amsg, wmsg);
    printf("'%s'\n", strrev(str));
    return 0;
}
```

Using TCHAR.H Data Types with _MBCS

As the table of generic-text routine mappings indicates (see Appendix B, "Generic-Text Mappings"), when the manifest constant **_MBCS** is defined, a given generic-text routine maps to one of the following kinds of routines:

- An SBCS routine that handles multibyte bytes, characters, and strings appropriately. In this case, the string arguments are expected to be of type **char***. For example, **_tprintf** maps to **printf**; the string arguments to **printf** are of type **char***. If you use the **_TCHAR** generic-text data type for your string types, the formal and actual parameter types for **printf** match because **_TCHAR*** maps to **char***.
- An MBCS-specific routine. In this case, the string arguments are expected to be of type **unsigned char***. For example, **_tcsrev** maps to **_mbsrev**, which expects and returns a string of type **unsigned char***. Again, if you use the **_TCHAR** generic-

text data type for your string types, there is a potential type conflict because **_TCHAR** maps to type **char**.

Following are three solutions for preventing this type conflict (and the C compiler warnings or C++ compiler errors that would result):

- Use the default behavior. TCHAR.H provides generic-text routine prototypes for routines in the run-time libraries, as in the following example.

  ```
  char *_tcsrev(char *);
  ```

  In the default case, the prototype for **_tcsrev** maps to **_mbsrev** through a thunk in LIBC.LIB. This changes the types of the **_mbsrev** incoming parameters and outgoing return value from **_TCHAR *** (i.e., **char ***) to **unsigned char ***. This method ensures type matching when you are using **_TCHAR**, but it is relatively slow because of the function call overhead.

- Use function inlining by incorporating the following preprocessor statement in your code.

  ```
  #define _USE_INLINING
  ```

  This method causes an inline function thunk, provided in TCHAR.H, to map the generic-text routine directly to the appropriate MBCS routine. The following code excerpt from TCHAR.H provides an example of how this is done.

  ```
  __inline char *_tcsrev(char *_s1)
  {return (char *)_mbsrev((unsigned char *)_s1);}
  ```

  If you can use inlining, this is the best solution, because it guarantees type matching and has no additional time cost.

- Use "direct mapping" by incorporating the following preprocessor statement in your code.

  ```
  #define _MB_MAP_DIRECT
  ```

  This approach provides a fast alternative if you do not want to use the default behavior or cannot use inlining. It causes the generic-text routine to be mapped by a macro directly to the MBCS version of the routine, as in the following example from TCHAR.H.

  ```
  #define _tcschr _mbschr
  ```

When you take this approach, you must be careful to ensure that appropriate data types are used for string arguments and string return values. You can use type casting to ensure proper type matching or you can use the **_TXCHAR** generic-text data type. **_TXCHAR** maps to type **char** in SBCS code but maps to type **unsigned char** in MBCS code. For more information about generic-text macros, see Appendix B, "Generic-Text Mappings."

END Microsoft Specific

Memory Allocation

Use these routines to allocate, free, and reallocate memory.

Memory-Allocation Routines

Routine	Use
_alloca	Allocate memory from stack
calloc	Allocate storage for array, initializing every byte in allocated block to 0
_calloc_dbg	Debug version of **calloc**; only available in the debug versions of the run-time libraries
_expand	Expand or shrink block of memory without moving it
_expand_dbg	Debug version of **_expand**; only available in the debug versions of the run-time libraries
free	Free allocated block
_free_dbg	Debug version of **free**; only available in the debug versions of the run-time libraries
_heapadd	Add memory to heap
_heapchk	Check heap for consistency
_heapmin	Release unused memory in heap
_heapset	Fill free heap entries with specified value
_heapwalk	Return information about each entry in heap
malloc	Allocate block of memory from heap
_malloc_dbg	Debug version of **malloc**; only available in the debug versions of the run-time libraries
_msize	Return size of allocated block
_msize_dbg	Debug version of **_msize**; only available in the debug versions of the run-time libraries
_query_new_handler	Return address of current new handler routine as set by **_set_new_handler**
_query_new_mode	Return integer indicating new handler mode set by **_set_new_mode** for **malloc**
realloc	Reallocate block to new size
_realloc_dbg	Debug version of **realloc**; only available in the debug versions of the run-time libraries
_set_new_handler	Enable error-handling mechanism when **new** operator fails (to allocate memory) and enable compilation of Standard Template Libraries (STL)
_set_new_mode	Set new handler mode for **malloc**

Process and Environment Control

Use the process-control routines to start, stop, and manage processes from within a program. Use the environment-control routines to get and change information about the operating-system environment.

Process and Environment Control Functions

Routine	Use
abort	Abort process without flushing buffers or calling functions registered by **atexit** and **_onexit**
assert	Test for logic error
_ASSERT, **_ASSERTE** macros	Similar to **assert**, but only available in the debug versions of the run-time libraries
atexit	Schedule routines for execution at program termination
_beginthread, **_beginthreadex**	Create a new thread on a Windows NT or Windows 95 process
_cexit	Perform **exit** termination procedures (such as flushing buffers), then return control to calling program without terminating process
_c_exit	Perform **_exit** termination procedures, then return control to calling program without terminating process
_cwait	Wait until another process terminates
_endthread, **_endthreadex**	Terminate a Windows NT or Windows 95 thread
_execl, **_wexecl**	Execute new process with argument list
_execle, **_wexecle**	Execute new process with argument list and given environment
_execlp, **_wexeclp**	Execute new process using **PATH** variable and argument list
_execlpe, **_wexeclpe**	Execute new process using **PATH** variable, given environment, and argument list
_execv, **_wexecv**	Execute new process with argument array
_execve, **_wexecve**	Execute new process with argument array and given environment
_execvp, **_wexecvp**	Execute new process using **PATH** variable and argument array
_execvpe, **_wexecvpe**	Execute new process using **PATH** variable, given environment, and argument array
exit	Call functions registered by **atexit** and **_onexit**, flush all buffers and close all open files, and terminate process
_exit	Terminate process immediately without calling **atexit** or **_onexit** or flushing buffers
getenv, **_wgetenv**	Get value of environment variable
_getpid	Get process ID number
longjmp	Restore saved stack environment; use it to execute a nonlocal **goto**

Process and Environment Control Functions *(continued)*

Routine	Use
_onexit	Schedule routines for execution at program termination; use for compatibility with Microsoft C/C++ version 7.0 and earlier
_pclose	Wait for new command processor and close stream on associated pipe
perror, _wperror	Print error message
_pipe	Create pipe for reading and writing
_popen, _wpopen	Create pipe and execute command
_putenv, _wputenv	Add or change value of environment variable
raise	Send signal to calling process
setjmp	Save stack environment; use to execute nonlocal **goto**
signal	Handle interrupt signal
_spawnl, _wspawnl	Create and execute new process with specified argument list
_spawnle, _wspawnle	Create and execute new process with specified argument list and environment
_spawnlp, _wspawnlp	Create and execute new process using **PATH** variable and specified argument list
_spawnlpe, _wspawnlpe	Create and execute new process using **PATH** variable, specified environment, and argument list
_spawnv, _wspawnv	Create and execute new process with specified argument array
_spawnve, _wspawnve	Create and execute new process with specified environment and argument array
_spawnvp, _wspawnvp	Create and execute new process using **PATH** variable and specified argument array
_spawnvpe, _wspawnvpe	Create and execute new process using **PATH** variable, specified environment, and argument array
system, _wsystem	Execute operating-system command

In Windows NT and Windows 95, the spawned process is equivalent to the spawning process. Therefore, the OS/2® **wait** function, which allows a parent process to wait for its children to terminate, is not available. Instead, any process can use **_cwait** to wait for any other process for which the process ID is known.

The difference between the **_exec** and **_spawn** families is that a **_spawn** function can return control from the new process to the calling process. In a **_spawn** function, both the calling process and the new process are present in memory unless **_P_OVERLAY** is specified. In an **_exec** function, the new process overlays the calling process, so control cannot return to the calling process unless an error occurs in the attempt to start execution of the new process.

The differences among the functions in the **_exec** family, as well as among those in the **_spawn** family, involve the method of locating the file to be executed as the new process, the form in which arguments are passed to the new process, and the method of setting the environment, as shown in the following table. Use a function that passes an argument list when the number of arguments is constant or is known at compile time. Use a function that passes a pointer to an array containing the arguments when the number of arguments is to be determined at run time. The information in the following table also applies to the wide-character counterparts of the **_spawn** and **_exec** functions.

_spawn and _exec Function Families

Functions	Use PATH Variable to Locate File	Argument-Passing Convention	Environment Settings
_execl, **_spawnl**	No	List	Inherited from calling process
_execle, **_spawnle**	No	List	Pointer to environment table for new process passed as last argument
_execlp, **_spawnlp**	Yes	List	Inherited from calling process
_execlpe, **_spawnlpe**	Yes	List	Pointer to environment table for new process passed as last argument
_execv, **_spawnv**	No	Array	Inherited from calling process
_execve, **_spawnve**	No	Array	Pointer to environment table for new process passed as last argument
_execvp, **_spawnvp**	Yes	Array	Inherited from calling process
_execvpe, **_spawnvpe**	Yes	Array	Pointer to environment table for new process passed as last argument

Searching and Sorting

Use the following functions for searching and sorting:

Searching and Sorting Functions

Function	Search or Sort
bsearch	Binary search
_lfind	Linear search for given value
_lsearch	Linear search for given value, which is added to array if not found
qsort	Quick sort

String Manipulation

These routines operate on null-terminated single-byte character, wide-character, and multibyte-character strings. Use the buffer-manipulation routines, described in Buffer Manipulation, to work with character arrays that do not end with a null character.

String-Manipulation Routines

Routine	Use
_mbscoll, **_mbsicoll**, **_mbsncoll**, **_mbsnicoll**	Compare two multibyte-character strings using multibyte code page information (**_mbsicoll** and **_mbsnicoll** are case-insensitive)
_mbsdec, _strdec, _wcsdec	Move string pointer back one character
_mbsinc, _strinc, _wcsinc	Advance string pointer by one character
_mbslen	Get number of multibyte characters in multibyte-character string; dependent upon OEM code page
_mbsnbcat	Append, at most, first *n* bytes of one multibyte-character string to another
_mbsnbcmp	Compare first *n* bytes of two multibyte-character strings
_mbsnbcnt	Return number of multibyte-character bytes within supplied character count
_mbsnbcpy	Copy *n* bytes of string
_mbsnbicmp	Compare *n* bytes of two multibyte-character strings, ignoring case
_mbsnbset	Set first *n* bytes of multibyte-character string to specified character
_mbsnccnt	Return number of multibyte characters within supplied byte count
_mbsnextc, _strnextc, _wcsnextc	Find next character in string
_mbsninc. _strninc, _wcsninc	Advance string pointer by *n* characters
_mbsspnp, _strspnp, _wcsspnp	Return pointer to first character in given string not in another given string
_mbstrlen	Get number of multibyte characters in multibyte-character string; locale-dependent
strcat, wcscat, _mbscat	Append one string to another
strchr, wcschr, _mbschr	Find first occurrence of specified character in string
strcmp, wcscmp, _mbscmp	Compare two strings
strcoll, wcscoll, **_stricoll, _wcsicoll**, **_strncoll, _wcsncoll**, **_strnicoll, _wcsnicoll**	Compare two strings using current locale code page information (**_stricoll**, **_wcsicoll**, **_strnicoll**, and **_wcsnicoll** are case-insensitive)
strcpy, wcscpy, _mbscpy	Copy one string to another

String-Manipulation Routines *(continued)*

Routine	Use
strcspn, wcscspn, _mbscspn,	Find first occurrence of character from specified character set in string
_strdup, _wcsdup, _mbsdup	Duplicate string
strerror	Map error number to message string
_strerror	Map user-defined error message to string
strftime, wcsftime	Format date-and-time string
_stricmp, _wcsicmp, _mbsicmp	Compare two strings without regard to case
strlen, wcslen, _mbslen, _mbstrlen	Find length of string
_strlwr, _wcslwr, _mbslwr	Convert string to lowercase
strncat, wcsncat, _mbsncat	Append characters of string
strncmp, wcsncmp, _mbsncmp	Compare characters of two strings
strncpy, wcsncpy, _mbsncpy	Copy characters of one string to another
_strnicmp, _wcsnicmp, _mbsnicmp	Compare characters of two strings without regard to case
_strnset, _wcsnset, _mbsnset	Set first *n* characters of string to specified character
strpbrk, wcspbrk, _mbspbrk	Find first occurrence of character from one string in another string
strrchr, wcsrchr,_mbsrchr	Find last occurrence of given character in string
_strrev, _wcsrev,_mbsrev	Reverse string
_strset, _wcsset, _mbsset	Set all characters of string to specified character
strspn, wcsspn, _mbsspn	Find first substring from one string in another string
strstr, wcsstr, _mbsstr	Find first occurrence of specified string in another string
strtok, wcstok, _mbstok	Find next token in string
_strupr, _wcsupr, _mbsupr	Convert string to uppercase
strxfrm, wcsxfrm	Transform string into collated form based on locale-specific information

System Calls

The following functions are Windows NT and Windows 95 operating-system calls:

System Call Functions

Function	Use
_findclose	Release resources from previous find operations
_findfirst, _findfirsti64, _wfindfirst, _wfindfirsti64	Find file with specified attributes
_findnext, _findnexti64, _wfindnext, _wfindnexti64	Find next file with specified attributes

Time Management

Use these functions to get the current time and convert, adjust, and store it as necessary. The current time is the system time.

The **_ftime** and **localtime** routines use the **TZ** environment variable. If **TZ** is not set, the run-time library attempts to use the time-zone information specified by the operating system. If this information is unavailable, these functions use the default value of PST8PDT. For more information on **TZ**, see "**_tzset**;" also see "_daylight, timezone, and _tzname" on page 40.

Time Routines

Function	Use
asctime, _wasctime	Convert time from type **struct tm** to character string
clock	Return elapsed CPU time for process
ctime, _wctime	Convert time from type **time_t** to character string
difftime	Compute difference between two times
_ftime	Store current system time in variable of type **struct _timeb**
_futime	Set modification time on open file
gmtime	Convert time from type **time_t** to **struct tm**
localtime	Convert time from type **time_t** to **struct tm** with local correction
mktime	Convert time to calendar value
_strdate, _wstrdate	Return current system date as string
strftime, wcsftime	Format date-and-time string for international use

Time Routines *(continued)*

Function	Use
_strtime, _wstrtime	Return current system time as string
time	Get current system time as type **time_t**
_tzset	Set external time variables from environment time variable **TZ**
_utime, _wutime	Set modification time for specified file using either current time or time value stored in structure

Note In all versions of Microsoft C/C++ except Microsoft C/C++ version 7.0, and in all versions of Microsoft Visual C++, the **time** function returns the current time as the number of seconds elapsed since midnight on January 1, 1970. In Microsoft C/C++ version 7.0, **time** returned the current time as the number of seconds elapsed since midnight on December 31, 1899.

CHAPTER 2

Global Variables and Standard Types

The Microsoft run-time library contains definitions for global variables, control flags, and standard types used by library routines. Access these variables, flags, and types by declaring them in your program or by including the appropriate header files.

Global Variables

The Microsoft run-time library provides the following global variables.

Variable	Description
_amblksiz	Controls memory heap granularity
daylight, _timezone, _tzname	Adjust for local time; used in some date and time functions
_doserrno, errno, _sys_errlist, _sys_nerr	Store error codes and related information
_environ, _wenviron	Pointers to arrays of pointers to strings that constitute process environment
_fileinfo	Specifies whether information regarding open files of a process is passed to new processes
_fmode	Sets default file-translation mode
_osver, _winmajor, _winminor, _winver	Store build and version numbers of operating system
_pgmptr, _wpgmptr	Initialized at program startup to value such as program name, filename, relative path, or full path

_amblksiz

_amblksiz controls memory heap granularity. It is declared in MALLOC.H as

extern unsigned int _amblksiz;

The value of **_amblksiz** specifies the size of blocks allocated by the operating system for the heap. The initial requested size for a segment of heap memory is just enough to satisfy the current allocation request (for example, a call to **malloc**) plus memory required for heap manager overhead. The value of **_amblksiz** should represent a trade-off between the number of times the operating system is to be called to increase the heap to required size and the amount of memory potentially wasted (available but not used) at the end of the heap.

The default value of **_amblksiz** is 8K. You can change this value by direct assignment in your program. For example:

```
_amblksiz = 2045;
```

If you assign a value to **_amblksiz,** the actual value used internally by the heap manager is the assigned value rounded up to the nearest whole power of 2. Thus, in the previous example, the heap manager would reset the value of **_amblksize** to 2048.

_daylight, _timezone, and _tzname

_daylight, **_timezone**, and **_tzname** are used in some time and date routines to make local-time adjustments. They are declared in TIME.H as

extern int _daylight;
extern long _timezone;
extern char *_tzname[2];

On a call to **_ftime**, **localtime**, or **_tzset**, the values of **_daylight**, **_timezone**, and **_tzname** are determined from the value of the **TZ** environment variable. If you do not explicitly set the value of **TZ**, **_tzname[0]** and **_tzname[1]** contain empty strings, but the time-manipulation functions (**_tzset**, **_ftime**, and **localtime**) attempt to set the values of **_daylight** and **_timezone** using the time-zone information specified in the Windows NT or Windows 95 Control Panel Date/Time application. If the time-zone information cannot be obtained from the operating system, the time-management functions use the default value PST8PDT. The time-zone global variable values are as follows.

Variable	Value
_daylight	Nonzero if daylight-saving-time zone (DST) is specified in **TZ**; otherwise, 0. Default value is 1.
_timezone	Difference in seconds between coordinated universal time and local time. Default value is 28,800.
_tzname[0]	Three-letter time-zone name derived from **TZ** environment variable.
_tzname[1]	Three-letter DST zone name derived from **TZ** environment variable. Default value is PDT (Pacific daylight time). If DST zone is omitted from **TZ**, **_tzname[1]** is empty string.

_doserrno, errno, _sys_errlist, and _sys_nerr

These global variables hold error codes used by the **perror** and **strerror** functions for printing error messages. Manifest constants for these variables are declared in STDLIB.H as follows:

extern int _doserrno;
extern int errno;
extern char *_sys_errlist[ ];
extern int _sys_nerr;

errno is set on an error in a system-level call. Because **errno** holds the value for the last call that set it, this value may be changed by succeeding calls. Always check **errno** immediately before and after a call that may set it. All **errno** values, defined as manifest constants in ERRNO.H, are UNIX-compatible. The values valid for 32-bit Windows applications are a subset of these UNIX values.

On an error, **errno** is not necessarily set to the same value as the error code returned by a system call. For I/O operations only, use **_doserrno** to access the operating-system error-code equivalents of **errno** codes. For other operations the value of **_doserrno** is undefined.

Each **errno** value is associated with an error message that can be printed using **perror** or stored in a string using **strerror**. **perror** and **strerror** use the **_sys_errlist** array and **_sys_nerr**, the number of elements in **_sys_errlist**, to process error information.

Library math routines set **errno** by calling **_matherr**. To handle math errors differently, write your own routine according to the **_matherr** reference description and name it **_matherr**.

The following **errno** values are compatible with 32-bit Windows applications. Only **ERANGE** and **EDOM** are specified in the ANSI standard.

Constant	System Error Message	Value
E2BIG	Argument list too long	7
EACCES	Permission denied	13
EAGAIN	No more processes or not enough memory or maximum nesting level reached	11
EBADF	Bad file number	9
ECHILD	No spawned processes	10
EDEADLOCK	Resource deadlock would occur	36
EDOM	Math argument	33
EEXIST	File exists	17
EINVAL	Invalid argument	22

Constant	System Error Message	Value
EMFILE	Too many open files	24
ENOENT	No such file or directory	2
ENOEXEC	Exec format error	8
ENOMEM	Not enough memory	12
ENOSPC	No space left on device	28
ERANGE	Result too large	34
EXDEV	Cross-device link	18

_environ, _wenviron

The **_environ** variable is a pointer to an array of pointers to the multibyte-character strings that constitute the process environment. **_environ** is declared in STDLIB.H as

extern char **_environ;

In a program that uses the **main** function, **_environ** is initialized at program startup according to settings taken from the operating-system environment. The environment consists of one or more entries of the form

ENVVARNAME=*string*

getenv and **_putenv** use the **_environ** variable to access and modify the environment table. When **_putenv** is called to add or delete environment settings, the environment table changes size. Its location in memory may also change, depending on the program's memory requirements. The value of **_environ** is automatically adjusted accordingly.

The **_wenviron** variable, declared in STDLIB.H as

extern wchar_t **_wenviron;

is a wide-character version of **_environ**. In a program that uses the **wmain** function, **_wenviron** is initialized at program startup according to settings taken from the operating-system environment.

In a program that uses **main**, **_wenviron** is initially **NULL**, because the environment is composed of multibyte-character strings. On the first call to **_wgetenv** or **_wputenv**, a corresponding wide-character string environment is created and is pointed to by **_wenviron**.

Similarly, in a program that uses **wmain**, **_environ** is initially **NULL** because the environment is composed of wide-character strings. On the first call to **_getenv** or **_putenv**, a corresponding wide-character string environment is created and is pointed to by **_environ**.

When two copies of the environment (MBCS and Unicode) exist simultaneously in a program, the run-time system must maintain both copies, resulting in slower execution time. For example, whenever you call **_putenv**, a call to **_wputenv** is also executed automatically, so that the two environment strings correspond.

Caution In rare instances, when the run-time system is maintaining both a Unicode version and a multibyte version of the environment, these two environment versions may not correspond exactly. This is because, although any unique multibyte-character string maps to a unique Unicode string, the mapping from a unique Unicode string to a multibyte-character string is not necessarily unique. Therefore, two distinct Unicode strings may map to the same multibyte string.

The following pseudocode illustrates how this can happen.

```
int i, j;
i = _wputenv( "env_var_x=string1" );  // results in the implicit call:
                                      // putenv ("env_var_z=string1")
j = _wputenv( "env_var_y=string2" );  // also results in implicit call:
                                      // putenv("env_var_z=string2")
```

In the notation used for this example, the character strings are not C string literals; rather they are placeholders that represent Unicode environment string literals in the **_wputenv** call and multibyte environment strings in the **putenv** call. The character-placeholders '*x*' and '*y*' in the two distinct Unicode enviroment strings do not map uniquely to characters in the current MBCS; instead, both map to some MBCS character '*z*' that is the default result of the attempt to convert the strings.

Thus in the multibyte environment the value of "*env_var_z*" after the first implicit call to **putenv** would be "*string1*", but this value would be overwritten on the second implicit call to **putenv**, when the value of "*env_var_z*" is set to "*string2*". The Unicode environment (in **_wenviron**) and the multibyte environment (in **_environ**) would therefore differ following this series of calls.

_fileinfo

The **_fileinfo** variable determines whether information about the open files of a process is passed to new processes by functions such as **_spawn**. **_fileinfo** is declared in STDLIB.H as

extern int _fileinfo;

- If **_fileinfo** is 0 (the default), information about open files is not passed to new processes; otherwise the information is passed. You can modify the default value of **_fileinfo** by setting the **_fileinfo** variable to a nonzero value in your program.

_fmode

The **_fmode** variable sets the default file-translation mode for text or binary translation. It is declared in STDLIB.H as

extern int _fmode;

The default setting of **_fmode** is **_O_TEXT**, for text-mode translation. **_O_BINARY** is the setting for binary mode.

You can change the value of **_fmode** in either of two ways:

- Link with BINMODE.OBJ. This changes the initial setting of **_fmode** to **_O_BINARY**, causing all files except **stdin**, **stdout**, and **stderr** to be opened in binary mode.
- Change the value of **_fmode** directly by setting it in your program.

_osver, _winmajor, _winminor, _winver

These variables store build and version numbers of the 32-bit Windows operating systems. Declarations for these variables in STDLIB.H are as follows:

extern unsigned int _osver;
extern unsigned int _winmajor;
extern unsigned int _winminor;
extern unsigned int _winver;

These variables are useful in programs that run in different versions of Windows NT or Windows 95.

Variable	Description
_osver	Current build number
_winmajor	Major version number
_winminor	Minor version number
_winver	Holds value of **_winmajor** in high byte and value of **_winminor** in low byte

_pgmptr, _wpgmptr

When a program is run from the command interpreter (CMD.EXE), **_pgmptr** is automatically initialized to the full path of the executable file. For example, if HELLO.EXE is in C:\BIN and C:\BIN is in the path, **_pgmptr** is set to C:\BIN\HELLO.EXE when you execute

```
C> hello
```

When a program is not run from the command line, **_pgmptr** may be initialized to the program name (the file's base name without the extension), or to a filename, a relative path, or a full path.

_wpgmptr is the wide-character counterpart of **_pgmptr** for use with programs that use **wmain. _pgmptr** and **_wpgmptr** are declared in STDLIB.H as

extern char *_pgmptr;
extern wchar_t *_pgmptr;

The following program demonstrates the use of **_pgmptr**.

```
/*
 * PGMPTR.C: The following program demonstrates the use of _pgmptr.
 */

#include <stdio.h>
#include <stdlib.h>
void main( void )
{
   printf("The full path of the executing program is : %Fs\n",
      _pgmptr);
}
```

Control Flags

The debug version of the Microsoft C run-time library uses the following flags to control the heap allocation and reporting process. For more information, see Chapter 4, "Debug Version of the C Run-Time Library."

Flag	Description
CRTDBG_MAP_ALLOC	Maps the base heap functions to their debug version counterparts
_DEBUG	Enables the use of the debugging versions of the run-time functions
_crtDbgFlag	Controls how the debug heap manager tracks allocations

These flags can be defined with a /D command-line option or with a **#define** directive. When the flag is defined with **#define**, the directive must appear before the header file include statement for the routine declarations.

_CRTDBG_MAP_ALLOC

When the **_CRTDBG_MAP_ALLOC** flag is defined in the debug version of an application, the base version of the heap functions are directly mapped to their debug versions. This flag is declared in CRTDBG.H. This flag is only available when the **_DEBUG** flag has been defined in the application.

For more information about using the debug version versus the base version of a heap function, see "Using the Debug Version Versus the Base Version" on page 84 in Chapter 4.

_DEBUG

When the **_DEBUG** flag is defined, the application is built with the debug version of the C run-time library. This flag is declared in CRTDBG.H.

For more information, see Chapter 4, "Debug Version of the C Run-Time Library."

_crtDbgFlag

The **_crtDbgFlag** flag consists of five bit fields that control how memory allocations on the debug version of the heap are tracked, verified, reported, and dumped. The bit fields of the flag are set using the **_CrtSetDbgFlag** function. This flag and its bit fields are declared in CRTDBG.H. This flag is only available when the **_DEBUG** flag has been defined in the application.

For more information about using this flag in conjunction with other debug functions, see "Heap State Reporting Functions" on page 83 in Chapter 4.

Standard Types

The Microsoft run-time library defines the following standard types.

Type	Description	Declared In
clock_t structure	Stores time values; used by **clock**.	TIME.H
_complex structure	Stores real and imaginary parts of complex numbers; used by **_cabs**.	MATH.H
_dev_t short or unsigned integer	Represents device handles.	SYS\TYPES.H
div_t, ldiv_t structures	Store values returned by **div** and **ldiv**, respectively.	STDLIB.H
_exception structure	Stores error information for **_matherr**.	MATH.H
FILE structure	Stores information about current state of stream; used in all stream I/O operations.	STDIO.H

Type	Description	Declared In
_finddata_t, _wfinddata_t structures	**_finddata_t** stores file-attribute information returned by **_findfirst** and **_findnext**. **_wfinddata_t** stores file-attribute information returned by **_wfindfirst** and **_wfindnext**.	**_finddata_t**: IO.H **_wfinddata_t**: IO.H, WCHAR.H
_FPIEEE_RECORD structure	Contains information pertaining to IEEE floating-point exception; passed to user-defined trap handler by **_fpieee_flt**.	FPIEEE.H
fpos_t long integer	Used by **fgetpos** and **fsetpos** to record information for uniquely specifying every position within a file.	STDIO.H
_HEAPINFO structure	Contains information about next heap entry for **_heapwalk**.	MALLOC.H
jmp_buf array	Used by **setjmp** and **longjmp** to save and restore program environment.	SETJMP.H
lconv structure	Contains formatting rules for numeric values in different countries.	LOCALE.H
_off_t long integer	Represents file-offset value.	SYS\TYPES.H
_onexit_t pointer	Returned by **_onexit**.	STDLIB.H
_PNH pointer to function	Type of argument to **_set_new_handler**.	NEW.H
ptrdiff_t integer	Result of subtraction of two pointers.	STDDEF.H
sig_atomic_t integer	Type of object that can be modified as atomic entity, even in presence of asynchronous interrupts; used with **signal**.	SIGNAL.H
size_t unsigned integer	Result of **sizeof** operator.	STDDEF.H and other include files
_stat structure	Contains file-status information returned by **_stat** and **_fstat**.	SYS\STAT.H
time_t long integer	Represents time values in **mktime** and **time**.	TIME.H
_timeb structure	Used by **_ftime** to store current system time.	SYS\TIMEB.H
tm structure	Used by **asctime**, **gmtime**, **localtime**, **mktime**, and **strftime** to store and retrieve time information.	TIME.H
_utimbuf structure	Stores file access and modification times used by **_utime** to change file-modification dates.	SYS\UTIME.H

Type	Description	Declared In
va_list structure	Used to hold information needed by **va_arg** and **va_end** macros. Called function declares variable of type **va_list** that can be passed as argument to another function.	STDARG.H
wchar_t internal type of a wide character	Useful for writing portable programs for international markets.	STDDEF.H, STDLIB.H
wctype_t integer	Can represent all characters of any national character set.	STDDEF.H, STDLIB.H
wint_t integer	Type of data object that can hold any wide character or wide end-of-file value.	WCHAR.H

CHAPTER 3

Global Constants

The Microsoft run-time library contains definitions for global constants used by library routines. To use these constants, include the appropriate header files as indicated in the description for each constant. The global constants are listed in the following table.

BUFSIZ	**__LOCAL_SIZE**
CLOCKS_PER_SEC, CLK_TCK	Locale Categories
Commit-To-Disk Constants	**_locking** Constants
Data Type Constants	Math Error Constants
EOF	**MB_CUR_MAX**
errno	**NULL**
Exception-Handling Constants	Path Field Limits
EXIT_SUCCESS, EXIT_FAILURE	**RAND_MAX**
File Attribute Constants	**setvbuf** Constants
File Constants	Sharing Constants
File Permission Constants	**signal** Constants
File Read/Write Access Constants	**signal** Action Constants
File Translation Constants	**_spawn** Constants
FILENAME_MAX	**_stat** Structure **st_mode** Field Constants
FOPEN_MAX, _SYS_OPEN	**stdin, stdout, stderr**
_FREEENTRY, _USEDENTRY	**TMP_MAX, L_tmpnam**
fseek, _lseek	Translation Mode Constants
Heap Constants	**_WAIT_CHILD, _WAIT_GRANDCHILD**
_HEAP_MAXREQ	32-bit Windows Time/Date Formats
HUGE_VAL	

BUFSIZ

#include <stdio.h>

Remarks

BUFSIZ is the required user-allocated buffer for the **setvbuf** routine.

See Also Stream I/O

CLOCKS_PER_SEC, CLK_TCK

#include <time.h>

Remarks

The time in seconds is the value returned by the **clock** function, divided by **CLOCKS_PER_SEC**. **CLK_TCK** is equivalent, but considered obsolete.

See Also **clock**

Commit-To-Disk Constants

Microsoft Specific →

#include <stdio.h>

Remarks

These Microsoft-specific constants specify whether the buffer associated with the open file is flushed to operating system buffers or to disk. The mode is included in the string specifying the type of read/write access (**"r"**, **"w"**, **"a"**, **"r+"**, **"w+"**, **"a+"**).

The commit-to-disk modes are as follows:

c Writes the unwritten contents of the specified buffer to disk. This commit-to-disk functionality only occurs at explicit calls to either the **fflush** or the **_flushall** function. This mode is useful when dealing with sensitive data. For example, if your program terminates after a call to **fflush** or **_flushall**, you can be sure that your data reached the operating system's buffers. However, unless a file is opened with the **c** option, the data might never make it to disk if the operating system also terminates.

n Writes the unwritten contents of the specified buffer to the operating system's buffers. The operating system can cache data and then determine an optimal time to write to disk. Under many conditions, this behavior makes for efficient program behavior. However, if the retention of data is critical (such as bank transactions or airline ticket information) consider using the **c** option. The **n** mode is the default.

Note The **c** and **n** options are not part of the ANSI standard for **fopen**, but are Microsoft extensions and should not be used where ANSI portability is desired.

Using the Commit-to-Disk Feature with Existing Code

By default, calls to the **fflush** or **_flushall** library functions write data to buffers maintained by the operating system; the operating system determines the optimal time to actually write the data to disk. The commit-to-disk feature of the run-time library lets you ensure that critical data is written directly to disk rather than to the operating system's buffers. You can give this capability to an existing program without rewriting it by linking its object files with COMMODE.OBJ.

In the resulting executable file, calls to **fflush** write the contents of the buffer directly to disk, and calls to **_flushall** write the contents of all buffers to disk. These two functions are the only ones affected by COMMODE.OBJ.

END Microsoft Specific

See Also Stream I/O, **_fdopen**, **fopen**

Data Type Constants

Remarks

These are implementation-dependent ranges of values allowed for integral data types. The constants listed below give the ranges for the integral data types and are defined in LIMITS.H.

Note The /J compiler option changes the default **char** type to **unsigned**.

Constant	Value	Meaning
SCHAR_MAX	127	Maximum signed **char** value
SCHAR_MIN	–128	Minimum signed **char** value
UCHAR_MAX	255 (0xff)	Maximum **unsigned char** value
CHAR_BIT	8	Number of bits in a **char**
USHRT_MAX	65535 (0xffff)	Maximum **unsigned short** value
SHRT_MAX	32767	Maximum (signed) **short** value
SHRT_MIN	–32768	Minimum (signed) **short** value
UINT_MAX	4294967295 (0xffffffff)	Maximum **unsigned int** value
ULONG_MAX	4294967295 (0xffffffff)	Maximum **unsigned long** value
INT_MAX	2147483647	Maximum (signed) **int** value
INT_MIN	–2147483647–1	Minimum (signed) **int** value

Constant	Value	Meaning
LONG_MAX	2147483647	Maximum (signed) **long** value
LONG_MIN	–2147483647–1	Minimum (signed) **long** value
CHAR_MAX	127 (255 if /J option used)	Maximum **char** value
CHAR_MIN	–128 (0 if /J option used)	Minimum **char** value
MB_LEN_MAX	2	Maximum number of bytes in multibyte **char**

The following constants give the range and other characteristics of the **double** and **float** data types, and are defined in FLOAT.H:

Constant	Value	Description
DBL_DIG	15	# of decimal digits of precision
DBL_EPSILON	2.2204460492503131e-016	Smallest such that 1.0+**DBL_EPSILON** !=1.0
DBL_MANT_DIG	53	# of bits in mantissa
DBL_MAX	1.7976931348623158e+308	Maximum value
DBL_MAX_10_EXP	308	Maximum decimal exponent
DBL_MAX_EXP	1024	Maximum binary exponent
DBL_MIN	2.2250738585072014e-308	Minimum positive value
DBL_MIN_10_EXP	(-307)	Minimum decimal exponent
DBL_MIN_EXP	(–1021)	Minimum binary exponent
_DBL_RADIX	2	Exponent radix
_DBL_ROUNDS	1	Addition rounding: near
FLT_DIG	6	Number of decimal digits of precision
FLT_EPSILON	1.192092896e-07F	Smallest such that 1.0+**FLT_EPSILON** !=1.0
FLT_MANT_DIG	24	Number of bits in mantissa
FLT_MAX	3.402823466e+38F	Maximum value
FLT_MAX_10_EXP	38	Maximum decimal exponent
FLT_MAX_EXP	128	Maximum binary exponent
FLT_MIN	1.175494351e-38F	Minimum positive value
FLT_MIN_10_EXP	(–37)	Minimum decimal exponent
FLT_MIN_EXP	(–125)	Minimum binary exponent
FLT_RADIX	2	Exponent radix
FLT_ROUNDS	1	Addition rounding: near

EOF

Remarks

This value is returned by an I/O routine when the end-of-file (or in some cases, an error) is encountered.

See Also **putc**, **ungetc**, **scanf**, **fflush**, **_fcloseall**, **_ungetch**, **_putch**, **__isascii**

---

errno Constants

#include <errno.h>

Remarks

The **errno** values are constants assigned to **errno** in the event of various error conditions.

ERRNO.H contains the definitions of the **errno** values. However, not all the definitions given in ERRNO.H are used in 32-bit Windows operating systems. Some of the values in ERRNO.H are present to maintain compatibility with the UNIX family of operating systems.

The **errno** values in a 32-bit Windows operating system, are a subset of the values for **errno** in XENIX systems. Thus, the **errno** value is not necessarily the same as the actual error code returned by a Windows NT or Windows 95 system call. To access the actual operating system error code, use the **_doserrno** variable, which contains this value.

The following **errno** values are supported:

ECHILD No spawned processes.

EAGAIN No more processes. An attempt to create a new process failed because there are no more process slots, or there is not enough memory, or thc maximum nesting level has been reached.

E2BIG Argument list too long.

EACCES Permission denied. The file's permission setting does not allow the specified access. This error signifies that an attempt was made to access a file (or, in some cases, a directory) in a way that is incompatible with the file's attributes.

For example, the error can occur when an attempt is made to read from a file that is not open, to open an existing read-only file for writing, or to open a directory instead of a file. Under MS-DOS operating system versions 3.0 and later, **EACCES** may also indicate a locking or sharing violation.

The error can also occur in an attempt to rename a file or directory or to remove an existing directory.

EBADF Bad file number. There are two possible causes: 1) The specified file handle is not a valid file-handle value or does not refer to an open file. 2) An attempt was made to write to a file or device opened for read-only access.

EDEADLOCK Resource deadlock would occur. The argument to a math function is not in the domain of the function.

EDOM Math argument.

EEXIST Files exist. An attempt has been made to create a file that already exists. For example, the **_O_CREAT** and **_O_EXCL** flags are specified in an **_open** call, but the named file already exists.

EINVAL Invalid argument. An invalid value was given for one of the arguments to a function. For example, the value given for the origin when positioning a file pointer (by means of a call to **fseek**) is before the beginning of the file.

EMFILE Too many open files. No more file handles are available, so no more files can be opened.

ENOENT No such file or directory. The specified file or directory does not exist or cannot be found. This message can occur whenever a specified file does not exist or a component of a path does not specify an existing directory.

ENOEXEC Exec format error. An attempt was made to execute a file that is not executable or that has an invalid executable-file format.

ENOMEM Not enough core. Not enough memory is available for the attempted operator. For example, this message can occur when insufficient memory is available to execute a child process, or when the allocation request in a **_getcwd** call cannot be satisfied.

ENOSPC No space left on device. No more space for writing is available on the device (for example, when the disk is full).

ERANGE Result too large. An argument to a math function is too large, resulting in partial or total loss of significance in the result. This error can also occur in other functions when an argument is larger than expected (for example, when the *buffer* argument to **_getcwd** is longer than expected).

EXDEV Cross-device link. An attempt was made to move a file to a different device (using the **rename** function).

Exception-Handling Constants

Remarks

The constant **EXCEPTION_CONTINUE_SEARCH**, **EXCEPTION_CONTINUE_EXECUTION**, or **EXCEPTION_EXECUTE_HANDLER** is returned when an exception occurs during execution of the guarded section of a **try-except** statement. The return value determines how the exception is handled. For more information, see "try-except Statement" in *C Language Reference*.

EXIT_SUCCESS, EXIT_FAILURE

#include <stdlib.h>

Remarks

These are arguments for the **exit** and **_exit** functions and the return values for the **atexit** and **_onexit** functions.

See Also **atexit**, **exit**, **_onexit**

File Attribute Constants

#include <io.h>

Remarks

These constants specify the current attributes of the file or directory specified by the function.

The attributes are represented by the following manifest constants:

_A_ARCH Archive. Set whenever the file is changed, and cleared by the BACKUP command. Value: 0x20

_A_HIDDEN Hidden file. Not normally seen with the DIR command, unless the /AH option is used. Returns information about normal files as well as files with this attribute. Value: 0x02

_A_NORMAL Normal. File can be read or written to without restriction. Value: 0x00

_A_RDONLY Read-only. File cannot be opened for writing, and a file with the same name cannot be created. Value: 0x01

_A_SUBDIR Subdirectory. Value: 0x10

_A_SYSTEM System file. Not normally seen with the DIR command, unless the /AS option is used. Value: 0x04

Multiple constants can be combined with the OR operator (|).

See Also **_find** Functions

File Constants

#include <fcntl.h>

Remarks

The integer expression formed from one or more of these constants determines the type of reading or writing operations permitted. It is formed by combining one or more constants with a translation-mode constant.

The file constants are as follows:

_O_APPEND Repositions the file pointer to the end of the file before every write operation.

_O_CREAT Creates and opens a new file for writing; this has no effect if the file specified by *filename* exists.

_O_EXCL Returns an error value if the file specified by *filename* exists. Only applies when used with **_O_CREAT**.

_O_RDONLY Opens file for reading only; if this flag is given, neither **_O_RDWR** nor **_O_WRONLY** can be given.

_O_RDWR Opens file for both reading and writing; if this flag is given, neither **_O_RDONLY** nor **_O_WRONLY** can be given.

_O_TRUNC Opens and truncates an existing file to zero length; the file must have write permission. The contents of the file are destroyed. If this flag is given, you cannot specify **_O_RDONLY**.

_O_WRONLY Opens file for writing only; if this flag is given, neither **_O_RDONLY** nor **_O_RDWR** can be given.

See Also **_open**, **_sopen**

File Permission Constants

#include <sys/stat.h>

Remarks

One of these constants is required when **_O_CREAT** (**_open**, **_sopen**) is specified.

The *pmode* argument specifies the file's permission settings as follows.

Constant	Meaning
_S_IREAD	Reading permitted
_S_IWRITE	Writing permitted
_S_IREAD | _S_IWRITE	Reading and writing permitted

When used as the *pmode* argument for **_umask**, the manifest constant sets the permission setting, as follows.

Constant	Meaning
_S_IREAD	Writing not permitted (file is read-only)
_S_IWRITE	Reading not permitted (file is write-only)
_S_IREAD | _S_IWRITE	Neither reading nor writing permitted

See Also **_open**, **_sopen**, **_umask**, **_stat structure**

File Read/Write Access Constants

#include <stdio.h>

Remarks

These constants specify the access type ("a", "r", or "w") requested for the file. Both the translation mode ("b" or "t") and the commit-to-disk mode ("c" or "n") can be specified with the type of access.

The access types are described below.

"a" Opens for writing at the end of the file (appending); creates the file first if it does not exist. All write operations occur at the end of the file. Although the file pointer can be repositioned using **fseek** or **rewind**, it is always moved back to the end of the file before any write operation is carried out.

"a+" Same as above, but also allows reading.

"r" Opens for reading. If the file does not exist or cannot be found, the call to open the file will fail.

"r+" Opens for both reading and writing. If the file does not exist or cannot be found, the call to open the file will fail.

"w" Opens an empty file for writing. If the given file exists, its contents are destroyed.

"w+" Opens an empty file for both reading and writing. If the given file exists, its contents are destroyed.

When the "r+", "w+", or "a+" type is specified, both reading and writing are allowed (the file is said to be open for "update"). However, when you switch between reading and writing, there must be an intervening **fflush**, **fsetpos**, **fseek**, or **rewind** operation. The current position can be specified for the **fsetpos** or **fseek** operation.

See Also **_fdopen**, **fopen**, **freopen**, **_fsopen**, **_popen**

File Translation Constants

#include <stdio.h>

Remarks

These constants specify the mode of translation (**"b"** or **"t"**). The mode is included in the string specifying the type of access (**"r"**, **"w"**, **"a"**, **"r+"**, **"w+"**, **"a+"**).

The translation modes are as follows:

t Opens in text (translated) mode. In this mode, carriage-return/linefeed (CR-LF) combinations are translated into single linefeeds (LF) on input, and LF characters are translated into CR-LF combinations on output. Also, CTRL+Z is interpreted as an end-of-file character on input. In files opened for reading or reading/writing, **fopen** checks for CTRL+Z at the end of the file and removes it, if possible. This is done because using the **fseek** and **ftell** functions to move within a file ending with CTRL+Z may cause **fseek** to behave improperly near the end of the file.

Note The **t** option is not part of the ANSI standard for **fopen** and **freopen** it is a Microsoft extension and should not be used where ANSI portability is desired.

b Opens in binary (untranslated) mode. The above translations are suppressed.

If **t** or **b** is not given in *mode*, the translation mode is defined by the default-mode variable **_fmode**. For more information about using text and binary modes, see "Text and Binary Mode File I/O" on page 15 in Chapter 1.

See Also **_fdopen**, **fopen**, **freopen**, **_fsopen**

FILENAME_MAX

#include <stdio.h>

Remarks

This is the maximum permissible length for *filename*.

See Also Path Field Limits

FOPEN_MAX, _SYS_OPEN

#include <stdio.h>

Remarks

This is the maximum number of files that can be opened simultaneously. **FOPEN_MAX** is the ANSI-compatible name. **_SYS_OPEN** is provided for compatibility with existing code.

_FREEENTRY, _USEDENTRY

#include <malloc.h>

Remarks

These constants represent values assigned by the **_heapwalk** routines to the **_useflag** element of the **_HEAPINFO** structure. They indicate the status of the heap entry.

See Also **_heapwalk**

---

fseek, _lseek Constants

#include <stdio.h>

Remarks

The *origin* argument specifies the initial position and can be one of the manifest constants shown below:

Constant	Meaning
SEEK_END	End of file
SEEK_CUR	Current position of file pointer
SEEK_SET	Beginning of file

See Also **fseek, _lseek, _lseeki64**

Heap Constants

#include <malloc.h>

Remarks

These constants give the return value indicating status of the heap.

Constant	Meaning
_HEAPBADBEGIN	Initial header information was not found or was invalid.
_HEAPBADNODE	Bad node was found, or heap is damaged.
_HEAPBADPTR	**_pentry** field of **_HEAPINFO** structure does not contain valid pointer into heap (**_heapwalk** routine only).
_HEAPEMPTY	Heap has not been initialized.

Constant	Meaning
_HEAPEND	End of heap was reached successfully (**_heapwalk** routine only).
_HEAPOK	Heap is consistent (**_heapset** and **_heapchk** routines only). No errors so far; **_HEAPINFO** structure contains information about next entry (**_heapwalk** routine only).

See Also **_heapchk**, **_heapset**, **_heapwalk**

_HEAP_MAXREQ

#include <malloc.h>

Remarks

The maximum size of a user request for memory that can possibly be granted.

See Also **malloc**, **calloc**

HUGE_VAL

#include <math.h>

Remarks

HUGE_VAL is the largest representable double value. This value is returned by many run-time math functions when an error occurs. For some functions, –**HUGE_VAL** is returned.

_ _LOCAL_SIZE

Remarks

The compiler provides a symbol, **_ _LOCAL_SIZE**, for use in the inline assembler block of function prolog code. This symbol is used to allocate space for local variables on the stack frame in your custom prolog code.

The compiler determines the value of **_ _LOCAL_SIZE**. Its value is the total number of bytes of all user-defined locals as well as compiler-generated temporary variables.

_ _LOCAL_SIZE can be used as an immediate operand; it cannot be used in an expression. You must not change or redefine the value of this symbol. For example:

```
mov      eax, __LOCAL_SIZE           ;Immediate operand
mov      eax, [ebp - __LOCAL_SIZE]   ;Expression
```

The following is a example of a naked function containing custom prolog and epilog sequences using the _ _**LOCAL_SIZE** symbol in the prolog sequence:

For more information, see "naked Functions" and "**naked**" in *C Language Reference*.

Locale Categories

#include <locale.h>

Remarks

Locale categories are manifest constants used by the localization routines to specify which portion of a program's locale information will be used. The locale refers to the locality (or country) for which certain aspects of your program can be customized. Locale-dependent areas include, for example, the formatting of dates or the display format for monetary values

Locale Category	Parts of Program Affected
LC_ALL	All locale-specific behavior (all categories)
LC_COLLATE	Behavior of **strcoll** and **strxfrm** functions
LC_CTYPE	Behavior of character-handling functions (except **isdigit**, **isxdigit**, **mbstowcs**, and **mbtowc**, which are unaffected)
LC_MAX	Same as **LC_TIME**
LC_MIN	Same as **LC_ALL**
LC_MONETARY	Monetary formatting information returned by the **localeconv** function
LC_NUMERIC	Decimal-point character for formatted output routines (for example, **printf**), data conversion routines, and nonmonetary formatting information returned by **localeconv** function
LC_TIME	Behavior of **strftime** function

See Also **localeconv**, **setlocale**, **strcoll** Functions, **strftime**, **strxfrm**

_locking Constants

#include <sys/locking.h>

Remarks

The *mode* argument in the call to the **_locking** function specifies the locking action to be performed.

The *mode* argument must be one of the following manifest constants:

_LK_LOCK Locks the specified bytes. If the bytes cannot be locked, the function tries again after one second. If, after ten attempts, the bytes cannot be locked, the function returns an error.

_LK_RLCK Same as **_LK_LOCK**.

_LK_NBLCK Locks the specified bytes. If bytes cannot be locked, the function returns an error.

_LK_NBRLCK Same as **_LK_NBLCK**.

_LK_UNLCK Unlocks the specified bytes. (The bytes must have been previously locked.)

See Also **_locking**

Math Error Constants

#include <math.h>

Remarks

The math error constants can be generated by the math routines of the run-time library.

These errors, described as follows, correspond to the exception types defined in MATH.H and are returned by the **_matherr** function when a math error occurs.

Constant	Meaning
_DOMAIN	Argument to function is outside domain of function.
_OVERFLOW	Result is too large to be represented in function's return type.
_PLOSS	Partial loss of significance occurred.
_SING	Argument singularity: argument to function has illegal value. (For example, value 0 is passed to function that requires nonzero value.)
_TLOSS	Total loss of significance occurred.
_UNDERFLOW	Result is too small to be represented.

See Also **_matherr**

MB_CUR_MAX

#include <stdlib.h>

Context: ANSI multibyte- and wide-character conversion functions

Remarks

The value of **MB_CUR_MAX** is the maximum number of bytes in a multibyte character for the current locale.

See Also **mblen**, **mbstowcs**, **mbtowc**, **wchar_t**, **wcstombs**, **wctomb**, Data Type

NULL

Remarks

NULL is the null-pointer value used with many pointer operations and functions.

Path Field Limits

#include <stdlib.h>

Remarks

These constants define the maximum length for the path and for the individual fields within the path.

Constant	Meaning
_MAX_DIR	Maximum length of directory component
_MAX_DRIVE	Maximum length of drive component
_MAX_EXT	Maximum length of extension component
_MAX_FNAME	Maximum length of filename component
_MAX_PATH	Maximum length of full path

The sum of the fields should not exceed **_MAX_PATH**.

RAND_MAX

#include <stdlib.h>

Remarks

The constant **RAND_MAX** is the maximum value that can be returned by the **rand** function. **RAND_MAX** is defined as the value 0x7fff.

See Also **rand**

setvbuf Constants

#include <stdio.h>

Remarks

These constants represent the type of buffer for **setvbuf**.

The possible values are given by the following manifest constants:

Constant	Meaning
_IOFBF	Full buffering: Buffer specified in call to **setvbuf** is used and its size is as specified in **setvbuf** call. If buffer pointer is **NULL**, automatically allocated buffer of specified size is used.
_IOLBF	Same as **_IOFBF**.
_IONBF	No buffer is used, regardless of arguments in call to **setvbuf**.

See Also **setbuf**

Sharing Constants

#include <share.h>

Remarks

The *shflag* argument determines the sharing mode, which consists of one or more manifest constants. These can be combined with the *oflag* arguments (see "File Constants" on page 56).

The constants and their meanings are listed below:

Constant	Meaning
_SH_COMPAT	Sets compatibility mode
_SH_DENYRW	Denies read and write access to file
_SH_DENYWR	Denies write access to file
_SH_DENYRD	Denies read access to file
_SH_DENYNO	Permits read and write access

See Also **_sopen**, **_fsopen**

signal Constants

#include <signal.h>

Remarks

The *sig* argument must be one of the manifest constants listed below (defined in SIGNAL.H).

SIGABRT Abnormal termination. The default action terminates the calling program with exit code 3.

SIGFPE Floating-point error, such as overflow, division by zero, or invalid operation. The default action terminates the calling program. **SIGFPE** is the only signal constant available when the **_WINDOWS** constant is defined. The **_WINDOWS** constant is defined by CL options /GA, /GD, /GE, /GW, /Gw, and /Mq. The CL.EXE tool controls the Microsoft C and C++ compilers and linker.

SIGILL Illegal instruction. The default action terminates the calling program.

SIGINT CTRL+C interrupt. The default action issues **INT 23H**.

SIGSEGV Illegal storage access. The default action terminates the calling program.

SIGTERM Termination request sent to the program. The default action terminates the calling program.

See Also **signal**, **raise**

---

signal Action Constants

#include <signal.h>

Remarks

The action taken when the interrupt signal is received depends on the value of *func*.

The *func* argument must be either a function address or one of the manifest constants listed below and defined in SIGNAL.H.

SIG_DFL Uses system-default response. If the calling program uses stream I/O, buffers created by the run-time library are not flushed.

SIG_IGN Ignores interrupt signal. This value should never be given for **SIGFPE**, since the floating-point state of the process is left undefined.

See Also **signal**

_spawn Constants

#include <process.h>

Remarks

The *mode* argument determines the action taken by the calling process before and during a spawn operation. The following values for *mode* are possible:

Constant	Meaning
_P_OVERLAY	Overlays calling process with new process, destroying calling process (same effect as **_exec** calls).
_P_WAIT	Suspends calling process until execution of new process is complete (synchronous **_spawn**).
_P_NOWAIT or **_P_NOWAITO**	Continues to execute calling process concurrently with new process (asynchronous **_spawn**, valid only in 32-bit Windows applications).
_P_DETACH	Continues to execute calling process; new process is run in background with no access to console or keyboard. Calls to **_cwait** against new process will fail. This is an asynchronous **_spawn** and is valid only in 32-bit Windows applications.

See Also **_spawn** Functions

_stat Structure st_mode Field Constants

#include <sys/stat.h>

Remarks

These constants are used to indicate file type in the **st_mode** field of the **_stat structure**.

The bit mask constants are described below:

Constant	Meaning
_S_IFMT	File type mask
_S_IFDIR	Directory
_S_IFCHR	Character special (indicates a device if set)
_S_IFREG	Regular
_S_IREAD	Read permission, owner
_S_IWRITE	Write permission, owner
_S_IEXEC	Execute/search permission, owner

See Also **_stat**, **_fstat**, Standard Types

stdin, stdout, stderr

FILE *stdin;
FILE *stdout;
FILE *stderr;

#include <stdio.h>

Remarks

These are standard streams for input, output, and error output.

By default, standard input is read from the keyboard, while standard output and standard error are printed to the screen.

The following stream pointers are available to access the standard streams:

Pointer	Stream
stdin	Standard input
stdout	Standard output
stderr	Standard error

These pointers can be used as arguments to functions. Some functions, such as **getchar** and **putchar**, use **stdin** and **stdout** automatically.

These pointers are constants, and cannot be assigned new values. The **freopen** function can be used to redirect the streams to disk files or to other devices. The operating system allows you to redirect a program's standard input and output at the command level.

See Also Stream I/O

TMP_MAX, L_tmpnam

#include <stdio.h>

Remarks

TMP_MAX is the maximum number of unique filenames that the **tmpnam** function can generate. **L_tmpnam** is the length of temporary filenames generated by **tmpnam**.

Translation Mode Constants

#include <fcntl.h>

Remarks

The **_O_BINARY** and **_O_TEXT** manifest constants determine the translation mode for files (**_open** and **_sopen**) or the translation mode for streams (**_setmode**).

The allowed values are:

_O_TEXT Opens file in text (translated) mode. Carriage return–linefeed (CR-LF) combinations are translated into a single linefeed (LF) on input. Linefeed characters are translated into CR-LF combinations on output. Also, CTRL+Z is interpreted as an end-of-file character on input. In files opened for reading and reading/writing, **fopen** checks for CTRL+Z at the end of the file and removes it, if possible. This is done because using the **fseek** and **ftell** functions to move within a file ending with CTRL+Z may cause **fseek** to behave improperly near the end of the file.

_O_BINARY Opens file in binary (untranslated) mode. The above translations are suppressed.

_O_RAW Same as **_O_BINARY**. Supported for C 2.0 compatibility.

For more information, see "Text and Binary Mode File I/O" on page 15 in Chapter 1 and "File Translation Constants" on page 58.

See Also **_open**, **_pipe**, **_sopen**, **_setmode**

_WAIT_CHILD, _WAIT_GRANDCHILD

#include <process.h>

Remarks

The **_cwait** function can be used by any process to wait for any other process (if the process ID is known). The action argument can be one of the following values:

Constant	Meaning
_WAIT_CHILD	Calling process waits until specified new process terminates.
_WAIT_GRANDCHILD	Calling process waits until specified new process, and all processes created by that new process, terminate.

See Also **_cwait**

32-bit Windows Time/Date Formats

Remarks

The file time and the date are stored individually, using unsigned integers as bit fields. File time and date are packed as follows:

Time

Bit Position:	**0 1 2 3 4**	**5 6 7 8 9 A**	**B C D E F**
Length:	5	6	5
Contents:	hours	minutes	2-second increments
Value Range:	0–23	0–59	0–29 in 2-second intervals

Date

Bit Position:	**0 1 2 3 4 5 6**	**7 8 9 A**	**B C D E F**
Length:	7	4	5
Contents:	year	month	day
Value Range:	0–119		
(relative to 1980)	1–12	1–31	

Example

The following code sample extracts the components of a date from a variable **wr_date** containing a date packed in the format described above. You can use similar methods to extract the time from a variable containing a packed time.

CHAPTER 4

Debug Version of the C Run-Time Library

Visual C++ version 4.0 adds extensive debug support to the C run-time library, letting you step directly into run-time functions when debugging an application. The library also provides a variety of tools to keep track of heap allocations, locate memory leaks, and track down other memory-related problems.

Much of the heap-checking technology included in the debug version of the C run-time library has been moved from the Microsoft Foundation Class library. To continue to use the technology, debug builds of MFC applications must now be linked with a debug version of the run-time library.

The C run-time debug functions are available for Windows 95, Windows NT, and the Power Macintosh. However, the 68K Macintosh platform is not supported.

The following sections of this chapter describe the new debug components of the C run-time library and explain how to take advantage of the debugging services they provide:

- Source Code for the Run-Time Functions
- C Run-Time Debug Libraries
- Debug Reporting Functions of the C Run-Time Library
- Using Macros for Verification and Reporting
- Memory Management and the Debug Heap
- Writing Your Own Debug Hook Functions
- Example Programs

Source Code for the Run-Time Functions

Visual C++ introduces source code availability for most of the C run-time library functions. You can now use the debugger to step into the source code for the run-time functions by linking your application with a debug version of the run-time library.

During the debugging process, source code availability allows you to confirm that the run-time functions are working as expected, check for bad parameters and memory states, and examine your code for other errors.

Because the C run-time library has been designed to achieve the highest possible performance, the release versions of the functions rarely verify parameters, confirm internal states, or perform other checking that might slow program execution. As a result, an incorrect call to a run-time function can result in serious problems accompanied by too little information to resolve the situation. For example, passing a bad pointer to the **strcpy** function usually results in a simple "General Protection Fault" error message. The ability to step into the run-time source code provides you with a method for controlling the type of verifications and how many to perform, as well as the opportunity to trace through the execution of your application to resolve specific problems.

The Setup program gives you the option of installing the C run-time library source code on your hard disk. Even if you choose to leave the source files on the CD-ROM, you can step into run-time functions while you are debugging, as long as the CD-ROM is loaded in the drive.

The main definitions and macros that control the debugging process are contained in the CRTDBG.H header file. Experienced programmers should examine this file to understand how to take full advantage of the flexibility that the new debug libraries offer.

Source code for the debug run-time functions is contained in source files whose names begin with **dbg**. Source code for the other C run-time functions is contained in files whose names reflect the function names. However, Microsoft considers some run-time technology to be proprietary and does not provide source code for the exception handling, floating point, and a few other routines. For a complete list of these routines, see "Debug Routines" on page 6 in Chapter 1.

C Run-Time Debug Libraries

The following table lists the debug versions of the C run-time library files shipped with Visual C++. For each library, a compiler option that makes it the default library is identified, together with the environment variables that are automatically defined by the compiler when that option is used. For a list of the release versions of these libraries, see "C Run-Time Libraries" on page ix in the Introduction.

Library	Characteristics	Option	Defined
LIBCD.LIB	Single threaded, static link	/MLd	_DEBUG
LIBCMTD.LIB	Multithreaded, static link	/MTd	_DEBUG, _MT
MSVCRTD.LIB	Multithreaded, dynamic link (import library for msvcrx0d.dll[1])	/MDd	_DEBUG, _MT, _DLL

1 In place of the "x0" in the DLL name, substitute the major version numeral of Visual C++ that you are using. For example, if you are using Visual C++ version 4, then the library name would be MSVCR40D.DLL.

The debug versions of the library functions differ from the release versions mainly in that debug information was included when they were compiled (using the /Z7 or /Zi compiler option), optimization was turned off, and source code is available. A few of the debug library functions also contain asserts that verify parameter validity.

Using one of these debug libraries is as simple as linking it to your application with the /DEBUG:FULL linker option set. You can then step directly into almost any run-time function call.

Debug Reporting Functions of the C Run-Time Library

The run-time library includes three new debug reporting functions that provide extensive flexibility for reporting warnings and errors during execution of a debug build of an application. The main reporting function is **_CrtDbgReport**. Two configuration functions, **_CrtSetReportMode** and **_CrtSetReportFile**, can be used at any point to specify the destinations to which different kinds of reports will be sent. The following list summarizes the operation of these three functions:

_CrtDbgReport Reports from within an application. The programmer determines the destination(s) to which the report is sent by specifying its category (**_CRT_WARN**, **_CRT_ERROR**, and **_CRT_ASSERT**). The report may also include a message string, a source file name and line number, and one or more arguments to be formatted into the message string.

_CrtSetReportMode Specifies the general destination(s) to which a given category of report output should be sent. The three categories of report output are **_CRT_WARN**, **_CRT_ERROR**, and **_CRT_ASSERT**. Possible destinations include the debugger, a message window, and/or a file or stream.

_CrtSetReportFile When **_CrtSetReportMode** has specified that a given category of report output will be directed to a file or stream, **_CrtSetReportFile** identifies that specific file or stream.

For detailed information about the syntax and usage of these functions, see the function descriptions at the end of this chapter.

Debug reports can be assigned to three different categories, depending on the urgency of the messages they contain:

_CRT_WARN Warnings, messages, and information not needing immediate attention.

_CRT_ERROR Errors, unrecoverable problems, and information needing immediate attention.

_CRT_ASSERT Assertion failure (an asserted expression evaluated as FALSE).

A different destination can be specified for each of these report categories. Usually one destination is sufficient for a category, but each category can be sent to more than one destination. Up to three of the following bit-flags can be combined in the *reportMode* argument passed to **_CrtReportMode** to specify the destination(s) for a given report category:

_CRTDBG_MODE_DEBUG Reports are sent to the debugger or debug monitor, using the Win32 **OutputDebugString** API.

_CRTDBG_MODE_FILE Reports are sent to a file (including the **stderr** and **stdout** streams) using the Win32 **WriteFile** API.

_CRTDBG_MODE_WNDW Reports are sent to a message window using the Win32 **MessageBox** API.

To turn off a given category of report, pass **_CrtReportMode** a *reportMode* value of zero.

Report destinations are handled somewhat differently on the Macintosh. If your application will be targeting the Macintosh as well as systems running Windows operating software, be sure to check the documentation for the Visual C++ Macintosh Cross-Platform Edition to see how these destinations are implemented on the Macintosh.

By default, errors and assertion failures are directed to a message window, since they generally signal serious problems that you want to know about right away. Warnings from Windows applications are sent to the debugger, and warnings from console applications are directed to **stderr**. You only need to use the **_CrtSetReport...** functions when you want to change these destinations. For example, the following code causes assertion failures to be sent both to a message window and to **stderr**:

```
_CrtSetReportMode( _CRT_ASSERT, _CRTDBG_MODE_FILE |
                   _CRTDBG_MODE_WNDW );
_CrtSetReportFile( _CRT_ASSERT, _CRTDBG_FILE_STDERR );
```

To send a debug report, you use **_CrtDbgReport** and control the destination by specifying the category of the report. If you need more flexibility, you can write your own reporting function and hook it into the C run-time library reporting mechanism using **_CrtSetReportHook**, as described later in this chapter.

Whereas messages that go to a file or the debugger are generally single lines that can include a filename and line number, the message window contains considerably more information. It identifies the error and the program more fully, along with message text, and can also display a file name and line number. Assert message windows contain additional information particular to asserts.

The following is an example of an assert message box under Windows NT:

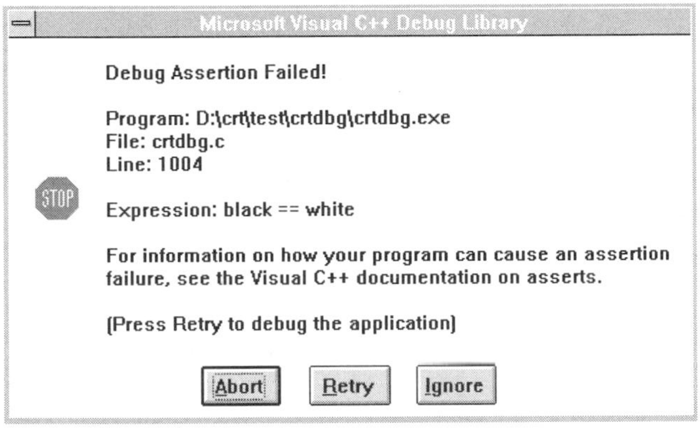

All message windows display Abort/Retry/Ignore buttons. Choosing Abort causes the program to stop execution immediately, Ignore causes execution to continue, and Retry invokes the debugger, provided that "just-in-time" debugging is enabled. Choosing Ignore when an error condition exists often results in "undefined behavior."

Using Macros for Verification and Reporting

A common way of keeping track of what is going on in an application during the debugging process is to use **printf** statements in code such as the following:

```
#ifdef _DEBUG
   if ( someVar > MAX_SOMEVAR )
      printf( "OVERFLOW! In NameOfThisFunc( ),
               someVar=%d,
            otherVar=%d.\n",
               someVar, otherVar );
#endif
```

The **_ASSERT**, **_ASSERTE**, **_RPT*n*** and **_RPTF*n*** macros defined in the CRTDBG.H header file provide a variety of more concise and flexible ways to accomplish the same task. These macros automatically disappear in your release build when **_DEBUG** is not defined, so there is no need to enclose them in **#ifdef**s. For debug builds, they provide a range of reporting options that can be directed to any of the debugging destinations described above. The following table summarizes these options:

Macro	Reporting Option
_ASSERT	If an asserted expression evaluates to FALSE, the macro reports the filename and line number of the **_ASSERT**, under the **_CRT_ASSERT** report category.
_ASSERTE	Same as **_ASSERT**, except that it also reports a string representation of the expression that was asserted to be true but was evaluated to be false.
_RPT*n* (where ***n*** is 0, 1, 2, 3, or 4)	These five macros send a message string and from zero to four arguments to the report category of your choice. In the cases of macros **_RPT1** through **_RPT4**, the message string serves as a **printf**-style formatting string for the arguments.
_RPTF*n* (where ***n*** is 0, 1, 2, 3, or 4)	Same as **_RPT*n*** , except that these macros also include in each report the filename and line number at which the macro was executed.

Asserts are used to check specific assumptions you make in your code. **_ASSERTE** is a little more convenient to use because it reports the asserted expression that turned out to be false. Often this tells you enough to identify the problem without going back to your source code. A disadvantage, however, is that every expression asserted using **_ASSERTE** must be included in the debug version of your application as a string constant. If you use so many asserts that these string expressions take up a significant amount of memory, you may prefer to use **_ASSERT** instead.

Examining the definitions of these macros in the CRTDBG.H header file can give you a detailed understanding of how they work. When **_DEBUG** is defined, for example, the **_ASSERTE** macro is defined essentially as follows:

```
#define _ASSERTE(expr) \
   do { \
      if (!(expr) && (1 == _CrtDbgReport( \
          _CRT_ASSERT, __FILE__, __LINE__, #expr))) \
         _CrtDbgBreak(); \
    } while (0)
```

If *expr* evaluates to TRUE, execution continues uninterrupted, but if *expr* evaluates to FALSE, **_CrtDbgReport** is called to report the assertion failure. If the destination is a message window in which you choose Retry, **_CrtDbgReport** returns 1 and **_CrtDbgBreak** calls the debugger.

A single call to **_ASSERTE** could be used to replace the **printf** code at the beginning of this section:

```
_ASSERTE(someVar <= MAX_SOMEVAR);
```

If **_CRT_ASSERT** reports were being directed to message boxes (the default), or to the debugger, then program execution would be interrupted when `someVar` exceeded `MAX_SOMEVAR`.

Asserts can also be used as a simple debugging error handling mechanism for any function that returns FALSE when it fails. For example, in the following code, the assertion will fail if corruption is detected in the heap:

```
_ASSERTE(_CrtCheckMemory());
```

The following memory checking functions can be used in asserts of this kind to verify pointers, memory ranges, and specific memory blocks:

_CrtIsValidHeapPointer Verifies that a given pointer points to memory in the local heap; "local" here refers to the particular heap created and managed by this instance of the C run-time library. A dynamic-link library (DLL) could have its own instance of the library, and therefore its own heap, independent of your application's local heap. Note that this routine catches not only null or out-of-bounds addresses, but also pointers to static variables, stack variables, and any other non-local memory.

_CrtIsValidPointer Verifies that a given memory range is valid for reading or writing.

_CrtIsMemoryBlock Verifies that a specified block of memory is in the "local" heap and has a valid block type. This function can actually do more than check a block's validity, however. If you pass it non-null values for the request number, filename and/or line number, it sets the value in the block's header accordingly.

For more information on how these and other assertion checking routines can be used during the debugging process, see "Debugging Assertions" in Chapter 17 of the *Visual C++ User's Guide*.

The **printf** code at the start of this section reported actual values of `someVar` and `otherVar` to **stdout**. If these values were useful in the debugging process, one of the

_RPTn or **_RPTFn** macros could be used to report them. The **_RPTF2** macro, for example, is defined essentially as follows in CRTDBG.H:

```
#define _RPTF2(rptno, msg, arg1, arg2) \
   do { \
      if (1 == _CrtDbgReport(rptno, __FILE__, \
              __LINE__, msg, arg1, arg2)) \
         _CrtDbgBreak(); \
   } while (0)
```

The following call to **_RPTF2** would report the values of `someVar` and `otherVar`, together with the filename and line number, every time the function that contained the macro was executed:

```
_RPTF2(_CRT_WARN, "In NameOfThisFunc( ), someVar= %d,
       otherVar= %d\n",
        someVar, otherVar);
```

Of course, you may only be interested in knowing the values of `someVar` and `otherVar` under the circumstance that `someVar` has exceeded its maximum permitted value. By using an assert, as described above, you could halt program execution and then use the debugger to examine the values of these variables. Alternatively, you could use a variant of the original **printf** code, enclosing a conditional call to the **_RPTF2** macro in **#ifdef**s:

```
#ifdef _DEBUG
   if (someVar > MAX_SOMEVAR)
      _RPTF2(_CRT_WARN,
"In NameOfThisFunc( ), someVar= %d, otherVar= %d\n",

            someVar, otherVar );
#endif
```

Of course, if you find that a particular application needs a kind of debug reporting that the macros supplied with the C run-time library do not provide, you can write a macro designed specifically to fit your own requirements. In one of your header files, for example, you could include code like the following to define a macro called ALERT_IF2:

```
#ifndef _DEBUG                   /* For RELEASE builds */
#define  ALERT_IF2(expr, msg, arg1, arg2)  ((void)0)
#else                            /* For DEBUG builds   */
#define  ALERT_IF2(expr, msg, arg1, arg2) \
   do { \
      if ((expr) && \
          (1 == _CrtDbgReport(_CRT_ERROR, \
               __FILE__, __LINE__, msg, arg1, arg2))) \
          _CrtDbgBreak( ); \
   } while (0)
#endif
```

One call to ALERT_IF2 could perform all the functions of the **printf** code at the start of this section:

```
ALERT_IF2(someVar > MAX_SOMEVAR, "OVERFLOW! In NameOfThisFunc( ),
      someVar=%d, otherVar=%d.\n", someVar, otherVar );
```

This approach can be particularly useful as your debugging requirements evolve, because a custom macro can easily be changed to report more or less information to different destinations, depending on what is most convenient.

Memory Management and the Debug Heap

Two of the most common and intractable problems that programmers encounter are overwriting the end of an allocated buffer and leaking memory (failing to free allocations after they are no longer needed). The debug heap provides powerful tools to solve memory allocation problems of this kind.

The debug versions of the heap functions call the standard or base versions used in release builds. When you request a memory block, the debug heap manager allocates from the base heap a slightly larger block of memory than requested and returns a pointer to your portion of that block. For example, suppose your application contains the call: `malloc( 10 )`. In a release build, **malloc** would call the base heap allocation routine requesting an allocation of 10 bytes. In a debug build, however, **malloc** would call **_malloc_dbg**, which would then call the base heap allocation routine requesting an allocation of 10 bytes plus approximately 36 bytes of additional memory. All the resulting memory blocks in the debug heap are connected in a single linked list, ordered according to when they were allocated:

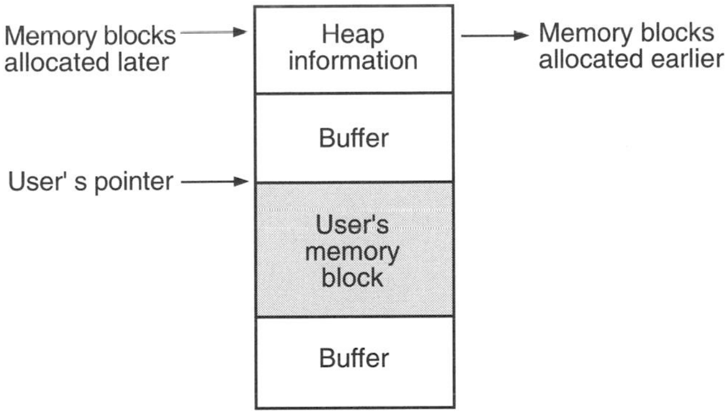

The additional memory allocated by the debug heap routines is used for bookkeeping information, for pointers that link debug memory blocks together, and for small buffers on either side of your data to catch overwrites of the allocated region.

Currently, the block header structure used to store the debug heap's bookkeeping information is declared as follows in the DBGINT.H header file:

```
typedef struct _CrtMemBlockHeader
{
// Pointer to the block allocated just before this one:
   struct _CrtMemBlockHeader *pBlockHeaderNext;
// Pointer to the block allocated just after this one:
   struct _CrtMemBlockHeader *pBlockHeaderPrev;
   char *szFileName;    // File name
   int nLine;           // Line number
   size_t nDataSize;    // Size of user block
   int nBlockUse;       // Type of block
   long lRequest;       // Allocation number
// Buffer just before (lower than) the user's memory:
   unsigned char gap[nNoMansLandSize];
} _CrtMemBlockHeader;

/* In an actual memory block in the debug heap,
 * this structure is followed by:
 *    unsigned char data[nDataSize];
 *    unsigned char anotherGap[nNoMansLandSize];
 */
```

The "NoMansLand" buffers on either side of the user data area of the block are currently 4 bytes in size, and are filled with a known byte value used by the debug heap routines to verify that the limits of the user's memory block have not been overwritten. The debug heap also fills new memory blocks with a known value, and if you elect to keep freed blocks in the heap's linked list as explained below, these freed blocks are also filled with a known value. Currently, the actual byte values used are as follows:

NoMansLand (0xFD)   The "NoMansLand" buffers on either side of the memory used by an application are currently filled with 0xFD.

Freed blocks (0xDD)   The freed blocks kept unused in the debug heap's linked list when the **_CRTDBG_DELAY_FREE_MEM_DF** flag is set are currently filled with 0xDD.

New objects (0xCD)   New objects are filled with 0xCD when they are allocated.

Types of Blocks on the Debug Heap

Every memory block in the debug heap is assigned to one of five allocation types. These types are tracked and reported differently for purposes of leak detection and state reporting. You can specify a block's type by allocating it using a direct call to one of the debug heap allocation functions such as **_malloc_dbg**. The five types of memory blocks in the debug heap (set in the **nBlockUse** member of the **_CrtMemBlockHeader** structure) are as follows:

_NORMAL_BLOCK   A call to **malloc** or **calloc** creates a Normal block. If you intend to use Normal blocks only, and have no need for Client blocks, you may want to define **_CRTDBG_MAP_ALLOC**, which causes all heap allocation calls to be mapped to their debug equivalents in debug builds. This will allow filename and line number information about each allocation call to be stored in the corresponding block header.

_CRT_BLOCK The memory blocks allocated internally by many run-time library functions are marked as Crt blocks, so that they can be handled separately. As a result, leak detection and other operations need not be affected by them. An allocation must never allocate, reallocate, or free any block of Crt type.

_CLIENT_BLOCK An application can keep special track of a given group of allocations for debugging purposes by allocating them as this type, using explicit calls to the debug heap functions. MFC, for example, allocates all CObjects as Client blocks; other applications might keep different memory objects in Client blocks. Subtypes of Client blocks can also be specified for greater tracking granularity. A client-supplied hook function for dumping the objects stored in Client blocks can be installed using **_CrtSetDumpClient**, and will then be called whenever a Client block is dumped by a debug function. Also, **_CrtDoForAllClientObjects** can be used to call a given function supplied by the application for every Client block in the debug heap.

_FREE_BLOCK Normally, blocks that are freed are removed from the list. To check that freed memory is not still being written to, or to simulate low memory conditions, you can choose to keep freed blocks on the linked list, marked as Free and filled with a known byte value (currently 0xDD).

_IGNORE_BLOCK It is possible to turn off the debug heap operations for a period of time. During this time, memory blocks are kept on the list, but are marked as Ignore blocks.

Using the Debug Heap

To use the debug heap, link the debug build of your application with a debug version of the C run-time library. All calls to heap functions such as **malloc**, **free**, **calloc**, **realloc**, **new** and **delete** resolve to debug versions of those functions that operate in the debug heap. When you free a memory block, the debug heap automatically checks the integrity of the buffers on either side of your allocated area and issues an error report if overwriting has occurred.

Many of the debug heap's features, however, must be accessed from within your code. You can use a call to **_CrtCheckMemory**, for example, to check the heap's integrity at any point. This function inspects every memory block in the heap, verifies that the memory block header information is valid, and confirms that the buffers have not been modified. You can control how the debug heap keeps track of allocations using an internal flag, **_crtDbgFlag**, which can be read and set using the **_CrtSetDbgFlag** function. By changing this flag, you can instruct the debug heap to check for memory leaks when the program exits, and report any leaks that are detected. Similarly, you can specify that freed memory blocks not be removed from the linked list, to simulate low memory situations. When the heap is checked, these freed blocks are inspected in their entirety to ensure that they have not been disturbed.

The **_crtDbgFlag** flag contains the following bit fields:

_CRTDBG_ALLOC_MEM_DF (On by default)   Turns on debug allocation. When this bit is off, allocations remain chained together but their block type is **_IGNORE_BLOCK**.

_CRTDBG_DELAY_FREE_MEM_DF (Off by default)   Prevents memory from actually being freed, as for simulating low-memory conditions. When this bit is on, freed blocks are kept in the debug heap's linked list but are marked as **_FREE_BLOCK** and filled with a special byte value.

_CRTDBG_CHECK_ALWAYS_DF (Off by default)   Causes **_CrtCheckMemory** to be called at every allocation and deallocation. This slows execution, but catches errors quickly.

_CRTDBG_CHECK_CRT_DF (Off by default)   Causes blocks marked as type **_CRT_BLOCK** to be included in leak detection and state difference operations. When this bit is off, the memory used internally by the run-time library is ignored during such operations.

_CRTDBG_LEAK_CHECK_DF (Off by default)   Causes leak checking to be performed at program exit via a call to **_CrtDumpMemoryLeaks**. An error report is generated if the application has failed to free all the memory that it allocated.

To change one or more of these bit fields and create a new state for the flag, follow these steps:

1. Call **_CrtSetDbgFlag** with the *newFlag* parameter set to **_CRTDBG_REPORT_FLAG** to obtain the current **_crtDbgFlag** state and store the returned value in a temporary variable.
2. Turn on any bits by OR-ing (bitwise | symbol) the temporary variable with the corresponding bitmasks (represented in the application code by manifest constants).
3. Turn off the other bits by AND-ing (bitwise & symbol) the variable with a NOT (bitwise ~ symbol) of the appropriate bitmasks.
4. Call **_CrtSetDbgFlag** with the *newFlag* parameter set to the value stored in the temporary variable to create the new state for **_crtDbgFlag**.

For example, the following lines of code turn on automatic leak detection and turn off checking for blocks of type **_CRT_BLOCK**:

```
// Get current flag
int tmpFlag = _CrtSetDbgFlag( _CRTDBG_REPORT_FLAG );

// Turn on leak-checking bit
tmpFlag |= _CRTDBG_LEAK_CHECK_DF;
```

```
// Turn off CRT block checking bit
tmpFlag &= ~_CRTDBG_CHECK_CRT_DF;

// Set flag to the new value
_CrtSetDbgFlag( tmpFlag );
```

Heap State Reporting Functions

Several new functions report the contents of the debug heap at a given moment. To capture a summary snapshot of the state of the heap at a given time, they use the **_CrtMemState** structure defined in CRTDBG.H:

```
typedef struct _CrtMemState
{
// Pointer to the most recently allocated block:
   struct _CrtMemBlockHeader * pBlockHeader;
// A counter for each of the 5 types of block:
   long lCounts[_MAX_BLOCKS];
// Total bytes allocated in each block type:
   long lSizes[_MAX_BLOCKS];
// The most bytes allocated at a time up to now:
   long lHighWaterCount;
// The total bytes allocated at present:
   long lTotalCount;
} _CrtMemState;
```

This structure saves a pointer to the first (most recently allocated) block in the debug heap's linked list. Then, in two arrays, it records how many of each type of memory block (**_NORMAL_BLOCK**, **_CLIENT_BLOCK**, **_FREE_BLOCK**, and so forth) there are in the list, and the number of bytes allocated in each type of block. Finally, it records the highest number of bytes allocated in the heap as a whole up to that point, and the number of bytes currently allocated.

The following functions report the state and contents of the heap, and use the information to help detect memory leaks and other problems:

Function	Description
_CrtMemCheckpoint	Saves a snapshot of the heap in a **_CrtMemState** structure supplied by the application.
_CrtMemDifference	Compares two memory state structures, saves the difference between them in a third state structure, and returns TRUE if the two states are different.
_CrtMemDumpStatistics	Dumps a given **_CrtMemState** structure. The structure may contain a snapshot of the state of the debug heap at a given moment, or the difference between two snapshots. "Dumping" means reporting the data in a form that a person can understand.

Function	Description
_CrtMemDumpAllObjectsSince	Dumps information about all objects allocated since a given snapshot was taken of the heap, or from the start of execution. Every time it dumps a **_CLIENT_BLOCK** block, it calls a hook function supplied by the application, if one has been installed using **_CrtSetDumpClient**.
_CrtDumpMemoryLeaks	Determines whether any memory leaks occurred since the start of program execution, and if so, it dumps all allocated objects. Every time it dumps a **_CLIENT_BLOCK** block, it calls a hook function supplied by the application, if one has been installed using **_CrtSetDumpClient**.

Using the Debug Version Versus the Base Version

The run-time library now contains special debug versions of the heap allocation functions that use the same names as the base versions and add the **_dbg** ending. This section describes the differences in behavior between the debug version and the base version in a debug build of an application. The information in this section is presented using **malloc** and **_malloc_dbg** as the example, but is applicable to all of the heap allocation functions discussed in this chapter.

Applications that contain existing calls to **malloc** do not need to convert their calls to **_malloc_dbg** to obtain the debugging features. When **_DEBUG** is defined, all calls to **malloc** are resolved to **_malloc_dbg**. However, explicitly calling **_malloc_dbg** allows the application to perform additional debugging tasks: it can separately track **_CLIENT_BLOCK** type allocations, and it can include the source file and line number where the allocation request occurred in the bookkeeping information stored in the debug header.

Because the base versions of the allocation functions are implemented as wrappers, the source file name and line number of each heap allocation request is not available by explicitly calling the base version. Applications that do not want to convert their **malloc** calls to **_malloc_dbg** can obtain the source file information by defining the **_CRTDBG_MAP_ALLOC** environment variable. Defining this variable causes the preprocessor to directly map all calls to **malloc** to **_malloc_dbg**, thereby providing the additional information. To track particular types of allocations separately in client blocks, **_malloc_dbg** must be called directly and the *blockType* parameter must be set to **_CLIENT_BLOCK**.

When **_DEBUG** is *not* defined, calls to **malloc** are not disturbed, calls to **_malloc_dbg** are resolved to **malloc**, the **_CRTDBG_MAP_ALLOC** environment variable is ignored, and source file information pertaining to the allocation request is not provided. Because **malloc** does not have a block type parameter, requests for **_CLIENT_BLOCK** types are treated as standard allocations.

Tracking Heap Allocation Requests

Although pinpointing the source file name and line number at which an assert or reporting macro executes is often very useful in locating the cause of a problem, the same is not as likely to be true of heap allocation functions. Whereas macros can be inserted at many appropriate points in an application's logic tree, an allocation is often buried in a special routine that is called from many different places at many different times. The question is usually not what line of code made a bad allocation, but rather which one of the thousands of allocations made by that line of code was bad, and why.

The simplest way to identify the specific heap allocation call that went bad is to take advantage of the unique allocation request number associated with each block in the debug heap. When information about a block is reported by one of the dump functions, this allocation request number is enclosed in curly brackets (for example, "{36}").

Once you know the allocation request number of an improperly allocated block, you can pass this number to **_CrtSetBreakAlloc** to create a breakpoint. Execution will break just prior to allocating the block, and you can backtrack to determine what routine was responsible for the bad call. To avoid recompiling, you can accomplish the same thing in the debugger by setting **_crtBreakAlloc** to the allocation request number you are interested in.

A somewhat more complicated approach is to create debug versions of your own allocation routines, comparable to the **_dbg** versions of the heap allocation functions. You can then pass source file and line number arguments through to the underlying heap allocation routines, and you will immediately be able to see where a bad allocation originated.

For example, suppose your application contains a commonly used routine something like the following:

```
int addNewRecord(struct RecStruct * prevRecord,
                 int recType, int recAccess)
{
   /* ...code omitted through actual allocation... */
   if ((newRec = malloc(recSize)) == NULL)
   /* ... rest of routine omitted too ... */
}
```

In a header file, you could add code such as the following:

```
#ifdef _DEBUG
#define  addNewRecord(p, t, a) \
         addNewRecord(p, t, a, __FILE__, __LINE__)
#endif
```

Next, you could change the allocation in your record-creation routine as follows:

```
int addNewRecord(struct RecStruct *prevRecord,
                  int recType, int recAccess
#ifdef _DEBUG
                 , const char *srcFile, int srcLine
#endif
   )
{
   /* ... code omitted through actual allocation ... */
   if ((newRec = _malloc_dbg(recSize, _NORMAL_BLOCK,
        srcFile, scrLine)) == NULL)
   /* ... rest of routine omitted too ... */
}
```

Now the source file name and line number where `addNewRecord` was called will be stored in each resulting block allocated in the debug heap, and will be reported when that block is examined.

Using the Debug Heap from C++

The debug versions of the C run-time library contain debug versions of the C++ **new** and **delete** operators. Unless you intend to make special use of the **_CLIENT_BLOCK** allocation type, be sure to define **_CRTDBG_MAP_ALLOC** when you are using C++. This environment variable causes all instances of **new** in your code to be mapped properly to the debug version of **new** so as to record source file and line number information. If you intend to use the **_CLIENT_BLOCK** type, do not define **_CRTDBG_MAP_ALLOC**, but instead include code like the following in an include file:

```
#ifdef _DEBUG
inline void* __cdecl operator new( unsigned int s )
   { return ::operator new( s, _CLIENT_BLOCK, __FILE__,
                            __LINE__ ); }
#endif
```

The debug version of the **delete** operator works with all block types and should require no changes in your program.

Writing Your Own Debug Hook Functions

You may need special features and tools when debugging a complex application. In many cases, you can add exactly the capabilities you want by taking advantage of the debug hooks in the C run-time library.

Client Block Hook Functions

If you are interested in validating or reporting the contents of the data that you are storing in **_CLIENT_BLOCK** blocks, you can write a function specifically for this purpose. The function that you write must have a prototype similar to the following, as defined in CRTDBG.H:

```
void YourClientDump(void *, size_t)
```

In other words, your hook function should accept a **void** pointer to the beginning of the user's section of the allocation block, together with a **size_t** type value indicating the size of the allocation, and return **void**. Other than that, its contents are up to you.

Once you have installed it using **_CrtSetDumpClient**, your hook function will be called every time a **_CLIENT_BLOCK** block is dumped.

The pointer to your function that you pass to **_CrtSetDumpClient** is of type **_CRT_DUMP_CLIENT**, as defined in CRTDBG.H:

```
typedef void (__cdecl *_CRT_DUMP_CLIENT)
   (void *, size_t);
```

Allocation Hook Functions

An allocation hook function, installed using **_CrtSetAllocHook**, is called every time memory is allocated, re-allocated, or freed. This type of hook can be used for many different purposes. Use it to test how an application handles insufficient memory situations, for example, or to examine allocation patterns, or to log allocation information for later analysis. Be aware of the restriction described below about using C run-time library functions in an allocation hook function.

An allocation hook function should have a prototype like the following:

```
int YourAllocHook(int nAllocType, void *pvData,
      size_t nSize, int nBlockUse, long lRequest,
      const unsigned char * szFileName, int nLine )
```

The pointer that you pass to **_CrtSetAllocHook** is of type **_CRT_ALLOC_HOOK**, as defined in CRTDBG.H:

```
typedef int (__cdecl * _CRT_ALLOC_HOOK)
   (int, void *, size_t, int, long, const char *, int);
```

When the run-time library calls your hook, the *nAllocType* argument indicates what allocation operation is about to be performed (**_HOOK_ALLOC**, **_HOOK_REALLOC**, or **_HOOK_FREE**). In the case of a free or a reallocation, `pvData` contains a pointer to the user section of the block about to be freed, but in the case of an allocation this pointer is null, since the allocation has not yet occurred. The remaining arguments contain the size of the allocation in question, its block type, the sequential request number associated with it, and a pointer to the filename and line number in which the allocation was made, if available. After the hook function performs whatever analysis and other tasks its author wants, it must return either TRUE, indicating that the allocation operation can continue, or FALSE, indicating that the operation should fail. A simple hook of this type might check the amount of memory allocated so far, and return FALSE if that amount exceeded a small limit. The application would then experience the kind of allocation errors that would normally only occur when available memory was very low. More complex hooks might keep track of allocation patterns, analyze memory use, or report when specific situations occur.

Using C Run-time Library Functions in Allocation Hooks

A very important restriction on allocation hook functions is that they must explicitly ignore **_CRT_BLOCK** blocks (the memory allocations made internally by C run-time library functions) if they make any calls to C run-time library functions that allocate internal memory. **_CRT_BLOCK** blocks can be ignored by including code such as the following at the beginning of your allocation hook function:

```
if ( nBlockUse == _CRT_BLOCK )
   return( TRUE );
```

If your allocation hook does not ignore **_CRT_BLOCK** blocks, then any C run-time library function called in your hook can trap the program in an endless loop. For example, **printf** makes an internal allocation. If your hook code calls **printf**, then the resulting allocation will cause your hook to be called again, which will call **printf** again, and so on until the stack overflows. If you need to report **_CRT_BLOCK** allocation operations, one way to circumvent this restriction is to use Windows API functions for formatting and output rather than C run-time functions. Because the Windows APIs do not use the C run-time library heap, they will not trap your allocation hook in an endless loop.

If you examine the run-time library source files, you will see that the default allocation hook function, **CrtDefaultAllocHook** (which simply returns TRUE), is located in a separate file of its own, DBGHOOK.C. If you want your allocation hook to be called even for the allocations made by the run-time startup code that is executed before your application's **main** function, you can replace this default function with one of your own, instead of using **_CrtSetAllocHook**.

Report Hook Functions

A report hook function, installed using **_CrtSetReportHook**, is called every time **_CrtDbgReport** generates a debug report. You can use it, among other things, for filtering reports so as to focus on specific types of allocations. A report hook function should have a prototype like the following:

```
int YourReportHook(int nRptType, char *szMsg, int *retVal);
```

The pointer that you pass to **_CrtSetReportHook** is of type **_CRT_REPORT_HOOK**, as defined in CRTDBG.H:

```
typedef int (__cdecl *_CRT_REPORT_HOOK)(int, char *, int *);
```

When the run-time library calls your hook function, the *nRptType* argument contains the category of the report (**_CRT_WARN**, **_CRT_ERROR**, or **_CRT_ASSERT**), *szMsg* contains a pointer to a fully assembled report message string, and *retVal* specifies the value that should be returned by **_CrtDbgReport**. If the hook handles the message in question completely, so that no further reporting is required, it should return FALSE. If it returns TRUE, then **_CrtDbgReport** will report the message in the normal way.

Example Programs

Build these example programs as Win32 console applications. Your command line should look like the following:

```
cl -D_DEBUG /MTd -Od -Zi -W3 t.c -link -verbose:lib -debug:full
```

In console applications such as the following examples, debugging is complicated by the fact that errors do not interrupt execution of the program, as they normally would when directed to a message window.

First Example Program

This simple program illustrates most of the basic debugging features of the C run-time library, and the kind of debug output that results.

```
/****************************************************************
 *  EXAMPLE 1                                                   *
 *  This simple program illustrates the basic debugging features *
 *  of the C runtime libraries, and the kind of debug output    *
 *  that these features generate.                               *
 ****************************************************************/

#include <stdio.h>
#include <string.h>
#include <malloc.h>
#include <crtdbg.h>
```

```
// This routine place comments at the head of a section of debug output
void OutputHeading( const char * explanation )
{
   _RPT1( _CRT_WARN, "\n\n%s:\n**************************************\
************************************\n", explanation );
}

// The following macros set and clear, respectively, given bits
// of the C runtime library debug flag, as specified by a bitmask.
#ifdef   _DEBUG
#define  SET_CRT_DEBUG_FIELD(a) \
            _CrtSetDbgFlag((a) | _CrtSetDbgFlag(_CRTDBG_REPORT_FLAG))
#define  CLEAR_CRT_DEBUG_FIELD(a) \
            _CrtSetDbgFlag(~(a) & _CrtSetDbgFlag(_CRTDBG_REPORT_FLAG))
#else
#define  SET_CRT_DEBUG_FIELD(a)   ((void) 0)
#define  CLEAR_CRT_DEBUG_FIELD(a) ((void) 0)
#endif


void main( )
{
   char *p1, *p2;
   _CrtMemState s1, s2, s3;

   // Send all reports to STDOUT
   _CrtSetReportMode( _CRT_WARN, _CRTDBG_MODE_FILE );
   _CrtSetReportFile( _CRT_WARN, _CRTDBG_FILE_STDOUT );
   _CrtSetReportMode( _CRT_ERROR, _CRTDBG_MODE_FILE );
   _CrtSetReportFile( _CRT_ERROR, _CRTDBG_FILE_STDOUT );
   _CrtSetReportMode( _CRT_ASSERT, _CRTDBG_MODE_FILE );
   _CrtSetReportFile( _CRT_ASSERT, _CRTDBG_FILE_STDOUT );

   // Allocate 2 memory blocks and store a string in each
   p1 = malloc( 34 );
   strcpy( p1, "This is the p1 string (34 bytes)." );

   p2 = malloc( 34 );
   strcpy( p2, "This is the p2 string (34 bytes)." );


   OutputHeading(
      "Use _ASSERTE to check that the two strings are identical" );
   _ASSERTE( strcmp( p1, p2 ) == 0 );

   OutputHeading(
      "Use a _RPT macro to report the string contents as a warning" );
   _RPT2( _CRT_WARN, "p1 points to '%s' and \np2 points to '%s'\n", p1, p2 );
```

```
OutputHeading(
   "Use _CRTMemDumpAllObjectsSince to check the p1 and p2 allocations" );
_CrtMemDumpAllObjectsSince( NULL );

free( p2 );

OutputHeading(
   "Having freed p2, dump allocation information about p1 only" );
_CrtMemDumpAllObjectsSince( NULL );

// Store a memory checkpoint in the s1 memory-state structure
_CrtMemCheckpoint( &s1 );

// Allocate another block, pointed to by p2
p2 = malloc( 38 );
strcpy( p2, "This new p2 string occupies 38 bytes.");

// Store a 2nd memory checkpoint in s2
_CrtMemCheckpoint( &s2 );

OutputHeading(
   "Dump the changes that occurred between two memory checkpoints" );
if ( _CrtMemDifference( &s3, &s1, &s2 ) )
   _CrtMemDumpStatistics( &s3 );

// Free p2 again and store a new memory checkpoint in s2
free( p2 );
_CrtMemCheckpoint( &s2 );

OutputHeading(
   "Now the memory state at the two checkpoints is the same" );
if ( _CrtMemDifference( &s3, &s1, &s2 ) )
   _CrtMemDumpStatistics( &s3 );

strcpy( p1, "This new p1 string is over 34 bytes" );
OutputHeading( "Free p1 after overwriting the end of the allocation" );
free( p1 );

// Set the debug-heap flag so that freed blocks are kept on the
// linked list, to catch any inadvertent use of freed memory
SET_CRT_DEBUG_FIELD( _CRTDBG_DELAY_FREE_MEM_DF );

p1 = malloc( 10 );
free( p1 );
strcpy( p1, "Oops" );

OutputHeading( "Perform a memory check after corrupting freed memory" );
_CrtCheckMemory( );
```

```
   // Use explicit calls to _malloc_dbg to save file name and line number
   // information, and also to allocate Client type blocks for tracking
   p1 = _malloc_dbg( 40, _NORMAL_BLOCK, __FILE__, __LINE__ );
   p2 = _malloc_dbg( 40, _CLIENT_BLOCK, __FILE__, __LINE__ );
   strcpy( p1, "p1 points to a Normal allocation block" );
   strcpy( p2, "p2 points to a Client allocation block" );

   // You must use _free_dbg to free a Client block
   OutputHeading(
      "Using free( ) to free a Client block causes an assertion failure" );
   free( p1 );
   free( p2 );

   p1 = malloc( 10 );
   OutputHeading( "Examine outstanding allocations (dump memory leaks)" );
   _CrtDumpMemoryLeaks( );

   // Set the debug-heap flag so that memory leaks are reported when
   // the process terminates. Then, exit.
   OutputHeading( "Program exits without freeing a memory block" );
   SET_CRT_DEBUG_FIELD( _CRTDBG_LEAK_CHECK_DF );
}
```

Output

```
Use _ASSERTE to check that the two strings are identical:
**************************************************************************
C:\DEV\EXAMPLE1.C(56) : Assertion failed: strcmp( p1, p2 ) == 0


Use a _RPT macro to report the string contents as a warning:
**************************************************************************
p1 points to 'This is the p1 string (34 bytes).' and
p2 points to 'This is the p2 string (34 bytes).'


Use _CRTMemDumpAllObjectsSince to check the p1 and p2 allocations:
**************************************************************************
Dumping objects ->
{13} normal block at 0x00660B5C, 34 bytes long
 Data: <This is the p2 s> 54 68 69 73 20 69 73 20 74 68 65 20 70 32 20 73
{12} normal block at 0x00660B10, 34 bytes long
 Data: <This is the p1 s> 54 68 69 73 20 69 73 20 74 68 65 20 70 31 20 73
Object dump complete.


Having freed p2, dump allocation information about p1 only:
**************************************************************************
Dumping objects ->
{12} normal block at 0x00660B10, 34 bytes long
 Data: <This is the p1 s> 54 68 69 73 20 69 73 20 74 68 65 20 70 31 20 73
Object dump complete.
```

```
Dump the changes that occurred between two memory checkpoints:
**************************************************************************
0 bytes in 0 Free Blocks.
38 bytes in 1 Normal Blocks.
0 bytes in 0 CRT Blocks.
0 bytes in 0 IgnoreClient Blocks.
0 bytes in 0 (null) Blocks.
Largest number used: 4 bytes.
Total allocations: 38 bytes.

Now the memory state at the two checkpoints is the same:
**************************************************************************

Free p1 after overwriting the end of the allocation:
**************************************************************************
memory check error at 0x00660B32 = 0x73, should be 0xFD.
memory check error at 0x00660B33 = 0x00, should be 0xFD.
DAMAGE: after Normal block (#12) at 0x00660B10.

Perform a memory check after corrupting freed memory:
**************************************************************************
memory check error at 0x00660B10 = 0x4F, should be 0xDD.
memory check error at 0x00660B11 = 0x6F, should be 0xDD.
memory check error at 0x00660B12 = 0x70, should be 0xDD.
memory check error at 0x00660B13 = 0x73, should be 0xDD.
memory check error at 0x00660B14 = 0x00, should be 0xDD.
DAMAGE: on top of Free block at 0x00660B10.
DAMAGED located at 0x00660B10 is 10 bytes long.


Using free( ) to free a Client block causes an assertion failure:
**************************************************************************
dbgheap.c(1039) : Assertion failed: pHead->nBlockUse == nBlockUse


Examine outstanding allocations (dump memory leaks):
**************************************************************************
Detected memory leaks!
Dumping objects ->
{18} normal block at 0x00660BE4, 10 bytes long
 Data: <          > CD CD CD CD CD CD CD CD CD CD
Object dump complete.


Program exits without freeing a memory block:
**************************************************************************
Detected memory leaks!
Dumping objects ->
{18} normal block at 0x00660BE4, 10 bytes long
 Data: <          > CD CD CD CD CD CD CD CD CD CD
Object dump complete.
```

Second Example Program

This program illustrates several ways to use debugging hook functions with the new debug versions of the C run-time library. To add some realism, it has a few elements of an actual application, including two bugs.

The program stores birth date information in a linked list of Client blocks. A Client-dump hook function validates the birthday data and reports the contents of the Client blocks. An allocation hook function logs heap operations to a text file, and the report hook function logs selected reports to the same text file.

Note that the allocation hook function explicitly excludes Crt blocks (the memory allocated internally by the C run-time library) from its log. The hook function uses **fprintf** to write to the log file, and **fprintf** allocates a CRT block. If CRT blocks were not excluded in this case, an endless loop would overflow the stack: **fprintf** would cause the hook function to be called, the hook would in turn call **fprintf**, which would in turn cause the hook to be called again, and so forth.

To be able to report CRT-type blocks in your allocation hook, Windows API functions could be used instead of C run-time functions. Since the Windows APIs do not use the CRT heap, they would not trap the hook in an endless loop.

The debug heap catches two bugs and a data error in the second example. One bug is that the birthday name field is not large enough to hold several of the test names. The field should be larger, and **strncpy** should be used instead of **strcpy**. The second bug is that the 'while' loop in the `printRecords` function should not end until the `HeadPtr` itself is equal to null. This bug results not only in an incomplete display of birthdays, but also in a memory leak. Finally, Gauss' birthday should be April 30, not April 32.

```
/*****************************************************************
 *  EXAMPLE 2                                                    *
 *  ----------                                                   *
 *  This program illustrates several ways to use debugging hook  *
 *  functions with the new debug versions of the C runtime       *
 *  libraries. To add some realism, it has a few elements of an  *
 *  actual application, including two bugs.                      *
 *                                                               *
 *  The program stores birthdate information in a linked list    *
 *  of Client blocks. A Client-dump hook function validates the  *
 *  birthday data and reports the contents of the Client blocks. *
 *  An allocation hook function logs heap operations to a text   *
 *  file, and the report hook function logs reports to the same  *
 *  text file.                                                   *
 *                                                               *
```

```
 *  NOTE: The allocation hook function explicitly excludes CRT    *
 *        blocks (the memory allocated internally by the C        *
 *        runtime library) from its log. It is important to      *
 *        understand why! The hook function uses fprintf( ) to    *
 *        write to the log file, and fprintf( ) allocates a CRT   *
 *        block. If CRT blocks were not excluded in this case,    *
 *        an endless loop would be created in which fprintf( )    *
 *        would cause the hook function to be called, and the     *
 *        hook would in turn call fprintf( ), which would cause   *
 *        the hook to be called again, and so on. The moral is:   *
 *                                                                *
 *   -->  IF YOUR ALLOCATION HOOK USES ANY C RUNTIME FUNCTION     *
 *        THAT ALLOCATES MEMORY, THE HOOK MUST IGNORE CRT-TYPE    *
 *        ALLOCATION OPERATIONS!                                  *
 *                                                                *
 *  HINT: If you want to be able to report CRT-type blocks in     *
 *        your allocation hook, use Windows API functions for     *
 *        formatting and output, instead of C runtime functions.  *
 *        Since the Windows APIs do not use the CRT heap, they    *
 *        will not trap your hook in an endless loop.             *
 *                                                                *
 *  BUGS: There are two bugs in the program below, which the      *
 *        debug heap features identify in several ways. One bug   *
 *        is that the birthDay.Name field is not large enough     *
 *        to hold several of the test names. The field should     *
 *        be larger, and strncpy( ) should be used in place of    *
 *        strcpy( ). The second bug is that the while( ) loop     *
 *        in the printRecords( ) function should not end until    *
 *        HeadPtr itself == NULL. This bug results not only in    *
 *        an incomplete display of birthdays, but also in a       *
 *        memory leak. In addition to these two bugs, Gauss'      *
 *        birthday data is out of range (April 30, not 32).       *
 *                                                                *
 ******************************************************************/

#include <stdio.h>
#include <stdlib.h>
#include <string.h>
#include <malloc.h>
#include <time.h>
#include <crtdbg.h>

/******************************************************************
 *  DATA DECLARATIONS AND DEFINES                                 *
 ******************************************************************/

// The following arrays provide test data for the example program:
```

```
const char * Names[] =
{
   "George Washington",
   "Thomas Jefferson",
   "Carl Friedrich Gauss",
   "Ludwig van Beethoven",
   "Thomas Carlyle"
} ;

const int Dates[] =
{
   1732,  2, 11,
   1743,  4, 13,
   1777,  4, 32,
   1795, 12,  4,
   1770, 12, 16
} ;

#define  TEST_RECS            5
// A generic sort of linked-list data structure, in this case for birthdays:
typedef struct BirthdayStruct
{
   struct BirthdayStruct * NextRec;
   int   Year;
   int   Month;
   int   Day;
   char  Name[20];
} birthDay;

birthDay * HeadPtr;
birthDay * TailPtr;

#define  FILE_IO_ERROR        0
#define  OUT_OF_MEMORY        1

#define  TRUE                 7
#define  FALSE                0

// Macros for setting or clearing bits in the CRT debug flag
#ifdef _DEBUG
#define  SET_CRT_DEBUG_FIELD(a)   _CrtSetDbgFlag((a) |
_CrtSetDbgFlag(_CRTDBG_REPORT_FLAG))
#define  CLEAR_CRT_DEBUG_FIELD(a) _CrtSetDbgFlag(~(a) &
_CrtSetDbgFlag(_CRTDBG_REPORT_FLAG))
#else
#define  SET_CRT_DEBUG_FIELD(a)   ((void) 0)
#define  CLEAR_CRT_DEBUG_FIELD(a) ((void) 0)
#endif
```

```
/******************************************************************
 *  SPECIAL-PURPOSE ROUTINES                                      *
 ******************************************************************/

/* ERROR HANDLER
   -------------
   Handling serious errors gracefully is a real test of craftsmanship.
   This function is just a stub; it doesn't really handle errors.
*/
void FatalError( int ErrType )
{
   exit( 1 );
}


/* MEMORY ALLOCATION FUNCTION
   --------------------------
   The createRecord function allocates memory for a new birthday record,
   fills in the structure members, and then adds the record to a linked list.
   In debug builds, it makes these allocations in Client blocks. If memory
   is not available, it calls the error handler.
*/
void createRecord(
   const int    Year,
   const int    Month,
   const int    Day,
   const char * Name
#ifdef _DEBUG
,  const unsigned char * szFileName, int nLine
#endif
   )
{
   birthDay * ptr;
   size_t n;

   n = sizeof( struct BirthdayStruct );
   ptr = (birthDay *) _malloc_dbg( n, _CLIENT_BLOCK, szFileName, nLine );
   if( ptr == NULL )
      FatalError( OUT_OF_MEMORY );
   ptr->Year = Year;
   ptr->Month = Month;
   ptr->Day = Day;
   strcpy( ptr->Name, Name );

   ptr->NextRec = NULL;
   if ( HeadPtr == NULL )      // If this is the first record in the linked list
      HeadPtr = ptr;
   else
      TailPtr->NextRec = ptr;
   TailPtr = ptr;
}
```

```
/* BIRTHDAY DISPLAY FUNCTION
   -------------------------
   This function traverses the linked list, displays the birthday data,
   and then frees the memory blocks used to store the birthdays.
*/
void printRecords( )
{
   birthDay * ptr;
   char *months[] = {
      "", "January", "February", "March", "April", "May", "June", "July",
      "August", "September", "October", "November", "December" };

   if ( HeadPtr == NULL )         // Do nothing if list is empty
      return;

   printf( "\n\nThis is the birthday list:\n" );
   while ( HeadPtr->NextRec != NULL )
   {
      printf( "   %s was born on %s %d, %d.\n",
              HeadPtr->Name, months[HeadPtr->Month], HeadPtr->Day, HeadPtr->Year );
      ptr = HeadPtr->NextRec;
      _free_dbg( HeadPtr, _CLIENT_BLOCK );
      HeadPtr = ptr;
   }
}


/*******************************************************************
 *  DEBUG C RUNTIME LIBRARY HOOK FUNCTIONS AND DEFINES             *
 *******************************************************************/
#ifdef _DEBUG
#define  createRecord(a, b, c, d) \
         createRecord(a, b, c, d, __FILE__, __LINE__)
FILE *logFile;                    // Used to log allocation information
const char lineStr[] = { "---------------------------------------\
--------------------------------------\n"  };

/* CLIENT DUMP HOOK FUNCTION
   -------------------------
   A hook function for dumping a Client block usually reports some
   or all of the contents of the block in question.  The function
   below also checks the data in several ways, and reports corruption
   or inconsistency as an assertion failure.
*/
void __cdecl MyDumpClientHook(
   void * pUserData,
   size_t nBytes
   )
{
   birthDay * bday;

   bday = (birthDay *) pUserData;
```

```
   _RPT4( _CRT_WARN, "   The birthday of %s is %d/%d/%d.\n",
          bday->Name, bday->Month, bday->Day, bday->Year );
   _ASSERTE( ( bday->Day > 0 ) && ( bday->Day < 32 ) );
   _ASSERTE( ( bday->Month > 0 ) && ( bday->Month < 13 ) );
   _ASSERTE( ( bday->Year > 0 ) && ( bday->Year < 1996 ) );
}


/* ALLOCATION HOOK FUNCTION
   -------------------------
   An allocation hook function can have many, many different
   uses. This one simply logs each allocation operation in a file.
*/
int __cdecl MyAllocHook(
   int      nAllocType,
   void   * pvData,
   size_t   nSize,
   int      nBlockUse,
   long     lRequest,
   const unsigned char * szFileName,
   int      nLine
   )
{
   char *operation[] = { "", "allocating", "re-allocating", "freeing" };
   char *blockType[] = { "Free", "Normal", "CRT", "Ignore", "Client" };

   if ( nBlockUse == _CRT_BLOCK )   // Ignore internal C runtime library allocations
      return( TRUE );

   _ASSERT( ( nAllocType > 0 ) && ( nAllocType < 4 ) );
   _ASSERT( ( nBlockUse >= 0 ) && ( nBlockUse < 5 ) );

   fprintf( logFile,
            "Memory operation in %s, line %d: %s a %d-byte '%s' block (# %ld)\n",
            szFileName, nLine, operation[nAllocType], nSize,
            blockType[nBlockUse], lRequest );
   if ( pvData != NULL )
      fprintf( logFile, " at %X", pvData );

   return( TRUE );         // Allow the memory operation to proceed
}


/* REPORT HOOK FUNCTION
   --------------------
   Again, report hook functions can serve a very wide variety of purposes.
   This one logs error and assertion failure debug reports in the
   log file, along with 'Damage' reports about overwritten memory.

   By setting the retVal parameter to zero, we are instructing _CrtDbgReport
   to return zero, which causes execution to continue. If we want the function
   to start the debugger, we should have _CrtDbgReport return one.
*/
```

```
int MyReportHook(
   int   nRptType,
   char *szMsg,
   int  *retVal
   )
{
   char *RptTypes[] = { "Warning", "Error", "Assert" };

   if ( ( nRptType > 0 ) || ( strstr( szMsg, "DAMAGE" ) ) )
      fprintf( logFile, "%s: %s", RptTypes[nRptType], szMsg );

   retVal = 0;

   return( TRUE );         // Allow the report to be made as usual

}
#endif                     // End of #ifdef _DEBUG


/*****************************************************************
 *  MAIN FUNCTION                                                *
 *****************************************************************/
void main( )
{
   int i, j;

#ifdef _DEBUG
   _CrtMemState checkPt1;
   char timeStr[10], dateStr[10];         // Used to set up log file

   // Send all reports to STDOUT, since this example is a console app
   _CrtSetReportMode(_CRT_WARN, _CRTDBG_MODE_FILE);
   _CrtSetReportFile(_CRT_WARN, _CRTDBG_FILE_STDOUT);
   _CrtSetReportMode(_CRT_ERROR, _CRTDBG_MODE_FILE);
   _CrtSetReportFile(_CRT_ERROR, _CRTDBG_FILE_STDOUT);
   _CrtSetReportMode(_CRT_ASSERT, _CRTDBG_MODE_FILE);
   _CrtSetReportFile(_CRT_ASSERT, _CRTDBG_FILE_STDOUT);

   // Set the debug heap to report memory leaks when the process terminates,
   // and to keep freed blocks in the linked list.
   SET_CRT_DEBUG_FIELD( _CRTDBG_LEAK_CHECK_DF | _CRTDBG_DELAY_FREE_MEM_DF );

   // Open a log file for the hook functions to use
   logFile = fopen( "MEM-LOG.TXT", "w" );
   if ( logFile == NULL )
      FatalError( FILE_IO_ERROR );
   _strtime( timeStr );
   _strdate( dateStr );
   fprintf( logFile,
            "Memory Allocation Log File for Example Program, run at %s on %s.\n",
            timeStr, dateStr );
   fputs( lineStr, logFile );
```

```
   // Install the hook functions
   _CrtSetDumpClient( MyDumpClientHook );
   _CrtSetAllocHook( MyAllocHook );
   _CrtSetReportHook( MyReportHook );

#endif                       // End of #ifdef _DEBUG

   HeadPtr = NULL;

   // Create a trial birthday record.
   createRecord( 1749, 3, 23, "Pierre de Laplace" );

   // Check the debug heap, and dump the new birthday record. --Note that
   // debug C runtime library functions such as _CrtCheckMemory( ) and
   // _CrtMemDumpAllObjectsSince( ) automatically disappear in a release build.
   _CrtMemDumpAllObjectsSince( NULL );
   _CrtCheckMemory( );
   _CrtMemCheckpoint( &checkPt1 );

   // Since everything has worked so far, create more records
   for ( i = 0, j = 0; i < TEST_RECS; i++, j+=3 )
      createRecord( Dates[j], Dates[j+1], Dates[j+2], Names[i] );

   // Examine the results
   _CrtMemDumpAllObjectsSince( &checkPt1 );
   _CrtMemCheckpoint( &checkPt1 );
   _CrtMemDumpStatistics( &checkPt1 );
   _CrtCheckMemory( );

   // This fflush needs to be removed...
   fflush( logFile );

   // Now try displaying the records, which frees the memory being used
   printRecords( );

   // OK, time to go. Did I forget to turn out any lights? I could check
   // explicitly using _CrtDumpMemoryLeaks( ), but I have set
   // _CRTDBG_LEAK_CHECK_DF, so the C runtime library debug heap will
   // automatically alert me at exit of any memory leaks.

#ifdef _DEBUG
   fclose( logFile );
#endif
}
```

Output

Screen output:

```
Dumping objects ->
C:\DEV\EXAMPLE2.C(327) : {13} client block at 0x00661B38, subtype 0, 36 bytes long:
   The birthday of Pierre de Laplace is 3/23/1749.
Object dump complete.
Dumping objects ->
```

```
C:\DEV\EXAMPLE2.C(338) : {18} client block at 0x00661CB4, subtype 0, 36 bytes long:
   The birthday of Thomas Carlyle is 12/16/1770.
C:\DEV\EXAMPLE2.C(338) : {17} client block at 0x00661C68, subtype 0, 36 bytes long:
   The birthday of Ludwig van Beethoven is 12/4/1795.
C:\DEV\EXAMPLE2.C(338) : {16} client block at 0x00661C1C, subtype 0, 36 bytes long:
   The birthday of Carl Friedrich Gauss is 4/32/1777.
C:\DEV\EXAMPLE2.C(219) : Assertion failed: ( bday->Day > 0 ) && ( bday->Day < 32 )
C:\DEV\EXAMPLE2.C(338) : {15} client block at 0x00661BD0, subtype 0, 36 bytes long:
   The birthday of Thomas Jefferson is 4/13/1743.
C:\DEV\EXAMPLE2.C(338) : {14} client block at 0x00661B84, subtype 0, 36 bytes long:
   The birthday of George Washington is 2/11/1732.
Object dump complete.
0 bytes in 0 Free Blocks.
0 bytes in 0 Normal Blocks.
6442 bytes in 12 CRT Blocks.
0 bytes in 0 IgnoreClient Blocks.
216 bytes in 6 (null) Blocks.
Largest number used: 6658 bytes.
Total allocations: 6658 bytes.
memory check error at 0x00661C8C = 0x00, should be 0xFD.
DAMAGE: after (null) block (#17) at 0x00661C68.
(null) allocated at file C:\DEV\EXAMPLE2.C(338).
(null) located at 0x00661C68 is 36 bytes long.
memory check error at 0x00661C40 = 0x00, should be 0xFD.
DAMAGE: after (null) block (#16) at 0x00661C1C.
(null) allocated at file C:\DEV\EXAMPLE2.C(338).
(null) located at 0x00661C1C is 36 bytes long.
memory check error at 0x00661C40 = 0x00, should be 0xFD.
DAMAGE: after (null) block (#16) at 0x00661C1C.
memory check error at 0x00661C8C = 0x00, should be 0xFD.
DAMAGE: after (null) block (#17) at 0x00661C68.


This is the birthday list:
   Pierre de Laplace was born on March 23, 1749.
   George Washington was born on February 11, 1732.
   Thomas Jefferson was born on April 13, 1743.
   Carl Friedrich Gauss was born on April 32, 1777.
   Ludwig van Beethoven was born on December 4, 1795.
Detected memory leaks!
Dumping objects ->
C:\DEV\EXAMPLE2.C(338) : {18} client block at 0x00661CB4, subtype 0, 36 bytes long:
   The birthday of Thomas Carlyle is 12/16/1770.
Object dump complete.
```

Log file output:

```
Memory Allocation Log File for Example Program, run at 14:11:01 on 04/28/95.
-----------------------------------------------------------------------------
Memory operation in C:\DEV\EXAMPLE2.C, line 327:
                                   allocating a 36-byte 'Client' block (# 13)
Memory operation in C:\DEV\EXAMPLE2.C, line 338:
                                    allocating a 36-byte 'Client' block (# 14)
```

```
Memory operation in C:\DEV\EXAMPLE2.C, line 338:
                                    allocating a 36-byte 'Client' block (# 15)
Memory operation in C:\DEV\EXAMPLE2.C, line 338:
                                    allocating a 36-byte 'Client' block (# 16)
Memory operation in C:\DEV\EXAMPLE2.C, line 338:
                                    allocating a 36-byte 'Client' block (# 17)
Memory operation in C:\DEV\EXAMPLE2.C, line 338:
                                    allocating a 36-byte 'Client' block (# 18)
Assert: C:\DEV\EXAMPLE2.C(219) : Assertion failed:
                                    ( bday->Day > 0 ) && ( bday->Day < 32 )
Warning: DAMAGE: after (null) block (#17) at 0x00661C68.
Warning: DAMAGE: after (null) block (#16) at 0x00661C1C.
Memory operation in (null), line 0: freeing a 0-byte 'Client' block (# 0)
 at 661B38Memory operation in (null), line 0:
                                    freeing a 0-byte 'Client' block (# 0)
 at 661B84Memory operation in (null), line 0:
                                    freeing a 0-byte 'Client' block (# 0)
 at 661BD0Memory operation in (null), line 0:
                                    freeing a 0-byte 'Client' block (# 0)
 at 661C1CError: DAMAGE: after (null) block (#16) at 0x00661C1C.
Memory operation in (null), line 0: freeing a 0-byte 'Client' block (# 0)
 at 661C68Error: DAMAGE: after (null) block (#17) at 0x00661C68.
```

_ASSERT, _ASSERTE Macros

Evaluate an expression and generate a debug report when the result is FALSE (debug version only)

_ASSERT(*booleanExpression* **);**
_ASSERTE(*booleanExpression* **);**

Macro	Required Header	Optional Headers	Compatibility
_ASSERT	<crtdbg.h>		Win NT, Win 95, PMac
_ASSERTE	<crtdbg.h>		Win NT, Win 95, PMac

For additional compatibility information, see "Compatibility" on page ix in the Introduction.

Libraries

LIBCD.LIB	Single thread static library, debug version
LIBCMTD.LIB	Multithread static library, debug version
MSVCRTD.LIB	Import library for MSVCRx0D.DLL, debug version
MSVCRx0D.DLL	Multithread DLL library, debug version

Although **_ASSERT** and **_ASSERTE** are macros and are obtained by including CRTDBG.H, the application must link with one of the libraries listed above because these macros call other run-time functions.

Return Value

None

Parameter

booleanExpression Expression (including pointers) that evaluates to nonzero or 0

Remarks

The **_ASSERT** and **_ASSERTE** macros provide an application with a clean and simple mechanism for checking assumptions during the debugging process. They are very flexible because they do not need to be enclosed in **#ifdef** statements to prevent them from being called in a retail build of an application. This flexibility is achieved by using the **_DEBUG** macro. **_ASSERT** and **_ASSERTE** are only available when **_DEBUG** is defined. When **_DEBUG** is not defined, calls to these macros are removed during preprocessing.

_ASSERT and **_ASSERTE** evaluate their *booleanExpression* argument and when the result is FALSE (0), they print a diagnostic message and call **_CrtDbgReport** to generate a debug report. The **_ASSERT** macro prints a simple diagnostic message, while **_ASSERTE** includes a string representation of the failed expression in the message. These macros do nothing when *booleanExpression* evaluates to nonzero.

Because the **_ASSERTE** macro specifies the failed expression in the generated report, it enables users to identify the problem without referring to the application source code. However, a disadvantage exists in that every expression evaluated by **_ASSERTE** must be included in the debug version of your application as a string constant. Therefore, if a large number of calls are made to **_ASSERTE**, these expressions can take up a significant amount of space.

_CrtDbgReport generates the debug report and determines its destination(s), based on the current report mode(s) and file defined for the **_CRT_ASSERT** report type. By default, assertion failures and errors are directed to a debug message window. The **_CrtSetReportMode** and **_CrtSetReportFile** functions are used to define the destination(s) for each report type.

When the destination is a debug message window and the user chooses the Retry button, **_CrtDbgReport** returns 1, causing the **_ASSERT** and **_ASSERTE** macros to start the debugger, provided that "just-in-time" (JIT) debugging is enabled. See page 75 for an example of an assert message box under Windows NT.

For more information about the reporting process, see the **_CrtDbgReport** function and the section "Debug Reporting Functions of the C Run-Time Library" on page 73. For more information about resolving assertion failures and using these macros as a debugging error handling mechanism, see "Using Macros for Verification and Reporting" on page 75.

The **_RPT, _RPTF** debug macros are also available for generating a debug report, but they do not evaluate an expression. The **_RPT** macros generate a simple report and the **_RPTF** macros include the source file and line number where the report macro was called, in the generated report. In addition to the **_ASSERTE** macros, the ANSI **assert** routine can also be used to verify program logic. This routine is available in both the debug and release versions of the libraries.

Example

```
/*
 * DBGMACRO.C
 * In this program, calls are made to the _ASSERT and _ASSERTE
 * macros to test the condition 'string1 == string2'.  If the
 * condition fails, these macros print a diagnostic message.
 * The _RPTn and _RPTFn group of macros are also exercised in
 * this program, as an alternative to the printf function.
 */

#include <stdio.h>
#include <string.h>
#include <malloc.h>
#include <crtdbg.h>

int main()
{
    char *p1, *p2;

    /*
     * The Reporting Mode and File must be specified
     * before generating a debug report via an assert
     * or report macro.
     * This program sends all report types to STDOUT
     */
    _CrtSetReportMode(_CRT_WARN, _CRTDBG_MODE_FILE);
    _CrtSetReportFile(_CRT_WARN, _CRTDBG_FILE_STDOUT);
    _CrtSetReportMode(_CRT_ERROR, _CRTDBG_MODE_FILE);
    _CrtSetReportFile(_CRT_ERROR, _CRTDBG_FILE_STDOUT);
    _CrtSetReportMode(_CRT_ASSERT, _CRTDBG_MODE_FILE);
    _CrtSetReportFile(_CRT_ASSERT, _CRTDBG_FILE_STDOUT);

    /*
     * Allocate and assign the pointer variables
     */
    p1 = malloc(10);
    strcpy(p1, "I am p1");
    p2 = malloc(10);
    strcpy(p2, "I am p2");
```

```
    /*
     * Use the report macros as a debugging
     * warning mechanism, similar to printf.
     *
     * Use the assert macros to check if the
     * p1 and p2 variables are equivalent.
     *
     * If the expression fails, _ASSERTE will
     * include a string representation of the
     * failed expression in the report.
     * _ASSERT does not include the
     * expression in the generated report.
     */
    _RPT0(_CRT_WARN, "\n\n Use the assert macros to evaluate the expression p1 ==
p2.\n");
    _RPTF2(_CRT_WARN, "\n Will _ASSERT find '%s' == '%s' ?\n", p1, p2);
    _ASSERT(p1 == p2);

    _RPTF2(_CRT_WARN, "\n\n Will _ASSERTE find '%s' == '%s' ?\n", p1, p2);
    _ASSERTE(p1 == p2);

    _RPT2(_CRT_ERROR, "\n \n '%s' != '%s'\n", p1, p2);

    free(p2);
    free(p1);

    return 0;
}
```

Output

```
Use the assert macros to evaluate the expression p1 == p2.

dbgmacro.c(54) : Will _ASSERT find 'I am p1' == 'I am p2' ?
dbgmacro.c(55) : Assertion failed

dbgmacro.c(57) : Will _ASSERTE find 'I am p1' == 'I am p2' ?
dbgmacro.c(58) : Assertion failed: p1 == p2

'I am p1' != 'I am p2'
```

See Also **_RPT, _RPTF**

_calloc_dbg

Allocates a number of memory blocks in the heap with additional space for a debugging header and overwrite buffers (debug version only).

void *_**calloc_dbg(size_t** *num*, **size_t** *size*, **int** *blockType*, **const char** **filename*, **int** *linenumber* **);**

Routine	Required Header	Optional Headers	Compatibility
_calloc_dbg	<crtdbg.h>		Win NT, Win 95, PMac

For additional compatibility information, see "Compatibility" on page ix in the Introduction.

Libraries	
LIBCD.LIB	Single thread static library, debug version
LIBCMTD.LIB	Multithread static library, debug version
MSVCRTD.LIB	Import library for MSVCRx0D.DLL, debug version
MSVCRx0D.DLL	Multithread DLL library, debug version

Return Value

Upon successful completion, this function either returns a pointer to the user portion of the last allocated memory block, calls the new handler function, or returns NULL. See the following Remarks section for a complete description of the return behavior. See the **calloc** function for more information on how the new handler function is used.

Parameters

num Requested number of memory blocks

size Requested size of each memory block (bytes)

blockType Requested type of memory block: **_CLIENT_BLOCK** or **_NORMAL_BLOCK**

filename Pointer to name of source file that requested allocation operation or NULL

linenumber Line number in source file where allocation operation was requested or NULL

The *filename* and *linenumber* parameters are only available when **_calloc_dbg** has been called explicitly or the **_CRTDBG_MAP_ALLOC** environment variable has been defined.

Remarks

_calloc_dbg is a debug version of the **calloc** function. When **_DEBUG** is not defined, calls to **_calloc_dbg** are removed during preprocessing. Both **calloc** and **_calloc_dbg** allocate *num* memory blocks in the base heap, but **_calloc_dbg** offers several debugging features: buffers on either side of the user portion of the block to test for leaks, a block type parameter to track specific allocation types, and *filename/linenumber* information to determine the origin of allocation requests.

_calloc_dbg allocates each memory block with slightly more space than the requested *size*. The additional space is used by the debug heap manager to link the debug memory blocks together and to provide the application with debug header information and overwrite buffers. When the block is allocated, the user portion of the block is filled with the value 0xCD and each of the overwrite buffers are filled with 0xFD.

For information about how memory blocks are allocated, initialized, and managed in the debug version of the base heap, see "Memory Management and the Debug Heap" on page 79. For information about the allocation block types and how they are used, see "Types of Blocks on the Debug Heap" on page 80. For information on the differences between calling a standard heap function versus its debug version in a debug build of an application, see "Using the Debug Version Versus the Base Version" on page 84.

Example

```
/*
 * CALLOCD.C
 * This program uses _calloc_dbg to allocate space for
 * 40 long integers. It initializes each element to zero.
 */
#include <stdio.h>
#include <malloc.h>
#include <crtdbg.h>

void main( void )
{
        long *bufferN, *bufferC;

        /*
         * Call _calloc_dbg to include the filename and line number
         * of our allocation request in the header and also so we can
         * allocate CLIENT type blocks specifically
         */
        bufferN = (long *)_calloc_dbg( 40, sizeof(long), _NORMAL_BLOCK, __FILE__,
__LINE__ );
        bufferC = (long *)_calloc_dbg( 40, sizeof(long), _CLIENT_BLOCK, __FILE__,
__LINE__ );
        if( bufferN != NULL && bufferC != NULL )
              printf( "Allocated memory successfully\n" );
        else
              printf( "Problem allocating memory\n" );

        /*
         * _free_dbg must be called to free CLIENT type blocks
         */
        free( bufferN );
        _free_dbg( bufferC, _CLIENT_BLOCK );
}
```

Output

```
Allocated memory successfully
```

See Also **calloc**, **_malloc_dbg**, **_DEBUG**

_CrtCheckMemory

Confirms the integrity of the memory blocks allocated in the debug heap (debug version only).

int _CrtCheckMemory(void);

Routine	Required Header	Optional Headers	Compatibility
_CrtCheckMemory	<crtdbg.h>		Win NT, Win 95, PMac

For additional compatibility information, see "Compatibility" on page ix in the Introduction.

Libraries	
LIBCD.LIB	Single thread static library, debug version
LIBCMTD.LIB	Multithread static library, debug version
MSVCRTD.LIB	Import library for MSVCRx0D.DLL, debug version
MSVCRx0D.DLL	Multithread DLL library, debug version

Return Value

If successful, **_CrtCheckMemory** returns TRUE; otherwise, the function returns FALSE.

Remarks

The **_CrtCheckMemory** function validates memory allocated by the debug heap manager by verifying the underlying base heap and inspecting every memory block. If an error or memory inconsistency is encountered in the underlying base heap, the debug header information, or the overwrite buffers, **_CrtCheckMemory** generates a debug report with information describing the error condition. When **_DEBUG** is not defined, calls to **_CrtCheckMemory** are removed during preprocessing.

The behavior of **_CrtCheckMemory** can be controlled by setting the bit fields of the **_crtDbgFlag** flag using the **_CrtSetDbgFlag** function. Turning the **_CRTDBG_CHECK_ALWAYS_DF** bit field ON results in **_CrtCheckMemory** being called every time a memory allocation operation is requested. Although this method slows down execution, it is useful for catching errors quickly. Turning the **_CRTDBG_ALLOC_MEM_DF** bit field OFF causes **_CrtCheckMemory** to not verify the heap and immediately return TRUE.

Because this function returns TRUE or FALSE, it can be passed to one of the **_ASSERT** macros to create a simple debugging error handling mechanism. The following example will cause an assertion failure if corruption is detected in the heap:

```
_ASSERTE( _CrtCheckMemory( ) );
```

For more information about how **_CrtCheckMemory** can be used with other debug functions, see "Heap State Reporting Functions" on page 83. For an overview of memory management and the debug heap, see "Memory Management and the Debug Heap" on page 79.

Example

See "First Example Program" on page 89.

See Also **_crtDbgFlag**, **_CrtSetDbgFlag**

_CrtDbgReport

Generates a report with a debugging message and sends the report to three possible destinations (debug version only).

int _CrtDbgReport(**int** *reportType*, **const char** **filename*, **int** *linenumber*, **const char** **moduleName*, **const char** **format* [, *argument*] ... **);**

Routine	Required Header	Optional Headers	Compatibility
_CrtDbgReport	<crtdbg.h>		Win NT, Win 95, PMac

For additional compatibility information, see "Compatibility" on page ix in the Introduction.

Libraries	
LIBCD.LIB	Single thread static library, debug version
LIBCMTD.LIB	Multithread static library, debug version
MSVCRTD.LIB	Import library for MSVCRx0D.DLL, debug version
MSVCRx0D.DLL	Multithread DLL library, debug version

Return Value

For all report destinations, **_CrtDbgReport** returns –1 if an error occurs and 0 if no errors are encountered. However, when the report destination is a debug message window and the user chooses the Retry button, **_CrtDbgReport** returns 1. If the user chooses the Abort button in the debug message window, **_CrtDbgReport** immediately aborts and does not return a value.

The **_ASSERT[E]** and **_RPT, _RPTF** debug macros call **_CrtDbgReport** to generate their debug report. When **_CrtDbgReport** returns 1, these macros start the debugger, provided that "just-in-time" (JIT) debugging is enabled.

Parameters

reportType Report type: **_CRT_WARN**, **_CRT_ERROR**, **_CRT_ASSERT**

filename Pointer to name of source file where assert/report occurred or NULL

linenumber Line number in source file where assert/report occured or NULL

moduleName Pointer to name of module (.EXE or .DLL) where assert/report occurred

format Pointer to format-control string used to create the user message

argument Optional substitution arguments used by *format*

Remarks

The **_CrtDbgReport** function is similar to the **printf** function, as it can be used to report warnings, errors, and assert information to the user during the debugging process. However, this function is more flexible than **printf** because it does not need to be enclosed in **#ifdef** statements to prevent it from being called in a retail build of an application. This is achieved by using the **_DEBUG** flag: When **_DEBUG** is not defined, calls to **_CrtDbgReport** are removed during preprocessing.

_CrtDbgReport can send the debug report to three different destinations: a debug report file, a debug monitor (the Visual C++ debugger), or a debug message window. Two configuration functions, **_CrtSetReportMode** and **_CrtSetReportFile**, are used to specify the destination(s) for each report type. These functions allow the reporting destination(s) for each report type to be separately controlled. For example, it is possible to specify that a *reportType* of **_CRT_WARN** only be sent to the debug monitor, while a *reportType* of **_CRT_ASSERT** be sent to a debug message window and a user-defined report file.

_CrtDbgReport creates the user message for the debug report by substituting the *argument*[*n*] arguments into the *format* string, using the same rules defined by the **printf** function. **_CrtDbgReport** then generates the debug report and determines the destination(s), based on the current report modes and file defined for *reportType*. When the report is sent to a debug message window, the *filename*, *lineNumber*, and *moduleName* are included in the information displayed in the window.

The following table lists the available choices for the report mode(s) and file and the resulting behavior of **_CrtDbgReport**. These options are defined as bit-flags in CRTDBG.H.

Report Mode	Report File	_CrtDbgReport Behavior
CRTDBG-MODE_DEBUG	Not applicable	Writes message to Windows **OutputDebugString** API.
CRTDBG-MODE_WNDW	Not applicable	Calls Windows **MessageBox** API to create message box to display the message along with Abort, Retry, and Ignore buttons. If user selects Abort, **_CrtDbgReport** immediately aborts. If user selects Retry, it returns 1. If user selects Ignore, execution continues and **_CrtDbgReport** returns 0. Note that choosing Ignore when an error condition exists often results in "undefined behavior."
CRTDBG-MODE_FILE	**__HFILE**	Writes message to user-supplied **HANDLE**, using the Windows **WriteFile** API, and does not verify validity of file handle; the application is responsible for opening the report file and passing a valid file handle.
CRTDBG-MODE_FILE	**_CRTDBG_-FILE_STDERR**	Writes message to **stderr**.
CRTDBG-MODE_FILE	**_CRTDBG_-FILE_STDOUT**	Writes message to **stdout**.

The report may be sent to one, two, or three destinations, or no destination at all. For more information about specifying the report mode(s) and report file, see the **_CrtSetReportMode** and **_CrtSetReportFile** functions. For more information about using the debug macros and reporting functions, see "Using Macros for Verification and Reporting" on page 75 and "Debug Reporting Functions of the C Run-Time Library" on page 73.

If your application needs more flexibility than that provided by **_CrtDbgReport**, you can write your own reporting function and hook it into the C run-time library reporting mechanism by using the **_CrtSetReportHook** function.

Example

```
/*
 * REPORT.C:
 * In this program, calls are made to the _CrtSetReportMode,
 * _CrtSetReportFile, and _CrtSetReportHook functions.
 * The _ASSERT macros are called to evaluate their expression.
 * When the condition fails, these macros print a diagnostic message
 * and call _CrtDbgReport to generate a debug report and the
 * client-defined reporting function is called as well.
 * The _RPTn and _RPTFn group of macros are also exercised in
 * this program, as an alternative to the printf function.
 * When these macros are called, the client-defined reporting function
 * takes care of all the reporting - _CrtDbgReport won't be called.
 */
```

```
#include <stdio.h>
#include <string.h>
#include <malloc.h>
#include <crtdbg.h>

/*
 * Define our own reporting function.
 * We'll hook it into the debug reporting
 * process later using _CrtSetReportHook.
 *
 * Define a global int to keep track of
 * how many assertion failures occur.
 */
int gl_num_asserts=0;
int OurReportingFunction( int reportType, char *userMessage, int *retVal )
{
    /*
     * Tell the user our reporting function is being called.
     * In other words - verify that the hook routine worked.
     */
    fprintf("Inside the client-defined reporting function.\n", STDOUT);
    fflush(STDOUT);

    /*
     * When the report type is for an ASSERT,
     * we'll report some information, but we also
     * want _CrtDbgReport to get called -
     * so we'll return TRUE.
     *
     * When the report type is a WARNing or ERROR,
     * we'll take care of all of the reporting. We don't
     * want _CrtDbgReport to get called -
     * so we'll return FALSE.
     */
    if (reportType == _CRT_ASSERT)
    {
        gl_num_asserts++;
        fprintf("This is the number of Assertion failures that have occurred: %d \n",
gl_num_asserts, STDOUT);
        fflush(STDOUT);
        fprintf("Returning TRUE from the client-defined reporting function.\n",
STDOUT);
        fflush(STDOUT);
        return(TRUE);
    } else {
        fprintf("This is the debug user message: %s \n", userMessage, STDOUT);
        fflush(STDOUT);
        fprintf("Returning FALSE from the client-defined reporting function.\n",
STDOUT);
        fflush(STDOUT);
        return(FALSE);
    }
```

```
    /*
     * By setting retVal to zero, we are instructing _CrtDbgReport
     * to continue with normal execution after generating the report.
     * If we wanted _CrtDbgReport to start the debugger, we would set
     * retVal to one.
     */
    retVal = 0;
}

int main()
{
        char *p1, *p2;

    /*
     * Hook in our client-defined reporting function.
     * Every time a _CrtDbgReport is called to generate
     * a debug report, our function will get called first.
     */
    _CrtSetReportHook( OurReportingFunction );

    /*
     * Define the report destination(s) for each type of report
     * we are going to generate.  In this case, we are going to
     * generate a report for every report type: _CRT_WARN,
     * _CRT_ERROR, and _CRT_ASSERT.
     * The destination(s) is defined by specifying the report mode(s)
     * and report file for each report type.
     * This program sends all report types to STDOUT.
     */
    _CrtSetReportMode(_CRT_WARN, _CRTDBG_MODE_FILE);
    _CrtSetReportFile(_CRT_WARN, _CRTDBG_FILE_STDOUT);
    _CrtSetReportMode(_CRT_ERROR, _CRTDBG_MODE_FILE);
    _CrtSetReportFile(_CRT_ERROR, _CRTDBG_FILE_STDOUT);
    _CrtSetReportMode(_CRT_ASSERT, _CRTDBG_MODE_FILE);
    _CrtSetReportFile(_CRT_ASSERT, _CRTDBG_FILE_STDOUT);

    /*
     * Allocate and assign the pointer variables
     */
    p1 = malloc(10);
    strcpy(p1, "I am p1");
    p2 = malloc(10);
    strcpy(p2, "I am p2");

    /*
     * Use the report macros as a debugging
     * warning mechanism, similar to printf.
     *
     * Use the assert macros to check if the
     * p1 and p2 variables are equivalent.
     *
```

```
      * If the expression fails, _ASSERTE will
      * include a string representation of the
      * failed expression in the report.
      *
      *  _ASSERT does not include the
      * expression in the generated report.
      */
    _RPT0(_CRT_WARN, "\n\n Use the assert macros to evaluate the expression p1 ==
p2.\n");
    _RPTF2(_CRT_WARN, "\n Will _ASSERT find '%s' == '%s' ?\n", p1, p2);
    _ASSERT(p1 == p2);

    _RPTF2(_CRT_WARN, "\n\n Will _ASSERTE find '%s' == '%s' ?\n", p1, p2);
    _ASSERTE(p1 == p2);

    _RPT2(_CRT_ERROR, "\n \n '%s' != '%s'\n", p1, p2);

    free(p2);
    free(p1);

    return 0;
}
```

Output

```
Inside the client-defined reporting function.
This is the debug user message: Use the assert macros to evaluate the expression p1 ==
p2
Returning FALSE from the client-defined reporting function.
Inside the client-defined reporting function.
This is the debug user message: dbgmacro.c(54) : Will _ASSERT find 'I am p1' == 'I am
p2' ?
Returning FALSE from the client-defined reporting function.
Inside the client-defined reporting function.
This is the number of Assertion failures that have occurred: 1
Returning TRUE from the client-defined reporting function.
dbgmacro.c(55) : Assertion failed
Inside the client-defined reporting function.
This is the debug user message: dbgmacro.c(57) : Will _ASSERTE find 'I am p1' == 'I am
p2' ?
Returning FALSE from the client-defined reporting function.
Inside the client-defined reporting function.
This is the number of Assertion failures that have occurred: 2
Returning TRUE from the client-defined reporting function.
dbgmacro.c(58) : Assertion failed: p1 == p2
Inside the client-defined reporting function.
This is the debug user message: 'I am p1' != 'I am p2'
Returning FALSE from the client-defined reporting function.
```

See Also **_CrtSetReportMode**, **_CrtSetReportFile**, **printf**, **_DEBUG**

_CrtDoForAllClientObjects

Calls an application-supplied function for all **_CLIENT_BLOCK** types in the heap (debug version only).

void _CrtDoForAllClientObjects(void (*pfn)(void *, void *), void **context* **);**

Routine	Required Header	Optional Headers	Compatibility
_CrtDoForAllClientObjects	<crtdbg.h>		Win NT, Win 95, PMac

For additional compatibility information, see "Compatibility" on page ix in the Introduction.

Libraries	
LIBCD.LIB	Single thread static library, debug version
LIBCMTD.LIB	Multithread static library, debug version
MSVCRTD.LIB	Import library for MSVCRx0D.DLL, debug version
MSVCRx0D.DLL	Multithread DLL library, debug version

Return Value

None

Parameters

*void (*pfn)(void *, void *)* Pointer to the application-supplied function to call

context Pointer to the application-supplied context to pass to the application-supplied function

Remarks

The **_CrtDoForAllClientObjects** function searches the heap's linked list for memory blocks with the **_CLIENT_BLOCK** type and calls the application-supplied function when a block of this type is found. The found block and the *context* parameter are passed as arguments to the application-supplied function. During debugging, an application can track a specific group of allocations by explicitly calling the debug heap functions to allocate the memory and specifying that the blocks be assigned the **_CLIENT_BLOCK** block type. These blocks can then be tracked separately and reported on differently during leak detection and memory state reporting.

If the **_CRTDBG_ALLOC_MEM_DF** bit field of the **_crtDbgFlag** flag is not turned on, **_CrtDoForAllClientObjects** immediately returns. When **_DEBUG** is not defined, calls to **_CrtDoForAllClientObjects** are removed during preprocessing.

For more information about the **_CLIENT_BLOCK** type and how it can be used by other debug functions, see "Types of Blocks on the Debug Heap" on page 80. For information about how memory blocks are allocated, initialized, and managed in the debug version of the base heap, see "Memory Management and the Debug Heap" on page 79.

Example

```
/*
 * DFACOBJS.C
 * This program allocates some CLIENT type blocks of memory
 * and then calls _CrtDoForAllClientObjects to print out the contents
 * of each client block found on the heap.
 */

#include <stdio.h>
#include <malloc.h>
#include <stdlib.h>
#include <crtdbg.h>

/*
 * My Memory Block linked-list data structure
 */
typedef struct MyMemoryBlockStruct
{
    struct MyMemoryBlockStruct *NextPtr;
    int blockType;
    int allocNum;
} aMemoryBlock;
aMemoryBlock *HeadPtr;
aMemoryBlock *TailPtr;

/*
 * CreateMemoryBlock
 * allocates a block of memory, fills in the data structure
 * and adds the new block to the linked list
 * Returns 1 if successful, otherwise 0
 */
int CreateMemoryBlock(
    int allocNum,
    int blockType
    )
{
    aMemoryBlock *blockPtr;
    size_t size;

    size = sizeof( struct MyMemoryBlockStruct );
    if ( blockType == _CLIENT_BLOCK )
        blockPtr = (aMemoryBlock *) _malloc_dbg( size, _CLIENT_BLOCK, __FILE__,
__LINE__ );
    else
        blockPtr = (aMemoryBlock *) _malloc_dbg( size, _NORMAL_BLOCK, __FILE__,
__LINE__ );

    if ( blockPtr == NULL )
        return(0);
```

```
    blockPtr->allocNum = allocNum;
    blockPtr->blockType = blockType;

    blockPtr->NextPtr = NULL;
    if ( HeadPtr == NULL )
        HeadPtr = blockPtr;
    else
        TailPtr->NextPtr = blockPtr;
    TailPtr = blockPtr;
    return(1);
}

/*
 * RestoreMemoryToHeap
 * restores all of the memory that we allocated on the heap
 */
void RestoreMemoryToHeap( )
{
    aMemoryBlock *blockPtr;

    while ( HeadPtr != NULL )
    {
        blockPtr = HeadPtr->NextPtr;
        if  ( blockPtr->blockType == _CLIENT_BLOCK )
            _free_dbg( HeadPtr, _CLIENT_BLOCK );
        else
            _free_dbg( HeadPtr, _NORMAL_BLOCK );

        HeadPtr = blockPtr;
    }
}

/*
 * MyClientObjectHook
 * A hook function for performing some action on all
 * client blocks found on the heap - In this case, print
 * out the value stored at each memory address.
 */
void __cdecl MyClientObjectHook(
    void * pUserData,
    void * ignored
    )
{
    aMemoryBlock *blockPtr;
    long allocReqNum;
    int success;

    blockPtr = (aMemoryBlock *) pUserData;
```

```
    /*
     * Let's retrieve the actual object allocation order request number
     * and see if it's different from the allocation number we stored in
     * in our data structure.
     */
    success = _CrtIsMemoryBlock((const void *) blockPtr,
                (unsigned int) sizeof( struct MyMemoryBlockStruct ), &allocReqNum,
                NULL, NULL );
    if ( success )
    printf( "Block #%d \t Type: %d \t Allocation Number: %d\n", blockPtr->allocNum,
            blockPtr->blockType, allocReqNum);
    else
    {
            printf("ERROR: not a valid memory block.\n");
            exit( 1 );
    }
}

void main( void )
{
    div_t div_result;
    int i, success, tmpFlag;

    /*
     * Set the _crtDbgFlag to turn debug type allocations.
     * This will enable us to specify that blocks of type
     * _CLIENT_BLOCK can be allocated and tracked separately.
     * Turn off checking for internal CRT blocks.
     */
    tmpFlag = _CrtSetDbgFlag( _CRTDBG_REPORT_FLAG );
    tmpFlag |= _CRTDBG_ALLOC_MEM_DF;
    tmpFlag &= _CRTDBG_CHECK_CRT_DF;
    _CrtSetDbgFlag( tmpFlag );

    /*
     * We're going to allocate 22 blocks and every other block is
     * going to be of type _CLIENT_BLOCK.
     * Blocks numbered 2, 4, 6, 8, 10, 12, 14, 16, 18, 20, and 22
     * should all be _CLIENT_BLOCKS.
     */
    HeadPtr = NULL;
    printf("Allocating the memory ");
    for (i=1; i < 23; i++)
    {
            div_result = div( i, 2);
    if ( div_result.rem > 0 )
        success = CreateMemoryBlock( i, _NORMAL_BLOCK );
    else
        success = CreateMemoryBlock( i, _CLIENT_BLOCK );
```

```
        if ( !success )
        {
                printf(" ERROR.\n");
                    exit( 1 );
            }
        else
            printf(".");
        }
        printf(" done.\n");

        /*
         * We're going to call _CrtDoForAllClientObjects to
         * make sure that only blocks numbered 2, 4, 6, 8, 10, 12, 14, 16, 18, 20, and 22
         * got allocated as _CLIENT_BLOCKS.
         */
        _CrtDoForAllClientObjects( MyClientObjectHook, NULL );

        /*
         * Restore the memory to the heap
         */
        RestoreMemoryToHeap();
        exit( 0 );
    }
```

Output

```
The instruction at "0x00401153" referenced memory at "0x00000004". The memory could not
be "read".
```

See Also **_CrtSetDbgFlag**

_CrtDumpMemoryLeaks

Dumps all of the memory blocks in the debug heap when a memory leak has occurred (debug version only).

int _CrtDumpMemoryLeaks(void);

Routine	Required Header	Optional Headers	Compatibility
_CrtDumpMemoryLeaks	<crtdbg.h>		Win NT, Win 95, PMac

For additional compatibility information, see "Compatibility" on page ix in the Introduction.

Libraries

LIBCD.LIB	Single thread static library, debug version
LIBCMTD.LIB	Multithread static library, debug version
MSVCRTD.LIB	Import library for MSVCRx0D.DLL, debug version
MSVCRx0D.DLL	Multithread DLL library, debug version

Return Value

_CrtDumpMemoryLeaks returns TRUE if a memory leak is found; otherwise, the function returns FALSE.

Remarks

The **_CrtDumpMemoryLeaks** function determines whether a memory leak has occurred since the start of program execution. When a leak is found, the debug header information for all of the objects in the heap is dumped in a user-readable form. When **_DEBUG** is not defined, calls to **_CrtDumpMemoryLeaks** are removed during preprocessing.

_CrtDumpMemoryLeaks is frequently called at the end of program execution to verify that all memory allocated by the application has been freed. The function can be called automatically at program termination by turning on the **_CRTDBG_ALLOC_MEM_DF** bit field of the **_crtDbgFlag** flag using the **_CrtSetDbgFlag** function.

_CrtDumpMemoryLeaks calls **_CrtMemCheckpoint** to obtain the current state of the heap and then scans the state for blocks that have not been freed. When an unfreed block is encountered, **_CrtDumpMemoryLeaks** calls **_CrtMemDumpAllObjectsSince** to dump information for all of the objects allocated in the heap from the start of program execution.

By default, internal C run-time blocks (**_CRT_BLOCK**) are not included in memory dump operations. The **_CrtSetDbgFlag** function can be used to turn on the **_CRTDBG_CHECK_CRT_DF** bit of **_crtDbgFlag** to include these blocks in the leak detection process.

For more information about heap state functions and the **_CrtMemState** structure, see "Heap State Reporting Functions" on page 83. For information about how memory blocks are allocated, initialized, and managed in the debug version of the base heap, see "Memory Management and the Debug Heap" on page 79.

Example

See "First Example Program" on page 89.

_CrtIsValidHeapPointer

Verifies that a specified pointer is in the local heap (debug version only).

int _CrtIsValidHeapPointer(const void **userData* **);**

Routine	Required Header	Optional Headers	Compatibility
_CrtIsValidHeapPointer	<crtdbg.h>		Win NT, Win 95, PMac

For additional compatibility information, see "Compatibility" on page ix in the Introduction.

Libraries	
LIBCD.LIB	Single thread static library, debug version
LIBCMTD.LIB	Multithread static library, debug version
MSVCRTD.LIB	Import library for MSVCRx0D.DLL, debug version
MSVCRx0D.DLL	Multithread DLL library, debug version

Return Value

_CrtIsValidHeapPointer returns TRUE if the specified pointer is in the local heap; otherwise, the function returns FALSE.

Parameter

userData Pointer for determining the heap location

Remarks

The **_CrtIsValidHeapPointer** function is used to ensure that a specific memory address is within the local heap. The "local" heap refers to the heap created and managed by a particular instance of the C run-time library. If a dynamically linked library (DLL) contains a static link to the run-time library, then it has its own instance of the run-time heap, and therefore its own heap, independent of the application's local heap. When **_DEBUG** is not defined, calls to **_CrtIsValidHeapPointer** are removed during preprocessing.

Because this function returns TRUE or FALSE, it can be passed to one of the **_ASSERT** macros to create a simple debugging error handling mechanism. The following example will cause an assertion failure if the specified address is not located within the local heap:

```
_ASSERTE( _CrtIsValidHeapPointer( userData ) );
```

For more information about how **_CrtIsValidHeapPointer** can be used with other debug functions and macros, see "Using Macros for Verification and Reporting" on page 75. For information about how memory blocks are allocated, initialized, and managed in the debug version of the base heap, see "Memory Management and the Debug Heap" on page 79.

Example

See the example for **_CrtIsValidPointer**.

_CrtIsMemoryBlock

Verifies that a specified memory block is in the local heap and that it has a valid debug heap block type identifier (debug version only).

int _CrtIsMemoryBlock(const void **userData*, **unsigned int** *size*, **long** **requestNumber*, **char** ***filename*, **int** **linenumber* **);**

Routine	Required Header	Optional Headers	Compatibility
_CrtIsMemoryBlock	<crtdbg.h>		Win NT, Win 95, PMac

For additional compatibility information, see "Compatibility" on page ix in the Introduction.

Libraries	
LIBCD.LIB	Single thread static library, debug version
LIBCMTD.LIB	Multithread static library, debug version
MSVCRTD.LIB	Import library for MSVCRx0D.DLL, debug version
MSVCRx0D.DLL	Multithread DLL library, debug version

Return Value

_CrtIsMemoryBlock returns TRUE if the specified memory block is located within the local heap and has a valid debug heap block type identifier; otherwise, the function returns FALSE.

Parameter

userData Pointer to the beginning of the memory block to verify

size Size of the specified block (bytes)

requestNumber Pointer to the allocation number of the block or NULL

filename Pointer to name of source file that requested the block or NULL

linenumber Pointer to the line number in the source file or NULL

Remarks

The **_CrtIsMemoryBlock** function verifies that a specified memory block is located within the application's local heap and that it has a valid block type identifier. This function can also be used to obtain the object allocation order number and source file name/line number where the memory block allocation was originally requested.

Passing non-NULL values for the *requestNumber*, *filename*, and/or *linenumber* parameters causes **_CrtIsMemoryBlock** to set these parameters to the values in the memory block's debug header, if it finds the block in the local heap. When **_DEBUG** is not defined, calls to **_CrtIsMemoryBlock** are removed during preprocessing.

Because this function returns TRUE or FALSE, it can be passed to one of the **_ASSERT** macros to create a simple debugging error handling mechanism. The following example will cause an assertion failure if the specified address is not located within the local heap:

```
_ASSERTE( _CrtIsMemoryBlock( userData, size, &requestNumber, &filename,
   &linenumber ) );
```

For more information about how **_CrtIsMemoryBlock** can be used with other debug functions and macros, see "Using Macros for Verification and Reporting" on page 75. For information about how memory blocks are allocated, initialized, and managed in the debug version of the base heap, see "Memory Management and the Debug Heap" on page 79.

Example

See the example for **_CrtIsValidPointer**.

_CrtIsValidPointer

Verifies that a specified memory range is valid for reading and writing (debug version only).

int _CrtIsValidPointer(const void **address*, **unsigned int** *size*, **int** *access* **);**

Routine	Required Header	Optional Headers	Compatibility
_CrtIsValidPointer	<crtdbg.h>		Win NT, Win 95, PMac

For additional compatibility information, see "Compatibility" on page ix in the Introduction.

Libraries	
LIBCD.LIB	Single thread static library, debug version
LIBCMTD.LIB	Multithread static library, debug version
MSVCRTD.LIB	Import library for MSVCRx0D.DLL, debug version
MSVCRx0D.DLL	Multithread DLL library, debug version

Return Value

_CrtIsValidPointer returns TRUE if the specified memory range is valid for the specified operation(s); otherwise, the function returns FALSE.

Parameter

address Points to the beginning of the memory range to test for validity

size Size of the specified memory range (bytes)

access Read/Write accessibility to determine for the memory range

Remarks

The **_CrtIsValidPointer** function verifies that the memory range beginning at *address* and extending for *size* bytes, is valid for the specified accessibility operation(s). When *access* is set to TRUE, the memory range is verified for both reading and writing. When *address* is FALSE, the memory range is only validated for reading. When **_DEBUG** is not defined, calls to **_CrtIsValidPointer** are removed during preprocessing.

Because this function returns TRUE or FALSE, it can be passed to one of the **_ASSERT** macros to create a simple debugging error handling mechanism. The following example will cause an assertion failure if the memory range is not valid for both reading and writing operations:

```
_ASSERTE( _CrtIsValidPointer( address, size, TRUE ) );
```

For more information about how **_CrtIsValidPointer** can be used with other debug functions and macros, see "Using Macros for Verification and Reporting" on page 75. For information about how memory blocks are allocated, initialized, and managed in the debug version of the base heap, see "Memory Management and the Debug Heap" on page 79.

Example

```
/*
 * ISVALID.C
 * This program allocates a block of memory using _malloc_dbg
 * and then tests the validity of this memory by calling _CrtIsMemoryBlock,
 * _CrtIsValidPointer, and _CrtIsValidHeapPointer.
 */

#include <stdio.h>
#include <string.h>
#include <malloc.h>
#include <crtdbg.h>

#define  TRUE   1
#define  FALSE  0

void main( void )
{
        char *my_pointer;
```

```
        /*
         * Call _malloc_dbg to include the filename and line number
         * of our allocation request in the header information
         */
        my_pointer = (char *)_malloc_dbg( sizeof(char) * 10, _NORMAL_BLOCK, __FILE__,
__LINE__ );

        /*
         * Ensure that the memory got allocated correctly
         */
        _CrtIsMemoryBlock((const void *)my_pointer, sizeof(char) * 10, NULL, NULL, NULL
);

        /*
         * Test for read/write accessibility
         */
        if (_CrtIsValidPointer((const void *)my_pointer, sizeof(char) * 10, TRUE))
                printf("my_pointer has read and write accessibility.\n");
        else
                printf("my_pointer only has read access.\n");

        /*
         * Make sure my_pointer is within the local heap
         */
        if (_CrtIsValidHeapPointer((const void *)my_pointer))
                printf("my_pointer is within the local heap.\n");
        else
                printf("my_pointer is not located within the local heap.\n");

        free(my_pointer);
}
```

Output

```
my_pointer has read and write accessibility.
my_pointer is within the local heap.
```

_CrtMemCheckpoint

Obtains the current state of the debug heap and stores in an application-supplied **_CrtMemState** structure (debug version only).

void _CrtMemCheckpoint(_CrtMemState ***state*** **);**

Routine	Required Header	Optional Headers	Compatibility
_CrtMemCheckpoint	<crtdbg.h>		Win NT, Win 95, PMac

For additional compatibility information, see “Compatibility” on page ix in the Introduction.

Libraries	
LIBCD.LIB	Single thread static library, debug version
LIBCMTD.LIB	Multithread static library, debug version
MSVCRTD.LIB	Import library for MSVCRx0D.DLL, debug version
MSVCRx0D.DLL	Multithread DLL library, debug version

Return Value

None

Parameter

state Pointer to **_CrtMemState** structure to fill with the memory checkpoint

Remarks

The **_CrtMemCheckpoint** function creates a snapshot of the current state of the debug heap at any given moment, which can be used by other heap state functions to help detect memory leaks and other problems. When **_DEBUG** is not defined, calls to **_CrtMemState** are removed during preprocessing.

The application must pass a pointer to a previously allocated instance of the **_CrtMemState** structure, defined in CRTDBG.H, in the *state* parameter. If **_CrtMemCheckpoint** encounters an error during the checkpoint creation, the function generates a **_CRT_WARN** debug report describing the problem.

For more information about heap state functions and the **_CrtMemState** structure, see "Heap State Reporting Functions" on page 83. For information about how memory blocks are allocated, initialized, and managed in the debug version of the base heap, see "Memory Management and the Debug Heap" on page 79.

Example

See "First Example Program" on page 89.

_CrtMemDifference

Compares two memory states and returns their differences (debug version only).

int _CrtMemDifference(_CrtMemState **stateDiff*, **const _CrtMemState** **oldState*, **const _CrtMemState** **newState* **);**

Routine	Required Header	Optional Headers	Compatibility
_CrtMemDifference	<crtdbg.h>		Win NT, Win 95, PMac

For additional compatibility information, see "Compatibility" on page ix in the Introduction.

Libraries

LIBCD.LIB	Single thread static library, debug version
LIBCMTD.LIB	Multithread static library, debug version
MSVCRTD.LIB	Import library for MSVCRx0D.DLL, debug version
MSVCRx0D.DLL	Multithread DLL library, debug version

Return Value

If the memory states are significantly different, **_CrtMemDifference** returns TRUE; otherwise, the function returns FALSE.

Parameters

stateDiff Pointer to a **_CrtMemState** structure that will be used to store the differences between the two memory states (returned)

oldState Pointer to an earlier memory state (**_CrtMemState** structure)

newState Pointer to a later memory state (**_CrtMemState** structure)

Remarks

The **_CrtMemDifference** function compares *oldState* and *newState* and stores their differences in *stateDiff*, which can then be used by the application to detect memory leaks and other memory problems. When **_DEBUG** is not defined, calls to **_CrtMemDifference** are removed during preprocessing.

newState and *oldState* must each be a valid pointer to a **_CrtMemState** structure, defined in CRTDBG.H, that has been filled in by **_CrtMemCheckpoint** before calling **_CrtMemDifference**. *stateDiff* must be a pointer to a previously allocated instance of the **_CrtMemState** structure.

_CrtMemDifference compares the **_CrtMemState** field values of the blocks in *oldState* to those in *newState* and stores the result in *stateDiff*. When the number of allocated block types or total number of allocated blocks for each type differs between the two memory states, the states are said to be significantly different. The difference between the two states' high water count and total allocations is also stored in *stateDiff*.

By default, internal C run-time blocks (**_CRT_BLOCK**) are not included in memory state operations. The **_CrtSetDbgFlag** function can be used to turn on the **_CRTDBG_CHECK_CRT_DF** bit of **_crtDbgFlag** to include these blocks in leak detection and other memory state operations. Freed memory blocks (**_FREE_BLOCK**) do not cause **_CrtMemDifference** to return TRUE.

For more information about heap state functions and the **_CrtMemState** structure, see "Heap State Reporting Functions" on page 83. For information about how memory blocks are allocated, initialized, and managed in the debug version of the base heap, see "Memory Management and the Debug Heap" on page 79.

Example

See "First Example Program" on page 89.

See Also **_crtDbgFlag**

_CrtMemDumpAllObjectsSince

Dumps information about objects in the heap from the start of program execution or from a specified heap state (debug version only).

void _CrtMemDumpAllObjectsSince(const _CrtMemState ****state* **);**

Routine	Required Header	Optional Headers	Compatibility
_CrtMemDumpAll-ObjectsSince	<crtdbg.h>		Win NT, Win 95, PMac

For additional compatibility information, see "Compatibility" on page ix in the Introduction.

Libraries	
LIBCD.LIB	Single thread static library, debug version
LIBCMTD.LIB	Multithread static library, debug version
MSVCRTD.LIB	Import library for MSVCRx0D.DLL, debug version
MSVCRx0D.DLL	Multithread DLL library, debug version

Return Value

None

Parameter

state Pointer to the heap state to begin dumping from or NULL

Remarks

The **_CrtMemDumpAllObjectsSince** function dumps the debug header information of objects allocated in the heap in a user-readable form. The dump information can be used by the application to track allocations and detect memory problems. When **_DEBUG** is not defined, calls to **_CrtMemDumpAllObjectsSince** are removed during preprocessing.

_CrtMemDumpAllObjectsSince uses the value of the *state* parameter to determine where to initiate the dump operation. To begin dumping from a specified heap state, the *state* parameter must be a pointer to a **_CrtMemState** structure that has been filled in by **_CrtMemCheckpoint** before **_CrtMemDumpAllObjectsSince** was called. When *state* is NULL, the function begins the dump from the start of program execution.

If the application has installed a dump hook function by calling **_CrtSetDumpClient**, then every time **_CrtMemDumpAllObjectsSince** dumps information about a **_CLIENT_BLOCK** type of block, it calls the application-supplied dump function as well. By default, internal C run-time blocks (**_CRT_BLOCK**) are not included in memory dump operations. The **_CrtSetDbgFlag** function can be used to turn on the **_CRTDBG_CHECK_CRT_DF** bit of **_crtDbgFlag** to include these blocks. In addition, blocks marked as freed or ignored (**_FREE_BLOCK**, **_IGNORE_BLOCK**) are not included in the memory dump.

For more information about heap state functions and the **_CrtMemState** structure, see "Heap State Reporting Functions" on page 83. For information about how memory blocks are allocated, initialized, and managed in the debug version of the base heap, see "Memory Management and the Debug Heap" on page 79.

Example

See "Second Example Program" on page 94.

See Also **_crtDbgFlag**

_CrtMemDumpStatistics

Dumps the debug header information for a specified heap state in a user-readable form (debug version only).

void _CrtMemDumpStatistics(const _CrtMemState ***state*** **);**

Routine	Required Header	Optional Headers	Compatibility
_CrtMemDumpStatistics	<crtdbg.h>		Win NT, Win 95, PMac

For additional compatibility information, see "Compatibility" on page ix in the Introduction.

Libraries	
LIBCD.LIB	Single thread static library, debug version
LIBCMTD.LIB	Multithread static library, debug version
MSVCRTD.LIB	Import library for MSVCRx0D.DLL, debug version
MSVCRx0D.DLL	Multithread DLL library, debug version

Return Value

None

Parameter

state Pointer to the heap state to dump

Remarks

The **_CrtMemDumpStatistics** function dumps the debug header information for a specified state of the heap in a user-readable form. The dump statistics can be used by the application to track allocations and detect memory problems. The memory state may contain a specific heap state, or the difference between two states. When **_DEBUG** is not defined, calls to **_CrtMemDumpStatistics** are removed during preprocessing.

The *state* parameter must be a pointer to a **_CrtMemState** structure that has been filled in by **_CrtMemCheckpoint** or returned by **_CrtMemDifference** before **_CrtMemDumpStatistics** is called.

For more information about heap state functions and the **_CrtMemState** structure, see "Heap State Reporting Functions" on page 83. For information about how memory blocks are allocated, initialized, and managed in the debug version of the base heap, see "Memory Management and the Debug Heap" on page 79.

Example

See "First Example Program" on page 89.

_CrtSetAllocHook

Installs a client-defined allocation function by hooking it into the C run-time debug memory allocation process (debug version only).

_CRT_ALLOC_HOOK _CrtSetAllocHook(_CRT_ALLOC_HOOK *allocHook* **);**

Routine	Required Header	Optional Headers	Compatibility
_CrtSetAllocHook	<crtdbg.h>		Win NT, Win 95, PMac

For additional compatibility information, see "Compatibility" on page ix in the Introduction.

Libraries	
LIBCD.LIB	Single thread static library, debug version
LIBCMTD.LIB	Multithread static library, debug version
MSVCRTD.LIB	Import library for MSVCRx0D.DLL, debug version
MSVCRx0D.DLL	Multithread DLL library, debug version

Return Value

_CrtSetAllocHook returns the previously defined allocation hook function.

Parameter

allocHook New client-defined allocation function to hook into the C run-time debug memory allocation process

Remarks

_CrtSetAllocHook allows an application to hook its own allocation function into the C run-time debug library memory allocation process. As a result, every call to a debug allocation function to allocate, reallocate, or free a memory block triggers a call to the application's hook function. **_CrtSetAllocHook** provides an application with an easy method for testing how the application handles insufficient memory situations, the ability to examine allocation patterns, and the opportunity to log allocation information for later analysis. When **_DEBUG** is not defined, calls to **_CrtSetAllocHook** are removed during preprocessing.

The **_CrtSetAllocHook** function installs the new client-defined allocation function specified in *allocHook* and returns the previously defined hook function. The following example demonstrates how a client-defined allocation hook should be prototyped:

```
int YourAllocHook( int allocType, void *userData, size_t size, int blockType,
   long requestNumber, const unsigned char *filename, int lineNumber);
```

The `allocType` argument specifies the type of allocation operation (**_HOOK_ALLOC**, **_HOOK_REALLOC**, **_HOOK_FREE**) that triggered the call to the allocation's hook function. When the triggering allocation type is **_HOOK_FREE**, `userData` is a pointer to the user data section of the memory block about to be freed. However, when the triggering allocation type is **_HOOK_ALLOC** or **_HOOK_REALLOC**, `userData` is NULL because the memory block has not been allocated yet.

`size` specifies the size of the memory block in bytes, `blockType` indicates the type of the memory block, `requestNumber` is the object allocation order number of the memory block, and if available, `filename` and `lineNumber` specify the source file name and line number where the triggering allocation operation was initiated.

After the hook function has finished processing, it must return a Boolean value, which tells the main C run-time allocation process how to continue. When the hook function wants the main allocation process to continue as if the hook function had never been called, then the hook function should return TRUE. This causes the original triggering allocation operation to be executed. Using this implementation, the hook function can gather and save allocation information for later analysis, without interfering with the current allocation operation or state of the debug heap.

When the hook function wants the main allocation process to continue as if the triggering allocation operation was called and it failed, then the hook function should return TRUE. Using this implementation, the hook function can simulate a wide range of memory conditions and debug heap states to test how the application handles each situation.

For more information about how **_CrtSetAllocHook** can be used with other memory management functions or how to write your own client-defined hook functions, see "Writing Your Own Debug Hook Functions" on page 86.

Example

See "Second Example Program" on page 94.

_CrtSetBreakAlloc

Sets a breakpoint on a specified object allocation order number (debug version only).

long _CrtSetBreakAlloc(long *lBreakAlloc* **);**

Routine	Required Header	Optional Headers	Compatibility
_CrtSetBreakAlloc	<crtdbg.h>		Win NT, Win 95, PMac

For additional compatibility information, see "Compatibility" on page ix in the Introduction.

Libraries	
LIBCD.LIB	Single thread static library, debug version
LIBCMTD.LIB	Multithread static library, debug version
MSVCRTD.LIB	Import library for MSVCRx0D.DLL, debug version
MSVCRx0D.DLL	Multithread DLL library, debug version

Return Value

_CrtSetBreakAlloc returns the previous object allocation order number that had a breakpoint set.

Parameter

lBreakAlloc Allocation order number, for which to set the breakpoint

Remarks

_CrtSetBreakAlloc allows an application to perform memory leak detection by breaking at a specific point of memory allocation and tracing back to the origin of the request. The function uses the sequential object allocation order number assigned to the memory block when it was allocated in the heap. When **_DEBUG** is not defined, calls to **_CrtSetBreakAlloc** are removed during preprocessing.

The object allocation order number is stored in the *lRequest* field of the **_CrtMemBlockHeader** structure, defined in CRTDBG.H. When information about a memory block is reported by one of the debug dump functions, this number is enclosed in curly brackets; for example, {36}.

For more information about how **_CrtSetBreakAlloc** can be used with other memory management functions, see "Tracking Heap Allocation Requests" on page 85.

Example

```
/*
 * SETBRKAL.C
 * In this program, a call is made to the _CrtSetBreakAlloc routine
 * to verify that the debugger halts program execution when it reaches
 * a specified allocation number.
 */

#include <malloc.h>
#include <crtdbg.h>

void main( )
{
        long allocReqNum;
        char *my_pointer;

        /*
         * Allocate "my_pointer" for the first
         * time and ensure that it gets allocated correctly
         */
        my_pointer = malloc(10);
        _CrtIsMemoryBlock(my_pointer, 10, &allocReqNum, NULL, NULL);

        /*
         * Set a breakpoint on the allocation request
         * number for "my_pointer"
         */
        _CrtSetBreakAlloc(allocReqNum+2);
        _crtBreakAlloc = allocReqNum+2;

        /*
         * Alternate freeing and reallocating "my_pointer"
         * to verify that the debugger halts program execution
         * when it reaches the allocation request
         */
        free(my_pointer);
        my_pointer = malloc(10);
        free(my_pointer);
        my_pointer = malloc(10);
        free(my_pointer);
}
```

Output

```
The exception Breakpoint
A breakpoint has been reached.
(0x0000003) occurred in the application at location 0x00401255.
```

_CrtSetDbgFlag

Retrieves and/or modifies the state of the **_crtDbgFlag** flag to control the allocation behavior of the debug heap manager (debug version only).

int _CrtSetDbgFlag(int *newFlag* **);**

Routine	Required Header	Optional Headers	Compatibility
_CrtSetDbgFlag	<crtdbg.h>		Win NT, Win 95, PMac

For additional compatibility information, see "Compatibility" on page ix in the Introduction.

Libraries	
LIBCD.LIB	Single thread static library, debug version
LIBCMTD.LIB	Multithread static library, debug version
MSVCRTD.LIB	Import library for MSVCRx0D.DLL, debug version
MSVCRx0D.DLL	Multithread DLL library, debug version

_CrtSetDbgFlag returns the previous state of **_crtDbgFlag**.

Parameter

newFlag New state for the **_crtDbgFlag**

Remarks

The **_CrtSetDbgFlag** function allows the application to control how the debug heap manager tracks memory allocations by modifying the bit fields of the **_crtDbgFlag** flag. By setting the bits (turning on), the application can instruct the debug heap manager to perform special debugging operations, including checking for memory leaks when the application exits and reporting if any are found, simulating low memory conditions by specifying that freed memory blocks should remain in the heap's linked list, and verifying the integrity of the heap by inspecting each memory block at every allocation request. When **_DEBUG** is not defined, calls to **_CrtSetDbgFlag** are removed during preprocessing.

The following table lists the bit fields for **_crtDbgFlag** and describes their behavior. Because setting the bits results in increased diagnostic output and reduced program execution speed, most of the bits are not set (turned off) by default. For more information about these bit fields, see "Using the Debug Heap" on page 81.

Bit field	Default	Description
_CRTDBG_ALLOC-_MEM_DF	ON	ON: Enable debug heap allocations and use of memory block type identifiers, such as **_CLIENT_BLOCK**. OFF: Add new allocations to heap's linked list, but set block type to **_IGNORE_BLOCK**.
_CRTDBG_CHECK-_ALWAYS_DF	OFF	ON: Call **_CrtCheckMemory** at every allocation and deallocation request. OFF: **_CrtCheckMemory** must be called explicitly.
_CRTDBG_CHECK-_CRT_DF	OFF	ON: Include **_CRT_BLOCK** types in leak detection and memory state difference operations. OFF: Memory used internally by the run-time library is ignored by these operations.
_CRTDBG_DELAY-_FREE_MEM_DF	OFF	ON: Keep freed memory blocks in the heap's linked list, assign them the **_FREE_BLOCK** type, and fill them with the byte value 0xDD. OFF: Do not keep freed blocks in the heap's linked list.
_CRTDBG_LEAK-_CHECK_DF	OFF	ON: Perform automatic leak checking at program exit via a call to **_CrtDumpMemoryLeaks** and generate an error report if the application failed to free all the memory it allocated. OFF: Do not automatically perform leak checking at program exit.

newFlag is the new state to apply to the **_crtDbgFlag** and is a combination of the values for each of the bit fields. To change one or more of these bit fields and create a new state for the flag, follow these steps:

1. Call **_CrtSetDbgFlag** with *newFlag* equal to **_CRTDBG_REPORT_FLAG** to obtain the current **_crtDbgFlag** state and store the returned value in a temporary variable.
2. Turn on any bits by OR-ing the temporary variable with the corresponding bitmasks (represented in the application code by manifest constants).
3. Turn off the other bits by AND-ing the variable with a bitwise NOT of the appropriate bitmasks.
4. Call **_CrtSetDbgFlag** with *newFlag* equal to the value stored in the temporary variable to set the new state for **_crtDbgFlag**.

The following lines of code demonstrate how to simulate low memory conditions by keeping freed memory blocks in the heap's linked list and prevent **_CrtCheckMemory** from being called at every allocation request:

```
// Get the current state of the flag
// and store it in a temporary variable
int tmpFlag = _CrtSetDbgFlag( _CRTDBG_REPORT_FLAG );

// Turn On (OR) - Keep freed memory blocks in the
// heap's linked list and mark them as freed
tmpFlag |= _CRTDBG_DELAY_FREE_MEM_DF;

// Turn Off (AND) - prevent _CrtCheckMemory from
// being called at every allocation request
tmpFlag &= ~_CRTDBG_CHECK_ALWAYS_DF;

// Set the new state for the flag
_CrtSetDbgFlag( tmpFlag );
```

For an overview of memory management and the debug heap, see "Memory Management and the Debug Heap" on page 79.

Example

```
/*
 * SETDFLAG.C
 * This program concentrates on allocating and freeing memory
 * blocks to test the functionality of the _crtDbgFlag flag..
 */

#include <string.h>
#include <malloc.h>
#include <crtdbg.h>

void main( )
{
        char *p1, *p2;
        int tmpDbgFlag;

        /*
         * Set the debug-heap flag to keep freed blocks in the
         * heap's linked list - This will allow us to catch any
         * inadvertent use of freed memory
         */
        tmpDbgFlag = _CrtSetDbgFlag(_CRTDBG_REPORT_FLAG);
        tmpDbgFlag |= _CRTDBG_DELAY_FREE_MEM_DF;
        tmpDbgFlag |= _CRTDBG_LEAK_CHECK_DF;
        _CrtSetDbgFlag(tmpDbgFlag);

        /*
         * Allocate 2 memory blocks and store a string in each
         */
        p1 = malloc( 34 );
        p2 = malloc( 38 );
        strcpy( p1, "p1 points to a Normal allocation block" );
        strcpy( p2, "p2 points to a Client allocation block" );
```

```
        /*
         * Free both memory blocks
         */
        free( p2 );
        free( p1 );

        /*
         * Set the debug-heap flag to no longer keep freed blocks in the
         * heap's linked list and turn on Debug type allocations (CLIENT)
         */
        tmpDbgFlag = _CrtSetDbgFlag(_CRTDBG_REPORT_FLAG);
        tmpDbgFlag |= _CRTDBG_ALLOC_MEM_DF;
        tmpDbgFlag &= _CRTDBG_DELAY_FREE_MEM_DF;
        _CrtSetDbgFlag(tmpDbgFlag);

        /*
         * Explicitly call _malloc_dbg to obtain the filename and line number
         * of our allocation request and also so we can allocate CLIENT type
         * blocks specifically for tracking
         */
        p1 = _malloc_dbg( 40, _NORMAL_BLOCK, __FILE__, __LINE__ );
        p2 = _malloc_dbg( 40, _CLIENT_BLOCK, __FILE__, __LINE__ );
        strcpy( p1, "p1 points to a Normal allocation block" );
        strcpy( p2, "p2 points to a Client allocation block" );

        /*
         * _free_dbg must be called to free the CLIENT block
         */
        _free_dbg( p2, _CLIENT_BLOCK );
        free( p1 );

        /*
         * Allocate p1 again and then exit - this will leave unfreed
         * memory on the heap
         */
        p1 = malloc( 10 );
}
```

Output

```
Debug Error!
Program: C:\code\setdflag.exe
DAMAGE: after Normal block (#31) at 0x002D06A8.
Press Retry to debug the application.
```

See Also **_crtDbgFlag**, **_CrtCheckMemory**

_CrtSetDumpClient

Installs an application-defined function to dump **_CLIENT_BLOCK** type memory blocks (debug version only).

_CRT_DUMP_CLIENT _CrtSetDumpClient(_CRT_DUMP_CLIENT *dumpClient* **);**

Routine	Required Header	Optional Headers	Compatibility
_CrtSetDumpClient	<crtdbg.h>		Win NT, Win 95, PMac

For additional compatibility information, see "Compatibility" on page ix in the Introduction.

Libraries	
LIBCD.LIB	Single thread static library, debug version
LIBCMTD.LIB	Multithread static library, debug version
MSVCRTD.LIB	Import library for MSVCRx0D.DLL, debug version
MSVCRx0D.DLL	Multithread DLL library, debug version

Return Value

_CrtSetDumpClient returns the previously defined client block dump function.

Parameter

dumpClient New client-defined memory dump function to hook into the C run-time debug memory dump process

Remarks

The **_CrtSetDumpClient** function allows the application to hook its own function to dump objects stored in **_CLIENT_BLOCK** memory blocks into the C run-time debug memory dump process. As a result, every time a debug dump function such as **_CrtMemDumpAllObjectsSince** or **_CrtDumpMemoryLeaks** dumps a **_CLIENT_BLOCK** memory block, the application's dump function will be called as well. **_CrtSetDumpClient** provides an application with an easy method for detecting memory leaks in and validating or reporting the contents of data stored in **_CLIENT_BLOCK** blocks. When **_DEBUG** is not defined, calls to **_CrtSetDumpClient** are removed during preprocessing.

The **_CrtSetDumpClient** function installs the new application-defined dump function specified in *dumpClient* and returns the previously defined dump function. An example of a client block dump function is as follows:

```
void DumpClientFunction( void *userPortion, size_t blockSize );
```

The `userPortion` argument is a pointer to the beginning of the user data portion of the memory block and `blockSize` specifies the size of the allocated memory block in bytes. The client block dump function must return **void**. The pointer to the client dump function that is passed to **_CrtSetDumpClient** is of type **_CRT_DUMP_CLIENT**, as defined in CRTDBG.H:

```
typedef void (__cdecl *_CRT_DUMP_CLIENT)( void *, size_t );
```

For an example of how to implement an application-defined dump function, see "Second Example Program" on page 94. For more information about functions that operate on **_CLIENT_BLOCK** type memory blocks, see "Client Block Hook Functions" on page 87.

Example

See "Second Example Program" on page 94.

_CrtSetReportFile

Identifies the file or stream to be used by **_CrtDbgReport** as a destination for a specific report type (debug version only).

_HFILE _CrtSetReportFile(int *reportType*, **_HFILE** *reportFile* **);**

Routine	Required Header	Optional Headers	Compatibility
_CrtSetReportFile	<crtdbg.h>		Win NT, Win 95, PMac

For additional compatibility information, see "Compatibility" on page ix in the Introduction.

Libraries	
LIBCD.LIB	Single thread static library, debug version
LIBCMTD.LIB	Multithread static library, debug version
MSVCRTD.LIB	Import library for MSVCRx0D.DLL, debug version
MSVCRx0D.DLL	Multithread DLL library, debug version

Return Value

Upon successful completion, **_CrtSetReportFile** returns the previous report file defined for the report type specified in *reportType*. If an error occurs, the report file for *reportType* is not modified and**_CrtSetReportFile** returns **_CRTDBG_HFILE_ERROR**.

Parameters

reportType Report type: **_CRT_WARN**, **_CRT_ERROR**, **_CRT_ASSERT**

reportFile New report file for *reportType*, see the following table

Remarks

_CrtSetReportFile is used in conjunction with the **_CrtSetReportMode** function to define the destination(s) for a specific report type generated by **_CrtDbgReport**. When **_CrtSetReportMode** has been called to assign the **_CRTDBG_MODE_FILE** reporting mode for a specific report type, **_CrtSetReportFile** should then be called to define the specific file or stream to use as the destination. When **_DEBUG** is not defined, calls to **_CrtSetReportFile** are removed during preprocessing.

The **_CrtSetReportFile** function assigns the new report file specified in *reportFile* to the report type specified in *reportType* and returns the previously defined report file for *reportType*. Thc following table lists the available choices for *reportFile* and the resulting behavior of **_CrtDbgReport**. These options are defined as bit-flags in CRTDBG.H.

Report File	_CrtDbgReport Behavior
_HFILE	**_CrtDbgReport** writes the message to a user-supplied **HANDLE** and does not verify the validity of the file handle. The application is responsible for opening and closing the report file and passing a valid file handle.
_CRTDBG_FILE_STDERR	**_CrtDbgReport** writes message to **stderr**.
_CRTDBG_FILE_STDOUT	**_CrtDbgReport** writes message to **stdout**.
_CRTDBG_REPORT_FILE	**_CrtDbgReport** is not called and the report file for *reportType* is not modified. **_CrtSetReportFile** simply returns the current report file for *reportType*.

When the report destination is a file, **_CrtSetReportMode** is called to set the file bit-flag and **_CrtSetReportFile** is called to define the specific file to use. The following code fragment demonstrates this configuration:

```
_CrtSetReportMode( _CRT_ASSERT, _CRTDBG_MODE_FILE );
_CrtSetReportFile( _CRT_ASSERT, _CRTDBG_FILE_STDERR );
```

The report file used by each report type can be separately controlled. For example, it is possible to specify that a *reportType* of **_CRT_ERROR** be reported to **stderr**, while a *reportType* of **_CRT_ASSERT** be reported to a user-defined file handle or stream.

For more information about defining the report mode(s) and file for a specific report type, see **_CrtDbgReport**, **_CrtSetReportMode** and the section "Debug Reporting Functions of the C Run-Time Library" on page 73.

Example

```
/*
 * REPORT.C:
 * In this program, calls are made to the _CrtSetReportMode,
 * _CrtSetReportFile, and _CrtSetReportHook functions.
 * The _ASSERT macros are called to evaluate their expression.
 * When the condition fails, these macros print a diagnostic message
```

```
 * and call _CrtDbgReport to generate a debug report and the
 * client-defined reporting function is called as well.
 * The _RPTn and _RPTFn group of macros are also exercised in
 * this program, as an alternative to the printf function.
 * When these macros are called, the client-defined reporting function
 * takes care of all the reporting - _CrtDbgReport won't be called.
 */

#include <stdio.h>
#include <string.h>
#include <malloc.h>
#include <crtdbg.h>

/*
 * Define our own reporting function.
 * We'll hook it into the debug reporting
 * process later using _CrtSetReportHook.
 *
 * Define a global int to keep track of
 * how many assertion failures occur.
 */
int gl_num_asserts=0;
int OurReportingFunction( int reportType, char *userMessage, int *retVal )
{
    /*
     * Tell the user our reporting function is being called.
     * In other words - verify that the hook routine worked.
     */
    fprintf("Inside the client-defined reporting function.\n", STDOUT);
    fflush(STDOUT);

    /*
     * When the report type is for an ASSERT,
     * we'll report some information, but we also
     * want _CrtDbgReport to get called -
     * so we'll return TRUE.
     *
     * When the report type is a WARNing or ERROR,
     * we'll take care of all of the reporting. We don't
     * want _CrtDbgReport to get called -
     * so we'll return FALSE.
     */
    if (reportType == _CRT_ASSERT)
    {
        gl_num_asserts++;
        fprintf("This is the number of Assertion failures that have occurred: %d \n",
gl_num_asserts, STDOUT);
        fflush(STDOUT);
        fprintf("Returning TRUE from the client-defined reporting function.\n",
STDOUT);
        fflush(STDOUT);
        return(TRUE);
```

```
    } else {
        fprintf("This is the debug user message: %s \n", userMessage, STDOUT);
        fflush(STDOUT);
        fprintf("Returning FALSE from the client-defined reporting function.\n",
STDOUT);
        fflush(STDOUT);
        return(FALSE);
    }

    /*
     * By setting retVal to zero, we are instructing _CrtDbgReport
     * to continue with normal execution after generating the report.
     * If we wanted _CrtDbgReport to start the debugger, we would set
     * retVal to one.
     */
    retVal = 0;
}

int main()
{
        char *p1, *p2;

    /*
     * Hook in our client-defined reporting function.
     * Every time a _CrtDbgReport is called to generate
     * a debug report, our function will get called first.
     */
    _CrtSetReportHook( OurReportingFunction );

    /*
     * Define the report destination(s) for each type of report
     * we are going to generate.  In this case, we are going to
     * generate a report for every report type: _CRT_WARN,
     * _CRT_ERROR, and _CRT_ASSERT.
     * The destination(s) is defined by specifying the report mode(s)
     * and report file for each report type.
     * This program sends all report types to STDOUT.
     */
    _CrtSetReportMode(_CRT_WARN, _CRTDBG_MODE_FILE);
    _CrtSetReportFile(_CRT_WARN, _CRTDBG_FILE_STDOUT);
    _CrtSetReportMode(_CRT_ERROR, _CRTDBG_MODE_FILE);
    _CrtSetReportFile(_CRT_ERROR, _CRTDBG_FILE_STDOUT);
    _CrtSetReportMode(_CRT_ASSERT, _CRTDBG_MODE_FILE);
    _CrtSetReportFile(_CRT_ASSERT, _CRTDBG_FILE_STDOUT);

    /*
     * Allocate and assign the pointer variables
     */
    p1 = malloc(10);
    strcpy(p1, "I am p1");
    p2 = malloc(10);
    strcpy(p2, "I am p2");
```

```
    /*
     * Use the report macros as a debugging
     * warning mechanism, similar to printf.
     *
     * Use the assert macros to check if the
     * p1 and p2 variables are equivalent.
     *
     * If the expression fails, _ASSERTE will
     * include a string representation of the
     * failed expression in the report.
     *
     *  _ASSERT does not include the
     * expression in the generated report.
     */
    _RPT0(_CRT_WARN, "\n\n Use the assert macros to evaluate the expression p1 ==
p2.\n");
    _RPTF2(_CRT_WARN, "\n Will _ASSERT find '%s' == '%s' ?\n", p1, p2);
    _ASSERT(p1 == p2);

    _RPTF2(_CRT_WARN, "\n\n Will _ASSERTE find '%s' == '%s' ?\n", p1, p2);
    _ASSERTE(p1 == p2);

    _RPT2(_CRT_ERROR, "\n \n '%s' != '%s'\n", p1, p2);

    free(p2);
    free(p1);

    return 0;
}
```

Output

```
Inside the client-defined reporting function.
This is the debug user message: Use the assert macros to evaluate the expression p1 ==
p2
Returning FALSE from the client-defined reporting function.
Inside the client-defined reporting function.
This is the debug user message: dbgmacro.c(54) : Will _ASSERT find 'I am p1' == 'I am
p2' ?
Returning FALSE from the client-defined reporting function.
Inside the client-defined reporting function.
This is the number of Assertion failures that have occurred: 1
Returning TRUE from the client-defined reporting function.
dbgmacro.c(55) : Assertion failed
Inside the client-defined reporting function.
This is the debug user message: dbgmacro.c(57) : Will _ASSERTE find 'I am p1' == 'I am
p2' ?
Returning FALSE from the client-defined reporting function.
Inside the client-defined reporting function.
This is the number of Assertion failures that have occurred: 2
```

```
Returning TRUE from the client-defined reporting function.
dbgmacro.c(58) : Assertion failed: p1 == p2
Inside the client-defined reporting function.
This is the debug user message: 'I am p1' != 'I am p2'
Returning FALSE from the client-defined reporting function.
```

See Also **_CrtDbgReport**

_CrtSetReportHook

Installs a client-defined reporting function by hooking it into the C run-time debug reporting process (debug version only).

_CRT_REPORT_HOOK _CrtSetReportHook(_CRT_REPORT_HOOK *reportHook* **);**

Routine	Required Header	Optional Headers	Compatibility
_CrtSetReportHook	<crtdbg.h>		Win NT, Win 95, PMac

For additional compatibility information, see "Compatibility" on page ix in the Introduction.

Libraries	
LIBCD.LIB	Single thread static library, debug version
LIBCMTD.LIB	Multithread static library, debug version
MSVCRTD.LIB	Import library for MSVCRx0D.DLL, debug version
MSVCRx0D.DLL	Multithread DLL library, debug version

Return Value

_CrtSetReportHook returns the previous client-defined reporting function.

Parameter

reportHook New client-defined reporting function to hook into the C run-time debug reporting process

Remarks

_CrtSetReportHook allows an application to use its own reporting function into the C run-time debug library reporting process. As a result, whenever **_CrtDbgReport** is called to generate a debug report, the application's reporting function is called first. This functionality enables an application to perform operations such as filtering debug reports so it can focus on specific allocation types or send a report to destinations not available by using **_CrtDbgReport**. When **_DEBUG** is not defined, calls to **_CrtSetReportHook** are removed during preprocessing.

The **_CrtSetReportHook** function installs the new client-defined reporting function specified in *reportHook* and returns the previous client-defined hook. The following example demonstrates how a client-defined report hook should be prototyped:

```
int YourReportHook( int reportType, char *message, int *returnValue );
```

where `reportType` is the debug report type (**_CRT_WARN**, **_CRT_ERROR**, **_CRT_ASSERT**), `message` is the fully assembled debug user message to be contained in the report, and `returnValue` is the value specified by the client-defined reporting function that should be returned by **_CrtDbgReport**. See the **_CrtSetReportMode** function for a complete description of the available report types.

If the client-defined reporting function completely handles the debug message such that no further reporting is required, then the function should return FALSE. When the function returns TRUE, **_CrtDbgReport** will be called to generate the debug report using the current settings for the report type, mode, and file. In addition, by specifying the **_CrtDbgReport** return value in `returnValue`, the application can also control whether a debug break occurs. See **_CrtSetReportMode**, **_CrtSetReportFile**, and **_CrtDbgReport** for a complete description of how the debug report is configured and generated.

For more information about other hook-capable run-time functions and writing your own client-defined hook functions, see "Writing Your Own Debug Hook Functions" on page 86.

Example

```
/*
 * REPORT.C:
 * In this program, calls are made to the _CrtSetReportMode,
 * _CrtSetReportFile, and _CrtSetReportHook functions.
 * The _ASSERT macros are called to evaluate their expression.
 * When the condition fails, these macros print a diagnostic message
 * and call _CrtDbgReport to generate a debug report and the
 * client-defined reporting function is called as well.
 * The _RPTn and _RPTFn group of macros are also exercised in
 * this program, as an alternative to the printf function.
 * When these macros are called, the client-defined reporting function
 * takes care of all the reporting - _CrtDbgReport won't be called.
 */

#include <stdio.h>
#include <string.h>
#include <malloc.h>
#include <crtdbg.h>

/*
 * Define our own reporting function.
 * We'll hook it into the debug reporting
 * process later using _CrtSetReportHook.
 *
```

```
 * Define a global int to keep track of
 * how many assertion failures occur.
 */
int gl_num_asserts=0;
int OurReportingFunction( int reportType, char *userMessage, int *retVal )
{
    /*
     * Tell the user our reporting function is being called.
     * In other words - verify that the hook routine worked.
     */
    fprintf("Inside the client-defined reporting function.\n", STDOUT);
    fflush(STDOUT);

    /*
     * When the report type is for an ASSERT,
     * we'll report some information, but we also
     * want _CrtDbgReport to get called -
     * so we'll return TRUE.
     *
     * When the report type is a WARNing or ERROR,
     * we'll take care of all of the reporting. We don't
     * want _CrtDbgReport to get called -
     * so we'll return FALSE.
     */
    if (reportType == _CRT_ASSERT)
    {
        gl_num_asserts++;
        fprintf("This is the number of Assertion failures that have occurred: %d \n",
gl_num_asserts, STDOUT);
        fflush(STDOUT);
        fprintf("Returning TRUE from the client-defined reporting function.\n",
STDOUT);
        fflush(STDOUT);
        return(TRUE);
    } else {
        fprintf("This is the debug user message: %s \n", userMessage, STDOUT);
        fflush(STDOUT);
        fprintf("Returning FALSE from the client-defined reporting function.\n",
STDOUT);
        fflush(STDOUT);
        return(FALSE);
    }

    /*
     * By setting retVal to zero, we are instructing _CrtDbgReport
     * to continue with normal execution after generating the report.
     * If we wanted _CrtDbgReport to start the debugger, we would set
     * retVal to one.
     */
    retVal = 0;
}
```

```
int main()
{
        char *p1, *p2;

    /*
     * Hook in our client-defined reporting function.
     * Every time a _CrtDbgReport is called to generate
     * a debug report, our function will get called first.
     */
    _CrtSetReportHook( OurReportingFunction );

    /*
     * Define the report destination(s) for each type of report
     * we are going to generate.  In this case, we are going to
     * generate a report for every report type: _CRT_WARN,
     * _CRT_ERROR, and _CRT_ASSERT.
     * The destination(s) is defined by specifying the report mode(s)
     * and report file for each report type.
     * This program sends all report types to STDOUT.
     */
    _CrtSetReportMode(_CRT_WARN, _CRTDBG_MODE_FILE);
    _CrtSetReportFile(_CRT_WARN, _CRTDBG_FILE_STDOUT);
    _CrtSetReportMode(_CRT_ERROR, _CRTDBG_MODE_FILE);
    _CrtSetReportFile(_CRT_ERROR, _CRTDBG_FILE_STDOUT);
    _CrtSetReportMode(_CRT_ASSERT, _CRTDBG_MODE_FILE);
    _CrtSetReportFile(_CRT_ASSERT, _CRTDBG_FILE_STDOUT);

    /*
     * Allocate and assign the pointer variables
     */
    p1 = malloc(10);
    strcpy(p1, "I am p1");
    p2 = malloc(10);
    strcpy(p2, "I am p2");

    /*
     * Use the report macros as a debugging
     * warning mechanism, similar to printf.
     *
     * Use the assert macros to check if the
     * p1 and p2 variables are equivalent.
     *
     * If the expression fails, _ASSERTE will
     * include a string representation of the
     * failed expression in the report.
     *
     *  _ASSERT does not include the
     * expression in the generated report.
     */
    _RPT0(_CRT_WARN, "\n\n Use the assert macros to evaluate the expression p1 ==
p2.\n");
    _RPTF2(_CRT_WARN, "\n Will _ASSERT find '%s' == '%s' ?\n", p1, p2);
    _ASSERT(p1 == p2);
```

```
    _RPTF2(_CRT_WARN, "\n\n Will _ASSERTE find '%s' == '%s' ?\n", p1, p2);
    _ASSERTE(p1 == p2);

    _RPT2(_CRT_ERROR, "\n \n '%s' != '%s'\n", p1, p2);

    free(p2);
    free(p1);

    return 0;
}
```

Output

```
Inside the client-defined reporting function.
This is the debug user message: Use the assert macros to evaluate the expression p1 ==
p2
Returning FALSE from the client-defined reporting function.
Inside the client-defined reporting function.
This is the debug user message: dbgmacro.c(54) : Will _ASSERT find 'I am p1' == 'I am
p2' ?
Returning FALSE from the client-defined reporting function.
Inside the client-defined reporting function.
This is the number of Assertion failures that have occurred: 1
Returning TRUE from the client-defined reporting function.
dbgmacro.c(55) : Assertion failed
Inside the client-defined reporting function.
This is the debug user message: dbgmacro.c(57) : Will _ASSERTE find 'I am p1' == 'I am
p2' ?
Returning FALSE from the client-defined reporting function.
Inside the client-defined reporting function.
This is the number of Assertion failures that have occurred: 2
Returning TRUE from the client-defined reporting function.
dbgmacro.c(58) : Assertion failed: p1 == p2
Inside the client-defined reporting function.
This is the debug user message: 'I am p1' != 'I am p2'
Returning FALSE from the client-defined reporting function.
```

_CrtSetReportMode

Specifies the general destination(s) for a specific report type generated by **_CrtDbgReport** (debug version only).

int _CrtSetReportMode(int *reportType*, **int** *reportMode* **);**

Routine	Required Header	Optional Headers	Compatibility
_CrtSetReportMode	<crtdbg.h>		Win NT, Win 95, PMac

For additional compatibility information, see "Compatibility" on page ix in the Introduction.

Libraries	
LIBCD.LIB	Single thread static library, debug version
LIBCMTD.LIB	Multithread static library, debug version
MSVCRTD.LIB	Import library for MSVCRx0D.DLL, debug version
MSVCRx0D.DLL	Multithread DLL library, debug version

Return Value

Upon successful completion, **_CrtSetReportMode** returns the previous report mode(s) for the report type specified in *reportType*. If an error occurs, the report mode(s) for *reportType* are not modified and**_CrtSetReportMode** returns –1.

Parameters

reportType Report type: **_CRT_WARN**, **_CRT_ERROR**, **_CRT_ASSERT**

reportMode New report mode(s) for *reportType*, see the table in the Remarks section

Remarks

_CrtSetReportMode is used in conjunction with the **_CrtSetReportFile** function to define the destination(s) for a specific report type generated by **_CrtDbgReport**. If **_CrtSetReportMode** and **_CrtSetReportFile** are not called to define the reporting method(s) for a specific report type, then **_CrtDbgReport** generates the report type using default destinations: Assertion failures and errors are directed to a debug message window, warnings from Windows applications are sent to the debugger, and warnings from console applications are directed to **stderr**. When **_DEBUG** is not defined, calls to **_CrtSetReportMode** are removed during preprocessing.

The following table lists the report types defined in CRTDBG.H.

Report Type	Description
_CRT_WARN	Warnings, messages, and information that does not need immediate attention.
_CRT_ERROR	Errors, unrecoverable problems, and issues that require immediate attention.
_CRT_ASSERT	Assertion failures (asserted expressions that evaluate to FALSE).

The **_CrtSetReportMode** function assigns the new report mode specified in *reportMode* to the report type specified in *reportType* and returns the previously defined report mode for *reportType*. The following table lists the available choices for *reportMode* and the resulting behavior of **_CrtDbgReport**. These options are defined as bit-flags in CRTDBG.H.

Report Mode	_CrtDbgReport Behavior
_CRTDBG_MODE_DEBUG	Writes the message to an output debug string.
_CRTDBG_MODE_FILE	Writes the message to a user-supplied file handle. **_CrtSetReportFile** should be called to define the specific file or stream to use as the destination.
_CRTDBG_MODE_WNDW	Creates a message box to display the message along with the Abort, Retry, and Ignore buttons.
_CRTDBG_REPORT_MODE	It is not called, and the report mode for *reportType* is not modified. **_CrtSetReportMode** simply returns the current report mode for *reportType*.

Each report type may be reported using one, two, or three modes, or no mode at all. Therefore, it is possible to have more than one destination defined for a single report type. For example, the following code fragment causes assertion failures to be sent to both a debug message window and to **stderr**:

```
_CrtSetReportMode( _CRT_ASSERT, _CRTDBG_MODE_FILE | _CRTDBG_MODE_WNDW );
_CrtSetReportFile( _CRT_ASSERT, _CRTDBG_FILE_STDERR );
```

In addition, the reporting mode(s) for each report type can be separately controlled. For example, it is possible to specify that a *reportType* of **_CRT_WARN** be sent to an output debug string, while **_CRT_ASSERT** be displayed using a a debug message window and sent to **stderr**, as illustrated above.

For more information about defining the report mode(s) and file for a specific report type, see **_CrtDbgReport**, **_CrtSetReportFile** and the section “Debug Reporting Functions of the C Run-Time Library” on page 73.

Example

```
/*
 * REPORT.C:
 * In this program, calls are made to the _CrtSetReportMode,
 * _CrtSetReportFile, and _CrtSetReportHook functions.
 * The _ASSERT macros are called to evaluate their expression.
 * When the condition fails, these macros print a diagnostic message
 * and call _CrtDbgReport to generate a debug report and the
 * client-defined reporting function is called as well.
 * The _RPTn and _RPTFn group of macros are also exercised in
 * this program, as an alternative to the printf function.
 * When these macros are called, the client-defined reporting function
 * takes care of all the reporting - _CrtDbgReport won't be called.
 */

#include <stdio.h>
#include <string.h>
#include <malloc.h>
#include <crtdbg.h>
```

```
/*
 * Define our own reporting function.
 * We'll hook it into the debug reporting
 * process later using _CrtSetReportHook.
 *
 * Define a global int to keep track of
 * how many assertion failures occur.
 */
int gl_num_asserts=0;
int OurReportingFunction( int reportType, char *userMessage, int *retVal )
{
    /*
     * Tell the user our reporting function is being called.
     * In other words - verify that the hook routine worked.
     */
    fprintf("Inside the client-defined reporting function.\n", STDOUT);
    fflush(STDOUT);

    /*
     * When the report type is for an ASSERT,
     * we'll report some information, but we also
     * want _CrtDbgReport to get called -
     * so we'll return TRUE.
     *
     * When the report type is a WARNing or ERROR,
     * we'll take care of all of the reporting. We don't
     * want _CrtDbgReport to get called -
     * so we'll return FALSE.
     */
    if (reportType == _CRT_ASSERT)
    {
        gl_num_asserts++;
        fprintf("This is the number of Assertion failures that have occurred: %d \n",
gl_num_asserts, STDOUT);
        fflush(STDOUT);
        fprintf("Returning TRUE from the client-defined reporting function.\n",
STDOUT);
        fflush(STDOUT);
        return(TRUE);
    } else {
        fprintf("This is the debug user message: %s \n", userMessage, STDOUT);
        fflush(STDOUT);
        fprintf("Returning FALSE from the client-defined reporting function.\n",
STDOUT);
        fflush(STDOUT);
        return(FALSE);
    }
```

```
    /*
     * By setting retVal to zero, we are instructing _CrtDbgReport
     * to continue with normal execution after generating the report.
     * If we wanted _CrtDbgReport to start the debugger, we would set
     * retVal to one.
     */
    retVal = 0;
}

int main()
{
        char *p1, *p2;

    /*
     * Hook in our client-defined reporting function.
     * Every time a _CrtDbgReport is called to generate
     * a debug report, our function will get called first.
     */
    _CrtSetReportHook( OurReportingFunction );

    /*
     * Define the report destination(s) for each type of report
     * we are going to generate.  In this case, we are going to
     * generate a report for every report type: _CRT_WARN,
     * _CRT_ERROR, and _CRT_ASSERT.
     * The destination(s) is defined by specifying the report mode(s)
     * and report file for each report type.
     * This program sends all report types to STDOUT.
     */
     CrtSetReportMode(_CRT_WARN, _CRTDBG_MODE_FILE);
    _CrtSetReportFile(_CRT_WARN, _CRTDBG_FILE_STDOUT);
    _CrtSetReportMode(_CRT_ERROR, _CRTDBG_MODE_FILE);
    _CrtSetReportFile(_CRT_ERROR, _CRTDBG_FILE_STDOUT);
    _CrtSetReportMode(_CRT_ASSERT, _CRTDBG_MODE_FILE);
    _CrtSetReportFile(_CRT_ASSERT, _CRTDBG_FILE_STDOUT);

    /*
     * Allocate and assign the pointer variables
     */
    p1 = malloc(10);
    strcpy(p1, "I am p1");
    p2 = malloc(10);
    strcpy(p2, "I am p2");

    /*
     * Use the report macros as a debugging
     * warning mechanism, similar to printf.
     *
     * Use the assert macros to check if the
     * p1 and p2 variables are equivalent.
     *
```

```
    * If the expression fails, _ASSERTE will
    * include a string representation of the
    * failed expression in the report.
    *
    *  _ASSERT does not include the
    * expression in the generated report.
    */
   _RPT0(_CRT_WARN, "\n\n Use the assert macros to evaluate the expression p1 ==
p2.\n");
   _RPTF2(_CRT_WARN, "\n Will _ASSERT find '%s' == '%s' ?\n", p1, p2);
   _ASSERT(p1 == p2);

   _RPTF2(_CRT_WARN, "\n\n Will _ASSERTE find '%s' == '%s' ?\n", p1, p2);
   _ASSERTE(p1 == p2);

   _RPT2(_CRT_ERROR, "\n \n '%s' != '%s'\n", p1, p2);

   free(p2);
   free(p1);

   return 0;
}
```

Output

```
Inside the client-defined reporting function.
This is the debug user message: Use the assert macros to evaluate the expression p1 ==
p2
Returning FALSE from the client-defined reporting function.
Inside the client-defined reporting function.
This is the debug user message: dbgmacro.c(54) : Will _ASSERT find 'I am p1' == 'I am
p2' ?
Returning FALSE from the client-defined reporting function.
Inside the client-defined reporting function.
This is the number of Assertion failures that have occurred: 1
Returning TRUE from the client-defined reporting function.
dbgmacro.c(55) : Assertion failed
Inside the client-defined reporting function.
This is the debug user message: dbgmacro.c(57) : Will _ASSERTE find 'I am p1' == 'I am
p2' ?
Returning FALSE from the client-defined reporting function.
Inside the client-defined reporting function.
This is the number of Assertion failures that have occurred: 2
Returning TRUE from the client-defined reporting function.
dbgmacro.c(58) : Assertion failed: p1 == p2
Inside the client-defined reporting function.
This is the debug user message: 'I am p1' != 'I am p2'
Returning FALSE from the client-defined reporting function.
```

_expand_dbg

Resizes a specified block of memory in the heap by expanding or contracting the block (debug version only).

void *_expand_dbg(void **userData*, **size_t** *newSize*, **int** *blockType*, **const char** **filename*, **int** *linenumber* **);**

Routine	Required Header	Optional Headers	Compatibility
_expand_dbg	<crtdbg.h>		Win NT, Win 95, PMac

For additional compatibility information, see "Compatibility" on page ix in the Introduction.

Libraries	
LIBCD.LIB	Single thread static library, debug version
LIBCMTD.LIB	Multithread static library, debug version
MSVCRTD.LIB	Import library for MSVCRx0D.DLL, debug version
MSVCRx0D.DLL	Multithread DLL library, debug version

Return Value

Upon successful completion, **_expand_dbg** returns a pointer to the resized memory block, otherwise it returns NULL.

Parameters

userData Pointer to the previously allocated memory block

newSize Requested new size for block (bytes)

blockType Requested type for resized block: **_CLIENT_BLOCK** or **_NORMAL_BLOCK**

filename Pointer to name of source file that requested expand operation or NULL

linenumber Line number in source file where expand operation was requested or NULL

The *filename* and *linenumber* parameters are only available when **_expand_dbg** has been called explicitly or the **_CRTDBG_MAP_ALLOC** environment variable has been defined.

Remarks

The **_expand_dbg** function is a debug version of the **_expand** function. When **_DEBUG** is not defined, calls to **_expand_dbg** are removed during preprocessing. Both **_expand** and **_expand_dbg** resize a memory block in the base heap, but **_expand_dbg** accomodates several debugging features: buffers on either side of the user portion of the block to test for leaks, a block type parameter to track specific allocation types, and *filename/linenumber* information to determine the origin of allocation requests.

_expand_dbg resizes the specified memory block with slightly more space than the requested *newSize*. *newSize* may be greater or less than the size of the originally allocated memory block. The additional space is used by the debug heap manager to link the debug memory blocks together and to provide the application with debug header information and overwrite buffers. The resize is accomplished by either expanding or contracting the original memory block. **_expand_dbg** does *not* move the memory block, as does the **_realloc_dbg** function.

When *newSize* is greater than the original block size, the memory block is expanded. During an expansion, if the memory block cannot be expanded to accommodate the requested size, the block is expanded as much as possible. When *newSize* is less than the original block size, the memory block is contracted until the new size is obtained.

For information about how memory blocks are allocated, initialized, and managed in the debug version of the base heap, see "Memory Management and the Debug Heap" on page 79. For information about the allocation block types and how they are used, see "Types of Blocks on the Debug Heap" on page 80. For information on the differences between calling a standard heap function versus its debug version in a debug build of an application, see "Using the Debug Version Versus the Base Version" on page 84.

Example

```
/*
 * EXPANDD.C
 * This program allocates a block of memory using _malloc_dbg
 * and then calls _msize_dbg to display the size of that block.
 * Next, it uses _expand_dbg to expand the amount of
 * memory used by the buffer and then calls _msize_dbg again to
 * display the new amount of memory allocated to the buffer.
 */

#include <stdio.h>
#include <malloc.h>
#include <stdlib.h>
#include <crtdbg.h>

void main( void )
{
        long *buffer;
        size_t size;

        /*
         * Call _malloc_dbg to include the filename and line number
         * of our allocation request in the header
         */
        buffer = (long *)_malloc_dbg( 40 * sizeof(long), _NORMAL_BLOCK, __FILE__,
__LINE__ );
        if( buffer == NULL )
               exit( 1 );
```

```
        /*
         * Get the size of the buffer by calling _msize_dbg
         */
        size = _msize_dbg( buffer, _NORMAL_BLOCK );
        printf( "Size of block after _malloc_dbg of 40 longs: %u\n", size );

        /*
         * Expand the buffer using _expand_dbg and show the new size
         */
        buffer = _expand_dbg( buffer, size + (40 * sizeof(long)), _NORMAL_BLOCK,
__FILE__, __LINE__ );
        if( buffer == NULL )
               exit( 1 );
        size = _msize_dbg( buffer, _NORMAL_BLOCK );
        printf( "Size of block after _expand_dbg of 40 more longs: %u\n", size );

        free( buffer );
        exit( 0 );
}
```

Output

```
Size of block after _malloc_dbg of 40 longs: 160
Size of block after _expand_dbg of 40 more longs: 320
```

See Also **_malloc_dbg**

_free_dbg

Frees a block of memory in the heap (debug version only).

void _free_dbg(void **userData*, **int** *blockType* **);**

Routine	Required Header	Optional Headers	Compatibility
_free_dbg	<crtdbg.h>		Win NT, Win 95, PMac

For additional compatibility information, see "Compatibility" on page ix in the Introduction.

Libraries	
LIBCD.LIB	Single thread static library, debug version
LIBCMTD.LIB	Multithread static library, debug version
MSVCRTD.LIB	Import library for MSVCRx0D.DLL, debug version
MSVCRx0D.DLL	Multithread DLL library, debug version

Return Value

None

Parameters

userData Pointer to the allocated memory block to be freed

blockType Type of allocated memory block to be freed: **_CLIENT_BLOCK**, **_NORMAL_BLOCK**, or **_IGNORE_BLOCK**

Remarks

The **_free_dbg** function is a debug version of the **free** function. When **_DEBUG** is not defined, calls to **_free_dbg** are removed during preprocessing. Both **free** and **_free_dbg** free a memory block in the base heap, but **_free_dbg** accomodates two debugging features: the ability to keep freed blocks in the heap's linked list to simulate low memory conditions and a block type parameter to free specific allocation types.

_free_dbg performs a validity check on all specified files and block locations before performing the free operation—the application is not expected to provide this information. When a memory block is freed, the debug heap manager automatically checks the integrity of the buffers on either side of the user portion and issues an error report if overwriting has occurred. If the **_CRTDBG_DELAY_FREE_MEM_DF** bit field of the **_crtDbgFlag** flag is set, the freed block is filled with the value 0xDD, assigned the **_FREE_BLOCK** block type, and kept in the heap's linked list of memory blocks.

For information about how memory blocks are allocated, initialized, and managed in the debug version of the base heap, see "Memory Management and the Debug Heap" on page 79. For information about the allocation block types and how they are used, see "Types of Blocks on the Debug Heap" on page 80. For information on the differences between calling a standard heap function versus its debug version in a debug build of an application, see "Using the Debug Version Versus the Base Version" on page 84.

Example

See "Second Example Program" on page 94.

See Also **_malloc_dbg**

_malloc_dbg

Allocates a block of memory in the heap with additional space for a debugging header and overwrite buffers (debug version only).

void *_malloc_dbg(size_t *size*, **int** *blockType*, **const char** **filename*, **int** *linenumber* **);**

Routine	Required Header	Optional Headers	Compatibility
_malloc_dbg	<crtdbg.h>		Win NT, Win 95, PMac

For additional compatibility information, see "Compatibility" on page ix in the Introduction.

Libraries

LIBCD.LIB	Single thread static library, debug version
LIBCMTD.LIB	Multithread static library, debug version
MSVCRTD.LIB	Import library for MSVCRx0D.DLL, debug version
MSVCRx0D.DLL	Multithread DLL library, debug version

Return Value

Upon successful completion, this function either returns a pointer to the user portion of the allocated memory block, calls the new handler function, or returns NULL. See the following Remarks section for a complete description of the return behavior. See the **malloc** function for more information on how the new handler function is used.

Parameters

size Requested size of memory block (bytes)

blockType Requested type of memory block: **_CLIENT_BLOCK** or **_NORMAL_BLOCK**

filename Pointer to name of source file that requested allocation operation or NULL

linenumber Line number in source file where allocation operation was requested or NULL

The *filename* and *linenumber* parameters are only available when **_malloc_dbg** has been called explicitly or the **_CRTDBG_MAP_ALLOC** environment variable has been defined.

Remarks

_malloc_dbg is a debug version of the **malloc** function. When **_DEBUG** is not defined, calls to **_malloc_dbg** are removed during preprocessing. Both **malloc** and **_malloc_dbg** allocate a block of memory in the base heap, but **_malloc_dbg** offers several debugging features: buffers on either side of the user portion of the block to test for leaks, a block type parameter to track specific allocation types, and *filename*/*linenumber* information to determine the origin of allocation requests.

_malloc_dbg allocates the memory block with slightly more space than the requested *size*. The additional space is used by the debug heap manager to link the debug memory blocks together and to provide the application with debug header information and overwrite buffers. When the block is allocated, the user portion of the block is filled with the value 0xCD and each of the overwrite buffers are filled with 0xFD.

For information about how memory blocks are allocated, initialized, and managed in the debug version of the base heap, see "Memory Management and the Debug Heap" on page 79. For information about the allocation block types and how they are used, see "Types of Blocks on the Debug Heap" on page 80. For information on the differences between calling a standard heap function versus its debug version in a debug build of an application, see "Using the Debug Version Versus the Base Version" on page 84.

Example

See "First Example Program" on page 89.

_msize_dbg

Calculates the size of a block of memory in the heap (debug version only).

size_t _msize_dbg(void **userData*, **int** *blockType* **);**

Routine	Required Header	Optional Headers	Compatibility
_msize_dbg	<crtdbg.h>		Win NT, Win 95, PMac

For additional compatibility information, see "Compatibility" on page ix in the Introduction.

Libraries	
LIBCD.LIB	Single thread static library, debug version
LIBCMTD.LIB	Multithread static library, debug version
MSVCRTD.LIB	Import library for MSVCRx0D.DLL, debug version
MSVCRx0D.DLL	Multithread DLL library, debug version

Return Value

Upon successful completion, **_msize_dbg** returns the size (bytes) of the specified memory block, otherwise it returns NULL.

Parameters

userData Pointer to the memory block for which to determine the size

blockType Type of the specified memory block: **_CLIENT_BLOCK** or **_NORMAL_BLOCK**

Remarks

_msize_dbg is a debug version of the **_msize** function. When **_DEBUG** is not defined, calls to **_msize_dbg** are removed during preprocessing. Both **_msize** and **_msize_dbg** calculate the size of a memory block in the base heap, but **_msize_dbg** adds two debugging features: It includes the buffers on either side of the user portion of the memory block in the returned size, and it allows size calculations for specific block types.

For information about how memory blocks are allocated, initialized, and managed in the debug version of the base heap, see "Memory Management and the Debug Heap" on page 79. For information about the allocation block types and how they are used, see "Types of Blocks on the Debug Heap" on page 80. For information on the differences between calling a standard heap function versus its debug version in a debug build of an application, see "Using the Debug Version Versus the Base Version" on page 84.

Example

See the example for **_realloc_dbg**.

See Also **_malloc_dbg**

_realloc_dbg

Reallocates a specified block of memory in the heap by moving and/or resizing the block (debug version only).

void ***_realloc_dbg(void** **userData*, **size_t** *newSize*, **int** *blockType*, **const char** **filename*, **int** *linenumber* **);**

Routine	Required Header	Optional Headers	Compatibility
_realloc_dbg	<crtdbg.h>		Win NT, Win 95, PMac

For additional compatibility information, see "Compatibility" on page ix in the Introduction.

Libraries	
LIBCD.LIB	Single thread static library, debug version
LIBCMTD.LIB	Multithread static library, debug version
MSVCRTD.LIB	Import library for MSVCRx0D.DLL, debug version
MSVCRx0D.DLL	Multithread DLL library, debug version

Return Value

Upon successful completion, this function either returns a pointer to the user portion of the reallocated memory block, calls the new handler function, or returns NULL. See the following Remarks section for a complete description of the return behavior. See the **realloc** function for more information on how the new handler function is used.

Parameters

userData Pointer to the previously allocated memory block

newSize Requested size for reallocated block (bytes)

blockType Requested type for reallocated block: **_CLIENT_BLOCK** or **_NORMAL_BLOCK** *filename* Pointer to name of source file that requested **realloc** operation or NULL

linenumber Line number in source file where **realloc** operation was requested or NULL

The *filename* and *linenumber* parameters are only available when **_realloc_dbg** has been called explicitly or the **_CRTDBG_MAP_ALLOC** environment variable has been defined.

Remarks

_realloc_dbg is a debug version of the **realloc** function. When **_DEBUG** is not defined, calls to **_realloc_dbg** are removed during preprocessing. Both **realloc** and **_realloc_dbg** reallocate a memory block in the base heap, but **_realloc_dbg** accommodates several debugging features: buffers on either side of the user portion of the block to test for leaks, a block type parameter to track specific allocation types, and *filename*/*linenumber* information to determine the origin of allocation requests.

_realloc_dbg reallocates the specified memory block with slightly more space than the requested *newSize*. *newSize* may be greater or less than the size of the originally allocated memory block. The additional space is used by the debug heap manager to link the debug memory blocks together and to provide the application with debug header information and overwrite buffers. The reallocation may result in moving the original memory block to a different location in the heap, as well as changing the size of the memory block. If the memory block is moved, the contents of the original block are copied over.

For information about how memory blocks are allocated, initialized, and managed in the debug version of the base heap, see "Memory Management and the Debug Heap" on page 79. For information about the allocation block types and how they are used, see "Types of Blocks on the Debug Heap" on page 80. For information on the differences between calling a standard heap function versus its debug version in a debug build of an application, see "Using the Debug Version Versus the Base Version" on page 84.

Example

```
/* REALLOCD.C
 * This program allocates a block of memory using _malloc_dbg
 * and then calls _msize_dbg to display the size of that block.
 * Next, it uses _realloc_dbg to expand the amount of
 * memory used by the buffer and then calls _msize_dbg again to
 * display the new amount of memory allocated to the buffer.
 */
#include <stdio.h>
#include <malloc.h>
#include <stdlib.h>
#include <crtdbg.h>

void main( void ) {
        long *buffer;
        size_t size;
```

```
        /* Call _malloc_dbg to include the filename and line number
         * of our allocation request in the header */
        buffer = (long *)_malloc_dbg( 40 * sizeof(long), _NORMAL_BLOCK, __FILE__,
__LINE__ );
        if( buffer == NULL )
               exit( 1 );

        /* Get the size of the buffer by calling _msize_dbg */
        size = _msize_dbg( buffer, _NORMAL_BLOCK );
        printf( "Size of block after _malloc_dbg of 40 longs: %u\n", size );

        /* Reallocate the buffer using _realloc_dbg and show the new size */
        buffer = _realloc_dbg( buffer, size + (40 * sizeof(long)), _NORMAL_BLOCK,
__FILE__, __LINE__ );
        if( buffer == NULL )
               exit( 1 );
        size = _msize_dbg( buffer, _NORMAL_BLOCK );
        printf( "Size of block after _realloc_dbg of 40 more longs: %u\n", size );

        free( buffer );
        exit( 0 );
}
```

Output

```
Size of block after _malloc_dbg of 40 longs: 160
Size of block after _realloc_dbg of 40 more longs: 320
```

See Also **_malloc_dbg**

_RPT, _RPTF Macros

Track an application's progress by generating a debug report (debug version only).

_RPT0(*reportType*, *format* **);**
_RPT1(*reportType*, *format*, *arg1* **);**
_RPT2(*reportType*, *format*, *arg1*, *arg2* **);**
_RPT3(*reportType*, *format*, *arg1*, *arg2*, *arg3* **);**
_RPT4(*reportType*, *format*, *arg1*, *arg2*, *arg3*, *arg4* **);**
_RPTF0(*reportType*, *format* **);**
_RPTF1(*reportType*, *format*, *arg1* **);**
_RPTF2(*reportType*, *format*, *arg1*, *arg2* **);**
_RPTF3(*reportType*, *format*, *arg1*, *arg2*, *arg3* **);**
_RPTF4(*reportType*, *format*, *arg1*, *arg2*, *arg3*, *arg4* **);**

Macro	Required Header	Optional Headers	Compatibility
_RPT Macros	<crtdbg.h>		Win NT, Win 95, PMac
_RPTF Macros	<crtdbg.h>		Win NT, Win 95, PMac

For additional compatibility information, see "Compatibility" on page ix in the Introduction.

Libraries

LIBCD.LIB	Single thread static library, debug version
LIBCMTD.LIB	Multithread static library, debug version
MSVCRTD.LIB	Import library for MSVCRx0D.DLL, debug version
MSVCRx0D.DLL	Multithread DLL library, debug version

Although these are macros and are obtained by including CRTDBG.H, the application must link with one of the libraries listed above because these macros call other run-time functions.

Return Value

None

Parameters

reportType Report type: **_CRT_WARN**, **_CRT_ERROR**, **_CRT_ASSERT**

format Format-control string used to create the user message

arg1 Name of first substitution argument used by *format*

arg2 Name of second substitution argument used by *format*

arg3 Name of third substitution argument used by *format*

arg4 Name of fourth substitution argument used by *format*

All of these macros take the *reportType* and *format* parameters. In addition, they might also take *arg1* through *arg4*, signified by the number appended to the macro name. For example, **_RPT0** and **_RPTF0** take no additional arguments, **_RPT1** and **_RPTF1** take *arg1*, **_RPT2** and **_RPTF2** take *arg1* and *arg2*, and so on.

Remarks

The **_RPT** and **_RPTF** macros are similar to the **printf** function, as they can be used to track an application's progress during the debugging process. However, these macros are more flexible than **printf** because they do not need to be enclosed in **#ifdef** statements to prevent them from being called in a retail build of an application. This flexibility is achieved by using the **_DEBUG** macro. The **_RPT** and **_RPTF** macros are only available when the **_DEBUG** flag is defined. When **_DEBUG** is not defined, calls to these macros are removed during preprocessing.

The **_RPT** macros call the **_CrtDbgReport** function to generate a debug report with a user message. The **_RPTF** macros create a debug report with the source file and line number where the report macro was called, in addition to the user message. The user message is created by substituting the *arg*[*n*] arguments into the *format* string, using the same rules defined by the **printf** function.

_CrtDbgReport generates the debug report and determines its destination(s), based on the current report modes and file defined for *reportType*. The

_CrtSetReportMode and **_CrtSetReportFile** functions are used to define the destination(s) for each report type.

When the destination is a debug message window and the user chooses the Retry button, **_CrtDbgReport** returns 1, causing these macros to start the debugger, provided that "just-in-time" (JIT) debugging is enabled. For more information about using these macros as a debugging error handling mechanism, see "Using Macros for Verification and Reporting" on page 75.

Two other macros exist that generate a debug report. The **_ASSERT** macro generates a report, but only when its expression argument evaluates to FALSE. **_ASSERTE** is exactly like **_ASSERT**, but includes the failed expression in the generated report.

Example

```
/*
 * DBGMACRO.C
 * In this program, calls are made to the _ASSERT and _ASSERTE
 * macros to test the condition 'string1 == string2'.  If the
 * condition fails, these macros print a diagnostic message.
 * The _RPTn and _RPTFn group of macros are also exercised in
 * this program, as an alternative to the printf function.
 */

#include <stdio.h>
#include <string.h>
#include <malloc.h>
#include <crtdbg.h>

int main()
{
    char *p1, *p2;

    /*
     * The Reporting Mode and File must be specified
     * before generating a debug report via an assert
     * or report macro.
     * This program sends all report types to STDOUT
     */
    _CrtSetReportMode(_CRT_WARN, _CRTDBG_MODE_FILE);
    _CrtSetReportFile(_CRT_WARN, _CRTDBG_FILE_STDOUT);
    _CrtSetReportMode(_CRT_ERROR, _CRTDBG_MODE_FILE);
    _CrtSetReportFile(_CRT_ERROR, _CRTDBG_FILE_STDOUT);
    _CrtSetReportMode(_CRT_ASSERT, _CRTDBG_MODE_FILE);
    _CrtSetReportFile(_CRT_ASSERT, _CRTDBG_FILE_STDOUT);

    /*
     * Allocate and assign the pointer variables
     */
    p1 = malloc(10);
    strcpy(p1, "I am p1");
    p2 = malloc(10);
    strcpy(p2, "I am p2");
```

```
    /*
     * Use the report macros as a debugging
     * warning mechanism, similar to printf.
     *
     * Use the assert macros to check if the
     * p1 and p2 variables are equivalent.
     *
     * If the expression fails, _ASSERTE will
     * include a string representation of the
     * failed expression in the report.
     * _ASSERT does not include the
     * expression in the generated report.
     */
    _RPT0(_CRT_WARN, "\n\n Use the assert macros to evaluate the expression p1 ==
p2.\n");
    _RPTF2(_CRT_WARN, "\n Will _ASSERT find '%s' == '%s' ?\n", p1, p2);
    _ASSERT(p1 == p2);

    _RPTF2(_CRT_WARN, "\n\n Will _ASSERTE find '%s' == '%s' ?\n", p1, p2);
    _ASSERTE(p1 == p2);

    _RPT2(_CRT_ERROR, "\n \n '%s' != '%s'\n", p1, p2);

    free(p2);
    free(p1);

    return 0;
}
```

Output

```
Use the assert macros to evaluate the expression p1 == p2.

dbgmacro.c(54) : Will _ASSERT find 'I am p1' == 'I am p2' ?
dbgmacro.c(55) : Assertion failed

dbgmacro.c(57) : Will _ASSERTE find 'I am p1' == 'I am p2' ?
dbgmacro.c(58) : Assertion failed: p1 == p2

'I am p1' != 'I am p2'
```

About the Alphabetic Reference

The following topics describe, in alphabetical order, the functions and macros in the Microsoft run-time library. In some cases, related routines are clustered in the same description. For example, the standard, wide-character, and multibyte versions of **strchr** are discussed in the same place, as are the various forms of the **exec** functions. Differences are noted where appropriate. To locate any function that does not appear in the expected position within the alphabetic reference, choose Search from the Help menu and type the name of the function you are looking for.

abort

Aborts the current process and returns an error code.

void abort(void);

Routine	Required Header	Optional Headers	Compatibility
abort	<process.h> or <stdlib.h>		ANSI, Win 95, Win NT, Win32s, 68K, PMac

For additional compatibility information, see "Compatibility" on page ix in the Introduction.

Libraries	
LIBC.LIB	Single thread static library, retail version
LIBCMT.LIB	Multithread static library, retail version
MSVCRT.LIB	Import library for MSVCRTx0.DLL, retail version
MSVCRTx0.DLL	Multithread DLL library, retail version

Return Value

abort does not return control to the calling process. By default, it terminates the current process and returns an exit code of 3.

Remarks

The **abort** routine prints the message "`abnormal program termination`" and then calls **raise(SIGABRT)**. The action taken in response to the **SIGABRT** signal depends on what action has been defined for that signal in a prior call to the **signal** function. The default **SIGABRT** action is for the calling process to terminate with exit code 3, returning control to the calling process or operating system. **abort** does not flush stream buffers or do **atexit/_onexit** processing.

abort determines the destination of the message based on the type of application that called the routine. Console applications always receive the message via **stderr**. In a single or multithreaded Windows application, **abort** calls the Windows **MessageBox** API to create a message box to display the message along with an OK button. When the user selects OK, the program aborts immediately.

When the application is linked with a debug version of the run-time libraries, **abort** creates a message box with three buttons: Abort, Retry, and Ignore. If the user selects Abort, the program aborts immediately. If the user selects Retry, the debugger is called and the user can debug the program if Just-In-Time (JIT) debugging is enabled. If the user selects Ignore, **abort** continues with its normal execution: creating the message box with the OK button. For more information, see Chapter 4, "Debug Version of the C Run-Time Library."

Example

```
/* ABORT.C:  This program tries to open a
 * file and aborts if the attempt fails.
 */

#include  <stdio.h>
#include  <stdlib.h>

void main( void )
{
   FILE *stream;

   if( (stream = fopen( "NOSUCHF.ILE", "r" )) == NULL )
   {
      perror( "Couldn't open file" );
      abort();
   }
   else
      fclose( stream );
}
```

Output

```
Couldn't open file: No such file or directory

abnormal program termination
```

See Also **_exec** Functions, **exit**, **raise**, **signal**, **_spawn** Functions, **_DEBUG**

abs

Calculates the absolute value.

int abs(int *n* **);**

Routine	Required Header	Optional Headers	Compatibility
abs	<stdlib.h> or <math.h>		ANSI, Win 95, Win NT, Win32s, 68K, PMac

For additional compatibility information, see "Compatibility" on page ix in the Introduction.

Libraries	
LIBC.LIB	Single thread static library, retail version
LIBCMT.LIB	Multithread static library, retail version
MSVCRT.LIB	Import library for MSVCRTx0.DLL, retail version
MSVCRTx0.DLL	Multithread DLL library, retail version

Return Value

The **abs** function returns the absolute value of its parameter. There is no error return.

Parameter

n Integer value

Example

```
/* ABS.C: This program computes and displays
 * the absolute values of several numbers.
 */

#include  <stdio.h>
#include  <math.h>
#include  <stdlib.h>

void main( void )
{
   int    ix = -4, iy;
   long   lx = -41567L, ly;
   double dx = -3.141593, dy;

   iy = abs( ix );
   printf( "The absolute value of %d is %d\n", ix, iy);

   ly = labs( lx );
   printf( "The absolute value of %ld is %ld\n", lx, ly);
```

```
    dy = fabs( dx );
    printf( "The absolute value of %f is %f\n", dx, dy );
}
```

Output

```
The absolute value of -4 is 4
The absolute value of -41567 is 41567
The absolute value of -3.141593 is 3.141593
```

See Also **_cabs, fabs, labs**

_access, _waccess

Determine file-access permission.

int _access(const char ****path*, **int** *mode* **);**
int _waccess(const wchar_t ****path*, **int** *mode* **);**

Routine	Required Header	Optional Headers	Compatibility
_access	<io.h>	<errno.h>	Win 95, Win NT, Win32s, 68K, PMac
_waccess	<wchar.h> or <io.h>	<errno.h>	Win NT

For additional compatibility information, see “Compatibility” on page ix in the Introduction.

Libraries	
LIBC.LIB	Single thread static library, retail version
LIBCMT.LIB	Multithread static library, retail version
MSVCRT.LIB	Import library for MSVCRTx0.DLL, retail version
MSVCRTx0.DLL	Multithread DLL library, retail version

Return Value

Each of these functions returns 0 if the file has the given mode. The function returns –1 if the named file does not exist or is not accessible in the given mode; in this case, **errno** is set as follows:

EACCES Access denied: file’s permission setting does not allow specified access.

ENOENT Filename or path not found.

Parameters

path File or directory path

mode Permission setting

Remarks

When used with files, the **_access** function determines whether the specified file exists and can be accessed as specified by the value of *mode*. When used with directories, **_access** determines only whether the specified directory exists; in Windows NT, all directories have read and write access.

mode Value	Checks File For
00	Existence only
02	Write permission
04	Read permission
06	Read and write permission

_waccess is a wide-character version of **_access**; the *path* argument to **_waccess** is a wide-character string. **_waccess** and **_access** behave identically otherwise.

Example

```
/* ACCESS.C: This example uses _access to check the
 * file named "ACCESS.C" to see if it exists and if
 * writing is allowed.
 */

#include  <io.h>
#include  <stdio.h>
#include  <stdlib.h>

void main( void )
{
   /* Check for existence */
   if( (_access( "ACCESS.C", 0 )) != -1 )
   {
      printf( "File ACCESS.C exists\n" );
      /* Check for write permission */
      if( (_access( "ACCESS.C", 2 )) != -1 )
         printf( "File ACCESS.C has write permission\n" );
   }
}
```

Output

```
File ACCESS.C exists
File ACCESS.C has write permission
```

See Also **_chmod**, **_fstat**, **_open**, **_stat**

acos

Calculates the arccosine.

double acos(double *x* **);**

Routine	Required Header	Optional Headers	Compatibility
acos	<math.h>	<errno.h>	ANSI, Win 95, Win NT, Win32s, 68K, PMac

For additional compatibility information, see "Compatibility" on page ix in the Introduction.

Libraries	
LIBC.LIB	Single thread static library, retail version
LIBCMT.LIB	Multithread static library, retail version
MSVCRT.LIB	Import library for MSVCRTx0.DLL, retail version
MSVCRTx0.DLL	Multithread DLL library, retail version

Return Value

The **acos** function returns the arccosine of *x* in the range 0 to π radians. If *x* is less than –1 or greater than 1, **acos** returns an indefinite (same as a quiet NaN). You can modify error handling with the **_matherr** routine.

Parameter

x Value between –1 and 1 whose arccosine is to be calculated

Example

```
/* ASINCOS.C: This program prompts for a value in the range
 * -1 to 1. Input values outside this range will produce
 * _DOMAIN error messages.If a valid value is entered, the
 * program prints the arcsine and the arccosine of that value.
 */

#include <math.h>
#include <stdio.h>
#include <stdlib.h>
#include <errno.h>

void main( void )
{
   double x, y;
```

```
    printf( "Enter a real number between -1 and 1: " );
    scanf( "%lf", &x );
    y = asin( x );
    printf( "Arcsine of %f = %f\n", x, y );
    y = acos( x );
    printf( "Arccosine of %f = %f\n", x, y );
}
```

Output

```
Enter a real number between -1 and 1: .32696
Arcsine of 0.326960 = 0.333085
Arccosine of 0.326960 = 1.237711
```

See Also **asin**, **atan**, **cos**, **_matherr**, **sin**, **tan**

_alloca

Allocates memory on the stack.

void *_alloca(size_t *size* **);**

Routine	Required Header	Optional Headers	Compatibility
_alloca	<malloc.h>		Win 95, Win NT, Win32s, 68K, PMac

For additional compatibility information, see "Compatibility" on page ix in the Introduction.

Libraries	
LIBC.LIB	Single thread static library, retail version
LIBCMT.LIB	Multithread static library, retail version
MSVCRT.LIB	Import library for MSVCRTx0.DLL, retail version
MSVCRTx0.DLL	Multithread DLL library, retail version

Return Value

The **_alloca** routine returns a **void** pointer to the allocated space, which is guaranteed to be suitably aligned for storage of any type of object. To get a pointer to a type other than **char**, use a type cast on the return value. A stack overflow exception is generated if the space cannot be allocated.

Parameter

size Bytes to be allocated from stack

Remarks

_alloca allocates *size* bytes from the program stack. The allocated space is automatically freed when the calling function exits. Therefore, do not pass the pointer value returned by **_alloca** as an argument to **free**.

See Also **calloc**, **malloc**, **realloc**

asctime, _wasctime

Converts a **tm** time structure to a character string.

char *asctime(const struct tm ***timeptr*** **);**
wchar_t *_wasctime(const struct tm ***timeptr*** **);**

Routine	Required Header	Optional Headers	Compatibility
asctime	<time.h>		ANSI, Win 95, Win NT, Win32s, 68K, PMac
_wasctime	<time.h> or <wchar.h>		Win 95, Win NT, Win32s

For additional compatibility information, see "Compatibility" on page ix in the Introduction.

Libraries	
LIBC.LIB	Single thread static library, retail version
LIBCMT.LIB	Multithread static library, retail version
MSVCRT.LIB	Import library for MSVCRTx0.DLL, retail version
MSVCRTx0.DLL	Multithread DLL library, retail version

Return Value

asctime returns a pointer to the character string result; **_wasctime** returns a pointer to the wide-character string result. There is no error return value.

Parameter

timeptr Time/date structure

Remarks

The **asctime** function converts a time stored as a structure to a character string. The *timeptr* value is usually obtained from a call to **gmtime** or **localtime**, which both return a pointer to a **tm** structure, defined in TIME.H.

timeptr Field	Value
tm_hour	Hours since midnight (0–23)
tm_isdst	Positive if daylight saving time is in effect; 0 if daylight saving time is not in effect; negative if status of daylight saving time is unknown.
tm_mday	Day of month (1–31)
tm_min	Minutes after hour (0–59)
tm_mon	Month (0–11; January = 0)
tm_sec	Seconds after minute (0–59)
tm_wday	Day of week (0–6; Sunday = 0)
tm_yday	Day of year (0–365; January 1 = 0)
tm_year	Year (current year minus 1900)

The converted character string is also adjusted according to the local time zone settings. See the **time**, **_ftime**, and **localtime** functions for information on configuring the local time and the **_tzset** function for details about defining the time zone environment and global variables.

The string result produced by **asctime** contains exactly 26 characters and has the form `Wed Jan 02 02:03:55 1980\n\0`. A 24-hour clock is used. All fields have a constant width. The newline character and the null character occupy the last two positions of the string. **asctime** uses a single, statically allocated buffer to hold the return string. Each call to this function destroys the result of the previous call.

_wasctime is a wide-character version of **_asctime**. **_wasctime** and **_asctime** behave identically otherwise.

Example

```
/* ASCTIME.C: This program places the system time
 * in the long integer aclock, translates it into the
 * structure newtime and then converts it to string
 * form for output, using the asctime function.
 */

#include <time.h>
#include <stdio.h>

struct tm *newtime;
time_t aclock;

void main( void )
{
   time( &aclock );                 /* Get time in seconds */

   newtime = localtime( &aclock );  /* Convert time to struct */
                                    /* tm form */
```

```
    /* Print local time as a string */
    printf( "The current date and time are: %s", asctime( newtime ) );
}
```

Output

```
The current date and time are: Sun May 01 20:27:01 1994
```

See Also **ctime**, **_ftime**, **gmtime**, **localtime**, **time**, **_tzset**

asin

Calculates the arcsine.

double asin(double *x* **);**

Routine	Required Header	Optional Headers	Compatibility
asin	<math.h>		ANSI, Win 95, Win NT, Win32s, 68K, PMac

For additional compatibility information, see "Compatibility" on page ix in the Introduction.

Libraries	
LIBC.LIB	Single thread static library, retail version
LIBCMT.LIB	Multithread static library, retail version
MSVCRT.LIB	Import library for MSVCRTx0.DLL, retail version
MSVCRTx0.DLL	Multithread DLL library, retail version

Return Value

The **asin** function returns the arcsine of *x* in the range $-\pi/2$ to $\pi/2$ radians. If *x* is less than –1 or greater than 1, **asin** returns an indefinite (same as a quiet NaN). You can modify error handling with the **_matherr** routine.

Parameter

x Value whose arcsine is to be calculated

Example

See the example for **acos**.

See Also **acos**, **atan**, **cos**, **_matherr**, **sin**, **tan**

assert

Evaluates an expression and when the result is FALSE, prints a diagnostic message and aborts the program.

void assert(int *expression* **);**

Routine	Required Header	Optional Headers	Compatibility
assert	<assert.h>		ANSI, Win 95, Win NT, Win32s, 68K, PMac

For additional compatibility information, see "Compatibility" on page ix in the Introduction.

Libraries	
LIBC.LIB	Single thread static library, retail version
LIBCMT.LIB	Multithread static library, retail version
MSVCRT.LIB	Import library for MSVCRTx0.DLL, retail version
MSVCRTx0.DLL	Multithread DLL library, retail version

Return Value

None

Parameter

expression Expression (including pointers) that evaluates to nonzero or 0

Remarks

The ANSI **assert** macro is typically used to identify logic errors during program development, by implementing the *expression* argument to evaluate to false only when the program is operating incorrectly. After debugging is complete, assertion checking can be turned off without modifying the source file by defining the identifier **NDEBUG**. **NDEBUG** can be defined with a /D command-line option or with a **#define** directive. If **NDEBUG** is defined with **#define**, the directive must appear before ASSERT.H is included.

assert prints a diagnostic message when *expression* evaluates to false (0) and calls **abort** to terminate program execution. No action is taken if *expression* is true (nonzero). The diagnostic message includes the failed expression and the name of the source file and line number where the assertion failed.

The destination of the diagnostic message depends on the type of application that called the routine. Console applications always receive the message via **stderr**. In a single- or multithreaded Windows application, **assert** calls the Windows **MessageBox** API to create a message box to display the message along with an OK button. When the user chooses OK, the program aborts immediately.

When the application is linked with a debug version of the run-time libraries, **assert** creates a message box with three buttons: Abort, Retry, and Ignore. If the user selects Abort, the program aborts immediately. If the user selects Retry, the debugger is called and the user can debug the program if Just-In-Time (JIT) debugging is enabled. If the user selects Ignore, **assert** continues with its normal execution: creating the message box with the OK button. Note that choosing Ignore when an error condition exists can result in "undefined behavior." For more information, see Chapter 4, "Debug Version of the C Run-Time Library."

The **assert** routine is available in both the release and debug versions of the C run-time libraries. Two other assertion macros, **_ASSERT** and **_ASSERTE**, are also available, but only when the **_DEBUG** flag has been defined. For more information about using these macros and the debug version of the C run-time library, see Chapter 4, "Debug Version of the C Run-Time Library."

Example

```
/* ASSERT.C: In this program, the analyze_string function uses
 * the assert function to test several conditions related to
 * string and length. If any of the conditions fails, the program
 * prints a message indicating what caused the failure.
 */

#include <stdio.h>
#include <assert.h>
#include <string.h>

void analyze_string( char *string );   /* Prototype */

void main( void )
{
   char  test1[] = "abc", *test2 = NULL, test3[] = "";

   printf ( "Analyzing string '%s'\n", test1 );
   analyze_string( test1 );
   printf ( "Analyzing string '%s'\n", test2 );
   analyze_string( test2 );
   printf ( "Analyzing string '%s'\n", test3 );
   analyze_string( test3 );
}

/* Tests a string to see if it is NULL, */
/*   empty, or longer than 0 characters */
void analyze_string( char * string )
{
   assert( string != NULL );        /* Cannot be NULL */
   assert( *string != '\0' );       /* Cannot be empty */
   assert( strlen( string ) > 2 );  /* Length must exceed 2 */
}
```

Output

```
Analyzing string 'abc'
Analyzing string '(null)'
Assertion failed: string != NULL, file assert.c, line 24

abnormal program termination
```

See Also **abort**, **raise**, **signal**, **_ASSERT**, **_ASSERTE**, **_DEBUG**

atan, atan2

Calculates the arctangent of *x* (**atan**) or the arctangent of *y*/*x* (**atan2**).

double atan(double *x* **);**
double atan2(double *y*, **double** *x* **);**

Routine	Required Header	Optional Headers	Compatibility
atan	<math.h>		ANSI, Win 95, Win NT, Win32s, 68K, PMac
atan2	<math.h>		ANSI, Win 95, Win NT, Win32s, 68K, PMac

For additional compatibility information, see "Compatibility" on page ix in the Introduction.

Libraries	
LIBC.LIB	Single thread static library, retail version
LIBCMT.LIB	Multithread static library, retail version
MSVCRT.LIB	Import library for MSVCRTx0.DLL, retail version
MSVCRTx0.DLL	Multithread DLL library, retail version

Return Value

atan returns the arctangent of *x*. **atan2** returns the arctangent of *y*/*x*. If *x* is 0, **atan** returns 0. If both parameters of **atan2** are 0, the function returns 0. You can modify error handling by using the **_matherr** routine. **atan** returns a value in the range $-\pi/2$ to $\pi/2$ radians; **atan2** returns a value in the range $-\pi$ to π radians, using the signs of both parameters to determine the quadrant of the return value.

Parameters

x, *y* Any numbers

Remarks

The **atan** function calculates the arctangent of *x*. **atan2** calculates the arctangent of *y*/*x*. **atan2** is well defined for every point other than the origin, even if *x* equals 0 and *y* does not equal 0.

Example

```
/* ATAN.C: This program calculates
 * the arctangent of 1 and -1.
 */

#include <math.h>
#include <stdio.h>
#include <errno.h>

void main( void )
{
   double x1, x2, y;

   printf( "Enter a real number: " );
   scanf( "%lf", &x1 );
   y = atan( x1 );
   printf( "Arctangent of %f: %f\n", x1, y );
   printf( "Enter a second real number: " );
   scanf( "%lf", &x2 );
   y = atan2( x1, x2 );
   printf( "Arctangent of %f / %f: %f\n", x1, x2, y );
}
```

Output

```
Enter a real number: -862.42
Arctangent of -862.420000: -1.569637
Enter a second real number: 78.5149
Arctangent of -862.420000 / 78.514900: -1.480006
```

See Also **acos**, **asin**, **cos**, **_matherr**, **sin**, **tan**

---

atexit

Processes the specified function at exit.

int atexit(void (__cdecl ***func*** **)(void));**

Routine	Required Header	Optional Headers	Compatibility
atexit	<stdlib.h>		ANSI, Win 95, Win NT, Win32s, 68K, PMac

For additional compatibility information, see "Compatibility" on page ix in the Introduction.

Libraries

LIBC.LIB	Single thread static library, retail version
LIBCMT.LIB	Multithread static library, retail version
MSVCRT.LIB	Import library for MSVCRTx0.DLL, retail version
MSVCRTx0.DLL	Multithread DLL library, retail version

To generate an ANSI-compliant application, use the ANSI-standard **atexit** function (rather than the similar **_onexit** function).

Return Value

atexit returns 0 if successful, or a nonzero value if an error occurs.

Parameter

func Function to be called

Remarks

The **atexit** function is passed the address of a function (*func*) to be called when the program terminates normally. Successive calls to **atexit** create a register of functions that are executed in LIFO (last-in-first-out) order. The functions passed to **atexit** cannot take parameters. **atexit** and **_onexit** use the heap to hold the register of functions. Thus, the number of functions that can be registered is limited only by heap memory.

Example

```
/* ATEXIT.C: This program pushes four functions onto
 * the stack of functions to be executed when atexit
 * is called. When the program exits, these programs
 * are executed on a "last in, first out" basis.
 */

#include <stdlib.h>
#include <stdio.h>

void fn1( void ), fn2( void ), fn3( void ), fn4( void );

void main( void )
{
   atexit( fn1 );
   atexit( fn2 );
   atexit( fn3 );
   atexit( fn4 );
   printf( "This is executed first.\n" );
}

void fn1()
{
   printf( "next.\n" );
}
```

```
void fn2()
{
   printf( "executed " );
}

void fn3()
{
   printf( "is " );
}

void fn4()
{
   printf( "This " );
}
```

Output

```
This is executed first.
This is executed next.
```

See Also **abort**, **exit**, **_onexit**

atof, atoi, atol

Convert strings to double (**atof**), integer (**integer**), or long (**atol**).

double atof(const char ****string* **);
int atoi(const char ****string* **);
long atol(const char ****string* **);

Routine	Required Header	Optional Headers	Compatibility
atof	<math.h> and <stdlib.h>		ANSI, Win 95, Win NT, Win32s, 68K, PMac
atoi	<stdlib.h>		ANSI, Win 95, Win NT, Win32s, 68K, PMac
atol	<stdlib.h>		ANSI, Win 95, Win NT, Win32s, 68K, PMac

For additional compatibility information, see "Compatibility" on page ix in the Introduction.

Libraries	
LIBC.LIB	Single thread static library, retail version
LIBCMT.LIB	Multithread static library, retail version
MSVCRT.LIB	Import library for MSVCRTx0.DLL, retail version
MSVCRTx0.DLL	Multithread DLL library, retail version

Return Value

Each function returns the **double**, **int**, or **long** value produced by interpreting the input characters as a number. The return value is 0 (for **atoi**), 0L (for **atol**), or 0.0 (for **atof**) if the input cannot be converted to a value of that type. The return value is undefined in case of overflow.

Parameter

string String to be converted

Remarks

These functions convert a character string to a double-precision floating-point value (**atof**), an integer value (**atoi**), or a long integer value (**atol**). The input string is a sequence of characters that can be interpreted as a numerical value of the specified type. The output value is affected by the setting of the **LC_NUMERIC** category in the current locale. For more information on the **LC_NUMERIC** category, see **setlocale**.The longest string size that **atof** can handle is 100 characters. The function stops reading the input string at the first character that it cannot recognize as part of a number. This character may be the null character ('\0') terminating the string.

The *string* argument to **atof** has the following form:

[*whitespace*] [*sign*] [*digits*] [*.digits*] [{**d** | **D** | **e** | **E** }[*sign*]*digits*]

A *whitespace* consists of space and/or tab characters, which are ignored; *sign* is either plus (+) or minus (–); and *digits* are one or more decimal digits. If no digits appear before the decimal point, at least one must appear after the decimal point. The decimal digits may be followed by an exponent, which consists of an introductory letter (**d**, **D**, **e**, or **E**) and an optionally signed decimal integer.

atoi and **atol** do not recognize decimal points or exponents. The *string* argument for these functions has the form:

[*whitespace*] [*sign*]*digits*

where *whitespace*, *sign*, and *digits* are exactly as described above for **atof**.

Example

```
/* ATOF.C: This program shows how numbers stored
 * as strings can be converted to numeric values
 * using the atof, atoi, and atol functions.
 */

#include <stdlib.h>
#include <stdio.h>

void main( void )
{
   char *s; double x; int i; long l;
```

```
    s = "  -2309.12E-15";     /* Test of atof */
    x = atof( s );
    printf( "atof test: ASCII string: %s\tfloat:  %e\n", s, x );

    s = "7.8912654773d210";  /* Test of atof */
    x = atof( s );
    printf( "atof test: ASCII string: %s\tfloat:  %e\n", s, x );

    s = "  -9885 pigs";      /* Test of atoi */
    i = atoi( s );
    printf( "atoi test: ASCII string: %s\t\tinteger: %d\n", s, i );

    s = "98854 dollars";     /* Test of atol */
    l = atol( s );
    printf( "atol test: ASCII string: %s\t\tlong: %ld\n", s, l );
}
```

Output

```
atof test: ASCII string:   -2309.12E-15 float:  -2.309120e-012
atof test: ASCII string: 7.8912654773d210  float:  7.891265e+210
atoi test: ASCII string:   -9885 pigs      integer: -9885
atol test: ASCII string: 98854 dollars     long: 98854
```

See Also **_ecvt, _fcvt, _gcvt, setlocale, strtod, wcstol, strtoul**

_beginthread, _beginthreadex

Create a thread.

unsigned long _beginthread(void(****start_address*)(void *), unsigned** *stack_size*, **void ****arglist* **);**
unsigned long _beginthreadex(void ****security*, **unsigned *stack_size*, **unsigned (*** *start_address* **) (void *), void ****arglist*, **unsigned** *initflag*, **unsigned ****thrdaddr* **);**

Routine	Required Header	Optional Headers	Compatibility
_beginthread	<process.h>		Win 95, Win NT
_beginthreadex	<process.h>		Win 95, Win NT

For additional compatibility information, see "Compatibility" on page ix in the Introduction.

Libraries	
LIBCMT.LIB	Multithread static library, retail version
MSVCRT.LIB	Import library for MSVCRTx0.DLL, retail version
MSVCRTx0.DLL	Multithread DLL library, retail version

To use **_beginthread** or **_beginthreadex**, the application must link with one of the multithreaded C run-time libraries.

Return Value

If successful, each of these functions returns a handle to the newly created thread. **_beginthread** returns –1 on an error, in which case **errno** is set to **EAGAIN** if there are too many threads, or to **EINVAL** if the argument is invalid or the stack size is incorrect. **_beginthreadex** returns 0 on an error, in which case **errno** and **doserrno** are set.

Parameters

start_address Start address of routine that begins execution of new thread

stack_size Stack size for new thread or 0

arglist Argument list to be passed to new thread or NULL

security Security descriptor for new thread; must be NULL for Windows 95 applications

initflag Initial state of new thread (running or suspended)

thrdaddr Address of new thread

Remarks

The **_beginthread** function creates a thread that begins execution of a routine at *start_address*. The routine at *start_address* should have no return value. When the thread returns from that routine, it is terminated automatically.

_beginthreadex resembles the Win32 **CreateThread** API more closely than does **_beginthread**. **_beginthreadex** differs from **_beginthread** in the following ways:

- **_beginthreadex** has three additional parameters: *initflag, security*, *threadaddr*. The new thread can be created in a suspended state, with a specified security (Windows NT only), and can be accessed using *thrdaddr*, which is the thread identifier.
- The routine at *start_address* passed to **_beginthreadex** must use the **__stdcall** calling convention and must return a thread exit code.
- **_beginthreadex** returns 0 on failure, rather than –1.
- A thread created with **_beginthreadex** is terminated by a call to **_endthreadex.**

You can call **_endthread** or **_endthreadex** explicitly to terminate a thread; however, **_endthread** or **_endthreadex** is called automatically when the thread returns from the routine passed as a parameter. Terminating a thread with a call to **endthread** or **_endthreadex** helps to ensure proper recovery of resources allocated for the thread.

_endthread automatically closes the thread handle (whereas **_endthreadex** does not). Therefore, when using **_beginthread** and **_endthread**, do not explicitly close the thread handle by calling the Win32 **CloseHandle** API. This behavior differs from the Win32 **ExitThread** API.

Note For an executable file linked with LIBCMT.LIB, do not call the Win32 **ExitThread** API; this prevents the run-time system from reclaiming allocated resources. **_endthread** and **_endthreadex** reclaim allocated thread resources and then call **ExitThread**.

The operating system handles the allocation of the stack when either **_beginthread** or **_beginthreadex** is called; you do not need to pass the address of the thread stack to either of these functions. In addition, the *stack_size* argument can be 0, in which case the operating system uses the same value as the stack specified for the main thread.

arglist is a parameter to be passed to the newly created thread. Typically it is the address of a data item, such as a character string. *arglist* may be NULL if it is not needed, but **_beginthread** and **_beginthreadex** must be provided with some value to pass to the new thread. All threads are terminated if any thread calls **abort**, **exit**, **_exit**, or **ExitProcess**.

Example

```
/* BEGTHRD.C illustrates multiple threads using functions:
 *
 *      _beginthread            _endthread
 *
 *
 * This program requires the multithreaded library. For example,
 * compile with the following command line:
 *     CL /MT /D "_X86_" BEGTHRD.C
 *

 * If you are using the Visual C++ development environment, select the
 * Multi-Threaded runtime library in the compiler Project Settings
 * dialog box.
 *
 */

#include <windows.h>
#include <process.h>    /* _beginthread, _endthread */
#include <stddef.h>
#include <stdlib.h>
#include <conio.h>

void Bounce( void *ch );
void CheckKey( void *dummy );

/* GetRandom returns a random integer between min and max. */
#define GetRandom( min, max ) ((rand() % (int)(((max) + 1) - (min))) + (min))

BOOL repeat = TRUE;     /* Global repeat flag and video variable */
HANDLE hStdOut;         /* Handle for console window */
CONSOLE_SCREEN_BUFFER_INFO csbi;    /* Console information structure */

void main()
```

```
{
    CHAR    ch = 'A';

    hStdOut = GetStdHandle( STD_OUTPUT_HANDLE );

    /* Get display screen's text row and column information. */
   GetConsoleScreenBufferInfo( hStdOut, &csbi );

    /* Launch CheckKey thread to check for terminating keystroke. */
    _beginthread( CheckKey, 0, NULL );

    /* Loop until CheckKey terminates program. */
    while( repeat )
    {
        /* On first loops, launch character threads. */
        _beginthread( Bounce, 0, (void *) (ch++)  );

        /* Wait one second between loops. */
        Sleep( 1000L );
    }
}

/* CheckKey - Thread to wait for a keystroke, then clear repeat flag. */
void CheckKey( void *dummy )
{
    _getch();
    repeat = 0;    /* _endthread implied */

}

/* Bounce - Thread to create and and control a colored letter that moves
 * around on the screen.
 *
 * Params: ch - the letter to be moved
 */
void Bounce( void *ch )
{
    /* Generate letter and color attribute from thread argument. */
    char    blankcell = 0x20;
    char    blockcell = (char) ch;
    BOOL    first = TRUE;
   COORD   oldcoord, newcoord;
   DWORD   result;


    /* Seed random number generator and get initial location. */
    srand( _threadid );
    newcoord.X = GetRandom( 0, csbi.dwSize.X - 1 );
    newcoord.Y = GetRandom( 0, csbi.dwSize.Y - 1 );
    while( repeat )
```

```
    {
        /* Pause between loops. */
        Sleep( 100L );

        /* Blank out our old position on the screen, and draw new letter. */
        if( first )
            first = FALSE;
        else
         WriteConsoleOutputCharacter( hStdOut, &blankcell, 1, oldcoord, &result );
         WriteConsoleOutputCharacter( hStdOut, &blockcell, 1, newcoord, &result );

        /* Increment the coordinate for next placement of the block. */
        oldcoord.X = newcoord.X;
        oldcoord.Y = newcoord.Y;
        newcoord.X += GetRandom( -1, 1 );
        newcoord.Y += GetRandom( -1, 1 );

        /* Correct placement (and beep) if about to go off the screen. */
        if( newcoord.X < 0 )
            newcoord.X = 1;
        else if( newcoord.X == csbi.dwSize.X )
            newcoord.X = csbi.dwSize.X - 2;
        else if( newcoord.Y < 0 )
            newcoord.Y = 1;
        else if( newcoord.Y == csbi.dwSize.Y )
            newcoord.Y = csbi.dwSize.Y - 2;

        /* If not at a screen border, continue, otherwise beep. */
        else
            continue;
        Beep( ((char) ch - 'A') * 100, 175 );
    }
    /* _endthread given to terminate */
    _endthread();
}
```

See Also **_endthread**, **abort**, **exit**

Bessel Functions

The Bessel functions are commonly used in the mathematics of electromagnetic wave theory.

_j0, _j1, _jn These routines return Bessel functions of the first kind: orders 0, 1, and *n*, respectively.

_y0, _y1, _yn These routines return Bessel functions of the second kind: orders 0, 1, and *n*, respectively.

Example

```
/* BESSEL.C: This program illustrates Bessel functions,
 * including:    _j0   _j1   _jn   _y0   _y1   _yn
 */

#include <math.h>
#include <stdio.h>

void main( void )
{
   double x = 2.387;
   int n = 3, c;

   printf( "Bessel functions for x = %f:\n", x );
   printf( " Kind\t\tOrder\tFunction\tResult\n\n" );
   printf( " First\t\t0\t_j0( x )\t%f\n", _j0( x ) );
   printf( " First\t\t1\t_j1( x )\t%f\n", _j1( x ) );
   for( c = 2; c < 5; c++ )
      printf( " First\t\t%d\t_jn( n, x )\t%f\n", c, _jn( c, x ) );
   printf( " Second\t0\t_y0( x )\t%f\n", _y0( x ) );
   printf( " Second\t1\t_y1( x )\t%f\n", _y1( x ) );
   for( c = 2; c < 5; c++ )
      printf( " Second\t%d\t_yn( n, x )\t%f\n", c, _yn( c, x ) );
}
```

Output

```
Bessel functions for x = 2.387000:
  Kind       Order   Function    Result

  First       0    _j0( x )    0.009288
  First       1    _j1( x )    0.522941
  First       2    _jn( n, x )    0.428870
  First       3    _jn( n, x )    0.195734
  First       4    _jn( n, x )    0.063131
  Second    0    _y0( x )    0.511681
  Second    1    _y1( x )    0.094374
  Second    2    _yn( n, x )    -0.432608
  Second    3    _yn( n, x )    -0.819314
  Second    4    _yn( n, x )    -1.626833
```

See Also **_matherr**

Bessel Functions: _j0, _j1, _jn

Compute the Bessel function.

double _j0(double *x* **);**
double _j1(double *x* **);**
double _jn(int *n*, **double** *x* **);**

Routine	Required Header	Optional Headers	Compatibility
_j0	<math.h>		Win 95, Win NT, Win32s, 68K, PMac
_j1	<math.h>		Win 95, Win NT, Win32s, 68K, PMac
_jn	<math.h>		Win 95, Win NT, Win32s, 68K, PMac

For additional compatibility information, see "Compatibility" on page ix in the Introduction.

Libraries	
LIBC.LIB	Single thread static library, retail version
LIBCMT.LIB	Multithread static library, retail version
MSVCRT.LIB	Import library for MSVCRTx0.DLL, retail version
MSVCRTx0.DLL	Multithread DLL library, retail version

Return Value

Each of these routines returns a Bessel function of *x*. You can modify error handling by using **_matherr**.

Parameters

x Floating-point value

n Integer order of Bessel function

Remarks

The **_j0**, **_j1**, and **_jn** routines return Bessel functions of the first kind: orders 0, 1, and n, respectively.

See Also **_matherr**

Bessel Functions: _y0, _y1, _yn

Compute the Bessel function.

double _y0(double *x* **);**
double _y1(double *x* **);**
double _yn(int *n*, **double** *x* **);**

Routine	Required Header	Optional Headers	Compatibility
_y0	<math.h>		Win 95, Win NT, Win32s, 68K, PMac
_y1	<math.h>		Win 95, Win NT, Win32s, 68K, PMac
_yn	<math.h>		Win 95, Win NT, Win32s, 68K, PMac

For additional compatibility information, see "Compatibility" on page ix in the Introduction.

Libraries

LIBC.LIB	Single thread static library, retail version
LIBCMT.LIB	Multithread static library, retail version
MSVCRT.LIB	Import library for MSVCRTx0.DLL, retail version
MSVCRTx0.DLL	Multithread DLL library, retail version

Return Value

Each of these routines returns a Bessel function of *x*. If *x* is negative, the routine sets **errno** to **EDOM**, prints a **_DOMAIN** error message to **stderr**, and returns **_HUGE_VAL**. You can modify error handling by using **_matherr**.

Parameters

x Floating-point value

n Integer order of Bessel function

Remarks

The **_y0**, **_y1**, and **_yn** routines return Bessel functions of the second kind: orders 0, 1, and n, respectively.

See Also **_matherr**

bsearch

Performs a binary search of a sorted array.

void *bsearch(const void ****key*, const void ****base***, size_t** *num***, size_t** *width***, int (__cdecl ****compare* **) (const void ****elem1***, const void ****elem2* **));**

Routine	Required Header	Optional Headers	Compatibility
bsearch	<stdlib.h> and <search.h>		ANSI, Win 95, Win NT, Win32s, 68K, PMac

For additional compatibility information, see "Compatibility" on page ix in the Introduction.

Libraries

LIBC.LIB	Single thread static library, retail version
LIBCMT.LIB	Multithread static library, retail version
MSVCRT.LIB	Import library for MSVCRTx0.DLL, retail version
MSVCRTx0.DLL	Multithread DLL library, retail version

Return Value

bsearch returns a pointer to an occurrence of *key* in the array pointed to by *base*. If *key* is not found, the function returns **NULL**. If the array is not in ascending sort order or contains duplicate records with identical keys, the result is unpredictable.

Parameters

key Object to search for

base Pointer to base of search data

num Number of elements

width Width of elements

compare Function that compares two elements: *elem1* and *elem2*

elem1 Pointer to the key for the search

elem2 Pointer to the array element to be compared with the key

Remarks

The **bsearch** function performs a binary search of a sorted array of *num* elements, each of *width* bytes in size. The *base* value is a pointer to the base of the array to be searched, and *key* is the value being sought. The *compare* parameter is a pointer to a user-supplied routine that compares two array elements and returns a value specifying their relationship. **bsearch** calls the *compare* routine one or more times during the search, passing pointers to two array elements on each call. The *compare* routine compares the elements, then returns one of the following values:

Value Returned by *compare* Routine	Description
< 0	*elem1* less than *elem2*
0	*elem1* equal to *elem2*
> 0	*elem1* greater than *elem2*

Example

```
/* BSEARCH.C: This program reads the command-line
 * parameters, sorting them with qsort, and then
 * uses bsearch to find the word "cat."
 */

#include <search.h>
#include <string.h>
#include <stdio.h>

int compare( char **arg1, char **arg2 ); /* Declare a function for compare */

void main( int argc, char **argv )
{
   char **result;
   char *key = "cat";
   int i;
```

```
   /* Sort using Quicksort algorithm: */
   qsort( (void *)argv, (size_t)argc, sizeof( char * ), (int (*)(const
   void*, const void*))compare );

   for( i = 0; i < argc; ++i )    /* Output sorted list */
      printf( "%s ", argv[i] );

   /* Find the word "cat" using a binary search algorithm: */
   result = (char **)bsearch( (char *) &key, (char *)argv, argc,
                              sizeof( char * ), (int (*)(const void*, const
void*))compare );
   if( result )
      printf( "\n%s found at %Fp\n", *result, result );
   else
      printf( "\nCat not found!\n" );
}

int compare( char **arg1, char **arg2 )
{
   /* Compare all of both strings: */
   return _strcmpi( *arg1, *arg2 );
}
```

Output

```
[C:\work]bsearch dog pig horse cat human rat cow goat
bsearch cat cow dog goat horse human pig rat
cat found at 002D0008
```

See Also **_lfind**, **_lsearch**, **qsort**

_cabs

Calculates the absolute value of a complex number.

double _cabs(struct _complex *z* **);**

Routine	Required Header	Optional Headers	Compatibility
_cabs	<math.h>		Win 95, Win NT, Win32s, 68K, PMac

For additional compatibility information, see “Compatibility” on page ix in the Introduction.

Libraries	
LIBC.LIB	Single thread static library, retail version
LIBCMT.LIB	Multithread static library, retail version
MSVCRT.LIB	Import library for MSVCRTx0.DLL, retail version
MSVCRTx0.DLL	Multithread DLL library, retail version

Return Value

_cabs returns the absolute value of its argument if successful. On overflow **_cabs** returns **HUGE_VAL** and sets **errno** to **ERANGE**. You can change error handling with **_matherr**.

Parameter

z Complex number

Remarks

The **_cabs** function calculates the absolute value of a complex number, which must be a structure of type **_complex**. The structure *z* is composed of a real component *x* and an imaginary component *y*. A call to **_cabs** produces a value equivalent to that of the expression **sqrt(** *z.x**z.x* + *z.y**z.y* **)**.

Example

```
/* CABS.C: Using _cabs, this program calculates
 * the absolute value of a complex number.
 */
#include <math.h>
#include <stdio.h>

void main( void )
{
   struct _complex number = { 3.0, 4.0 };
   double d;

   d = _cabs( number );
   printf( "The absolute value of %f + %fi is %f\n",
           number.x, number.y, d );
}
```

Output

```
The absolute value of 3.000000 + 4.000000i is 5.000000
```

See Also **abs**, **fabs**, **labs**

calloc

Allocates an array in memory with elements initialized to 0.

void *calloc(size_t *num*, **size_t** *size* **);**

Routine	Required Header	Optional Headers	Compatibility
calloc	<stdlib.h> and <malloc.h>		ANSI, Win 95, Win NT, Win32s, 68K, PMac

For additional compatibility information, see “Compatibility” on page ix in the Introduction.

Libraries

LIBC.LIB	Single thread static library, retail version
LIBCMT.LIB	Multithread static library, retail version
MSVCRT.LIB	Import library for MSVCRTx0.DLL, retail version
MSVCRTx0.DLL	Multithread DLL library, retail version

Return Value

calloc returns a pointer to the allocated space. The storage space pointed to by the return value is guaranteed to be suitably aligned for storage of any type of object. To get a pointer to a type other than **void**, use a type cast on the return value.

Parameters

num Number of elements

size Length in bytes of each element

Remarks

The **calloc** function allocates storage space for an array of *num* elements, each of length *size* bytes. Each element is initialized to 0.

calloc calls **malloc** in order to use the C++ **_set_new_mode** function to set the new handler mode. The new handler mode indicates whether, on failure, **malloc** is to call the new handler routine as set by **_set_new_handler**. By default, **malloc** does not call the new handler routine on failure to allocate memory. You can override this default behavior so that, when **calloc** fails to allocate memory, **malloc** calls the new handler routine in the same way that the **new** operator does when it fails for the same reason. To override the default, call

```
_set_new_mode(1)
```

early in your program, or link with NEWMODE.OBJ.

When the application is linked with a debug version of the C run-time libraries, **calloc** resolves to **_calloc_dbg**. For more information about how the heap is managed during the debugging process, see Chapter 4, "Debug Version of the C Run-Time Library."

Example

```
/* CALLOC.C: This program uses calloc to allocate space for
 * 40 long integers. It initializes each element to zero.
 */
#include <stdio.h>
#include <malloc.h>

void main( void )
{
   long *buffer;
```

```
    buffer = (long *)calloc( 40, sizeof( long ) );
    if( buffer != NULL )
       printf( "Allocated 40 long integers\n" );
    else
       printf( "Can't allocate memory\n" );
    free( buffer );
}
```

Output

```
Allocated 40 long integers
```

See Also **free**, **malloc**, **realloc**

ceil

Calculates the ceiling of a value.

double ceil(double *x* **);**

Routine	Required Header	Optional Headers	Compatibility
ceil	<math.h>		ANSI, Win 95, Win NT, Win32s, 68K, PMac

For additional compatibility information, see “Compatibility” on page ix in the Introduction.

Libraries	
LIBC.LIB	Single thread static library, retail version
LIBCMT.LIB	Multithread static library, retail version
MSVCRT.LIB	Import library for MSVCRTx0.DLL, retail version
MSVCRTx0.DLL	Multithread DLL library, retail version

Return Value

The **ceil** function returns a **double** value representing the smallest integer that is greater than or equal to *x*. There is no error return.

Parameter

x Floating-point value

Example

See the example for **floor**.

See Also **floor**, **fmod**

_cexit, _c_exit

Perform cleanup operations and return without terminating the process.

void _cexit(void);
void _c_exit(void);

Routine	Required Header	Optional Headers	Compatibility
_cexit	<process.h>		Win 95, Win NT, Win32s, 68K, PMac
_c_exit	<process.h>		Win 95, Win NT, Win32s, 68K, PMac

For additional compatibility information, see "Compatibility" on page ix in the Introduction.

Libraries	
LIBC.LIB	Single thread static library, retail version
LIBCMT.LIB	Multithread static library, retail version
MSVCRT.LIB	Import library for MSVCRTx0.DLL, retail version
MSVCRTx0.DLL	Multithread DLL library, retail version

Return Value

None

Remarks

The **_cexit** function calls, in last-in-first-out (LIFO) order, the functions registered by **atexit** and **_onexit**. Then **_cexit** flushes all I/O buffers and closes all open streams before returning. **_c_exit** is the same as **_exit** but returns to the calling process without processing **atexit** or **_onexit** or flushing stream buffers. The behavior of **exit, _exit**, **_cexit**, and **_c_exit** is as follows:

Function	Behavior
exit	Performs complete C library termination procedures, terminates process, and exits with supplied status code
_exit	Performs "quick" C library termination procedures, terminates process, and exits with supplied status code
_cexit	Performs complete C library termination procedures and returns to caller, but does not terminate process
_c_exit	Performs "quick" C library termination procedures and returns to caller, but does not terminate process

See Also **abort**, **atexit**, **_exec** Functions, **exit**, **_onexit**, **_spawn** Functions, **system**

_cgets

Gets a character string from the console.

char *_cgets(char ***buffer* **);

Routine	Required Header	Optional Headers	Compatibility
_cgets	<conio.h>		Win 95, Win NT, Win32s

For additional compatibility information, see "Compatibility" on page ix in the Introduction.

Libraries	
LIBC.LIB	Single thread static library, retail version
LIBCMT.LIB	Multithread static library, retail version
MSVCRT.LIB	Import library for MSVCRTx0.DLL, retail version
MSVCRTx0.DLL	Multithread DLL library, retail version

Return Value

_cgets returns a pointer to the start of the string, at *buffer*[2]. There is no error return.

Parameter

buffer Storage location for data

Remarks

The **_cgets** function reads a string of characters from the console and stores the string and its length in the location pointed to by *buffer*. The *buffer* parameter must be a pointer to a character array. The first element of the array, *buffer*[0], must contain the maximum length (in characters) of the string to be read. The array must contain enough elements to hold the string, a terminating null character ('\0'), and two additional bytes. The function reads characters until a carriagereturn–linefeed (CR-LF) combination or the specified number of characters is read. The string is stored starting at *buffer*[2]. If the function reads a CR-LF, it stores the null character ('\0'). **_cgets** then stores the actual length of the string in the second array element, *buffer* [1]. Because all editing keys are active when **_cgets** is called, pressing F3 repeats the last entry.

Example

```
/* CGETS.C: This program creates a buffer and initializes
 * the first byte to the size of the buffer: 2. Next, the
 * program accepts an input string using _cgets and displays
 * the size and text of that string.
 */

#include <conio.h>
#include <stdio.h>
```

```
void main( void )
{
   char buffer[82] = { 80 };  /* Maximum characters in 1st byte */
   char *result;

   printf( "Input line of text, followed by carriage return:\n");
   result = _cgets( buffer );  /* Input a line of text */
   printf( "\nLine length = %d\nText = %s\n", buffer[1], result );
}
```

Output

```
Input line of text, followed by carriage return:
This is a line of text

Line length = 22
Text = This is a line of text.
```

See Also **_getch**

_chdir, _wchdir

Change the current working directory.

int _chdir(const char ***dirname*** **);**
int _wchdir(const wchar_t ***dirname*** **);**

Routine	Required Header	Optional Headers	Compatibility
_chdir	<direct.h>	<errno.h>	Win 95, Win NT, Win32s, 68K, PMac
_wchdir	<direct.h> or <wchar.h>	<errno.h>	Win NT

For additional compatibility information, see "Compatibility" on page ix in the Introduction.

Libraries	
LIBC.LIB	Single thread static library, retail version
LIBCMT.LIB	Multithread static library, retail version
MSVCRT.LIB	Import library for MSVCRTx0.DLL, retail version
MSVCRTx0.DLL	Multithread DLL library, retail version

Return Value

Each of these functions returns a value of 0 if successful. A return value of –1 indicates that the specified path could not be found, in which case **errno** is set to **ENOENT**.

Parameter

dirname   Path of new working directory

Remarks

The **_chdir** function changes the current working directory to the directory specified by *dirname*. The *dirname* parameter must refer to an existing directory. This function can change the current working directory on any drive and if a new drive letter is specified in *dirname*, the default drive letter will be changed as well. For example, if A is the default drive letter and \BIN is the current working directory, the following call changes the current working directory for drive C and establishes C as the new default drive:

```
_chdir("c:\\temp");
```

When you use the optional backslash character (\) in paths, you must place two backslashes (\\) in a C string literal to represent a single backslash (\).

_wchdir is a wide-character version of **_chdir**; the *dirname* argument to **_wchdir** is a wide-character string. **_wchdir** and **_chdir** behave identically otherwise.

Example

```
/* CHGDIR.C: This program uses the _chdir function to verify
 * that a given directory exists.
 */

#include <direct.h>
#include <stdio.h>
#include <stdlib.h>

void main( int argc, char *argv[] )
{
   if( _chdir( argv[1] )   )
      printf( "Unable to locate the directory: %s\n", argv[1] );
   else
      system( "dir *.wri");
}
```

Output

```
 Volume in drive C is CDRIVE
 Volume Serial Number is 0E17-1702

 Directory of C:\msdev

04/29/94  01:06p                 3,200 ERRATA.WRI
04/29/94  01:06p                 2,816 README.WRI
               2 File(s)          6,016 bytes
                             86,433,792 bytes free
```

See Also   **_mkdir**, **_rmdir**, **system**

_chdrive

Changes the current working drive.

int _chdrive(int *drive* **);**

Routine	Required Header	Optional Headers	Compatibility
_chdrive	<direct.h>		Win 95, Win NT, Win32s

For additional compatibility information, see "Compatibility" on page ix in the Introduction.

Libraries	
LIBC.LIB	Single thread static library, retail version
LIBCMT.LIB	Multithread static library, retail version
MSVCRT.LIB	Import library for MSVCRTx0.DLL, retail version
MSVCRTx0.DLL	Multithread DLL library, retail version

Return Value

_chdrive returns a value of 0 if the working drive is successfully changed. A return value of –1 indicates an error.

Parameter

drive Number of new working drive

Remarks

The **_chdrive** function changes the current working drive to the drive specified by *drive*. The *drive* parameter uses an integer to specify the new working drive (1=A, 2=B, and so forth). This function changes only the working drive; **_chdir** changes the working directory.

Example

See the example for **_getdrive**.

See Also **_chdir**, **_fullpath**, **_getcwd**, **_getdrive**, **_mkdir**, **_rmdir**, **system**

_chgsign

Reverses the sign of a double-precision floating-point argument.

double _chgsign(double *x* **);**

Routine	Required Header	Optional Headers	Compatibility
_chgsign	<float.h>		Win 95, Win NT, Win32s, 68K, PMac

For additional compatibility information, see "Compatibility" on page ix in the Introduction.

Libraries

LIBC.LIB	Single thread static library, retail version
LIBCMT.LIB	Multithread static library, retail version
MSVCRT.LIB	Import library for MSVCRTx0.DLL, retail version
MSVCRTx0.DLL	Multithread DLL library, retail version

Return Value

_chgsign returns a value equal to its double-precision floating-point argument *x*, but with its sign reversed. There is no error return.

Parameter

x Double-precision floating-point value to be changed

See Also **fabs**, **_copysign**

_chmod, _wchmod

Change the file-permission settings.

int _chmod(const char ***filename*****, int** *pmode* **);**
int _wchmod(const wchar_t ***filename*****, int** *pmode* **);**

Routine	Required Header	Optional Headers	Compatibility
_chmod	<io.h>	<sys/types.h>, <sys/stat.h>, <errno.h>	Win 95, Win NT, Win32s, 68K, PMac
_wchmod	<io.h> or <wchar.h>	<sys/types.h>, <sys/stat.h>, <errno.h>	Win NT

For additional compatibility information, see "Compatibility" on page ix in the Introduction.

Libraries

LIBC.LIB	Single thread static library, retail version
LIBCMT.LIB	Multithread static library, retail version
MSVCRT.LIB	Import library for MSVCRTx0.DLL, retail version
MSVCRTx0.DLL	Multithread DLL library, retail version

Return Value

Each of these functions returns 0 if the permission setting is successfully changed. A return value of –1 indicates that the specified file could not be found, in which case **errno** is set to **ENOENT**.

Parameters

filename Name of existing file

pmode Permission setting for file

Remarks

The **_chmod** function changes the permission setting of the file specified by *filename*. The permission setting controls read and write access to the file. The integer expression *pmode* contains one or both of the following manifest constants, defined in SYS\STAT.H:

_S_IWRITE Writing permitted

_S_IREAD Reading permitted

_S_IREAD | _S_IWRITE Reading and writing permitted

Any other values for *pmode* are ignored. When both constants are given, they are joined with the bitwise-OR operator (**|**). If write permission is not given, the file is read-only. Note that all files are always readable; it is not possible to give write-only permission. Thus the modes **_S_IWRITE** and **_S_IREAD | _S_IWRITE** are equivalent.

_wchmod is a wide-character version of **_chmod**; the *filename* argument to **_wchmod** is a wide-character string. **_wchmod** and **_chmod** behave identically otherwise.

Example

```
/* CHMOD.C: This program uses _chmod to
 * change the mode of a file to read-only.
 * It then attempts to modify the file.
 */

#include <sys/types.h>
#include <sys/stat.h>
#include <io.h>
#include <stdio.h>
#include <stdlib.h>

void main( void )
{
   /* Make file read-only: */
   if( _chmod( "CHMOD.C", _S_IREAD ) == -1 )
      perror( "File not found\n" );
   else
      printf( "Mode changed to read-only\n" );
   system( "echo /* End of file */ >> CHMOD.C" );

   /* Change back to read/write: */
   if( _chmod( "CHMOD.C", _S_IWRITE ) == -1 )
      perror( "File not found\n" );
```

```
    else
       printf( "Mode changed to read/write\n" );
    system( "echo /* End of file */ >> CHMOD.C" );
}
```

Output

```
Mode changed to read-only
Access is denied
Mode changed to read/write
```

See Also **_access**, **_creat**, **_fstat**, **_open**, **_stat**

_chsize

Changes the file size.

int _chsize(int *handle*, **long** *size* **);**

Routine	Required Header	Optional Headers	Compatibility
_chsize	<io.h>	<errno.h>	Win 95, Win NT, Win32s, 68K, PMac

For additional compatibility information, see "Compatibility" on page ix in the Introduction.

Libraries	
LIBC.LIB	Single thread static library, retail version
LIBCMT.LIB	Multithread static library, retail version
MSVCRT.LIB	Import library for MSVCRTx0.DLL, retail version
MSVCRTx0.DLL	Multithread DLL library, retail version

Return Value

_chsize returns the value 0 if the file size is successfully changed. A return value of –1 indicates an error: **errno** is set to **EACCES** if the specified file is locked against access, to **EBADF** if the specified file is read-only or the handle is invalid, or to **ENOSPC** if no space is left on the device.

Parameters

handle Handle referring to open file

size New length of file in bytes

Remarks

The **_chsize** function extends or truncates the file associated with *handle* to the length specified by *size*. The file must be open in a mode that permits writing. Null characters ('\0') are appended if the file is extended. If the file is truncated, all data from the end of the shortened file to the original length of the file is lost.

Example

```
/* CHSIZE.C: This program uses _filelength to report the size
 * of a file before and after modifying it with _chsize.
 */

#include <io.h>
#include <fcntl.h>
#include <sys/types.h>
#include <sys/stat.h>
#include <stdio.h>

void main( void )
{
   int fh, result;
   unsigned int nbytes = BUFSIZ;

   /* Open a file */
   if( (fh = _open( "data", _O_RDWR | _O_CREAT, _S_IREAD
                    | _S_IWRITE ))  != -1 )
   {
      printf( "File length before: %ld\n", _filelength( fh ) );
      if( ( result = _chsize( fh, 329678 ) ) == 0 )
         printf( "Size successfully changed\n" );
      else
         printf( "Problem in changing the size\n" );
      printf( "File length after:  %ld\n", _filelength( fh ) );
      _close( fh );
   }
}
```

Output

```
File length before: 0
Size successfully changed
File length after:  329678
```

See Also **_close, _creat, _open**

_clear87, _clearfp

Get and clear the floating-point status word.

unsigned int _clear87(void);
unsigned int _clearfp(void);

Routine	Required Header	Optional Headers	Compatibility
_clear87	<float.h>		Win 95, Win NT, Win32s
_clearfp	<float.h>		Win 95, Win NT, Win32s, 68K, PMac

For additional compatibility information, see "Compatibility" on page ix in the Introduction.

Libraries

LIBC.LIB	Single thread static library, retail version
LIBCMT.LIB	Multithread static library, retail version
MSVCRT.LIB	Import library for MSVCRTx0.DLL, retail version
MSVCRTx0.DLL	Multithread DLL library, retail version

Return Value

The bits in the value returned indicate the floating-point status. See FLOAT.H for a complete definition of the bits returned by **_clear87**. Many of the math library functions modify the 8087/80287 status word, with unpredictable results. Return values from **_clear87** and **_status87** become more reliable as fewer floating-point operations are performed between known states of the floating-point status word.

Remarks

The **_clear87** function clears the exception flags in the floating-point status word, sets the busy bit to 0, and returns the status word. The floating-point status word is a combination of the 8087/80287 status word and other conditions detected by the 8087/80287 exception handler, such as floating-point stack overflow and underflow.

_clearfp is a platform-independent, portable version of the **_clear87** routine. It is identical to **_clear87** on Intel® (x86) platforms and is also supported by the MIPS® and ALPHA platforms. To ensure that your floating-point code is portable to MIPS or ALPHA, use **_clearfp**. If you are only targeting x86 platforms, you can use either **_clear87** or **_clearfp**.

Example

```
/* CLEAR87.C: This program creates various floating-point
 * problems, then uses _clear87 to report on these problems.
 * Compile this program with Optimizations disabled (/Od).
 * Otherwise the optimizer will remove the code associated with
 * the unused floating-point values.
 */

#include <stdio.h>
#include <float.h>

void main( void )
{
   double a = 1e-40, b;
   float x, y;

   printf( "Status: %.4x - clear\n", _clear87()  );

   /* Store into y is inexact and underflows: */
   y = a;
   printf( "Status: %.4x - inexact, underflow\n", _clear87() );
```

```
   /* y is denormal: */
   b = y;
   printf( "Status: %.4x - denormal\n", _clear87() );
}
```

Output

```
Status: 0000 - clear
Status: 0003 - inexact, underflow
Status: 80000 - denormal
```

See Also **_control87**, **_status87**

clearerr

Resets the error indicator for a stream

void clearerr(FILE ****stream*);**

Routine	Required Header	Optional Headers	Compatibility
clearerr	<stdio.h>		ANSI, Win 95, Win NT, Win32s, 68K, PMac

For additional compatibility information, see "Compatibility" on page ix in the Introduction.

Libraries	
LIBC.LIB	Single thread static library, retail version
LIBCMT.LIB	Multithread static library, retail version
MSVCRT.LIB	Import library for MSVCRTx0.DLL, retail version
MSVCRTx0.DLL	Multithread DLL library, retail version

Return Value

None

Parameter

stream Pointer to **FILE** structure

Remarks

The **clearerr** function resets the error indicator and end-of-file indicator for *stream*. Error indicators are not automatically cleared; once the error indicator for a specified stream is set, operations on that stream continue to return an error value until **clearerr**, **fseek**, **fsetpos**, or **rewind** is called.

Example

```
/* CLEARERR.C: This program creates an error
 * on the standard input stream, then clears
 * it so that future reads won't fail.
 */

#include <stdio.h>

void main( void )
{
   int c;
   /* Create an error by writing to standard input. */
   putc( 'c', stdin );
   if( ferror( stdin ) )
   {
      perror( "Write error" );
      clearerr( stdin );
   }

   /* See if read causes an error. */
   printf( "Will input cause an error? " );
   c = getc( stdin );
   if( ferror( stdin ) )
   {
      perror( "Read error" );
      clearerr( stdin );
   }
}
```

Output

```
Write error: No error
Will input cause an error? n
```

See Also **_eof**, **feof**, **ferror**, **perror**

clock

Calculates the time used by the calling process.

clock_t clock(void);

Routine	Required Header	Optional Headers	Compatibility
clock	<time.h>		ANSI, Win 95, Win NT, Win32s, 68K, PMac

For additional compatibility information, see "Compatibility" on page ix in the Introduction.

Libraries

LIBC.LIB	Single thread static library, retail version
LIBCMT.LIB	Multithread static library, retail version
MSVCRT.LIB	Import library for MSVCRTx0.DLL, retail version
MSVCRTx0.DLL	Multithread DLL library, retail version

Return Value

clock returns a time value in seconds. The returned value is the product of the amount of time that has elapsed since the start of a process and the value of the **CLOCKS_PER_SEC** constant. If the amount of elapsed time is unavailable, the function returns –1, cast as a **clock_t**.

Note The amount of time that has elapsed since the start of the calling process is not necessarily equal to the actual amount of processor time that that process has used.

Remarks

The **clock** function tells how much processor time the calling process has used. The time in seconds is approximated by dividing the clock return value by the value of the **CLOCKS_PER_SEC** constant. In other words, **clock** returns the number of processor timer ticks that have elapsed. A timer tick is approximately equal to 1/**CLOCKS_PER_SEC** second. In versions of Microsoft C before 6.0, the **CLOCKS_PER_SEC** constant was called **CLK_TCK**.

Example

```
/* CLOCK.C: This example prompts for how long
 * the program is to run and then continuously
 * displays the elapsed time for that period.
 */

#include <stdio.h>
#include <stdlib.h>
#include <time.h>

void sleep( clock_t wait );

void main( void )
{
   long    i = 600000L;
   clock_t start, finish;
   double  duration;

   /* Delay for a specified time. */
   printf( "Delay for three seconds\n" );
   sleep( (clock_t)3 * CLOCKS_PER_SEC );
   printf( "Done!\n" );
```

```
    /* Measure the duration of an event. */
    printf( "Time to do %ld empty loops is ", i );
    start = clock();
    while( i-- )
        ;
    finish = clock();
    duration = (double)(finish - start) / CLOCKS_PER_SEC;
    printf( "%2.1f seconds\n", duration );
}

/* Pauses for a specified number of milliseconds. */
void sleep( clock_t wait )
{
    clock_t goal;
    goal = wait + clock();
    while( goal > clock() )
        ;
}
```

Output

```
Delay for three seconds
Done!
Time to do 600000 empty loops is 0.1 seconds
```

See Also **difftime**, **time**

_close

Closes a file.

int _close(int *handle* **);**

Routine	Required Header	Optional Headers	Compatibility
_close	<io.h>	<errno.h>	Win 95, Win NT, Win32s, 68K, PMac

For additional compatibility information, see "Compatibility" on page ix in the Introduction.

Libraries	
LIBC.LIB	Single thread static library, retail version
LIBCMT.LIB	Multithread static library, retail version
MSVCRT.LIB	Import library for MSVCRTx0.DLL, retail version
MSVCRTx0.DLL	Multithread DLL library, retail version

Return Value

_close returns 0 if the file was successfully closed. A return value of –1 indicates an error, in which case **errno** is set to **EBADF**, indicating an invalid file-handle parameter.

Parameter

handle Handle referring to open file

Remarks

The **_close** function closes the file associated with *handle*.

Example

See the example for **_open**.

See Also **_chsize**, **_creat**, **_dup**, **_open**, **_unlink**

_commit

Flushes a file directly to disk.

int _commit(int *handle* **);**

Routine	Required Header	Optional Headers	Compatibility
_commit	<io.h>	<errno.h>	Win 95, Win NT, Win32s, 68K, PMac

For additional compatibility information, see "Compatibility" on page ix in the Introduction.

Libraries	
LIBC.LIB	Single thread static library, retail version
LIBCMT.LIB	Multithread static library, retail version
MSVCRT.LIB	Import library for MSVCRTx0.DLL, retail version
MSVCRTx0.DLL	Multithread DLL library, retail version

Return Value

_commit returns 0 if the file was successfully flushed to disk. A return value of –1 indicates an error, and **errno** is set to **EBADF**, indicating an invalid file-handle parameter.

Parameter

handle Handle referring to open file

Remarks

The **_commit** function forces the operating system to write the file associated with *handle* to disk. This call ensures that the specified file is flushed immediately, not at the operating system's discretion.

Example

```
/* COMMIT.C illustrates low-level file I/O functions including:
 *
 *     _close    _commit    memset    _open    _write
 *
 * This is example code; to keep the code simple and readable
 * return values are not checked.
 */

#include <io.h>
#include <stdio.h>
#include <fcntl.h>
#include <memory.h>
#include <errno.h>

#define MAXBUF 32

int log_receivable( int );

void main( void )
{
    int fhandle;
    fhandle = _open( "TRANSACT.LOG", _O_APPEND | _O_CREAT |
                                     _O_BINARY | _O_RDWR );
    log_receivable( fhandle );
    _close( fhandle );
}

int log_receivable( int fhandle )
{
/* The log_receivable function prompts for a name and a monetary
 * amount and places both values into a buffer (buf). The _write
 * function writes the values to the operating system and the
 * _commit function ensures that they are written to a disk file.
 */

    int i;
    char  buf[MAXBUF];

    memset( buf, '\0', MAXBUF );
    /* Begin Transaction. */
    printf( "Enter name: " );
    gets( buf );
    for( i = 1; buf[i] != '\0'; i++ );
    /* Write the value as a '\0' terminated string. */
    _write( fhandle, buf, i+1 );
    printf( "\n" );

    memset( buf, '\0', MAXBUF );
    printf( "Enter amount: $" );
    gets( buf );
    for( i = 1; buf[i] != '\0'; i++ );
```

```
    /* Write the value as a '\0' terminated string. */
    _write( fhandle, buf, i+1 );
    printf( "\n" );

    /* The _commit function ensures that two important pieces of
     * data are safely written to disk. The return value of the
     * _commit function is returned to the calling function.
     */
    return _commit( fhandle );
}
```

See Also **_creat**, **_open**, **_read**, **_write**

_control87, _controlfp

Get and set the floating-point control word.

unsigned int _control87(unsigned int *new*, **unsigned int** *mask* **);**
unsigned int _controlfp(unsigned int *new*, **unsigned int** *mask* **);**

Routine	Required Header	Optional Headers	Compatibility
_control87	<float.h>		Win 95, Win NT, Win32s
_controlfp	<float.h>		Win 95, Win NT, Win32s, 68K, PMac

For additional compatibility information, see "Compatibility" on page ix in the Introduction.

Libraries	
LIBC.LIB	Single thread static library, retail version
LIBCMT.LIB	Multithread static library, retail version
MSVCRT.LIB	Import library for MSVCRTx0.DLL, retail version
MSVCRTx0.DLL	Multithread DLL library, retail version

Return Value

The bits in the value returned indicate the floating-point control state. See FLOAT.H for a complete definition of the bits returned by **_control87**.

Parameters

new New control-word bit values

mask Mask for new control-word bits to set

Remarks

The **_control87** function gets and sets the floating-point control word. The floating-point control word allows the program to change the precision, rounding, and infinity modes in the floating-point math package. You can also mask or unmask floating-point exceptions using **_control87**. If the value for *mask* is equal to 0, **_control87** gets the floating-point control word. If *mask* is nonzero, a new value for the control word is set: For any bit that is on (equal to 1) in *mask*, the corresponding bit in *new* is used to update the control word. In other words, *fpcntrl* **= ((***fpcntrl* **& ~mask) | (new & mask))** where *fpcntrl* is the floating-point control word.

Note The run-time libraries mask all floating-point exceptions by default.

_controlfp is a platform-independent, portable version of **_control87**. It is nearly identical to the **_control87** function on Intel (x86) platforms and is also supported by the MIPS and ALPHA platforms. To ensure that your floating-point code is portable to MIPS or ALPHA, use **_controlfp**. If you are targeting x86 platforms, use either **_control87** or **_controlfp**.

The only other difference between **_control87** and **_controlfp** is that **_controlfp** does not interfere with the DENORMAL OPERAND exception mask. The following example demonstrates the difference:

```
_control87( _EM_INVALID, _MCW_EM ); // DENORMAL is unmasked by this call
_controlfp( _EM_INVALID, _MCW_EM ); // DENORMAL exception mask remains unchanged
```

The possible values for the mask constant (*mask*) and new control values (*new*) are shown in Table R.1. Use the portable constants listed below (**_MCW_EM**, **_EM_INVALID**, and so forth) as arguments to these functions, rather than supplying the hexadecimal values explicitly.

Table R.1 Hexadecimal Values

Mask	Hex Value	Constant	Hex Value
_MCW_EM (Interrupt exception)	0x0008001F		
		_EM_INVALID	0x00000010
		_EM_DENORMAL	0x00080000
		_EM_ZERODIVIDE	0x00000008
		_EM_OVERFLOW	0x00000004
		_EM_UNDERFLOW	0x00000002
		_EM_INEXACT	0x00000001
_MCW_IC (Infinity control)	0x00040000		
		_IC_AFFINE	0x00040000
		_IC_PROJECTIVE	0x00000000

Table R.1 Hexadecimal Values *(continued)*

Mask	Hex Value	Constant	Hex Value
_MCW_RC (Rounding control)	0x00000300		
		_RC_CHOP	0x00000300
		_RC_UP	0x00000200
		_RC_DOWN	0x00000100
		_RC_NEAR	0x00000000
_MCW_PC (Precision control)	0x00030000		
		_PC_24 (24 bits)	0x00020000
		_PC_53 (53 bits)	0x00010000
		_PC_64 (64 bits)	0x00000000

Example

```
/* CNTRL87.C: This program uses _control87 to output the control
 * word, set the precision to 24 bits, and reset the status to
 * the default.
 */

#include <stdio.h>
#include <float.h>

void main( void )
{
   double a = 0.1;

   /* Show original control word and do calculation. */
   printf( "Original: 0x%.4x\n", _control87( 0, 0 ) );
   printf( "%1.1f * %1.1f = %.15e\n", a, a, a * a );

   /* Set precision to 24 bits and recalculate. */
   printf( "24-bit:   0x%.4x\n", _control87( _PC_24, MCW_PC ) );
   printf( "%1.1f * %1.1f = %.15e\n", a, a, a * a );

   /* Restore to default and recalculate. */
   printf( "Default:  0x%.4x\n",
           _control87( _CW_DEFAULT, 0xfffff ) );
   printf( "%1.1f * %1.1f = %.15e\n", a, a, a * a );
}
```

Output

```
Original: 0x9001f
0.1 * 0.1 = 1.000000000000000e-002
24-bit:   0xa001f
0.1 * 0.1 = 9.999999776482582e-003
Default:  0x001f
0.1 * 0.1 = 1.000000000000000e-002
```

See Also **_clear87**, **_status87**

_copysign

Return one value with the sign of another.

double _copysign(double *x*, **double** *y* **);**

Routine	Required Header	Optional Headers	Compatibility
_copysign	<float.h>		Win 95, Win NT, Win32s, 68K, PMac

For additional compatibility information, see "Compatibility" on page ix in the Introduction.

Libraries	
LIBC.LIB	Single thread static library, retail version
LIBCMT.LIB	Multithread static library, retail version
MSVCRT.LIB	Import library for MSVCRTx0.DLL, retail version
MSVCRTx0.DLL	Multithread DLL library, retail version

Return Value

_copysign returns its double-precision floating point argument *x* with the same sign as its double-precision floating-point argument *y*. There is no error return.

Parameters

x Double-precision floating-point value to be changed

y Double-precision floating-point value

See Also **fabs**, **_chgsign**

cos, cosh

Calculate the cosine (**cos**) or hyperbolic cosine (**cosh**).

double cos(double *x* **);**
double cosh(double *x* **);**

Routine	Required Header	Optional Headers	Compatibility
cos	<math.h>		ANSI, Win 95, Win NT, Win32s, 68K, PMac
cosh	<math.h>		ANSI, Win 95, Win NT, Win32s, 68K, PMac

For additional compatibility information, see "Compatibility" on page ix in the Introduction.

Libraries	
LIBC.LIB	Single thread static library, retail version
LIBCMT.LIB	Multithread static library, retail version
MSVCRT.LIB	Import library for MSVCRTx0.DLL, retail version
MSVCRTx0.DLL	Multithread DLL library, retail version

Return Value

The **cos** and **cosh** functions return the cosine and hyperbolic cosine, respectively, of *x*. If *x* is greater than or equal to 2^{63}, or less than or equal to -2^{63}, a loss of significance in the result of a call to **cos** occurs, in which case the function generates a **_TLOSS** error and returns an indefinite (same as a quiet NaN).

If the result is too large in a **cosh** call, the function returns **HUGE_VAL** and sets **errno** to **ERANGE**. You can modify error handling with **_matherr**.

Parameter

x Angle in radians

Example

See the example for **sin**.

See Also **acos**, **asin**, **atan**, **_matherr**, **sin**, **tan**

_cprintf

Formats and prints to the console.

int _cprintf(const char ***format*** **[, *argument*] ...);**

Routine	Required Header	Optional Headers	Compatibility
_cprintf	<conio.h>		Win 95, Win NT, Win32s

For additional compatibility information, see "Compatibility" on page ix in the Introduction.

Libraries	
LIBC.LIB	Single thread static library, retail version
LIBCMT.LIB	Multithread static library, retail version
MSVCRT.LIB	Import library for MSVCRTx0.DLL, retail version
MSVCRTx0.DLL	Multithread DLL library, retail version

Return Value

_cprintf returns the number of characters printed.

Parameters

format Format-control string

argument Optional parameters

Remarks

The **_cprintf** function formats and prints a series of characters and values directly to the console, using the **_putch** function to output characters. Each *argument* (if any) is converted and output according to the corresponding format specification in *format*. The format has the same form and function as the *format* parameter for the **printf** function; for a description of the format and parameters, see **printf**. Unlike the **fprintf**, **printf**, and **sprintf** functions, **_cprintf** does not translate linefeed characters into carriage return–linefeed (CR-LF) combinations on output.

Example

```
/* CPRINTF.C: This program displays
 * some variables to the console.
 */

#include <conio.h>

void main( void )
{
   int      i = -16, h = 29;
   unsigned u = 62511;
   char     c = 'A';
   char     s[] = "Test";

   /* Note that console output does not translate \n as
    * standard output does. Use \r\n instead.
    */
   _cprintf( "%d  %.4x  %u  %c %s\r\n", i, h, u, c, s );
}
```

Output

```
-16  001d  62511  A Test
```

See Also **_cscanf**, **fprintf**, **printf**, **sprintf**, **vfprintf**

_cputs

Puts a string to the console.

int _cputs(const char ***string* **);

Routine	Required Header	Optional Headers	Compatibility
_cputs	<conio.h>		Win 95, Win NT, Win32s

For additional compatibility information, see "Compatibility" on page ix in the Introduction.

Libraries	
LIBC.LIB	Single thread static library, retail version
LIBCMT.LIB	Multithread static library, retail version
MSVCRT.LIB	Import library for MSVCRTx0.DLL, retail version
MSVCRTx0.DLL	Multithread DLL library, retail version

Return Value

If successful, **_cputs** returns a 0. If the function fails, it returns a nonzero value.

Parameter

string Output string

Remarks

The **_cputs** function writes the null-terminated string pointed to by *string* directly to the console. A carriage return–linefeed (CR-LF) combination is not automatically appended to the string.

Example

```
/* CPUTS.C: This program first displays
 * a string to the console.
 */

#include <conio.h>

void main( void )
{
   /* String to print at console.
    * Note the \r (return) character.
    */
   char *buffer = "Hello world (courtesy of _cputs)!\r\n";

   _cputs( buffer );
}
```

Output

```
Hello world (courtesy of _cputs)!
```

See Also **_putch**

_creat, _wcreat

Creates a new file.

int _creat(const char **filename*, **int** *pmode* **);**
int _wcreat(const wchar_t **filename*, **int** *pmode* **);**

Routine	Required Header	Optional Headers	Compatibility
_creat	<io.h>	<sys/types.h>, <sys/stat.h>, <errno.h>	Win 95, Win NT, Win32s, 68K, PMac
_wcreat	<io.h> or <wchar.h>	<sys/types.h>, <sys/stat.h>, <errno.h>	Win NT

For additional compatibility information, see "Compatibility" on page ix in the Introduction.

Libraries	
LIBC.LIB	Single thread static library, retail version
LIBCMT.LIB	Multithread static library, retail version
MSVCRT.LIB	Import library for MSVCRTx0.DLL, retail version
MSVCRTx0.DLL	Multithread DLL library, retail version

Return Value

Each of these functions, if successful, returns a handle to the created file. Otherwise the function returns –1 and sets **errno** as follows.

errno Setting	Description
EACCES	Filename specifies an existing read-only file or specifies a directory instead of a file
EMFILE	No more file handles are available
ENOENT	The specified file could not be found

Parameters

filename Name of new file

pmode Permission setting

Remarks

The **_creat** function creates a new file or opens and truncates an existing one. **_wcreat** is a wide-character version of **_creat**; the *filename* argument to **_wcreat** is a wide-character string. **_wcreat** and **_creat** behave identically otherwise.

If the file specified by *filename* does not exist, a new file is created with the given permission setting and is opened for writing. If the file already exists and its permission setting allows writing, **_creat** truncates the file to length 0, destroying the previous contents, and opens it for writing. The permission setting, *pmode*, applies to newly created files only. The new file receives the specified permission setting after it is closed for the first time. The integer expression *pmode* contains one or both of the manifest constants **_S_IWRITE** and **_S_IREAD**, defined in SYS\STAT.H. When both constants are given, they are joined with the bitwise-OR operator (|). The *pmode* parameter is set to one of the following values:

_S_IWRITE Writing permitted

_S_IREAD Reading permitted

_S_IREAD | _S_IWRITE Reading and writing permitted

If write permission is not given, the file is read-only. All files are always readable; it is impossible to give write-only permission. Thus the modes **_S_IWRITE** and **_S_IREAD | _S_IWRITE** are equivalent. Files opened using **_creat** are always opened in compatibility mode (see **_sopen**) with **_SH_DENYNO**.

_creat applies the current file-permission mask to *pmode* before setting the permissions (see **_umask**). **_creat** is provided primarily for compatibility with previous libraries. A call to **_open** with **_O_CREAT** and **_O_TRUNC** in the *oflag* parameter is equivalent to **_creat** and is preferable for new code.

Example

```
/* CREAT.C: This program uses _creat to create
 * the file (or truncate the existing file)
 * named data and open it for writing.
 */

#include <sys/types.h>
#include <sys/stat.h>
#include <io.h>
#include <stdio.h>
#include <stdlib.h>

void main( void )
{
   int fh;

   fh = _creat( "data", _S_IREAD | _S_IWRITE );
   if( fh == -1 )
      perror( "Couldn't create data file" );
   else
```

```
        {
            printf( "Created data file.\n" );
            _close( fh );
        }
    }
```

Output

```
Created data file.
```

See Also **_chmod**, **_chsize**, **_close**, **_dup**, **_open**, **_sopen**, **_umask**

_cscanf

Reads formatted data from the console.

int _cscanf(const char ****format* [,** *argument*] ... **);**

Routine	Required Header	Optional Headers	Compatibility
_cscanf	<conio.h>		Win 95, Win NT, Win32s

For additional compatibility information, see "Compatibility" on page ix in the Introduction.

Libraries	
LIBC.LIB	Single thread static library, retail version
LIBCMT.LIB	Multithread static library, retail version
MSVCRT.LIB	Import library for MSVCRTx0.DLL, retail version
MSVCRTx0.DLL	Multithread DLL library, retail version

Return Value

_cscanf returns the number of fields that were successfully converted and assigned. The return value does not include fields that were read but not assigned. The return value is **EOF** for an attempt to read at end of file. This can occur when keyboard input is redirected at the operating-system command-line level. A return value of 0 means that no fields were assigned.

Parameters

format Format-control string

argument Optional parameters

Remarks

The **_cscanf** function reads data directly from the console into the locations given by *argument*. The **_getche** function is used to read characters. Each optional parameter must be a pointer to a variable with a type that corresponds to a type specifier in *format*. The format controls the interpretation of the input fields and has the same form and function as the *format* parameter for the **scanf** function; for a description of *format,* see **scanf**. While **_cscanf** normally echoes the input character, it does not do so if the last call was to **_ungetch**.

Example

```
/* CSCANF.C: This program prompts for a string
 * and uses _cscanf to read in the response.
 * Then _cscanf returns the number of items
 * matched, and the program displays that number.
 */

#include <stdio.h>
#include <conio.h>

void main( void )
{
   int   result, i[3];

   _cprintf( "Enter three integers: ");
   result = _cscanf( "%i %i %i", &i[0], &i[1], &i[2] );
   _cprintf( "\r\nYou entered " );
   while( result-- )
      _cprintf( "%i ", i[result] );
   _cprintf( "\r\n" );
}
```

Output

```
Enter three integers: 1  2  3
You entered 3 2 1
```

See Also **_cprintf**, **fscanf**, **scanf**, **sscanf**

---

ctime, _wctime

Convert a time value to a string and adjust for local time zone settings.

char *ctime(const time_t ****timer* **);
wchar_t *_wctime(const time_t ****timer* **);

Routine	Required Header	Optional Headers	Compatibility
ctime	<time.h>		ANSI, Win 95, Win NT, Win32s, 68K, PMac
_wctime	<time.h> or <wchar.h>		Win 95, Win NT, Win32s

For additional compatibility information, see “Compatibility” on page ix in the Introduction.

Libraries

LIBC.LIB	Single thread static library, retail version
LIBCMT.LIB	Multithread static library, retail version
MSVCRT.LIB	Import library for MSVCRTx0.DLL, retail version
MSVCRTx0.DLL	Multithread DLL library, retail version

Return Value

Each of these functions returns a pointer to the character string result. If *time* represents a date before midnight, January 1, 1970, UTC, the function returns **NULL**.

Parameter

timer Pointer to stored time

Remarks

The **ctime** function converts a time value stored as a **time_t** structure into a character string. The *timer* value is usually obtained from a call to **time**, which returns the number of seconds elapsed since midnight (00:00:00), January 1, 1970, coordinated universal time (UTC). The string result produced by **ctime** contains exactly 26 characters and has the form:

```
Wed Jan 02 02:03:55 1980\n\0
```

A 24-hour clock is used. All fields have a constant width. The newline character ('\n') and the null character ('\0') occupy the last two positions of the string.

The converted character string is also adjusted according to the local time zone settings. See the **time**, **_ftime**, and **localtime** functions for information on configuring the local time and the **_tzset** function for details about defining the time zone environment and global variables.

A call to **ctime** modifies the single statically allocated buffer used by the **gmtime** and **localtime** functions. Each call to one of these routines destroys the result of the previous call. **ctime** shares a static buffer with the **asctime** function. Thus, a call to **ctime** destroys the results of any previous call to **asctime**, **localtime**, or **gmtime**.

_wctime is a wide-character version of **ctime**; **_wctime** returns a pointer to a wide-character string. **_wctime** and **ctime** behave identically otherwise.

Example

```
/* CTIME.C: This program gets the current
 * time in time_t form, then uses ctime to
 * display the time in string form.
 */

#include <time.h>
#include <stdio.h>
```

```
void main( void )
{
   time_t ltime;

   time( &ltime );
   printf( "The time is %s\n", ctime( &ltime ) );
}
```

Output

```
The time is Fri Apr 29 12:25:12 1994
```

See Also **asctime**, **_ftime**, **gmtime**, **localtime**, **time**

_cwait

Waits until another process terminates.

int _cwait(int ***termstat*****, int** *procHandle***, int** *action* **);**

Routine	Required Header	Optional Headers	Compatibility
_cwait	<process.h>	<errno.h>	Win 95, Win NT, Win32s

For additional compatibility information, see "Compatibility" on page ix in the Introduction.

Libraries	
LIBC.LIB	Single thread static library, retail version
LIBCMT.LIB	Multithread static library, retail version
MSVCRT.LIB	Import library for MSVCRTx0.DLL, retail version
MSVCRTx0.DLL	Multithread DLL library, retail version

Return Value

When the specified process has "successfully" completed, **_cwait** returns the handle of the specified process and sets *termstat* to the result code returned by the specified process. Otherwise, **_cwait** returns –1 and sets **errno** as follows.

Value	Description
ECHILD	No specified process exists, *procHandle* is invalid, or the call to the **GetExitCodeProcess** or **WaitForSingleObject** API failed
EINVAL	*action* is invalid

Parameters

termstat Pointer to a buffer where the result code of the specified process will be stored, or NULL

procHandle Handle to the current process or thread

action NULL: Ignored by Windows NT and Windows 95 applications; for other applications: action code to perform on *procHandle*

Remarks

The **_cwait** function waits for the termination of the process ID of the specified process that is provided by *procHandle*. The value of *procHandle* passed to **_cwait** should be the value returned by the call to the **_spawn** function that created the specified process. If the process ID terminates before **_cwait** is called, **_cwait** returns immediately. **_cwait** can be used by any process to wait for any other known process for which a valid handle (*procHandle*) exists.

termstat points to a buffer where the return code of the specified process will be stored. The value of *termstat* indicates whether the specified process terminated "normally" by calling the Windows NT **ExitProcess** API. **ExitProcess** is called internally if the specified process calls **exit** or **_exit**, returns from **main**, or reaches the end of **main**. See **GetExitCodeProcess** for more information regarding the value passed back through *termstat*. If **_cwait** is called with a NULL value for *termstat*, the return code of the specified process will not be stored.

The *action* parameter is ignored by Windows NT and Windows 95 because parent-child relationships are not implemented in these environments. Therefore, the OS/2 **wait** function, which allows a parent process to wait for any of its immediate children to terminate, is not available.

Example

```
/* CWAIT.C: This program launches several processes and waits
 * for a specified process to finish.
 */

#include <windows.h>
#include <process.h>
#include <stdlib.h>
#include <stdio.h>
#include <time.h>

/* Macro to get a random integer within a specified range */
#define getrandom( min, max ) (( rand() % (int)((( max ) + 1 ) - ( min ))) + ( min ))

struct PROCESS
{

   int      nPid;
   char     name[40];

} process[4] = { { 0, "Ann" }, { 0, "Beth" }, { 0, "Carl" }, { 0, "Dave" } };
```

```
void main( int argc, char *argv[] )
{

   int termstat, c;

   srand( (unsigned)time( NULL ) );    /* Seed randomizer */
   /* If no arguments, this is the calling process */
   if( argc == 1 )
   {

      /* Spawn processes in numeric order */
      for( c = 0; c < 4; c++ ){
         _flushall();
         process[c].nPid = spawnl( _P_NOWAIT, argv[0], argv[0],
                               process[c].name, NULL );
      }

      /* Wait for randomly specified process, and respond when done */
      c = getrandom( 0, 3 );
      printf( "Come here, %s.\n", process[c].name );
      _cwait( &termstat, process[c].nPid, _WAIT_CHILD );
      printf( "Thank you, %s.\n", process[c].name );

   }

   /* If there are arguments, this must be a spawned process */
   else
   {

      /* Delay for a period determined by process number */
      Sleep( (argv[1][0] - 'A' + 1) * 1000L );
      printf( "Hi, Dad. It's %s.\n", argv[1] );

   }

}
```

Output

```
Hi, Dad. It's Ann.
Come here, Ann.
Thank you, Ann.
Hi, Dad. It's Beth.
Hi, Dad. It's Carl.
Hi, Dad. It's Dave.
```

See Also **_spawn** Functions

difftime

Finds the difference between two times.

double difftime(time_t *timer1*, **time_t** *timer0* **);**

Routine	Required Header	Optional Headers	Compatibility
difftime	<time.h>		ANSI, Win 95, Win NT, Win32s, 68K, PMac

For additional compatibility information, see "Compatibility" on page ix in the Introduction.

Libraries	
LIBC.LIB	Single thread static library, retail version
LIBCMT.LIB	Multithread static library, retail version
MSVCRT.LIB	Import library for MSVCRTx0.DLL, retail version
MSVCRTx0.DLL	Multithread DLL library, retail version

Return Value

difftime returns the elapsed time in seconds, from *timer0* to *timer1*. The value returned is a double-precision floating-point number.

Parameters

timer1 Ending time

timer0 Beginning time

Remarks

The **difftime** function computes the difference between the two supplied time values *timer0* and *timer1*.

Example

```
/* DIFFTIME.C: This program calculates the amount of time
 * needed to do a floating-point multiply 10 million times.
 */

#include <stdio.h>
#include <stdlib.h>
#include <time.h>

void main( void )
{
   time_t   start, finish;
   long loop;
   double   result, elapsed_time;
```

```
   printf( "Multiplying 2 floating point numbers 10 million times...\n" );

   time( &start );
   for( loop = 0; loop < 10000000; loop++ )
      result = 3.63 * 5.27;
   time( &finish );

   elapsed_time = difftime( finish, start );
   printf( "\nProgram takes %6.0f seconds.\n", elapsed_time );
}
```

Output

```
Multiplying 2 floats 10 million times...

Program takes      2 seconds.
```

See Also **time**

div

Computes the quotient and the remainder of two integer values.

div_t div(int *numer*, **int** *denom* **);**

Routine	Required Header	Optional Headers	Compatibility
div	<stdlib.h>		ANSI, Win 95, Win NT, Win32s, 68K, PMac

For additional compatibility information, see "Compatibility" on page ix in the Introduction.

Libraries	
LIBC.LIB	Single thread static library, retail version
LIBCMT.LIB	Multithread static library, retail version
MSVCRT.LIB	Import library for MSVCRTx0.DLL, retail version
MSVCRTx0.DLL	Multithread DLL library, retail version

Return Value

div returns a structure of type **div_t**, comprising the quotient and the remainder. The structure is defined in STDLIB.H.

Parameters

numer Numerator

denom Denominator

Remarks

The **div** function divides *numer* by *denom*, computing the quotient and the remainder. The **div_t** structure contains **int quot**, the quotient, and **int rem**, the remainder. The sign of the quotient is the same as that of the mathematical quotient. Its absolute value is the largest integer that is less than the absolute value of the mathematical quotient. If the denominator is 0, the program terminates with an error message.

Example

```
/* DIV.C: This example takes two integers as command-line
 * arguments and displays the results of the integer
 * division. This program accepts two arguments on the
 * command line following the program name, then calls
 * div to divide the first argument by the second.
 * Finally, it prints the structure members quot and rem.
 */

#include <stdlib.h>
#include <stdio.h>
#include <math.h>

void main( int argc, char *argv[] )
{
   int x,y;
   div_t div_result;

   x = atoi( argv[1] );
   y = atoi( argv[2] );

   printf( "x is %d, y is %d\n", x, y );
   div_result = div( x, y );
   printf( "The quotient is %d, and the remainder is %d\n",
           div_result.quot, div_result.rem );
}
```

Output

```
x is 876, y is 13
The quotient is 67, and the remainder is 5
```

See Also **ldiv**

_dup, _dup2

Create a second handle for an open file (**_dup**), or reassign a file handle (**_dup2**).

int_dup(int *handle* **);**
int _dup2(int *handle1*, **int** *handle2* **);**

Routine	Required Header	Optional Headers	Compatibility
_dup	<io.h>		Win 95, Win NT, Win32s, 68K, PMac
_dup2	<io.h>		Win 95, Win NT, Win32s, 68K, PMac

For additional compatibility information, see "Compatibility" on page ix in the Introduction.

Libraries	
LIBC.LIB	Single thread static library, retail version
LIBCMT.LIB	Multithread static library, retail version
MSVCRT.LIB	Import library for MSVCRTx0.DLL, retail version
MSVCRTx0.DLL	Multithread DLL library, retail version

Return Value

_dup returns a new file handle. **_dup2** returns 0 to indicate success. If an error occurs, each function returns –1 and sets **errno** to **EBADF** if the file handle is invalid, or to **EMFILE** if no more file handles are available.

Parameters

handle, *handle1* Handles referring to open file

handle2 Any handle value

Remarks

The **_dup** and **_dup2** functions associate a second file handle with a currently open file. These functions can be used to associate a predefined file handle, such as that for **stdout**, with a different file. Operations on the file can be carried out using either file handle. The type of access allowed for the file is unaffected by the creation of a new handle. **_dup** returns the next available file handle for the given file. **_dup2** forces *handle2* to refer to the same file as *handle1*. If *handle2* is associated with an open file at the time of the call, that file is closed.

Both **_dup** and **_dup2** accept file handles as parameters. To pass a stream **(FILE *)** to either of these functions, use **_fileno**. The **fileno** routine returns the file handle currently associated with the given stream. The following example shows how to associate **stderr** (defined as **FILE *** in STDIO.H) with a handle:

```
cstderr = _dup( _fileno( stderr ));
```

Example

```
/* DUP.C: This program uses the variable old to save
 * the original stdout. It then opens a new file named
 * new and forces stdout to refer to it. Finally, it
 * restores stdout to its original state.
 */

#include <io.h>
#include <stdlib.h>
#include <stdio.h>
```

```
void main( void )
{
   int old;
   FILE *new;

   old = _dup( 1 );   /* "old" now refers to "stdout" */
                      /* Note:  file handle 1 == "stdout" */
   if( old == -1 )
   {
      perror( "_dup( 1 ) failure" );
      exit( 1 );
   }
   write( old, "This goes to stdout first\r\n", 27 );
   if( ( new = fopen( "data", "w" ) ) == NULL )
   {
      puts( "Can't open file 'data'\n" );
      exit( 1 );
   }

   /* stdout now refers to file "data" */
   if( -1 == _dup2( _fileno( new ), 1 ) )
   {
      perror( "Can't _dup2 stdout" );
      exit( 1 );
   }
   puts( "This goes to file 'data'\r\n" );

   /* Flush stdout stream buffer so it goes to correct file */
   fflush( stdout );
   fclose( new );

   /* Restore original stdout */
   _dup2( old, 1 );
   puts( "This goes to stdout\n" );
   puts( "The file 'data' contains:" );
   system( "type data" );
}
```

Output

```
This goes to stdout first
This goes to file 'data'

This goes to stdout

The file 'data' contains:

This goes to file 'data'
```

See Also **_close, _creat, _open**

_ecvt

Converts a **double** number to a string.

char *_ecvt(double *value*, **int** *count*, **int** **dec*, **int** **sign* **);**

Function	Required Header	Optional Headers	Compatibility
_ecvt	<stdlib.h>		Win 95, Win NT, Win32s, 68K, PMac

For additional compatibility information, see "Compatibility" on page ix in the Introduction.

Libraries	
LIBC.LIB	Single thread static library, retail version
LIBCMT.LIB	Multithread static library, retail version
MSVCRT.LIB	Import library for MSVCRTx0.DLL, retail version
MSVCRTx0.DLL	Multithread DLL library, retail version

Return Value

_ecvt returns a pointer to the string of digits. There is no error return.

Parameters

value Number to be converted

count Number of digits stored

dec Stored decimal-point position

sign Sign of converted number

Remarks

The **_ecvt** function converts a floating-point number to a character string. The *value* parameter is the floating-point number to be converted. This function stores up to *count* digits of *value* as a string and appends a null character ('\0'). If the number of digits in *value* exceeds *count,* the low-order digit is rounded. If there are fewer than *count* digits, the string is padded with zeros.

Only digits are stored in the string. The position of the decimal point and the sign of *value* can be obtained from *dec* and *sign* after the call. The *dec* parameter points to an integer value giving the position of the decimal point with respect to the beginning of the string. A 0 or negative integer value indicates that the decimal point lies to the left of the first digit. The *sign* parameter points to an integer that indicates the sign of the converted number. If the integer value is 0, the number is positive. Otherwise, the number is negative.

_ecvt and **_fcvt** use a single statically allocated buffer for the conversion. Each call to one of these routines destroys the result of the previous call.

Example

```
/* ECVT.C: This program uses _ecvt to convert a
 * floating-point number to a character string.
 */

#include <stdlib.h>
#include <stdio.h>

void main( void )
{
   int     decimal,   sign;
   char    *buffer;
   int     precision = 10;
   double  source = 3.1415926535;

   buffer = _ecvt( source, precision, &decimal, &sign );
   printf( "source: %2.10f   buffer: '%s'  decimal: %d  sign: %d\n",
           source, buffer, decimal, sign );
}
```

Output

```
source: 3.1415926535   buffer: '3141592654'  decimal: 1   sign: 0
```

See Also **atof**, **_fcvt**, **_gcvt**

_endthread, _endthreadex

void _endthread(void);
void _endthreadex(unsigned *retval* **);**

Function	Required Header	Optional Headers	Compatibility
_endthread	<process.h>		Win 95, Win NT
_endthreadex	<process.h>		Win 95, Win NT

For additional compatibility information, see "Compatibility" on page ix in the Introduction.

Libraries	
LIBCMT.LIB	Multithread static library, retail version
MSVCRT.LIB	Import library for MSVCRTx0.DLL, retail version
MSVCRTx0.DLL	Multithread DLL library, retail version

Return Value

None

Parameter

retval Thread exit code

Remarks

The **_endthread** and **_endthreadex** functions terminate a thread created by **_beginthread** or **_beginthreadex**, respectively. You can call **_endthread** or **_endthreadex** explicitly to terminate a thread; however, **_endthread** or **_endthreadex** is called automatically when the thread returns from the routine passed as a parameter to **_beginthread** or **_beginthreadex**. Terminating a thread with a call to **endthread** or **_endthreadex** helps to ensure proper recovery of resources allocated for the thread.

Note For an executable file linked with LIBCMT.LIB, do not call the Win32 **ExitThread** API; this prevents the run-time system from reclaiming allocated resources. **_endthread** and **_endthreadex** reclaim allocated thread resources and then call **ExitThread**.

_endthread automatically closes the thread handle. (This behavior differs from the Win32 **ExitThread** API.) Therefore, when you use **_beginthread** and **_endthread**, do not explicitly close the thread handle by calling the Win32 **CloseHandle** API.

Like the Win32 **ExitThread** API, **_endthreadex** does not close the thread handle. Therefore, when you use **_beginthreadex** and **_endthreadex**, you must close the thread handle by calling the Win32 **CloseHandle** API.

Example

See the example for **_beginthread**.

See Also **_beginthread**

_eof

Tests for end-of-file.

int _eof(int *handle* **);**

Function	Required Header	Optional Headers	Compatibility
_eof	<io.h>	<errno.h>	Win 95, Win NT, Win32s, 68K, PMac

For additional compatibility information, see "Compatibility" on page ix in the Introduction.

Libraries	
LIBC.LIB	Single thread static library, retail version
LIBCMT.LIB	Multithread static library, retail version
MSVCRT.LIB	Import library for MSVCRTx0.DLL, retail version
MSVCRTx0.DLL	Multithread DLL library, retail version

Return Value

_eof returns 1 if the current position is end of file, or 0 if it is not. A return value of –1 indicates an error; in this case, **errno** is set to **EBADF**, which indicates an invalid file handle.

Parameter

handle   Handle referring to open file

Remarks

The **_eof** function determines whether the end of the file associated with *handle* has been reached.

Example

```
/* EOF.C: This program reads data from a file
 * ten bytes at a time until the end of the
 * file is reached or an error is encountered.
 */
#include <io.h>
#include <fcntl.h>
#include <stdio.h>
#include <stdlib.h>
void main( void )
{
   int  fh, count, total = 0;
   char buf[10];
   if( (fh = _open( "eof.c", _O_RDONLY )) == - 1 )
   {
        perror( "Open failed");
        exit( 1 );
   }
   /* Cycle until end of file reached: */
   while( !_eof( fh ) )
   {
      /* Attempt to read in 10 bytes: */
      if( (count = _read( fh, buf, 10 )) == -1 )
      {
         perror( "Read error" );
         break;
      }
      /* Total actual bytes read */
      total += count;
   }
   printf( "Number of bytes read = %d\n", total );
   _close( fh );
}
```

Output

```
Number of bytes read = 754
```

See Also   **clearerr**, **feof**, **ferror**, **perror**

_exec, _wexec Functions

Each of the functions in this family loads and executes a new process.

_execl, _wexecl	**_execv, _wexecv**
_execle, _wexecle	**_execve, _wexecve**
_execlp, _wexeclp	**_execvp, _wexecvp**
_execlpe, _wexeclpe	**_execvpe, _wexecvpe**

The letter(s) at the end of the function name determine the variation.

_exec Function Suffix	Description
e	*envp*, array of pointers to environment settings, is passed to new process.
l	Command-line arguments are passed individually to **_exec** function. Typically used when number of parameters to new process is known in advance.
p	**PATH** environment variable is used to find file to execute.
v	*argv,* array of pointers to command-line arguments, is passed to **_exec**. Typically used when number of parameters to new process is variable.

Remarks

Each of the **_exec** functions loads and execute a new process. All **_exec** functions use the same operating-system function. The **_exec** functions automatically handle multibyte-character string arguments as appropriate, recognizing multibyte-character sequences according to the multibyte code page currently in use. The **_wexec** functions are wide-character versions of the **_exec** functions. The **_wexec** functions behave identically to their **_exec** family counterparts except that they do not handle multibyte-character strings.

When a call to an **_exec** function is successful, the new process is placed in the memory previously occupied by the calling process. Sufficient memory must be available for loading and executing the new process.

The *cmdname* parameter specifies the file to be executed as the new process. It can specify a full path (from the root), a partial path (from the current working directory), or a filename. If *cmdname* does not have a filename extension or does not end with a period (.), the **_exec** function searches for the named file. If the search is unsuccessful, it tries the same base name with the .COM extension and then with the .EXE, .BAT, and .CMD extensions. If *cmdname* has an extension, only that extension is used in the search. If *cmdname* ends with a period, the **_exec** function searches for *cmdname* with no extension. **_execlp**, **_execlpe**, **_execvp**, and **_execvpe** search for *cmdname* (using the same procedures) in the directories specified by the **PATH** environment variable. If *cmdname* contains a drive specifier or any slashes (that is, if it is a relative path), the **_exec** call searches only for the specified file; the path is not searched.

Parameters are passed to the new process by giving one or more pointers to character strings as parameters in the **_exec** call. These character strings form the parameter list for the new process. The combined length of the inherited environment settings and the strings forming the parameter list for the new process must not exceed 32K bytes. The terminating null character (`'\0'`) for each string is not included in the count, but space characters (inserted automatically to separate the parameters) are counted.

The argument pointers can be passed as separate parameters (in **_execl**, **_execle**, **_execlp**, and **_execlpe**) or as an array of pointers (in **_execv**, **_execve**, **_execvp**, and **_execvpe**). At least one parameter, *arg0*, must be passed to the new process; this parameter is *argv*[0] of the new process. Usually, this parameter is a copy of *cmdname*. (A different value does not produce an error.)

The **_execl**, **_execle**, **_execlp**, and **_execlpe** calls are typically used when the number of parameters is known in advance. The parameter *arg0* is usually a pointer to *cmdname*. The parameters *arg1* through *argn* point to the character strings forming the new parameter list. A null pointer must follow *argn* to mark the end of the parameter list.

The **_execv**, **_execve**, **_execvp**, and **_execvpe** calls are useful when the number of parameters to the new process is variable. Pointers to the parameters are passed as an array, *argv*. The parameter *argv*[0] is usually a pointer to *cmdname*. The parameters *argv*[1] through *argv*[*n*] point to the character strings forming the new parameter list. The parameter *argv*[*n*+1] must be a **NULL** pointer to mark the end of the parameter list.

Files that are open when an **_exec** call is made remain open in the new process. In **_execl**, **_execlp**, **_execv**, and **_execvp** calls, the new process inherits the environment of the calling process. **_execle**, **_execlpe**, **_execve**, and **_execvpe** calls alter the environment for the new process by passing a list of environment settings through the *envp* parameter. *envp* is an array of character pointers, each element of which (except for the final element) points to a null-terminated string defining an environment variable. Such a string usually has the form *NAME=value* where *NAME* is the name of an environment variable and *value* is the string value to which that variable is set. (Note that *value* is not enclosed in double quotation marks.) The final element of the *envp* array should be **NULL**. When *envp* itself is **NULL**, the new process inherits the environment settings of the calling process.

A program executed with one of the **_exec** functions is always loaded into memory as if the "maximum allocation" field in the program's .EXE file header were set to the default value of 0xFFFFH. You can use the EXEHDR utility to change the maximum allocation field of a program; however, such a program invoked with one of the **_exec** functions may behave differently from a program invoked directly from the operating-system command line or with one of the **_spawn** functions.

The **_exec** calls do not preserve the translation modes of open files. If the new process must use files inherited from the calling process, use the **_setmode** routine to set the translation mode of these files to the desired mode. You must explicitly flush (using **fflush** or **_flushall**) or close any stream before the **_exec** function call. Signal settings are not preserved in new processes that are created by calls to **_exec** routines. The signal settings are reset to the default in the new process.

Example

```
/* EXEC.C illustrates the different versions of exec including:
 *      _execl          _execle          _execlp          _execlpe
 *      _execv          _execve          _execvp          _execvpe
 *
 * Although EXEC.C can exec any program, you can verify how
 * different versions handle arguments and environment by
 * compiling and specifying the sample program ARGS.C. See
 * SPAWN.C for examples of the similar spawn functions.
 */

#include <stdio.h>
#include <conio.h>
#include <process.h>

char *my_env[] =                /* Environment for exec?e */
{
   "THIS=environment will be",
   "PASSED=to new process by",
   "the EXEC=functions",
   NULL
};

void main()
{
   char *args[4], prog[80];
   int ch;

   printf( "Enter name of program to exec: " );
   gets( prog );
   printf( " 1. _execl  2. _execle  3. _execlp  4. _execlpe\n" );
   printf( " 5. _execv  6. _execve  7. _execvp  8. _execvpe\n" );
   printf( "Type a number from 1 to 8 (or 0 to quit): " );
   ch = _getche();
   if( (ch < '1') || (ch > '8') )
       exit( 1 );
   printf( "\n\n" );

   /* Arguments for _execv? */
   args[0] = prog;
   args[1] = "exec??";
   args[2] = "two";
   args[3] = NULL;
```

```
   switch( ch )
   {
   case '1':
      _execl( prog, prog, "_execl", "two", NULL );
      break;
   case '2':
      _execle( prog, prog, "_execle", "two", NULL, my_env );
      break;
   case '3':
      _execlp( prog, prog, "_execlp", "two", NULL );
      break;
   case '4':
      _execlpe( prog, prog, "_execlpe", "two", NULL, my_env );
      break;
   case '5':
      _execv( prog, args );
      break;
   case '6':
      _execve( prog, args, my_env );
      break;
   case '7':
      _execvp( prog, args );
      break;
   case '8':
      _execvpe( prog, args, my_env );
      break;
   default:
      break;
   }

   /* This point is reached only if exec fails. */
   printf( "\nProcess was not execed." );
   exit( 0 );
}
```

See Also **abort**, **atexit**, **exit**, **_onexit**, **_spawn** Functions, **system**

_execl, _wexecl

Load and execute new child processes.

int _execl(const char ****cmdname*, const char ****arg0***, ... const char ****argn***, NULL);**
int _wexecl(const wchar_t ****cmdname*, const wchar_t ****arg0***, ... const wchar_t ****argn***, NULL);**

Function	Required Header	Optional Headers	Compatibility
_execl	<process.h>	<errno.h>	Win 95, Win NT, Win32s
_wexecl	<process.h> or <wchar.h>	<errno.h>	Win NT

For additional compatibility information, see "Compatibility" on page ix in the Introduction.

Libraries	
LIBC.LIB	Single thread static library, retail version
LIBCMT.LIB	Multithread static library, retail version
MSVCRT.LIB	Import library for MSVCRTx0.DLL, retail version
MSVCRTx0.DLL	Multithread DLL library, retail version

Return Value

If successful, these functions do not return to the calling process. A return value of –1 indicates an error, in which case the **errno** global variable is set.

errno Value	Description
E2BIG	The space required for the arguments and environment settings exceeds 32K.
EACCES	The specified file has a locking or sharing violation.
EMFILE	Too many files open (the specified file must be opened to determine whether it is executable).
ENOENT	File or path not found.
ENOEXEC	The specified file is not executable or has an invalid executable-file format.
ENOMEM	Not enough memory is available to execute the new process; or the available memory has been corrupted; or an invalid block exists, indicating that the calling process was not allocated properly.

Parameters

cmdname Path of file to be executed

arg0, ... argn List of pointers to parameters

Remarks

Each of these functions loads and executes a new process, passing each command-line argument as a separate parameter.

See Also **abort**, **atexit**, **exit**, **_onexit**, **_spawn** Functions, **system**

_execle, _wexecle

Load and execute new child processes.

int _execle(const char ***_cmdname_, const char ***_arg0_**, ... const char ***_argn_**, NULL, const char *const ***_envp_**);**

int _wexecle(const wchar_t ***_cmdname_, const wchar_t ***_arg0_**, ... const wchar_t ***_argn_**, NULL, const char *const ***_envp_**);**

Function	Required Header	Optional Headers	Compatibility
_execle	<process.h>	<errno.h>	Win 95, Win NT, Win32s
_wexecle	<process.h> or <wchar.h>	<errno.h>	Win NT

For additional compatibility information, see "Compatibility" on page ix in the Introduction.

Libraries	
LIBC.LIB	Single thread static library, retail version
LIBCMT.LIB	Multithread static library, retail version
MSVCRT.LIB	Import library for MSVCRTx0.DLL, retail version
MSVCRTx0.DLL	Multithread DLL library, retail version

Return Value

If successful, these functions do not return to the calling process. A return value of –1 indicates an error, in which case the **errno** global variable is set.

errno Value	Description
E2BIG	The space required for the arguments and environment settings exceeds 32K.
EACCES	The specified file has a locking or sharing violation.
EMFILE	Too many files open (the specified file must be opened to determine whether it is executable).
ENOENT	File or path not found.
ENOEXEC	The specified file is not executable or has an invalid executable-file format.
ENOMEM	Not enough memory is available to execute the new process; or the available memory has been corrupted; or an invalid block exists, indicating that the calling process was not allocated properly.

Parameters

cmdname Path of file to execute

arg0, ... argn List of pointers to parameters

envp Array of pointers to environment settings

Remarks

Each of these functions loads and executes a new process, passing each command-line argument as a separate parameter and also passing an array of pointers to environment settings.

See Also **abort**, **atexit**, **exit**, **_onexit**, **_spawn** Functions, **system**

_execlp, _wexeclp

Load and execute new child processes.

int _execlp(const char ****cmdname*, **const char** ****arg0*, **... const char** ****argn*, **NULL);**
int _wexeclp(const wchar_t ****cmdname*, **const wchar_t** ****arg0*, **... const wchar_t** ****argn*, **NULL);**

Function	Required Header	Optional Headers	Compatibility
_execlp	<process.h>	<errno.h>	Win 95, Win NT, Win32s
_wexeclp	<process.h> or <wchar.h>	<errno.h>	Win NT

For additional compatibility information, see "Compatibility" on page ix in the Introduction.

Libraries	
LIBC.LIB	Single thread static library, retail version
LIBCMT.LIB	Multithread static library, retail version
MSVCRT.LIB	Import library for MSVCRTx0.DLL, retail version
MSVCRTx0.DLL	Multithread DLL library, retail version

Return Value

If successful, these functions do not return to the calling process. A return value of –1 indicates an error, in which case the **errno** global variable is set.

errno Value	Description
E2BIG	The space required for the arguments and environment settings exceeds 32K.
EACCES	The specified file has a locking or sharing violation.
EMFILE	Too many files open (the specified file must be opened to determine whether it is executable).
ENOENT	File or path not found.
ENOEXEC	The specified file is not executable or has an invalid executable-file format.
ENOMEM	Not enough memory is available to execute the new process; or the available memory has been corrupted; or an invalid block exists, indicating that the calling process was not allocated properly.

Parameters

cmdname Path of file to execute

arg0, ... argn List of pointers to parameters

Remarks

Each of these functions loads and executes a new process, passing each command-line argument as a separate parameter and using the **PATH** environment variable to find the file to execute.

See Also **abort**, **atexit**, **exit**, **_onexit**, **_spawn** Functions, **system**

_execlpe, _wexeclpe

Load and execute new child processes.

int _execlpe(const char **cmdname*, **const char** **arg0*, ... **const char** **argn*, **NULL, const char *const** **envp* **);**

int _wexeclpe(const wchar_t **cmdname*, **const wchar_t** **arg0*, ... **const wchar_t** **argn*, **NULL, const wchar_t *const** **envp* **);**

Function	Required Header	Optional Headers	Compatibility
_execlpe	<process.h>	<errno.h>	Win 95, Win NT, Win32s
_wexeclpe	<process.h> or <wchar.h>	<errno.h>	Win NT

For additional compatibility information, see "Compatibility" on page ix in the Introduction.

Libraries	
LIBC.LIB	Single thread static library, retail version
LIBCMT.LIB	Multithread static library, retail version
MSVCRT.LIB	Import library for MSVCRTx0.DLL, retail version
MSVCRTx0.DLL	Multithread DLL library, retail version

Return Value

If successful, these functions do not return to the calling process. A return value of –1 indicates an error, in which case the **errno** global variable is set.

errno Value	Description
E2BIG	The space required for the arguments and environment settings exceeds 32K.
EACCES	The specified file has a locking or sharing violation.
EMFILE	Too many files open (the specified file must be opened to determine whether it is executable).

errno Value	Description
ENOENT	File or path not found.
ENOEXEC	The specified file is not executable or has an invalid executable-file format.
ENOMEM	Not enough memory is available to execute the new process; or the available memory has been corrupted; or an invalid block exists, indicating that the calling process was not allocated properly.

Parameters

cmdname Path of file to execute

arg0, ... argn List of pointers to parameters

envp Array of pointers to environment settings

Remarks

Each of these functions loads and executes a new process, passing each command-line argument as a separate parameter and also passing an array of pointers to environment settings. These functions use the **PATH** environment variable to find the file to execute.

See Also **abort**, **atexit**, **exit**, **_onexit**, **_spawn** Functions, **system**

_execv, _wexecv

Load and execute new child processes.

int _execv(const char ****cmdname*, **const char *const** **argv* **);**
int _wexecv(const wchar_t **cmdname*, **const wchar_t *const** **argv* **);**

Function	Required Header	Optional Headers	Compatibility
_execv	<process.h>	<errno.h>	Win 95, Win NT, Win32s
_wexecv	<process.h> or <wchar.h>	<errno.h>	Win NT

For additional compatibility information, see "Compatibility" on page ix in the Introduction.

Libraries	
LIBC.LIB	Single thread static library, retail version
LIBCMT.LIB	Multithread static library, retail version
MSVCRT.LIB	Import library for MSVCRTx0.DLL, retail version
MSVCRTx0.DLL	Multithread DLL library, retail version

Return Value

If successful, these functions do not return to the calling process. A return value of –1 indicates an error, in which case the **errno** global variable is set.

errno Value	Description
E2BIG	The space required for the arguments and environment settings exceeds 32K.
EACCES	The specified file has a locking or sharing violation.
EMFILE	Too many files open (the specified file must be opened to determine whether it is executable).
ENOENT	File or path not found.
ENOEXEC	The specified file is not executable or has an invalid executable-file format.
ENOMEM	Not enough memory is available to execute the new process; or the available memory has been corrupted; or an invalid block exists, indicating that the calling process was not allocated properly.

Parameters

cmdname Path of file to execute

argv Array of pointers to parameters

Remarks

Each of these functions loads and executes a new process, passing an array of pointers to command-line arguments.

See Also **abort**, **atexit**, **exit**, **_onexit**, **_spawn** Functions, **system**

_execve, _wexecve

Load and execute new child processes.

int _execve(const char ****cmdname*, const char *const ****argv***, const char *const ****envp***);**
int _wexecve(const wchar_t ****cmdname*, const wchar_t *const ****argv***, const wchar_t *const ****envp***);**

Function	Required Header	Optional Headers	Compatibility
_execve	<process.h>	<errno.h>	Win 95, Win NT, Win32s
_wexecve	<process.h> or <wchar.h>	<errno.h>	Win NT

For additional compatibility information, see “Compatibility” on page ix in the Introduction.

Libraries	
LIBC.LIB	Single thread static library, retail version
LIBCMT.LIB	Multithread static library, retail version
MSVCRT.LIB	Import library for MSVCRTx0.DLL, retail version
MSVCRTx0.DLL	Multithread DLL library, retail version

Return Value

If successful, these functions do not return to the calling process. A return value of –1 indicates an error, in which case the **errno** global variable is set.

errno Value	Description
E2BIG	The space required for the arguments and environment settings exceeds 32K.
EACCES	The specified file has a locking or sharing violation.
EMFILE	Too many files open (the specified file must be opened to determine whether it is executable).
ENOENT	File or path not found.
ENOEXEC	The specified file is not executable or has an invalid executable-file format.
ENOMEM	Not enough memory is available to execute the new process; or the available memory has been corrupted; or an invalid block exists, indicating that the calling process was not allocated properly.

Parameters

cmdname Path of file to execute

argv Array of pointers to parameters

envp Array of pointers to environment settings

Remarks

Each of these functions loads and executes a new process, passing an array of pointers to command-line arguments and an array of pointers to environment settings.

See Also **abort**, **atexit**, **exit**, **_onexit**, **_spawn** Functions, **system**

_execvp, _wexecvp

Load and execute new child processes.

int _execvp(const char ***_cmdname_, const char *const ***_argv_ **);**
int _wexecvp(const wchar_t ***_cmdname_, const wchar_t *const ***_argv_ **);**

Function	Required Header	Optional Headers	Compatibility
_execvp	<process.h>	<errno.h>	Win 95, Win NT, Win32s
_wexecvp	<process.h> or <wchar.h>	<errno.h>	Win NT

For additional compatibility information, see "Compatibility" on page ix in the Introduction.

Libraries	
LIBC.LIB	Single thread static library, retail version
LIBCMT.LIB	Multithread static library, retail version
MSVCRT.LIB	Import library for MSVCRTx0.DLL, retail version
MSVCRTx0.DLL	Multithread DLL library, retail version

Return Value

If successful, these functions do not return to the calling process. A return value of –1 indicates an error, in which case the **errno** global variable is set.

errno Value	Description
E2BIG	The space required for the arguments and environment settings exceeds 32K.
EACCES	The specified file has a locking or sharing violation.
EMFILE	Too many files open (the specified file must be opened to determine whether it is executable).
ENOENT	File or path not found.
ENOEXEC	The specified file is not executable or has an invalid executable-file format.
ENOMEM	Not enough memory is available to execute the new process; or the available memory has been corrupted; or an invalid block exists, indicating that the calling process was not allocated properly.

Parameters

cmdname Path of file to execute

argv Array of pointers to parameters

Remarks

Each of these functions loads and executes a new process, passing an array of pointers to command-line arguments and using the **PATH** environment variable to find the file to execute.

See Also **abort**, **atexit**, **exit**, **_onexit**, **_spawn** Functions, **system**

_execvpe, _wexecvpe

Load and execute new child processes.

int _execvpe(const char ***cmdname*****, const char *const** ***argv*****, const char *const** ***envp*);**
int _wexecvpe(const wchar_t ***cmdname*****, const wchar_t *const** ***argv*****, const wchar_t *const** ***envp*);**

Function	Required Header	Optional Headers	Compatibility
_execvpe	<process.h>	<errno.h>	Win 95, Win NT, Win32s
_wexecvpe	<process.h> or <wchar.h>	<errno.h>	Win NT

For additional compatibility information, see "Compatibility" on page ix in the Introduction.

Libraries	
LIBC.LIB	Single thread static library, retail version
LIBCMT.LIB	Multithread static library, retail version
MSVCRT.LIB	Import library for MSVCRTx0.DLL, retail version
MSVCRTx0.DLL	Multithread DLL library, retail version

Return Value

If successful, these functions do not return to the calling process. A return value of –1 indicates an error, in which case the **errno** global variable is set.

errno Value	Description
E2BIG	The space required for the arguments and environment settings exceeds 32K.
EACCES	The specified file has a locking or sharing violation.
EMFILE	Too many files open (the specified file must be opened to determine whether it is executable).

errno Value	Description
ENOENT	File or path not found.
ENOEXEC	The specified file is not executable or has an invalid executable-file format.
ENOMEM	Not enough memory is available to execute the new process; or the available memory has been corrupted; or an invalid block exists, indicating that the calling process was not allocated properly.

Parameters

cmdname Path of file to execute

argv Array of pointers to parameters

envp Array of pointers to environment settings

Remarks

Each of these functions loads and executes a new process, passing an array of pointers to command-line arguments and an array of pointers to environment settings. These functions use the **PATH** environment variable to find the file to execute.

See Also **abort**, **atexit**, **exit**, **_onexit**, **_spawn** Functions, **system**

exit, _exit

Terminate the calling process after cleanup (**exit**) or immediately (**_exit**).

void exit(int *status* **);**
void _exit(int *status* **);**

Function	Required Header	Optional Headers	Compatibility
exit	<process.h> or <stdlib.h>		ANSI, Win 95, Win NT, Win32s, 68K, PMac
_exit	<process.h> or <stdlib.h>		Win 95, Win NT, Win32s, 68K, PMac

For additional compatibility information, see "Compatibility" on page ix in the Introduction.

Libraries	
LIBC.LIB	Single thread static library, retail version
LIBCMT.LIB	Multithread static library, retail version
MSVCRT.LIB	Import library for MSVCRTx0.DLL, retail version
MSVCRTx0.DLL	Multithread DLL library, retail version

Return Value

None

Parameter

status Exit status

Remarks

The **exit** and **_exit** functions terminate the calling process. **exit** calls, in last-in-first-out (LIFO) order, the functions registered by **atexit** and **_onexit**, then flushes all file buffers before terminating the process. **_exit** terminates the process without processing **atexit** or **_onexit** or flushing stream buffers. The *status* value is typically set to 0 to indicate a normal exit and set to some other value to indicate an error.

Although the **exit** and **_exit** calls do not return a value, the low-order byte of *status* is made available to the waiting calling process, if one exists, after the calling process exits. The *status* value is available to the operating-system batch command **ERRORLEVEL** and is represented by one of two constants: **EXIT_SUCCESS**, which represents a value of 0, or **EXIT_FAILURE**, which represents a value of 1. The behavior of **exit**, **_exit**, **_cexit**, and **_c_exit** is as follows.

Function	Description
exit	Performs complete C library termination procedures, terminates the process, and exits with the supplied status code.
_exit	Performs "quick" C library termination procedures, terminates the process, and exits with the supplied status code.
_cexit	Performs complete C library termination procedures and returns to the caller, but does not terminate the process.
_c_exit	Performs "quick" C library termination procedures and returns to the caller, but does not terminate the process.

Example

```
/* EXITER.C: This program prompts the user for a yes
 * or no and returns an exit code of 1 if the
 * user answers Y or y; otherwise it returns 0. The
 * error code could be tested in a batch file.
 */

#include <conio.h>
#include <stdlib.h>

void main( void )
{
   int ch;
```

```
    _cputs( "Yes or no? " );
    ch = _getch();
    _cputs( "\r\n" );
    if( toupper( ch ) == 'Y' )
       exit( 1 );
    else
       exit( 0 );
}
```

See Also **abort**, **atexit**, **_cexit**, **_exec** Functions, **_onexit**, **_spawn** Functions, **system**

exp

Calculates the exponential.

double exp(double *x* **);**

Function	Required Header	Optional Headers	Compatibility
exp	<math.h>		ANSI, Win 95, Win NT, Win32s, 68K, PMac

For additional compatibility information, see "Compatibility" on page ix in the Introduction.

Libraries	
LIBC.LIB	Single thread static library, retail version
LIBCMT.LIB	Multithread static library, retail version
MSVCRT.LIB	Import library for MSVCRTx0.DLL, retail version
MSVCRTx0.DLL	Multithread DLL library, retail version

Return Value

The **exp** function returns the exponential value of the floating-point parameter, *x*, if successful. On overflow, the function returns INF (infinite) and on underflow, **exp** returns 0.

Parameter

x Floating-point value

Example

```
/* EXP.C */

#include <math.h>
#include <stdio.h>

void main( void )
{
   double x = 2.302585093, y;
```

```
   y = exp( x );
   printf( "exp( %f ) = %f\n", x, y );
}
```

Output

```
exp( 2.302585 ) = 10.000000
```

See Also **log**

_expand

Changes the size of a memory block.

void *_expand(void ***memblock*****, size_t** *size* **);**

Function	Required Header	Optional Headers	Compatibility
_expand	<malloc.h>		Win 95, Win NT, Win32s, 68K, PMac

For additional compatibility information, see "Compatibility" on page ix in the Introduction.

Libraries	
LIBC.LIB	Single thread static library, retail version
LIBCMT.LIB	Multithread static library, retail version
MSVCRT.LIB	Import library for MSVCRTx0.DLL, retail version
MSVCRTx0.DLL	Multithread DLL library, retail version

Return Value

_expand returns a void pointer to the reallocated memory block. **_expand**, unlike **realloc**, cannot move a block to change its size. Thus, if there is sufficient memory available to expand the block without moving it, the *memblock* parameter to **_expand** is the same as the return value.

_expand returns **NULL** if there is insufficient memory available to expand the block to the given size without moving it. The item pointed to by *memblock* is expanded as much as possible in its current location.

The return value points to a storage space that is guaranteed to be suitably aligned for storage of any type of object. To check the new size of the item, use **_msize**. To get a pointer to a type other than **void**, use a type cast on the return value.

Parameters

memblock Pointer to previously allocated memory block

size New size in bytes

Remarks

The **_expand** function changes the size of a previously allocated memory block by trying to expand or contract the block without moving its location in the heap. The *memblock* parameter points to the beginning of the block. The *size* parameter gives the new size of the block, in bytes. The contents of the block are unchanged up to the shorter of the new and old sizes. *memblock* can also point to a block that has been freed, as long as there has been no intervening call to **calloc**, **_expand**, **malloc**, or **realloc**. If *memblock* points to a freed block, the block remains free after a call to **_expand**.

When the application is linked with a debug version of the C run-time libraries, **_expand** resolves to **_expand_dbg**. For more information about how the heap is managed during the debugging process, see Chapter 4, "Debug Version of the C Run-Time Library."

Example

```
/* EXPAND.C */

#include <stdio.h>
#include <malloc.h>
#include <stdlib.h>

void main( void )
{
   char *bufchar;
   printf( "Allocate a 512 element buffer\n" );
   if( (bufchar = (char *)calloc( 512, sizeof( char ) )) == NULL )
      exit( 1 );
   printf( "Allocated %d bytes at %Fp\n",
         _msize( bufchar ), (void *)bufchar );
   if( (bufchar = (char *)_expand( bufchar, 1024 )) == NULL )
      printf( "Can't expand" );
   else
      printf( "Expanded block to %d bytes at %Fp\n",
            _msize( bufchar ), (void *)bufchar );
   /* Free memory */
   free( bufchar );
   exit( 0 );
}
```

Output

```
Allocate a 512 element buffer
Allocated 512 bytes at 002C12BC
Expanded block to 1024 bytes at 002C12BC
```

See Also **calloc**, **free**, **malloc**, **_msize**, **realloc**

fabs

Calculates the absolute value of the floating-point argument.

double fabs(double *x* **);**

Function	Required Header	Optional Headers	Compatibility
fabs	<math.h>		ANSI, Win 95, Win NT, Win32s, 68K, PMac

For additional compatibility information, see "Compatibility" on page ix in the Introduction.

Libraries	
LIBC.LIB	Single thread static library, retail version
LIBCMT.LIB	Multithread static library, retail version
MSVCRT.LIB	Import library for MSVCRTx0.DLL, retail version
MSVCRTx0.DLL	Multithread DLL library, retail version

Return Value

fabs returns the absolute value of its argument. There is no error return.

Parameter

x Floating-point value

Example

See the example for **abs**.

See Also **abs**, **_cabs**, **labs**

fclose, _fcloseall

Closes a stream (**fclose**) or closes all open streams (**_fcloseall**).

int fclose(FILE ***stream*** **);**
int _fcloseall(void);

Function	Required Header	Optional Headers	Compatibility
fclose	<stdio.h>		ANSI, Win 95, Win NT, Win32s, 68K, PMac
_fcloseall	<stdio.h>		ANSI, Win 95, Win NT, Win32s, 68K, PMac

For additional compatibility information, see "Compatibility" on page ix in the Introduction.

Libraries

LIBC.LIB	Single thread static library, retail version
LIBCMT.LIB	Multithread static library, retail version
MSVCRT.LIB	Import library for MSVCRTx0.DLL, retail version
MSVCRTx0.DLL	Multithread DLL library, retail version

Return Value

fclose returns 0 if the stream is successfully closed. **_fcloseall** returns the total number of streams closed. Both functions return **EOF** to indicate an error.

Parameter

stream Pointer to **FILE** structure

Remarks

The **fclose** function closes *stream*. **_fcloseall** closes all open streams except **stdin**, **stdout**, **stderr** (and, in MS-DOS®, **_stdaux** and **_stdprn**). It also closes and deletes any temporary files created by **tmpfile**. In both functions, all buffers associated with the stream are flushed prior to closing. System-allocated buffers are released when the stream is closed. Buffers assigned by the user with **setbuf** and **setvbuf** are not automatically released.

Example

See the example for **fopen**.

See Also **_close**, **_fdopen**, **fflush**, **fopen**, **freopen**

_fcvt

Converts a floating-point number to a string.

char *_fcvt(double *value*, **int** *count*, **int ****dec*, **int ****sign* **);**

Function	Required Header	Optional Headers	Compatibility
_fcvt	<stdlib.h>		Win 95, Win NT, Win32s, 68K, PMac

For additional compatibility information, see "Compatibility" on page ix in the Introduction.

Libraries

LIBC.LIB	Single thread static library, retail version
LIBCMT.LIB	Multithread static library, retail version
MSVCRT.LIB	Import library for MSVCRTx0.DLL, retail version
MSVCRTx0.DLL	Multithread DLL library, retail version

Return Value

_fcvt returns a pointer to the string of digits. There is no error return.

Parameters

value Number to be converted

count Number of digits after decimal point

dec Pointer to stored decimal-point position

sign Pointer to stored sign indicator

Remarks

The **_fcvt** function converts a floating-point number to a null-terminated character string. The *value* parameter is the floating-point number to be converted. **_fcvt** stores the digits of *value* as a string and appends a null character ('\0'). The *count* parameter specifies the number of digits to be stored after the decimal point. Excess digits are rounded off to *count* places. If there are fewer than *count* digits of precision, the string is padded with zeros.

Only digits are stored in the string. The position of the decimal point and the sign of *value* can be obtained from *dec* and *sign* after the call. The *dec* parameter points to an integer value; this integer value gives the position of the decimal point with respect to the beginning of the string. A zero or negative integer value indicates that the decimal point lies to the left of the first digit. The parameter *sign* points to an integer indicating the sign of *value*. The integer is set to 0 if *value* is positive and is set to a nonzero number if *value* is negative.

_ecvt and **_fcvt** use a single statically allocated buffer for the conversion. Each call to one of these routines destroys the results of the previous call.

Example

```
/* FCVT.C: This program converts the constant
 * 3.1415926535 to a string and sets the pointer
 * *buffer to point to that string.
 */

#include <stdlib.h>
#include <stdio.h>
```

```
void main( void )
{
   int  decimal, sign;
   char *buffer;
   double source = 3.1415926535;

   buffer = _fcvt( source, 7, &decimal, &sign );
   printf( "source: %2.10f   buffer: '%s'   decimal: %d   sign: %d\n",
            source, buffer, decimal, sign );
}
```

Output

```
source: 3.1415926535   buffer: '31415927'   decimal: 1   sign: 0
```

See Also **atof**, **_ecvt**, **_gcvt**

_fdopen, _wfdopen

Associate a stream with a file that was previously opened for low-level I/O.

FILE *_fdopen(int *handle*, **const char** **mode* **);**
FILE *_wfdopen(int *handle*, **const wchar_t** **mode* **);**

Function	Required Header	Optional Headers	Compatibility
_fdopen	<stdio.h>		Win 95, Win NT, Win32s, 68K, PMac
_wfdopen	<stdio.h> or <wchar.h>		Win 95, Win NT, Win32s

For additional compatibility information, see "Compatibility" on page ix in the Introduction.

Libraries	
LIBC.LIB	Single thread static library, retail version
LIBCMT.LIB	Multithread static library, retail version
MSVCRT.LIB	Import library for MSVCRTx0.DLL, retail version
MSVCRTx0.DLL	Multithread DLL library, retail version

Return Value

Each of these functions returns a pointer to the open stream. A null pointer value indicates an error.

Parameters

handle Handle to open file

mode Type of file access

Remarks

The **_fdopen** function associates an I/O stream with the file identified by *handle*, thus allowing a file opened for low-level I/O to be buffered and formatted. **_wfdopen** is a wide-character version of **_fdopen**; the *mode* argument to **_wfdopen** is a wide-character string. **_wfdopen** and **_fdopen** behave identically otherwise.

The *mode* character string specifies the type of file and file access.

The character string *mode* specifies the type of access requested for the file, as follows:

"r" Opens for reading. If the file does not exist or cannot be found, the **fopen** call fails.

"w" Opens an empty file for writing. If the given file exists, its contents are destroyed.

"a" Opens for writing at the end of the file (appending); creates the file first if it doesn't exist.

"r+" Opens for both reading and writing. (The file must exist.)

"w+" Opens an empty file for both reading and writing. If the given file exists, its contents are destroyed.

"a+" Opens for reading and appending; creates the file first if it doesn't exist.

When a file is opened with the **"a"** or **"a+"** access type, all write operations occur at the end of the file. The file pointer can be repositioned using **fseek** or **rewind**, but is always moved back to the end of the file before any write operation is carried out. Thus, existing data cannot be overwritten. When the **"r+"**, **"w+"**, or **"a+"** access type is specified, both reading and writing are allowed (the file is said to be open for "update"). However, when you switch between reading and writing, there must be an intervening **fflush**, **fsetpos**, **fseek**, or **rewind** operation. The current position can be specified for the **fsetpos** or **fseek** operation, if desired.

In addition to the above values, the following characters can be included in *mode* to specify the translation mode for newline characters:

t Open in text (translated) mode. In this mode, carriage return–linefeed (CR-LF) combinations are translated into single linefeeds (LF) on input, and LF characters are translated to CR-LF combinations on output. Also, CTRL+Z is interpreted as an end-of-file character on input. In files opened for reading/writing, **fopen** checks for a CTRL+Z at the end of the file and removes it, if possible. This is done because using the **fseek** and **ftell** functions to move within a file that ends with a CTRL+Z may cause **fseek** to behave improperly near the end of the file.

b Open in binary (untranslated) mode; the above translations are suppressed.

c Enable the commit flag for the associated *filename* so that the contents of the file buffer are written directly to disk if either **fflush** or **_flushall** is called.

n Reset the commit flag for the associated *filename* to "no-commit." This is the default. It also overrides the global commit flag if you link your program with COMMODE.OBJ. The global commit flag default is "no-commit" unless you explicitly link your program with COMMODE.OBJ.

The **t**, **c**, and **n** *mode* options are Microsoft extensions for **fopen** and **_fdopen** and should not be used where ANSI portability is desired.

If **t** or **b** is not given in *mode*, the default translation mode is defined by the global variable **_fmode**. If **t** or **b** is prefixed to the argument, the function fails and returns **NULL**. For a discussion of text and binary modes, see "Text and Binary Mode File I/O" on page 15.

Valid characters for the *mode* string used in **fopen** and **_fdopen** correspond to *oflag* arguments used in **_open** and **_sopen**, as follows.

Characters in *mode* String	Equivalent *oflag* Value for _open/_sopen
a	**_O_WRONLY | _O_APPEND** (usually **_O_WRONLY | _O_CREAT | _O_APPEND**)
a+	**_O_RDWR | _O_APPEND** (usually **_O_RDWR | _O_APPEND | _O_CREAT**)
r	**_O_RDONLY**
r+	**_O_RDWR**
w	**_O_WRONLY** (usually **_O_WRONLY | _O_CREAT | _O_TRUNC**)
w+	**_O_RDWR** (usually **_O_RDWR | _O_CREAT | _O_TRUNC**)
b	**_O_BINARY**
t	**_O_TEXT**
c	None
n	None

Example

```
/* _FDOPEN.C: This program opens a file using low-
 * level I/O, then uses _fdopen to switch to stream
 * access. It counts the lines in the file.
 */

#include <stdlib.h>
#include <stdio.h>
#include <fcntl.h>
#include <io.h>

void main( void )
```

```
{
   FILE *stream;
   int  fh, count = 0;
   char inbuf[128];

   /* Open a file handle. */
   if( (fh = _open( "_fdopen.c", _O_RDONLY )) == -1 )
      exit( 1 );

   /* Change handle access to stream access. */
   if( (stream = _fdopen( fh, "r" )) == NULL )
      exit( 1 );

   while( fgets( inbuf, 128, stream ) != NULL )
      count++;

   /* After _fdopen, close with fclose, not _close. */
   fclose( stream );
   printf( "Lines in file: %d\n", count );
}
```

Output

```
Lines in file: 32
```

See Also **_dup**, **fclose**, **fopen**, **freopen**, **_open**

feof

Tests for end-of-file on a stream.

int feof(FILE ***stream*** **);**

Function	Required Header	Optional Headers	Compatibility
feof	<stdio.h>		ANSI, Win 95, Win NT, Win32s, 68K, PMac

For additional compatibility information, see “Compatibility” on page ix in the Introduction.

Libraries	
LIBC.LIB	Single thread static library, retail version
LIBCMT.LIB	Multithread static library, retail version
MSVCRT.LIB	Import library for MSVCRTx0.DLL, retail version
MSVCRTx0.DLL	Multithread DLL library, retail version

Return Value

The **feof** function returns a nonzero value after the first read operation that attempts to read past the end of the file. It returns 0 if the current position is not end of file. There is no error return.

Parameter

stream Pointer to **FILE** structure

Remarks

The **feof** routine (implemented both as a function and as a macro) determines whether the end of *stream* has been reached. When end of file is reached, read operations return an end-of-file indicator until the stream is closed or until **rewind**, **fsetpos**, **fseek**, or **clearerr** is called against it.

Example

```
/* FEOF.C: This program uses feof to indicate when
 * it reaches the end of the file FEOF.C. It also
 * checks for errors with ferror.
 */

#include <stdio.h>
#include <stdlib.h>

void main( void )
{
   int  count, total = 0;
   char buffer[100];
   FILE *stream;

   if( (stream = fopen( "feof.c", "r" )) == NULL )
      exit( 1 );

   /* Cycle until end of file reached: */
   while( !feof( stream ) )
   {
      /* Attempt to read in 10 bytes: */
      count = fread( buffer, sizeof( char ), 100, stream );
      if( ferror( stream ) )      {
         perror( "Read error" );
         break;
      }

      /* Total up actual bytes read */
      total += count;
   }
   printf( "Number of bytes read = %d\n", total );
   fclose( stream );
}
```

Output

```
Number of bytes read = 745
```

See Also **clearerr**, **_eof**, **ferror**, **perror**

ferror

Tests for an error on a stream.

int ferror(FILE ****stream* **);

Function	Required Header	Optional Headers	Compatibility
ferror	<stdio.h>		ANSI, Win 95, Win NT, Win32s, 68K, PMac

For additional compatibility information, see "Compatibility" on page ix in the Introduction.

Libraries	
LIBC.LIB	Single thread static library, retail version
LIBCMT.LIB	Multithread static library, retail version
MSVCRT.LIB	Import library for MSVCRTx0.DLL, retail version
MSVCRTx0.DLL	Multithread DLL library, retail version

Return Value

If no error has occurred on *stream*, **ferror** returns 0. Otherwise, it returns a nonzero value.

Parameter

stream Pointer to **FILE** structure

Remarks

The **ferror** routine (implemented both as a function and as a macro) tests for a reading or writing error on the file associated with *stream*. If an error has occurred, the error indicator for the stream remains set until the stream is closed or rewound, or until **clearerr** is called against it.

Example

See the example for **feof**.

See Also **clearerr**, **_eof**, **feof**, **fopen**, **perror**

fflush

Flushes a stream.

int fflush(**FILE** ***stream*** **);**

Function	Required Header	Optional Headers	Compatibility
fflush	<stdio.h>		ANSI, Win 95, Win NT, Win32s, 68K, PMac

For additional compatibility information, see "Compatibility" on page ix in the Introduction.

Libraries	
LIBC.LIB	Single thread static library, retail version
LIBCMT.LIB	Multithread static library, retail version
MSVCRT.LIB	Import library for MSVCRTx0.DLL, retail version
MSVCRTx0.DLL	Multithread DLL library, retail version

Return Value

fflush returns 0 if the buffer was successfully flushed. The value 0 is also returned in cases in which the specified stream has no buffer or is open for reading only. A return value of **EOF** indicates an error.

Note If **fflush** returns **EOF**, data may have been lost due to a write failure. When setting up a critical error handler, it is safest to turn buffering off with the **setvbuf** function or to use low-level I/O routines such as **_open**, **_close**, and **_write** instead of the stream I/O functions.

Parameter

stream Pointer to **FILE** structure

Remarks

The **fflush** function flushes a stream. If the file associated with *stream* is open for output, **fflush** writes to that file the contents of the buffer associated with the stream. If the stream is open for input, **fflush** clears the contents of the buffer. **fflush** negates the effect of any prior call to **ungetc** against *stream*. Also, **fflush(NULL)** flushes all streams opened for output. The stream remains open after the call. **fflush** has no effect on an unbuffered stream.

Buffers are normally maintained by the operating system, which determines the optimal time to write the data automatically to disk: when a buffer is full, when a stream is closed, or when a program terminates normally without closing the stream. The commit-to-disk feature of the run-time library lets you ensure that critical data is written directly to disk rather than to the operating-system buffers. Without rewriting an existing program, you can enable this feature by linking the program's object files with COMMODE.OBJ. In the resulting executable file, calls to **_flushall** write the contents of all buffers to disk. Only **_flushall** and **fflush** are affected by COMMODE.OBJ.

For information about controlling the commit-to-disk feature, see "Stream I/O" on page 16, **fopen**, and **_fdopen**.

Example

```
/* FFLUSH.C */

#include <stdio.h>
#include <conio.h>

void main( void )
{
   int integer;
   char string[81];

   /* Read each word as a string. */
   printf( "Enter a sentence of four words with scanf: " );
   for( integer = 0; integer < 4; integer++ )
   {
      scanf( "%s", string );
      printf( "%s\n", string );
   }

   /* You must flush the input buffer before using gets. */
   fflush( stdin );
   printf( "Enter the same sentence with gets: " );
   gets( string );
   printf( "%s\n", string );
}
```

Output

```
Enter a sentence of four words with scanf: This is a test
This
is
a
test
Enter the same sentence with gets: This is a test
This is a test
```

See Also **fclose**, **_flushall**, **setvbuf**

fgetc, fgetwc, _fgetchar, _fgetwchar

Read a character from a stream (**fgetc**, **fgetwc**) or **stdin** (**_fgetchar**, **_fgetwchar**).

int fgetc(FILE ****stream* **);
wint_t fgetwc(FILE ****stream* **);
int _fgetchar(void);
wint_t _fgetwchar(void);

Function	Required Header	Optional Headers	Compatibility
fgetc	<stdio.h>		ANSI, Win 95, Win NT, Win32s, 68K, PMac
fgetwc	<stdio.h> or <wchar.h>		ANSI, Win 95, Win NT, Win32s
_fgetchar	<stdio.h>		Win 95, Win NT, Win32s, 68K, PMac
_fgetwchar	<stdio.h> or <wchar.h>		Win 95, Win NT, Win32s

For additional compatibility information, see "Compatibility" on page ix in the Introduction.

Libraries	
LIBC.LIB	Single thread static library, retail version
LIBCMT.LIB	Multithread static library, retail version
MSVCRT.LIB	Import library for MSVCRTx0.DLL, retail version
MSVCRTx0.DLL	Multithread DLL library, retail version

Return Value

fgetc and **_fgetchar** return the character read as an **int** or return **EOF** to indicate an error or end of file. **fgetwc** and **_fgetwchar** return, as a **wint_t**, the wide character that corresponds to the character read or return **WEOF** to indicate an error or end of file. For all four functions, use **feof** or **ferror** to distinguish between an error and an end-of-file condition. For **fgetc** and **fgetwc**, if a read error occurs, the error indicator for the stream is set.

Parameter

stream Pointer to **FILE** structure

Remarks

Each of these functions reads a single character from the current position of a file; in the case of **fgetc** and **fgetwc**, this is the file associated with *stream*. The function then increments the associated file pointer (if defined) to point to the next character. If the stream is at end of file, the end-of-file indicator for the stream is set. Routine-specific remarks follow.

Routine	Remarks
fgetc	Equivalent to **getc**, but implemented only as a function, rather than as a function and a macro.
fgetwc	Wide-character version of **fgetc**. Reads *c* as a multibyte character or a wide character according to whether *stream* is opened in text mode or binary mode.
_fgetchar	Equivalent to **fgetc(stdin)**. Also equivalent to **getchar**, but implemented only as a function, rather than as a function and a macro. Microsoft-specific; not ANSI-compatible.
_fgetwchar	Wide-character version of **_fgetchar**. Reads c as a multibyte character or a wide character according to whether stream is opened in text mode or binary mode. Microsoft-specific; not ANSI-compatible.

For more information about processing wide characters and multibyte characters in text and binary modes, see "Unicode Stream I/O in Text and Binary Modes" on page 15.

Example

```
/* FGETC.C: This program uses getc to read the first
 * 80 input characters (or until the end of input)
 * and place them into a string named buffer.
 */

#include <stdio.h>
#include <stdlib.h>

void main( void )
{
   FILE *stream;
   char buffer[81];
   int  i, ch;

   /* Open file to read line from: */
   if( (stream = fopen( "fgetc.c", "r" )) == NULL )
      exit( 0 );

   /* Read in first 80 characters and place them in "buffer": */
   ch = fgetc( stream );
   for( i=0; (i < 80 ) && ( feof( stream ) == 0 ); i++ )
   {
      buffer[i] = (char)ch;
      ch = fgetc( stream );
   }
```

```
    /* Add null to end string */
    buffer[i] = '\0';
    printf( "%s\n", buffer );
    fclose( stream );
}
```

Output

```
/* FGETC.C: This program uses getc to read the first
 * 80 input characters (or
```

See Also **fputc**, **getc**

fgetpos

Gets a stream's file-position indicator.

int fgetpos(FILE ***stream*****, fpos_t** ***pos*** **);**

Function	Required Header	Optional Headers	Compatibility
fgetpos	<stdio.h>		ANSI, Win 95, Win NT, Win32s, 68K, PMac

For additional compatibility information, see "Compatibility" on page ix in the Introduction.

Libraries	
LIBC.LIB	Single thread static library, retail version
LIBCMT.LIB	Multithread static library, retail version
MSVCRT.LIB	Import library for MSVCRTx0.DLL, retail version
MSVCRTx0.DLL	Multithread DLL library, retail version

Return Value

If successful, **fgetpos** returns 0. On failure, it returns a nonzero value and sets **errno** to one of the following manifest constants (defined in STDIO.H): **EBADF**, which means the specified stream is not a valid file handle or is not accessible, or **EINVAL**, which means the *stream* value is invalid.

Parameters

stream Target stream

pos Position-indicator storage

Remarks

The **fgetpos** function gets the current value of the *stream* argument's file-position indicator and stores it in the object pointed to by *pos*. The **fsetpos** function can later use information stored in *pos* to reset the *stream* argument's pointer to its position at the time **fgetpos** was called. The *pos* value is stored in an internal format and is intended for use only by **fgetpos** and **fsetpos**.

Example

```
/* FGETPOS.C: This program opens a file and reads
 * bytes at several different locations.
 */

#include <stdio.h>

void main( void )
{
   FILE   *stream;
   fpos_t pos;
   char   buffer[20];

   if( (stream = fopen( "fgetpos.c", "rb" )) == NULL )
      printf( "Trouble opening file\n" );
   else
   {
      /* Read some data and then check the position. */
      fread( buffer, sizeof( char ), 10, stream );
      if( fgetpos( stream, &pos ) != 0 )
         perror( "fgetpos error" );
      else
      {
         fread( buffer, sizeof( char ), 10, stream );
         printf( "10 bytes at byte %ld: %.10s\n", pos, buffer );
      }

   /* Set a new position and read more data */
   pos = 140;
   if( fsetpos( stream, &pos ) != 0 )
      perror( "fsetpos error" );

   fread( buffer, sizeof( char ), 10, stream );
   printf( "10 bytes at byte %ld: %.10s\n", pos, buffer );
   fclose( stream );
   }
}
```

Output

```
10 bytes at byte 10: .C: This p
10 bytes at byte 140:
{
   FIL
```

See Also **fsetpos**

fgets, fgetws

Get a string from a stream.

char *fgets(char ***string*, int** *n***, FILE ***stream* **);**
wchar_t *fgetws(wchar_t ***string*, int** *n***, FILE ***stream* **);**

Function	Required Header	Optional Headers	Compatibility
fgets	<stdio.h>		ANSI, Win 95, Win NT, Win32s, 68K, PMac
fgetws	<stdio.h> or <wchar.h>		ANSI, Win 95, Win NT, Win32s

For additional compatibility information, see "Compatibility" on page ix in the Introduction.

Libraries	
LIBC.LIB	Single thread static library, retail version
LIBCMT.LIB	Multithread static library, retail version
MSVCRT.LIB	Import library for MSVCRTx0.DLL, retail version
MSVCRTx0.DLL	Multithread DLL library, retail version

Return Value

Each of these functions returns *string*. **NULL** is returned to indicate an error or an end-of-file condition. Use **feof** or **ferror** to determine whether an error occurred.

Parameters

string Storage location for data

n Maximum number of characters to read

stream Pointer to **FILE** structure

Remarks

The **fgets** function reads a string from the input *stream* argument and stores it in *string*. **fgets** reads characters from the current stream position to and including the first newline character, to the end of the stream, or until the number of characters read is equal to *n*–1, whichever comes first. The result stored in *string* is appended with a null character. The newline character, if read, is included in the string.

fgets is similar to the **gets** function; however, **gets** replaces the newline character with **NULL**. **fgetws** is a wide-character version of **fgets**.

fgetws reads the wide-character argument *string* as a multibyte-character string or a wide-character string according to whether *stream* is opened in text mode or binary mode, respectively. For more information about using text and binary modes in Unicode and multibyte stream-I/O, see "Text and Binary Mode File I/O" and "Unicode Stream I/O in Text and Binary Modes" on page 15.

Example

```
/* FGETS.C: This program uses fgets to display
 * a line from a file on the screen.
 */

#include <stdio.h>

void main( void )
{
   FILE *stream;
   char line[100];

   if( (stream = fopen( "fgets.c", "r" )) != NULL )
   {
      if( fgets( line, 100, stream ) == NULL)
         printf( "fgets error\n" );
      else
         printf( "%s", line);
      fclose( stream );
   }
}
```

Output

```
/* FGETS.C: This program uses fgets to display
```

See Also **fputs**, **gets**, **puts**

_filelength, _filelengthi64

Get the length of a file.

long _filelength(int *handle* **);**
_ _int64 _filelengthi64(int *handle* **);**

Function	Required Header	Optional Headers	Compatibility
_filelength	<io.h>		Win 95, Win NT, Win32s, 68K, PMac
_filelengthi64	<io.h>		Win 95, Win NT, Win32s

For additional compatibility information, see "Compatibility" on page ix in the Introduction.

Libraries

LIBC.LIB	Single thread static library, retail version
LIBCMT.LIB	Multithread static library, retail version
MSVCRT.LIB	Import library for MSVCRTx0.DLL, retail version
MSVCRTx0.DLL	Multithread DLL library, retail version

Return Value

Both **_filelength** and **_filelengthi64** return the file length, in bytes, of the target file associated with *handle*. Both functions return a value of –1L to indicate an error, and an invalid handle sets **errno** to **EBADF**.

Parameter

handle Target file handle

Example

See the example for **_chsize**.

See Also **_chsize**, **_fileno**, **_fstat**, **_fstati64**, **_stat**, **_stati64**

_fileno

Gets the file handle associated with a stream.

int _fileno(FILE ****stream* **);

Function	Required Header	Optional Headers	Compatibility
_fileno	<stdio.h>		Win 95, Win NT, Win32s, 68K, PMac

For additional compatibility information, see "Compatibility" on page ix in the Introduction.

Libraries

LIBC.LIB	Single thread static library, retail version
LIBCMT.LIB	Multithread static library, retail version
MSVCRT.LIB	Import library for MSVCRTx0.DLL, retail version
MSVCRTx0.DLL	Multithread DLL library, retail version

Return Value

_fileno returns the file handle. There is no error return. The result is undefined if *stream* does not specify an open file.

Parameter

stream Pointer to **FILE** structure

Remarks

The **_fileno** routine returns the file handle currently associated with *stream*. This routine is implemented both as a function and as a macro. For details on choosing either implementation, see "Choosing Between Functions and Macros" on page xii.

Example

```
/* FILENO.C: This program uses _fileno to obtain
 * the file handle for some standard C streams.
 */

#include <stdio.h>

void main( void )
{
   printf( "The file handle for stdin is %d\n", _fileno( stdin ) );
   printf( "The file handle for stdout is %d\n", _fileno( stdout ) );
   printf( "The file handle for stderr is %d\n", _fileno( stderr ) );
}
```

Output

```
The file handle for stdin is 0
The file handle for stdout is 1
The file handle for stderr is 2
```

See Also **_fdopen, _filelength, fopen, freopen**

_find, _wfind Functions

These functions search for and close searches for specified filenames.

- **_findclose**
- **_findnext, _findnexti64, _wfindnext, _wfindnexti64**
- **_findfirst, _findfirsti64, _wfindfirst, _wfindfirsti64**

Remarks

The **_findfirst** function provides information about the first instance of a filename that matches the file specified in the *filespec* argument. Any wildcard combination supported by the host operating system can be used in *filespec*. File information is returned in a **_finddata_t** structure, defined in IO.H. The **_finddata_t** structure includes the following elements:

unsigned attrib File attribute

time_t time_create Time of file creation (–1L for FAT file systems)

time_t time_access Time of last file access (–1L for FAT file systems)

time_t time_write Time of last write to file

_fsize_t size Length of file in bytes

char name[**_MAX_FNAME**] Null-terminated name of matched file/directory, without the path

In file systems that do not support the creation and last access times of a file, such as the FAT system, the **time_create** and **time_access** fields are always –1L.

_MAX_FNAME is defined in STDLIB.H as 256 bytes.

You cannot specify target attributes (such as **_A_RDONLY**) by which to limit the find operation. This attribute is returned in the **attrib** field of the **_finddata_t** structure and can have the following values (defined in IO.H).

_A_ARCH Archive. Set whenever the file is changed, and cleared by the BACKUP command. Value: 0x20

_A_HIDDEN Hidden file. Not normally seen with the DIR command, unless the /AH option is used. Returns information about normal files as well as files with this attribute. Value: 0x02

_A_NORMAL Normal. File can be read or written to without restriction. Value: 0x00

_A_RDONLY Read-only. File cannot be opened for writing, and a file with the same name cannot be created. Value: 0x01

_A_SUBDIR Subdirectory. Value: 0x10

_A_SYSTEM System file. Not normally seen with the DIR command, unless the /A or /A:S option is used. Value: 0x04

_findnext finds the next name, if any, that matches the *filespec* argument specified in a prior call to **_findfirst**. The *fileinfo* argument should point to a structure initialized by a previous call to **_findfirst**. If a match is found, the *fileinfo* structure contents are altered as described above. **_findclose** closes the specified search handle and releases all associated resources. The handle returned by **_findfirst** must first be passed to **_findclose**, before modification operations such as deleting can be performed on the directories that form the path passed to **_findfirst**.

The **_find** functions allow nested calls. For example, if the file found by a call to **_findfirst** or **_findnext** is a subdirectory, a new search can be initiated with another call to **_findfirst** or **_findnext**.

_wfindfirst and **_wfindnext** are wide-character versions of **_findfirst** and **_findnext**. The structure argument of the wide-character versions has the **_wfinddata_t** data type, which is defined in IO.H and in WCHAR.H. The fields of this data type are the same as those of the **_finddata_t** data type, except that in **_wfinddata_t** the name field is of type **wchar_t** rather than type **char**. Otherwise **_wfindfirst** and

_wfindnext behave identically to **_findfirst** and **_findnext**. Functions **_findfirsti64**, **_findnexti64**, **_wfindfirsti64**, and **_wfindnexti64** also behave identically except they use and return 64-bit file lengths.

Example

```
/* FFIND.C: This program uses the 32-bit _find functions to print
 * a list of all files (and their attributes) with a .C extension
 * in the current directory.
 */

#include <stdio.h>
#include <io.h>
#include <time.h>

void main( void )
{
    struct _finddata_t c_file;
    long hFile;

    /* Find first .c file in current directory */
    if( (hFile = _findfirst( "*.c", &c_file )) == -1L )
       printf( "No *.c files in current directory!\n" );
   else
   {
            printf( "Listing of .c files\n\n" );
            printf( "\nRDO HID SYS ARC  FILE         DATE %25c SIZE\n", ' ' );
            printf( "--- --- --- ---  ----         ---- %25c ----\n", ' ' );
            printf( ( c_file.attrib & _A_RDONLY ) ? " Y  " : " N  " );
            printf( ( c_file.attrib & _A_SYSTEM ) ? " Y  " : " N  " );
            printf( ( c_file.attrib & _A_HIDDEN ) ? " Y  " : " N  " );
            printf( ( c_file.attrib & _A_ARCH )   ? " Y  " : " N  " );
            printf( " %-12s %.24s  %9ld\n",
               c_file.name, ctime( &( c_file.time_write ) ), c_file.size );

            /* Find the rest of the .c files */
            while( _findnext( hFile, &c_file ) == 0 )
            {
                printf( ( c_file.attrib & _A_RDONLY ) ? " Y  " : " N  " );
                printf( ( c_file.attrib & _A_SYSTEM ) ? " Y  " : " N  " );
                printf( ( c_file.attrib & _A_HIDDEN ) ? " Y  " : " N  " );
                printf( ( c_file.attrib & _A_ARCH )   ? " Y  " : " N  " );
                printf( " %-12s %.24s  %9ld\n",
                   c_file.name, ctime( &( c_file.time_write ) ), c_file.size );
            }

       _findclose( hFile );
   }
}
```

Output

```
Listing of .c files

RDO HID SYS ARC  FILE          DATE                          SIZE
--- --- --- ---  ----          ----                          ----
 N   N   N   Y   CWAIT.C       Tue Jun 01 04:07:26 1993      1611
 N   N   N   Y   SPRINTF.C     Thu May 27 04:59:18 1993       617
 N   N   N   Y   CABS.C        Thu May 27 04:58:46 1993       359
 N   N   N   Y   BEGTHRD.C     Tue Jun 01 04:00:48 1993      3726
```

_findclose

Closes the specified search handle and releases associated resources.

int _findclose(long *handle* **);**

Function	Required Header	Optional Headers	Compatibility
_findclose	<io.h>		Win 95, Win NT, Win32s

For additional compatibility information, see "Compatibility" on page ix in the Introduction.

Libraries	
LIBC.LIB	Single thread static library, retail version
LIBCMT.LIB	Multithread static library, retail version
MSVCRT.LIB	Import library for MSVCRTx0.DLL, retail version
MSVCRTx0.DLL	Multithread DLL library, retail version

Return Value

If successful, **_findclose** returns 0. Otherwise, it returns –1 and sets **errno** to **ENOENT**, indicating that no more matching files could be found.

Parameter

handle Search handle returned by a previous call to **_findfirst**

_findfirst, _findfirsti64, _wfindfirst, _wfindfirsti64

Provides information about the first instance of a filename that matches the file specified in the *filespec* argument.

long _findfirst(char **filespec*, **struct _finddata_t** **fileinfo* **);**
_ _int64 _findfirsti64(char **filespec*, **struct _finddata_t** **fileinfo* **);**
long _wfindfirst(wchar_t **filespec*, **struct _wfinddata_t** **fileinfo* **);**
_ _int64 _wfindfirsti64(wchar_t **filespec*, **struct _wfinddata_t** **fileinfo* **);**

Function	Required Header	Optional Headers	Compatibility
_findfirst	<io.h>		Win 95, Win NT, Win32s
_findfirsti64	<io.h>		Win 95, Win NT, Win32s
_wfindfirst	<io.h> or <wchar.h>		Win NT
_wfindfirsti64	<io.h> or <wchar.h>		Win NT

For additional compatibility information, see "Compatibility" on page ix in the Introduction.

Libraries	
LIBC.LIB	Single thread static library, retail version
LIBCMT.LIB	Multithread static library, retail version
MSVCRT.LIB	Import library for MSVCRTx0.DLL, retail version
MSVCRTx0.DLL	Multithread DLL library, retail version

Return Value

If successful, **_findfirst** and **_wfindfirst** return a unique search handle identifying the file or group of files matching the *filespec* specification, which can be used in a subsequent call to **_findnext** or **_wfindnext**, respectively, or to **_findclose**. Otherwise, **_findfirst** and **_wfindfirst** return –1 and set **errno** to one of the following values:

ENOENT File specification that could not be matched

EINVAL Invalid filename specification

Parameters

filespec Target file specification (may include wildcards)

fileinfo File information buffer

_findnext, _findnexti64, _wfindnext, _wfindnexti64

Find the next name, if any, that matches the *filespec* argument in a previous call to **_findfirst**, and then alters the *fileinfo* structure contents accordingly.

int _findnext(long *handle*, **struct _finddata_t** **fileinfo* **);**
_ _int64 _findnexti64(long *handle*, **struct _finddata_t** **fileinfo* **);**
int _wfindnext(long *handle*, **struct _wfinddata_t** **fileinfo* **);**
_ _int64 _wfindnexti64(long *handle*, **struct _wfinddata_t** **fileinfo* **);**

Function	Required Header	Optional Headers	Compatibility
_findnext	<io.h>		Win 95, Win NT, Win32s
_findnexti64	<io.h>		Win 95, Win NT, Win32s
_wfindnext	<io.h> or <wchar.h>		Win NT
_wfindnexti64	<io.h> or <wchar.h>		Win NT

For additional compatibility information, see "Compatibility" on page ix in the Introduction.

Libraries	
LIBC.LIB	Single thread static library, retail version
LIBCMT.LIB	Multithread static library, retail version
MSVCRT.LIB	Import library for MSVCRTx0.DLL, retail version
MSVCRTx0.DLL	Multithread DLL library, retail version

Return Value

If successful, **_findnext** and **_wfindnext** return 0. Otherwise, they return –1 and set **errno** to **ENOENT**, indicating that no more matching files could be found.

Parameters

handle Search handle returned by a previous call to **_findfirst**

fileinfo File information buffer

_finite

Determines whether given double-precision floating point value is finite.

int _finite(double *x* **);**

Function	Required Header	Optional Headers	Compatibility
_finite	<float.h>		Win 95, Win NT, Win32s, 68K, PMac

For additional compatibility information, see "Compatibility" on page ix in the Introduction.

Libraries	
LIBC.LIB	Single thread static library, retail version
LIBCMT.LIB	Multithread static library, retail version
MSVCRT.LIB	Import library for MSVCRTx0.DLL, retail version
MSVCRTx0.DLL	Multithread DLL library, retail version

Return Value

_finite returns a nonzero value (TRUE) if its argument *x* is not infinite, that is, if –INF < *x* < +INF. It returns 0 (FALSE) if the argument is infinite or a NaN.

Parameter

x Double-precision floating-point value

See Also **_isnan**, **_fpclass**

floor

Calculates the floor of a value.

double floor(double *x* **);**

Function	Required Header	Optional Headers	Compatibility
floor	<math.h>		ANSI, Win 95, Win NT, Win32s, 68K, PMac

For additional compatibility information, see "Compatibility" on page ix in the Introduction.

Libraries	
LIBC.LIB	Single thread static library, retail version
LIBCMT.LIB	Multithread static library, retail version
MSVCRT.LIB	Import library for MSVCRTx0.DLL, retail version
MSVCRTx0.DLL	Multithread DLL library, retail version

Return Value

The **floor** function returns a floating-point value representing the largest integer that is less than or equal to *x*.There is no error return.

Parameter

x Floating-point value

Example

```
/* FLOOR.C: This example displays the largest integers
 * less than or equal to the floating-point values 2.8
 * and -2.8. It then shows the smallest integers greater
 * than or equal to 2.8 and -2.8.
 */

#include <math.h>
#include <stdio.h>

void main( void )
{
   double y;

   y = floor( 2.8 );
   printf( "The floor of 2.8 is %f\n", y );
   y = floor( -2.8 );
   printf( "The floor of -2.8 is %f\n", y );
```

```
    y = ceil( 2.8 );
    printf( "The ceil of 2.8 is %f\n", y );
    y = ceil( -2.8 );
    printf( "The ceil of -2.8 is %f\n", y );
}
```

Output

```
The floor of 2.8 is 2.000000
The floor of -2.8 is -3.000000
The ceil of 2.8 is 3.000000
The ceil of -2.8 is -2.000000
```

See Also **ceil**, **fmod**

_flushall

Flushes all streams; clears all buffers.

int _flushall(void);

Function	Required Header	Optional Headers	Compatibility
_flushall	<stdio.h>		Win 95, Win NT, Win32s, 68K, PMac

For additional compatibility information, see "Compatibility" on page ix in the Introduction.

Libraries	
LIBC.LIB	Single thread static library, retail version
LIBCMT.LIB	Multithread static library, retail version
MSVCRT.LIB	Import library for MSVCRTx0.DLL, retail version
MSVCRTx0.DLL	Multithread DLL library, retail version

Return Value

_flushall returns the number of open streams (input and output). There is no error return.

Remarks

By default, the **_flushall** function writes to appropriate files the contents of all buffers associated with open output streams. All buffers associated with open input streams are cleared of their current contents. (These buffers are normally maintained by the operating system, which determines the optimal time to write the data automatically to disk: when a buffer is full, when a stream is closed, or when a program terminates normally without closing streams.)

If a read follows a call to **_flushall**, new data is read from the input files into the buffers. All streams remain open after the call to **_flushall**.

The commit-to-disk feature of the run-time library lets you ensure that critical data is written directly to disk rather than to the operating system buffers. Without rewriting an existing program, you can enable this feature by linking the program's object files with COMMODE.OBJ. In the resulting executable file, calls to **_flushall** write the contents of all buffers to disk. Only **_flushall** and **fflush** are affected by COMMODE.OBJ.

For information about controlling the commit-to-disk feature, see "Stream I/O" on page 16, **fopen**, and **_fdopen**.

Example

```
/* FLUSHALL.C: This program uses _flushall
 * to flush all open buffers.
 */

#include <stdio.h>

void main( void )
{
   int numflushed;

   numflushed = _flushall();
   printf( "There were %d streams flushed\n", numflushed );
}
```

Output

```
There were 3 streams flushed
```

See Also **_commit**, **fclose**, **fflush**, **_flushall**, **setvbuf**

fmod

Calculates the floating-point remainder.

double fmod(double *x*, **double** *y* **);**

Function	Required Header	Optional Headers	Compatibility
fmod	<math.h>		ANSI, Win 95, Win NT, Win32s, 68K, PMac

For additional compatibility information, see "Compatibility" on page ix in the Introduction.

Libraries	
LIBC.LIB	Single thread static library, retail version
LIBCMT.LIB	Multithread static library, retail version

Libraries

MSVCRT.LIB	Import library for MSVCRTx0.DLL, retail version
MSVCRTx0.DLL	Multithread DLL library, retail version

Return Value

fmod returns the floating-point remainder of *x* / *y*. If the value of *y* is 0.0, **fmod** returns a quiet NaN. For information about representation of a quiet NaN by the **printf** family, see **printf**.

Parameters

x, *y* Floating-point values

Remarks

The **fmod** function calculates the floating-point remainder *f* of *x* / *y* such that $x = i * y + f$, where *i* is an integer, *f* has the same sign as *x*, and the absolute value of *f* is less than the absolute value of *y*.

Example

```
/* FMOD.C: This program displays a
 * floating-point remainder.
 */

#include <math.h>
#include <stdio.h>

void main( void )
{
   double w = -10.0, x = 3.0, y = 0.0, z;

   z = fmod( x, y );
   printf( "The remainder of %.2f / %.2f is %f\n", w, x, z );
   printf( "The remainder of %.2f / %.2f is %f\n", x, y, z );

}
```

Output

```
The remainder of -10.00 / 3.00 is -1.000000
```

See Also **ceil**, **fabs**, **floor**

fopen, _wfopen

Open a file.

FILE *fopen(const char ****filename*, const char ****mode***);**
FILE *_wfopen(const wchar_t ****filename*, const wchar_t ****mode***);**

Function	Required Header	Optional Headers	Compatibility
fopen	<stdio.h>		ANSI, Win 95, Win NT, Win32s, 68K, PMac
_wfopen	<stdio.h> or <wchar.h>		Win NT

For additional compatibility information, see "Compatibility" on page ix in the Introduction.

Libraries	
LIBC.LIB	Single thread static library, retail version
LIBCMT.LIB	Multithread static library, retail version
MSVCRT.LIB	Import library for MSVCRTx0.DLL, retail version
MSVCRTx0.DLL	Multithread DLL library, retail version

The **c**, **n**, and **t** *mode* options are Microsoft extensions for **fopen** and **_fdopen** and should not be used where ANSI portability is desired.

Return Value

Each of these functions returns a file handle for the opened file. A return value of –1 indicates an error, in which case **errno** is set to one of the following values:

EACCES Tried to open read-only file for writing, or file's sharing mode does not allow specified operations, or given path is directory

EEXIST **_O_CREAT** and **_O_EXCL** flags specified, but *filename* already exists

EINVAL Invalid *oflag* or *pmode* argument

ENOENT File or path not found

Parameters

filename Filename

mode Type of access permitted

Remarks

The **fopen** function opens the file specified by *filename*. **_wfopen** is a wide-character version of **fopen**; the arguments to **_wfopen** are wide-character strings. **_wfopen** and **fopen** behave identically otherwise.

The character string *mode* specifies the type of access requested for the file, as follows:

"r" Opens for reading. If the file does not exist or cannot be found, the **fopen** call fails.

"w" Opens an empty file for writing. If the given file exists, its contents are destroyed.

"a" Opens for writing at the end of the file (appending) without removing the EOF marker before writing new data to the file; creates the file first if it doesn't exist.

"r+" Opens for both reading and writing. (The file must exist.)

"w+" Opens an empty file for both reading and writing. If the given file exists, its contents are destroyed.

"a+" Opens for reading and appending; the appending operation includes the removal of the EOF marker before new data is written to the file and the EOF marker is restored after writing is complete; creates the file first if it doesn't exist.

When a file is opened with the **"a"** or **"a+"** access type, all write operations occur at the end of the file. The file pointer can be repositioned using **fseek** or **rewind**, but is always moved back to the end of the file before any write operation is carried out. Thus, existing data cannot be overwritten.

The **"a"** mode does not remove the EOF marker before appending to the file. After appending has occurred, the MS-DOS TYPE command only shows data up to the original EOF marker and not any data appended to the file. The **"a+"** mode does remove the EOF marker before appending to the file. After appending, the MS-DOS TYPE command shows all data in the file. The **"a+"** mode is required for appending to a stream file that is terminated with the CTRL+Z EOF marker.

When the **"r+"**, **"w+"**, or **"a+"** access type is specified, both reading and writing are allowed (the file is said to be open for "update"). However, when you switch between reading and writing, there must be an intervening **fflush**, **fsetpos**, **fseek**, or **rewind** operation. The current position can be specified for the **fsetpos** or **fseek** operation, if desired.

In addition to the above values, the following characters can be included in *mode* to specify the translation mode for newline characters:

t Open in text (translated) mode. In this mode, CTRL+Z is interpreted as an end-of-file character on input. In files opened for reading/writing with **"a+"**, **fopen** checks for a CTRL+Z at the end of the file and removes it, if possible. This is done because using **fseek** and **ftell** to move within a file that ends with a CTRL+Z, may cause **fseek** to behave improperly near the end of the file.

Also, in text mode, carriage return–linefeed combinations are translated into single linefeeds on input, and linefeed characters are translated to carriage return–linefeed combinations on output. When a Unicode stream-I/O function operates in text mode (the default), the source or destination stream is assumed to be a sequence of multibyte characters. Therefore, the Unicode stream-input functions convert multibyte characters to wide characters (as if by a call to the **mbtowc** function). For the same reason, the Unicode stream-output functions convert wide characters to multibyte characters (as if by a call to the **wctomb** function).

b Open in binary (untranslated) mode; translations involving carriage-return and linefeed characters are suppressed.

If **t** or **b** is not given in *mode*, the default translation mode is defined by the global variable **_fmode**. If **t** or **b** is prefixed to the argument, the function fails and returns **NULL**.

For more information about using text and binary modes in Unicode and multibyte stream-I/O, see "Text and Binary Mode File I/O" and "Unicode Stream I/O in Text and Binary Modes" on page 15.

c Enable the commit flag for the associated *filename* so that the contents of the file buffer are written directly to disk if either **fflush** or **_flushall** is called.

n Reset the commit flag for the associated *filename* to "no-commit." This is the default. It also overrides the global commit flag if you link your program with COMMODE.OBJ. The global commit flag default is "no-commit" unless you explicitly link your program with COMMODE.OBJ.

Valid characters for the *mode* string used in **fopen** and **_fdopen** correspond to *oflag* arguments used in **_open** and **_sopen**, as follows.

Characters in mode String	Equivalent *oflag* Value for _open/_sopen
a	**_O_WRONLY | _O_APPEND** (usually **_O_WRONLY | _O_CREAT | _O_APPEND**)
a+	**_O_RDWR | _O_APPEND** (usually **_O_RDWR | _O_APPEND | _O_CREAT**)
r	**_O_RDONLY**
r+	**_O_RDWR**
w	**_O_WRONLY** (usually **_O_WRONLY | _O_CREAT | _O_TRUNC**)
w+	**_O_RDWR** (usually **_O_RDWR | _O_CREAT | _O_TRUNC**)
b	**_O_BINARY**
t	**_O_TEXT**
c	None
n	None

Example

```
/* FOPEN.C: This program opens files named "data"
 * and "data2".It  uses fclose to close "data" and
 * _fcloseall to close all remaining files.
 */

#include <stdio.h>

FILE *stream, *stream2;

void main( void )
{
   int numclosed;
```

```
   /* Open for read (will fail if file "data" does not exist) */
   if( (stream  = fopen( "data", "r" )) == NULL )
      printf( "The file 'data' was not opened\n" );
   else
      printf( "The file 'data' was opened\n" );

   /* Open for write */
   if( (stream2 = fopen( "data2", "w+" )) == NULL )
      printf( "The file 'data2' was not opened\n" );
   else
      printf( "The file 'data2' was opened\n" );

   /* Close stream */
   if( fclose( stream ) )
      printf( "The file 'data' was not closed\n" );

   /* All other files are closed: */
   numclosed = _fcloseall( );
   printf( "Number of files closed by _fcloseall: %u\n", numclosed );
}
```

Output

```
The file 'data' was opened
The file 'data2' was opened
Number of files closed by _fcloseall: 1
```

See Also **fclose**, **_fdopen**, **ferror**, **_fileno**, **freopen**, **_open**, **_setmode**

_fpclass

Returns status word containing information on floating-point class.

int _fpclass(double *x* **);**

Function	Required Header	Optional Headers	Compatibility
_fpclass	<float.h>		Win 95, Win NT, Win32s

For additional compatibility information, see "Compatibility" on page ix in the Introduction.

Libraries	
LIBC.LIB	Single thread static library, retail version
LIBCMT.LIB	Multithread static library, retail version
MSVCRT.LIB	Import library for MSVCRTx0.DLL, retail version
MSVCRTx0.DLL	Multithread DLL library, retail version

Return Value

_fpclass returns an integer value that indicates the floating-point class of its argument *x*. The status word may have one of the following values, defined in FLOAT.H.

Value	Meaning
_FPCLASS_SNAN	Signaling NaN
_FPCLASS_QNAN	Quiet NaN
_FPCLASS_NINF	Negative infinity (–INF)
_FPCLASS_NN	Negative normalized non-zero
_FPCLASS_ND	Negative denormalized
_FPCLASS_NZ	Negative zero (–0)
_FPCLASS_PZ	Positive 0 (+0)
_FPCLASS_PD	Positive denormalized
_FPCLASS_PN	Positive normalized non-zero
_FPCLASS_PINF	Positive infinity (+INF)

Parameter

x Double-precision floating-point value

See Also **_isnan**

_fpieee_flt

Invokes user-defined trap handler for IEEE floating-point exceptions.

int _fpieee_flt(unsigned long *exc_code*, **struct _EXCEPTION_POINTERS** **exc_info*, **int** *handler*(**_FPIEEE_RECORD *));**

Function	Required Header	Optional Headers	Compatibility
_fpieee_flt	<fpieee.h>		Win 95, Win NT, Win32s

For additional compatibility information, see "Compatibility" on page ix in the Introduction.

Libraries	
LIBC.LIB	Single thread static library, retail version
LIBCMT.LIB	Multithread static library, retail version
MSVCRT.LIB	Import library for MSVCRTx0.DLL, retail version
MSVCRTx0.DLL	Multithread DLL library, retail version

Return Value

The return value of **_fpieee_flt** is the value returned by *handler.* As such, the IEEE filter routine may be used in the except clause of a structured exception-handling (SEH) mechanism.

Parameters

exc_code Exception code

exc_info Pointer to the Windows NT exception information structure

handler Pointer to user's IEEE trap-handler routine

Remarks

The **_fpieee_flt** function invokes a user-defined trap handler for IEEE floating-point exceptions and provides it with all relevant information. This routine serves as an exception filter in the SEH mechanism, which invokes your own IEEE exception handler when necessary.

The **_FPIEEE_RECORD** structure, defined in FPIEEE.H, contains information pertaining to an IEEE floating-point exception. This structure is passed to the user-defined trap handler by **_fpieee_flt**.

_FPIEEE_RECORD Field	Description
unsigned int RoundingMode, **unsigned int Precision**	These fields contain information on the floating-point environment at the time the exception occurred.
unsigned int Operation	Indicates the type of operation that caused the trap. If the type is a comparison (**_FpCodeCompare**), you can supply one of the special **_FPIEEE_COMPARE_RESULT** values (as defined in FPIEEE.H) in the **Result.Value** field. The conversion type (**_FpCodeConvert**) indicates that the trap occurred during a floating-point conversion operation. You can look at the **Operand1** and **Result** types to determine the type of conversion being attempted.
_FPIEEE_VALUE Operand1, **_FPIEEE_VALUE Operand2**, **_FPIEEE_VALUE Result**	These structures indicate the types and values of the proposed result and operands: **OperandValid** Flag indicating whether the responding value is valid. **Format** Data type of the corresponding value. The format type may be returned even if the corresponding value is not valid. **Value** Result or operand data value.

Example

```
/* FPIEEE.C: This program demonstrates the implementation of
 * a user-defined floating-point exception handler using the
 * _fpieee_flt function.
 */
```

```
#include <fpieee.h>
#include <excpt.h>
#include <float.h>

int fpieee_handler( _FPIEEE_RECORD * );

int fpieee_handler( _FPIEEE_RECORD *pieee )
{
   // user-defined ieee trap handler routine:
   // there is one handler for all
   // IEEE exceptions

   // Assume the user wants all invalid
   // operations to return 0.

   if ((pieee->Cause.InvalidOperation) &&
       (pieee->Result.Format == _FpFormatFp32))
   {
        pieee->Result.Value.Fp32Value = 0.0F;

        return EXCEPTION_CONTINUE_EXECUTION;
   }
   else
      return EXCEPTION_EXECUTE_HANDLER;
}

#define _EXC_MASK     \
    _EM_UNDERFLOW  + \
    _EM_OVERFLOW   + \
    _EM_ZERODIVIDE + \
    _EM_INEXACT

void main( void )
{
   // ...

   __try {
      // unmask invalid operation exception
      _controlfp(_EXC_MASK, _MCW_EM);

      // code that may generate
      // fp exceptions goes here
   }
   __except ( _fpieee_flt( GetExceptionCode(),
                 GetExceptionInformation(),
                 fpieee_handler ) ){

      // code that gets control
```

```
        // if fpieee_handler returns
        // EXCEPTION_EXECUTE_HANDLER goes here
    }

    // ...
}
```

See Also **_control87**

_fpreset

Resets the floating-point package.

void _fpreset(void);

Function	Required Header	Optional Headers	Compatibility
_fpreset	<float.h>		Win 95, Win NT, Win32s, 68K, PMac

For additional compatibility information, see "Compatibility" on page ix in the Introduction.

Libraries	
LIBC.LIB	Single thread static library, retail version
LIBCMT.LIB	Multithread static library, retail version
MSVCRT.LIB	Import library for MSVCRTx0.DLL, retail version
MSVCRTx0.DLL	Multithread DLL library, retail version

Return Value

None

Remarks

The **_fpreset** function reinitializes the floating-point math package. **_fpreset** is usually used with **signal**, **system**, or the **_exec** or **_spawn** functions. If a program traps floating-point error signals (**SIGFPE**) with **signal**, it can safely recover from floating-point errors by invoking **_fpreset** and using **longjmp**.

Example

```
/* FPRESET.C: This program uses signal to set up a
 * routine for handling floating-point errors.
 */
#include <stdio.h>
#include <signal.h>
#include <setjmp.h>
#include <stdlib.h>
#include <float.h>
#include <math.h>
#include <string.h>
```

```
#pragma warning(disable : 4113) /* C4113 warning expected */

jmp_buf mark;              /* Address for long jump to jump to */
int     fperr;             /* Global error number */

void __cdecl fphandler( int sig, int num );   /* Prototypes */
void fpcheck( void );

void main( void )
{
   double n1, n2, r;
   int jmpret;
   /* Unmask all floating-point exceptions. */
    _control87( 0, _MCW_EM );
   /* Set up floating-point error handler. The compiler
    * will generate a warning because it expects
    * signal-handling functions to take only one argument.
    */
    if( signal( SIGFPE, fphandler ) == SIG_ERR )

   {
      fprintf( stderr, "Couldn't set SIGFPE\n" );
      abort();   }

   /* Save stack environment for return in case of error. First
    * time through, jmpret is 0, so true conditional is executed.
    * If an error occurs, jmpret will be set to -1 and false
    * conditional will be executed.
    */
   jmpret = setjmp( mark );
   if( jmpret == 0 )
   {
      printf( "Test for invalid operation - " );
      printf( "enter two numbers: " );
      scanf( "%lf %lf", &n1, &n2 );
      r = n1 / n2;
      /* This won't be reached if error occurs. */
      printf( "\n\n%4.3g / %4.3g = %4.3g\n", n1, n2, r );

      r = n1 * n2;
      /* This won't be reached if error occurs. */
      printf( "\n\n%4.3g * %4.3g = %4.3g\n", n1, n2, r );
   }
   else
      fpcheck();
}
/* fphandler handles SIGFPE (floating-point error) interrupt. Note
 * that this prototype accepts two arguments and that the
 * prototype for signal in the run-time library expects a signal
 * handler to have only one argument.
 *
```

```
 * The second argument in this signal handler allows processing of
 * _FPE_INVALID, _FPE_OVERFLOW, _FPE_UNDERFLOW, and
 * _FPE_ZERODIVIDE, all of which are Microsoft-specific symbols
 * that augment the information provided by SIGFPE. The compiler
 * will generate a warning, which is harmless and expected.

 */
void fphandler( int sig, int num )
{
   /* Set global for outside check since we don't want
    * to do I/O in the handler.
    */
   fperr = num;
   /* Initialize floating-point package. */
   _fpreset();
   /* Restore calling environment and jump back to setjmp. Return
    * -1 so that setjmp will return false for conditional test.
    */
   longjmp( mark, -1 );
}
void fpcheck( void )
{
   char fpstr[30];
   switch( fperr )
   {
   case _FPE_INVALID:
       strcpy( fpstr, "Invalid number" );
       break;
   case _FPE_OVERFLOW:
       strcpy( fpstr, "Overflow" );

       break;
   case _FPE_UNDERFLOW:
       strcpy( fpstr, "Underflow" );
       break;
   case _FPE_ZERODIVIDE:
       strcpy( fpstr, "Divide by zero" );
       break;
   default:
       strcpy( fpstr, "Other floating point error" );
       break;
   }
   printf( "Error %d: %s\n", fperr, fpstr );
}
```

Output

```
Test for invalid operation - enter two numbers: 5 0
Error 131: Divide by zero
```

See Also **_exec** Functions, **signal**, **_spawn** Functions, **system**

fprintf, fwprintf

Print formatted data to a stream.

int fprintf(FILE ****stream*, const char ****format* [, *argument*]...**);**
int fwprintf(FILE ****stream*, const wchar_t ****format* [, *argument*]...**);**

Function	Required Header	Optional Headers	Compatibility
fprintf	<stdio.h>		ANSI, Win 95, Win NT, 68K, PMac
fwprintf	<stdio.h> or <wchar.h>		ANSI, Win 95, Win NT

For additional compatibility information, see "Compatibility" on page ix in the Introduction.

Libraries	
LIBC.LIB	Single thread static library, retail version
LIBCMT.LIB	Multithread static library, retail version
MSVCRT.LIB	Import library for MSVCRTx0.DLL, retail version
MSVCRTx0.DLL	Multithread DLL library, retail version

Return Value

fprintf returns the number of bytes written. **fwprintf** returns the number of wide characters written. Each of these functions returns a negative value instead when an output error occurs.

Parameters

stream Pointer to **FILE** structure

format Format-control string

argument Optional arguments

Remarks

fprintf formats and prints a series of characters and values to the output *stream.* Each function *argument* (if any) is converted and output according to the corresponding format specification in *format.* For **fprintf**, the *format* argument has the same syntax and use that it has in **printf**.

fwprintf is a wide-character version of **fprintf**; in **fwprintf**, *format* is a wide-character string. These functions behave identically otherwise.

For more information, see **printf**.

Example

```
/* FPRINTF.C: This program uses fprintf to format various
 * data and print it to the file named FPRINTF.OUT. It
 * then displays FPRINTF.OUT on the screen using the system
 * function to invoke the operating-system TYPE command.
 */

#include <stdio.h>
#include <process.h>

FILE *stream;

void main( void )
{
   int    i = 10;
   double fp = 1.5;
   char   s[] = "this is a string";
   char   c = '\n';

   stream = fopen( "fprintf.out", "w" );
   fprintf( stream, "%s%c", s, c );
   fprintf( stream, "%d\n", i );
   fprintf( stream, "%f\n", fp );
   fclose( stream );
   system( "type fprintf.out" );
}
```

Output

```
this is a string
10
1.500000
```

See Also **_cprintf**, **fscanf**, **sprintf**

fputc, fputwc, _fputchar, _fputwchar

Writes a character to a stream (**fputc**, **fputwc**) or to **stdout** (**_fputchar**, **_fputwchar**).

int fputc(int *c*, **FILE ****stream* **);**
wint_t fputwc(wint_t *c*, **FILE ****stream* **);**
int _fputchar(int *c* **);**
wint_t _fputwchar(wint_t *c* **);**

Function	Required Header	Optional Headers	Compatibility
fputc	<stdio.h>		ANSI, Win 95, Win NT, Win32s, 68K, PMac
fputwc	<stdio.h> or <wchar.h>		ANSI, Win 95, Win NT, Win32s

Function	Required Header	Optional Headers	Compatibility
_fputchar	<stdio.h>		Win 95, Win NT, Win32s, 68K, PMac
_fputwchar	<stdio.h> or <wchar.h>		Win 95, Win NT, Win32s

For additional compatibility information, see "Compatibility" on page ix in the Introduction.

Libraries	
LIBC.LIB	Single thread static library, retail version
LIBCMT.LIB	Multithread static library, retail version
MSVCRT.LIB	Import library for MSVCRTx0.DLL, retail version
MSVCRTx0.DLL	Multithread DLL library, retail version

Return Value

Each of these functions returns the character written. For **fputc** and **_fputchar**, a return value of **EOF** indicates an error. For **fputwc** and **_fputwchar**, a return value of **WEOF** indicates an error.

Parameters

c Character to be written

stream Pointer to **FILE** structure

Remarks

Each of these functions writes the single character *c* to a file at the position indicated by the associated file position indicator (if defined) and advances the indicator as appropriate. In the case of **fputc** and **fputwc**, the file is associated with *stream.* If the file cannot support positioning requests or was opened in append mode, the character is appended to the end of the stream. Routine-specific remarks follow.

Routine	Remarks
fputc	Equivalent to **putc**, but implemented only as a function, rather than as a function and a macro.
fputwc	Wide-character version of **fputc**. Writes *c* as a multibyte character or a wide character according to whether *stream* is opened in text mode or binary mode.
_fputchar	Equivalent to **fputc(stdout)**. Also equivalent to **putchar**, but implemented only as a function, rather than as a function and a macro. Microsoft-specific; not ANSI-compatible.
_fputwchar	Wide-character version of **_fputchar**. Writes *c* as a multibyte character or a wide character according to whether *stream* is opened in text mode or binary mode. Microsoft-specific; not ANSI-compatible.

Example

```
/* FPUTC.C: This program uses fputc and _fputchar
 * to send a character array to stdout.
 */

#include <stdio.h>

void main( void )
{
   char strptr1[] = "This is a test of fputc!!\n";
   char strptr2[] = "This is a test of _fputchar!!\n";
   char *p;

   /* Print line to stream using fputc. */
   p = strptr1;
   while( (*p != '\0') && fputc( *(p++), stdout ) != EOF ) ;

   /* Print line to stream using _fputchar. */
   p = strptr2;
   while( (*p != '\0') && _fputchar( *(p++) ) != EOF )
      ;
}
```

See Also **fgetc**, **putc**

fputs, fputws

Write a string to a stream.

int fputs(const char ***string*****, FILE** ***stream*** **);**
int fputws(const wchar_t ***string*****, FILE** ***stream*** **);**

Function	Required Header	Optional Headers	Compatibility
fputs	<stdio.h>		ANSI, Win 95, Win NT, Win32s, 68K, PMac
fputws	<stdio.h> or <wchar.h>		ANSI, Win 95, Win NT, Win32s

For additional compatibility information, see "Compatibility" on page ix in the Introduction.

Libraries	
LIBC.LIB	Single thread static library, retail version
LIBCMT.LIB	Multithread static library, retail version
MSVCRT.LIB	Import library for MSVCRTx0.DLL, retail version
MSVCRTx0.DLL	Multithread DLL library, retail version

Return Value

Each of these functions returns a nonnegative value if it is successful. On an error, **fputs** returns **EOF**, and **fputws** returns **WEOF**.

Parameters

string Output string

stream Pointer to **FILE** structure

Remarks

Each of these functions copies *string* to the output *stream* at the current position. **fputws** copies the wide-character argument *string* to *stream* as a multibyte-character string or a wide-character string according to whether *stream* is opened in text mode or binary mode, respectively. Neither function copies the terminating null character.

Example

```
/* FPUTS.C: This program uses fputs to write
 * a single line to the stdout stream.
 */

#include <stdio.h>

void main( void )
{
   fputs( "Hello world from fputs.\n", stdout );
}
```

Output

```
Hello world from fputs.
```

See Also **fgets**, **gets**, **puts**, **_putws**

fread

Reads data from a stream.

size_t fread(void ***buffer*, **size_t** *size*, **size_t** *count*, **FILE** ***stream* **);**

Function	Required Header	Optional Headers	Compatibility
fread	<stdio.h>		ANSI, Win 95, Win NT, Win32s, 68K, PMac

For additional compatibility information, see "Compatibility" on page ix in the Introduction.

Libraries

LIBC.LIB	Single thread static library, retail version
LIBCMT.LIB	Multithread static library, retail version
MSVCRT.LIB	Import library for MSVCRTx0.DLL, retail version
MSVCRTx0.DLL	Multithread DLL library, retail version

Return Value

fread returns the number of full items actually read, which may be less than *count* if an error occurs or if the end of the file is encountered before reaching *count*. Use the **feof** or **ferror** function to distinguish a read error from an end-of-file condition. If *size* or *count* is 0, **fread** returns 0 and the buffer contents are unchanged.

Parameters

buffer Storage location for data

size Item size in bytes

count Maximum number of items to be read

stream Pointer to **FILE** structure

Remarks

The **fread** function reads up to *count* items of *size* bytes from the input *stream* and stores them in *buffer*. The file pointer associated with *stream* (if there is one) is increased by the number of bytes actually read. If the given stream is opened in text mode, carriage return–linefeed pairs are replaced with single linefeed characters. The replacement has no effect on the file pointer or the return value. The file-pointer position is indeterminate if an error occurs. The value of a partially read item cannot be determined.

Example

```
/* FREAD.C: This program opens a file named FREAD.OUT and
 * writes 25 characters to the file. It then tries to open
 * FREAD.OUT and read in 25 characters. If the attempt succeeds,
 * the program displays the number of actual items read.
 */

#include <stdio.h>

void main( void )
{
   FILE *stream;
   char list[30];
   int  i, numread, numwritten;

   /* Open file in text mode: */
   if( (stream = fopen( "fread.out", "w+t" )) != NULL )
```

```
   {
      for ( i = 0; i < 25; i++ )
         list[i] = (char)('z' - i);
      /* Write 25 characters to stream */
      numwritten = fwrite( list, sizeof( char ), 25, stream );
      printf( "Wrote %d items\n", numwritten );
      fclose( stream );

   }
   else
      printf( "Problem opening the file\n" );

   if( (stream = fopen( "fread.out", "r+t" )) != NULL )
   {
      /* Attempt to read in 25 characters */
      numread = fread( list, sizeof( char ), 25, stream );
      printf( "Number of items read = %d\n", numread );
      printf( "Contents of buffer = %.25s\n", list );
      fclose( stream );
   }
   else
      printf( "File could not be opened\n" );
}
```

Output

```
Wrote 25 items
Number of items read = 25
Contents of buffer = zyxwvutsrqponmlkjihgfedcb
```

See Also **fwrite**, **_read**

---

free

Deallocates or frees a memory block.

void free(void ***memblock*** **);**

Function	Required Header	Optional Headers	Compatibility
free	<stdlib.h> and <malloc.h>		ANSI, Win 95, Win NT, Win32s, 68K, PMac

For additional compatibility information, see “Compatibility” on page ix in the Introduction.

Libraries	
LIBC.LIB	Single thread static library, retail version
LIBCMT.LIB	Multithread static library, retail version
MSVCRT.LIB	Import library for MSVCRTx0.DLL, retail version
MSVCRTx0.DLL	Multithread DLL library, retail version

Return Value

None

Parameter

memblock Previously allocated memory block to be freed

Remarks

The **free** function deallocates a memory block (*memblock*) that was previously allocated by a call to **calloc**, **malloc**, or **realloc**. The number of freed bytes is equivalent to the number of bytes requested when the block was allocated (or reallocated, in the case of **realloc**). If *memblock* is **NULL**, the pointer is ignored and **free** immediately returns. Attempting to free an invalid pointer (a pointer to a memory block that was not allocated by **calloc**, **malloc**, or **realloc**) may affect subsequent allocation requests and cause errors. After a memory block has been freed, **_heapmin** minimizes the amount of free memory on the heap by coalescing the unused regions and releasing them back to the operating system. Freed memory that is not released to the operating system is restored to the free pool and is available for allocation again.

When the application is linked with a debug version of the C run-time libraries, **free** resolves to **_free_dbg**. For more information about how the heap is managed during the debugging process, see Chapter 4, "Debug Version of the C Run-Time Library."

Example

See the example for **malloc**.

See Also **_alloca**, **calloc**, **malloc**, **realloc**, **_free_dbg**, **_heapmin**

freopen, _wfreopen

Reassign a file pointer.

FILE *freopen(const char **path*, **const char** **mode*, **FILE** **stream* **);**
FILE *_wfreopen(const wchar_t **path*, **const wchar_t** **mode*, **FILE** **stream* **);**

Function	Required Header	Optional Headers	Compatibility
freopen	<stdio.h>		ANSI, Win 95, Win NT, Win32s, 68K, PMac
_wfreopen	<stdio.h> or <wchar.h>		Win NT

For additional compatibility information, see "Compatibility" on page ix in the Introduction.

Libraries

LIBC.LIB	Single thread static library, retail version
LIBCMT.LIB	Multithread static library, retail version
MSVCRT.LIB	Import library for MSVCRTx0.DLL, retail version
MSVCRTx0.DLL	Multithread DLL library, retail version

Return Value

Each of these functions returns a pointer to the newly opened file. If an error occurs, the original file is closed and the function returns a **NULL** pointer value.

Parameters

path Path of new file

mode Type of access permitted

stream Pointer to **FILE** structure

Remarks

The **freopen** function closes the file currently associated with *stream* and reassigns *stream* to the file specified by *path.* **_wfreopen** is a wide-character version of **_freopen**; the *path* and *mode* arguments to **_wfreopen** are wide-character strings. **_wfreopen** and **_freopen** behave identically otherwise.

freopen is typically used to redirect the pre-opened files **stdin**, **stdout**, and **stderr** to files specified by the user. The new file associated with *stream* is opened with *mode,* which is a character string specifying the type of access requested for the file, as follows:

"r" Opens for reading. If the file does not exist or cannot be found, the **freopen** call fails.

"w" Opens an empty file for writing. If the given file exists, its contents are destroyed.

"a" Opens for writing at the end of the file (appending) without removing the EOF marker before writing new data to the file; creates the file first if it does not exist.

"r+" Opens for both reading and writing. (The file must exist.)

"w+" Opens an empty file for both reading and writing. If the given file exists, its contents are destroyed.

"a+" Opens for reading and appending; the appending operation includes the removal of the EOF marker before new data is written to the file and the EOF marker is restored after writing is complete; creates the file first if it does not exist.

Use the **"w"** and **"w+"** types with care, as they can destroy existing files.

When a file is opened with the **"a"** or **"a+"** access type, all write operations take place at the end of the file. Although the file pointer can be repositioned using **fseek** or **rewind**, the file pointer is always moved back to the end of the file before any write operation is carried out. Thus, existing data cannot be overwritten.

The **"a"** mode does not remove the EOF marker before appending to the file. After appending has occurred, the MS-DOS TYPE command only shows data up to the original EOF marker and not any data appended to the file. The **"a+"** mode does remove the EOF marker before appending to the file. After appending, the MS-DOS TYPE command shows all data in the file. The **"a+"** mode is required for appending to a stream file that is terminated with the CTRL+Z EOF marker.

When the **"r+"**, **"w+"**, or **"a+"** access type is specified, both reading and writing are allowed (the file is said to be open for "update"). However, when you switch between reading and writing, there must be an intervening **fsetpos**, **fseek**, or **rewind** operation. The current position can be specified for the **fsetpos** or **fseek** operation, if desired. In addition to the above values, one of the following characters may be included in the *mode* string to specify the translation mode for new lines.

t Open in text (translated) mode; carriage return–linefeed (CR-LF) combinations are translated into single linefeed (LF) characters on input; LF characters are translated to CR-LF combinations on output. Also, CTRL+Z is interpreted as an end-of-file character on input. In files opened for reading or for writing and reading with **"a+"**, the run-time library checks for a CTRL+Z at the end of the file and removes it, if possible. This is done because using **fseek** and **ftell** to move within a file may cause **fseek** to behave improperly near the end of the file. The **t** option is a Microsoft extension that should not be used where ANSI portability is desired.

b Open in binary (untranslated) mode; the above translations are suppressed.

If **t** or **b** is not given in the *mode* string, the translation mode is defined by the default mode variable **_fmode**.

For a discussion of text and binary modes, see "Text and Binary Mode File I/O" on page 15.

Example

```
/* FREOPEN.C: This program reassigns stderr to the file
 * named FREOPEN.OUT and writes a line to that file.
 */

#include <stdio.h>
#include <stdlib.h>

FILE *stream;

void main( void )
```

```
{
   /* Reassign "stderr" to "freopen.out": */
   stream = freopen( "freopen.out", "w", stderr );

   if( stream == NULL )
      fprintf( stdout, "error on freopen\n" );
   else
   {
      fprintf( stream, "This will go to the file 'freopen.out'\n" );
      fprintf( stdout, "successfully reassigned\n" );
      fclose( stream );
   }
   system( "type freopen.out" );
}
```

Output

```
successfully reassigned
This will go to the file 'freopen.out'
```

See Also **fclose**, **_fdopen**, **_fileno**, **fopen**, **_open**, **_setmode**

frexp

Gets the mantissa and exponent of a floating-point number.

double frexp(double *x*, **int** **expptr* **);**

Function	Required Header	Optional Headers	Compatibility
frexp	<math.h>		ANSI, Win 95, Win NT, Win32s, 68K, PMac

For additional compatibility information, see "Compatibility" on page ix in the Introduction.

Libraries	
LIBC.LIB	Single thread static library, retail version
LIBCMT.LIB	Multithread static library, retail version
MSVCRT.LIB	Import library for MSVCRTx0.DLL, retail version
MSVCRTx0.DLL	Multithread DLL library, retail version

Return Value

frexp returns the mantissa. If *x* is 0, the function returns 0 for both the mantissa and the exponent. There is no error return.

Parameters

x Floating-point value

expptr Pointer to stored integer exponent

Remarks

The **frexp** function breaks down the floating-point value (*x*) into a mantissa (*m*) and an exponent (*n*), such that the absolute value of *m* is greater than or equal to 0.5 and less than 1.0, and $x = m*2^n$. The integer exponent *n* is stored at the location pointed to by *expptr*.

Example

```
/* FREXP.C: This program calculates frexp( 16.4, &n )
 * then displays y and n.
 */

#include <math.h>
#include <stdio.h>

void main( void )
{
   double x, y;
   int n;

   x = 16.4;
   y = frexp( x, &n );
   printf( "frexp( %f, &n ) = %f, n = %d\n", x, y, n );
}
```

Output

```
frexp( 16.400000, &n ) = 0.512500, n = 5
```

See Also **ldexp**, **modf**

fscanf, fwscanf

Read formatted data from a stream.

int fscanf(FILE ****stream*, const char ****format* [, *argument*]... **);**
int fwscanf(FILE ****stream*, const wchar_t ****format* [, *argument*]... **);**

Function	Required Header	Optional Headers	Compatibility
fscanf	<stdio.h>		ANSI, Win 95, Win NT, Win32s, 68K, PMac
fwscanf	<stdio.h> or <wchar.h>		ANSI, Win 95, Win NT, Win32s

For additional compatibility information, see “Compatibility” on page ix in the Introduction.

Libraries

LIBC.LIB	Single thread static library, retail version
LIBCMT.LIB	Multithread static library, retail version
MSVCRT.LIB	Import library for MSVCRTx0.DLL, retail version
MSVCRTx0.DLL	Multithread DLL library, retail version

Return Value

Each of these functions returns the number of fields successfully converted and assigned; the return value does not include fields that were read but not assigned. A return value of 0 indicates that no fields were assigned. If an error occurs, or if the end of the file stream is reached before the first conversion, the return value is **EOF** for fscanf or **WEOF** for **fwscanf**.

Parameters

stream Pointer to **FILE** structure

format Format-control string

argument Optional arguments

Remarks

The **fscanf** function reads data from the current position of *stream* into the locations given by *argument* (if any). Each *argument* must be a pointer to a variable of a type that corresponds to a type specifier in *format*. *format* controls the interpretation of the input fields and has the same form and function as the *format* argument for **scanf**; see **scanf** for a description of *format*. If copying takes place between strings that overlap, the behavior is undefined.

fwscanf is a wide-character version of **fscanf**; the format argument to **fwscanf** is a wide-character string. These functions behave identically otherwise.

For more information, see "**scanf** Format Specification Fields" on page 517.

Example

```
/* FSCANF.C: This program writes formatted
 * data to a file. It then uses fscanf to
 * read the various data back from the file.
 */

#include <stdio.h>

FILE *stream;

void main( void )
{
   long l;
   float fp;
   char s[81];
   char c;
```

```
    stream = fopen( "fscanf.out", "w+" );
    if( stream == NULL )
       printf( "The file fscanf.out was not opened\n" );
    else
    {
       fprintf( stream, "%s %ld %f%c", "a-string",
                65000, 3.14159, 'x' );

       /* Set pointer to beginning of file: */
       fseek( stream, 0L, SEEK_SET );

       /* Read data back from file: */
       fscanf( stream, "%s", s );
       fscanf( stream, "%ld", &l );

       fscanf( stream, "%f", &fp );
       fscanf( stream, "%c", &c );

       /* Output data read: */
       printf( "%s\n", s );
       printf( "%ld\n", l );
       printf( "%f\n", fp );
       printf( "%c\n", c );

       fclose( stream );
    }
}
```

Output

```
a-string
65000
3.141590
x
```

See Also **_cscanf**, **fprintf**, **scanf**, **sscanf**

fseek

Moves the file pointer to a specified location.

int fseek(FILE ***stream*****, long** ***offset*****, int** ***origin*** **);**

Function	Required Header	Optional Headers	Compatibility
fseek	<stdio.h>		ANSI, Win 95, Win NT, Win32s, 68K, PMac

For additional compatibility information, see "Compatibility" on page ix in the Introduction.

Libraries

LIBC.LIB	Single thread static library, retail version
LIBCMT.LIB	Multithread static library, retail version
MSVCRT.LIB	Import library for MSVCRTx0.DLL, retail version
MSVCRTx0.DLL	Multithread DLL library, retail version

Return Value

If successful, **fseek** returns 0. Otherwise, it returns a nonzero value. On devices incapable of seeking, the return value is undefined.

Parameters

stream Pointer to **FILE** structure

offset Number of bytes from *origin*

origin Initial position

Remarks

The **fseek** function moves the file pointer (if any) associated with *stream* to a new location that is *offset* bytes from *origin*. The next operation on the stream takes place at the new location. On a stream open for update, the next operation can be either a read or a write. The argument origin must be one of the following constants, defined in STDIO.H:

SEEK_CUR Current position of file pointer

SEEK_END End of file

SEEK_SET Beginning of file

You can use **fseek** to reposition the pointer anywhere in a file. The pointer can also be positioned beyond the end of the file. **fseek** clears the end-of-file indicator and negates the effect of any prior **ungetc** calls against *stream*.

When a file is opened for appending data, the current file position is determined by the last I/O operation, not by where the next write would occur. If no I/O operation has yet occurred on a file opened for appending, the file position is the start of the file.

For streams opened in text mode, **fseek** has limited use, because carriage return–linefeed translations can cause **fseek** to produce unexpected results. The only **fseek** operations guaranteed to work on streams opened in text mode are:

- Seeking with an offset of 0 relative to any of the origin values.
- Seeking from the beginning of the file with an offset value returned from a call to **ftell**.

Also in text mode, CTRL+Z is interpreted as an end-of-file character on input. In files opened for reading/writing, **fopen** and all related routines check for a CTRL+Z at the end of the file and remove it if possible. This is done because using **fseek** and **ftell** to move within a file that ends with a CTRL+Z may cause **fseek** to behave improperly near the end of the file.

Example

```
/* FSEEK.C: This program opens the file FSEEK.OUT and
 * moves the pointer to the file's beginning.
 */

#include <stdio.h>

void main( void )
{
   FILE *stream;
   char line[81];
   int  result;

   stream = fopen( "fseek.out", "w+" );
   if( stream == NULL )
      printf( "The file fseek.out was not opened\n" );
   else
   {
      fprintf( stream, "The fseek begins here: "
                       "This is the file 'fseek.out'.\n" );
      result = fseek( stream, 23L, SEEK_SET);
      if( result )
         perror( "Fseek failed" );
      else
      {
         printf( "File pointer is set to middle of first line.\n" );
         fgets( line, 80, stream );
         printf( "%s", line );

      }
      fclose( stream );
   }
}
```

Output

```
File pointer is set to middle of first line.
This is the file 'fseek.out'.
```

See Also **ftell**, **_lseek**, **rewind**

fsetpos

Sets the stream-position indicator.

int fsetpos(FILE ****stream*, **const fpos_t ****pos*);**

Function	Required Header	Optional Headers	Compatibility
fsetpos	<stdio.h>		ANSI, Win 95, Win NT, Win32s, 68K, PMac

For additional compatibility information, see "Compatibility" on page ix in the Introduction.

Libraries	
LIBC.LIB	Single thread static library, retail version
LIBCMT.LIB	Multithread static library, retail version
MSVCRT.LIB	Import library for MSVCRTx0.DLL, retail version
MSVCRTx0.DLL	Multithread DLL library, retail version

Return Value

If successful, **fsetpos** returns 0. On failure, the function returns a nonzero value and sets **errno** to one of the following manifest constants (defined in ERRNO.H): **EBADF**, which means the file is not accessible or the object that *stream* points to is not a valid file handle; or **EINVAL**, which means an invalid stream value was passed.

Parameters

stream Pointer to **FILE** structure

pos Position-indicator storage

Remarks

The **fsetpos** function sets the file-position indicator for *stream* to the value of *pos,* which is obtained in a prior call to **fgetpos** against *stream.* The function clears the end-of-file indicator and undoes any effects of **ungetc** on *stream.* After calling **fsetpos**, the next operation on *stream* may be either input or output.

Example

See the example for **fgetpos**.

See Also **fgetpos**

_fsopen, _wfsopen

Open a stream with file sharing.

FILE *_fsopen(const char ***_filename_, const char ***_mode_**, int** _shflag_ **);**
FILE *_wfsopen(const wchar_t ***_filename_, const wchar_t ***_mode_**, int** _shflag_ **);**

Function	Required Header	Optional Headers	Compatibility
_fsopen	<stdio.h>	<share.h>[1]	Win 95, Win NT, Win32s, 68K, PMac
_wfsopen	<stdio.h> or <wchar.h>	<share.h>[1]	Win NT

[1] For manifest constant for *shflag* parameter.

For additional compatibility information, see "Compatibility" on page ix in the Introduction.

Libraries	
LIBC.LIB	Single thread static library, retail version
LIBCMT.LIB	Multithread static library, retail version
MSVCRT.LIB	Import library for MSVCRTx0.DLL, retail version
MSVCRTx0.DLL	Multithread DLL library, retail version

Return Value

Each of these functions returns a pointer to the stream. A **NULL** pointer value indicates an error.

Parameters

filename Name of file to open

mode Type of access permitted

shflag Type of sharing allowed

Remarks

The **_fsopen** function opens the file specified by *filename* as a stream and prepares the file for subsequent shared reading or writing, as defined by the mode and *shflag* arguments. **_wfsopen** is a wide-character version of **_fsopen**; the *filename* and *mode* arguments to **_wfsopen** are wide-character strings. **_wfsopen** and **_fsopen** behave identically otherwise.

The character string *mode* specifies the type of access requested for the file, as follows:

"r" Opens for reading. If the file does not exist or cannot be found, the **_fsopen** call fails.

"w" Opens an empty file for writing. If the given file exists, its contents are destroyed.

"a" Opens for writing at the end of the file (appending); creates the file first if it does not exist.

"r+" Opens for both reading and writing. (The file must exist.)

"w+" Opens an empty file for both reading and writing. If the given file exists, its contents are destroyed.

"a+" Opens for reading and appending; creates the file first if it does not exist.

Use the **"w"** and **"w+"** types with care, as they can destroy existing files.

When a file is opened with the **"a"** or **"a+"** access type, all write operations occur at the end of the file. The file pointer can be repositioned using **fseek** or **rewind**, but is always moved back to the end of the file before any write operation is carried out. Thus existing data cannot be overwritten. When the **"r+"**, **"w+"**, or **"a+"** access type is specified, both reading and writing are allowed (the file is said to be open for "update"). However, when switching between reading and writing, there must be an intervening **fsetpos**, **fseek**, or **rewind** operation. The current position can be specified for the **fsetpos** or **fseek** operation, if desired. In addition to the above values, one of the following characters can be included in *mode* to specify the translation mode for new lines:

t Opens a file in text (translated) mode. In this mode, carriage return–linefeed (CR-LF) combinations are translated into single linefeeds (LF) on input and LF characters are translated to CR-LF combinations on output. Also, CTRL+Z is interpreted as an end-of-file character on input. In files opened for reading or reading/writing, **_fsopen** checks for a CTRL+Z at the end of the file and removes it, if possible. This is done because using **fseek** and **ftell** to move within a file that ends with a CTRL+Z may cause **fseek** to behave improperly near the end of the file.

b Opens a file in binary (untranslated) mode; the above translations are suppressed.

If **t** or **b** is not given in *mode,* the translation mode is defined by the default-mode variable **_fmode**. If **t** or **b** is prefixed to the argument, the function fails and returns **NULL**. For a discussion of text and binary modes, see "Text and Binary Mode File I/O" on page 15.

The argument *shflag* is a constant expression consisting of one of the following manifest constants, defined in SHARE.H:

_SH_COMPAT Sets Compatibility mode for 16-bit applications

_SH_DENYNO Permits read and write access

_SH_DENYRD Denies read access to file

_SH_DENYRW Denies read and write access to file

_SH_DENYWR Denies write access to file

Example

```
/* FSOPEN.C:
 */

#include <stdio.h>
#include <stdlib.h>
#include <share.h>

void main( void )
{
   FILE *stream;

   /* Open output file for writing. Using _fsopen allows us to
    * ensure that no one else writes to the file while we are
    * writing to it.
    */
   if( (stream = _fsopen( "outfile", "wt", _SH_DENYWR )) != NULL )
   {
      fprintf( stream, "No one else in the network can write "
                       "to this file until we are done.\n" );
      fclose( stream );
   }
   /* Now others can write to the file while we read it. */
   system( "type outfile" );
}
```

Output

```
No one else in the network can write to this file until we are done.
```

See Also **fclose**, **_fdopen**, **ferror**, **_fileno**, **fopen**, **freopen**, **_open**, **_setmode**, **_sopen**

_fstat, _fstati64

Get information about an open file.

int _fstat(**int** *handle*, **struct _stat** **buffer* **);**
__int64 _fstati64(**int** *handle*, **struct _stat** **buffer* **);**

Function	Required Header	Optional Headers	Compatibility
_fstat	<sys/stat.h> and <sys/types.h>		Win 95, Win NT, Win32s, 68K, PMac
_fstati64	<sys/stat.h> and <sys/types.h>		Win 95, Win NT, Win32s

For additional compatibility information, see "Compatibility" on page ix in the Introduction.

Libraries

LIBC.LIB	Single thread static library, retail version
LIBCMT.LIB	Multithread static library, retail version
MSVCRT.LIB	Import library for MSVCRTx0.DLL, retail version
MSVCRTx0.DLL	Multithread DLL library, retail version

Return Value

_fstat and **_fstati64** return 0 if the file-status information is obtained. A return value of –1 indicates an error, in which case **errno** is set to **EBADF**, indicating an invalid file handle.

Parameters

handle Handle of open file

buffer Pointer to structure to store results

Remarks

The **_fstat** function obtains information about the open file associated with *handle* and stores it in the structure pointed to by *buffer*. The **_stat** structure, defined in SYS\STAT.H, contains the following fields:

st_atime Time of last file access.

st_ctime Time of creation of file.

st_dev If a device, *handle*; otherwise 0.

st_mode Bit mask for file-mode information. The **_S_IFCHR** bit is set if *handle* refers to a device. The **_S_IFREG** bit is set if *handle* refers to an ordinary file. The read/write bits are set according to the file's permission mode. **_S_IFCHR** and other constants are defined in SYS\STAT.H.

st_mtime Time of last modification of file.

st_nlink Always 1 on non-NTFS file systems.

st_rdev If a device, *handle*; otherwise 0.

st_size Size of the file in bytes.

If *handle* refers to a device, the **st_atime**, **st_ctime**, and **st_mtime** and **st_size** fields are not meaningful.

Because STAT.H uses the **_dev_t** type, which is defined in TYPES.H, you must include TYPES.H before STAT.H in your code.

Example

```
/* FSTAT.C: This program uses _fstat to report
 * the size of a file named F_STAT.OUT.
 */
```

```
#include <io.h>
#include <fcntl.h>
#include <time.h>
#include <sys/types.h>
#include <sys/stat.h>
#include <stdio.h>
#include <stdlib.h>
#include <string.h>

void main( void )
{
   struct _stat buf;
   int fh, result;
   char buffer[] = "A line to output";

   if( (fh = _open( "f_stat.out", _O_CREAT | _O_WRONLY |
                                  _O_TRUNC )) ==  -1 )
   _write( fh, buffer, strlen( buffer ) );

   /* Get data associated with "fh": */
   result = _fstat( fh, &buf );

   /* Check if statistics are valid: */
   if( result != 0 )
      printf( "Bad file handle\n" );
   else
   {
      printf( "File size     : %ld\n", buf.st_size );

      printf( "Time modified : %s", ctime( &buf.st_ctime ) );
   }
   _close( fh );
}
```

Output

```
File size     : 0
Time modified : Tue Mar 21 15:23:08 1995
```

See Also **_access**, **_chmod**, **_filelength**, **_stat**

ftell

Gets the current position of a file pointer.

long ftell(FILE ****stream* **);

Function	Required Header	Optional Headers	Compatibility
ftell	<stdio.h>	<errno.h>	ANSI, Win 95, Win NT, Win32s, 68K, PMac

For additional compatibility information, see "Compatibility" on page ix in the Introduction.

Libraries

LIBC.LIB	Single thread static library, retail version
LIBCMT.LIB	Multithread static library, retail version
MSVCRT.LIB	Import library for MSVCRTx0.DLL, retail version
MSVCRTx0.DLL	Multithread DLL library, retail version

Return Value

ftell returns the current file position. The value returned by **ftell** may not reflect the physical byte offset for streams opened in text mode, because text mode causes carriage return–linefeed translation. Use **ftell** with **fseek** to return to file locations correctly. On error, **ftell** returns –1L and **errno** is set to one of two constants, defined in ERRNO.H. The **EBADF** constant means the *stream* argument is not a valid file-handle value or does not refer to an open file. **EINVAL** means an invalid *stream* argument was passed to the function. On devices incapable of seeking (such as terminals and printers), or when *stream* does not refer to an open file, the return value is undefined.

Parameter

stream Target **FILE** structure

Remarks

The **ftell** function gets the current position of the file pointer (if any) associated with *stream*. The position is expressed as an offset relative to the beginning of the stream.

Note that when a file is opened for appending data, the current file position is determined by the last I/O operation, not by where the next write would occur. For example, if a file is opened for an append and the last operation was a read, the file position is the point where the next read operation would start, not where the next write would start. (When a file is opened for appending, the file position is moved to end of file before any write operation.) If no I/O operation has yet occurred on a file opened for appending, the file position is the beginning of the file.

In text mode, CTRL+Z is interpreted as an end-of-file character on input. In files opened for reading/writing, **fopen** and all related routines check for a CTRL+Z at the end of the file and remove it if possible. This is done because using **ftell** and **fseek** to move within a file that ends with a CTRL+Z may cause **ftell** to behave improperly near the end of the file.

Example

```
/* FTELL.C: This program opens a file named FTELL.C
 * for reading and tries to read 100 characters. It
 * then uses ftell to determine the position of the
 * file pointer and displays this position.
 */
```

```
#include <stdio.h>

FILE *stream;

void main( void )
{
   long position;
   char list[100];
   if( (stream = fopen( "ftell.c", "rb" )) != NULL )
   {
      /* Move the pointer by reading data: */
      fread( list, sizeof( char ), 100, stream );
      /* Get position after read: */
      position = ftell( stream );
      printf( "Position after trying to read 100 bytes: %ld\n",
              position );
      fclose( stream );
   }
}
```

Output

```
Position after trying to read 100 bytes: 100
```

See Also **fgetpos**, **fseek**, **_lseek**, **_tell**

_ftime

Gets the current time.

void _ftime(struct _timeb ***timeptr*** **);**

Function	Required Header	Optional Headers	Compatibility
_ftime	<sys/types.h> and <sys/timeb.h>		Win 95, Win NT, Win32s, 68K, PMac

For additional compatibility information, see "Compatibility" on page ix in the Introduction.

Libraries	
LIBC.LIB	Single thread static library, retail version
LIBCMT.LIB	Multithread static library, retail version
MSVCRT.LIB	Import library for MSVCRTx0.DLL, retail version
MSVCRTx0.DLL	Multithread DLL library, retail version

Return Value

_ftime does not return a value, but fills in the fields of the structure pointed to by *timeptr*.

Parameter

timeptr Pointer to **_timeb** structure

Remarks

The **_ftime** function gets the current local time and stores it in the structure pointed to by *timeptr.* The **_timeb** structure is defined in SYS\TIMEB.H. It contains four fields:

dstflag Nonzero if daylight savings time is currently in effect for the local time zone. (See **_tzset** for an explanation of how daylight savings time is determined.)

millitm Fraction of a second in milliseconds.

time Time in seconds since midnight (00:00:00), January 1, 1970, coordinated universal time (UTC).

timezone Difference in minutes, moving westward, between UTC and local time. The value of *timezone* is set from the value of the global variable **_timezone** (see **_tzset**).

Example

```
/* FTIME.C: This program uses _ftime to obtain the current
 * time and then stores this time in timebuffer.
 */

#include <stdio.h>
#include <sys/timeb.h>
#include <time.h>

void main( void )
{
   struct _timeb timebuffer;
   char *timeline;

   _ftime( &timebuffer );
   timeline = ctime( & ( timebuffer.time ) );

   printf( "The time is %.19s.%hu %s", timeline, timebuffer.millitm, &timeline[20] );
}
```

Output

```
The time is Tue Mar 21 15:26:41.341 1995
```

See Also **asctime**, **ctime**, **gmtime**, **localtime**, **time**

_fullpath, _wfullpath

Create an absolute or full path name for the specified relative path name.

char *_fullpath(char *absPath*, **const char** *relPath*, **size_t** *maxLength* **);**
wchar_t *_wfullpath(wchar_t *absPath*, **const wchar_t** *relPath*, **size_t** *maxLength* **);**

Function	Required Header	Optional Headers	Compatibility
_fullpath	<stdlib.h>		Win 95, Win NT, Win32s, 68K, PMac
_wfullpath	<stdlib.h> or <wchar.h>		Win NT

For additional compatibility information, see "Compatibility" on page ix in the Introduction.

Libraries	
LIBC.LIB	Single thread static library, retail version
LIBCMT.LIB	Multithread static library, retail version
MSVCRT.LIB	Import library for MSVCRTx0.DLL, retail version
MSVCRTx0.DLL	Multithread DLL library, retail version

Return Value

Each of these functions returns a pointer to a buffer containing the absolute path name (*absPath*). If there is an error (for example, if the value passed in *relPath* includes a drive letter that is not valid or cannot be found, or if the length of the created absolute path name (*absPath*) is greater than *maxLength*) the function returns **NULL**.

Parameters

absPath Pointer to a buffer containing the absolute or full path name

relPath Relative path name

maxLength Maximum length of the absolute path name buffer (*absPath*)

Remarks

The **_fullpath** function expands the relative path name in *relPath* to its fully qualified or "absolute" path, and stores this name in *absPath.* A relative path name specifies a path to another location from the current location (such as the current working directory: "."). An absolute path name is the expansion of a relative path name that states the entire path required to reach the desired location from the root of the file system. Unlike **_makepath**, **_fullpath** can be used to obtain the absolute path name for relative paths (*relPath*) that include "./" or "../" in their names.

For example, to use C run-time routines, the application must include the header files that contain the declarations for the routines. Each header file include statement references the location of the file in a relative manner (from the application's working directory):

```
#include <stdlib.h>
```

when the absolute path (actual filesystem location) of the file may be:

```
\\machine\shareName\msvcSrc\crt\headerFiles\stdlib.h
```

_fullpath automatically handles multibyte-character string arguments as appropriate, recognizing multibyte-character sequences according to the multibyte code page currently in use. **_wfullpath** is a wide-character version of **_fullpath**; the string arguments to **_wfullpath** are wide-character strings. **_wfullpath** and **_fullpath** behave identically except that **_wfullpath** does not handle multibyte-character strings.

If the *absPath* buffer is **NULL**, **_fullpath** calls **malloc** to allocate a buffer of size **_MAX_PATH** and ignores the *maxLength* argument. It is the caller's responsibility to deallocate this buffer (using **free**) as appropriate. If the *relPath* argument specifies a disk drive, the current directory of this drive is combined with the path.

Example

```
/* FULLPATH.C: This program demonstrates how _fullpath
 * creates a full path from a partial path.
 */

#include <stdio.h>
#include <conio.h>
#include <stdlib.h>
#include <direct.h>

char full[_MAX_PATH], part[_MAX_PATH];

void main( void )
{
   while( 1 )
   {
      printf( "Enter partial path or ENTER to quit: " );
      gets( part );
      if( part[0] == 0 )
         break;

      if( _fullpath( full, part, _MAX_PATH ) != NULL )
         printf( "Full path is: %s\n", full );
      else
         printf( "Invalid path\n" );
   }
}
```

See Also **_getcwd**, **_getdcwd**, **_makepath**, **_splitpath**

_futime

Sets modification time on an open file.

int _futime(int *handle***, struct _utimbuf ***filetime* **);**

Function	Required Header	Optional Headers	Compatibility
_futime	<sys/utime.h>	<errno.h>	Win 95, Win NT, Win32s

For additional compatibility information, see "Compatibility" on page ix in the Introduction.

Libraries	
LIBC.LIB	Single thread static library, retail version
LIBCMT.LIB	Multithread static library, retail version
MSVCRT.LIB	Import library for MSVCRTx0.DLL, retail version
MSVCRTx0.DLL	Multithread DLL library, retail version

Return Value

_futime returns 0 if successful. If an error occurs, this function returns –1 and **errno** is set to **EBADF**, indicating an invalid file handle.

Parameters

handle Handle to open file

filetime Pointer to structure containing new modification date

Remarks

The **_futime** routine sets the modification date and the access time on the open file associated with *handle*. **_futime** is identical to **_utime**, except that its argument is the handle to an open file, rather than the name of a file or a path to a file. The **_utimbuf** structure contains fields for the new modification date and access time. Both fields must contain valid values.

Example

```
/* FUTIME.C: This program uses _futime to set the
 * file-modification time to the current time.
 */

#include <stdio.h>
#include <stdlib.h>
#include <fcntl.h>
#include <io.h>
#include <sys/types.h>
#include <sys/stat.h>
#include <sys/utime.h>
```

```
void main( void )
{

   int hFile;

   /* Show file time before and after. */
   system( "dir futime.c" );

   hFile = _open("futime.c", _O_RDWR);

   if( _futime( hFile, NULL ) == -1 )
      perror( "_futime failed\n" );
   else
      printf( "File time modified\n" );

   close (hFile);

   system( "dir futime.c" );

}
```

Output

```
 Volume in drive C is CDRIVE
 Volume Serial Number is 1D37-7A7A

 Directory of C:\code

05/03/95  01:30p                    601 futime.c
               1 File(s)              601 bytes
                               16,269,312 bytes free
 Volume in drive C is CDRIVE
 Volume Serial Number is 1D37-7A7A

 Directory of C:\code

05/03/95  01:36p                    601 futime.c
               1 File(s)              601 bytes
                               16,269,312 bytes free
File time modified
```

fwrite

Writes data to a stream.

size_t fwrite(const void ****buffer*, size_t** *size***, size_t** *count***, FILE ****stream* **);**

Function	Required Header	Optional Headers	Compatibility
fwrite	<stdio.h>		ANSI, Win 95, Win NT, Win32s, 68K, PMac

For additional compatibility information, see "Compatibility" on page ix in the Introduction.

Libraries

LIBC.LIB	Single thread static library, retail version
LIBCMT.LIB	Multithread static library, retail version
MSVCRT.LIB	Import library for MSVCRTx0.DLL, retail version
MSVCRTx0.DLL	Multithread DLL library, retail version

Return Value

fwrite returns the number of full items actually written, which may be less than *count* if an error occurs. Also, if an error occurs, the file-position indicator cannot be determined.

Parameters

buffer Pointer to data to be written

size Item size in bytes

count Maximum number of items to be written

stream Pointer to **FILE** structure

Remarks

The **fwrite** function writes up to *count* items, of *size* length each, from *buffer* to the output *stream.* The file pointer associated with *stream* (if there is one) is incremented by the number of bytes actually written. If *stream* is opened in text mode, each carriage return is replaced with a carriage-return–linefeed pair. The replacement has no effect on the return value.

Example

See the example for **fread**.

See Also **fread**, **_write**

_gcvt

Converts a floating-point value to a string, which it stores in a buffer.

char *_gcvt(double *value*, **int** *digits*, **char** **buffer* **);**

Routine	Required Header	Optional Headers	Compatibility
_gcvt	<stdlib.h>		Win 95, Win NT, Win32s, 68K, PMac

For additional compatibility information, see "Compatibility" on page ix in the Introduction.

Libraries

LIBC.LIB	Single thread static library, retail version
LIBCMT.LIB	Multithread static library, retail version
MSVCRT.LIB	Import library for MSVCRTx0.DLL, retail version
MSVCRTx0.DLL	Multithread DLL library, retail version

Return Value

_gcvt returns a pointer to the string of digits. There is no error return.

Parameters

value Value to be converted

digits Number of significant digits stored

buffer Storage location for result

Remarks

The **_gcvt** function converts a floating-point *value* to a character string (which includes a decimal point and a possible sign byte) and stores the string in *buffer*. The *buffer* should be large enough to accommodate the converted value plus a terminating null character, which is appended automatically. If a buffer size of *digits* + 1 is used, the function overwrites the end of the buffer. This is because the converted string includes a decimal point and can contain sign and exponent information. There is no provision for overflow. **_gcvt** attempts to produce *digits* digits in decimal format. If it cannot, it produces *digits* digits in exponential format. Trailing zeros may be suppressed in the conversion.

Example

```
/* _GCVT.C: This program converts -3.1415e5
 * to its string representation.
 */

#include <stdlib.h>
#include <stdio.h>

void main( void )
{
   char buffer[50];
   double source = -3.1415e5;
   _gcvt( source, 7, buffer );
   printf( "source: %f  buffer: '%s'\n", source, buffer );
   _gcvt( source, 7, buffer );
   printf( "source: %e  buffer: '%s'\n", source, buffer );
}
```

Output

```
source: -314150.000000  buffer: '-314150.'
source: -3.141500e+005  buffer: '-314150.'
```

See Also **atof**, **_ecvt**, **_fcvt**

getc, getwc, getchar, getwchar

Read a character from a stream (**getc**, **getwc**), or get a character from **stdin** (**getchar**, **getwchar**).

int getc(FILE ****stream* **);
wint_t getwc(FILE ****stream* **);
int getchar(void);
wint_t getwchar(void);

Routine	Required Header	Optional Headers	Compatibility
getc	<stdio.h>		ANSI, Win 95, Win NT, Win32s, 68K, PMac
getwc	<stdio.h> or <wchar.h>		ANSI, Win 95, Win NT, Win32s
getchar	<stdio.h>		ANSI, Win 95, Win NT, Win32s, 68K, PMac
getwchar	<stdio.h> or <wchar.h>		ANSI, Win 95, Win NT, Win32s

For additional compatibility information, see "Compatibility" on page ix in the Introduction.

Libraries	
LIBC.LIB	Single thread static library, retail version
LIBCMT.LIB	Multithread static library, retail version
MSVCRT.LIB	Import library for MSVCRTx0.DLL, retail version
MSVCRTx0.DLL	Multithread DLL library, retail version

Return Value

Each of these functions returns the character read. To indicate an read error or end-of-file condition, **getc** and **getchar** return **EOF**, and **getwc** and **getwchar** return **WEOF**. For **getc** and **getchar**, use **ferror** or **feof** to check for an error or for end of file.

Parameter

stream Input stream

Remarks

Each of these routines reads a single character from a file at the current position and increments the associated file pointer (if defined) to point to the next character. In the case of **getc** and **getwc**, the file is associated with *stream* (see "Choosing Between Functions and Macros" on page xii). Routine-specific remarks follow.

Routine	Remarks
getc	Same as **fgetc**, but implemented as a function and as a macro.
getwc	Wide-character version of **getc**. Reads a multibyte character or a wide character according to whether *stream* is opened in text mode or binary mode.
getchar	Same as **_fgetchar**, but implemented as a function and as a macro.
getwchar	Wide-character version of **getchar**. Reads a multibyte character or a wide character according to whether *stream* is opened in text mode or binary mode.

Example

```
/* GETC.C: This program uses getchar to read a single line
 * of input from stdin, places this input in buffer, then
 * terminates the string before printing it to the screen.
 */

#include <stdio.h>

void main( void )
{
   char buffer[81];
   int i, ch;

   printf( "Enter a line: " );

   /* Read in single line from "stdin": */
   for( i = 0; (i < 80) &&  ((ch = getchar()) != EOF)
                        && (ch != '\n'); i++ )
      buffer[i] = (char)ch;

   /* Terminate string with null character: */
   buffer[i] = '\0';
   printf( "%s\n", buffer );
}
```

Output

```
Enter a line: This is a test
This is a test
```

See Also **fgetc**, **_getch**, **putc**, **ungetc**

_getch, _getche

Get a character from the console without echo (**_getch**) or with echo (**_getche**).

int _getch(void);
int _getche(void);

Routine	Required Header	Optional Headers	Compatibility
_getch	<conio.h>		Win 95, Win NT, Win32s
_getche	<conio.h>		Win 95, Win NT, Win32s

For additional compatibility information, see "Compatibility" on page ix in the Introduction.

Libraries	
LIBC.LIB	Single thread static library, retail version
LIBCMT.LIB	Multithread static library, retail version
MSVCRT.LIB	Import library for MSVCRTx0.DLL, retail version
MSVCRTx0.DLL	Multithread DLL library, retail version

Return Value

Both **_getch** and **_getche** return the character read. There is no error return.

Remarks

The **_getch** function reads a single character from the console without echoing. **_getche** reads a single character from the console and echoes the character read. Neither function can be used to read CTRL+C. When reading a function key or an arrow key, **_getch** and **_getche** must be called twice; the first call returns 0 or 0xE0, and the second call returns the actual key code.

Example

```
/* GETCH.C: This program reads characters from
 * the keyboard until it receives a 'Y' or 'y'.
 */

#include <conio.h>
#include <ctype.h>

void main( void )
{
   int ch;

   _cputs( "Type 'Y' when finished typing keys: " );
   do
```

```
    {
        ch = _getch();
        ch = toupper( ch );
    } while( ch != 'Y' );

    _putch( ch );
    _putch( '\r' );    /* Carriage return */
    _putch( '\n' );    /* Line feed       */
}
```

Output

```
Type 'Y' when finished typing keys: Y
```

See Also **_cgets**, **getc**, **_ungetch**

_getcwd, _wgetcwd

Get the current working directory.

char *_getcwd(char ****buffer*, int** *maxlen* **);**
wchar_t *_wgetcwd(wchar_t ****buffer*, int** *maxlen* **);**

Routine	Required Header	Optional Headers	Compatibility
_getcwd	<direct.h>		Win 95, Win NT, Win32s, 68K, PMac
_wgetcwd	<direct.h> or <wchar.h>		Win NT

For additional compatibility information, see "Compatibility" on page ix in the Introduction.

Libraries	
LIBC.LIB	Single thread static library, retail version
LIBCMT.LIB	Multithread static library, retail version
MSVCRT.LIB	Import library for MSVCRTx0.DLL, retail version
MSVCRTx0.DLL	Multithread DLL library, retail version

Return Value

Each of these functions returns a pointer to *buffer*. A **NULL** return value indicates an error, and **errno** is set either to **ENOMEM**, indicating that there is insufficient memory to allocate *maxlen* bytes (when a **NULL** argument is given as *buffer*), or to **ERANGE**, indicating that the path is longer than *maxlen* characters.

Parameters

buffer Storage location for path

maxlen Maximum length of path

Remarks

The **_getcwd** function gets the full path of the current working directory for the default drive and stores it at *buffer*. The integer argument *maxlen* specifies the maximum length for the path. An error occurs if the length of the path (including the terminating null character) exceeds *maxlen*. The *buffer* argument can be **NULL**; a buffer of at least size *maxlen* (more only if necessary) will automatically be allocated, using **malloc**, to store the path. This buffer can later be freed by calling **free** and passing it the **_getcwd** return value (a pointer to the allocated buffer).

_getcwd returns a string that represents the path of the current working directory. If the current working directory is the root, the string ends with a backslash (\). If the current working directory is a directory other than the root, the string ends with the directory name and not with a backslash.

_wgetcwd is a wide-character version of **_getcwd**; the *buffer* argument and return value of **_wgetcwd** are wide-character strings. **_wgetcwd** and **_getcwd** behave identically otherwise.

Example

```
// GETCWD.C
/* This program places the name of the current directory in the
 * buffer array, then displays the name of the current directory
 * on the screen. Specifying a length of _MAX_PATH leaves room
 * for the longest legal path name.
 */

#include <direct.h>
#include <stdlib.h>
#include <stdio.h>

void main( void )
{
   char buffer[_MAX_PATH];

   /* Get the current working directory: */
   if( _getcwd( buffer, _MAX_PATH ) == NULL )
      perror( "_getcwd error" );
   else
      printf( "%s\n", buffer );
}
```

Output

```
C:\code
```

See Also **_chdir**, **_mkdir**, **_rmdir**

_getdcwd, _wgetdcwd

Get full path name of current working directory on the specified drive.

char *_getdcwd(int *drive*, **char** **buffer*, **int** *maxlen* **);**
wchar_t *_wgetdcwd(int *drive*, **wchar_t** **buffer*, **int** *maxlen* **);**

Routine	Required Header	Optional Headers	Compatibility
_getdcwd	<direct.h>		Win 95, Win NT, Win32s
_wgetdcwd	<direct.h> or <wchar.h>		Win NT

For additional compatibility information, see "Compatibility" on page ix in the Introduction.

Libraries	
LIBC.LIB	Single thread static library, retail version
LIBCMT.LIB	Multithread static library, retail version
MSVCRT.LIB	Import library for MSVCRTx0.DLL, retail version
MSVCRTx0.DLL	Multithread DLL library, retail version

Return Value

Each of these functions returns *buffer*. A **NULL** return value indicates an error, and **errno** is set either to **ENOMEM**, indicating that there is insufficient memory to allocate *maxlen* bytes (when a **NULL** argument is given as *buffer*), or to **ERANGE**, indicating that the path is longer than *maxlen* characters.

Parameters

drive Disk drive

buffer Storage location for path

maxlen Maximum length of path

Remarks

The **_getdcwd** function gets the full path of the current working directory on the specified drive and stores it at *buffer*. An error occurs if the length of the path (including the terminating null character) exceeds *maxlen*. The *drive* argument specifies the drive (0 = default drive, 1 = A, 2 = B, and so on). The *buffer* argument can be **NULL**; a buffer of at least size *maxlen* (more only if necessary) will automatically be allocated, using **malloc**, to store the path. This buffer can later be freed by calling **free** and passing it the **_getdcwd** return value (a pointer to the allocated buffer).

_getdcwd returns a string that represents the path of the current working directory. If the current working directory is set to the root, the string ends with a backslash (\ ). If the current working directory is set to a directory other than the root, the string ends with the name of the directory and not with a backslash.

_wgetdcwd is a wide-character version of **_getdcwd**; the *buffer* argument and return value of **_wgetdcwd** are wide-character strings. **_wgetdcwd** and **_getdcwd** behave identically otherwise.

Example

See the example for **_getdrive**.

See Also **_chdir**, **_getcwd**, **_getdrive**, **_mkdir**, **_rmdir**

_getdrive

Gets the current disk drive.

int _getdrive(void);

Routine	Required Header	Optional Headers	Compatibility
_getdrive	<direct.h>		Win 95, Win NT, Win32s

For additional compatibility information, see "Compatibility" on page ix in the Introduction.

Libraries	
LIBC.LIB	Single thread static library, retail version
LIBCMT.LIB	Multithread static library, retail version
MSVCRT.LIB	Import library for MSVCRTx0.DLL, retail version
MSVCRTx0.DLL	Multithread DLL library, retail version

Return Value

_getdrive returns the current (default) drive (1=A, 2=B, and so on). There is no error return.

Example

```
/* GETDRIVE.C illustrates drive functions including:
 *      _getdrive       _chdrive        _getdcwd
 */

#include <stdio.h>
#include <conio.h>
#include <direct.h>
#include <stdlib.h>
#include <ctype.h>

void main( void )
```

```
{
   int ch, drive, curdrive;
   static char path[_MAX_PATH];

   /* Save current drive. */
   curdrive = _getdrive();

   printf( "Available drives are: \n" );

   /* If we can switch to the drive, it exists. */
   for( drive = 1; drive <= 26; drive++ )
      if( !_chdrive( drive ) )
         printf( "%c: ", drive + 'A' - 1 );

   while( 1 )
   {
      printf( "\nType drive letter to check or ESC to quit: " );
      ch = _getch();
      if( ch == 27 )
         break;
      if( isalpha( ch ) )
         _putch( ch );
      if( _getdcwd( toupper( ch ) - 'A' + 1, path, _MAX_PATH ) != NULL )
         printf( "\nCurrent directory on that drive is %s\n", path );
   }

   /* Restore original drive.*/
   _chdrive( curdrive );
   printf( "\n" );
}
```

Output

```
Available drives are:
A: B: C: L: M: O: U: V:
Type drive letter to check or ESC to quit: c
Current directory on that drive is C:\CODE

Type drive letter to check or ESC to quit: m
Current directory on that drive is M:\

Type drive letter to check or ESC to quit:
```

See Also **_chdrive**, **_getcwd**, **_getdcwd**

getenv, _wgetenv

Get a value from the current environment.

char *getenv(const char *varname* **);**
wchar_t *_wgetenv(const wchar_t *varname* **);**

Routine	Required Header	Optional Headers	Compatibility
getenv	<stdlib.h>		ANSI, Win 95, Win NT, Win32s, 68K, PMac
_wgetenv	<stdlib.h> or <wchar.h>		Win 95, Win NT, Win32s

For additional compatibility information, see "Compatibility" on page ix in the Introduction.

Libraries	
LIBC.LIB	Single thread static library, retail version
LIBCMT.LIB	Multithread static library, retail version
MSVCRT.LIB	Import library for MSVCRTx0.DLL, retail version
MSVCRTx0.DLL	Multithread DLL library, retail version

Return Value

Each of these functions returns a pointer to the environment table entry containing *varname*. It is not safe to modify the value of the environment variable using the returned pointer. Use the **_putenv** function to modify the value of an environment variable. The return value is **NULL** if *varname* is not found in the environment table.

Parameter

varname Environment variable name

Remarks

The **getenv** function searches the list of environment variables for *varname*. **getenv** is not case sensitive in Windows NT and Windows 95. **getenv** and **_putenv** use the copy of the environment pointed to by the global variable **_environ** to access the environment. **getenv** operates only on the data structures accessible to the run-time library and not on the environment "segment" created for the process by the operating system. Therefore, programs that use the *envp* argument to **main** or **wmain** may retrieve invalid information. For more information on **wmain**, see "Using **wmain**" in *C Language Reference*.

_wgetenv is a wide-character version of **getenv**; the argument and return value of **_wgetenv** are wide-character strings. The **_wenviron** global variable is a wide-character version of **_environ**.

In an MBCS program (for example, in an SBCS ASCII program), **_wenviron** is initially **NULL** because the environment is composed of multibyte-character strings. Then, on the first call to **_wputenv**, or on the first call to **_wgetenv** if an (MBCS) environment already exists, a corresponding wide-character string environment is created and is then pointed to by **_wenviron**.

Similarly in a Unicode (**_wmain**) program, **_environ** is initially **NULL** because the environment is composed of wide-character strings. Then, on the first call to **_putenv**, or on the first call to **getenv** if a (Unicode) environment already exists, a corresponding MBCS environment is created and is then pointed to by **_environ**.

When two copies of the environment (MBCS and Unicode) exist simultaneously in a program, the run-time system must maintain both copies, resulting in slower execution time. For example, whenever you call **_putenv**, a call to **_wputenv** is also executed automatically, so that the two environment strings correspond.

Caution In rare instances, when the run-time system is maintaining both a Unicode version and a multibyte version of the environment, these two environment versions may not correspond exactly. This is because, although any unique multibyte-character string maps to a unique Unicode string, the mapping from a unique Unicode string to a multibyte-character string is not necessarily unique. For more information, see "**_environ, _wenviron**" on page 42.

To check or change the value of the **TZ** environment variable, use **getenv**, **_putenv** and **_tzset** as necessary. For more information about **TZ**, see **_tzset** and see "**_daylight**, **timezone**, and **_tzname**" on page 40.

Example

```
/* GETENV.C: This program uses getenv to retrieve
 * the LIB environment variable and then uses
 * _putenv to change it to a new value.
 */

#include <stdlib.h>
#include <stdio.h>

void main( void )
{
   char *libvar;

   /* Get the value of the LIB environment variable. */
   libvar = getenv( "LIB" );

   if( libvar != NULL )
      printf( "Original LIB variable is: %s\n", libvar );
```

```
    /* Attempt to change path. Note that this only affects the environment
     * variable of the current process. The command processor's environment
     * is not changed.
     */
    _putenv( "LIB=c:\\mylib;c:\\yourlib" );

    /* Get new value. */
    libvar = getenv( "LIB" );

    if( libvar != NULL )
       printf( "New LIB variable is: %s\n", libvar );
}
```

Output

```
Original LIB variable is: C:\MSDEV
New LIB variable is: c:\mylib;c:\yourlib
```

See Also **_putenv**

_getmbcp

int _getmbcp(void);

Routine	Required Header	Optional Headers	Compatibility
_getmbcp	<mbctype.h>		Win 95, Win NT, Win32s, 68K, PMac

For additional compatibility information, see "Compatibility" on page ix in the Introduction.

Libraries	
LIBC.LIB	Single thread static library, retail version
LIBCMT.LIB	Multithread static library, retail version
MSVCRT.LIB	Import library for MSVCRTx0.DLL, retail version
MSVCRTx0.DLL	Multithread DLL library, retail version

Return Value

_getmbcp returns the current multibyte code page. A return value of 0 indicates that a single byte code page is in use.

See Also **_setmbcp**

_get_osfhandle

Gets operating-system file handle associated with existing stream **FILE** pointer.

long _get_osfhandle(int *filehandle* **);**

Routine	Required Header	Optional Headers	Compatibility
_get_osfhandle	<io.h>		Win 95, Win NT, Win32s, 68K, PMac

For additional compatibility information, see "Compatibility" on page ix in the Introduction.

Libraries	
LIBC.LIB	Single thread static library, retail version
LIBCMT.LIB	Multithread static library, retail version
MSVCRT.LIB	Import library for MSVCRTx0.DLL, retail version
MSVCRTx0.DLL	Multithread DLL library, retail version

Return Value

If successful, **_get_osfhandle** returns an operating-system file handle corresponding to *filehandle*. Otherwise, it returns –1 and sets **errno** to **EBADF**, indicating an invalid file handle.

Parameter

filehandle User file handle

Remarks

The **_get_osfhandle** function returns *filehandle* if it is in range and if it is internally marked as free.

See Also **_close**, **_creat**, **_dup**, **_open**

_getpid

Gets the process identification.

int _getpid(void);

Routine	Required Header	Optional Headers	Compatibility
_getpid	<process.h>		Win 95, Win NT, Win32s, 68K, PMac

For additional compatibility information, see "Compatibility" on page ix in the Introduction.

Libraries

LIBC.LIB	Single thread static library, retail version
LIBCMT.LIB	Multithread static library, retail version
MSVCRT.LIB	Import library for MSVCRTx0.DLL, retail version
MSVCRTx0.DLL	Multithread DLL library, retail version

Return Value

_getpid returns the process ID obtained from the system. There is no error return.

Remarks

The **_getpid** function obtains the process ID from the system. The process ID uniquely identifies the calling process.

Example

```
/* GETPID.C: This program uses _getpid to obtain
 * the process ID and then prints the ID.
 */

#include <stdio.h>
#include <process.h>

void main( void )
{
   /* If run from command line, shows different ID for
    * command line than for operating system shell.
    */
   printf( "\nProcess id: %d\n", _getpid() );
}
```

Output

```
Process id: 193
```

See Also **_mktemp**

gets, getws

Get a line from the **stdin** stream.

char *gets(char ***buffer* **);
wchar_t *getws(wchar_t ***buffer* **);

Routine	Required Header	Optional Headers	Compatibility
gets	<stdio.h>		ANSI, Win 95, Win NT, Win32s, 68K, PMac
getws	<stdio.h> or <wchar.h>		ANSI, Win 95, Win NT, Win32s

For additional compatibility information, see "Compatibility" on page ix in the Introduction.

Libraries

LIBC.LIB	Single thread static library, retail version
LIBCMT.LIB	Multithread static library, retail version
MSVCRT.LIB	Import library for MSVCRTx0.DLL, retail version
MSVCRTx0.DLL	Multithread DLL library, retail version

Return Value

Each of these functions returns its argument if successful. A **NULL** pointer indicates an error or end-of-file condition. Use **ferror** or **feof** to determine which one has occurred.

Parameter

buffer Storage location for input string

Remarks

The **gets** function reads a line from the standard input stream **stdin** and stores it in *buffer*. The line consists of all characters up to and including the first newline character ('\n'). **gets** then replaces the newline character with a null character ('\0') before returning the line. In contrast, the **fgets** function retains the newline character. **getws** is a wide-character version of **gets**; its argument and return value are wide-character strings.

Example

```
/* GETS.C */

#include <stdio.h>

void main( void )
{
   char line[81];

   printf( "Input a string: " );
   gets( line );
   printf( "The line entered was: %s\n", line );
}
```

Output

```
Input a string: Hello!
The line entered was: Hello!
```

See Also **fgets**, **fputs**, **puts**

_getw

Gets an integer from a stream.

int _getw(FILE ***stream*** **);**

Routine	Required Header	Optional Headers	Compatibility
_getw	<stdio.h>		Win 95, Win NT, Win32s, 68K, PMac

For additional compatibility information, see "Compatibility" on page ix in the Introduction.

Libraries	
LIBC.LIB	Single thread static library, retail version
LIBCMT.LIB	Multithread static library, retail version
MSVCRT.LIB	Import library for MSVCRTx0.DLL, retail version
MSVCRTx0.DLL	Multithread DLL library, retail version

Return Value

_getw returns the integer value read. A return value of **EOF** indicates either an error or end of file. However, because the **EOF** value is also a legitimate integer value, use **feof** or **ferror** to verify an end-of-file or error condition.

Parameter

stream Pointer to **FILE** structure

Remarks

The **_getw** function reads the next binary value of type **int** from the file associated with *stream* and increments the associated file pointer (if there is one) to point to the next unread character. **_getw** does not assume any special alignment of items in the stream. Problems with porting may occur with **_getw** because the size of the **int** type and the ordering of bytes within the **int** type differ across systems.

Example

```
/* GETW.C: This program uses _getw to read a word
 * from a stream, then performs an error check.
 */

#include <stdio.h>
#include <stdlib.h>

void main( void )
{
   FILE *stream;
   int i;
```

```
    if( (stream = fopen( "getw.c", "rb" )) == NULL )
       printf( "Couldn't open file\n" );
    else
    {
       /* Read a word from the stream: */
       i = _getw( stream );

       /* If there is an error... */
       if( ferror( stream ) )
       {
          printf( "_getw failed\n" );
          clearerr( stream );
       }
       else
          printf( "First data word in file: 0x%.4x\n", i );
       fclose( stream );
    }
}
```

Output

```
First data word in file: 0x47202a2f
```

See Also **_putw**

gmtime

Converts a time value to a structure.

struct tm *gmtime(const time_t ***timer*** **);**

Routine	Required Header	Optional Headers	Compatibility
gmtime	<time.h>		ANSI, Win 95, Win NT, Win32s, 68K, PMac

For additional compatibility information, see "Compatibility" on page ix in the Introduction.

Libraries	
LIBC.LIB	Single thread static library, retail version
LIBCMT.LIB	Multithread static library, retail version
MSVCRT.LIB	Import library for MSVCRTx0.DLL, retail version
MSVCRTx0.DLL	Multithread DLL library, retail version

Return Value

gmtime returns a pointer to a structure of type **tm**. The fields of the returned structure hold the evaluated value of the *timer* argument in UTC rather than in local time. Each of the structure fields is of type **int**, as follows:

tm_sec Seconds after minute (0–59)

tm_min Minutes after hour (0–59)

tm_hour Hours since midnight (0–23)

tm_mday Day of month (1–31)

tm_mon Month (0–11; January = 0)

tm_year Year (current year minus 1900)

tm_wday Day of week (0–6; Sunday = 0)

tm_yday Day of year (0–365; January 1 = 0)

tm_isdst Always 0 for **gmtime**

The **gmtime**, **mktime**, and **localtime** functions use the same single, statically allocated structure to hold their results. Each call to one of these functions destroys the result of any previous call. If *timer* represents a date before midnight, January 1, 1970, **gmtime** returns **NULL**. There is no error return.

Parameter

timer Pointer to stored time. The time is represented as seconds elapsed since midnight (00:00:00), January 1, 1970, coordinated universal time (UTC).

Remarks

The **gmtime** function breaks down the *timer* value and stores it in a statically allocated structure of type **tm**, defined in TIME.H. The value of *timer* is usually obtained from a call to the **time** function.

Note The target environment should try to determine whether daylight savings time is in effect.

Example

```
/* GMTIME.C: This program uses gmtime to convert a long-
 * integer representation of coordinated universal time
 * to a structure named newtime, then uses asctime to
 * convert this structure to an output string.
 */

#include <time.h>
#include <stdio.h>

void main( void )
{
   struct tm *newtime;
   long ltime;

   time( &ltime );
```

```
   /* Obtain coordinated universal time: */
   newtime = gmtime( &ltime );
   printf( "Coordinated universal time is %s\n",
                               asctime( newtime ) );
}
```

Output

```
Coordinated universal time is Tue Mar 23 02:00:56 1993
```

See Also **asctime**, **ctime**, **_ftime**, **localtime**, **mktime**, **time**

_heapadd

Adds memory to the heap.

int _heapadd(**void** ***memblock*, size_t** *size* **);**

Routine	Required Header	Optional Headers	Compatibility
_heapadd	<malloc.h>	<errno.h>	68K, PMac

For additional compatibility information, see "Compatibility" on page ix in the Introduction.

Libraries	
LIBC.LIB	Single thread static library, retail version
LIBCMT.LIB	Multithread static library, retail version
MSVCRT.LIB	Import library for MSVCRTx0.DLL, retail version
MSVCRTx0.DLL	Multithread DLL library, retail version

Return Value

If successful, **_heapadd** returns 0; otherwise, the function returns –1 and sets **errno** to **ENOSYS**.

Parameters

memblock Pointer to heap memory

size Size in bytes of memory to add

Remarks

The **_heapadd** function adds an unused piece of memory to the heap.

Note In Visual C++ Version 4.0, the underlying heap structure has been moved to the C run-time libraries to support the new debugging features. As a result, **_heapadd** is no longer supported on any Win32 platform and will immediately return –1 when called from an application of this type.

See Also **free**, **_heapchk**, **_heapmin**, **_heapset**, **_heapwalk**, **malloc**, **realloc**

_heapchk

Runs consistency checks on the heap.

int _heapchk(void);

Routine	Required Header	Optional Headers	Compatibility
_heapchk	<malloc.h>	<errno.h>	Win NT, 68K, PMac

For additional compatibility information, see "Compatibility" on page ix in the Introduction.

Libraries	
LIBC.LIB	Single thread static library, retail version
LIBCMT.LIB	Multithread static library, retail version
MSVCRT.LIB	Import library for MSVCRTx0.DLL, retail version
MSVCRTx0.DLL	Multithread DLL library, retail version

Return Value

_heapchk returns one of the following integer manifest constants defined in MALLOC.H:

_HEAPBADBEGIN Initial header information is bad or cannot be found

_HEAPBADNODE Bad node has been found or heap is damaged

_HEAPBADPTR Pointer into heap is not valid

_HEAPEMPTY Heap has not been initialized

_HEAPOK Heap appears to be consistent

In addition, if an error occurs, **_heapchk** sets **errno** to **ENOSYS**.

Remarks

The **_heapchk** function helps debug heap-related problems by checking for minimal consistency of the heap.

Note In Visual C++ Version 4.0, the underlying heap structure has been moved to the C run-time libraries to support the new debugging features. As a result, the only Win32 platform that is supported by **_heapchk** is Windows NT. The function returns **_HEAPOK** and sets **errno** to **ENOSYS**, when it is called by any other Win32 platform.

Example

```
/* HEAPCHK.C: This program checks the heap for
 * consistency and prints an appropriate message.
 */

#include <malloc.h>
#include <stdio.h>
```

```
void main( void )
{
   int  heapstatus;
   char *buffer;

   /* Allocate and deallocate some memory */
   if( (buffer = (char *)malloc( 100 )) != NULL )
      free( buffer );

   /* Check heap status */
   heapstatus = _heapchk();
   switch( heapstatus )
   {
   case _HEAPOK:
      printf(" OK - heap is fine\n" );
      break;
   case _HEAPEMPTY:
      printf(" OK - heap is empty\n" );
      break;
   case _HEAPBADBEGIN:
      printf( "ERROR - bad start of heap\n" );
      break;
   case _HEAPBADNODE:
      printf( "ERROR - bad node in heap\n" );
      break;
   }
}
```

Output

```
OK - heap is fine
```

See Also **_heapadd**, **_heapmin**, **_heapset**, **_heapwalk**

_heapmin

Releases unused heap memory to the operating system.

int _heapmin(void);

Routine	Required Header	Optional Headers	Compatibility
_heapmin	<malloc.h>	<errno.h>	Win NT, 68K, PMac

For additional compatibility information, see "Compatibility" on page ix in the Introduction.

Libraries	
LIBC.LIB	Single thread static library, retail version
LIBCMT.LIB	Multithread static library, retail version
MSVCRT.LIB	Import library for MSVCRTx0.DLL, retail version
MSVCRTx0.DLL	Multithread DLL library, retail version

Return Value

If successful, **_heapmin** returns 0; otherwise, the function returns –1 and sets **errno** to **ENOSYS**.

Remarks

The **_heapmin** function minimizes the heap by releasing unused heap memory to the operating system.

Note In Visual C++ Version 4.0, the underlying heap structure has been moved to the C run-time libraries to support the new debugging features. As a result, the only Win32 platform that is supported by **_heapmin** is Windows NT. The function returns –1 and sets **errno** to **ENOSYS**, when it is called by any other Win32 platform.

See Also **free**, **_heapadd**, **_heapchk**, **_heapset**, **_heapwalk**, **malloc**

_heapset

Checks heaps for minimal consistency and sets the free entries to a specified value.

int _heapset(unsigned int ***fill*** **);**

Routine	Required Header	Optional Headers	Compatibility
_heapset	<malloc.h>	<errno.h>	Win NT, 68K, PMac

For additional compatibility information, see "Compatibility" on page ix in the Introduction.

Libraries	
LIBC.LIB	Single thread static library, retail version
LIBCMT.LIB	Multithread static library, retail version
MSVCRT.LIB	Import library for MSVCRTx0.DLL, retail version
MSVCRTx0.DLL	Multithread DLL library, retail version

Return Value

_heapset returns one of the following integer manifest constants defined in MALLOC.H:

_HEAPBADBEGIN Initial header information invalid or not found

_HEAPBADNODE Heap damaged or bad node found

_HEAPEMPTY Heap not initialized

_HEAPOK Heap appears to be consistent

In addition, if an error occurs, **_heapset** sets **errno** to **ENOSYS**.

Parameter

fill Fill character

Remarks

The **_heapset** function shows free memory locations or nodes that have been unintentionally overwritten.

_heapset checks for minimal consistency on the heap, then sets each byte of the heap's free entries to the *fill* value. This known value shows which memory locations of the heap contain free nodes and which contain data that were unintentionally written to freed memory.

Note In Visual C++ Version 4.0, the underlying heap structure has been moved to the C run-time libraries to support the new debugging features. As a result, the only Win32 platform that is supported by **_heapset** is Windows NT. The function returns **_HEAPOK** and sets **errno** to **ENOSYS**, when it is called by any other Win32 platform.

Example

```
/* HEAPSET.C: This program checks the heap and
 * fills in free entries with the character 'Z'.
 */

#include <malloc.h>
#include <stdio.h>
#include <stdlib.h>

void main( void )
{
   int heapstatus;
   char *buffer;

   if( (buffer = malloc( 1 )) == NULL ) /* Make sure heap is */
      exit( 0 );                        /*    initialized    */
   heapstatus = _heapset( 'Z' );        /* Fill in free entries */
   switch( heapstatus )
   {
   case _HEAPOK:
      printf( "OK - heap is fine\n" );
      break;
   case _HEAPEMPTY:
      printf( "OK - heap is empty\n" );
      break;
   case _HEAPBADBEGIN:
      printf( "ERROR - bad start of heap\n" );
      break;
```

```
      case _HEAPBADNODE:
         printf( "ERROR - bad node in heap\n" );
         break;
   }
   free( buffer );
}
```

Output

```
OK - heap is fine
```

See Also **_heapadd**, **_heapchk**, **_heapmin**, **_heapwalk**

_heapwalk

Traverses the heap and returns information about the next entry.

int _heapwalk(_HEAPINFO ***_entryinfo_ **);

Routine	Required Header	Optional Headers	Compatibility
_heapwalk	<malloc.h>	<errno.h>	Win NT, 68K, PMac

For additional compatibility information, see "Compatibility" on page ix in the Introduction.

Libraries	
LIBC.LIB	Single thread static library, retail version
LIBCMT.LIB	Multithread static library, retail version
MSVCRT.LIB	Import library for MSVCRTx0.DLL, retail version
MSVCRTx0.DLL	Multithread DLL library, retail version

Return Value

_heapwalk returns one of the following integer manifest constants defined in MALLOC.H:

_HEAPBADBEGIN Initial header information invalid or not found

_HEAPBADNODE Heap damaged or bad node found

_HEAPBADPTR **_pentry** field of **_HEAPINFO** structure does not contain valid pointer into heap

_HEAPEND End of heap reached successfully

_HEAPEMPTY Heap not initialized

_HEAPOK No errors so far; **_HEAPINFO** structure contains information about next entry.

In addition, if an error occurs, **_heapwalk** sets **errno** to **ENOSYS**.

Parameter

entryinfo Buffer to contain heap information

Remarks

The **_heapwalk** function helps debug heap-related problems in programs. The function walks through the heap, traversing one entry per call, and returns a pointer to a structure of type **_HEAPINFO** that contains information about the next heap entry. The **_HEAPINFO** type, defined in MALLOC.H, contains the following elements:

int *_pentry Heap entry pointer

size_t _size Size of heap entry

int _useflag Flag that indicates whether heap entry is in use

A call to **_heapwalk** that returns **_HEAPOK** stores the size of the entry in the **_size** field and sets the **_useflag** field to either **_FREEENTRY** or **_USEDENTRY** (both are constants defined in MALLOC.H). To obtain this information about the first entry in the heap, pass **_heapwalk** a pointer to a **_HEAPINFO** structure whose **_pentry** member is **NULL**.

Note In Visual C++ Version 4.0, the underlying heap structure has been moved to the C run-time libraries to support the new debugging features. As a result, the only Win32 platform that is supported by **_heapwalk** is Windows NT. The function returns **_HEAPOK** and sets **errno** to **ENOSYS**, when it is called by any other Win32 platform.

Example

```
/* HEAPWALK.C: This program "walks" the heap, starting
 * at the beginning (_pentry = NULL). It prints out each
 * heap entry's use, location, and size. It also prints
 * out information about the overall state of the heap as
 * soon as _heapwalk returns a value other than _HEAPOK.
 */

#include <stdio.h>
#include <malloc.h>

void heapdump( void );

void main( void )
{
   char *buffer;

   heapdump();
   if( (buffer = malloc( 59 )) != NULL )
   {
      heapdump();
      free( buffer );
   }
   heapdump();
}
```

```
void heapdump( void )
{
   _HEAPINFO hinfo;
   int heapstatus;
   hinfo._pentry = NULL;
   while( ( heapstatus = _heapwalk( &hinfo ) ) == _HEAPOK )
   { printf( "%6s block at %Fp of size %4.4X\n",
         ( hinfo._useflag == _USEDENTRY ? "USED" : "FREE" ),
           hinfo._pentry, hinfo._size );
   }

   switch( heapstatus )
   {
   case _HEAPEMPTY:
      printf( "OK - empty heap\n" );
      break;
   case _HEAPEND:
      printf( "OK - end of heap\n" );
      break;
   case _HEAPBADPTR:
      printf( "ERROR - bad pointer to heap\n" );
      break;
   case _HEAPBADBEGIN:
      printf( "ERROR - bad start of heap\n" );
      break;
   case _HEAPBADNODE:
      printf( "ERROR - bad node in heap\n" );
      break;
   }
}
```

Output

```
USED block at 002C0004 of size 0014
USED block at 002C001C of size 0054
USED block at 002C0074 of size 0024
USED block at 002C009C of size 0010
USED block at 002C00B0 of size 0018
USED block at 002C00CC of size 000C
USED block at 002C00DC of size 001C
USED block at 002C00FC of size 0010
USED block at 002C0110 of size 0014
USED block at 002C0128 of size 0010
USED block at 002C013C of size 0028
USED block at 002C0168 of size 0088
USED block at 002C01F4 of size 001C
USED block at 002C0214 of size 0014
USED block at 002C022C of size 0010
USED block at 002C0240 of size 0014
USED block at 002C0258 of size 0010
USED block at 002C026C of size 000C
USED block at 002C027C of size 0010
USED block at 002C0290 of size 0014
USED block at 002C02A8 of size 0010
```

```
  USED block at 002C02BC of size 0010
  USED block at 002C02D0 of size 1000
  FREE block at 002C12D4 of size ED2C
OK - end of heap
```

See Also **_heapadd**, **_heapchk**, **_heapmin**, **_heapset**

_hypot

Calculates the hypotenuse.

double _hypot(double *x*, **double** *y* **);**

Routine	Required Header	Optional Headers	Compatibility
_hypot	<math.h>		Win 95, Win NT, Win32s, 68K, PMac

For additional compatibility information, see "Compatibility" on page ix in the Introduction.

Libraries	
LIBC.LIB	Single thread static library, retail version
LIBCMT.LIB	Multithread static library, retail version
MSVCRT.LIB	Import library for MSVCRTx0.DLL, retail version
MSVCRTx0.DLL	Multithread DLL library, retail version

Return Value

_hypot returns the length of the hypotenuse if successful or INF (infinity) on overflow. The **errno** variable is set to **ERANGE** on overflow. You can modify error handling with **_matherr**.

Parameters

x, *y* Floating-point values

Remarks

The **_hypot** function calculates the length of the hypotenuse of a right triangle, given the length of the two sides *x* and *y*. A call to **_hypot** is equivalent to the square root of $x^2 + y^2$.

Example

```
/* HYPOT.C: This program prints the
 * hypotenuse of a right triangle.
 */

#include <math.h>
#include <stdio.h>
```

```
void main( void )
{
   double x = 3.0, y = 4.0;

   printf( "If a right triangle has sides %2.1f and %2.1f, "
           "its hypotenuse is %2.1f\n", x, y, _hypot( x, y ) );
}
```

Output

```
If a right triangle has sides 3.0 and 4.0, its hypotenuse is 5.0
```

See Also **_cabs**, **_matherr**

_inp, _inpw, _inpd

Input a byte (**_inp**), a word (**_inpw**), or a double word (**_inpd**) from a port.

int _inp(unsigned short *port* **);**
unsigned short _inpw(unsigned short *port* **);**
unsigned long _inpd(unsigned short *port* **);**

Routine	Required Header	Optional Headers	Compatibility
_inp	<conio.h>		Win 95, Win32s
_inpw	<conio.h>		Win 95, Win32s
_inpd	<conio.h>		Win 95, Win32s

For additional compatibility information, see "Compatibility" on page ix in the Introduction.

Libraries	
LIBC.LIB	Single thread static library, retail version
LIBCMT.LIB	Multithread static library, retail version
MSVCRT.LIB	Import library for MSVCRTx0.DLL, retail version
MSVCRTx0.DLL	Multithread DLL library, retail version

Return Value

The functions return the byte, word, or double word read from *port*. There is no error return.

Parameter

port Port number

Remarks

The **_inp**, **_inpw**, and **_inpd** functions read a byte, a word, and a double word, respectively, from the specified input port. The input value can be any unsigned short integer in the range 0–65,535.

See Also _**outp**

is, isw Routines

isalnum, iswalnum	**islower, iswlower**
isalpha, iswalpha	**isprint, iswprint**
_ _isascii, iswascii	**ispunct, iswpunct**
iscntrl, iswcntrl	**isspace, iswspace**
_ _iscsym, _ _iscsymf	**isupper, iswupper**
isdigit, iswdigit	**isxdigit, iswxdigit**
isgraph, iswgraph	**iswctype**

Remarks

These routines test characters for specified conditions.

The **is** routines produce meaningful results for any integer argument from –1 (**EOF**) to **UCHAR_MAX** (0xFF), inclusive. The expected argument type is **int**.

Warning For the **is** routines, passing an argument of type **char** may yield unpredictable results. An SBCS or MBCS single-byte character of type **char** with a value greater than 0x7F is negative. If a **char** is passed, the compiler may convert the value to a signed **int** or a signed **long**. This value may be sign-extended by the compiler, with unexpected results.

The **isw** routines produce meaningful results for any integer value from – 1 (**WEOF**) to 0xFFFF, inclusive. The **wint_t** data type is defined in WCHAR.H as an **unsigned short**; it can hold any wide character or the wide-character end-of-file (**WEOF**) value.

For each of the **is** routines, the result of the test for the specified condition depends on the **LC_CTYPE** category setting of the current locale; see **setlocale** for more information. In the "C" locale, the test conditions for the **is** routines are as follows:

isalnum Alphanumeric (A–Z, a–z, or 0–9)

isalpha Alphabetic (A–Z or a–z)

_ _isascii ASCII character (0x00–0x7F)

iscntrl Control character (0x00–0x1F or 0x7F)

_ _iscsym Letter, underscore, or digit

_ _iscsymf Letter or underscore

isdigit Decimal digit (0–9)

isgraph Printable character except space ( )

islower Lowercase letter (a–z)

isprint Printable character including space (0x20–0x7E)

ispunct Punctuation character

isspace White-space character (0x09–0x0D or 0x20)

isupper Uppercase letter (A–Z)

isxdigit Hexadecimal digit (A–F, a–f, or 0–9)

For the **isw** routines, the result of the test for the specified condition is independent of locale. The test conditions for the **isw** functions are as follows:

iswalnum **iswalpha** or **iswdigit**

iswalpha Any wide character that is one of an implementation-defined set for which none of **iswcntrl**, **iswdigit**, **iswpunct**, or **iswspace** is true. **iswalpha** returns true only for wide characters for which **iswupper** or **iswlower** is true.

iswascii Wide-character representation of ASCII character (0x0000–0x007F).

iswcntrl Control wide character.

iswctype Character has property specified by the *desc* argument. For each valid value of the *desc* argument of **iswctype**, there is an equivalent wide-character classification routine, as shown in the following table:

Table R.2 Equivalence of iswctype(*c, desc*) to Other isw Testing Routines

Value of *desc* Argument	iswctype(*c, desc*) Equivalent
_ALPHA	**iswalpha(** *c* **)**
_ALPHA | _DIGIT	**iswalnum(** *c* **)**
_CONTROL	**iswcntrl(** *c* **)**
_DIGIT	**iswdigit(** *c* **)**
_ALPHA | _DIGIT | _PUNCT	**iswgraph(** *c* **)**
_LOWER	**iswlower(** *c* **)**
_ALPHA | _BLANK | _DIGIT | _PUNCT	**iswprint(** *c* **)**
_PUNCT	**iswpunct(** *c* **)**
_SPACE	**iswspace(** *c* **)**
_UPPER	**iswupper(** *c* **)**
_HEX	**iswxdigit(** *c* **)**

iswdigit Wide character corresponding to a decimal-digit character.

iswgraph Printable wide character except space wide character (L' ').

iswlower Lowercase letter, or one of implementation-defined set of wide characters for which none of **iswcntrl**, **iswdigit**, **iswpunct**, or **iswspace** is true. **iswlower** returns true only for wide characters that correspond to lowercase letters.

iswprint Printable wide character, including space wide character (L' ').

iswpunct Printable wide character that is neither space wide character (L' ') nor wide character for which **iswalnum** is true.

iswspace Wide character that corresponds to standard white-space character or is one of implementation defined set of wide characters for which **iswalnum** is false. Standard white-space characters are: space (L' '), formfeed (L'\f'), newline (L'\n'), carriage return (L'\r'), horizontal tab (L'\t'), and vertical tab (L'\v').

iswupper Wide character that is uppercase or is one of an implementation-defined set of wide characters for which none of **iswcntrl**, **iswdigit**, **iswpunct**, or **iswspace** is true. **iswupper** returns true only for wide characters that correspond to uppercase characters.

iswxdigit Wide character that corresponds to a hexadecimal-digit character.

Example

```
/* ISFAM.C: This program tests all characters between 0x0
 * and 0x7F, then displays each character with abbreviations
 * for the character-type codes that apply. The output has
 * been abridged to save space.

#include <stdio.h>
#include <ctype.h>

void main( void )
{
   int ch;
   for( ch = 0; ch <= 0x7F; ch++ )
   {
      printf( "%.2x  ", ch );
      printf( " %c", isprint( ch )  ? ch   : '\0' );
      printf( "%4s", isalnum( ch )  ? "AN" : "" );
      printf( "%3s", isalpha( ch )  ? "A"  : "" );
      printf( "%3s", __isascii( ch )  ? "AS" : "" );
      printf( "%3s", iscntrl( ch )  ? "C"  : "" );
      printf( "%3s", __iscsym( ch )  ? "CS "  : "" );
      printf( "%3s", __iscsymf( ch )  ? "CSF"  : "" );
      printf( "%3s", isdigit( ch )  ? "D"  : "" );
      printf( "%3s", isgraph( ch )  ? "G"  : "" );
      printf( "%3s", islower( ch )  ? "L"  : "" );
      printf( "%3s", ispunct( ch )  ? "PU" : "" );
      printf( "%3s", isspace( ch )  ? "S"  : "" );
      printf( "%3s", isprint( ch )  ? "PR" : "" );
      printf( "%3s", isupper( ch )  ? "U"  : "" );
      printf( "%3s", isxdigit( ch ) ? "X"  : "" );
      printf( "\n" );
   }
}
```

Output

```
00
01
02
.
.
.
20             AS                                S PR
21   !         AS                   G     PU       PR
22   "         AS                   G     PU       PR
.
.
.
30   0  AN     AS   CS        D  G                 PR      X
31   1  AN     AS   CS        D  G                 PR      X
32   2  AN     AS   CS        D  G                 PR      X
.
.
.
3f   ?         AS                   G     PU       PR
40   @         AS                   G     PU       PR
41   A  AN   A AS   CS CSF          G              PR   U  X
.
.
.
7d   }         AS                   G     PU       PR
7e   ~         AS                   G     PU       PR
7f
```

See Also **setlocale**, **to** Functions

isalnum, iswalnum

int isalnum(int *c* **);**
int iswalnum(wint_t *c* **);**

Each of these routines returns true if *c* is a particular representation of an alphanumeric character.

Routine	Required Header	Optional Headers	Compatibility
isalnum	<ctype.h>		ANSI, Win 95, Win NT, Win32s, 68K, PMac
iswalnum	<ctype.h> or <wchar.h>		ANSI, Win 95, Win NT, Win32s, 68K, PMac

For additional compatibility information, see "Compatibility" on page ix in the Introduction.

Libraries

LIBC.LIB	Single thread static library, retail version
LIBCMT.LIB	Multithread static library, retail version
MSVCRT.LIB	Import library for MSVCRTx0.DLL, retail version
MSVCRTx0.DLL	Multithread DLL library, retail version

Return Value

isalnum returns a non-zero value if either **isalpha** or **isdigit** is true for *c*, that is, if *c* is within the ranges A–Z, a–z, or 0–9. **iswalnum** returns a non-zero value if either **iswalpha** or **iswdigit** is true for *c*. Each of these routines returns 0 if *c* does not satisfy the test condition.

The result of the test condition for the **isalnum** function depends on the **LC_CTYPE** category setting of the current locale; see **setlocale** for more information. For **iswalnum**, the result of the test condition is independent of locale.

Parameter

c Integer to test

isalpha, iswalpha

int isalpha(int *c* **);**
int iswalpha(wint_t *c* **);**

Each of these routines returns true if *c* is a particular representation of an alphabetic character.

Routine	Required Header	Optional Headers	Compatibility
isalpha	<ctype.h>		ANSI, Win 95, Win NT, Win32s, 68K, PMac
iswalpha	<ctype.h> or <wchar.h>		ANSI, Win 95, Win NT, Win32s, 68K, PMac

For additional compatibility information, see "Compatibility" on page ix in the Introduction.

Libraries

LIBC.LIB	Single thread static library, retail version
LIBCMT.LIB	Multithread static library, retail version
MSVCRT.LIB	Import library for MSVCRTx0.DLL, retail version
MSVCRTx0.DLL	Multithread DLL library, retail version

Return Value

isalpha returns a non-zero value if *c* is within the ranges A–Z or a–z. **iswalpha** returns a non-zero value only for wide characters for which **iswupper** or **iswlower** is true, that is, for any wide character that is one of an implementation-defined set for which none of **iswcntrl**, **iswdigit**, **iswpunct**, or **iswspace** is true. Each of these routines returns 0 if *c* does not satisfy the test condition.

The result of the test condition for the **isalpha** function depends on the **LC_CTYPE** category setting of the current locale; see **setlocale** for more information. For **iswalpha**, the result of the test condition is independent of locale.

Parameter

c Integer to test

_ _isascii, iswascii

int _ _isascii(int *c* **);**
int iswascii(wint_t *c* **);**

Each of these routines returns true if *c* is a particular representation of an ASCII character.

Routine	Required Header	Optional Headers	Compatibility
_ _isascii	<ctype.h>		Win 95, Win NT, Win32s, 68K, PMac
iswascii	<ctype.h> or <wchar.h>		ANSI, Win 95, Win NT, Win32s, 68K, PMac

For additional compatibility information, see "Compatibility" on page ix in the Introduction.

Libraries	
LIBC.LIB	Single thread static library, retail version
LIBCMT.LIB	Multithread static library, retail version
MSVCRT.LIB	Import library for MSVCRTx0.DLL, retail version
MSVCRTx0.DLL	Multithread DLL library, retail version

Return Value

_ _isascii returns a non-zero value if *c* is an ASCII character (in the range 0x00–0x7F). **iswascii** returns a non-zero value if *c* is a wide-character representation of an ASCII character. Each of these routines returns 0 if *c* does not satisfy the test condition.

The result of the test condition for the **_ _isascii** function depends on the **LC_CTYPE** category setting of the current locale; see **setlocale** for more information. For **iswascii**, the result of the test condition is independent of locale.

Parameter

c Integer to test

iscntrl, iswcntrl

int iscntrl(int *c* **);**
int iswcntrl(wint_t *c* **);**

Each of these routines returns true if *c* is a particular representation of a control character.

Routine	Required Header	Optional Headers	Compatibility
iscntrl	<ctype.h>		ANSI, Win 95, Win NT, Win32s, 68K, PMac
iswcntrl	<ctype.h> or <wchar.h>		ANSI, Win 95, Win NT, Win32s, 68K, PMac

For additional compatibility information, see "Compatibility" on page ix in the Introduction.

Libraries	
LIBC.LIB	Single thread static library, retail version
LIBCMT.LIB	Multithread static library, retail version
MSVCRT.LIB	Import library for MSVCRTx0.DLL, retail version
MSVCRTx0.DLL	Multithread DLL library, retail version

Return Value

iscntrl returns a non-zero value if *c* is a control character (0x00–0x1F or 0x7F). **iswcntrl** returns a non-zero value if *c* is a control wide character. Each of these routines returns 0 if *c* does not satisfy the test condition.

The result of the test condition for the **iscntrl** function depends on the **LC_CTYPE** category setting of the current locale; see **setlocale** for more information. For **iswcntrl**, the result of the test condition is independent of locale.

Parameter

c Integer to test

__iscsym, __iscsymf

int __iscsym(int *c* **);**
int __iscsymf(int *c* **);**

Routine	Required Header	Optional Headers	Compatibility
__iscsym	<ctype.h>		Win 95, Win NT, Win32s, 68K, PMac
__iscsymf	<ctype.h>		Win 95, Win NT, Win32s, 68K, PMac

For additional compatibility information, see "Compatibility" on page ix in the Introduction.

Libraries

LIBC.LIB	Single thread static library, retail version
LIBCMT.LIB	Multithread static library, retail version
MSVCRT.LIB	Import library for MSVCRTx0.DLL, retail version
MSVCRTx0.DLL	Multithread DLL library, retail version

Return Value

_ _iscsym returns a non-zero value if *c* is a letter, underscore, or digit. **_ _iscsymf** returns a non-zero value if *c* is a letter or an underscore. Each of these routines returns 0 if *c* does not satisfy the test condition.

The result of the test condition for the **_ _iscsym** function depends on the **LC_CTYPE** category setting of the current locale; see **setlocale** for more information. For
_ _iscsymf, the result of the test condition is independent of locale.

Parameter

c Integer to test

isdigit, iswdigit

int isdigit(int *c* **);**
int iswdigit(wint_t *c* **);**

Each of these routines returns true if *c* is a particular representation of a decimal-digit character.

Routine	Required Header	Optional Headers	Compatibility
isdigit	<ctype.h>		ANSI, Win 95, Win NT, Win32s, 68K, PMac
iswdigit	<ctype.h> or <wchar.h>		ANSI, Win 95, Win NT, Win32s, 68K, PMac

For additional compatibility information, see "Compatibility" on page ix in the Introduction.

Libraries

LIBC.LIB	Single thread static library, retail version
LIBCMT.LIB	Multithread static library, retail version
MSVCRT.LIB	Import library for MSVCRTx0.DLL, retail version
MSVCRTx0.DLL	Multithread DLL library, retail version

Return Value

isdigit returns a non-zero value if *c* is a decimal digit (0–9). **iswdigit** returns a non-zero value if *c* is a wide character corresponding to a decimal-digit character. Each of these routines returns 0 if *c* does not satisfy the test condition.

The result of the test condition for the **isdigit** function depends on the **LC_CTYPE** category setting of the current locale; see **setlocale** for more information. For **iswdigit**, the result of the test condition is independent of locale.

Parameter

c Integer to test

isgraph, iswgraph

int isgraph(int *c* **);**
int iswgraph(wint_t *c* **);**

Each of these routines returns true if *c* is a particular representation of a printable character other than a space.

Routine	Required Header	Optional Headers	Compatibility
isgraph	<ctype.h>		ANSI, Win 95, Win NT, Win32s, 68K, PMac
iswgraph	<ctype.h> or <wchar.h>		ANSI, Win 95, Win NT, Win32s, 68K, PMac

For additional compatibility information, see "Compatibility" on page ix in the Introduction.

Libraries	
LIBC.LIB	Single thread static library, retail version
LIBCMT.LIB	Multithread static library, retail version
MSVCRT.LIB	Import library for MSVCRTx0.DLL, retail version
MSVCRTx0.DLL	Multithread DLL library, retail version

Return Value

isgraph returns a non-zero value if *c* is a printable character other than a space. **iswgraph** returns a non-zero value if *c* is a printable wide character other than a wide-character space. Each of these routines returns 0 if *c* does not satisfy the test condition.

The result of the test condition for the **isgraph** function depends on the **LC_CTYPE** category setting of the current locale; see **setlocale** for more information. For **iswgraph**, the result of the test condition is independent of locale.

Parameter

c Integer to test

islower, iswlower

int islower(int *c* **);**
int iswlower(wint_t *c* **);**

Each of these routines returns true if *c* is a particular representation of a lowercase character.

Routine	Required Header	Optional Headers	Compatibility
islower	<ctype.h>		ANSI, Win 95, Win NT, Win32s, 68K, PMac
iswlower	<ctype.h> or <wchar.h>		ANSI, Win 95, Win NT, Win32s, 68K, PMac

For additional compatibility information, see "Compatibility" on page ix in the Introduction.

Libraries	
LIBC.LIB	Single thread static library, retail version
LIBCMT.LIB	Multithread static library, retail version
MSVCRT.LIB	Import library for MSVCRTx0.DLL, retail version
MSVCRTx0.DLL	Multithread DLL library, retail version

Return Value

islower returns a non-zero value if *c* is a lowercase character (a–z). **iswlower** returns a non-zero value if *c* is a wide character that corresponds to a lowercase letter, or if *c* is one of an implementation-defined set of wide characters for which none of **iswcntrl**, **iswdigit**, **iswpunct**, or **iswspace** is true. Each of these routines returns 0 if *c* does not satisfy the test condition.

The result of the test condition for the **islower** function depends on the **LC_CTYPE** category setting of the current locale; see **setlocale** for more information. For **iswlower**, the result of the test condition is independent of locale.

Parameter

c Integer to test

isprint, iswprint

int isprint(int *c* **);**
int iswprint(wint_t *c* **);**

Each of these routines returns true if *c* is a particular representation of a printable character.

Routine	Required Header	Optional Headers	Compatibility
isprint	<ctype.h>		ANSI, Win 95, Win NT, Win32s, 68K, PMac
iswprint	<ctype.h> or <wchar.h>		ANSI, Win 95, Win NT, Win32s, 68K, PMac

For additional compatibility information, see "Compatibility" on page ix in the Introduction.

Libraries	
LIBC.LIB	Single thread static library, retail version
LIBCMT.LIB	Multithread static library, retail version
MSVCRT.LIB	Import library for MSVCRTx0.DLL, retail version
MSVCRTx0.DLL	Multithread DLL library, retail version

Return Value

isprint returns a nonzero value if *c* is a printable character, including the space character (0x20–0x7E). **iswprint** returns a nonzero value if *c* is a printable wide character, including the space wide character. Each of these routines returns 0 if *c* does not satisfy the test condition.

The result of the test condition for the **isprint** function depends on the **LC_CTYPE** category setting of the current locale; see **setlocale** for more information. For **iswprint**, the result of the test condition is independent of locale.

Parameter

c Integer to test

ispunct, iswpunct

int ispunct(int *c* **);**
int iswpunct(wint_t *c* **);**

Each of these routines returns true if *c* is a particular representation of a punctuation character.

Routine	Required Header	Optional Headers	Compatibility
ispunct	<ctype.h>		ANSI, Win 95, Win NT, Win32s, 68K, PMac
iswpunct	<ctype.h> or <wchar.h>		ANSI, Win 95, Win NT, Win32s, 68K, PMac

For additional compatibility information, see "Compatibility" on page ix in the Introduction.

Libraries

LIBC.LIB	Single thread static library, retail version
LIBCMT.LIB	Multithread static library, retail version
MSVCRT.LIB	Import library for MSVCRTx0.DLL, retail version
MSVCRTx0.DLL	Multithread DLL library, retail version

Return Value

ispunct returns a non-zero value for any printable character that is not a space character or a character for which **isalnum** is true. **iswpunct** returns a non-zero value for any printable wide character that is neither the space wide character nor a wide character for which **iswalnum** is true. Each of these routines returns 0 if *c* does not satisfy the test condition.

The result of the test condition for the **ispunct** function depends on the **LC_CTYPE** category setting of the current locale; see **setlocale** for more information. For **iswpunct**, the result of the test condition is independent of locale.

Parameter

c Integer to test

isspace, iswspace

int isspace(int *c* **);**
int iswspace(wint_t *c* **);**

Each of these routines returns true if *c* is a particular representation of a space character.

Routine	Required Header	Optional Headers	Compatibility
isspace	<ctype.h>		ANSI, Win 95, Win NT, Win32s, 68K, PMac
iswspace	<ctype.h> or <wchar.h>		ANSI, Win 95, Win NT, Win32s, 68K, PMac

For additional compatibility information, see "Compatibility" on page ix in the Introduction.

Libraries

LIBC.LIB	Single thread static library, retail version
LIBCMT.LIB	Multithread static library, retail version
MSVCRT.LIB	Import library for MSVCRTx0.DLL, retail version
MSVCRTx0.DLL	Multithread DLL library, retail version

Return Value

isspace returns a non-zero value if *c* is a white-space character (0x09–0x0D or 0x20). **iswspace** returns a non-zero value if *c* is a wide character that corresponds to a standard white-space character or is one of an implementation-defined set of wide characters for which **iswalnum** is false. Each of these routines returns 0 if *c* does not satisfy the test condition.

The result of the test condition for the **isspace** function depends on the **LC_CTYPE** category setting of the current locale; see **setlocale** for more information. For **iswspace**, the result of the test condition is independent of locale.

Parameter

c Integer to test

isupper, iswupper

int isupper(int *c* **);**
int iswupper(wint_t *c* **);**

Each of these routines returns true if *c* is a particular representation of an uppercase letter.

Routine	Required Header	Optional Headers	Compatibility
isupper	<ctype.h>		ANSI, Win 95, Win NT, Win32s, 68K, PMac
iswupper	<ctype.h> or <wchar.h>		ANSI, Win 95, Win NT, Win32s, 68K, PMac

For additional compatibility information, see "Compatibility" on page ix in the Introduction.

Libraries	
LIBC.LIB	Single thread static library, retail version
LIBCMT.LIB	Multithread static library, retail version
MSVCRT.LIB	Import library for MSVCRTx0.DLL, retail version
MSVCRTx0.DLL	Multithread DLL library, retail version

Return Value

isupper returns a non-zero value if *c* is an uppercase character (a–z). **iswupper** returns a non-zero value if *c* is a wide character that corresponds to an uppercase letter, or if *c* is one of an implementation-defined set of wide characters for which none of **iswcntrl**, **iswdigit**, **iswpunct**, or **iswspace** is true. Each of these routines returns 0 if *c* does not satisfy the test condition.

The result of the test condition for the **isupper** function depends on the **LC_CTYPE** category setting of the current locale; see **setlocale** for more information. For **iswupper**, the result of the test condition is independent of locale.

Parameter

c Integer to test

iswctype

int iswctype(wint_t *c*, **wctype_t** *desc* **);**

iswctype tests *c* for the property specified by the *desc* argument. For each valid value of *desc*, there is an equivalent wide-character classification routine.

Routine	Required Header	Optional Headers	Compatibility
iswctype	<ctype.h> or <wchar.h>		ANSI, Win 95, Win NT, Win32s, 68K, PMac

For additional compatibility information, see "Compatibility" on page ix in the Introduction.

Libraries	
LIBC.LIB	Single thread static library, retail version
LIBCMT.LIB	Multithread static library, retail version
MSVCRT.LIB	Import library for MSVCRTx0.DLL, retail version
MSVCRTx0.DLL	Multithread DLL library, retail version

Return Value

iswctype returns a nonzero value if *c* has the property specified by *desc*, or 0 if it does not. The result of the test condition is independent of locale.

Parameters

c Integer to test

desc Property to test for

isxdigit, iswxdigit

int isxdigit(int *c* **);**
int iswxdigit(wint_t *c* **);**

Each of these routines returns true if *c* is a particular representation of a hexadecimal digit.

Routine	Required Header	Optional Headers	Compatibility
isxdigit	<ctype.h>		ANSI, Win 95, Win NT, Win32s, 68K, PMac
iswxdigit	<ctype.h> or <wchar.h>		ANSI, Win 95, Win NT, Win32s, 68K, PMac

For additional compatibility information, see "Compatibility" on page ix in the Introduction.

Libraries	
LIBC.LIB	Single thread static library, retail version
LIBCMT.LIB	Multithread static library, retail version
MSVCRT.LIB	Import library for MSVCRTx0.DLL, retail version
MSVCRTx0.DLL	Multithread DLL library, retail version

Return Value

isxdigit returns a non-zero value if *c* is a hexadecimal digit (A–F, a–f, or 0–9). **iswxdigit** returns a non-zero value if *c* is a wide character that corresponds to a hexadecimal digit character. Each of these routines returns 0 if *c* does not satisfy the test condition.

The result of the test condition for the **isxdigit** function depends on the **LC_CTYPE** category setting of the current locale; see **setlocale** for more information. For the "C" locale, the **iswxdigit** function does not provide support for Unicode fullwidth hexadecimal characters. The result of the test condition for **iswxdigit** is independent of any other locale.

Parameter

c Integer to test

_isatty

int _isatty(int *handle* **);**

Routine	Required Header	Optional Headers	Compatibility
_isatty	<io.h>		Win 95, Win NT, Win32s, 68K, PMac

For additional compatibility information, see "Compatibility" on page ix in the Introduction.

Libraries

LIBC.LIB	Single thread static library, retail version
LIBCMT.LIB	Multithread static library, retail version
MSVCRT.LIB	Import library for MSVCRTx0.DLL, retail version
MSVCRTx0.DLL	Multithread DLL library, retail version

Return Value

_isatty returns a nonzero value handle is associated with a character device. Otherwise, **_isatty** returns 0.

Parameter

handle Handle referring to device to be tested

Remarks

The **_isatty** function determines whether *handle* is associated with a character device (a terminal, console, printer, or serial port).

Example

```
/* ISATTY.C: This program checks to see whether
 * stdout has been redirected to a file.
 */

#include <stdio.h>
#include <io.h>

void main( void )
{
   if( _isatty( _fileno( stdout ) ) )
      printf( "stdout has not been redirected to a file\n" );
   else
      printf( "stdout has been redirected to a file\n");
}
```

Output

```
stdout has been redirected to a file
```

isleadbyte

int isleadbyte(int *c* **);**

Routine	Required Header	Optional Headers	Compatibility
isleadbyte	<ctype.h>		ANSI, Win 95, Win NT, Win32s

For additional compatibility information, see "Compatibility" on page ix in the Introduction.

Libraries

LIBC.LIB	Single thread static library, retail version
LIBCMT.LIB	Multithread static library, retail version
MSVCRT.LIB	Import library for MSVCRTx0.DLL, retail version
MSVCRTx0.DLL	Multithread DLL library, retail version

Return Value

isleadbyte returns a nonzero value if the argument satisfies the test condition or 0 if it does not. In the "C" locale and in single-byte–character set (SBCS) locales, **isleadbyte** always returns 0.

Parameter

c Integer to test

Remarks

The **isleadbyte** macro returns a nonzero value if its argument is the first byte of a multibyte character. **isleadbyte** produces a meaningful result for any integer argument from –1 (**EOF**) to **UCHAR_MAX** (0xFF), inclusive. The result of the test depends upon the **LC_CTYPE** category setting of the current locale; see **setlocale** for more information.

The expected argument type of **isleadbyte** is **int**; if a signed character is passed, the compiler may convert it to an integer by sign extension, yielding unpredictable results.

See Also **_ismbb** Routines

_ismbb Routines

Each routine in the **_ismbb** family tests the given integer value *c* for a particular condition.

_ismbbalnum	**_ismbbkpunct**
_ismbbalpha	**_ismbblead**
_ismbbgraph	**_ismbbprint**
_ismbbkalnum	**_ismbbpunct**
_ismbbkana	**_ismbbtrail**
_ismbbkprint	

Remarks

Each routine in the **_ismbb** family tests the given integer value *c* for a particular condition. The test result depends on the multibyte code page in effect. By default, the multibyte code page is set to the system-default ANSI code page obtained from the operating system at program startup. You can query or change the multibyte code page in use with **_getmbcp** or **_setmbcp**, respectively.

The routines in the **_ismbb** family test the given integer *c* as follows.

Routine	Byte Test Condition
_ismbbalnum	**isalnum** || **_ismbbkalnum**
_ismbbalpha	**isalpha** || **_ismbbkalnum**
_ismbbgraph	Same as **_ismbbprint**, but **_ismbbgraph** does not include the space character (0x20).
_ismbbkalnum	Non-ASCII text symbol other than punctuation. For example, in code page 932 only, **_ismbbkalnum** tests for katakana alphanumeric.
_ismbbkana	Katakana (0xA1–0xDF). Specific to code page 932.
_ismbbkprint	Non-ASCII text or non-ASCII punctuation symbol. For example, in code page 932 only, **_ismbbkprint** tests for katakana alphanumeric or katakana punctuation (range: 0xA1–0xDF).
_ismbbkpunct	Non-ASCII punctuation. For example, in code page 932 only, **_ismbbkpunct** tests for katakana punctuation.
_ismbblead	First byte of multibyte character. For example, in code page 932 only, valid ranges are 0x81–0x9F, 0xE0–0xFC.
_ismbbprint	**isprint** || **_ismbbkprint**. **ismbbprint** includes the space character (0x20).
_ismbbpunct	**ispunct** || **_ismbbkpunct**
_ismbbtrail	Second byte of multibyte character. For example, in code page 932 only, valid ranges are 0x40–0x7E, 0x80–0xEC.

The following table shows the ORed values that compose the test conditions for these routines. The manifest constants **_BLANK**, **_DIGIT**, **_LOWER**, **_PUNCT**, and **_UPPER** are defined in CTYPE.H.

Routine	_BLANK	_DIGIT	LOWER	_PUNCT	UPPER	Non-ASCII Text	Non-ASCII Punct
_ismbbalnum	—	x	x	—	x	x	—
_ismbbalpha	—	—	x	—	x	x	—
_ismbbgraph	—	x	x	x	x	x	x
_ismbbkalnum	—	—	—	—	—	x	—
_ismbbkprint	—	—	—	—	—	x	x
_ismbbkpunct	—	—	—	—	—	—	x
_ismbbprint	x	x	x	x	x	x	x
_ismbbpunct	—	—	—	x	—	—	x

The **_ismbb** routines are implemented both as functions and as macros. For details on choosing either implementation, see "Choosing Between Functions and Macros" on page xii.

See Also **is, isw** Functions, **_mbbtombc**, **_mbctombb**

_ismbbalnum

int _ismbbalnum(unsigned int *c* **);**

Routine	Required Header	Optional Headers	Compatibility
_ismbbalnum	<mbctype.h>		Win 95, Win NT, Win32s, 68K, PMac

For additional compatibility information, see "Compatibility" on page ix in the Introduction.

Libraries	
LIBC.LIB	Single thread static library, retail version
LIBCMT.LIB	Multithread static library, retail version
MSVCRT.LIB	Import library for MSVCRTx0.DLL, retail version
MSVCRTx0.DLL	Multithread DLL library, retail version

Return Value

_ismbbalnum returns a nonzero value if the expression

```
isalnum || _ismbbkalnum
```

is true of *c*, or 0 if it is not.

Parameter

c Integer to be tested

_ismbbalpha

int _ismbbalpha(unsigned int *c* **);**

Routine	Required Header	Optional Headers	Compatibility
_ismbbalpha	<mbctype.h>		Win 95, Win NT, Win32s, 68K, PMac

For additional compatibility information, see "Compatibility" on page ix in the Introduction.

Libraries

LIBC.LIB	Single thread static library, retail version
LIBCMT.LIB	Multithread static library, retail version
MSVCRT.LIB	Import library for MSVCRTx0.DLL, retail version
MSVCRTx0.DLL	Multithread DLL library, retail version

Return Value

_ismbbalpha returns a nonzero value if the expression

```
isalpha || _ismbbkalnum
```

is true of *c*, or 0 if it is not.

Parameter

c Integer to be tested

_ismbbgraph

int _ismbbgraph (unsigned int *c* **);**

Routine	Required Header	Optional Headers	Compatibility
_ismbbgraph	<mbctype.h>		Win 95, Win NT, Win32s, 68K, PMac

For additional compatibility information, see "Compatibility" on page ix in the Introduction.

Libraries

LIBC.LIB	Single thread static library, retail version
LIBCMT.LIB	Multithread static library, retail version
MSVCRT.LIB	Import library for MSVCRTx0.DLL, retail version
MSVCRTx0.DLL	Multithread DLL library, retail version

Return Value

_ismbbgraph returns a nonzero value if the expression

```
( _PUNCT | _UPPER | _LOWER | _DIGIT ) || _ismbbkprint
```

is true of *c*, or 0 if it is not.

Parameter

c Integer to be tested

_ismbbkalnum

int _ismbbkalnum(unsigned int *c* **);**

Routine	Required Header	Optional Headers	Compatibility
_ismbbkalnum	<mbctype.h>		Win 95, Win NT, Win32s, 68K, PMac

For additional compatibility information, see "Compatibility" on page ix in the Introduction.

Libraries	
LIBC.LIB	Single thread static library, retail version
LIBCMT.LIB	Multithread static library, retail version
MSVCRT.LIB	Import library for MSVCRTx0.DLL, retail version
MSVCRTx0.DLL	Multithread DLL library, retail version

Return Value

_ismbbkalnum returns a nonzero value if the integer *c* is a non-ASCII text symbol other than punctuation, or 0 if it is not.

Parameter

c Integer to be tested

_ismbbkana

int _ismbbkana(unsigned int *c* **);**

_ismbbkana tests for a katakana symbol and is specific to code page 932.

Routine	Required Header	Optional Headers	Compatibility
_ismbbkana	<mbctype.h>		Win 95, Win NT, Win32s, 68K, PMac

For additional compatibility information, see "Compatibility" on page ix in the Introduction.

Libraries	
LIBC.LIB	Single thread static library, retail version
LIBCMT.LIB	Multithread static library, retail version
MSVCRT.LIB	Import library for MSVCRTx0.DLL, retail version
MSVCRTx0.DLL	Multithread DLL library, retail version

Return Value

_ismbbkana returns a nonzero value if the integer *c* is a katakana symbol, or 0 if it is not.

Parameter

c Integer to be tested

_ismbbkprint

int _ismbbkprint(unsigned int *c* **);**

Routine	Required Header	Optional Headers	Compatibility
_ismbbkprint	<mbctype.h>		Win 95, Win NT, Win32s, 68K, PMac

For additional compatibility information, see "Compatibility" on page ix in the Introduction.

Libraries	
LIBC.LIB	Single thread static library, retail version
LIBCMT.LIB	Multithread static library, retail version
MSVCRT.LIB	Import library for MSVCRTx0.DLL, retail version
MSVCRTx0.DLL	Multithread DLL library, retail version

Return Value

_ismbbkprint returns a nonzero value if the integer *c* is a non-ASCII text or non-ASCII punctuation symbol, or 0 if it is not. For example, in code page 932 only, **_ismbbkprint** tests for katakana alphanumeric or katakana punctuation (range: 0xA1–0xDF).

Parameter

c Integer to be tested

_ismbbkpunct

int _ismbbkpunct(unsigned int *c* **);**

Routine	Required Header	Optional Headers	Compatibility
_ismbbkpunct	<mbctype.h>		Win 95, Win NT, Win32s, 68K, PMac

For additional compatibility information, see "Compatibility" on page ix in the Introduction.

Libraries	
LIBC.LIB	Single thread static library, retail version
LIBCMT.LIB	Multithread static library, retail version
MSVCRT.LIB	Import library for MSVCRTx0.DLL, retail version
MSVCRTx0.DLL	Multithread DLL library, retail version

Return Value

_ismbbkpunct returns a nonzero value if the integer *c* is a non-ASCII punctuation symbol, or 0 if it is not. For example, in code page 932 only, **_ismbbkpunct** tests for katakana punctuation.

Parameter

c Integer to be tested

_ismbblead

int _ismbblead(unsigned int *c* **);**

Routine	Required Header	Optional Headers	Compatibility
_ismbblead	<mbctype.h> or <mbstring.h>	<ctype.h>,[1] <limits.h>, <stdlib.h>	Win 95, Win NT, Win32s, 68K, PMac

1 For manifest constants for the test conditions.

For additional compatibility information, see "Compatibility" on page ix in the Introduction.

Libraries	
LIBC.LIB	Single thread static library, retail version
LIBCMT.LIB	Multithread static library, retail version
MSVCRT.LIB	Import library for MSVCRTx0.DLL, retail version
MSVCRTx0.DLL	Multithread DLL library, retail version

Return Value

_ismbblead returns a nonzero value if the integer *c* is the first byte of a multibyte character. For example, in code page 932 only, valid ranges are 0x81–0x9F and 0xE0–0xFC.

Parameter

c Integer to be tested

_ismbbprint

int _ismbbprint(unsigned int *c* **);**

Routine	Required Header	Optional Headers	Compatibility
_ismbbprint	<mbctype.h>		Win 95, Win NT, Win32s, 68K, PMac

For additional compatibility information, see “Compatibility” on page ix in the Introduction.

Libraries	
LIBC.LIB	Single thread static library, retail version
LIBCMT.LIB	Multithread static library, retail version
MSVCRT.LIB	Import library for MSVCRTx0.DLL, retail version
MSVCRTx0.DLL	Multithread DLL library, retail version

Return Value

_ismbbprint returns a nonzero value if the expression

```
isprint || _ismbbkprint
```

is true of *c*, or 0 if it is not.

Parameter

c Integer to be tested

_ismbbpunct

int _ismbbpunct(unsigned int *c* **);**

Routine	Required Header	Optional Headers	Compatibility
_ismbbpunct	<mbctype.h>		Win 95, Win NT, Win32s, 68K, PMac

For additional compatibility information, see “Compatibility” on page ix in the Introduction.

Libraries	
LIBC.LIB	Single thread static library, retail version
LIBCMT.LIB	Multithread static library, retail version
MSVCRT.LIB	Import library for MSVCRTx0.DLL, retail version
MSVCRTx0.DLL	Multithread DLL library, retail version

Return Value

_ismbbpunct returns a nonzero value if the integer *c* is a non-ASCII punctuation symbol.

Parameter

c Integer to be tested

_ismbbtrail

int _ismbbtrail(unsigned int *c* **);**

Routine	Required Header	Optional Headers	Compatibility
_ismbbtrail	<mbctype.h> or <mbstring.h>	<ctype.h>,[1] <limits.h>, <stdlib.h>	Win 95, Win NT, Win32s, 68K, PMac

[1] For manifest constants for the test conditions.

For additional compatibility information, see "Compatibility" on page ix in the Introduction.

Libraries	
LIBC.LIB	Single thread static library, retail version
LIBCMT.LIB	Multithread static library, retail version
MSVCRT.LIB	Import library for MSVCRTx0.DLL, retail version
MSVCRTx0.DLL	Multithread DLL library, retail version

Return Value

_ismbbtrail returns a nonzero value if the integer *c* is the second byte of a multibyte character. For example, in code page 932 only, valid ranges are 0x40–0x7E and 0x80 –0xEC.

Parameter

c Integer to be tested

_ismbc Routines

Each of the **_ismbc** routines tests a given multibyte character *c* for a particular condition.

_ismbcalnum, _ismbcalpha, _ismbcdigit	**_ismbcl0, _ismbcl1, _ismbcl2**
_ismbcgraph, _ismbcprint, _ismbcpunct, _ismbcspace	**_ismbclegal, _ismbcsymbol**
_ismbchira, _ismbckata	**_ismbclower, _ismbcupper**

Remarks

The test result of each of the **_ismbc** routines depends on the multibyte code page in effect. Multibyte code pages have single byte alphabetic characters. By default, the multibyte code page is set to the system-default ANSI code page obtained from the operating system at program startup. You can query or change the multibyte code page in use with **_getmbcp** or **_setmbcp**, respectively.

Routine	Test Condition	Code Page 932 Example
_ismbcalnum	Alphanumeric	Returns true if and only if *c* is a single-byte representation of an ASCII English letter: See examples for **_ismbcdigit** and **_ismbcalpha**.
_ismbcalpha	Alphabetic	Returns true if and only if *c* is a single-byte representation of an ASCII English letter: See examples for **_ismbcupper** and **_ismbclower**; or a Katakana letter: 0xA6<=*c*<=0xDF.
_ismbcdigit	Digit	Returns true if and only if *c* is a single-byte representation of an ASCII digit: 0x30<=*c*<=0x39.
_ismbcgraph	Graphic	Returns true if and only if *c* is a single-byte representation of any ASCII or Katakana printable character except a white space ( ). See examples for **_ismbcdigit**, **_ismbcalpha**, and **_ismbcpunct**.
_ismbclegal	Valid multibyte character	Returns true if and only if the first byte of *c* is within ranges 0x81–0x9F or 0xE0–0xFC, while the second byte is within ranges 0x40–0x7E or 0x80–FC.
_ismbclower	Lowercase alphabetic	Returns true if and only if *c* is a single-byte representation of an ASCII lowercase English letter: 0x61<=*c*<=0x7A.
_ismbcprint	Printable	Returns true if and only if *c* is a single-byte representation of any ASCII or Katakana printable character including a white space ( ): See examples for **_ismbcspace**, **_ismbcdigit**, **_ismbcalpha**, and **_ismbcpunct**.
_ismbcpunct	Punctuation	Returns true if and only if *c* is a single-byte representation of any ASCII or Katakana punctuation character.
_ismbcspace	Whitespace	Returns true if and only if *c* is a whitespace character: *c*=0x20 or 0x09<=*c*<=0x0D.
_ismbcsymbol	Multibyte symbol	Returns true if and only if 0x8141<=*c*<=0x81AC.
_ismbcupper	Uppercase alphabetic	Returns true if and only if *c* is a single-byte representation of an ASCII uppercase English letter: 0x41<=*c*<=0x5A.

Code Page 932 Specific →

The following routines are specific to code page 932.

Routine	Test Condition (Code Page 932 Only)
_ismbchira	Double-byte Hiragana: 0x829F<=*c*<=0x82F1.
_ismbckata	Double-byte Katakana: 0x8340<=*c*<=0x8396.
_ismbcl0	JIS non-Kanji: 0x8140<=*c*<=0x889E.
_ismbcl1	JIS level-1: 0x889F<=*c*<=0x9872.
_ismbcl2	JIS level-2: 0x989F<=*c*<=0xEA9E.

_ismbcl0, **_ismbcl1**, and **_ismbcl2** check that the specified value *c* matches the test conditions described in the preceding table, but do not check that *c* is a valid multibyte character. If the lower byte is in the ranges 0x00–0x3F, 0x7F, or 0xFD–0xFF, these functions return a nonzero value, indicating that the character satisfies the test condition. Use **_ismbbtrail** to test whether the multibyte character is defined.

END Code Page 932 Specific

See Also **is, isw** Functions, **_ismbb** Functions

_ismbcalnum, _ismbcalpha, _ismbcdigit

int _ismbcalnum(unsigned int *c* **);**
int _ismbcalpha(unsigned int *c* **);**
int _ismbcdigit(unsigned int *c* **);**

Routine	Required Header	Optional Headers	Compatibility
_ismbcalnum	<mbstring.h>		Win 95, Win NT, Win32s, 68K, PMac
_ismbcalpha	<mbstring.h>		Win 95, Win NT, Win32s, 68K, PMac
_ismbcdigit	<mbstring.h>		Win 95, Win NT, Win32s, 68K, PMac

For additional compatibility information, see "Compatibility" on page ix in the Introduction.

Libraries

LIBC.LIB	Single thread static library, retail version
LIBCMT.LIB	Multithread static library, retail version
MSVCRT.LIB	Import library for MSVCRTx0.DLL, retail version
MSVCRTx0.DLL	Multithread DLL library, retail version

Return Value

Each of these routines returns a nonzero value if the character satisfies the test condition or 0 if it does not. If *c*<= 255 and there is a corresponding **_ismbb** routine (for example, **_ismbcalnum** corresponds to **_ismbbalnum**), the result is the return value of the corresponding **_ismbb** routine.

Parameter

c Character to be tested

Remarks

Each of these routines tests a given multibyte character for a given condition.

Routine	Test Condition	Code Page 932 Example
_ismbcalnum	Alphanumeric	Returns true if and only if *c* is a single-byte representation of an ASCII English letter: See examples for **_ismbcdigit** and **_ismbcalpha**.
_ismbcalpha	Alphabetic	Returns true if and only if *c* is a single-byte representation of an ASCII English letter: 0x41<=*c*<=0x5A or 0x61<=*c*<=0x7A; or a Katakana letter: 0xA6<=*c*<=0xDF.
_ismbcdigit	Digit	Returns true if and only if *c* is a single-byte representation of an ASCII digit: 0x30<=*c*<=0x39.

See Also **is, isw** Functions, **_ismbb** Functions

_ismbcgraph, _ismbcprint, _ismbcpunct, _ismbcspace

int _ismbcgraph(unsigned int *c* **);**
int _ismbcprint(unsigned int *c* **);**
int _ismbcpunct(unsigned int *c* **);**
int _ismbcspace(unsigned int *c* **);**

Routine	Required Header	Optional Headers	Compatibility
_ismbcgraph	<mbstring.h>		Win 95, Win NT, Win32s, 68K, PMac
_ismbcprint	<mbstring.h>		Win 95, Win NT, Win32s, 68K, PMac
_ismbcpunct	<mbstring.h>		Win 95, Win NT, Win32s, 68K, PMac
_ismbcspace	<mbstring.h>		Win 95, Win NT, Win32s, 68K, PMac

For additional compatibility information, see "Compatibility" on page ix in the Introduction.

Libraries

LIBC.LIB	Single thread static library, retail version
LIBCMT.LIB	Multithread static library, retail version
MSVCRT.LIB	Import library for MSVCRTx0.DLL, retail version
MSVCRTx0.DLL	Multithread DLL library, retail version

Return Value

Each of these routines returns a nonzero value if the character satisfies the test condition or 0 if it does not. If *c*<= 255 and there is a corresponding **_ismbb** routine (for example, **_ismbcalnum** corresponds to **_ismbbalnum**), the result is the return value of the corresponding **_ismbb** routine.

Parameter

c Character to be tested

Remarks

Each of these functions tests a given multibyte character for a given condition.

Routine	Test Condition	Code Page 932 Example
_ismbcgraph	Graphic	Returns true if and only if *c* is a single-byte representation of any ASCII or Katakana printable character except a white space ( ).
_ismbcprint	Printable	Returns true if and only if *c* is a single-byte representation of any ASCII or Katakana printable character including a white space ( ).
_ismbcpunct	Punctuation	Returns true if and only if *c* is a single-byte representation of any ASCII or Katakana punctuation character.
_ismbcspace	Whitespace	Returns true if and only if *c* is a whitespace character: *c*=0x20 or 0x09<=*c*<=0x0D.

See Also **is, isw** Functions, **_ismbb** Functions

_ismbchira, _ismbckata

Code Page 932 Specific →

int _ismbchira(unsigned int *c* **);**
int _ismbckata(unsigned int *c* **);**

Routine	Required Header	Optional Headers	Compatibility
_ismbchira	<mbstring.h>		Win 95, Win NT, Win32s, 68K, PMac
_ismbckata	<mbstring.h>		Win 95, Win NT, Win32s, 68K, PMac

For additional compatibility information, see "Compatibility" on page ix in the Introduction.

Libraries

LIBC.LIB	Single thread static library, retail version
LIBCMT.LIB	Multithread static library, retail version
MSVCRT.LIB	Import library for MSVCRTx0.DLL, retail version
MSVCRTx0.DLL	Multithread DLL library, retail version

Return Value

Each of these routines returns a nonzero value if the character satisfies the test condition or 0 if it does not. If *c*<= 255 and there is a corresponding **_ismbb** routine (for example, **_ismbcalnum** corresponds to **_ismbbalnum**), the result is the return value of the corresponding **_ismbb** routine.

Parameter

c Character to be tested

Remarks

Each of these functions tests a given multibyte character for a given condition.

Routine	Test Condition (Code Page 932 Only)
_ismbchira	Double-byte Hiragana: 0x829F<=*c*<=0x82F1.
_ismbckata	Double-byte Katakana: 0x8340<=*c*<=0x8396.

End Code Page 932 Specific

See Also **is, isw** Functions, **_ismbb** Functions

_ismbcl0, _ismbcl1, _ismbcl2

Code Page 932 Specific→

int _ismbcl0(unsigned int *c* **);**
int _ismbcl1(unsigned int *c* **);**
int _ismbcl2(unsigned int *c* **);**

Routine	Required Header	Optional Headers	Compatibility
_ismbcl0	<mbstring.h>		Win 95, Win NT, Win32s, 68K, PMac
_ismbcl1	<mbstring.h>		Win 95, Win NT, Win32s, 68K, PMac
_ismbcl2	<mbstring.h>		Win 95, Win NT, Win32s, 68K, PMac

For additional compatibility information, see "Compatibility" on page ix in the Introduction.

Libraries

LIBC.LIB	Single thread static library, retail version
LIBCMT.LIB	Multithread static library, retail version
MSVCRT.LIB	Import library for MSVCRTx0.DLL, retail version
MSVCRTx0.DLL	Multithread DLL library, retail version

Return Value

Each of these routines returns a nonzero value if the character satisfies the test condition or 0 if it does not. If *c*<= 255 and there is a corresponding **_ismbb** routine (for example, **_ismbcalnum** corresponds to **_ismbbalnum**), the result is the return value of the corresponding **_ismbb** routine.

Parameter

c Character to be tested

Remarks

Each of these functions tests a given multibyte character for a given condition.

Routine	Test Condition (Code Page 932 Only)
_ismbcl0	JIS non-Kanji: 0x8140<=*c*<=0x889E.
_ismbcl1	JIS level-1: 0x889F<=*c*<=0x9872.
_ismbcl2	JIS level-2: 0x989F<=*c*<=0xEA9E.

_ismbcl0, **_ismbcl1**, and **_ismbcl2** check that the specified value *c* matches the test conditions described above, but do not check that *c* is a valid multibyte character. If the lower byte is in the ranges 0x00–0x3F, 0x7F, or 0xFD–0xFF, these functions return a nonzero value, indicating that the character satisfies the test condition. Use **_ismbbtrail** to test whether the multibyte character is defined.

End Code Page 932 Specific

See Also **is, isw** Functions, **_ismbb** Functions

_ismbclegal, _ismbcsymbol

int _ismbclegal(unsigned int *c* **);**
int _ismbcsymbol(unsigned int *c* **);**

Routine	Required Header	Optional Headers	Compatibility
_ismbclegal	<mbstring.h>		Win 95, Win NT, Win32s, 68K, PMac
_ismbcsymbol	<mbstring.h>		Win 95, Win NT, Win32s, 68K, PMac

For additional compatibility information, see “Compatibility” on page ix in the Introduction.

Libraries

LIBC.LIB	Single thread static library, retail version
LIBCMT.LIB	Multithread static library, retail version
MSVCRT.LIB	Import library for MSVCRTx0.DLL, retail version
MSVCRTx0.DLL	Multithread DLL library, retail version

Return Value

Each of these routines returns a nonzero value if the character satisfies the test condition or 0 if it does not. If *c*<= 255 and there is a corresponding **_ismbb** routine (for example, **_ismbcalnum** corresponds to **_ismbbalnum**), the result is the return value of the corresponding **_ismbb** routine.

Parameter

c Character to be tested

Remarks

Each of these functions tests a given multibyte character for a given condition.

Routine	Test Condition	Code Page 932 Example
_ismbclegal	Valid multibyte	Returns true if and only if the first byte of *c* is within ranges 0x81–0x9F or 0xE0–0xFC, while the second byte is within ranges 0x40-0x7E or 0x80–FC.
_ismbcsymbol	Multibyte symbol	Returns true if and only if 0x8141<=*c*<=0x81AC.

See Also **is, isw** Functions, **_ismbb** Functions

_ismbclower, _ismbcupper

int _ismbclower(unsigned int *c* **);**
int _ismbcupper(unsigned int *c* **);**

Routine	Required Header	Optional Headers	Compatibility
_ismbclower	<mbstring.h>		Win 95, Win NT, Win32s, 68K, PMac
_ismbcupper	<mbstring.h>		Win 95, Win NT, Win32s, 68K, PMac

For additional compatibility information, see “Compatibility” on page ix in the Introduction.

Libraries

LIBC.LIB	Single thread static library, retail version
LIBCMT.LIB	Multithread static library, retail version
MSVCRT.LIB	Import library for MSVCRTx0.DLL, retail version
MSVCRTx0.DLL	Multithread DLL library, retail version

Return Value

Each of these routines returns a nonzero value if the character satisfies the test condition or 0 if it does not. If *c*<= 255 and there is a corresponding **_ismbb** routine (for example, **_ismbcalnum** corresponds to **_ismbbalnum**), the result is the return value of the corresponding **_ismbb** routine.

Parameter

c Character to be tested

Remarks

Each of these functions tests a given multibyte character for a given condition.

Routine	Test Condition	Code Page 932 Example
_ismbclower	Lowercase alphabetic	Returns true if and only if *c* is a single-byte representation of an ASCII lowercase English letter: 0x61<=*c*<=0x7A.
_ismbcupper	Uppercase alphabetic	Returns true if and only if *c* is a single-byte representation of an ASCII uppercase English letter: 0x41<=*c*<=0x5A.

See Also **is, isw** Functions, **_ismbb** Functions

_ismbslead, _ismbstrail

int _ismbslead(const unsigned char ***string*****, const unsigned char** ***current*** **);**
int _ismbstrail(const unsigned char ***string*****, const unsigned char** ***current*** **);**

Routine	Required Header	Optional Headers	Compatibility
_ismbslead	<mbctype.h> or <mbstring.h>	<ctype.h>,[1] <limits.h>, <stdlib.h>	Win 95, Win NT, Win32s, 68K, PMac
_ismbstrail	<mbctype.h> or <mbstring.h>	<ctype.h>,[1] <limits.h>, <stdlib.h>	Win 95, Win NT, Win32s, 68K, PMac

1 For manifest constants for the test conditions.

For additional compatibility information, see "Compatibility" on page ix in the Introduction.

Libraries	
LIBC.LIB	Single thread static library, retail version
LIBCMT.LIB	Multithread static library, retail version
MSVCRT.LIB	Import library for MSVCRTx0.DLL, retail version
MSVCRTx0.DLL	Multithread DLL library, retail version

Return Value

_ismbslead and **_ismbstrail** return –1 if the character is a lead or trail byte, respectively. Otherwise they return zero.

Parameters

string Pointer to start of string or previous known lead byte

current Pointer to position in string to be tested

Remarks

The **_ismbslead** and **_ismbstrail** routines perform context-sensitive tests for multibyte-character string lead and trail bytes; they determine whether a given substring pointer points to a lead byte or a trail byte. **_ismbslead** and **_ismbstrail** are slower than their **_ismbblead** and **_ismbbtrail** counterparts because they take the string context into account.

See Also **is, isw** Functions, **_ismbb** Functions

_isnan

Checks given double-precision floating-point value for not a number (NaN).

int _isnan(double *x* **);**

Routine	Required Header	Optional Headers	Compatibility
_isnan	<float.h>		Win 95, Win NT, Win32s, 68K, PMac

For additional compatibility information, see "Compatibility" on page ix in the Introduction.

Libraries	
LIBC.LIB	Single thread static library, retail version
LIBCMT.LIB	Multithread static library, retail version
MSVCRT.LIB	Import library for MSVCRTx0.DLL, retail version
MSVCRTx0.DLL	Multithread DLL library, retail version

Return Value

_isnan returns a nonzero value (TRUE) if the argument *x* is a NaN; otherwise it returns 0 (FALSE).

Parameter

x Double-precision floating-point value

Remarks

The **_isnan** function tests a given double-precision floating-point value *x*, returning a nonzero value if *x* is a NaN. A NaN is generated when the result of a floating-point operation cannot be represented in Institute of Electrical and Electronics Engineers (IEEE) format. For information about how a NaN is represented for output, see **printf**.

See Also **_finite**, **_fpclass**

_itoa, _itow

Convert an integer to a string.

char *_itoa(int *value*, **char ****string*, **int** *radix* **);**
wchar_t * _itow(int *value*, **wchar_t ****string*, **int** *radix* **);**

Routine	Required Header	Optional Headers	Compatibility
_itoa	<stdlib.h>		Win 95, Win NT, Win32s, 68K, PMac
_itow	<stdlib.h>		Win 95, Win NT, Win32s

For additional compatibility information, see "Compatibility" on page ix in the Introduction.

Libraries	
LIBC.LIB	Single thread static library, retail version
LIBCMT.LIB	Multithread static library, retail version
MSVCRT.LIB	Import library for MSVCRTx0.DLL, retail version
MSVCRTx0.DLL	Multithread DLL library, retail version

Return Value

Each of these functions returns a pointer to *string*. There is no error return.

Parameters

value Number to be converted

string String result

radix Base of *value*; must be in the range 2–36

Remarks

The **_itoa** function converts the digits of the given *value* argument to a null-terminated character string and stores the result (up to 17 bytes) in *string*. If *radix* equals 10 and *value* is negative, the first character of the stored string is the minus sign (–). **_itow** is a wide-character version of **_itoa**.

Example

```
/* ITOA.C: This program converts integers of various
 * sizes to strings in various radixes.
 */

#include <stdlib.h>
#include <stdio.h>

void main( void )
{
   char buffer[20];
   int  i = 3445;
   long l = -344115L;
   unsigned long ul = 1234567890UL;

   _itoa( i, buffer, 10 );
   printf( "String of integer %d (radix 10): %s\n", i, buffer );
   _itoa( i, buffer, 16 );
   printf( "String of integer %d (radix 16): 0x%s\n", i, buffer );
   _itoa( i, buffer, 2  );
   printf( "String of integer %d (radix 2): %s\n", i, buffer );

   _ltoa( l, buffer, 16 );
   printf( "String of long int %ld (radix 16): 0x%s\n", l,
                                                    buffer );

   _ultoa( ul, buffer, 16 );
   printf( "String of unsigned long %lu (radix 16): 0x%s\n", ul,
                                                    buffer );
}
```

Output

```
String of integer 3445 (radix 10): 3445
String of integer 3445 (radix 16): 0xd75
String of integer 3445 (radix 2): 110101110101
String of long int -344115 (radix 16): 0xfffabfcd
String of unsigned long 1234567890 (radix 16): 0x499602d2
```

See Also **_ltoa**, **_ultoa**

_kbhit

Checks the console for keyboard input.

int _kbhit(void);

Routine	Required Header	Optional Headers	Compatibility
_kbhit	<conio.h>		Win 95, Win NT, Win32s

For additional compatibility information, see "Compatibility" on page ix in the Introduction.

Libraries	
LIBC.LIB	Single thread static library, retail version
LIBCMT.LIB	Multithread static library, retail version
MSVCRT.LIB	Import library for MSVCRTx0.DLL, retail version
MSVCRTx0.DLL	Multithread DLL library, retail version

Return Value

_kbhit returns a nonzero value if a key has been pressed. Otherwise, it returns 0.

Remarks

The **_kbhit** function checks the console for a recent keystroke. If the function returns a nonzero value, a keystroke is waiting in the buffer. The program can then call **_getch** or **_getche** to get the keystroke.

Example

```
/* KBHIT.C: This program loops until the user
 * presses a key. If _kbhit returns nonzero, a
 * keystroke is waiting in the buffer. The program
 * can call _getch or _getche to get the keystroke.
 */

#include <conio.h>
#include <stdio.h>

void main( void )
{
   /* Display message until key is pressed. */
   while( !_kbhit() )
      _cputs( "Hit me!! " );

   /* Use _getch to throw key away. */
   printf( "\nKey struck was '%c'\n", _getch() );
   _getch();
}
```

Output

```
Hit me!! Hit me!! Hit me!! Hit me!! Hit me!! Hit me!! Hit me!!
Key struck was 'q'
```

labs

Calculates the absolute value of a long integer.

long labs(long *n* **);**

Routine	Required Header	Optional Headers	Compatibility
labs	<stdlib.h> and <math.h>		ANSI, Win 95, Win NT, Win32s, 68K, PMac

For additional compatibility information, see "Compatibility" on page ix in the Introduction.

Libraries	
LIBC.LIB	Single thread static library, retail version
LIBCMT.LIB	Multithread static library, retail version
MSVCRT.LIB	Import library for MSVCRTx0.DLL, retail version
MSVCRTx0.DLL	Multithread DLL library, retail version

Return Value

The **labs** function returns the absolute value of its argument. There is no error return.

Parameter

n Long-integer value

Example

See the example for **abs**.

See Also **abs**, **_cabs**, **fabs**

ldexp

Computes a real number from the mantissa and exponent.

double ldexp(double *x*, **int** *exp* **);**

Routine	Required Header	Optional Headers	Compatibility
ldexp	<math.h>		ANSI, Win 95, Win NT, Win32s, 68K, PMac

For additional compatibility information, see "Compatibility" on page ix in the Introduction.

Libraries	
LIBC.LIB	Single thread static library, retail version
LIBCMT.LIB	Multithread static library, retail version
MSVCRT.LIB	Import library for MSVCRTx0.DLL, retail version
MSVCRTx0.DLL	Multithread DLL library, retail version

Return Value

The **ldexp** function returns the value of $x * 2^{exp}$ if successful. On overflow (depending on the sign of *x*), **ldexp** returns +/–**HUGE_VAL**; the **errno** variable is set to **ERANGE**.

Parameters

x Floating-point value

exp Integer exponent

Example

```
/* LDEXP.C */

#include <math.h>
#include <stdio.h>

void main( void )
{
   double x = 4.0, y;
   int p = 3;

   y = ldexp( x, p );
   printf( "%2.1f times two to the power of %d is %2.1f\n", x, p, y );
}
```

Output

```
4.0 times two to the power of 3 is 32.0
```

See Also **frexp**, **modf**

ldiv

Computes the quotient and remainder of a long integer.

ldiv_t ldiv(long int *numer*, **long int** *denom* **);**

Routine	Required Header	Optional Headers	Compatibility
ldiv	<stdlib.h>		ANSI, Win 95, Win NT, Win32s, 68K, PMac

For additional compatibility information, see "Compatibility" on page ix in the Introduction.

Libraries	
LIBC.LIB	Single thread static library, retail version
LIBCMT.LIB	Multithread static library, retail version
MSVCRT.LIB	Import library for MSVCRTx0.DLL, retail version
MSVCRTx0.DLL	Multithread DLL library, retail version

Return Value

ldiv returns a structure of type **ldiv_t** that comprises both the quotient and the remainder.

Parameters

numer Numerator

denom Denominator

Remarks

The **ldiv** function divides *numer* by *denom*, computing the quotient and remainder. The sign of the quotient is the same as that of the mathematical quotient. The absolute value of the quotient is the largest integer that is less than the absolute value of the mathematical quotient. If the denominator is 0, the program terminates with an error message. **ldiv** is the same as **div**, except that the arguments of **ldiv** and the members of the returned structure are all of type **long int**.

The **ldiv_t** structure, defined in STDLIB.H, contains **long int quot**, the quotient, and **long int rem**, the remainder.

Example

```
/* LDIV.C: This program takes two long integers
 * as command-line arguments and displays the
 * results of the integer division.
 */

#include <stdlib.h>
#include <math.h>
#include <stdio.h>

void main( void )
{
   long x = 5149627, y = 234879;
   ldiv_t div_result;

   div_result = ldiv( x, y );
   printf( "For %ld / %ld, the quotient is ", x, y );
   printf( "%ld, and the remainder is %ld\n",
           div_result.quot, div_result.rem );
}
```

Output

```
For 5149627 / 234879, the quotient is 21, and the remainder is 217168
```

See Also **div**

_lfind

Performs a linear search for the specified key.

void *_lfind(const void ***key*****, const void** ***base*****, unsigned int** ***num*****, unsigned int** *width*, **int (_ _cdecl** ***compare*****)(const void** ***elem1*****, const void** ***elem2*****));**

Routine	Required Header	Optional Headers	Compatibility
_lfind	<search.h>		Win 95, Win NT, Win32s, 68K, PMac

For additional compatibility information, see "Compatibility" on page ix in the Introduction.

Libraries	
LIBC.LIB	Single thread static library, retail version
LIBCMT.LIB	Multithread static library, retail version
MSVCRT.LIB	Import library for MSVCRTx0.DLL, retail version
MSVCRTx0.DLL	Multithread DLL library, retail version

Return Value

If the key is found, **_lfind** returns a pointer to the element of the array at *base* that matches *key*. If the key is not found, **_lfind** returns **NULL**.

Parameters

key Object to search for

base Pointer to base of search data

num Number of array elements

width Width of array elements

compare Pointer to comparison routine

elem1 Pointer to key for search

elem2 Pointer to array element to be compared with key

Remarks

The **_lfind** function performs a linear search for the value *key* in an array of *num* elements, each of *width* bytes in size. Unlike **bsearch**, **_lfind** does not require the array to be sorted. The *base* argument is a pointer to the base of the array to be searched. The *compare* argument is a pointer to a user-supplied routine that compares two array elements and then returns a value specifying their relationship. **_lfind** calls the *compare* routine one or more times during the search, passing pointers to two array elements on each call. The *compare* routine must compare the elements then return nonzero, meaning the elements are different, or 0, meaning the elements are identical.

Example

```
/* LFIND.C: This program uses _lfind to search for
 * the word "hello" in the command-line arguments.
 */

#include <search.h>
#include <string.h>
#include <stdio.h>

int compare( const void *arg1, const void *arg2 );

void main( unsigned int argc, char **argv )
{
   char **result;
   char *key = "hello";

   result = (char **)_lfind( &key, argv,
                      &argc, sizeof(char *), compare );
   if( result )
      printf( "%s found\n", *result );
   else
      printf( "hello not found!\n" );
}
```

```
int compare(const void *arg1, const void *arg2 )
{
   return( _stricmp( * (char**)arg1, * (char**)arg2 ) );
}
```

Output

```
[C:\code]lfind Hello
Hello found
```

See Also **bsearch**, **_lsearch**, **qsort**

localeconv

Gets detailed information on locale settings.

struct lconv *localeconv(void);

Routine	Required Header	Optional Headers	Compatibility
localeconv	<locale.h>		ANSI, Win 95, Win NT, Win32s, 68K, PMac

For additional compatibility information, see "Compatibility" on page ix in the Introduction.

Libraries	
LIBC.LIB	Single thread static library, retail version
LIBCMT.LIB	Multithread static library, retail version
MSVCRT.LIB	Import library for MSVCRTx0.DLL, retail version
MSVCRTx0.DLL	Multithread DLL library, retail version

Return Value

localeconv returns a pointer to a filled-in object of type **struct lconv**. The values contained in the object can be overwritten by subsequent calls to **localeconv** and do not directly modify the object. Calls to **setlocale** with *category* values of **LC_ALL**, **LC_MONETARY**, or **LC_NUMERIC** overwrite the contents of the structure.

Remarks

The **localeconv** function gets detailed information about numeric formatting for the current locale. This information is stored in a structure of type **lconv**. The **lconv** structure, defined in LOCALE.H, contains the following members:

char *decimal_point Decimal-point character for nonmonetary quantities.

char *thousands_sep Character that separates groups of digits to left of decimal point for nonmonetary quantities.

char *grouping Size of each group of digits in nonmonetary quantities.

char *int_curr_symbol International currency symbol for current locale. First three characters specify alphabetic international currency symbol as defined in the *ISO 4217 Codes for the Representation of Currency and Funds* standard. Fourth character (immediately preceding null character) separates international currency symbol from monetary quantity.

char *currency_symbol Local currency symbol for current locale.

char *mon_decimal_point Decimal-point character for monetary quantities.

char *mon_thousands_sep Separator for groups of digits to left of decimal place in monetary quantities.

char *mon_grouping Size of each group of digits in monetary quantities.

char *positive_sign String denoting sign for nonnegative monetary quantities.

char *negative_sign String denoting sign for negative monetary quantities.

char int_frac_digits Number of digits to right of decimal point in internationally formatted monetary quantities.

char frac_digits Number of digits to right of decimal point in formatted monetary quantities.

char p_cs_precedes Set to 1 if currency symbol precedes value for nonnegative formatted monetary quantity. Set to 0 if symbol follows value.

char p_sep_by_space Set to 1 if currency symbol is separated by space from value for nonnegative formatted monetary quantity. Set to 0 if there is no space separation.

char n_cs_precedes Set to 1 if currency symbol precedes value for negative formatted monetary quantity. Set to 0 if symbol succeeds value.

char n_sep_by_space Set to 1 if currency symbol is separated by space from value for negative formatted monetary quantity. Set to 0 if there is no space separation.

char p_sign_posn Position of positive sign in nonnegative formatted monetary quantities.

char n_sign_posn Position of positive sign in negative formatted monetary quantities.

The **char *** members of the structure are pointers to strings. Any of these (other than **char *decimal_point**) that equals "" is either of zero length or is not supported in the current locale. The **char** members of the structure are nonnegative numbers. Any of these that equals **CHAR_MAX** is not supported in the current locale.

The elements of **grouping** and **mon_grouping** are interpreted according to the following rules.

CHAR_MAX Do not perform any further grouping.

0 Use previous element for each of remaining digits.

n Number of digits that make up current group. Next element is examined to determine size of next group of digits before current group.

The values for **int_curr_symbol** are interpreted according to the following rules:

- The first three characters specify the alphabetic international currency symbol as defined in the *ISO 4217 Codes for the Representation of Currency and Funds* standard.
- The fourth character (immediately preceding the null character) separates the international currency symbol from the monetary quantity.

The values for **p_cs_precedes** and **n_cs_precedes** are interpreted according to the following rules (the **n_cs_precedes** rule is in parentheses):

0 Currency symbol follows value for nonnegative (negative) formatted monetary value.

1 Currency symbol precedes value for nonnegative (negative) formatted monetary value.

The values for **p_sep_by_space** and **n_sep_by_space** are interpreted according to the following rules (the **n_sep_by_space** rule is in parentheses):

0 Currency symbol is separated from value by space for nonnegative (negative) formatted monetary value.

1 There is no space separation between currency symbol and value for nonnegative (negative) formatted monetary value.

The values for **p_sign_posn** and **n_sign_posn** are interpreted according to the following rules:

0 Parentheses surround quantity and currency symbol

1 Sign string precedes quantity and currency symbol

2 Sign string follows quantity and currency symbol

3 Sign string immediately precedes currency symbol

4 Sign string immediately follows currency symbol

See Also **setlocale**, **strcoll** Functions, **strftime**, **strxfrm**

localtime

Converts a time value and corrects for the local time zone.

struct tm *localtime(const time_t ***timer* **);

Routine	Required Header	Optional Headers	Compatibility
localtime	<time.h>		ANSI, Win 95, Win NT, Win32s, 68K, PMac

For additional compatibility information, see "Compatibility" on page ix in the Introduction.

Libraries	
LIBC.LIB	Single thread static library, retail version
LIBCMT.LIB	Multithread static library, retail version
MSVCRT.LIB	Import library for MSVCRTx0.DLL, retail version
MSVCRTx0.DLL	Multithread DLL library, retail version

Return Value

localtime returns a pointer to the structure result. If the value in *timer* represents a date before midnight, January 1, 1970, **localtime** returns **NULL**. The fields of the structure type **tm** store the following values, each of which is an **int**:

tm_sec Seconds after minute (0–59)

tm_min Minutes after hour (0–59)

tm_hour Hours after midnight (0–23)

tm_mday Day of month (1–31)

tm_mon Month (0–11; January = 0)

tm_year Year (current year minus 1900)

tm_wday Day of week (0–6; Sunday = 0)

tm_yday Day of year (0–365; January 1 = 0)

tm_isdst Positive value if daylight saving time is in effect; 0 if daylight saving time is not in effect; negative value if status of daylight saving time is unknown

Parameter

timer Pointer to stored time

Remarks

The **localtime** function converts a time stored as a **time_t** value and stores the result in a structure of type **tm**. The **long** value *timer* represents the seconds elapsed since midnight (00:00:00), January 1, 1970, coordinated universal time (UTC). This value is usually obtained from the **time** function.

gmtime, **mktime**, and **localtime** all use a single statically allocated **tm** structure for the conversion. Each call to one of these routines destroys the result of the previous call.

localtime corrects for the local time zone if the user first sets the global environment variable **TZ**. When **TZ** is set, three other environment variables (**_timezone**, **_daylight**, and **_tzname**) are automatically set as well. See **_tzset** for a description of these variables. **TZ** is a Microsoft extension and not part of the ANSI standard definition of **localtime**.

Note The target environment should try to determine whether daylight saving time is in effect.

Example

```
/* LOCALTIM.C: This program uses time to get the current time
 * and then uses localtime to convert this time to a structure
 * representing the local time. The program converts the result
 * from a 24-hour clock to a 12-hour clock and determines the
 * proper extension (AM or PM).
 */

#include <stdio.h>
#include <string.h>
#include <time.h>

void main( void )
{
        struct tm *newtime;
        char am_pm[] = "AM";
        time_t long_time;

        time( &long_time );                /* Get time as long integer. */
        newtime = localtime( &long_time ); /* Convert to local time. */

        if( newtime->tm_hour > 12 )        /* Set up extension. */
                strcpy( am_pm, "PM" );
        if( newtime->tm_hour > 12 )        /* Convert from 24-hour */
                newtime->tm_hour -= 12;    /*   to 12-hour clock.  */
        if( newtime->tm_hour == 0 )        /*Set hour to 12 if midnight. */
                newtime->tm_hour = 12;

        printf( "%.19s %s\n", asctime( newtime ), am_pm );
}
```

Output

```
Tue Mar 23 11:28:17 AM
```

See Also **asctime**, **ctime**, **_ftime**, **gmtime**, **time**, **_tzset**

_locking

Locks or unlocks bytes of a file.

int _locking(**int** *handle*, **int** *mode*, **long** *nbytes* **);**

Routine	Required Header	Optional Headers	Compatibility
_locking	<io.h> and <sys/locking.h>	<errno.h>	Win 95, Win NT, Win32s, 68K, PMac

For additional compatibility information, see "Compatibility" on page ix in the Introduction.

Libraries	
LIBC.LIB	Single thread static library, retail version
LIBCMT.LIB	Multithread static library, retail version
MSVCRT.LIB	Import library for MSVCRTx0.DLL, retail version
MSVCRTx0.DLL	Multithread DLL library, retail version

Return Value

_locking returns 0 if successful. A return value of –1 indicates failure, in which case **errno** is set to one of the following values:

EACCES Locking violation (file already locked or unlocked).

EBADF Invalid file handle.

EDEADLOCK Locking violation. Returned when the **_LK_LOCK** or **_LK_RLCK** flag is specified and the file cannot be locked after 10 attempts.

EINVAL An invalid argument was given to **_locking**.

Parameters

handle File handle

mode Locking action to perform

nbytes Number of bytes to lock

Remarks

The **_locking** function locks or unlocks *nbytes* bytes of the file specified by *handle*. Locking bytes in a file prevents access to those bytes by other processes. All locking or unlocking begins at the current position of the file pointer and proceeds for the next *nbytes* bytes. It is possible to lock bytes past end of file.

mode must be one of the following manifest constants, which are defined in LOCKING.H:

_LK_LOCK Locks the specified bytes. If the bytes cannot be locked, the program immediately tries again after 1 second. If, after 10 attempts, the bytes cannot be locked, the constant returns an error.

_LK_NBLCK Locks the specified bytes. If the bytes cannot be locked, the constant returns an error.

_LK_NBRLCK Same as **_LK_NBLCK**.

_LK_RLCK Same as **_LK_LOCK**.

_LK_UNLCK Unlocks the specified bytes, which must have been previously locked.

Multiple regions of a file that do not overlap can be locked. A region being unlocked must have been previously locked. **_locking** does not merge adjacent regions; if two locked regions are adjacent, each region must be unlocked separately. Regions should be locked only briefly and should be unlocked before closing a file or exiting the program.

Example

```
/* LOCKING.C: This program opens a file with sharing. It locks
 * some bytes before reading them, then unlocks them. Note that the
 * program works correctly only if the file exists.
 */

#include <io.h>
#include <sys/types.h>
#include <sys/stat.h>
#include <sys/locking.h>
#include <share.h>
#include <fcntl.h>
#include <stdio.h>
#include <stdlib.h>

void main( void )
{
   int  fh, numread;
   char buffer[40];

   /* Quit if can't open file or system doesn't
    * support sharing.
    */
   fh = _sopen( "locking.c", _O_RDWR, _SH_DENYNO,
                  _S_IREAD | _S_IWRITE );
   if( fh == -1 )
      exit( 1 );

   /* Lock some bytes and read them. Then unlock. */
   if( _locking( fh, LK_NBLCK, 30L ) != -1 )
```

```
    {
       printf( "No one can change these bytes while I'm reading them\n" );
       numread = _read( fh, buffer, 30 );
       printf( "%d bytes read: %.30s\n", numread, buffer );
       lseek( fh, 0L, SEEK_SET );
      _locking( fh, LK_UNLCK, 30L );
       printf( "Now I'm done. Do what you will with them\n" );
    }
    else
       perror( "Locking failed\n" );

    _close( fh );
}
```

Output

```
No one can change these bytes while I'm reading them
30 bytes read: /* LOCKING.C: This program ope
Now I'm done. Do what you will with them
```

See Also **_creat**, **_open**

log, log10

Calculates logarithms.

double log(double *x* **);**
double log10(double *x* **);**

Routine	Required Header	Optional Headers	Compatibility
log	<math.h>		ANSI, Win 95, Win NT, Win32s, 68K, PMac
log10	<math.h>		ANSI, Win 95, Win NT, Win32s, 68K, PMac

For additional compatibility information, see "Compatibility" on page ix in the Introduction.

Libraries	
LIBC.LIB	Single thread static library, retail version
LIBCMT.LIB	Multithread static library, retail version
MSVCRT.LIB	Import library for MSVCRTx0.DLL, retail version
MSVCRTx0.DLL	Multithread DLL library, retail version

Return Value

The **log** functions return the logarithm of *x* if successful. If *x* is negative, these functions return an indefinite (same as a quiet NaN). If *x* is 0, they return INF (infinite). You can modify error handling by using the **_matherr** routine.

Parameter

x Value whose logarithm is to be found

Example

```
/* LOG.C: This program uses log and log10
 * to calculate the natural logarithm and
 * the base-10 logarithm of 9,000.
 */

#include <math.h>
#include <stdio.h>

void main( void )
{
   double x = 9000.0;
   double y;

   y = log( x );
   printf( "log( %.2f ) = %f\n", x, y );
   y = log10( x );
   printf( "log10( %.2f ) = %f\n", x, y );
}
```

Output

```
log( 9000.00 ) = 9.104980
log10( 9000.00 ) = 3.954243
```

See Also **exp**, **_matherr**, **pow**

_logb

Extracts exponential value of double-precision floating-point argument.

double _logb(double *x* **);**

Routine	Required Header	Optional Headers	Compatibility
_logb	<float.h>		Win 95, Win NT, Win32s, 68K, PMac

For additional compatibility information, see "Compatibility" on page ix in the Introduction.

Libraries

LIBC.LIB	Single thread static library, retail version
LIBCMT.LIB	Multithread static library, retail version
MSVCRT.LIB	Import library for MSVCRTx0.DLL, retail version
MSVCRTx0.DLL	Multithread DLL library, retail version

Return Value

_logb returns the unbiased exponential value of *x*.

Parameter

x Double-precision floating-point value

Remarks

The **_logb** function extracts the exponential value of its double-precision floating-point argument *x*, as though *x* were represented with infinite range. If the argument *x* is denormalized, it is treated as if it were normalized.

See Also **frexp**

longjmp

Restores stack environment and execution locale.

void longjmp(jmp_buf *env*, **int** *value* **);**

Routine	Required Header	Optional Headers	Compatibility
longjmp	<setjmp.h>		ANSI, Win 95, Win NT, Win32s, 68K, PMac

For additional compatibility information, see "Compatibility" on page ix in the Introduction.

Libraries

LIBC.LIB	Single thread static library, retail version
LIBCMT.LIB	Multithread static library, retail version
MSVCRT.LIB	Import library for MSVCRTx0.DLL, retail version
MSVCRTx0.DLL	Multithread DLL library, retail version

Return Value

None

Parameters

env Variable in which environment is stored

value Value to be returned to **setjmp** call

Remarks

The **longjmp** function restores a stack environment and execution locale previously saved in *env* by **setjmp**. **setjmp** and **longjmp** provide a way to execute a nonlocal **goto**; they are typically used to pass execution control to error-handling or recovery code in a previously called routine without using the normal call and return conventions.

A call to **setjmp** causes the current stack environment to be saved in *env*. A subsequent call to **longjmp** restores the saved environment and returns control to the point immediately following the corresponding **setjmp** call. Execution resumes as if *value* had just been returned by the **setjmp** call. The values of all variables (except register variables) that are accessible to the routine receiving control contain the values they had when **longjmp** was called. The values of register variables are unpredictable. The value returned by **setjmp** must be nonzero. If *value* is passed as 0, the value 1 is substituted in the actual return.

Call **longjmp** before the function that called **setjmp** returns; otherwise the results are unpredictable.

Observe the following restrictions when using **longjmp**:

- Do not assume that the values of the register variables will remain the same. The values of register variables in the routine calling **setjmp** may not be restored to the proper values after **longjmp** is executed.
- Do not use **longjmp** to transfer control out of an interrupt-handling routine unless the interrupt is caused by a floating-point exception. In this case, a program may return from an interrupt handler via **longjmp** if it first reinitializes the floating-point math package by calling **_fpreset**.
- Be careful when using **setjmp** and **longjmp** in C++ programs. Because these functions do not support C++ object semantics, it is safer to use the C++ exception-handling mechanism.

Example

See the example for **_fpreset**.

See Also **setjmp**

_lrotl, _lrotr

Rotate bits to the left (**_lrotl**) or right (**_lrotr**).

unsigned long _lrotl(unsigned long *value*, **int** *shift* **);**
unsigned long _lrotr(unsigned long *value*, **int** *shift* **);**

Routine	Required Header	Optional Headers	Compatibility
_lrotl	<stdlib.h>		Win 95, Win NT, Win32s, 68K, PMac
_lrotr	<stdlib.h>		Win 95, Win NT, Win32s, 68K, PMac

For additional compatibility information, see "Compatibility" on page ix in the Introduction.

Libraries	
LIBC.LIB	Single thread static library, retail version
LIBCMT.LIB	Multithread static library, retail version
MSVCRT.LIB	Import library for MSVCRTx0.DLL, retail version
MSVCRTx0.DLL	Multithread DLL library, retail version

Return Value

Both functions return the rotated value. There is no error return.

Parameters

value Value to be rotated

shift Number of bits to shift *value*

Remarks

The **_lrotl** and **_lrotr** functions rotate *value* by *shift* bits. **_lrotl** rotates the value left. **_lrotr** rotates the value right. Both functions "wrap" bits rotated off one end of *value* to the other end.

Example

```
/* LROT.C */

#include <stdlib.h>
#include <stdio.h>

void main( void )
{
   unsigned long val = 0x0fac35791;
   printf( "0x%8.8lx rotated left eight times is 0x%8.8lx\n",
           val, _lrotl( val, 8 ) );
   printf( "0x%8.8lx rotated right four times is 0x%8.8lx\n",
           val, _lrotr( val, 4 ) );
}
```

Output

```
0xfac35791 rotated left eight times is 0xc35791fa
0xfac35791 rotated right four times is 0x1fac3579
```

See Also **_rotl**, **_rotr**

_lsearch

Performs a linear search for a value; adds to end of list if not found.

void *_lsearch(const void ***key*, void ***base***, unsigned int ***num***, unsigned int** *width***, int (_ _cdecl ***compare***)(const void ***elem1***, const void ***elem2***));**

Routine	Required Header	Optional Headers	Compatibility
_lsearch	<search.h>		Win 95, Win NT, Win32s, 68K, PMac

For additional compatibility information, see "Compatibility" on page ix in the Introduction.

Libraries	
LIBC.LIB	Single thread static library, retail version
LIBCMT.LIB	Multithread static library, retail version
MSVCRT.LIB	Import library for MSVCRTx0.DLL, retail version
MSVCRTx0.DLL	Multithread DLL library, retail version

Return Value

If the key is found, **_lsearch** returns a pointer to the element of the array at *base* that matches *key*. If the key is not found, **_lsearch** returns a pointer to the newly added item at the end of the array.

Parameters

key Object to search for

base Pointer to base of array to be searched

num Number of elements

width Width of each array element

compare Pointer to comparison routine

elem1 Pointer to key for search

elem2 Pointer to array element to be compared with key

Remarks

The **_lsearch** function performs a linear search for the value *key* in an array of *num* elements, each of *width* bytes in size. Unlike **bsearch**, **_lsearch** does not require the array to be sorted. If *key* is not found, **_lsearch** adds it to the end of the array and increments *num*.

The *compare* argument is a pointer to a user-supplied routine that compares two array elements and returns a value specifying their relationship. **_lsearch** calls the *compare* routine one or more times during the search, passing pointers to two array elements on each call. *compare* must compare the elements, then return either nonzero, meaning the elements are different, or 0, meaning the elements are identical.

Example

See the example for **_lfind**.

See Also **bsearch**, **_lfind**

_lseek, _lseeki64

Move a file pointer to the specified location.

long _lseek(int *handle*, **long** *offset*, **int** *origin* **);**
_ _int64 _lseeki64(int *handle*, **_ _int64** *offset*, **int** *origin* **);**

Routine	Required Header	Optional Headers	Compatibility
_lseek	<io.h>		Win 95, Win NT, Win32s, 68K, PMac
_lseeki64	<io.h>		Win 95, Win NT, Win32s

For additional compatibility information, see "Compatibility" on page ix in the Introduction.

Libraries	
LIBC.LIB	Single thread static library, retail version
LIBCMT.LIB	Multithread static library, retail version
MSVCRT.LIB	Import library for MSVCRTx0.DLL, retail version
MSVCRTx0.DLL	Multithread DLL library, retail version

Return Value

_lseek returns the offset, in bytes, of the new position from the beginning of the file. **_lseeki64** returns the offset in a 64-bit integer. The function returns –1L to indicate an error and sets **errno** either to **EBADF**, meaning the file handle is invalid, or to **EINVAL**, meaning the value for *origin* is invalid or the position specified by *offset* is before the beginning of the file. On devices incapable of seeking (such as terminals and printers), the return value is undefined.

Parameters

handle Handle referring to open file

offset Number of bytes from *origin*

origin Initial position

Remarks

The **_lseek** function moves the file pointer associated with *handle* to a new location that is *offset* bytes from *origin*. The next operation on the file occurs at the new location. The *origin* argument must be one of the following constants, which are defined in STDIO.H:

SEEK_SET Beginning of file

SEEK_CUR Current position of file pointer

SEEK_END End of file

You can use **_lseek** to reposition the pointer anywhere in a file or beyond the end of the file.

Example

```
/* LSEEK.C: This program first opens a file named LSEEK.C.
 * It then uses _lseek to find the beginning of the file,
 * to find the current position in the file, and to find
 * the end of the file.
 */

#include <io.h>
#include <fcntl.h>
#include <stdlib.h>
#include <stdio.h>

void main( void )
{
   int fh;
   long pos;               /* Position of file pointer */
   char buffer[10];

   fh = _open( "lseek.c", _O_RDONLY );

   /* Seek the beginning of the file: */
   pos = _lseek( fh, 0L, SEEK_SET );
   if( pos == -1L )
      perror( "_lseek to beginning failed" );
   else
      printf( "Position for beginning of file seek = %ld\n", pos );

   /* Move file pointer a little */
    _read( fh, buffer, 10 );
```

```
   /* Find current position: */
   pos = _lseek( fh, 0L, SEEK_CUR );
   if( pos == -1L )
      perror( "_lseek to current position failed" );
   else
      printf( "Position for current position seek = %ld\n", pos );

   /* Set the end of the file: */
   pos = _lseek( fh, 0L, SEEK_END );
   if( pos == -1L )
      perror( "_lseek to end failed" );
   else
      printf( "Position for end of file seek = %ld\n", pos );

   _close( fh );
}
```

Output

```
Position for beginning of file seek = 0
Position for current position seek = 10
Position for end of file seek = 1207
```

See Also **fseek**, **_tell**

_ltoa, _ltow

Convert a long integer to a string.

char *_ltoa(long *value*, **char** **string*, **int** *radix* **);**
wchar_t *_ltow(long *value*, **wchar_t** **string*, **int** *radix* **);**

Routine	Required Header	Optional Headers	Compatibility
_ltoa	<stdlib.h>		Win 95, Win NT, Win32s, 68K, PMac
_ltow	<stdlib.h>		Win 95, Win NT, Win32s

For additional compatibility information, see "Compatibility" on page ix in the Introduction.

Libraries	
LIBC.LIB	Single thread static library, retail version
LIBCMT.LIB	Multithread static library, retail version
MSVCRT.LIB	Import library for MSVCRTx0.DLL, retail version
MSVCRTx0.DLL	Multithread DLL library, retail version

Return Value

Each of these functions returns a pointer to *string*. There is no error return.

Parameters

value Number to be converted

string String result

radix Base of *value*

Remarks

The **_ltoa** function converts the digits of *value* to a null-terminated character string and stores the result (up to 33 bytes) in *string*. The *radix* argument specifies the base of *value*, which must be in the range 2–36. If *radix* equals 10 and *value* is negative, the first character of the stored string is the minus sign (–). **_ltow** is a wide-character version of **_ltoa**; the second argument and return value of **_ltow** are wide-character strings. Each of these functions is Microsoft-specific.

Example

See the example for **_itoa**.

See Also **_itoa**, **_ultoa**

_makepath, _wmakepath

Create a path name from components.

void _makepath(char **path*, **const char** **drive*, **const char** **dir*, **const char** **fname*, **const char** **ext* **);**

void _wmakepath(wchar_t **path*, **const wchar_t** **drive*, **const wchar_t** **dir*, **const wchar_t** **fname*, **const wchar_t** **ext* **);**

Routine	Required Header	Optional Headers	Compatibility
_makepath	<stdlib.h>		Win 95, Win NT, Win32s
_wmakepath	<stdlib.h> or <wchar.h>		Win 95, Win NT, Win32s

For additional compatibility information, see "Compatibility" on page ix in the Introduction.

Libraries	
LIBC.LIB	Single thread static library, retail version
LIBCMT.LIB	Multithread static library, retail version
MSVCRT.LIB	Import library for MSVCRTx0.DLL, retail version
MSVCRTx0.DLL	Multithread DLL library, retail version

Return Value

None

Parameters

path Full path buffer

drive Drive letter

dir Directory path

fname Filename

ext File extension

Remarks

The **_makepath** function creates a single path and stores it in *path*. The path may include a drive letter, directory path, filename, and filename extension. **_wmakepath** is a wide-character version of **_makepath**; the arguments to **_wmakepath** are wide-character strings. **_wmakepath** and **_makepath** behave identically otherwise.

The following arguments point to buffers containing the path elements:

drive Contains a letter (A, B, and so on) corresponding to the desired drive and an optional trailing colon. **_makepath** inserts the colon automatically in the composite path if it is missing. If *drive* is a null character or an empty string, no drive letter and colon appear in the composite *path* string.

dir Contains the path of directories, not including the drive designator or the actual filename. The trailing slash is optional, and either a forward slash (/) or a backslash (\) or both may be used in a single *dir* argument. If a trailing slash (/ or \) is not specified, it is inserted automatically. If *dir* is a null character or an empty string, no slash is inserted in the composite *path* string.

fname Contains the base filename without any extensions. If *fname* is **NULL** or points to an empty string, no filename is inserted in the composite *path* string.

ext Contains the actual filename extension, with or without a leading period (.). **_makepath** inserts the period automatically if it does not appear in *ext*. If *ext* is a null character or an empty string, no period is inserted in the composite *path* string.

The *path* argument must point to an empty buffer large enough to hold the complete path. Although there are no size limits on any of the fields that constitute *path*, the composite *path* must be no larger than the **_MAX_PATH** constant, defined in STDLIB.H. **_MAX_PATH** may be larger than the current operating-system version will handle.

Example

```
/* MAKEPATH.C */

#include <stdlib.h>
#include <stdio.h>
```

```
void main( void )
{
   char path_buffer[_MAX_PATH];
   char drive[_MAX_DRIVE];
   char dir[_MAX_DIR];
   char fname[_MAX_FNAME];
   char ext[_MAX_EXT];

   _makepath( path_buffer, "c", "\\sample\\crt\\", "makepath", "c" );
   printf( "Path created with _makepath: %s\n\n", path_buffer );
   _splitpath( path_buffer, drive, dir, fname, ext );
   printf( "Path extracted with _splitpath:\n" );
   printf( "  Drive: %s\n", drive );
   printf( "  Dir: %s\n", dir );
   printf( "  Filename: %s\n", fname );
   printf( "  Ext: %s\n", ext );
}
```

Output

```
Path created with _makepath: c:\sample\crt\makepath.c

Path extracted with _splitpath:
  Drive: c:
  Dir: \sample\crt\
  Filename: makepath
  Ext: .c
```

See Also **_fullpath**, **_splitpath**

malloc

Allocates memory blocks.

void *malloc(size_t *size* **);**

Routine	Required Header	Optional Headers	Compatibility
malloc	<stdlib.h> and <malloc.h>		ANSI, Win 95, Win NT, Win32s, 68K, PMac

For additional compatibility information, see "Compatibility" on page ix in the Introduction.

Libraries	
LIBC.LIB	Single thread static library, retail version
LIBCMT.LIB	Multithread static library, retail version
MSVCRT.LIB	Import library for MSVCRTx0.DLL, retail version
MSVCRTx0.DLL	Multithread DLL library, retail version

Return Value

malloc returns a void pointer to the allocated space, or **NULL** if there is insufficient memory available. To return a pointer to a type other than **void**, use a type cast on the return value. The storage space pointed to by the return value is guaranteed to be suitably aligned for storage of any type of object. If size is 0, **malloc** allocates a zero-length item in the heap and returns a valid pointer to that item. Always check the return from **malloc**, even if the amount of memory requested is small.

Parameter

size Bytes to allocate

Remarks

The **malloc** function allocates a memory block of at least *size* bytes. The block may be larger than *size* bytes because of space required for alignment and maintenance information.

The startup code uses **malloc** to allocate storage for the **_environ**, **envp**, and **argv** variables. The following functions and their wide-character counterparts also call **malloc**:

calloc	**fscanf**	**_getw**	**setvbuf**
_exec functions	**fseek**	**_popen**	**_spawn** functions
fgetc	**fsetpos**	**printf**	**_strdup**
_fgetchar	**_fullpath**	**putc**	**system**
fgets	**fwrite**	**putchar**	**_tempnam**
fprintf	**getc**	**_putenv**	**ungetc**
fputc	**getchar**	**puts**	**vfprintf**
_fputchar	**_getcwd**	**_putw**	**vprintf**
fputs	**_getdcwd**	**scanf**	
fread	**gets**	**_searchenv**	

The C++ **_set_new_mode** function sets the new handler mode for **malloc**. The new handler mode indicates whether, on failure, **malloc** is to call the new handler routine as set by **_set_new_handler**. By default, **malloc** does not call the new handler routine on failure to allocate memory. You can override this default behavior so that, when **malloc** fails to allocate memory, **malloc** calls the new handler routine in the same way that the **new** operator does when it fails for the same reason. To override the default, call

```
_set_new_mode(1)
```

early in your program, or link with NEWMODE.OBJ.

When the application is linked with a debug version of the C run-time libraries, **malloc** resolves to **_malloc_dbg**. For more information about how the heap is managed during the debugging process, see Chapter 4, "Debug Version of the C Run-Time Library."

Example

```
/* MALLOC.C: This program allocates memory with
 * malloc, then frees the memory with free.
 */

#include <stdlib.h>         /* For _MAX_PATH definition */
#include <stdio.h>
#include <malloc.h>

void main( void )
{
   char *string;

   /* Allocate space for a path name */
   string = malloc( _MAX_PATH );
   if( string == NULL )
      printf( "Insufficient memory available\n" );
   else
   {
      printf( "Memory space allocated for path name\n" );
      free( string );
      printf( "Memory freed\n" );
   }
}
```

Output

```
Memory space allocated for path name
Memory freed
```

See Also **calloc**, **free**, **realloc**

_matherr

Handles math errors.

int _matherr(struct _exception ***except*** **);**

Routine	Required Header	Optional Headers	Compatibility
_matherr	<math.h>		Win 95, Win NT, Win32s

For additional compatibility information, see "Compatibility" on page ix in the Introduction.

Libraries

LIBC.LIB	Single thread static library, retail version
LIBCMT.LIB	Multithread static library, retail version
MSVCRT.LIB	Import library for MSVCRTx0.DLL, retail version
MSVCRTx0.DLL	Multithread DLL library, retail version

Return Value

_matherr returns 0 to indicate an error or a non-zero value to indicate success. If **_matherr** returns 0, an error message can be displayed, and **errno** is set to an appropriate error value. If **_matherr** returns a nonzero value, no error message is displayed, and **errno** remains unchanged.

Parameter

except Pointer to structure containing error information

Remarks

The **_matherr** function processes errors generated by the floating-point functions of the math library. These functions call **_matherr** when an error is detected.

For special error handling, you can provide a different definition of **_matherr**. If you use the dynamically linked version of the C run-time library (MSVCRTx0.DLL), you can replace the default **_matherr** routine in a client executable with a user-defined version. However, you cannot replace the default **_matherr** routine in a DLL client of MSVCRTx0.DLL.

When an error occurs in a math routine, **_matherr** is called with a pointer to an **_exception** type structure (defined in MATH.H) as an argument. The **_exception** structure contains the following elements:

int type Exception type

char *name Name of function where error occurred

double arg1, **arg2** First and second (if any) arguments to function

double retval Value to be returned by function

The **type** specifies the type of math error. It is one of the following values, defined in MATH.H:

_DOMAIN Argument domain error.

_SING Argument singularity.

_OVERFLOW Overflow range error.

_PLOSS Partial loss of significance.

_TLOSS Total loss of significance.

_UNDERFLOW The result is too small to be represented. (This condition is not currently supported.)

The structure member **name** is a pointer to a null-terminated string containing the name of the function that caused the error. The structure members **arg1** and **arg2** specify the values that caused the error. (If only one argument is given, it is stored in **arg1**.)

The default return value for the given error is **retval**. If you change the return value, it must specify whether an error actually occurred.

Example

```
/* MATHERR.C illustrates writing an error routine for math
 * functions. The error function must be:
 *      _matherr
 */

#include <math.h>
#include <string.h>
#include <stdio.h>

void main()
{
    /* Do several math operations that cause errors. The _matherr
     * routine handles _DOMAIN errors, but lets the system handle
     * other errors normally.
     */
    printf( "log( -2.0 ) = %e\n", log( -2.0 ) );
    printf( "log10( -5.0 ) = %e\n", log10( -5.0 ) );
    printf( "log( 0.0 ) = %e\n", log( 0.0 ) );
}

/* Handle several math errors caused by passing a negative argument
 * to log or log10 (_DOMAIN errors). When this happens, _matherr
 * returns the natural or base-10 logarithm of the absolute value
 * of the argument and suppresses the usual error message.
 */
int _matherr( struct _exception *except )
{
    /* Handle _DOMAIN errors for log or log10. */
    if( except->type == _DOMAIN )
    {
        if( strcmp( except->name, "log" ) == 0 )
        {
            except->retval = log( -(except->arg1) );
            printf( "Special: using absolute value: %s: _DOMAIN "
                    "error\n", except->name );
            return 1;
        }
        else if( strcmp( except->name, "log10" ) == 0 )
```

```
        {
            except->retval = log10( -(except->arg1) );
            printf( "Special: using absolute value: %s: _DOMAIN "
                     "error\n", except->name );
            return 1;
        }
    }
    else
    {
        printf( "Normal: " );
        return 0;    /* Else use the default actions */
    }
}
```

Output

```
Special: using absolute value: log: _DOMAIN error
log( -2.0 ) = 6.931472e-001
Special: using absolute value: log10: _DOMAIN error
log10( -5.0 ) = 6.989700e-001
Normal: log( 0.0 ) = -1.#INF00e+000
```

_ _max

Returns the larger of two values.

type **_ _max(** *type a***,** *type b* **);**

Routine	Required Header	Optional Headers	Compatibility
_ _max	<stdlib.h>		Win 95, Win NT, Win32s, 68K, PMac

For additional compatibility information, see "Compatibility" on page ix in the Introduction.

Libraries	
LIBC.LIB	Single thread static library, retail version
LIBCMT.LIB	Multithread static library, retail version
MSVCRT.LIB	Import library for MSVCRTx0.DLL, retail version
MSVCRTx0.DLL	Multithread DLL library, retail version

Return Value

_ _max returns the larger of its arguments.

Parameters

type Any numeric data type

a, b Values of any numeric type to be compared

Remarks

The _ _**max** macro compares two values and returns the value of the larger one. The arguments can be of any numeric data type, signed or unsigned. Both arguments and the return value must be of the same data type.

Example

See the example for _ _**min**.

See Also _ _**min**

_mbbtombc

unsigned short _mbbtombc(unsigned short *c* **);**

Routine	Required Header	Optional Headers	Compatibility
_mbbtombc	<mbstring.h>		Win 95, Win NT, Win32s, 68K, PMac

For additional compatibility information, see "Compatibility" on page ix in the Introduction.

Libraries	
LIBC.LIB	Single thread static library, retail version
LIBCMT.LIB	Multithread static library, retail version
MSVCRT.LIB	Import library for MSVCRTx0.DLL, retail version
MSVCRTx0.DLL	Multithread DLL library, retail version

Return Value

If **_mbbtombc** successfully converts *c*, it returns a multibyte character; otherwise it returns *c*.

Parameter

c Single-byte character to convert.

Remarks

The **_mbbtombc** function converts a given single-byte multibyte character to a corresponding double-byte multibyte character. Characters must be within the range 0x20–0x7E or 0xA1–0xDF to be converted.

In earlier versions, **_mbbtombc** was called **hantozen**. For new code, use **_mbbtombc** instead.

See Also **_mbctombb**

_mbbtype

int _mbbtype(unsigned char *c*, **int** *type* **);**

Routine	Required Header	Optional Headers	Compatibility
_mbbtype	<mbstring.h>	<mbctype.h>[1]	Win 95, Win NT, Win32s, 68K, PMac

[1] For definitions of manifest constants used as return values.

For additional compatibility information, see "Compatibility" on page ix in the Introduction.

Libraries	
LIBC.LIB	Single thread static library, retail version
LIBCMT.LIB	Multithread static library, retail version
MSVCRT.LIB	Import library for MSVCRTx0.DLL, retail version
MSVCRTx0.DLL	Multithread DLL library, retail version

Return Value

_mbbtype returns the type of byte within a string. This decision is context-sensitive as specified by the value of *type*, which provides the control test condition. *type* is the type of the previous byte in the string.The manifest constants in the following table are defined in MBCTYPE.H.

Value of *type*	_mbbtype Tests For	Return Value	c
Any value except 1	Valid single byte or lead byte	**_MBC_SINGLE** (0)	Single byte (0x20–0x7E, 0xA1–0xDF)
Any value except 1	Valid single byte or lead byte	**_MBC_LEAD** (1)	Lead byte of multibyte character (0x81–0x9F, 0xE0–0xFC)
Any value except 1	Valid single-byte or lead byte	**_MBC_ILLEGAL** (–1)	Invalid character (any value except 0x20–0x7E, 0xA1–0xDF, 0x81–0x9F, 0xE0–0xFC
1	Valid trail byte	**_MBC_TRAIL** (2)	Trailing byte of multibyte character (0x40–0x7E, 0x80–0xFC)
1	Valid trail byte	**_MBC_ILLEGAL** (–1)	Invalid character (any value except 0x20–0x7E, 0xA1–0xDF, 0x81–0x9F, 0xE0–0xFC

Parameters

c Character to test

type Type of byte to test for

Remarks

The **_mbbtype** function determines the type of a byte in a multibyte character. If the value of *type* is any value except 1, **_mbbtype** tests for a valid single-byte or lead byte of a multibyte character. If the value of *type* is 1, **_mbbtype** tests for a valid trail byte of a multibyte character.

In earlier versions, **_mbbtype** was called **chkctype**. For new code, **_mbbtype** use instead.

_mbccpy

void _mbccpy(unsigned char ****dest*, const unsigned char ****src* **);**

Routine	Required Header	Optional Headers	Compatibility
_mbccpy	<mbctype.h>		Win 95, Win NT, Win32s, 68K, PMac

For additional compatibility information, see "Compatibility" on page ix in the Introduction.

Libraries	
LIBC.LIB	Single thread static library, retail version
LIBCMT.LIB	Multithread static library, retail version
MSVCRT.LIB	Import library for MSVCRTx0.DLL, retail version
MSVCRTx0.DLL	Multithread DLL library, retail version

Return Value

None

Parameters

dest Copy destination

src Multibyte character to copy

Remarks

The **_mbccpy** function copies one multibyte character from *src* to *dest*. If *src* does not point to the lead byte of a multibyte character as determined by an implicit call to **_ismbblead**, no copy is performed.

See Also **_mbclen**

_mbcjistojms, _mbcjmstojis

unsigned int _mbcjistojms(unsigned int *c* **);**
unsigned int _mbcjmstojis(unsigned int *c* **);**

Routine	Required Header	Optional Headers	Compatibility
_mbcjistojms	<mbstring.h>		Win 95, Win NT, Win32s, 68K, PMac
_mbcjmstojis	<mbstring.h>		Win 95, Win NT, Win32s, 68K, PMac

For additional compatibility information, see "Compatibility" on page ix in the Introduction.

Libraries	
LIBC.LIB	Single thread static library, retail version
LIBCMT.LIB	Multithread static library, retail version
MSVCRT.LIB	Import library for MSVCRTx0.DLL, retail version
MSVCRTx0.DLL	Multithread DLL library, retail version

Return Value

_mbcjistojms and **_mbcjmstojis** return a converted character. Otherwise they return 0.

Parameter

c Character to convert

Remarks

The **_mbcjistojms** function converts a Japan Industry Standard (JIS) character to a Microsoft Kanji (Shift JIS) character. The character is converted only if the lead and trail bytes are in the range 0x21–0x7E.

The **_mbcjmstojis** function converts a Shift JIS character to a JIS character. The character is converted only if the lead byte is in the range 0x81–0x9F or 0xE0–0xFC, and the trail byte is in the range 0x40–0x7E or 0x80–0xFC.

The value *c* should be a 16-bit value whose upper eight bits represent the lead byte of the character to convert and whose lower eight bits represent the trail byte.

In earlier versions, **_mbcjistojms** and **_mbcjmstojis** were called **jistojms** and **jmstojis**, repectively. **_mbcjistojms** and **_mbcjmstojis** should be used instead.

See Also **_ismbb** Routines

_mbclen, mblen

Get the length and determine the validity of a multibyte character.

size_t _mbclen(const unsigned char ***_c_ **);
int mblen(const char ***_mbstr_, size_t** _count_ **);**

Routine	Required Header	Optional Headers	Compatibility
_mbclen	<mbstring.h>		Win 95, Win NT, Win32s, 68K, PMac
mblen	<stdlib.h>		ANSI, Win 95, Win NT, Win32s, 68K, PMac

For additional compatibility information, see "Compatibility" on page ix in the Introduction.

Libraries

LIBC.LIB	Single thread static library, retail version
LIBCMT.LIB	Multithread static library, retail version
MSVCRT.LIB	Import library for MSVCRTx0.DLL, retail version
MSVCRTx0.DLL	Multithread DLL library, retail version

Return Value

_mbclen returns 1 or 2, according to whether the multibyte character *c* is one or two bytes long. There is no error return for **_mbclen**. If *mbstr* is not **NULL**, **mblen** returns the length, in bytes, of the multibyte character. If *mbstr* is **NULL**, or if it points to the wide-character null character, **mblen** returns 0. If the object that *mbstr* points to does not form a valid multibyte character within the first *count* characters, **mblen** returns –1.

Parameters

c Multibyte character

mbstr Address of multibyte-character byte sequence

count Number of bytes to check

Remarks

The **_mbclen** function returns the length, in bytes, of the multibyte character *c*. If *c* does not point to the lead byte of a multibyte character as determined by an implicit call to **_ismbblead**, the result of **_mbclen** is unpredictable.

mblen returns the length in bytes of *mbstr* if it is a valid multibyte character. It examines *count* or fewer bytes contained in *mbstr*, but not more than **MB_CUR_MAX** bytes. **mblen** determines multibyte-character validity according to the **LC_CTYPE** category setting of the current locale. For more information on the **LC_CTYPE** category, see **setlocale**.

Example

```
/* MBLEN.C illustrates the behavior of the mblen function
 */

#include <stdlib.h>
#include <stdio.h>

void main( void )
{
    int      i;
    char    *pmbc = (char *)malloc( sizeof( char ) );
    wchar_t  wc   = L'a';

    printf( "Convert wide character to multibyte character:\n" );
    i = wctomb( pmbc, wc );
    printf( "\tCharacters converted: %u\n", i );
    printf( "\tMultibyte character: %x\n\n", pmbc );

    i = mblen( pmbc, MB_CUR_MAX );
    printf( "Length in bytes of multibyte character %x: %u\n", pmbc, i );

    pmbc = NULL;
    i = mblen( pmbc, MB_CUR_MAX );
    printf( "Length in bytes of NULL multibyte character %x: %u\n", pmbc, i );
}
```

Output

```
Convert wide character to multibyte character:
    Characters converted: 1
    Multibyte character: 2c02cc

Length in bytes of multibyte character 2c02cc: 1
Length in bytes of NULL multibyte character 0: 0
```

See Also **_mbccpy**, **_mbslen**

_mbctohira, _mbctokata

unsigned int _mbctohira(unsigned int *c* **);**
unsigned int _mbctokata(unsigned int *c* **);**

Routine	Required Header	Optional Headers	Compatibility
_mbctohira	<mbstring.h>		Win 95, Win NT, Win32s, 68K, PMac
_mbctokata	<mbstring.h>		Win 95, Win NT, Win32s, 68K, PMac

For additional compatibility information, see "Compatibility" on page ix in the Introduction.

Libraries	
LIBC.LIB	Single thread static library, retail version
LIBCMT.LIB	Multithread static library, retail version
MSVCRT.LIB	Import library for MSVCRTx0.DLL, retail version
MSVCRTx0.DLL	Multithread DLL library, retail version

Return Value

Each of these functions returns the converted character *c*, if possible. Otherwise it returns the character *c* unchanged.

Parameter

c Multibyte character to convert

Remarks

The **_mbctohira** and **_mbctohira** functions test a character *c* and, if possible, apply one of the following conversions.

Routine	Converts
_mbctohira	Multibyte katakana to multibyte hiragana
_mbctokata	Multibyte hiragana to multibyte katakana

In previous versions, **_mbctohira** was called **jtohira** and **_mbctokata** was called **jtokata**. For new code, use the new names instead.

See Also **_mbcjistojms**, **_mbctolower**, **_mbctombb**

_mbctolower, _mbctoupper

unsigned int _mbctolower(unsigned int *c* **);**
unsigned int _mbctoupper(unsigned int *c* **);**

Routine	Required Header	Optional Headers	Compatibility
_mbctolower	<mbstring.h>		Win 95, Win NT, Win32s, 68K, PMac
_mbctoupper	<mbstring.h>		Win 95, Win NT, Win32s, 68K, PMac

For additional compatibility information, see "Compatibility" on page ix in the Introduction.

Libraries	
LIBC.LIB	Single thread static library, retail version
LIBCMT.LIB	Multithread static library, retail version
MSVCRT.LIB	Import library for MSVCRTx0.DLL, retail version
MSVCRTx0.DLL	Multithread DLL library, retail version

Return Value

Each of these functions returns the converted character *c*, if possible. Otherwise it returns the character *c* unchanged.

Parameter

c Multibyte character to convert

Remarks

The **_mbctolower** and **_mbctoupper** functions test a character *c* and, if possible, apply one of the following conversions.

Routine	Converts
_mbctolower	Uppercase character to lowercase character
_mbctoupper	Lowercase character to uppercase character

In previous versions, **_mbctolower** was called **jtolower**, and **_mbctoupper** was called **jtoupper**. For new code, use the new names instead.

See Also **_mbbtombc**, **_mbcjistojms**, **_mbctohira**, **_mbctombb**

_mbctombb

unsigned int _mbctombb(unsigned int *c* **);**

Routine	Required Header	Optional Headers	Compatibility
_mbctombb	<mbstring.h>		Win 95, Win NT, Win32s, 68K, PMac

For additional compatibility information, see "Compatibility" on page ix in the Introduction.

Libraries	
LIBC.LIB	Single thread static library, retail version
LIBCMT.LIB	Multithread static library, retail version
MSVCRT.LIB	Import library for MSVCRTx0.DLL, retail version
MSVCRTx0.DLL	Multithread DLL library, retail version

Return Value

If successful, **_mbctombb** returns the single-byte character that corresponds to *c*; otherwise it returns *c*.

Parameter

c Multibyte character to convert.

Remarks

The **_mbctombb** function converts a given multibyte character to a corresponding single-byte multibyte character. Characters must correspond to single-byte characters within the range 0x20–0x7E or 0xA1–0xDF to be converted.

In previous versions, **_mbctombb** was called **zentohan**. Use **_mbctombb** instead.

See Also **_mbbtombc**, **_mbcjistojms**, **_mbctohira**, **_mbctolower**

_mbsbtype

int _mbsbtype(const unsigned char **mbstr*, **size_t** *count* **);**

Routine	Required Header	Optional Headers	Compatibility
_mbsbtype	<mbstring.h>	<mbctype.h>[1]	Win 95, Win NT, Win32s, 68K, PMac

[1] For manifest constants used as return values.

For additional compatibility information, see "Compatibility" on page ix in the Introduction.

Libraries

LIBC.LIB	Single thread static library, retail version
LIBCMT.LIB	Multithread static library, retail version
MSVCRT.LIB	Import library for MSVCRTx0.DLL, retail version
MSVCRTx0.DLL	Multithread DLL library, retail version

Return Value

_mbsbtype returns an integer value indicating the result of the test on the specified byte. The manifest constants in the following table are defined in MBCTYPE.H.

Return Value	Byte Type
_MBC_SINGLE (0)	Single-byte character. For example, in code page 932, **_mbsbtype** returns 0 if the specified byte is within the range 0x20–0x7E or 0xA1–0xDF.
_MBC_LEAD (1)	Lead byte of multibyte character. For example, in code page 932, **_mbsbtype** returns 1 if the specified byte is within the range 0x81–0x9F or 0xE0–0xFC.

Return Value	Byte Type
_MBC_TRAIL (2)	Trailing byte of multibyte character. For example, in code page 932, **_mbsbtype** returns 2 if the specified byte is within the range 0x40–0x7E or 0x80–0xFC.
_MBC_ILLEGAL (–1)	Invalid character, or **NULL** byte found before the byte at offset *count* in *mbstr*.

Parameters

mbstr Address of a sequence of multibyte characters

count Byte offset from head of string

Remarks

The **_mbsbtype** function determines the type of a byte in a multibyte character string. The function examines only the byte at offset *count* in *mbstr*, ignoring invalid characters before the specified byte.

_mbsdec, _strdec, _wcsdec

unsigned char *_mbsdec(const unsigned char ***start*, const unsigned char ***current* **);**

Routine	Required Header	Optional Headers	Compatibility
_mbsdec	<mbstring.h>	<mbctype.h>	Win 95, Win NT, Win32s, 68K, PMac
_strdec	<tchar.h>		Win 95, Win NT, Win32s, 68K, PMac
_wcsdec	<tchar.h>		Win 95, Win NT, Win32s, 68K, PMac

For additional compatibility information, see “Compatibility” on page ix in the Introduction.

Libraries	
LIBC.LIB	Single thread static library, retail version
LIBCMT.LIB	Multithread static library, retail version
MSVCRT.LIB	Import library for MSVCRTx0.DLL, retail version
MSVCRTx0.DLL	Multithread DLL library, retail version

Return Value

Each of these routines returns a pointer to the character that immediately precedes *current*, or **NULL** if the value of *start* is greater than or equal to that of *current*. The return value from **_tcsdec** is undefined; thus, when using **_tcsdec**, you must ensure that you do not decrement the string pointer beyond *start*.

Parameters

start Pointer to first byte of any multibyte character in the source string; *start* must precede *current* in the source string

current Pointer to first byte of any multibyte character in the source string; *current* must follow *start* in the source string

Remarks

The **_mbsdec** function returns a pointer to the first byte of the multibyte-character that immediately precedes *current* in the string that contains *start*. **_mbsdec** recognizes multibyte-character sequences according to the multibyte code page currently in use.

The generic-text function **_tcsdec**, defined in TCHAR.H, maps to **_mbsdec** if **_MBCS** has been defined, or to **_wcsdec** if **_UNICODE** has been defined. Otherwise **_tcsdec** maps to **_strdec**. **_strdec** and **_wcsdec** are single-byte character and wide-character versions of **_mbsdec**. **_strdec** and **_wcsdec** are provided only for this mapping and should not be used otherwise.

For more information, see "Using Generic-Text Mappings" on page 25 and Appendix B, "Generic-Text Mappings."

See Also **_mbsinc**, **_mbsnextc**, **_mbsninc**

_mbsinc, _strinc, _wcsinc

unsigned char *_mbsinc(const unsigned char ***current* **);

Routine	Required Header	Optional Headers	Compatibility
_mbsinc	<mbstring.h>		Win 95, Win NT, Win32s, 68K, PMac
_strinc	<tchar.h>		Win 95, Win NT, Win32s, 68K, PMac
_wcsinc	<tchar.h>		Win 95, Win NT, Win32s, 68K, PMac

For additional compatibility information, see "Compatibility" on page ix in the Introduction.

Libraries	
LIBC.LIB	Single thread static library, retail version
LIBCMT.LIB	Multithread static library, retail version
MSVCRT.LIB	Import library for MSVCRTx0.DLL, retail version
MSVCRTx0.DLL	Multithread DLL library, retail version

Return Value

Each of these routines returns a pointer to the character that immediately follows *current*.

Parameter

current Character pointer

Remarks

The **_mbsinc** function returns a pointer to the first byte of the multibyte character that immediately follows *current*. **_mbsinc** recognizes multibyte-character sequences according to the multibyte code page currently in use.

The generic-text function **_tcsinc**, defined in TCHAR.H, maps to **_mbsinc** if **_MBCS** has been defined, or to **_wcsinc** if **_UNICODE** has been defined. Otherwise **_tcsinc** maps to **_strinc**. **_strinc** and **_wcsinc** are single-byte character and wide-character versions of **_mbsinc**. **_strinc** and **_wcsinc** are provided only for this mapping and should not be used otherwise.

For more information, see "Using Generic-Text Mappings" on page 25 and Appendix B, "Generic-Text Mappings."

See Also **_mbsdec**, **_mbsnextc**, **_mbsninc**

_mbsnbcat

unsigned char *_mbsnbcat(unsigned char ***dest*****, const unsigned char** ***src*****, size_t** *count* **);**

Routine	Required Header	Optional Headers	Compatibility
_mbsnbcat	<mbstring.h>		Win 95, Win NT, Win32s, 68K, PMac

For additional compatibility information, see "Compatibility" on page ix in the Introduction.

Libraries	
LIBC.LIB	Single thread static library, retail version
LIBCMT.LIB	Multithread static library, retail version
MSVCRT.LIB	Import library for MSVCRTx0.DLL, retail version
MSVCRTx0.DLL	Multithread DLL library, retail version

Return Value

_mbsnbcat returns a pointer to the destination string. No return value is reserved to indicate an error.

Parameters

dest Null-terminated multibyte-character destination string

src Null-terminated multibyte-character source string

count Number of bytes from *src* to append to *dest*

Remarks

The **_mbsnbcat** function appends, at most, the first *count* bytes of *src* to *dest*. If the byte immediately preceding the null character in *dest* is a lead byte, the initial byte of *src* overwrites this lead byte. Otherwise the initial byte of *src* overwrites the terminating null character of *dest*. If a null byte appears in *src* before *count* bytes are appended, **_mbsnbcat** appends all bytes from *src*, up to the null character. If *count* is greater than the length of *src*, the length of *src* is used in place of *count*. The resulting string is terminated with a null character. If copying takes place between strings that overlap, the behavior is undefined.

See Also **_mbsnbcmp**, **_mbsnbcnt, _mbsnccnt**, **_mbsnbcpy**, **_mbsnbicmp**, **_mbsnbset**, **strncat**

_mbsnbcmp

int _mbsnbcmp(const unsigned char ****string1*, const unsigned char** *string2***, size_t** *count* **);**

Routine	Required Header	Optional Headers	Compatibility
_mbsnbcmp	<mbstring.h>		Win 95, Win NT, Win32s, 68K, PMac

For additional compatibility information, see "Compatibility" on page ix in the Introduction.

Libraries	
LIBC.LIB	Single thread static library, retail version
LIBCMT.LIB	Multithread static library, retail version
MSVCRT.LIB	Import library for MSVCRTx0.DLL, retail version
MSVCRTx0.DLL	Multithread DLL library, retail version

Return Value

The return value indicates the relation of the substrings of *string1* and *string*.

Return Value	Description
< 0	*string1* substring less than *string2* substring
0	*string1* substring identical to *string2* substring
> 0	*string1* substring greater than *string2* substring

On an error, **_mbsnbcmp** returns **_NLSCMPERROR**, which is defined in STRING.H and MBSTRING.H.

Parameters

string1, *string2* Strings to compare

count Number of bytes to compare

Remarks

The **_mbsnbcmp** function lexicographically compares, at most, the first *count* bytes in *string1* and *string2* and returns a value indicating the relationship between the substrings. **_mbsnbcmp** is a case-sensitive version of **_mbsnbicmp**. Unlike **strcoll**, **_mbsnbcmp** is not affected by locale. **_mbsnbcmp** recognizes multibyte-character sequences according to the current multibyte code page. For more information, see "Code Pages" on page 22.

_mbsnbcmp is similar to **_mbsncmp**, except that **_mbsnbcmp** compares strings by characters rather than by bytes.

Example

```
/* STRNBCMP.C */
#include <mbstring.h>
#include <stdio.h>

char string1[] = "The quick brown dog jumps over the lazy fox";
char string2[] = "The QUICK brown fox jumps over the lazy dog";

void main( void )
{
   char tmp[20];
   int result;
   printf( "Compare strings:\n\t\t%s\n\t\t%s\n\n", string1, string2 );
   printf( "Function:\t_mbsnbcmp (first 10 characters only)\n" );
   result = _mbsncmp( string1, string2 , 10 );
   if( result > 0 )
      _mbscpy( tmp, "greater than" );
   else if( result < 0 )
      _mbscpy( tmp, "less than" );
   else
      _mbscpy( tmp, "equal to" );
   printf( "Result:\t\tString 1 is %s string 2\n\n", tmp );
   printf( "Function:\t_mbsnicmp _mbsnicmp (first 10 characters only)\n" );
   result = _mbsnicmp( string1, string2, 10 );
   if( result > 0 )
      _mbscpy( tmp, "greater than" );
   else if( result < 0 )
      _mbscpy( tmp, "less than" );
   else
      _mbscpy( tmp, "equal to" );
   printf( "Result:\t\tString 1 is %s string 2\n\n", tmp );
}
```

Output

```
Compare strings:
        The quick brown dog jumps over the lazy fox
        The QUICK brown fox jumps over the lazy dog

Function:    _mbsnbcmp (first 10 characters only)
Result:      String 1 is greater than string 2

Function:    _mbsnicmp (first 10 characters only)
Result:      String 1 is equal to string 2
```

See Also **_mbsnbcat**, **_mbsnbicmp**, **strncmp**, **_strnicmp**

_mbsnbcnt, _mbsnccnt, _strncnt, _wcsncnt

Return number of characters or bytes within a supplied count

size_t _mbsnbcnt(const unsigned char ***string*****, size_t** *number* **);**
size_t _mbsnccnt(const unsigned char ***string*****, size_t** *number* **);**

Routine	Required Header	Optional Headers	Compatibility
_mbsnbcnt	<mbstring.h>		Win 95, Win NT, Win32s, 68K, PMac
_mbsnccnt	<mbstring.h>		Win 95, Win NT, Win32s, 68K, PMac
_strncnt	<tchar.h>		Win 95, Win NT, Win32s, 68K, PMac
_wcsncnt	<tchar.h>		Win 95, Win NT, Win32s, 68K, PMac

For additional compatibility information, see "Compatibility" on page ix in the Introduction.

Libraries	
LIBC.LIB	Single thread static library, retail version
LIBCMT.LIB	Multithread static library, retail version
MSVCRT.LIB	Import library for MSVCRTx0.DLL, retail version
MSVCRTx0.DLL	Multithread DLL library, retail version

Return Value

_mbsnbcnt returns the number of bytes found in the first *number* of multibyte characters of *string*. **_mbsnccnt** returns the number of characters found in the first *number* of bytes of *string*. If a NULL character is encountered before the examination of *string* has completed, they return the number of bytes or characters found before the NULL character. If *string* consists of fewer than *number* characters or bytes, they return the number of characters or bytes in the string. If *number* is less than zero, they return 0. In previous versions, these functions had a return value of type **int** rather than **size_t**.

_strncnt returns the number of characters in the first *number* bytes of the single-byte string *string*. **_wcsncnt** returns the number of bytes in the first *number* wide characters of the wide-character string *string*.

Parameters

string String to be examined

number Number of characters or bytes to be examined in *string*

Remarks

_mbsnbcnt counts the number of bytes found in the first *number* of multibyte characters of *string*. **_mbsnbcnt** replaces **mtob**, and should be used in place of **mtob**.

_mbsnccnt counts the number of characters found in the first *number* of bytes of *string*. If **_mbsnccnt** encounters a NULL in the second byte of a double-byte character, the first byte is also considered to be NULL and is not included in the returned count value. **_mbsnccnt** replaces **btom**, and should be used in place of **btom**.

If **_MBCS** is defined, **_mbsnbcnt** is mapped to **_tcsnbcnt** and **_mbsnbcnt** is mapped to **_tcsnccnt**. These two mapping routines provide generic-text support and are defined in TCHAR.H. If **_UNICODE** is defined, both **_mbsnbcnt** and **_mbsnccnt** are mapped to the **_wcsncnt** macro. When **_MBCS** and **_UNICODE** are not defined, both **_tcsnbcnt** and **_tcsnccnt** are mapped to the **_strncnt** macro. **_strncnt** is the single-byte–character string version and **_wcsncnt** is the wide-character–string version of these mapping routines. **_strncnt** and **_wcsncnt** are provided only for generic-text mapping and should not be used otherwise. For more information, see "Using Generic-Text Mappings" on page 25 and see Appendix B, "Generic-Text Mappings."

Example

```
/* MBSNBCNT.C */

#include  <mbstring.h>
#include  <stdio.h>

void main( void )
{
   unsigned char str[] = "This is a multibyte-character string.";
   unsigned int char_count, byte_count;
   char_count = _mbsnccnt( str, 10 );
   byte_count = _mbsnbcnt( str, 10 );
   if ( byte_count - char_count )
      printf( "The first 10 characters contain %s multibyte characters", char_count );
   else
      printf( "The first 10 characters are single-byte.");
}
```

Output

```
The first 10 characters are single-byte.
```

See Also **_mbsnbcat**

_mbsnbcoll, _mbsnbicoll

int _mbsnbcoll(const unsigned char ****string1*, const unsigned char** *string2***, size_t** *count* **);**
int _mbsnbicoll(const unsigned char ****string1*, const unsigned char** *string2***, size_t** *count* **);**

Routine	Required Header	Optional Headers	Compatibility
_mbsnbcoll	<mbstring.h>		Win 95, Win NT, Win32s, 68K, PMac
_mbsnbicoll	<mbstring.h>		Win 95, Win NT, Win32s, 68K, PMac

For additional compatibility information, see "Compatibility" on page ix in the Introduction.

Libraries	
LIBC.LIB	Single thread static library, retail version
LIBCMT.LIB	Multithread static library, retail version
MSVCRT.LIB	Import library for MSVCRTx0.DLL, retail version
MSVCRTx0.DLL	Multithread DLL library, retail version

Return Value

The return value indicates the relation of the substrings of *string1* and *string2*.

Return Value	Description
< 0	*string1* substring less than *string2* substring
0	*string1* substring identical to *string2* substring
> 0	*string1* substring greater than *string2* substring

Each of these functions returns **_NLSCMPERROR** on an error. To use **_NLSCMPERROR**, include either STRING.H or MBSTRING.H.

Parameters

string1, *string2* Strings to compare

count Number of bytes to compare

Remarks

Each of these functions collates, at most, the first *count* bytes in *string1* and *string2* and returns a value indicating the relationship between the resulting substrings of *string1* and *string2*. If the final byte in the substring of *string1* or *string2* is a lead byte, it is not included in the comparison; these functions compare only complete characters in the substrings. **_mbsnbicoll** is a case-insensitive version of **_mbsnbcoll**. Like **_mbsnbcmp** and **_mbsnbicmp**, **_mbsnbcoll** and **_mbsnbicoll** collate the two multibyte-character strings according to the lexicographic order specified by the multibyte code page currently in use. For more information, see "Code Pages" on page 22.

For some code pages and corresponding character sets, the order of characters in the character set may differ from the lexicographic character order. In the "C" locale, this is not the case: the order of characters in the ASCII character set is the same as the lexicographic order of the characters. However, in certain European code pages, for example, the character 'a' (value 0x61) precedes the character 'ä' (value 0xE4) in the character set, but the character 'ä' precedes the character 'a' lexicographically. To perform a lexicographic comparison of strings by bytes in such an instance, use **_mbsnbcoll** rather than **_mbsnbcmp**; to check only for string equality, use **_mbsnbcmp**.

Because the **coll** functions collate strings lexicographically for comparison, whereas the **cmp** functions simply test for string equality, the **coll** functions are much slower than the corresponding **cmp** versions. Therefore, the **coll** functions should be used only when there is a difference between the character set order and the lexicographic character order in the current code page and this difference is of interest for the comparison.

See Also **_mbsnbcat**, **_mbsnbcmp**, **_mbsnbicmp**, **strcoll** Functions, **strncmp**, **_strnicmp**

_mbsnbcpy

unsigned char * _mbsnbcpy(unsigned char ***dest*, **const unsigned char ***src*, **size_t *count* **);**

Routine	Required Header	Optional Headers	Compatibility
_mbsnbcpy	<mbstring.h>		Win 95, Win NT, Win32s, 68K, PMac

For additional compatibility information, see "Compatibility" on page ix in the Introduction.

Libraries

LIBC.LIB	Single thread static library, retail version
LIBCMT.LIB	Multithread static library, retail version
MSVCRT.LIB	Import library for MSVCRTx0.DLL, retail version
MSVCRTx0.DLL	Multithread DLL library, retail version

Return Value

_mbsnbcpy returns a pointer to the character string that is to be copied.

Parameters

dest Destination for character string to be copied

src Character string to be copied

count Number of bytes to be copied

Remarks

The **_mbsnbcpy** function copies count bytes from *src* to *dest*. If *src* is shorter than *dest*, the string is padded with null characters. If *dest* is less than or equal to *count* it is not terminated with a null character.

See Also **_mbsnbcat**, **_mbsnbcmp**, **_mbsnbcnt,** **_mbsnccnt**, **_mbsnbicmp**, **_mbsnbset**, **_mbsncpy**

_mbsnbicmp

int _mbsnbicmp(const unsigned char ***string1*****, const unsigned char** ***string2*****, size_t** *count* **);**

Routine	Required Header	Optional Headers	Compatibility
_mbsnbicmp	<mbstring.h>		Win 95, Win NT, Win32s, 68K, PMac

For additional compatibility information, see "Compatibility" on page ix in the Introduction.

Libraries	
LIBC.LIB	Single thread static library, retail version
LIBCMT.LIB	Multithread static library, retail version
MSVCRT.LIB	Import library for MSVCRTx0.DLL, retail version
MSVCRTx0.DLL	Multithread DLL library, retail version

Return Value

The return value indicates the relationship between the substrings.

Return Value	Description
< 0	*string1* substring less than *string2* substring
0	*string1* substring identical to *string2* substring
> 0	*string1* substring greater than *string2* substring

On an error, **_mbsnbcmp** returns **_NLSCMPERROR**, which is defined in STRING.H and MBSTRING.H.

Parameters

string1, string2 Null-terminated strings to compare

count Number of bytes to compare

Remarks

The **_mbsnbicmp** function lexicographically compares, at most, the first *count* bytes of *string1* and *string2*. The comparison is performed without regard to case; **_mbsnbcmp** is a case-sensitive version of **_mbsnbicmp**. The comparison ends if a terminating null character is reached in either string before *count* characters are compared. If the strings are equal when a terminating null character is reached in either string before *count* characters are compared, the shorter string is lesser.

_mbsnbicmp is similar to **_mbsnicmp**, except that it compares strings by bytes instead of by characters.

Two strings containing characters located between `'Z'` and `'a'` in the ASCII table (`'['`, `'\'`, `']'`, `'^'`, `'_'`, and `'`'`) compare differently, depending on their case. For example, the two strings `"ABCDE"` and `"ABCD^"` compare one way if the comparison is lowercase (`"abcde"` > `"abcd^"`) and the other way (`"ABCDE"` < `"ABCD^"`) if it is uppercase.

_mbsnbicmp recognizes multibyte-character sequences according to the multibyte code page currently in use. It is not affected by the current locale setting.

Example

See the example for **_mbsnbcmp**.

See Also **_mbsnbcat**, **_mbsnbcmp**, **_stricmp**, **_strnicmp**

_mbsnbset

unsigned char *_mbsnbset(unsigned char ***string*, unsigned int** *c***, size_t** *count* **);**

Routine	Required Header	Optional Headers	Compatibility
_mbsnbset	<mbstring.h>		Win 95, Win NT, Win32s, 68K, PMac

For additional compatibility information, see "Compatibility" on page ix in the Introduction.

Libraries	
LIBC.LIB	Single thread static library, retail version
LIBCMT.LIB	Multithread static library, retail version
MSVCRT.LIB	Import library for MSVCRTx0.DLL, retail version
MSVCRTx0.DLL	Multithread DLL library, retail version

Return Value

_mbsnbset returns a pointer to the altered string.

Parameters

string String to be altered

c Single-byte or multibyte character setting

count Number of bytes to be set

Remarks

The **_mbsnbset** function sets, at most, the first *count* bytes of *string* to *c*. If *count* is greater than the length of *string*, the length of *string* is used instead of *count*. If *c* is a multibyte character and cannot be set entirely into the last byte specified by *count*, then the last byte will be padded with a blank character. **_mbsnbset** does not place a terminating null at the end of *string*.

_mbsnbset is similar to **_mbsnset**, except that it sets *count* bytes rather than *count* characters of *c*.

Example

```
/* MBSNBSET.C */

#include <mbstring.h>
#include <stdio.h>

void main( void )
{
   char string[15] = "This is a test";
   /* Set not more than 4 bytes of string to be *'s */
   printf( "Before: %s\n", string );
   _mbsnbset( string, '*', 4 );
   printf( "After:  %s\n", string );
}
```

Output

```
Before: This is a test
After:  **** is a test
```

See Also **_mbsnbcat**, **_mbsnset**, **_mbsset**

_mbsnextc, _strnextc, _wcsnextc

unsigned int _mbsnextc(const unsigned char ***string* **);

Routine	Required Header	Optional Headers	Compatibility
_mbsnextc	<mbstring.h>		Win 95, Win NT, Win32s, 68K, PMac
_strnextc	<tchar.h>		Win 95, Win NT, Win32s, 68K, PMac
_wcsnextc	<tchar.h>		Win 95, Win NT, Win32s, 68K, PMac

For additional compatibility information, see "Compatibility" on page ix in the Introduction.

Libraries	
LIBC.LIB	Single thread static library, retail version
LIBCMT.LIB	Multithread static library, retail version
MSVCRT.LIB	Import library for MSVCRTx0.DLL, retail version
MSVCRTx0.DLL	Multithread DLL library, retail version

Return Value

Each of these functions returns the integer value of the next character in *string*.

Parameter

string Source string

Remarks

The **_mbsnextc** function returns the integer value of the next multibyte-character in *string*, without advancing the string pointer. **_mbsnextc** recognizes multibyte-character sequences according to the multibyte code page currently in use.

The generic-text function **_tcsnextc**, defined in TCHAR.H, maps to **_mbsnextc** if **_MBCS** has been defined, or to **_wcsnextc** if **_UNICODE** has been defined. Otherwise **_tcsnextc** maps to **_strnextc**. **_strnextc** and **_wcsnextc** are single-byte–character string and wide-character string versions of **_mbsnextc**. **_wcsnextc** returns the integer value of the next wide character in *string*; **_strnextc** returns the integer value of the next single-byte character in *string*. **_strnextc** and **_wcsnextc** are provided only for this mapping and should not be used otherwise. For more information, see "Using Generic-Text Mappings" on page 25 and Appendix B, "Generic-Text Mappings."

See Also **_mbsdec**, **_mbsinc**, **_mbsninc**

_mbsninc, _strninc, _wcsninc

unsigned char *_mbsninc(const unsigned char ***_string_, size_t** _count_ **);**

Routine	Required Header	Optional Headers	Compatibility
_mbsninc	<mbstring.h>		Win 95, Win NT, Win32s, 68K, PMac
_strninc	<tchar.h>		Win 95, Win NT, Win32s, 68K, PMac
_wcsninc	<tchar.h>		Win 95, Win NT, Win32s, 68K, PMac

For additional compatibility information, see "Compatibility" on page ix in the Introduction.

Libraries	
LIBC.LIB	Single thread static library, retail version
LIBCMT.LIB	Multithread static library, retail version
MSVCRT.LIB	Import library for MSVCRTx0.DLL, retail version
MSVCRTx0.DLL	Multithread DLL library, retail version

Return Value

Each of these routines returns a pointer to *string* after *string* has been incremented by *count* characters, or **NULL** if the supplied pointer is **NULL**. If *count* is greater than or equal to the number of characters in *string,* the result is undefined.

Parameters

string Source string

count Number of characters to increment string pointer

Remarks

The **_mbsninc** function increments *string* by *count* multibyte characters. **_mbsninc** recognizes multibyte-character sequences according to the multibyte code page currently in use.

The generic-text function **_tcsninc**, defined in TCHAR.H, maps to **_mbsninc** if **_MBCS** has been defined, or to **_wcsninc** if **_UNICODE** has been defined. Otherwise **_tcsninc** maps to **_strninc**. **_strninc** and **_wcsninc** are single-byte–character string and wide-character string versions of **_mbsninc**. **_wcsninc** and **_strninc** are provided only for this mapping and should not be used otherwise. For more information, see "Using Generic-Text Mappings" on page 25 and Appendix B, "Generic-Text Mappings."

See Also **_mbsdec**, **_mbsinc**, **_mbsnextc**

_mbsspnp, _strspnp, _wcsspnp

unsigned char *_mbsspnp(const unsigned char ***string1,**
const unsigned char ***string2* **);

Routine	Required Header	Optional Headers	Compatibility
_mbsspnp	<mbstring.h>		Win 95, Win NT, Win32s, 68K, PMac
_strspnp	<tchar.h>		Win 95, Win NT, Win32s, 68K, PMac
_wcsspnp	<tchar.h>		Win 95, Win NT, Win32s

For additional compatibility information, see "Compatibility" on page ix in the Introduction.

Libraries	
LIBC.LIB	Single thread static library, retail version
LIBCMT.LIB	Multithread static library, retail version
MSVCRT.LIB	Import library for MSVCRTx0.DLL, retail version
MSVCRTx0.DLL	Multithread DLL library, retail version

Return Value

_strspnp, **_wcsspnp**, and **_mbsspnp** return a pointer to the first character in *string1* that does not belong to the set of characters in *string2*. Each of these functions returns **NULL** if *string1* consists entirely of characters from *string2*. For each of these routines, no return value is reserved to indicate an error.

Parameters

string1 Null-terminated string to search

string2 Null-terminated character set

Remarks

The **_mbsspnp** function returns a pointer to the multibyte character that is the first character in *string1* that does not belong to the set of characters in *string2*. **_mbsspnp** recognizes multibyte-character sequences according to the multibyte code page currently in use. The search does not include terminating null characters.

The generic-text function **_tcsspnp**, defined in TCHAR.H, maps to **_mbsspnp** if **_MBCS** has been defined, or to **_wcsspnp** if **_UNICODE** has been defined. Otherwise **_tcsspnp** maps to **_strspnp**. **_strspnp** and **_wcsspnp** are single-byte character and wide-character versions of **_mbsspnp**. **_strspnp** and **_wcsspnp** behave identically to **_mbsspnp** otherwise; they are provided only for this mapping and should not be used for any other reason. For more information, see "Using Generic-Text Mappings" on page 25 and Appendix B, "Generic-Text Mappings."

Example

See the example for **strspn**.

See Also **strspn**, **strcspn**, **strncat**, **strncmp**, **strncpy**, **_strnicmp**, **strrchr**

---

mbstowcs

Converts a sequence of multibyte characters to a corresponding sequence of wide characters.

size_t mbstowcs(wchar_t ***wcstr*****, const char** ***mbstr*****, size_t** *count* **);**

Routine	Required Header	Optional Headers	Compatibility
mbstowcs	<stdlib.h>		ANSI, Win 95, Win NT, Win32s, 68K, PMac

For additional compatibility information, see "Compatibility" on page ix in the Introduction.

Libraries	
LIBC.LIB	Single thread static library, retail version
LIBCMT.LIB	Multithread static library, retail version
MSVCRT.LIB	Import library for MSVCRTx0.DLL, retail version
MSVCRTx0.DLL	Multithread DLL library, retail version

Return Value

If **mbstowcs** successfully converts the source string, it returns the number of converted multibyte characters. If the *wcstr* argument is **NULL**, the function returns the required size of the destination string. If **mbstowcs** encounters an invalid multibyte character, it returns –1. If the return value is *count*, the wide-character string is not null-terminated.

Parameters

wcstr The address of a sequence of wide characters

mbstr The address of a sequence of multibyte characters

count The number of multibyte characters to convert

Remarks

The **mbstowcs** function converts *count* or fewer multibyte characters pointed to by *mbstr* to a string of corresponding wide characters that are determined by the current locale. It stores the resulting wide-character string at the address represented by *wcstr*. The result is similiar to a series of calls to **mbtowc**. If **mbstowcs** encounters the single-byte null character ('\0') either before or when *count* occurs, it converts the null character to a wide-character null character (L'\0') and stops. Thus the wide-character string at *wcstr* is null-terminated only if a null character is encountered during conversion. If the sequences pointed to by *wcstr* and *mbstr* overlap, the behavior is undefined.

If the *wcstr* argument is **NULL**, **mbstowcs** returns the required size of the destination string.

Example

```
/* MBSTOWCS.CPP illustrates the behavior of the mbstowcs function
 */

#include <stdlib.h>
#include <stdio.h>

void main( void )
{
    int i;
    char    *pmbnull  = NULL;
    char    *pmbhello = (char *)malloc( MB_CUR_MAX );
    wchar_t *pwchello = L"Hi";
    wchar_t *pwc      = (wchar_t *)malloc( sizeof( wchar_t ));

    printf( "Convert to multibyte string:\n" );
    i = wcstombs( pmbhello, pwchello, MB_CUR_MAX );
    printf( "\tCharacters converted: %u\n", i );
    printf( "\tHex value of first" );
    printf( " multibyte character: %#.4x\n\n", pmbhello );

    printf( "Convert back to wide-character string:\n" );
    i = mbstowcs( pwc, pmbhello, MB_CUR_MAX );
    printf( "\tCharacters converted: %u\n", i );
    printf( "\tHex value of first" );
    printf( " wide character: %#.4x\n\n", pwc );
}
```

Output

```
Convert to multibyte string:
   Characters converted: 1
   Hex value of first multibyte character: 0x0e1a

Convert back to wide-character string:
   Characters converted: 1
   Hex value of first wide character: 0x0e1e
```

See Also **mblen**, **mbtowc**, **wcstombs**, **wctomb**

mbtowc

Convert a multibyte character to a corresponding wide character.

int mbtowc(**wchar_t** **wchar*, **const char** **mbchar*, **size_t** *count* **);**

Routine	Required Header	Optional Headers	Compatibility
mbtowc	<stdlib.h>		ANSI, Win 95, Win NT, Win32s, 68K, PMac

For additional compatibility information, see "Compatibility" on page ix in the Introduction.

Libraries	
LIBC.LIB	Single thread static library, retail version
LIBCMT.LIB	Multithread static library, retail version
MSVCRT.LIB	Import library for MSVCRTx0.DLL, retail version
MSVCRTx0.DLL	Multithread DLL library, retail version

Return Value

If **mbchar** is not **NULL** and if the object that *mbchar* points to forms a valid multibyte character, **mbtowc** returns the length in bytes of the multibyte character. If *mbchar* is **NULL** or the object that it points to is a wide-character null character (`L'\0'`), the function returns 0. If the object that *mbchar* points to does not form a valid multibyte character within the first *count* characters, it returns –1.

Parameters

wchar Address of a wide character (type **wchar_t**)

mbchar Address of a sequence of bytes (a multibyte character)

count Number of bytes to check

Remarks

The **mbtowc** function converts *count* or fewer bytes pointed to by *mbchar*, if *mbchar* is not **NULL**, to a corresponding wide character. **mbtowc** stores the resulting wide character at *wchar,* if *wchar* is not **NULL. mbtowc** does not examine more than **MB_CUR_MAX** bytes.

Example

```
/* MBTOWC.CPP illustrates the behavior of the mbtowc function
 */

#include <stdlib.h>
#include <stdio.h>
```

```
void main( void )
{
    int      i;
    char    *pmbc    = (char *)malloc( sizeof( char ) );
    wchar_t  wc      = L'a';
    wchar_t *pwcnull = NULL;
    wchar_t *pwc     = (wchar_t *)malloc( sizeof( wchar_t ) );
    printf( "Convert a wide character to multibyte character:\n" );
    i = wctomb( pmbc, wc );
    printf( "\tCharacters converted: %u\n", i );
    printf( "\tMultibyte character: %x\n\n", pmbc );

    printf( "Convert multibyte character back to a wide "
            "character:\n" );
    i = mbtowc( pwc, pmbc, MB_CUR_MAX );
    printf( "\tBytes converted: %u\n", i );
    printf( "\tWide character: %x\n\n", pwc );
    printf( "Attempt to convert when target is NULL\n" );
    printf( "  returns the length of the multibyte character:\n" );
    i = mbtowc( pwcnull, pmbc, MB_CUR_MAX );
    printf( "\tLength of multibyte character: %u\n\n", i );

    printf( "Attempt to convert a NULL pointer to a" );
    printf( " wide character:\n" );
    pmbc = NULL;
    i = mbtowc( pwc, pmbc, MB_CUR_MAX );
    printf( "\tBytes converted: %u\n", i );
}
```

Output

```
Convert a wide character to multibyte character:
   Characters converted: 1
   Multibyte character: 2d02d4

Convert multibyte character back to a wide character:
   Bytes converted: 1
   Wide character: 2d02dc

Attempt to convert when target is NULL
  returns the length of the multibyte character:
   Length of multibyte character: 1

Attempt to convert a NULL pointer to a wide character:
   Bytes converted: 0
```

See Also **mblen, wcstombs, wctomb**

_memccpy

Copies characters from a buffer.

void *_memccpy(void ***dest*, const void ***src***, int** *c***, unsigned int** *count* **);**

Routine	Required Header	Optional Headers	Compatibility
_memccpy	<memory.h> or <string.h>		Win 95, Win NT, Win32s, 68K, PMac

For additional compatibility information, see "Compatibility" on page ix in the Introduction.

Libraries	
LIBC.LIB	Single thread static library, retail version
LIBCMT.LIB	Multithread static library, retail version
MSVCRT.LIB	Import library for MSVCRTx0.DLL, retail version
MSVCRTx0.DLL	Multithread DLL library, retail version

Return Value

If the character *c* is copied, **_memccpy** returns a pointer to the byte in *dest* that immediately follows the character. If *c* is not copied, it returns **NULL**.

Parameters

dest Pointer to destination

src Pointer to source

c Last character to copy

count Number of characters

Remarks

The **_memccpy** function copies 0 or more bytes of *src* to *dest*, halting when the character *c* has been copied or when *count* bytes have been copied, whichever comes first.

Example

```
/* MEMCCPY.C */

#include <memory.h>
#include <stdio.h>
#include <string.h>

char string1[60] = "The quick brown dog jumps over the lazy fox";
```

```
void main( void )
{
   char buffer[61];
   char *pdest;

   printf( "Function:\t_memccpy 60 characters or to character 's'\n" );
   printf( "Source:\t\t%s\n", string1 );
   pdest = _memccpy( buffer, string1, 's', 60 );
   *pdest = '\0';
   printf( "Result:\t\t%s\n", buffer );
   printf( "Length:\t\t%d characters\n\n", strlen( buffer ) );
}
```

Output

```
Function:   _memccpy 60 characters or to character 's'
Source:      The quick brown dog jumps over the lazy fox
Result:      The quick brown dog jumps
Length:      25 characters
```

See Also **memchr**, **memcmp**, **memcpy**, **memset**

---

memchr

Finds characters in a buffer.

void *memchr(const void ***buf*, **int *c*, **size_t** *count* **);**

Routine	Required Header	Optional Headers	Compatibility
memchr	<memory.h> or <string.h>		ANSI, Win 95, Win NT, Win32s, 68K, PMac

For additional compatibility information, see "Compatibility" on page ix in the Introduction.

Libraries	
LIBC.LIB	Single thread static library, retail version
LIBCMT.LIB	Multithread static library, retail version
MSVCRT.LIB	Import library for MSVCRTx0.DLL, retail version
MSVCRTx0.DLL	Multithread DLL library, retail version

Return Value

If successful, **memchr** returns a pointer to the first location of *c* in *buf*. Otherwise it returns **NULL**.

Parameters

buf Pointer to buffer

c Character to look for

count Number of characters to check

Remarks

The **memchr** function looks for the first occurrence of *c* in the first *count* bytes of *buf*. It stops when it finds *c* or when it has checked the first *count* bytes.

Example

```
/* MEMCHR.C */

#include <memory.h>
#include <stdio.h>

int  ch = 'r';
char str[] =    "lazy";
char string[] = "The quick brown dog jumps over the lazy fox";
char fmt1[] =   "         1         2         3         4         5";
char fmt2[] =   "12345678901234567890123456789012345678901234567890";

void main( void )
{
   char *pdest;
   int result;
   printf( "String to be searched:\n\t\t%s\n", string );
   printf( "\t\t%s\n\t\t%s\n\n", fmt1, fmt2 );

   printf( "Search char:\t%c\n", ch );
   pdest = memchr( string, ch, sizeof( string ) );
   result = pdest - string + 1;
   if( pdest != NULL )
      printf( "Result:\t\t%c found at position %d\n\n", ch, result );
   else
      printf( "Result:\t\t%c not found\n" );
}
```

Output

```
String to be searched:
      The quick brown dog jumps over the lazy fox
               1         2         3         4         5
      12345678901234567890123456789012345678901234567890

Search char:   r
Result:        r found at position 12
```

See Also **_memccpy**, **memcmp**, **memcpy**, **memset**, **strchr**

memcmp

Compare characters in two buffers.

int memcmp(const void ***_buf1_, const void ***_buf2_**, size_t** _count_ **);**

Routine	Required Header	Optional Headers	Compatibility
memcmp	<memory.h> or <string.h>		ANSI, Win 95, Win NT, Win32s, 68K, PMac

For additional compatibility information, see "Compatibility" on page ix in the Introduction.

Libraries	
LIBC.LIB	Single thread static library, retail version
LIBCMT.LIB	Multithread static library, retail version
MSVCRT.LIB	Import library for MSVCRTx0.DLL, retail version
MSVCRTx0.DLL	Multithread DLL library, retail version

Return Value

The return value indicates the relationship between the buffers.

Return Value	Relationship of First count Bytes of buf1 and buf2
< 0	*buf1* less than *buf2*
0	*buf1* identical to *buf2*
> 0	*buf1* greater than *buf2*

Parameters

buf1 First buffer

buf2 Second buffer

count Number of characters

Remarks

The **memcmp** function compares the first *count* bytes of *buf1* and *buf2* and returns a value indicating their relationship.

Example

```
/* MEMCMP.C: This program uses memcmp to compare
 * the strings named first and second. If the first
 * 19 bytes of the strings are equal, the program
 * considers the strings to be equal.
 */

#include <string.h>
#include <stdio.h>

void main( void )
```

```
{
   char first[]  = "12345678901234567890";
   char second[] = "12345678901234567891";
   int result;

   printf( "Compare '%.19s' to '%.19s':\n", first, second );
   result = memcmp( first, second, 19 );
   if( result < 0 )
      printf( "First is less than second.\n" );
   else if( result == 0 )
      printf( "First is equal to second.\n" );
   else if( result > 0 )
      printf( "First is greater than second.\n" );
   printf( "Compare '%.20s' to '%.20s':\n", first, second );
   result = memcmp( first, second, 20 );
   if( result < 0 )
      printf( "First is less than second.\n" );
   else if( result == 0 )
      printf( "First is equal to second.\n" );
   else if( result > 0 )
      printf( "First is greater than second.\n" );
}
```

Output

```
Compare '1234567890123456789' to '1234567890123456789':
First is equal to second.
Compare '12345678901234567890' to '12345678901234567891':
First is less than second.
```

See Also **_memccpy**, **memchr**, **memcpy**, **memset**, **strcmp**, **strncmp**

---

memcpy

Copies characters between buffers.

void *memcpy(void ***dest*****, const void** ***src*****, size_t** ***count*** **);**

Routine	Required Header	Optional Headers	Compatibility
memcpy	<memory.h> or <string.h>		ANSI, Win 95, Win NT, Win32s, 68K, PMac

For additional compatibility information, see "Compatibility" on page ix in the Introduction.

Libraries

LIBC.LIB	Single thread static library, retail version
LIBCMT.LIB	Multithread static library, retail version
MSVCRT.LIB	Import library for MSVCRTx0.DLL, retail version
MSVCRTx0.DLL	Multithread DLL library, retail version

Return Value

memcpy returns the value of *dest.*

Parameters

dest New buffer

src Buffer to copy from

count Number of characters to copy

Remarks

The **memcpy** function copies *count* bytes of *src* to *dest.* If the source and destination overlap, this function does not ensure that the original source bytes in the overlapping region are copied before being overwritten. Use **memmove** to handle overlapping regions.

Example

```
/* MEMCPY.C: Illustrate overlapping copy: memmove
 * handles it correctly; memcpy does not.
 */

#include <memory.h>
#include <string.h>
#include <stdio.h>

char string1[60] = "The quick brown dog jumps over the lazy fox";
char string2[60] = "The quick brown fox jumps over the lazy dog";
/*                           1         2         3         4         5
 *                  12345678901234567890123456789012345678901234567890
 */

void main( void )
{
   printf( "Function:\tmemcpy without overlap\n" );
   printf( "Source:\t\t%s\n", string1 + 40 );
   printf( "Destination:\t%s\n", string1 + 16 );
   memcpy( string1 + 16, string1 + 40, 3 );
   printf( "Result:\t\t%s\n", string1 );
   printf( "Length:\t\t%d characters\n\n", strlen( string1 ) );

   /* Restore string1 to original contents */
   memcpy( string1 + 16, string2 + 40, 3 );
```

```
    printf( "Function:\tmemmove with overlap\n" );
    printf( "Source:\t\t%s\n", string2 + 4 );
    printf( "Destination:\t%s\n", string2 + 10 );
    memmove( string2 + 10, string2 + 4, 40 );
    printf( "Result:\t\t%s\n", string2 );
    printf( "Length:\t\t%d characters\n\n", strlen( string2 ) );

    printf( "Function:\tmemcpy with overlap\n" );
    printf( "Source:\t\t%s\n", string1 + 4 );
    printf( "Destination:\t%s\n", string1 + 10 );
    memcpy( string1 + 10, string1 + 4, 40 );
    printf( "Result:\t\t%s\n", string1 );
    printf( "Length:\t\t%d characters\n\n", strlen( string1 ) );
}
```

Output

```
Function:   memcpy without overlap
Source:      fox
Destination:   dog jumps over the lazy fox
Result:      The quick brown fox jumps over the lazy fox
Length:      43 characters

Function:   memmove with overlap
Source:      quick brown fox jumps over the lazy dog
Destination:   brown fox jumps over the lazy dog
Result:      The quick quick brown fox jumps over the lazy dog
Length:      49 characters

Function:   memcpy with overlap
Source:      quick brown dog jumps over the lazy fox
Destination:   brown dog jumps over the lazy fox
Result:      The quick quick brown dog jumps over the lazy fox
Length:      49 characters
```

See Also **_memccpy, memchr, memcmp, memmove, memset, strcpy, strncpy**

_memicmp

Compares characters in two buffers (case-insensitive).

int _memicmp(const void *_buf1_, const void *_buf2_, unsigned int _count_);

Routine	Required Header	Optional Headers	Compatibility
_memicmp	<memory.h> or <string.h>		Win 95, Win NT, Win32s, 68K, PMac

For additional compatibility information, see "Compatibility" on page ix in the Introduction.

Libraries	
LIBC.LIB	Single thread static library, retail version
LIBCMT.LIB	Multithread static library, retail version
MSVCRT.LIB	Import library for MSVCRTx0.DLL, retail version
MSVCRTx0.DLL	Multithread DLL library, retail version

Return Value

The return value indicates the relationship between the buffers.

Return Value	Relationship of First count Bytes of buf1 and buf2
< 0	*buf1* less than *buf2*
0	*buf1* identical to *buf2*
> 0	*buf1* greater than *buf2*

Parameters

buf1 First buffer

buf2 Second buffer

count Number of characters

Remarks

The **_memicmp** function compares the first *count* characters of the two buffers *buf1* and *buf2* byte by byte. The comparison is not case sensitive.

Example

```
/* MEMICMP.C: This program uses _memicmp to compare
 * the first 29 letters of the strings named first and
 * second without regard to the case of the letters.
 */

#include <memory.h>
#include <stdio.h>
#include <string.h>

void main( void )
{
   int result;
   char first[] = "Those Who Will Not Learn from History";
   char second[] = "THOSE WHO WILL NOT LEARN FROM their mistakes";
   /* Note that the 29th character is right here ^ */

   printf( "Compare '%.29s' to '%.29s'\n", first, second );
   result = _memicmp( first, second, 29 );
   if( result < 0 )
      printf( "First is less than second.\n" );
   else if( result == 0 )
      printf( "First is equal to second.\n" );}
```

```
   else if( result > 0 )
      printf( "First is greater than second.\n" );
}
```

Output

```
Compare 'Those Who Will Not Learn from' to 'THOSE WHO WILL NOT LEARN FROM'
First is equal to second.
```

See Also **_memccpy**, **memchr**, **memcmp**, **memcpy**, **memset**, **_stricmp**, **_strnicmp**

---

memmove

Moves one buffer to another.

void *memmove(void ***dest*, const void ***src***, size_t** *count* **);**

Routine	Required Header	Optional Headers	Compatibility
memmove	<string.h> or <memory.h>		ANSI, Win 95, Win NT, Win32s, 68K, PMac

For additional compatibility information, see "Compatibility" on page ix in the Introduction.

Libraries	
LIBC.LIB	Single thread static library, retail version
LIBCMT.LIB	Multithread static library, retail version
MSVCRT.LIB	Import library for MSVCRTx0.DLL, retail version
MSVCRTx0.DLL	Multithread DLL library, retail version

Return Value

memmove returns the value of *dest.*

Parameters

dest Destination object

src Source object

count Number of bytes of characters to copy

Remarks

The **memmove** function copies *count* bytes of characters from *src* to *dest.* If some regions of the source area and the destination overlap, **memmove** ensures that the original source bytes in the overlapping region are copied before being overwritten.

Example

See the example for **memcpy**.

See Also **_memccpy**, **memcpy**, **strcpy**, **strncpy**

memset

Sets buffers to a specified character.

void *memset(void ***dest*, int** *c***, size_t** *count* **);**

Routine	Required Header	Optional Headers	Compatibility
memset	<memory.h> or <string.h>		ANSI, Win 95, Win NT, Win32s, 68K, PMac

For additional compatibility information, see "Compatibility" on page ix in the Introduction.

Libraries	
LIBC.LIB	Single thread static library, retail version
LIBCMT.LIB	Multithread static library, retail version
MSVCRT.LIB	Import library for MSVCRTx0.DLL, retail version
MSVCRTx0.DLL	Multithread DLL library, retail version

Return Value

memset returns the value of *dest.*

Parameters

dest Pointer to destination

c Character to set

count Number of characters

Remarks

The **memset** function sets the first *count* bytes of *dest* to the character *c.*

Example

```
/* MEMSET.C: This program uses memset to
 * set the first four bytes of buffer to "*".
 */

#include <memory.h>
#include <stdio.h>

void main( void )
{
   char buffer[] = "This is a test of the memset function";

   printf( "Before: %s\n", buffer );
   memset( buffer, '*', 4 );
   printf( "After:  %s\n", buffer );
}
```

Output

```
Before: This is a test of the memset function
After:  **** is a test of the memset function
```

See Also **_memccpy**, **memchr**, **memcmp**, **memcpy**, **_strnset**

_ _min

Returns the smaller of two values.

type **_ _min(** *type a*, *type b* **);**

Routine	Required Header	Optional Headers	Compatibility
_ _min	<stdlib.h>		Win 95, Win NT, Win32s, 68K, PMac

For additional compatibility information, see "Compatibility" on page ix in the Introduction.

Libraries	
LIBC.LIB	Single thread static library, retail version
LIBCMT.LIB	Multithread static library, retail version
MSVCRT.LIB	Import library for MSVCRTx0.DLL, retail version
MSVCRTx0.DLL	Multithread DLL library, retail version

Return Value

The smaller of the two arguments

Parameters

type Any numeric data type

a, b Values of any numeric type to be compared

Remarks

The **_ _min** macro compares two values and returns the value of the smaller one. The arguments can be of any numeric data type, signed or unsigned. Both arguments and the return value must be of the same data type.

Example

```
/* MINMAX.C */

#include <stdlib.h>
#include <stdio.h>
```

```
void main( void )
{
   int a = 10;
   int b = 21;

   printf( "The larger of %d and %d is %d\n",  a, b, __max( a, b ) );
   printf( "The smaller of %d and %d is %d\n", a, b, __min( a, b ) );
}
```

Output

```
The larger of 10 and 21 is 21
The smaller of 10 and 21 is 10
```

See Also **__max**

_mkdir, _wmkdir

Create a new directory.

int _mkdir(const char ****dirname* **);
int _wmkdir(const wchar_t ****dirname* **);

Routine	Required Header	Optional Headers	Compatibility
_mkdir	<direct.h>		Win 95, Win NT, Win32s, 68K, PMac
_wmkdir	<direct.h> or <wchar.h>		Win NT

For additional compatibility information, see "Compatibility" on page ix in the Introduction.

Libraries	
LIBC.LIB	Single thread static library, retail version
LIBCMT.LIB	Multithread static library, retail version
MSVCRT.LIB	Import library for MSVCRTx0.DLL, retail version
MSVCRTx0.DLL	Multithread DLL library, retail version

Return Value

Each of these functions returns the value 0 if the new directory was created. On an error the function returns –1 and sets **errno** as follows:

EACCES Directory was not created because *dirname* is the name of an existing file, directory, or device

ENOENT Path was not found

Parameter

dirname Path for new directory

Remarks

The **_mkdir** function creates a new directory with the specified *dirname*. **_mkdir** can create only one new directory per call, so only the last component of *dirname* can name a new directory. **_mkdir** does not translate path delimiters. In Windows NT, both the backslash (\) and the forward slash (/) are valid path delimiters in character strings in run-time routines.

_wmkdir is a wide-character version of **_mkdir**; the *dirname* argument to **_wmkdir** is a wide-character string. **_wmkdir** and **_mkdir** behave identically otherwise.

Example

```
/* MAKEDIR.C */

#include <direct.h>
#include <stdlib.h>
#include <stdio.h>

void main( void )
{
   if( _mkdir( "\\testtmp" ) == 0 )
   {
      printf( "Directory '\\testtmp' was successfully created\n" );
      system( "dir \\testtmp" );
      if( _rmdir( "\\testtmp" ) == 0 )
        printf( "Directory '\\testtmp' was successfully removed\n"  );
      else
         printf( "Problem removing directory '\\testtmp'\n" );
   }
   else
      printf( "Problem creating directory '\\testtmp'\n" );
}
```

Output

```
Directory '\testtmp' was successfully created
 Volume in drive C is CDRIVE
 Volume Serial Number is 0E17-1702

 Directory of C:\testtmp

05/03/94  12:30p        <DIR>           .
05/03/94  12:30p        <DIR>           ..
              2 File(s)          0 bytes
                            17,358,848 bytes free
Directory '\testtmp' was successfully removed
```

See Also **_chdir**, **_rmdir**

_mktemp, _wmktemp

Create a unique filename.

char *_mktemp(char ***_template_ **);
wchar_t *_wmktemp(wchar_t ***_template_ **);

Routine	Required Header	Optional Headers	Compatibility
_mktemp	<io.h>		Win 95, Win NT, Win32s, 68K, PMac
_wmktemp	<io.h> or <wchar.h>		Win 95, Win NT, Win32s

For additional compatibility information, see "Compatibility" on page ix in the Introduction.

Libraries	
LIBC.LIB	Single thread static library, retail version
LIBCMT.LIB	Multithread static library, retail version
MSVCRT.LIB	Import library for MSVCRTx0.DLL, retail version
MSVCRTx0.DLL	Multithread DLL library, retail version

Return Value

Each of these functions returns a pointer to the modified template. The function returns **NULL** if *template* is badly formed or no more unique names can be created from the given template.

Parameter

template Filename pattern

Remarks

The **_mktemp** function creates a unique filename by modifying the *template* argument. **_mktemp** automatically handles multibyte-character string arguments as appropriate, recognizing multibyte-character sequences according to the multibyte code page currently in use by the run-time system. **_wmktemp** is a wide-character version of **_mktemp**; the argument and return value of **_wmktemp** are wide-character strings. **_wmktemp** and **_mktemp** behave identically otherwise, except that **_wmktemp** does not handle multibyte-character strings.

template has the form *base*XXXXXX where *base* is the part of the new filename that you supply and each X is a placeholder for a character supplied by **_mktemp**. Each placeholder character in *template* must be an uppercase X. **_mktemp** preserves *base* and replaces the first trailing X with an alphabetic character. **_mktemp** replaces the following trailing X's with a five-digit value; this value is a unique number identifying the calling process, or in multi-threaded programs, the calling thread.

Each successful call to **_mktemp** modifies *template*. In each subsequent call from the same process or thread with the same *template* argument, **_mktemp** checks for filenames that match names returned by **_mktemp** in previous calls. If no file exists for a given name, **_mktemp** returns that name. If files exist for all previously returned names, **_mktemp** creates a new name by replacing the alphabetic character it used in the previously returned name with the next available lowercase letter, in order, from 'a' through 'z'. For example, if *base* is

```
fn
```

and the five-digit value supplied by **_mktemp** is 12345, the first name returned is

```
fna12345
```

If this name is used to create file FNA12345 and this file still exists, the next name returned on a call from the same process or thread with the same *base* for *template* will be

```
fnb12345
```

If FNA12345 does not exist, the next name returned will again be

```
fna12345
```

_mktemp can create a maximum of 27 unique filenames for any given combination of base and template values. Therefore, FNZ12345 is the last unique filename **_mktemp** can create for the *base* and *template* values used in this example.

Example

```
/* MKTEMP.C: The program uses _mktemp to create
 * five unique filenames. It opens each filename
 * to ensure that the next name is unique.
 */

#include <io.h>
#include <string.h>
#include <stdio.h>

char *template = "fnXXXXXX";
char *result;
char names[5][9];

void main( void )
{
   int i;
   FILE *fp;

   for( i = 0; i < 5; i++ )
   {
      strcpy( names[i], template );
      /* Attempt to find a unique filename: */
      result = _mktemp( names[i] );
      if( result == NULL )
         printf( "Problem creating the template" );
```

```
            else
            {
               if( (fp = fopen( result, "w" )) != NULL )
                  printf( "Unique filename is %s\n", result );
               else
                  printf( "Cannot open %s\n", result );
               fclose( fp );
            }
         }
      }
```

Output

```
Unique filename is fna00141
Unique filename is fnb00141
Unique filename is fnc00141
Unique filename is fnd00141
Unique filename is fne00141
```

See Also **fopen**, **_getmbcp**, **_getpid**, **_open**, **_setmbcp**, **_tempnam**, **tmpfile**

---

mktime

Converts the local time to a calendar value.

time_t mktime(struct tm **timeptr* **);**

Routine	Required Header	Optional Headers	Compatibility
mktime	<time.h>		ANSI, Win 95, Win NT, Win32s, 68K, PMac

For additional compatibility information, see "Compatibility" on page ix in the Introduction.

Libraries	
LIBC.LIB	Single thread static library, retail version
LIBCMT.LIB	Multithread static library, retail version
MSVCRT.LIB	Import library for MSVCRTx0.DLL, retail version
MSVCRTx0.DLL	Multithread DLL library, retail version

Return Value

mktime returns the specified calendar time encoded as a value of type **time_t**. If *timeptr* references a date before midnight, January 1, 1970, or if the calendar time cannot be represented, the function returns –1 cast to type **time_t**.

Parameter

timeptr Pointer to time structure

Remarks

The **mktime** function converts the supplied time structure (possibly incomplete) pointed to by *timeptr* into a fully defined structure with normalized values and then converts it to a **time_t** calendar time value. For description of **tm** structure fields, see **asctime**. The converted time has the same encoding as the values returned by the **time** function. The original values of the **tm_wday** and **tm_yday** components of the *timeptr* structure are ignored, and the original values of the other components are not restricted to their normal ranges.

mktime handles dates in any time zone from midnight, January 1, 1970, to midnight, February 5, 2036. If successful, **mktime** sets the values of **tm_wday** and **tm_yday** as appropriate and sets the other components to represent the specified calendar time, but with their values forced to the normal ranges; the final value of **tm_mday** is not set until **tm_mon** and **tm_year** are determined. When specifying a **tm** structure time, set the **tm_isdst** field to 0 to indicate that standard time is in effect, or to a value greater than 0 to indicate that daylight savings time is in effect, or to a value less than zero to have the C run-time library code compute whether standard time or daylight savings time is in effect. **tm_isdst** is a required field. If not set, its value is undefined and the return value from **mktime** is unpredictable. If *timeptr* points to a **tm** structure returned by a previous call to **asctime**, **gmtime**, or **localtime**, the **tm_isdst** field contains the correct value.

Note that **gmtime** and **localtime** use a single statically allocated buffer for the conversion. If you supply this buffer to **mktime**, the previous contents are destroyed.

Example

```
/* MKTIME.C: The example takes a number of days
 * as input and returns the time, the current
 * date, and the specified number of days.
 */

#include <time.h>
#include <stdio.h>

void main( void )
{
   struct tm when;
   time_t now, result;
   int    days;

   time( &now );
   when = *localtime( &now );
   printf( "Current time is %s\n", asctime( &when ) );
   printf( "How many days to look ahead: " );
   scanf( "%d", &days );
```

```
    when.tm_mday = when.tm_mday + days;
    if( (result = mktime( &when )) != (time_t)-1 )
       printf( "In %d days the time will be %s\n",
               days, asctime( &when ) );
    else
       perror( "mktime failed" );
}
```

Output

```
Current time is Tue May 03 12:45:47 1994

How many days to look ahead: 29
In 29 days the time will be Wed Jun 01 12:45:47 1994
```

See Also **asctime**, **gmtime**, **localtime**, **time**

modf

Splits a floating-point value into fractional and integer parts.

double modf(double *x*, **double** **intptr* **);**

Routine	Required Header	Optional Headers	Compatibility
modf	<math.h>		ANSI, Win 95, Win NT, Win32s, 68K, PMac

For additional compatibility information, see "Compatibility" on page ix in the Introduction.

Libraries	
LIBC.LIB	Single thread static library, retail version
LIBCMT.LIB	Multithread static library, retail version
MSVCRT.LIB	Import library for MSVCRTx0.DLL, retail version
MSVCRTx0.DLL	Multithread DLL library, retail version

Return Value

This function returns the signed fractional portion of *x*. There is no error return.

Parameters

x Floating-point value

intptr Pointer to stored integer portion

Remarks

The **modf** function breaks down the floating-point value *x* into fractional and integer parts, each of which has the same sign as *x*. The signed fractional portion of *x* is returned. The integer portion is stored as a floating-point value at *intptr*.

Example

```
/* MODF.C */

#include <math.h>
#include <stdio.h>

void main( void )
{
   double x, y, n;

   x = -14.87654321;      /* Divide x into its fractional */
   y = modf( x, &n );     /* and integer parts            */

   printf( "For %f, the fraction is %f and the integer is %.f\n",
           x, y, n );
}
```

Output

```
For -14.876543, the fraction is -0.876543 and the integer is -14
```

See Also **frexp**, **ldexp**

_msize

Returns the size of a memory block allocated in the heap.

size_t _msize(void **memblock* **);**

Routine	Required Header	Optional Headers	Compatibility
_msize	<malloc.h>		Win 95, Win NT, Win32s, 68K, PMac

For additional compatibility information, see "Compatibility" on page ix in the Introduction.

Libraries	
LIBC.LIB	Single thread static library, retail version
LIBCMT.LIB	Multithread static library, retail version
MSVCRT.LIB	Import library for MSVCRTx0.DLL, retail version
MSVCRTx0.DLL	Multithread DLL library, retail version

Return Value

_msize returns the size (in bytes) as an unsigned integer.

Parameter

memblock Pointer to memory block

Remarks

The **_msize** function returns the size, in bytes, of the memory block allocated by a call to **calloc**, **malloc**, or **realloc**.

When the application is linked with a debug version of the C run-time libraries, **_msize** resolves to **_msize_dbg**. For more information about how the heap is managed during the debugging process, see Chapter 4, "Debug Version of the C Run-Time Library."

Example

See the example for **realloc**.

See Also **calloc**, **_expand**, **malloc**, **realloc**

_nextafter

Returns next representable neighbor.

double _nextafter(double *x*, **double** *y* **);**

Routine	Required Header	Optional Headers	Compatibility
_nextafter	<float.h>		Win 95, Win NT, Win32s, 68K, PMac

For additional compatibility information, see "Compatibility" on page ix in the Introduction.

Libraries	
LIBC.LIB	Single thread static library, retail version
LIBCMT.LIB	Multithread static library, retail version
MSVCRT.LIB	Import library for MSVCRTx0.DLL, retail version
MSVCRTx0.DLL	Multithread DLL library, retail version

Return Value

If *x*=*y*, **_nextafter** returns *x*, with no exception triggered. If either *x* or *y* is a quiet NaN, then the return value is one or the other of the input NaNs.

Parameters

x, *y* Double-precision floating-point values

Remarks

The **_nextafter** function returns the closest representable neighbor of *x* in the direction toward *y*.

See Also **_isnan**

offsetof

Retrieves the offset of a member from the beginning of its parent structure.

size_t offsetof(*structName*, *memberName* **);**

Routine	Required Header	Optional Headers	Compatibility
offsetof	<stddef.h>		ANSI, Win 95, Win NT, Win32s, 68K, PMac

For additional compatibility information, see "Compatibility" on page ix in the Introduction.

Libraries	
LIBC.LIB	Single thread static library, retail version
LIBCMT.LIB	Multithread static library, retail version
MSVCRT.LIB	Import library for MSVCRTx0.DLL, retail version
MSVCRTx0.DLL	Multithread DLL library, retail version

Return Value

offsetof returns the offset in bytes of the specified member from the beginning of its parent data structure. It is undefined for bit fields.

Parameters

structName Name of the parent data structure

memberName Name of the member in the parent data structure for which to determine the offset

Remarks

The **offsetof** macro returns the offset in bytes of *memberName* from the beginning of the structure specified by *structName*. You can specify types with the **struct** keyword.

Note **offsetof** is not a function and cannot be described using a C prototype.

_onexit

Registers a routine to be called at exit time.

_onexit_t _onexit(_onexit_t *func* **);**

Routine	Required Header	Optional Headers	Compatibility
_onexit	<stdlib.h>		Win 95, Win NT, Win32s, 68K, PMac

For additional compatibility information, see "Compatibility" on page ix in the Introduction.

Libraries

LIBC.LIB	Single thread static library, retail version
LIBCMT.LIB	Multithread static library, retail version
MSVCRT.LIB	Import library for MSVCRTx0.DLL, retail version
MSVCRTx0.DLL	Multithread DLL library, retail version

Return Value

_onexit returns a pointer to the function if successful, or **NULL** if there is no space to store the function pointer.

Parameter

func Pointer to function to be called at exit

Remarks

The **_onexit** function is passed the address of a function (*func*) to be called when the program terminates normally. Successive calls to **_onexit** create a register of functions that are executed in LIFO (last-in-first-out) order. The functions passed to **_onexit** cannot take parameters.

_onexit is a Microsoft extension. For ANSI portability use **atexit**.

Example

```
/* ONEXIT.C */

#include <stdlib.h>
#include <stdio.h>

/* Prototypes */
int fn1(void), fn2(void), fn3(void), fn4 (void);

void main( void )
{
   _onexit( fn1 );
   _onexit( fn2 );
   _onexit( fn3 );
   _onexit( fn4 );
   printf( "This is executed first.\n" );
}

int fn1()
{
   printf( "next.\n" );
   return 0;
}
```

```
int fn2()
{
   printf( "executed " );
   return 0;
}

int fn3()
{
   printf( "is " );
   return 0;
}

int fn4()
{
   printf( "This " );
   return 0;
}
```

Output

```
This is executed first.
This is executed next.
```

See Also **atexit**, **exit**

_open, _wopen

Open a file.

int _open(const char ****filename*, **int** *oflag* [, **int** *pmode*] **);**
int _wopen(const wchar_t ****filename*, **int** *oflag* [, **int** *pmode*] **);**

Routine	Required Header	Optional Headers	Compatibility
_open	<io.h>	<fcntl.h>, <sys/types.h>, <sys/stat.h>	Win 95, Win NT, Win32s, 68K, PMac
_wopen	<io.h> or <wchar.h>	<fcntl.h>, <sys/types.h>, <sys/stat.h>	Win NT

For additional compatibility information, see "Compatibility" on page ix in the Introduction.

Libraries	
LIBC.LIB	Single thread static library, retail version
LIBCMT.LIB	Multithread static library, retail version
MSVCRT.LIB	Import library for MSVCRTx0.DLL, retail version
MSVCRTx0.DLL	Multithread DLL library, retail version

Return Value

Each of these functions returns a file handle for the opened file. A return value of –1 indicates an error, in which case **errno** is set to one of the following values:

EACCES Tried to open read-only file for writing, or file's sharing mode does not allow specified operations, or given path is directory

EEXIST **_O_CREAT** and **_O_EXCL** flags specified, but *filename* already exists

EINVAL Invalid *oflag* or *pmode* argument

EMFILE No more file handles available (too many open files)

ENOENT File or path not found

Parameters

filename Filename

oflag Type of operations allowed

pmode Permission mode

Remarks

The **_open** function opens the file specified by *filename* and prepares the file for reading or writing, as specified by *oflag*. **_wopen** is a wide-character version of **_open**; the *filename* argument to **_wopen** is a wide-character string. **_wopen** and **_open** behave identically otherwise.

oflag is an integer expression formed from one or more of the following manifest constants or constant combinations defined in FCNTL.H:

_O_APPEND Moves file pointer to end of file before every write operation.

_O_BINARY Opens file in binary (untranslated) mode. (See **fopen** for a description of binary mode.)

_O_CREAT Creates and opens new file for writing. Has no effect if file specified by *filename* exists. *pmode* argument is required when **_O_CREAT** is specified.

_O_CREAT | _O_SHORT_LIVED Create file as temporary and if possible do not flush to disk. *pmode* argument is required when **_O_CREAT** is specified.

_O_CREAT | _O_TEMPORARY Create file as temporary; file is deleted when last file handle is closed. *pmode* argument is required when **_O_CREAT** is specified.

_O_CREAT | _O_EXCL Returns error value if file specified by *filename* exists. Applies only when used with **_O_CREAT**.

_O_RANDOM Specifies primarily random access from disk

_O_RDONLY Opens file for reading only; cannot be specified with **_O_RDWR** or **_O_WRONLY**.

_O_RDWR Opens file for both reading and writing; you cannot specify this flag with **_O_RDONLY** or **_O_WRONLY**.

_O_SEQUENTIAL Specifies primarily sequential access from disk

_O_TEXT Opens file in text (translated) mode. (For more information, see "Text and Binary Mode File I/O" on page 15 and **fopen** on page 282.)

_O_TRUNC Opens file and truncates it to zero length; file must have write permission. You cannot specify this flag with **_O_RDONLY**. **_O_TRUNC** used with **_O_CREAT** opens an existing file or creates a new file.

Warning The **_O_TRUNC** flag destroys the contents of the specified file.

_O_WRONLY Opens file for writing only; cannot be specified with **_O_RDONLY** or **_O_RDWR**.

To specify the file access mode, you must specify either **_O_RDONLY**, **_O_RDWR**, or **_O_WRONLY**. There is no default value for the access mode.

When two or more manifest constants are used to form the *oflag* argument, the constants are combined with the bitwise-OR operator (**|**). See "Text and Binary Mode File I/O" on page 15 for a discussion of binary and text modes.

The *pmode* argument is required only when **_O_CREAT** is specified. If the file already exists, *pmode* is ignored. Otherwise, *pmode* specifies the file permission settings, which are set when the new file is closed the first time. **_open** applies the current file-permission mask to *pmode* before setting the permissions (for more information, see **_umask**). *pmode* is an integer expression containing one or both of the following manifest constants, defined in SYS\STAT.H:

_S_IREAD Reading only permitted

_S_IWRITE Writing permitted (effectively permits reading and writing)

_S_IREAD | _S_IWRITE Reading and writing permitted

When both constants are given, they are joined with the bitwise-OR operator (**|**). In Windows NT, all files are readable, so write-only permission is not available; thus the modes **_S_IWRITE** and **_S_IREAD | _S_IWRITE** are equivalent.

Example

```
/* OPEN.C: This program uses _open to open a file
 * named OPEN.C for input and a file named OPEN.OUT
 * for output. The files are then closed.
 */

#include <fcntl.h>
#include <sys/types.h>
#include <sys/stat.h>
#include <io.h>
#include <stdio.h>
```

```
void main( void )
{
   int fh1, fh2;

   fh1 = _open( "OPEN.C", _O_RDONLY );
   if( fh1 == -1 )
      perror( "open failed on input file" );
   else
   {
      printf( "open succeeded on input file\n" );
      _close( fh1 );
   }

   fh2 = _open( "OPEN.OUT", _O_WRONLY | _O_CREAT, _S_IREAD |
                            _S_IWRITE );
   if( fh2 == -1 )
      perror( "Open failed on output file" );
   else
   {
      printf( "Open succeeded on output file\n" );
      _close( fh2 );
   }
}
```

Output

```
Open succeeded on input file
Open succeeded on output file
```

See Also **_chmod**, **_close**, **_creat**, **_dup**, **fopen**, **_sopen**

_open_osfhandle

Associates a C run-time file handle with a existing operating-system file handle.

int _open_osfhandle (long *osfhandle*, **int** *flags* **);**

Routine	Required Header	Optional Headers	Compatibility
_open_osfhandle	<io.h>		Win 95, Win NT, Win32s, 68K, PMac

For additional compatibility information, see "Compatibility" on page ix in the Introduction.

Libraries

LIBC.LIB	Single thread static library, retail version
LIBCMT.LIB	Multithread static library, retail version
MSVCRT.LIB	Import library for MSVCRTx0.DLL, retail version
MSVCRTx0.DLL	Multithread DLL library, retail version

Return Value

If successful, **_open_osfhandle** returns a C run-time file handle. Otherwise, it returns –1.

Parameters

osfhandle Operating-system file handle

flags Types of operations allowed

Remarks

The **_open_osfhandle** function allocates a C run-time file handle and sets it to point to the operating-system file handle specified by *osfhandle*. The *flags* argument is an integer expression formed from one or more of the manifest constants defined in FCNTL.H. When two or more manifest constants are used to form the *flags* argument, the constants are combined with the bitwise-OR operator (|).

The FCNTL.H file defines the following manifest constants:

_O_APPEND Positions file pointer to end of file before every write operation.

_O_RDONLY Opens file for reading only

_O_TEXT Opens file in text (translated) mode

_outp, _outpw, _outpd

Output a byte(**_outp**), a word(**_outpw**), or a double word (**_outpd**) at a port.

int _outp(unsigned short *port*, **int** *databyte* **);**
unsigned short _outpw(unsigned short *port*, **unsigned short** *dataword* **);**
unsigned long _outpd(unsigned short *port*, **unsigned long** *dataword* **);**

Routine	Required Header	Optional Headers	Compatibility
_outp	<conio.h>		Win 95, Win32s
_outpw	<conio.h>		Win 95, Win32s
_outpd	<conio.h>		Win 95, Win32s

For additional compatibility information, see "Compatibility" on page ix in the Introduction.

Libraries

LIBC.LIB	Single thread static library, retail version
LIBCMT.LIB	Multithread static library, retail version
MSVCRT.LIB	Import library for MSVCRTx0.DLL, retail version
MSVCRTx0.DLL	Multithread DLL library, retail version

Return Value

The functions return the data output. There is no error return.

Parameters

port Port number

databyte, dataword Output values

Remarks

The **_outp**, **_outpw**, and **_outpd** functions write a byte, a word, and a double word, respectively, to the specified output port. The *port* argument can be any unsigned integer in the range 0–65,535; *databyte* can be any integer in the range 0–255; and *dataword* can be any value in the range of an integer, an unsigned short integer, and an unsigned long integer, respectively.

_pclose

Waits for new command processor and closes stream on associated pipe.

int _pclose(FILE ****stream* **);

Routine	Required Header	Optional Headers	Compatibility
_pclose	<stdio.h>		Win 95, Win NT

For additional compatibility information, see “Compatibility” on page ix in the Introduction.

Libraries

LIBC.LIB	Single thread static library, retail version
LIBCMT.LIB	Multithread static library, retail version
MSVCRT.LIB	Import library for MSVCRTx0.DLL, retail version
MSVCRTx0.DLL	Multithread DLL library, retail version

Return Value

_pclose returns the exit status of the terminating command processor, or –1 if an error occurs. The format of the return value is the same as that for **_cwait**, except the low-order and high-order bytes are swapped.

Parameter

stream Return value from previous call to **_popen**

Remarks

The **_pclose** function looks up the process ID of the command processor (CMD.EXE) started by the associated **_popen** call, executes a **_cwait** call on the new command processor, and closes the stream on the associated pipe.

See Also **_pipe**, **_popen**

---

perror, _wperror

Print an error message.

void perror(const char **string* **);**
void _wperror(const wchar_t **string* **);**

Routine	Required Header	Optional Headers	Compatibility
perror	<stdio.h> or <stdlib.h>		ANSI, Win 95, Win NT, 68K, PMac
_wperror	<stdio.h> or <wchar.h>		Win 95, Win NT

For additional compatibility information, see "Compatibility" on page ix in the Introduction.

Libraries	
LIBC.LIB	Single thread static library, retail version
LIBCMT.LIB	Multithread static library, retail version
MSVCRT.LIB	Import library for MSVCRTx0.DLL, retail version
MSVCRTx0.DLL	Multithread DLL library, retail version

Return Value

None

Parameter

string String message to print

Remarks

The **perror** function prints an error message to **stderr**. **_wperror** is a wide-character version of **_perror**; the *string* argument to **_wperror** is a wide-character string. **_wperror** and **_perror** behave identically otherwise.

string is printed first, followed by a colon, then by the system error message for the last library call that produced the error, and finally by a newline character. If *string* is a null pointer or a pointer to a null string, **perror** prints only the system error message.

The error number is stored in the variable **errno** (defined in ERRNO.H). The system error messages are accessed through the variable **_sys_errlist**, which is an array of messages ordered by error number. **perror** prints the appropriate error message using the **errno** value as an index to **_sys_errlist**. The value of the variable **_sys_nerr** is defined as the maximum number of elements in the **_sys_errlist** array.

For accurate results, call **perror** immediately after a library routine returns with an error. Otherwise, subsequent calls can overwrite the **errno** value.

In Windows NT and Windows 95, some **errno** values listed in ERRNO.H are unused. These values are reserved for use by the UNIX operating system. See "**_doserrno, errno, _sys_errlist**, and **_sys_nerr**" on page 41 for a listing of **errno** values used by Windows NT and Windows 95. **perror** prints an empty string for any **errno** value not used by these platforms.

Example

```
/* PERROR.C: This program attempts to open a file named
 * NOSUCHF.ILE. Because this file probably doesn't exist,
 * an error message is displayed. The same message is
 * created using perror, strerror, and _strerror.
 */

#include <fcntl.h>
#include <sys/types.h>
#include <sys/stat.h>
#include <io.h>
#include <stdlib.h>
#include <stdio.h>
#include <string.h>

void main( void )
{
   int  fh;

   if( (fh = _open( "NOSUCHF.ILE", _O_RDONLY )) == -1 )
   {
      /* Three ways to create error message: */
      perror( "perror says open failed" );
      printf( "strerror says open failed: %s\n", strerror( errno ) );
      printf( _strerror( "_strerror says open failed" ) );
   }
   else
   {
      printf( "open succeeded on input file\n" );
      _close( fh );
   }
}
```

Output

```
perror says open failed: No such file or directory

strerror says open failed: No such file or directory
_strerror says open failed: No such file or directory
```

See Also **clearerr**, **ferror**, **strerror**

_pipe

Creates a pipe for reading and writing.

int _pipe(int ***phandles*, unsigned int** *psize***, int** *textmode* **);**

Routine	Required Header	Optional Headers	Compatibility
_pipe	<io.h>	<fcntl.h>,[1] <errno.h>[2]	Win 95, Win NT, Win32s

1 For **_O_BINARY** and **_O_TEXT** definitions.

2 **errno** definitions.

For additional compatibility information, see "Compatibility" on page ix in the Introduction.

Libraries	
LIBC.LIB	Single thread static library, retail version
LIBCMT.LIB	Multithread static library, retail version
MSVCRT.LIB	Import library for **MSVCRTx0.DLL**, retail version
MSVCRTx0.DLL	Multithread DLL library, retail version

Return Value

_pipe returns 0 if successful. It returns –1 to indicate an error, in which case **errno** is set to one of two values: **EMFILE**, which indicates no more file handles available, or **ENFILE**, which indicates a system file table overflow.

Parameters

phandles[2] Array to hold read and write handles

psize Amount of memory to reserve

textmode File mode

Remarks

The **_pipe** function creates a pipe. A *pipe* is an artificial I/O channel that a program uses to pass information to other programs. A pipe is similar to a file in that it has a file pointer, a file descriptor, or both, and can be read from or written to using the standard library's input and output functions. However, a pipe does not represent a specific file or device. Instead, it represents temporary storage in memory that is independent of the program's own memory and is controlled entirely by the operating system.

_pipe is similar to **_open** but opens the pipe for reading and writing, returning two file handles instead of one. The program can use both sides of the pipe or close the one it does not need. For example, the command processor in Windows NT creates a pipe when executing a command such as

```
PROGRAM1 | PROGRAM2
```

The standard output handle of PROGRAM1 is attached to the pipe's write handle. The standard input handle of PROGRAM2 is attached to the pipe's read handle. This eliminates the need for creating temporary files to pass information to other programs.

The **_pipe** function returns two handles to the pipe in the *phandles* argument. The element *phandles*[0] contains the read handle, and the element *phandles*[1] contains the write handle. Pipe file handles are used in the same way as other file handles. (The low-level input and output functions **_read** and **_write** can read from and write to a pipe.) To detect the end-of-pipe condition, check for a **_read** request that returns 0 as the number of bytes read.

The *psize* argument specifies the amount of memory, in bytes, to reserve for the pipe. The *textmode* argument specifies the translation mode for the pipe. The manifest constant **_O_TEXT** specifies a text translation, and the constant **_O_BINARY** specifies binary translation. (See **fopen** for a description of text and binary modes.) If the *textmode* argument is 0, **_pipe** uses the default translation mode specified by the default-mode variable **_fmode**.

In multithreaded programs, no locking is performed. The handles returned are newly opened and should not be referenced by any thread until after the **_pipe** call is complete.

In Windows NT and Windows 95, a pipe is destroyed when all of its handles have been closed. (If all read handles on the pipe have been closed, writing to the pipe causes an error.) All read and write operations on the pipe wait until there is enough data or enough buffer space to complete the I/O request.

Example

```
/* PIPE.C: This program uses the _pipe function to pass streams of
 * text to spawned processes.
 */

#include <stdlib.h>
#include <stdio.h>
#include <io.h>
#include <fcntl.h>
#include <process.h>
#include <math.h>
```

```
enum PIPES { READ, WRITE }; /* Constants 0 and 1 for READ and WRITE */
#define NUMPROBLEM 8

void main( int argc, char *argv[] )
{

   int hpipe[2];
   char hstr[20];
   int pid, problem, c;
   int termstat;

   /* If no arguments, this is the spawning process */
   if( argc == 1 )
   {

      setvbuf( stdout, NULL, _IONBF, 0 );

      /* Open a set of pipes */
      if( _pipe( hpipe, 256, O_BINARY ) == -1 )
          exit( 1 );

      /* Convert pipe read handle to string and pass as argument
       * to spawned program. Program spawns itself (argv[0]).
       */
      itoa( hpipe[READ], hstr, 10 );
      if( ( pid = spawnl( P_NOWAIT, argv[0], argv[0],
            hstr, NULL ) ) == -1 )
          printf( "Spawn failed" );

      /* Put problem in write pipe. Since spawned program is
       * running simultaneously, first solutions may be done
       * before last problem is given.
       */
      for( problem = 1000; problem <= NUMPROBLEM * 1000; problem += 1000)
      {

         printf( "Son, what is the square root of %d?\n", problem );
         write( hpipe[WRITE], (char *)&problem, sizeof( int ) );

      }

      /* Wait until spawned program is done processing. */
      _cwait( &termstat, pid, WAIT_CHILD );
      if( termstat & 0x0 )
         printf( "Child failed\n" );

      close( hpipe[READ] );
      close( hpipe[WRITE] );

   }

   /* If there is an argument, this must be the spawned process. */
   else
```

```
    {

        /* Convert passed string handle to integer handle. */
        hpipe[READ] = atoi( argv[1] );

        /* Read problem from pipe and calculate solution. */
        for( c = 0; c < NUMPROBLEM; c++ )
        {

          read( hpipe[READ], (char *)&problem, sizeof( int ) );
          printf( "Dad, the square root of %d is %3.2f.\n",
                   problem, sqrt( ( double )problem ) );

        }
    }
}
```

Output

```
Son, what is the square root of 1000?
Son, what is the square root of 2000?
Son, what is the square root of 3000?
Son, what is the square root of 4000?
Son, what is the square root of 5000?
Son, what is the square root of 6000?
Son, what is the square root of 7000?
Son, what is the square root of 8000?
Dad, the square root of 1000 is 31.62.
Dad, the square root of 2000 is 44.72.
Dad, the square root of 3000 is 54.77.
Dad, the square root of 4000 is 63.25.
Dad, the square root of 5000 is 70.71.
Dad, the square root of 6000 is 77.46.
Dad, the square root of 7000 is 83.67.
Dad, the square root of 8000 is 89.44.
```

See Also **_open**

_popen, _wpopen

Creates a pipe and executes a command.

FILE *_popen(const char ****command*, **const char ****mode* **);
FILE *_wpopen(const wchar_t ****command*, **const wchar_t ****mode* **);

Routine	Required Header	Optional Headers	Compatibility
_popen	<stdio.h>		Win 95, Win NT
_wpopen	<stdio.h> or <wchar.h>		Win NT

For additional compatibility information, see "Compatibility" on page ix in the Introduction.

Libraries

LIBC.LIB	Single thread static library, retail version
LIBCMT.LIB	Multithread static library, retail version
MSVCRT.LIB	Import library for MSVCRTx0.DLL, retail version
MSVCRTx0.DLL	Multithread DLL library, retail version

Return Value

Each of these functions returns a stream associated with one end of the created pipe. The other end of the pipe is associated with the spawned command's standard input or standard output. The functions return **NULL** on an error.

Parameters

command Command to be executed

mode Mode of returned stream

Remarks

The **_popen** function creates a pipe and asynchronously executes a spawned copy of the command processor with the specified string *command*. The character string *mode* specifies the type of access requested, as follows:

"r" The calling process can read the spawned command's standard output via the returned stream.

"w" The calling process can write to the spawned command's standard input via the returned stream.

"b" Open in binary mode.

"t" Open in text mode.

_wpopen is a wide character version of **_popen**; the *path* argument to **_wpopen** is a wide-character string. **_wpopen** and **_popen** behave identically otherwise.

Example

```
/* POPEN.C: This program uses _popen and _pclose to receive a
 * stream of text from a system process.
 */

#include <stdio.h>
#include <stdlib.h>

void main( void )
{

   char   psBuffer[128];
   FILE   *chkdsk;
```

```
   /* Run DIR so that it writes its output to a pipe. Open this
    * pipe with read text attribute so that we can read it
    * like a text file.
    */
   if( (chkdsk = _popen( "dir *.c /on /p", "rt" )) == NULL )
      exit( 1 );

   /* Read pipe until end of file. End of file indicates that
    * CHKDSK closed its standard out (probably meaning it
    * terminated).
    */
   while( !feof( chkdsk ) )
   {
      if( fgets( psBuffer, 128, chkdsk ) != NULL )
         printf( psBuffer );
   }

   /* Close pipe and print return value of CHKDSK. */
   printf( "\nProcess returned %d\n", _pclose( chkdsk ) );
}
```

Output

```
 Volume in drive C is CDRIVE
 Volume Serial Number is 0E17-1702

 Directory of C:\dolphin\crt\code\pcode

05/02/94  01:05a                   805 perror.c
05/02/94  01:05a                 2,149 pipe.c
05/02/94  01:05a                   882 popen.c
05/02/94  01:05a                   206 pow.c
05/02/94  01:05a                 1,514 printf.c
05/02/94  01:05a                   454 putc.c
05/02/94  01:05a                   162 puts.c
05/02/94  01:05a                   654 putw.c
               8 File(s)          6,826 bytes
                             86,597,632 bytes free

Process returned 0
```

See Also **_pclose, _pipe**

pow

Calculates *x* raised to the power of *y*.

double pow(double *x*, **double** *y* **);**

Routine	Required Header	Optional Headers	Compatibility
pow	<math.h>		ANSI, Win 95, Win NT, Win32s, 68K, PMac

For additional compatibility information, see "Compatibility" on page ix in the Introduction.

Libraries	
LIBC.LIB	Single thread static library, retail version
LIBCMT.LIB	Multithread static library, retail version
MSVCRT.LIB	Import library for MSVCRTx0.DLL, retail version
MSVCRTx0.DLL	Multithread DLL library, retail version

Return Value

pow returns the value of *xy*. No error message is printed on overflow or underflow.

Values of x and y	Return Value of pow
x < > 0 and *y* = 0.0	1
x = 0.0 and *y* = 0.0	1
x = 0.0 and *y* < 0	INF

Parameters

x Base

y Exponent

Remarks

The **pow** function computes *x* raised to the power of *y*.

pow does not recognize integral floating-point values greater than 2^{64}, such as `1.0E100`.

Example

```
/* POW.C
 *
 */

#include <math.h>
#include <stdio.h>
```

```
void main( void )
{
   double x = 2.0, y = 3.0, z;

   z = pow( x, y );
   printf( "%.1f to the power of %.1f is %.1f\n", x, y, z );
}
```

Output

```
2.0 to the power of 3.0 is 8.0
```

See Also **exp**, **log**, **sqrt**

printf, wprintf

Print formatted output to the standard output stream.

int printf(const char ***format*** **[,** ***argument*****]...);**
int wprintf(const wchar_t ***format*** **[,** ***argument*****]...);**

Routine	Required Header	Optional Headers	Compatibility
printf	<stdio.h>		ANSI, Win 95, Win NT, 68K, PMac
wprintf	<stdio.h> or <wchar.h>		ANSI, Win 95, Win NT

For additional compatibility information, see "Compatibility" on page ix in the Introduction.

Libraries	
LIBC.LIB	Single thread static library, retail version
LIBCMT.LIB	Multithread static library, retail version
MSVCRT.LIB	Import library for MSVCRTx0.DLL, retail version
MSVCRTx0.DLL	Multithread DLL library, retail version

Return Value

Each of these functions returns the number of characters printed, or a negative value if an error occurs.

Parameters

format Format control

argument Optional arguments

Remarks

The **printf** function formats and prints a series of characters and values to the standard output stream, **stdout**. If arguments follow the *format* string, the *format* string must contain specifications that determine the output format for the arguments. **printf** and **fprintf** behave identically except that **printf** writes output to **stdout** rather than to a destination of type **FILE**.

wprintf is a wide-character version of **printf**; *format* is a wide-character string. **wprintf** and **printf** behave identically otherwise.

The *format* argument consists of ordinary characters, escape sequences, and (if arguments follow *format*) format specifications. The ordinary characters and escape sequences are copied to **stdout** in order of their appearance. For example, the line

```
printf("Line one\n\t\tLine two\n");
```

produces the output

```
Line one
        Line two
```

Format specifications always begin with a percent sign (%) and are read left to right. When **printf** encounters the first format specification (if any), it converts the value of the first argument after *format* and outputs it accordingly. The second format specification causes the second argument to be converted and output, and so on. If there are more arguments than there are format specifications, the extra arguments are ignored. The results are undefined if there are not enough arguments for all the format specifications.

Example

```
/* PRINTF.C: This program uses the printf and wprintf functions
 * to produce formatted output.
 */

#include <stdio.h>

void main( void )
{
   char   ch = 'h', *string = "computer";
   int    count = -9234;
   double fp = 251.7366;
   wchar_t wch = L'w', *wstring = L"Unicode";

   /* Display integers. */
   printf( "Integer formats:\n"
           "\tDecimal: %d  Justified: %.6d  Unsigned: %u\n",
           count, count, count, count );

   printf( "Decimal %d as:\n\tHex: %Xh  C hex: 0x%x  Octal: %o\n",
            count, count, count, count );

   /* Display in different radixes. */
   printf( "Digits 10 equal:\n\tHex: %i  Octal: %i  Decimal: %i\n",
            0x10, 010, 10 );

   /* Display characters. */
```

```
    printf("Characters in field (1):\n%10c%5hc%5C%5lc\n", ch, ch, wch, wch);
    wprintf(L"Characters in field (2):\n%10C%5hc%5c%5lc\n", ch, ch, wch, wch);

    /* Display strings. */

    printf("Strings in field (1):\n%25s\n%25.4hs\n\t%S%25.3ls\n",
    string, string, wstring, wstring);
    wprintf(L"Strings in field (2):\n%25S\n%25.4hs\n\t%s%25.3ls\n",
        string, string, wstring, wstring);

    /* Display real numbers. */
    printf( "Real numbers:\n\t%f %.2f %e %E\n", fp, fp, fp, fp );

    /* Display pointer. */
    printf( "\nAddress as:\t%p\n", &count);

    /* Count characters printed. */
    printf( "\nDisplay to here:\n" );
    printf( "1234567890123456%n78901234567890\n", &count );
    printf( "\tNumber displayed: %d\n\n", count );
}
```

Output

```
Integer formats:
    Decimal: -9234  Justified: -009234  Unsigned: 4294958062
Decimal -9234 as:
    Hex: FFFFDBEEh  C hex: 0xffffdbee  Octal: 37777755756
Digits 10 equal:
    Hex: 16  Octal: 8  Decimal: 10
Characters in field (1):
         h    h    w    w
Characters in field (2):
         h    h    w    w
Strings in field (1):
                 computer
                     comp
    Unicode                      Uni
Strings in field (2):
                 computer
                     comp
    Unicode                      Uni
Real numbers:
    251.736600 251.74 2.517366e+002 2.517366E+002

Address as: 0012FFAC

Display to here:
123456789012345678901234567890
    Number displayed: 16
```

See Also **fopen**, **fprintf**, **scanf**, **sprintf**, **vprintf** Functions

printf Format Specification Fields

A format specification, which consists of optional and required fields, has the following form:

%[*flags*] [*width*] [*.precision*] [{**h** | **l** | **L**}]*type*

Each field of the format specification is a single character or a number signifying a particular format option. The simplest format specification contains only the percent sign and a *type* character (for example, `%s`). If a percent sign is followed by a character that has no meaning as a format field, the character is copied to **stdout**. For example, to print a percent-sign character, use `%%`.

The optional fields, which appear before the *type* character, control other aspects of the formatting, as follows:

type Required character that determines whether the associated *argument* is interpreted as a character, a string, or a number (see Table R.3).

flags Optional character or characters that control justification of output and printing of signs, blanks, decimal points, and octal and hexadecimal prefixes (see Table R.4). More than one flag can appear in a format specification.

width Optional number that specifies the minimum number of characters output.

precision Optional number that specifies the maximum number of characters printed for all or part of the output field, or the minimum number of digits printed for integer values (see Table R.5).

h | **l** | **L** Optional prefixes to *type*-that specify the size of *argument* (see Table R.6).

printf Type Field Characters

The *type* character is the only required format field ; it appears after any optional format fields. The *type* character determines whether the associated argument is interpreted as a character, string, or number The types **c**, **C**, **s**, and **S** are Microsoft extensions and are not ANSI-compatible.

Table R.3 printf Type Field Characters

Character	Type	Output Format
c	**int** or **wint_t**	When used with **printf** functions, specifies a single-byte character; when used with **wprintf** functions, specifies a wide character.
C	**int** or **wint_t**	When used with **printf** functions, specifies a wide character; when used with **wprintf** functions, specifies a single-byte character.
d	**int**	Signed decimal integer.
i	**int**	Signed decimal integer.

Table R.3 printf Type Field Characters *(continued)*

Character	Type	Output Format
o	**int**	Unsigned octal integer.
u	**int**	Unsigned decimal integer.
x	**int**	Unsigned hexadecimal integer, using "abcdef."
X	**int**	Unsigned hexadecimal integer, using "ABCDEF."
e	**double**	Signed value having the form [–]*d***.***dddd* **e** [*sign*]*ddd* where *d* is a single decimal digit, *dddd* is one or more decimal digits, *ddd* is exactly three decimal digits, and *sign* is + or –.
E	**double**	Identical to the **e** format except that **E** rather than **e** introduces the exponent.
f	**double**	Signed value having the form [–]*dddd***.***dddd*, where *dddd* is one or more decimal digits. The number of digits before the decimal point depends on the magnitude of the number, and the number of digits after the decimal point depends on the requested precision.
g	**double**	Signed value printed in **f** or **e** format, whichever is more compact for the given value and precision. The **e** format is used only when the exponent of the value is less than –4 or greater than or equal to the precision argument. Trailing zeros are truncated, and the decimal point appears only if one or more digits follow it.
G	**double**	Identical to the **g** format, except that **E**, rather than **e**, introduces the exponent (where appropriate).
n	Pointer to integer	Number of characters successfully written so far to the stream or buffer; this value is stored in the integer whose address is given as the argument.
p	Pointer to **void**	Prints the address pointed to by the argument in the form *xxxx***:***yyyy* where *xxxx* is the segment and *yyyy* is the offset, and the digits *x* and *y* are uppercase hexadecimal digits.
s	String	When used with **printf** functions, specifies a single-byte–character string; when used with **wprintf** functions, specifies a wide-character string. Characters are printed up to the first null character or until the *precision* value is reached.
S	String	When used with **printf** functions, specifies a wide-character string; when used with **wprintf** functions, specifies a single-byte–character string. Characters are printed up to the first null character or until the *precision* value is reached.

printf Flag Directives

The first optional field of the format specification is *flags*. A flag directive is a character that justifies output and prints signs, blanks, decimal points, and octal and hexadecimal prefixes. More than one flag directive may appear in a format specification.

Table R.4 Flag Characters

Flag	Meaning	Default
–	Left align the result within the given field width.	Right align.
+	Prefix the output value with a sign (+ or –) if the output value is of a signed type.	Sign appears only for negative signed values (–).
0	If *width* is prefixed with **0**, zeros are added until the minimum width is reached. If 0 and – appear, the **0** is ignored. If **0** is specified with an integer format (**i**, **u**, **x**, **X**, **o**, **d**) the **0** is ignored.	No padding.
blank (' ')	Prefix the output value with a blank if the output value is signed and positive; the blank is ignored if both the blank and + flags appear.	No blank appears.
#	When used with the **o**, **x**, or **X** format, the # flag prefixes any nonzero output value with 0, 0x, or 0X, respectively.	No blank appears.
	When used with the **e**, **E**, or **f** format, the **#** flag forces the output value to contain a decimal point in all cases.	Decimal point appears only if digits follow it.
	When used with the **g** or **G** format, the **#** flag forces the output value to contain a decimal point in all cases and prevents the truncation of trailing zeros.	Decimal point appears only if digits follow it. Trailing zeros are truncated.
	Ignored when used with **c**, **d**, **i**, **u**, or **s**.	

printf Width Specification

The second optional field of the format specification is the width specification. The *width* argument is a nonnegative decimal integer controlling the minimum number of characters printed. If the number of characters in the output value is less than the specified width, blanks are added to the left or the right of the values—depending on whether the – flag (for left alignment) is specified—until the minimum width is reached. If *width* is prefixed with 0, zeros are added until the minimum width is reached (not useful for left-aligned numbers).

The width specification never causes a value to be truncated. If the number of characters in the output value is greater than the specified width, or if *width* is not given, all characters of the value are printed (subject to the precision specification).

If the width specification is an asterisk (*), an **int** argument from the argument list supplies the value. The *width* argument must precede the value being formatted in the argument list. A nonexistent or small field width does not cause the truncation of a field; if the result of a conversion is wider than the field width, the field expands to contain the conversion result.

printf Precision Specification

The third optional field of the format specification is the precision specification. It specifies a nonnegative decimal integer, preceded by a period (**.**), which specifies the number of characters to be printed, the number of decimal places, or the number of significant digits (see Table R.5). Unlike the width specification, the precision specification can cause either truncation of the output value or rounding of a floating-point value. If *precision* is specified as 0 and the value to be converted is 0, the result is no characters output, as shown below:

```
printf( "%.0d", 0 );      /* No characters output */
```

If the precision specification is an asterisk (*), an **int** argument from the argument list supplies the value. The *precision* argument must precede the value being formatted in the argument list.

The type determines the interpretation of *precision* and the default when *precision* is omitted, as shown in Table R.5.

Table R.5 How Precision Values Affect Type

Type	Meaning	Default
c, **C**	The precision has no effect.	Character is printed.
d, i, u, o, x, X	The precision specifies the minimum number of digits to be printed. If the number of digits in the argument is less than *precision*, the output value is padded on the left with zeros. The value is not truncated when the number of digits exceeds *precision*.	Default precision is 1.
e, E	The precision specifies the number of digits to be printed after the decimal point. The last printed digit is rounded.	Default precision is 6; if *precision* is 0 or the period (.) appears without a number following it, no decimal point is printed.

Table R.5 How Precision Values Affect Type *(continued)*

Type	Meaning	Default
f	The precision value specifies the number of digits after the decimal point. If a decimal point appears, at least one digit appears before it. The value is rounded to the appropriate number of digits.	Default precision is 6; if *precision* is 0, or if the period (.) appears without a number following it, no decimal point is printed.
g, G	The precision specifies the maximum number of significant digits printed.	Six significant digits are printed, with any trailing zeros truncated.
s, S	The precision specifies the maximum number of characters to be printed. Characters in excess of *precision* are not printed.	Characters are printed until a null character is encountered.

If the argument corresponding to a floating-point specifier is infinite, indefinite, or NaN, **printf** gives the following output.

Value	Output
+ infinity	**1.#INF***random-digits*
– infinity	**–1.#INF***random-digits*
Indefinite (same as quiet NaN)	*digit*.**#IND***random-digits*
NAN	*digit*.**#NAN***random-digits*

printf Size and Distance Specification

The optional prefixes to *type*, **h**, **l**, and **L**, specify the "size" of *argument* (long or short, single-byte character or wide character, depending upon the type specifier that they modify). These type-specifier prefixes are used with type characters in **printf** functions or **wprintf** functions to specify interpretation of arguments, as shown in the following table. These prefixes are Microsoft extensions and are not ANSI-compatible.

Table R.6 Size Prefixes for printf and wprintf Format-Type Specifiers

To Specify	Use Prefix	With Type Specifier
long int	**l**	**d**, **i**, **o**, **x**, or **X**
long unsigned int	**l**	**u**
short int	**h**	**d**, **i**, **o**, **x**, or **X**
short unsigned int	**h**	**u**
Single-byte character with **printf** functions	**h**	**c** or **C**
Single-byte character with **wprintf** functions	**h**	**c** or **C**
Wide character with **printf** functions	**l**	**c** or **C**

Table R.6 Size Prefixes for printf and wprintf Format-Type Specifiers *(continued)*

To Specify	Use Prefix	With Type Specifier
Wide character with **wprintf** functions	**l**	**c** or **C**
Single-byte–character string with **printf** functions	**h**	**s** or **S**
Single-byte–character string with **wprintf** functions	**h**	**s** or **S**
Wide-character string with **printf** functions	**l**	**s** or **S**
Wide-character string with **wprintf** functions	**l**	**s** or **S**

Thus to print single-byte or wide-characters with **printf** functions and **wprintf** functions, use format specifiers as follows.

To Print Character As	Use Function	With Format Specifier
single byte	printf	**c**, **hc**, or **hC**
single byte	wprintf	**C**, **hc**, or **hC**
wide	wprintf	**c**, **lc**, or **lC**
wide	printf	**C**, **lc**, or **lC**

To print strings with **printf** functions and **wprintf** functions, use the prefixes **h** and **l** analogously with format type-specifiers **s** and **S**.

putc, putwc, putchar, putwchar

Writes a character to a stream (**putc**, **putwc**) or to **stdout** (**putchar**, **putwchar**).

int putc(int *c*, **FILE ****stream* **);**
wint_t putwc(wint_t *c*, **FILE ****stream* **);**
int putchar(int *c* **);**
wint_t putwchar(wint_t *c* **);**

Routine	Required Header	Optional Headers	Compatibility
putc	<stdio.h>		ANSI, Win 95, Win NT, Win32s, 68K, PMac
putwc	<stdio.h> or <wchar.h>		ANSI, Win 95, Win NT, Win32s
putchar	<stdio.h>		ANSI, Win 95, Win NT, Win32s, 68K, PMac
putwchar	<stdio.h> or <wchar.h>		ANSI, Win 95, Win NT, Win32s

For additional compatibility information, see "Compatibility" on page ix in the Introduction.

Libraries

LIBC.LIB	Single thread static library, retail version
LIBCMT.LIB	Multithread static library, retail version
MSVCRT.LIB	Import library for MSVCRTx0.DLL, retail version
MSVCRTx0.DLL	Multithread DLL library, retail version

Return Value

Each of these functions returns the character written. To indicate an error or end-of-file condition, **putc** and **putchar** return **EOF**; **putwc** and **putwchar** return **WEOF**. For all four routines, use **ferror** or **feof** to check for an error or end of file.

Parameters

c Character to be written

stream Pointer to **FILE** structure

Remarks

The **putc** routine writes the single character *c* to the output *stream* at the current position. Any integer can be passed to **putc**, but only the lower 8 bits are written. The **putchar** routine is identical to **putc(** *c*, **stdout)**. For each routine, if a read error occurs, the error indicator for the stream is set. **putc** and **putchar** are similar to **fputc** and **_fputchar**, respectively, but are implemented both as functions and as macros (see "Choosing Between Functions and Macros" on page xii). **putwc** and **putwchar** are wide-character versions of **putc** and **putchar**, respectively.

Example

```
/* PUTC.C: This program uses putc to write buffer
 * to a stream. If an error occurs, the program
 * stops before writing the entire buffer.
 */

#include <stdio.h>

void main( void )
{
   FILE *stream;
   char *p, buffer[] = "This is the line of output\n";
   int  ch;

   /* Make standard out the stream and write to it. */
   stream = stdout;
   for( p = buffer; (ch != EOF) && (*p != '\0'); p++ )
      ch = putc( *p, stream );
}
```

Output

```
This is the line of output
```

See Also **fputc**, **getc**

_putch

Writes a character to the console.

int _putch(int *c* **);**

Routine	Required Header	Optional Headers	Compatibility
_putch	<conio.h>		Win 95, Win NT, Win32s

For additional compatibility information, see "Compatibility" on page ix in the Introduction.

Libraries	
LIBC.LIB	Single thread static library, retail version
LIBCMT.LIB	Multithread static library, retail version
MSVCRT.LIB	Import library for MSVCRTx0.DLL, retail version
MSVCRTx0.DLL	Multithread DLL library, retail version

Return Value

The function returns *c* if successful, and **EOF** if not.

Parameter

c Character to be output

Remarks

The **_putch** function writes the character *c* directly (without buffering) to the console.

Example

See the example for **_getch**.

See Also **_cprintf**, **_getch**

_putenv, _wputenv

Creates new environment variables; modifies or removes existing ones.

int _putenv(const char **envstring* **);**
int _wputenv(const wchar_t **envstring* **);**

Routine	Required Header	Optional Headers	Compatibility
_putenv	<stdlib.h>		Win 95, Win NT, Win32s, 68K, PMac
_wputenv	<stdlib.h> or <wchar.h>		Win NT

For additional compatibility information, see "Compatibility" on page ix in the Introduction.

Libraries	
LIBC.LIB	Single thread static library, retail version
LIBCMT.LIB	Multithread static library, retail version
MSVCRT.LIB	Import library for MSVCRTx0.DLL, retail version
MSVCRTx0.DLL	Multithread DLL library, retail version

Return Value

_putenv and **_wputenv** return 0 if successful, or –1 in the case of an error.

Parameter

envstring Environment-string definition

Remarks

The **_putenv** function adds new environment variables or modifies the values of existing environment variables. Environment variables define the environment in which a process executes (for example, the default search path for libraries to be linked with a program). **_wputenv** is a wide-character version of **_putenv**; the *envstring* argument to **_wputenv** is a wide-character string.

The *envstring* argument must be a pointer to a string of the form *varname=string*, where *varname* is the name of the environment variable to be added or modified and *string* is the variable's value. If *varname* is already part of the environment, its value is replaced by *string*; otherwise, the new *varname* variable and its *string* value are added to the environment. You can remove a variable from the environment by specifying an empty *string*—in other words, by specifying only *varname=*.

_putenv and **_wputenv** affect only the environment that is local to the current process; you cannot use them to modify the command-level environment. That is, these functions operate only on data structures accessible to the run-time library and not on the environment "segment" created for a process by the operating system. When the current process terminates, the environment reverts to the level of the calling process (in most cases, the operating-system level). However, the modified environment can be passed to any new processes created by **_spawn**, **_exec**, or **system**, and these new processes get any new items added by **_putenv** and **_wputenv**.

With regard to environment entries, observe the following cautions:

- Do not change an environment entry directly; instead, use **_putenv** or **_wputenv** to change it. To modify the return value of **_putenv** or **_wputenv** without affecting the environment table, use **_strdup** or **strcpy** to make a copy of the string.
- Never free a pointer to an environment entry, because the environment variable will then point to freed space. A similar problem can occur if you pass **_putenv** or **_wputenv** a pointer to a local variable, then exit the function in which the variable is declared.

getenv and **_putenv** use the global variable **_environ** to access the environment table; **_wgetenv** and **_wputenv** use **_wenviron**. **_putenv** and **_wputenv** may change the value of **_environ** and **_wenviron**, thus invalidating the *envp* argument to **main** and the_*wenvp* argument to **wmain**. Therefore, it is safer to use **_environ** or **_wenviron** to access the environment information. For more information about the relation of **_putenv** and **_wputenv** to global variables, see "**_environ, _wenviron**" on page 42.

Example

See the example for **getenv**.

See Also **getenv**, **_searchenv**

---

puts, _putws

Write a string to **stdout**.

int puts(const char ****string* **);
int _putws(const wchar_t ****string* **);

Routine	Required Header	Optional Headers	Compatibility
puts	<stdio.h>		ANSI, Win 95, Win NT, 68K, PMac
_putws	<stdio.h>		ANSI, Win 95, Win NT

For additional compatibility information, see "Compatibility" on page ix in the Introduction.

Libraries	
LIBC.LIB	Single thread static library, retail version
LIBCMT.LIB	Multithread static library, retail version
MSVCRT.LIB	Import library for MSVCRTx0.DLL, retail version
MSVCRTx0.DLL	Multithread DLL library, retail version

Return Value

Each of these returns a nonnegative value if successful. If **puts** fails it returns **EOF**; if **_putws** fails it returns **WEOF**.

Parameter

string Output string

Remarks

The **puts** function writes *string* to the standard output stream **stdout**, replacing the string's terminating null character ('\0') with a newline character ('\n') in the output stream.

Example

```
/* PUTS.C: This program uses puts
 * to write a string to stdout.
 */

#include <stdio.h>

void main( void )
{
   puts( "Hello world from puts!" );
}
```

Output

```
Hello world from puts!
```

See Also **fputs**, **gets**

_putw

Writes an integer to a stream.

int _putw(int *binint*, **FILE** **stream* **);**

Routine	Required Header	Optional Headers	Compatibility
_putw	<stdio.h>		Win 95, Win NT, Win32s, 68K, PMac

For additional compatibility information, see "Compatibility" on page ix in the Introduction.

Libraries	
LIBC.LIB	Single thread static library, retail version
LIBCMT.LIB	Multithread static library, retail version
MSVCRT.LIB	Import library for MSVCRTx0.DLL, retail version
MSVCRTx0.DLL	Multithread DLL library, retail version

Return Value

_putw returns the value written. A return value of **EOF** may indicate an error. Because **EOF** is also a legitimate integer value, use **ferror** to verify an error.

Parameters

binint Binary integer to be output

stream Pointer to **FILE** structure

Remarks

The **_putw** function writes a binary value of type **int** to the current position of *stream*. **_putw** does not affect the alignment of items in the stream, nor does it assume any special alignment. **_putw** is primarily for compatibility with previous libraries. Portability problems may occur with **_putw** because the size of an **int** and the ordering of bytes within an **int** differ across systems.

Example

```
/* PUTW.C: This program uses _putw to write a
 * word to a stream, then performs an error check.
 */

#include <stdio.h>
#include <stdlib.h>

void main( void )
{
   FILE *stream;
   unsigned u;
   if( (stream = fopen( "data.out", "wb" )) == NULL )
      exit( 1 );
   for( u = 0; u << 10; u++ )
   {
      _putw( u + 0x2132, stdout );
      _putw( u + 0x2132, stream );    /* Write word to stream. */
      if( ferror( stream ) )          /* Make error check. */
      {
         printf( "_putw failed" );
         clearerr( stream );
         exit( 1 );
      }
   }
   printf( "\nWrote ten words\n" );
   fclose( stream );
}
```

Output

```
Wrote ten words
```

See Also **_getw**

qsort

Performs a quick sort.

void qsort(void **base*, **size_t** *num*, **size_t** *width*, **int (__cdecl** **compare* **)(const void** **elem1*, **const void** **elem2* **));**

Routine	Required Header	Optional Headers	Compatibility
qsort	<stdlib.h> and <search.h>		ANSI, Win 95, Win NT, Win32s, 68K, PMac

For additional compatibility information, see "Compatibility" on page ix in the Introduction.

Libraries	
LIBC.LIB	Single thread static library, retail version
LIBCMT.LIB	Multithread static library, retail version
MSVCRT.LIB	Import library for MSVCRTx0.DLL, retail version
MSVCRTx0.DLL	Multithread DLL library, retail version

Return Value

None

Parameters

base Start of target array

num Array size in elements

width Element size in bytes

compare Comparison function

elem1 Pointer to the key for the search

elem2 Pointer to the array element to be compared with the key

Remarks

The **qsort** function implements a quick-sort algorithm to sort an array of *num* elements, each of *width* bytes. The argument *base* is a pointer to the base of the array to be sorted. **qsort** overwrites this array with the sorted elements. The argument *compare* is a pointer to a user-supplied routine that compares two array elements and returns a value specifying their relationship. **qsort** calls the *compare* routine one or more times during the sort, passing pointers to two array elements on each call:

compare(**(void *)** *elem1*, **(void *)** *elem2* **);**

The routine must compare the elements, then return one of the following values:

Return Value	Description
< 0	*elem1* less than *elem2*
0	*elem1* equivalent to *elem2*
> 0	*elem1* greater than *elem2*

The array is sorted in increasing order, as defined by the comparison function. To sort an array in decreasing order, reverse the sense of "greater than" and "less than" in the comparison function.

Example

```
/* QSORT.C: This program reads the command-line
 * parameters and uses qsort to sort them. It
 * then displays the sorted arguments.
 */

#include <stdlib.h>
#include <string.h>
#include <stdio.h>

int compare( const void *arg1, const void *arg2 );

void main( int argc, char **argv )
{
   int i;
   /* Eliminate argv[0] from sort: */
   argv++;
   argc--;

   /* Sort remaining args using Quicksort algorithm: */
   qsort( (void *)argv, (size_t)argc, sizeof( char * ), compare );

   /* Output sorted list: */
   for( i = 0; i < argc; ++i )
      printf( "%s ", argv[i] );
   printf( "\n" );
}

int compare( const void *arg1, const void *arg2 )
{
   /* Compare all of both strings: */
   return _stricmp( * ( char** ) arg1, * ( char** ) arg2 );
}
```

Output

```
[C:\code]qsort every good boy deserves favor
boy deserves every favor good
```

See Also **bsearch**, **_lsearch**

_query_new_handler

Returns address of current new handler routine.

_PNH _query_new_handler(void);

Routine	Required Header	Optional Headers	Compatibility
_query_new_handler	<new.h>		Win 95, Win NT, Win32s

For additional compatibility information, see "Compatibility" on page ix in the Introduction.

Libraries	
LIBC.LIB	Single thread static library, retail version
LIBCMT.LIB	Multithread static library, retail version
MSVCRT.LIB	Import library for MSVCRTx0.DLL, retail version
MSVCRTx0.DLL	Multithread DLL library, retail version

Return Value

_query_new_handler returns the address of the current new handler routine as set by **_set_new_handler**.

Remarks

The C++ **_query_new_handler** function returns the address of the current exception-handling function set by the C++ **_set_new_handler** function. **_set_new_handler** is used to specify an exception-handling function that is to gain control if the **new** operator fails to allocate memory. For more information, see the discussions of the **operator new** and **operator delete** functions in *C++ Language Reference*.

See Also **free**

_query_new_mode

Returns an integer indicating new handler mode set by **_set_new_mode** for **malloc**.

int _query_new_mode(void);

Routine	Required Header	Optional Headers	Compatibility
_query_new_mode	<new.h>		Win 95, Win NT, Win32s

For additional compatibility information, see "Compatibility" on page ix in the Introduction.

Libraries

LIBC.LIB	Single thread static library, retail version
LIBCMT.LIB	Multithread static library, retail version
MSVCRT.LIB	Import library for MSVCRTx0.DLL, retail version
MSVCRTx0.DLL	Multithread DLL library, retail version

Return Value

_query_new_mode returns the current new handler mode, namely 0 or 1, for **malloc**. A return value of 1 indicates that, on failure to allocate memory, **malloc** calls the new handler routine; a return value of 0 indicates that it does not.

Remarks

The C++ **_query_new_mode** function returns an integer that indicates the new handler mode that is set by the C++ **_set_new_mode** function for **malloc**. The new handler mode indicates whether, on failure to allocate memory, **malloc** is to call the new handler routine as set by **_set_new_handler**. By default, **malloc** does not call the new handler routine on failure. You can use **_set_new_mode** to override this behavior so that on failure **malloc** calls the new handler routine in the same way that the **new** operator does when it fails to allocate memory. For more information, see the **operator delete** and **operator new** functions in *C++ Language Reference*.

See Also **calloc**, **free**, **malloc**, **realloc**, **_query_new_handler**, **_set_new_handler**, **_set_new_mode**

raise

Sends a signal to the executing program.

int raise(int *sig* **);**

Routine	Required Header	Optional Headers	Compatibility
raise	<signal.h>		ANSI, Win 95, Win NT, Win32s, 68K, PMac

For additional compatibility information, see "Compatibility" on page ix in the Introduction.

Libraries

LIBC.LIB	Single thread static library, retail version
LIBCMT.LIB	Multithread static library, retail version
MSVCRT.LIB	Import library for MSVCRTx0.DLL, retail version
MSVCRTx0.DLL	Multithread DLL library, retail version

Return Value

If successful, **raise** returns 0. Otherwise, it returns a nonzero value.

Parameter

sig Signal to be raised

Remarks

The **raise** function sends *sig* to the executing program. If a previous call to **signal** has installed a signal-handling function for *sig*, **raise** executes that function. If no handler function has been installed, the default action associated with the signal value *sig* is taken, as follows.

Signal	Meaning	Default
SIGABRT	Abnormal termination	Terminates the calling program with exit code 3
SIGFPE	Floating-point error	Terminates the calling program
SIGILL	Illegal instruction	Terminates the calling program
SIGINT	CTRL+C interrupt	Terminates the calling program
SIGSEGV	Illegal storage access	Terminates the calling program
SIGTERM	Termination request sent to the program	Ignores the signal

See Also **abort**, **signal**

rand

Generates a pseudorandom number.

int rand(void);

Routine	Required Header	Optional Headers	Compatibility
rand	<stdlib.h>		ANSI, Win 95, Win NT, Win32s, 68K, PMac

For additional compatibility information, see "Compatibility" on page ix in the Introduction.

Libraries	
LIBC.LIB	Single thread static library, retail version
LIBCMT.LIB	Multithread static library, retail version
MSVCRT.LIB	Import library for MSVCRTx0.DLL, retail version
MSVCRTx0.DLL	Multithread DLL library, retail version

Return Value

rand returns a pseudorandom number, as described above. There is no error return.

Remarks

The **rand** function returns a pseudorandom integer in the range 0 to **RAND_MAX**. Use the **srand** function to seed the pseudorandom-number generator before calling **rand**.

Example

```
/* RAND.C: This program seeds the random-number generator
 * with the time, then displays 10 random integers.
 */

#include <stdlib.h>
#include <stdio.h>
#include <time.h>

void main( void )
{
   int i;

   /* Seed the random-number generator with current time so that
    * the numbers will be different every time we run.
    */
   srand( (unsigned)time( NULL ) );

   /* Display 10 numbers. */
   for( i = 0;   i < 10;i++ )
      printf( "  %6d\n", rand() );
}
```

Output

```
  6929
  8026
 21987
 30734
 20587
  6699
 22034
 25051
  7988
 10104
```

See Also **srand**

_read

Reads data from a file.

int _read(int *handle*, **void** **buffer*, **unsigned int** *count* **);**

Routine	Required Header	Optional Headers	Compatibility
_read	<io.h>		Win 95, Win NT, Win32s, 68K, PMac

For additional compatibility information, see "Compatibility" on page ix in the Introduction.

Libraries	
LIBC.LIB	Single thread static library, retail version
LIBCMT.LIB	Multithread static library, retail version
MSVCRT.LIB	Import library for MSVCRTx0.DLL, retail version
MSVCRTx0.DLL	Multithread DLL library, retail version

Return Value

_read returns the number of bytes read, which may be less than *count* if there are fewer than *count* bytes left in the file or if the file was opened in text mode, in which case each carriage return–linefeed (CR-LF) pair is replaced with a single linefeed character. Only the single linefeed character is counted in the return value. The replacement does not affect the file pointer.

If the function tries to read at end of file, it returns 0. If the *handle* is invalid, or the file is not open for reading, or the file is locked, the function returns –1 and sets **errno** to **EBADF**.

Parameters

handle Handle referring to open file

buffer Storage location for data

count Maximum number of bytes

Remarks

The **_read** function reads a maximum of *count* bytes into *buffer* from the file associated with *handle*. The read operation begins at the current position of the file pointer associated with the given file. After the read operation, the file pointer points to the next unread character.

If the file was opened in text mode, the read terminates when **_read** encounters a CTRL+Z character, which is treated as an end-of-file indicator. Use **_lseek** to clear the end-of-file indicator.

Example

```
/* READ.C: This program opens a file named
 * READ.C and tries to read 60,000 bytes from
 * that file using _read. It then displays the
 * actual number of bytes read from READ.C.
 */

#include <fcntl.h>      /* Needed only for _O_RDWR definition */
#include <io.h>
#include <stdlib.h>
#include <stdio.h>

char buffer[60000];

void main( void )
{
   int fh;
   unsigned int nbytes = 60000, bytesread;

   /* Open file for input: */
   if( (fh = _open( "read.c", _O_RDONLY )) == -1 )
   {
      perror( "open failed on input file" );
      exit( 1 );
   }

   /* Read in input: */
   if( ( bytesread = _read( fh, buffer, nbytes ) ) <= 0 )
      perror( "Problem reading file" );
   else
      printf( "Read %u bytes from file\n", bytesread );

   _close( fh );
}
```

Output

```
Read 775 bytes from file
```

See Also **_creat, fread, _open, _write**

---

realloc

Reallocate memory blocks.

void *realloc(void ***memblock*, **size_t *size* **);**

Routine	Required Header	Optional Headers	Compatibility
realloc	<stdlib.h> and <malloc.h>		ANSI, Win 95, Win NT, Win32s, 68K, PMac

For additional compatibility information, see “Compatibility” on page ix in the Introduction.

Libraries

LIBC.LIB	Single thread static library, retail version
LIBCMT.LIB	Multithread static library, retail version
MSVCRT.LIB	Import library for MSVCRTx0.DLL, retail version
MSVCRTx0.DLL	Multithread DLL library, retail version

Return Value

realloc returns a **void** pointer to the reallocated (and possibly moved) memory block. The return value is **NULL** if the size is zero and the buffer argument is not **NULL**, or if there is not enough available memory to expand the block to the given size. In the first case, the original block is freed. In the second, the original block is unchanged. The return value points to a storage space that is guaranteed to be suitably aligned for storage of any type of object. To get a pointer to a type other than **void**, use a type cast on the return value.

Parameters

memblock Pointer to previously allocated memory block

size New size in bytes

Remarks

The **realloc** function changes the size of an allocated memory block. The *memblock* argument points to the beginning of the memory block. If *memblock* is **NULL**, **realloc** behaves the same way as **malloc** and allocates a new block of *size* bytes. If *memblock* is not **NULL**, it should be a pointer returned by a previous call to **calloc**, **malloc**, or **realloc**.

The *size* argument gives the new size of the block, in bytes. The contents of the block are unchanged up to the shorter of the new and old sizes, although the new block can be in a different location. Because the new block can be in a new memory location, the pointer returned by **realloc** is not guaranteed to be the pointer passed through the *memblock* argument.

realloc calls **malloc** in order to use the C++ **_set_new_mode** function to set the new handler mode. The new handler mode indicates whether, on failure, **malloc** is to call the new handler routine as set by **_set_new_handler**. By default, **malloc** does not call the new handler routine on failure to allocate memory. You can override this default behavior so that, when **realloc** fails to allocate memory, **malloc** calls the new handler routine in the same way that the **new** operator does when it fails for the same reason. To override the default, call

```
_set_new_mode(1)
```

early in your program, or link with NEWMODE.OBJ.

When the application is linked with a debug version of the C run-time libraries, **realloc** resolves to **_realloc_dbg**. For more information about how the heap is managed during the debugging process, see Chapter 4, "Debug Version of the C Run-Time Library."

Example

```
/* REALLOC.C: This program allocates a block of memory for
 * buffer and then uses _msize to display the size of that
 * block. Next, it uses realloc to expand the amount of
 * memory used by buffer and then calls _msize again to
 * display the new amount of memory allocated to buffer.
 */

#include <stdio.h>
#include <malloc.h>
#include <stdlib.h>

void main( void )
{
   long *buffer;
   size_t size;

   if( (buffer = (long *)malloc( 1000 * sizeof( long ) )) == NULL )
      exit( 1 );
   size = _msize( buffer );
   printf( "Size of block after malloc of 1000 longs: %u\n", size );
   /* Reallocate and show new size: */
   if( (buffer = realloc( buffer, size + (1000 * sizeof( long )) ))
        == NULL )
      exit( 1 );
   size = _msize( buffer );
   printf( "Size of block after realloc of 1000 more longs: %u\n",
            size );
   free( buffer );
   exit( 0 );
}
```

Output

```
Size of block after malloc of 1000 longs: 4000
Size of block after realloc of 1000 more longs: 8000
```

See Also **calloc**, **free**, **malloc**

remove, _wremove

Delete a file.

int remove(const char ***path* **);
int _wremove(const wchar_t ***path* **);

Routine	Required Header	Optional Headers	Compatibility
remove	<stdio.h> or <io.h>		ANSI, Win 95, Win NT, Win32s, 68K, PMac
_wremove	<stdio.h> or <wchar.h>		Win NT

For additional compatibility information, see "Compatibility" on page ix in the Introduction.

Libraries	
LIBC.LIB	Single thread static library, retail version
LIBCMT.LIB	Multithread static library, retail version
MSVCRT.LIB	Import library for MSVCRTx0.DLL, retail version
MSVCRTx0.DLL	Multithread DLL library, retail version

Return Value

Each of these functions returns 0 if the file is successfully deleted. Otherwise, it returns –1 and sets **errno** either to **EACCES** to indicate that the path specifies a read-only file, or to **ENOENT** to indicate that the filename or path was not found or that the path specifies a directory.

Parameter

path Path of file to be removed

Remarks

The **remove** function deletes the file specified by *path*. **_wremove** is a wide-character version of **_remove**; the *path* argument to **_wremove** is a wide-character string. **_wremove** and **_remove** behave identically otherwise.

Example

```
/* REMOVE.C: This program uses remove to delete REMOVE.OBJ. */

#include <stdio.h>

void main( void )
{
   if( remove( "remove.obj" ) == -1 )
      perror( "Could not delete 'REMOVE.OBJ'" );
   else
      printf( "Deleted 'REMOVE.OBJ'\n" );
}
```

Output

```
Deleted 'REMOVE.OBJ'
```

See Also **_unlink**

rename, _wrename

Rename a file or directory.

int rename(const char ***oldname*****, const char** ***newname*);**
int _wrename(const wchar_t ***oldname*****, const wchar_t** ***newname*);**

Routine	Required Header	Optional Headers	Compatibility
rename	<io.h> or <stdio.h>		ANSI, Win 95, Win NT, Win32s, 68K, PMac
_wrename	<stdio.h> or <wchar.h>		Win NT

For additional compatibility information, see "Compatibility" on page ix in the Introduction.

Libraries	
LIBC.LIB	Single thread static library, retail version
LIBCMT.LIB	Multithread static library, retail version
MSVCRT.LIB	Import library for MSVCRTx0.DLL, retail version
MSVCRTx0.DLL	Multithread DLL library, retail version

Return Value

Each of these functions returns 0 if it is successful. On an error, the function returns a nonzero value and sets **errno** to one of the following values:

EACCES File or directory specified by *newname* already exists or could not be created (invalid path); or *oldname* is a directory and *newname* specifies a different path.

ENOENT File or path specified by *oldname* not found.

Parameters

oldname Pointer to old name

newname Pointer to new name

Remarks

The **rename** function renames the file or directory specified by *oldname* to the name given by *newname*. The old name must be the path of an existing file or directory. The new name must not be the name of an existing file or directory. You can use **rename** to move a file from one directory or device to another by giving a different path in the *newname* argument. However, you cannot use **rename** to move a directory. Directories can be renamed, but not moved.

_wrename is a wide-character version of **_rename**; the arguments to **_wrename** are wide-character strings. **_wrename** and **_rename** behave identically otherwise.

Example

```
/* RENAMER.C: This program attempts to rename a file
 * named RENAMER.OBJ to RENAMER.JBO. For this operation
 * to succeed, a file named RENAMER.OBJ must exist and
 * a file named RENAMER.JBO must not exist.
 */

#include <stdio.h>

void main( void )
{
   int  result;
   char old[] = "RENAMER.OBJ", new[] = "RENAMER.JBO";

   /* Attempt to rename file: */
   result = rename( old, new );
   if( result != 0 )
      printf( "Could not rename '%s'\n", old );
   else
      printf( "File '%s' renamed to '%s'\n", old, new );
}
```

Output

```
File 'RENAMER.OBJ' renamed to 'RENAMER.JBO'
```

rewind

Repositions the file pointer to the beginning of a file.

void rewind(FILE ***stream* **);

Routine	Required Header	Optional Headers	Compatibility
rewind	<stdio.h>		ANSI, Win 95, Win NT, Win32s, 68K, PMac

For additional compatibility information, see "Compatibility" on page ix in the Introduction.

Libraries

LIBC.LIB	Single thread static library, retail version
LIBCMT.LIB	Multithread static library, retail version
MSVCRT.LIB	Import library for MSVCRTx0.DLL, retail version
MSVCRTx0.DLL	Multithread DLL library, retail version

Return Value

None

Parameter

stream Pointer to **FILE** structure

Remarks

The **rewind** function repositions the file pointer associated with *stream* to the beginning of the file. A call to **rewind** is similar to

(void) fseek(*stream*, **0L, SEEK_SET);**

However, unlike **fseek**, **rewind** clears the error indicators for the stream as well as the end-of-file indicator. Also, unlike **fseek**, **rewind** does not return a value to indicate whether the pointer was successfully moved.

To clear the keyboard buffer, use **rewind** with the stream **stdin**, which is associated with the keyboard by default.

Example

```
/* REWIND.C: This program first opens a file named
 * REWIND.OUT for input and output and writes two
 * integers to the file. Next, it uses rewind to
 * reposition the file pointer to the beginning of
 * the file and reads the data back in.
 */

#include <stdio.h>

void main( void )
{
   FILE *stream;
   int data1, data2;
   data1 = 1;
   data2 = -37;

   if( (stream = fopen( "rewind.out", "w+" )) != NULL )
```

```
    {
        fprintf( stream, "%d %d", data1, data2 );
        printf( "The values written are: %d and %d\n", data1, data2 );
        rewind( stream );
        fscanf( stream, "%d %d", &data1, &data2 );
        printf( "The values read are: %d and %d\n", data1, data2 );
        fclose( stream );
    }
}
```

Output

```
The values written are: 1 and -37
The values read are: 1 and -37
```

_rmdir, _wrmdir

Delete a directory.

int _rmdir(const char ***dirname* **);
int _rmdir(const wchar_t ***dirname* **);

Routine	Required Header	Optional Headers	Compatibility
_rmdir	<direct.h>		Win 95, Win NT, Win32s, 68K, PMac
_wrmdir	<direct.h> or <wchar.h>		Win NT

For additional compatibility information, see "Compatibility" on page ix in the Introduction.

Libraries	
LIBC.LIB	Single thread static library, retail version
LIBCMT.LIB	Multithread static library, retail version
MSVCRT.LIB	Import library for MSVCRTx0.DLL, retail version
MSVCRTx0.DLL	Multithread DLL library, retail version

Return Value

Each of these functions returns 0 if the directory is successfully deleted. A return value of –1 indicates an error, and **errno** is set to one of the following values:

ENOTEMPTY Given path is not a directory; directory is not empty; or directory is either current working directory or root directory.

ENOENT Path is invalid.

Parameter

dirname Path of directory to be removed

Remarks

The **_rmdir** function deletes the directory specified by *dirname*. The directory must be empty, and it must not be the current working directory or the root directory.

_wrmdir is a wide-character version of **_rmdir**; the *dirname* argument to **_wrmdir** is a wide-character string. **_wrmdir** and **_rmdir** behave identically otherwise.

Example

See the example for **_mkdir**.

See Also **_chdir**, **_mkdir**

_rmtmp

Removes temporary files.

int _rmtmp(void);

Routine	Required Header	Optional Headers	Compatibility
_rmtmp	<stdio.h>		Win 95, Win NT, Win32s, 68K, PMac

For additional compatibility information, see "Compatibility" on page ix in the Introduction.

Libraries	
LIBC.LIB	Single thread static library, retail version
LIBCMT.LIB	Multithread static library, retail version
MSVCRT.LIB	Import library for MSVCRTx0.DLL, retail version
MSVCRTx0.DLL	Multithread DLL library, retail version

Return Value

_rmtmp returns the number of temporary files closed and deleted.

Remarks

The **_rmtmp** function cleans up all temporary files in the current directory. The function removes only those files created by **tmpfile**; use it only in the same directory in which the temporary files were created.

Example

See the example for **tmpfile**.

See Also **_flushall**, **tmpfile**, **tmpnam**

_rotl, _rotr

Rotate bits to the left (**_rotl**) or right (**_rotr**).

unsigned int _rotl(unsigned int *value*, **int** *shift* **);**
unsigned int _rotr(unsigned int *value*, **int** *shift* **);**

Routine	Required Header	Optional Headers	Compatibility
_rotl	<stdlib.h>		Win 95, Win NT, Win32s, 68K, PMac
_rotr	<stdlib.h>		Win 95, Win NT, Win32s, 68K, PMac

For additional compatibility information, see "Compatibility" on page ix in the Introduction.

Libraries	
LIBC.LIB	Single thread static library, retail version
LIBCMT.LIB	Multithread static library, retail version
MSVCRT.LIB	Import library for MSVCRTx0.DLL, retail version
MSVCRTx0.DLL	Multithread DLL library, retail version

Return Value

Both functions return the rotated value. There is no error return.

Parameters

value Value to be rotated

shift Number of bits to shift

Remarks

The **_rotl** and **_rotr** functions rotate the unsigned *value* by *shift* bits. **_rotl** rotates the value left. **_rotr** rotates the value right. Both functions "wrap" bits rotated off one end of *value* to the other end.

Example

```
/* ROT.C: This program uses _rotr and _rotl with
 * different shift values to rotate an integer.
 */

#include <stdlib.h>
#include <stdio.h>

void main( void )
```

```
{
   unsigned val = 0x0fd93;
   printf( "0x%4.4x rotated left three times is 0x%4.4x\n",
           val, _rotl( val, 3 ) );
   printf( "0x%4.4x rotated right four times is 0x%4.4x\n",
           val, _rotr( val, 4 ) );
}
```

Output

```
0xfd93 rotated left three times is 0x7ec98
0xfd93 rotated right four times is 0x30000fd9
```

See Also **_lrotl**

_scalb

Scales argument by a power of 2.

double _scalb(double *x*, **long** *exp* **);**

Routine	Required Header	Optional Headers	Compatibility
_scalb	<float.h>		Win 95, Win NT, Win32s, 68K, PMac

For additional compatibility information, see "Compatibility" on page ix in the Introduction.

Libraries	
LIBC.LIB	Single thread static library, retail version
LIBCMT.LIB	Multithread static library, retail version
MSVCRT.LIB	Import library for MSVCRTx0.DLL, retail version
MSVCRTx0.DLL	Multithread DLL library, retail version

Return Value

_scalb returns an exponential value if successful. On overflow (depending on the sign of *x*), **_scalb** returns **+/–HUGE_VAL**; the **errno** variable is set to **ERANGE**.

Parameters

x Double-precision floating-point value

exp Long integer exponent

Remarks

The **_scalb** function calculates the value of $x * 2^{exp}$.

See Also **ldexp**

scanf, wscanf

Read formatted data from the standard input stream.

int scanf(const char ***format* [,*argument*]... **);
int wscanf(const wchar_t ***format* [,*argument*]... **);

Routine	Required Header	Optional Headers	Compatibility
scanf	<stdio.h>		ANSI, Win 95, Win NT, Win32s, 68K, PMac
wscanf	<stdio.h> or <wchar.h>		ANSI, Win 95, Win NT, Win32s

For additional compatibility information, see "Compatibility" on page ix in the Introduction.

Libraries	
LIBC.LIB	Single thread static library, retail version
LIBCMT.LIB	Multithread static library, retail version
MSVCRT.LIB	Import library for MSVCRTx0.DLL, retail version
MSVCRTx0.DLL	Multithread DLL library, retail version

Return Value

Both **scanf** and **wscanf** return the number of fields successfully converted and assigned; the return value does not include fields that were read but not assigned. A return value of 0 indicates that no fields were assigned. The return value is **EOF** for an error or if the end-of-file character or the end-of-string character is encountered in the first attempt to read a character.

Parameters

format Format control string

argument Optional arguments

Remarks

The **scanf** function reads data from the standard input stream **stdin** and writes the data into the location given by *argument*. Each *argument* must be a pointer to a variable of a type that corresponds to a type specifier in *format*. If copying takes place between strings that overlap, the behavior is undefined.

wscanf is a wide-character version of **scanf**; the *format* argument to **wscanf** is a wide-character string. **wscanf** and **scanf** behave identically otherwise.

Example

```
/* SCANF.C: This program uses the scanf and wscanf functions
 * to read formatted input.
 */

#include <stdio.h>

void main( void )
{
   int   i, result;
   float fp;
   char  c, s[81];
   wchar_t wc, ws[81];

   printf( "\n\nEnter an int, a float, two chars and two strings\n");

   result = scanf( "%d %f %c %C %s %S", &i, &fp, &c, &wc, s, ws );
   printf( "\nThe number of fields input is %d\n", result );
   printf( "The contents are: %d %f %c %C %s %S\n", i, fp, c, wc, s, ws);

   wprintf( L"\n\nEnter an int, a float, two chars and two strings\n");

   result = wscanf( L"%d %f %hc %lc %S %ls", &i, &fp, &c, &wc, s, ws );
   wprintf( L"\nThe number of fields input is %d\n", result );
   wprintf( L"The contents are: %d %f %C %c %hs %s\n", i, fp, c, wc, s, ws);
}
```

Output

```
Enter an int, a float, two chars and two strings
71
98.6
h
z
Byte characters

The number of fields input is 6
The contents are: 71 98.599998 h z Byte characters

Enter an int, a float, two chars and two strings
36
92.3
y
n
Wide characters

The number of fields input is 6
The contents are: 456 92.300003 y n Wide characters
```

See Also **fscanf, printf, sprintf, sscanf**

scanf Format Specification Fields

A format specification has the following form:

%[*] [*width*] [{**h** | **l** | **L**}]*type*

The *format* argument specifies the interpretation of the input and can contain one or more of the following:

White-space characters: blank (`' '`); tab (`'\t'`); or newline (`'\n'`). A white-space character causes **scanf** to read, but not store, all consecutive white-space characters in the input up to the next non–white-space character. One white-space character in the format matches any number (including 0) and combination of white-space characters in the input.

- Non–white-space characters, except for the percent sign (%). A non–white-space character causes **scanf** to read, but not store, a matching non–white-space character. If the next character in **stdin** does not match, **scanf** terminates.
- Format specifications, introduced by the percent sign (%). A format specification causes **scanf** to read and convert characters in the input into values of a specified type. The value is assigned to an argument in the argument list.

The format is read from left to right. Characters outside format specifications are expected to match the sequence of characters in **stdin**; the matching characters in **stdin** are scanned but not stored. If a character in **stdin** conflicts with the format specification, **scanf** terminates, and the character is left in **stdin** as if it had not been read.

When the first format specification is encountered, the value of the first input field is converted according to this specification and stored in the location that is specified by the first *argument*. The second format specification causes the second input field to be converted and stored in the second *argument*, and so on through the end of the format string.

An input field is defined as all characters up to the first white-space character (space, tab, or newline), or up to the first character that cannot be converted according to the format specification, or until the field width (if specified) is reached. If there are too many arguments for the given specifications, the extra arguments are evaluated but ignored. The results are unpredictable if there are not enough arguments for the format specification.

Each field of the format specification is a single character or a number signifying a particular format option. The *type* character, which appears after the last optional format field, determines whether the input field is interpreted as a character, a string, or a number.

The simplest format specification contains only the percent sign and a *type* character (for example, `%s`). If a percent sign (%) is followed by a character that has no meaning as a format-control character, that character and the following characters (up to the next percent sign) are treated as an ordinary sequence of characters, that is, a sequence of characters that must match the input. For example, to specify that a percent-sign character is to be input, use `%%`.

An asterisk (*) following the percent sign suppresses assignment of the next input field, which is interpreted as a field of the specified type. The field is scanned but not stored.

scanf Width Specification

width is a positive decimal integer controlling the maximum number of characters to be read from **stdin**. No more than *width* characters are converted and stored at the corresponding *argument*. Fewer than *width* characters may be read if a white-space character (space, tab, or newline) or a character that cannot be converted according to the given format occurs before *width* is reached.

The optional prefixes **h**, **l**, and **L** indicate the "size" of the *argument* (long or short, single-byte character or wide character, depending upon the type character that they modify). These format-specification characters are used with type characters in **scanf** or **wscanf** functions to specify interpretation of arguments as shown in the Table R.7. The type prefixes **h**, **l**, and **L** are Microsoft extensions and are not ANSI-compatible. The type characters and their meanings are described in Table R.8.

Table R.7 Size Prefixes for scanf and wscanf Format-Type Specifiers

To Specify	Use Prefix	With Type Specifier
double	**l**	**e**, **E**, **f**, **g**, or **G**
long int	**l**	**d**, **i**, **o**, **x**, or **X**
long unsigned int	**l**	**u**
short int	**h**	**d**, **i**, **o**, **x**, or **X**
short unsigned int	**h**	**u**
Single-byte character with **scanf**	**h**	**c or C**
Single-byte character with **wscanf**	**h**	**c** or **C**
Wide character with **scanf**	**l**	**c** or **C**
Wide character with **wscanf**	**l**	**c**, or **C**
Single-byte–character string with **scanf**	**h**	**s** or **S**
Single-byte–character string with **wscanf**	**h**	**s** or **S**
Wide-character string with **scanf**	**l**	**s** or **S**
Wide-character string with **wscanf**	**l**	**s** or **S**

Following are examples of the use of **h** and **l** with **scanf**functions and **wscanf** functions:

```
scanf( "%ls", &x );     // Read a wide-character string
wscanf( "%lC", &x );     // Read a single-byte character
```

To read strings not delimited by space characters, a set of characters in brackets (**[ ]**) can be substituted for the **s** (string) type character. The corresponding input field is read up to the first character that does not appear in the bracketed character set. If the first character in the set is a caret (**^**), the effect is reversed: The input field is read up to the first character that does appear in the rest of the character set.

Note that **%[a-z]** and **%[z-a]** are interpreted as equivalent to **%[abcde...z]**. This is a common **scanf** function extension, but note that the ANSI standard does not require it.

To store a string without storing a terminating null character ('\0'), use the specification **%*n*c** where *n* is a decimal integer. In this case, the **c** type character indicates that the argument is a pointer to a character array. The next *n* characters are read from the input stream into the specified location, and no null character ('\0') is appended. If *n* is not specified, its default value is 1.

The **scanf** function scans each input field, character by character. It may stop reading a particular input field before it reaches a space character for a variety of reasons:

- The specified width has been reached.
- The next character cannot be converted as specified.
- The next character conflicts with a character in the control string that it is supposed to match.
- The next character fails to appear in a given character set.

For whatever reason, when the **scanf** function stops reading an input field, the next input field is considered to begin at the first unread character. The conflicting character, if there is one, is considered unread and is the first character of the next input field or the first character in subsequent read operations on **stdin**.

scanf Type Field Characters

The *type* character is the only required format field; it appears after any optional format fields. The *type* character determines whether the associated argument is interpreted as a character, string, or number.

Table R.8 Type Characters for scanf functions

Character	Type of Input Expected	Type of Argument
c	When used with **scanf** functions, specifies single-byte character; when used with **wscanf** functions, specifies wide character. White-space characters that are ordinarily skipped are read when **c** is specified. To read next non–white-space single-byte character, use **%1s**; to read next non–white-space wide character, use **%1ws**.	Pointer to **char** when used with **scanf** functions, pointer to **wchar_t** when used with **wscanf** functions.
C	When used with **scanf** functions, specifies wide character; when used with **wscanf** functions, specifies single-byte character. White-space characters that are ordinarily skipped are read when **C** is specified. To read next non–white-space single-byte character, use **%1s**; to read next non–white-space wide character, use **%1ws**.	Pointer to **wchar_t** when used with **scanf** functions, pointer to **char** when used with **wscanf** functions.
d	Decimal integer.	Pointer to **int**.
i	Decimal, hexadecimal, or octal integer.	Pointer to **int**.
o	Octal integer.	Pointer to **int**.
u	Unsigned decimal integer.	Pointer to **unsigned int**.
x	Hexadecimal integer.	Pointer to **int**.
e, E, f, g, G	Floating-point value consisting of optional sign (+ or –), series of one or more decimal digits containing decimal point, and optional exponent ("e" or "E") followed by an optionally signed integer value.	Pointer to **float**.
n	No input read from stream or buffer.	Pointer to **int**, into which is stored number of characters successfully read from stream or buffer up to that point in current call to **scanf** functions or **wscanf** functions.

Table R.8 Type Characters for scanf functions *(continued)*

Character	Type of Input Expected	Type of Argument
s	String, up to first white-space character (space, tab or newline). To read strings not delimited by space characters, use set of square brackets ([ ]), as discussed following Table R.7.	When used with **scanf** functions, signifies single-byte character array; when used with **wscanf** functions, signifies wide-character array. In either case, character array must be large enough for input field plus terminating null character, which is automatically appended.
S	String, up to first white-space character (space, tab or newline). To read strings not delimited by space characters, use set of square brackets ([ ]), as discussed preceding this table.	When used with **scanf** functions, signifies wide-character array; when used with **wscanf** functions, signifies single-byte–character array. In either case, character array must be large enough for input field plus terminating null character, which is automatically appended.

The types **c**, **C**, **s**, and **S** are Microsoft extensions and are not ANSI-compatible.

Thus, to read single-byte or wide characters with **scanf** functions and **wscanf** functions, use format specifiers as follows.

To Read Character As	Use This Function	With These Format Specifiers
single byte	**scanf** functions	**c**, **hc**, or **hC**
single byte	**wscanf** functions	**C**, **hc**, or **hC**
wide	**wscanf** functions	**c**, **lc**, or **lC**
wide	**scanf** functions	**C**, **lc**, or **lC**

To scan strings with **scanf** functions, and **wscanf** functions, use the prefixes **h** and **l** analogously with format type-specifiers **s** and **S**.

_searchenv, _wsearchenv

Searches for a file using environment paths.

void _searchenv(const char ***filename*****, const char** ***varname*****, char** ***pathname*);**
void _wsearchenv(const wchar_t ***filename*****, const wchar_t** ***varname*****, wchar_t** ***pathname*);**

Routine	Required Header	Optional Headers	Compatibility
_searchenv	<stdlib.h>		Win 95, Win NT, Win32s, 68K, PMac
_wsearchenv	<stdlib.h> or <wchar.h>		Win NT

For additional compatibility information, see "Compatibility" on page ix in the Introduction.

Libraries	
LIBC.LIB	Single thread static library, retail version
LIBCMT.LIB	Multithread static library, retail version
MSVCRT.LIB	Import library for MSVCRTx0.DLL, retail version
MSVCRTx0.DLL	Multithread DLL library, retail version

Return Value

None

Parameters

filename Name of file to search for

varname Environment to search

pathname Buffer to store complete path

Remarks

The **_searchenv** routine searches for the target file in the specified domain. The *varname* variable can be any environment or user-defined variable that specifies a list of directory paths, such as **PATH**, **LIB**, and **INCLUDE**. **_searchenv** is case sensitive, so *varname* should match the case of the environment variable.

The routine searches first for the file in the current working directory. If it does not find the file, it looks next through the directories specified by the environment variable. If the target file is in one of those directories, the newly created path is copied into *pathname*. If the *filename* file is not found, *pathname* contains an empty, null-terminated string.

The *pathname* buffer must be large enough to accomodate the full length of the constructed path name. Otherwise, **_searchenv** will overwite the *pathname* buffer resulting in unexpected behavior. This condition can be avoided by ensuring that the length of the constructed path name does not exceed the size of the *pathname* buffer, by calculating the maximum sum of the *filename* and *varname* lengths before calling **_searchenv**.

_wsearchenv is a wide-character version of **_searchenv**; the arguments to **_wsearchenv** are wide-character strings. **_wsearchenv** and **_searchenv** behave identically otherwise.

Example

```
/* SEARCHEN.C: This program searches for a file in
 * a directory specified by an environment variable.
 */

#include <stdlib.h>
#include <stdio.h>

void main( void )
{
   char pathbuffer[_MAX_PATH];
   char searchfile[] = "CL.EXE";
   char envvar[] = "PATH";

   /* Search for file in PATH environment variable: */
   _searchenv( searchfile, envvar, pathbuffer );
   if( *pathbuffer != '\0' )
      printf( "Path for %s: %s\n", searchfile, pathbuffer );
   else
      printf( "%s not found\n", searchfile );
}
```

Output

```
Path for CL.EXE: C:\msvcnt\c32\bin\CL.EXE
```

See Also **getenv**, **_putenv**

setbuf

Controls stream buffering.

void setbuf(FILE ****stream*, char ****buffer* **);**

Routine	Required Header	Optional Headers	Compatibility
setbuf	<stdio.h>		ANSI, Win 95, Win NT, Win32s, 68K, PMac

For additional compatibility information, see "Compatibility" on page ix in the Introduction.

Libraries

LIBC.LIB	Single thread static library, retail version
LIBCMT.LIB	Multithread static library, retail version
MSVCRT.LIB	Import library for MSVCRTx0.DLL, retail version
MSVCRTx0.DLL	Multithread DLL library, retail version

Return Value

None

Parameters

stream Pointer to **FILE** structure

buffer User-allocated buffer

Remarks

The **setbuf** function controls buffering for *stream*. The *stream* argument must refer to an open file that has not been read or written. If the *buffer* argument is **NULL**, the stream is unbuffered. If not, the buffer must point to a character array of length **BUFSIZ**, where **BUFSIZ** is the buffer size as defined in STDIO.H. The user-specified buffer, instead of the default system-allocated buffer for the given stream, is used for I/O buffering. The **stderr** stream is unbuffered by default, but you can use **setbuf** to assign buffers to **stderr**.

setbuf has been replaced by **setvbuf**, which is the preferred routine for new code. **setbuf** is retained for compatibility with existing code.

Example

```
/* SETBUF.C: This program first opens files named DATA1 and
 * DATA2. Then it uses setbuf to give DATA1 a user-assigned
 * buffer and to change DATA2 so that it has no buffer.
 */

#include <stdio.h>

void main( void )
{
   char buf[BUFSIZ];
   FILE *stream1, *stream2;

   if( ((stream1 = fopen( "data1", "a" )) != NULL) &&
       ((stream2 = fopen( "data2", "w" )) != NULL) )
   {
      /* "stream1" uses user-assigned buffer: */
      setbuf( stream1, buf );
      printf( "stream1 set to user-defined buffer at: %Fp\n", buf );
```

```
        /* "stream2" is unbuffered            */
        setbuf( stream2, NULL );
        printf( "stream2 buffering disabled\n" );
        _fcloseall();
    }
}
```

Output

```
stream1 set to user-defined buffer at: 0013FDA0
stream2 buffering disabled
```

See Also **fclose**, **fflush**, **fopen**, **setvbuf**

setjmp

Saves the current state of the program.

int setjmp(jmp_buf *env* **);**

Routine	Required Header	Optional Headers	Compatibility
setjmp	<setjmp.h>		ANSI, Win 95, Win NT, Win32s, 68K, PMac

For additional compatibility information, see "Compatibility" on page ix in the Introduction.

Libraries	
LIBC.LIB	Single thread static library, retail version
LIBCMT.LIB	Multithread static library, retail version
MSVCRT.LIB	Import library for MSVCRTx0.DLL, retail version
MSVCRTx0.DLL	Multithread DLL library, retail version

Return Value

setjmp returns 0 after saving the stack environment. If **setjmp** returns as a result of a **longjmp** call, it returns the *value* argument of **longjmp**, or if the *value* argument of **longjmp** is 0, **setjmp** returns 1. There is no error return.

Parameter

env Variable in which environment is stored

Remarks

The **setjmp** function saves a stack environment, which you can subsequently restore using **longjmp**. When used together, **setjmp** and **longjmp** provide a way to execute a "non-local goto." They are typically used to pass execution control to error-handling or recovery code in a previously called routine without using the normal calling or return conventions.

A call to **setjmp** saves the current stack environment in *env*. A subsequent call to **longjmp** restores the saved environment and returns control to the point just after the corresponding **setjmp** call. All variables (except register variables) accessible to the routine receiving control contain the values they had when **longjmp** was called.

setjmp and **longjmp** do not support C++ object semantics. In C++ programs, use the C++ exception-handling mechanism.

Example

See the example for **_fpreset**.

See Also **longjmp**

---

setlocale, _wsetlocale

Define the locale.

char *setlocale(int *category*, **const char** **locale* **);**
wchar_t *_wsetlocale(int *category*, **const wchar_t** **locale* **);**

Routine	Required Header	Optional Headers	Compatibility
setlocale	<locale.h>		ANSI, Win 95, Win NT, Win32s, 68K, PMac
_wsetlocale	<locale.h> or <wchar.h>		Win 95, Win NT, Win32s

For additional compatibility information, see "Compatibility" on page ix in the Introduction.

Libraries	
LIBC.LIB	Single thread static library, retail version
LIBCMT.LIB	Multithread static library, retail version
MSVCRT.LIB	Import library for MSVCRTx0.DLL, retail version
MSVCRTx0.DLL	Multithread DLL library, retail version

Return Value

If a valid locale and category are given, the function returns a pointer to the string associated with the specified locale and category. If the locale or category is invalid, the function returns a null pointer and the current locale settings of the program are not changed.

For example, the call

```
setlocale( LC_ALL, "English" );
```

sets all categories, returning only the string `English_USA.1252`. If all categories are not explicitly set by a call to **setlocale**, the function returns a string indicating the current setting of each of the categories, separated by semicolons. If the *locale* argument is a null pointer, **setlocale** returns a pointer to the string associated with the *category* of the program's locale; the program's current locale setting is not changed.

The null pointer is a special directive that tells **setlocale** to query rather than set the international environment. For example, the sequence of calls

```
// Set all categories and return "English_USA.1252"
setlocale( LC_ALL, "English" );
// Set only the LC_MONETARY category and return "French_France.1252"
setlocale( LC_MONETARY, "French" );
setlocale( LC_ALL, NULL );
```

returns

```
LC_COLLATE=English_USA.1252;
LC_CTYPE=English_USA.1252;
LC_MONETARY=French_France.1252;
LC_NUMERIC=English_USA.1252;
LC_TIME=English_USA.1252
```

which is the string associated with the **LC_ALL** category.

You can use the string pointer returned by **setlocale** in subsequent calls to restore that part of the program's locale information, assuming that your program does not alter the pointer or the string. Later calls to **setlocale** overwrite the string; you can use **_strdup** to save a specific locale string.

Parameters

category Category affected by locale

locale Locale name

Remarks

Use the **setlocale** function to set, change, or query some or all of the current program locale information specified by *locale* and *category*. "Locale" refers to the locality (country and language) for which you can customize certain aspects of your program. Some locale-dependent categories include the formatting of dates and the display format for monetary values.

_wsetlocale is a wide-character version of **setlocale**; the *locale* argument and return value of **_wsetlocale** are wide-character strings. **_wsetlocale** and **setlocale** behave identically otherwise.

The *category* argument specifies the parts of a program's locale information that are affected. The macros used for *category* and the parts of the program they affect are as follows:

LC_ALL All categories, as listed below

LC_COLLATE The **strcoll, _stricoll, wcscoll, _wcsicoll,** and **strxfrm** functions

LC_CTYPE The character-handling functions (except **isdigit**, **isxdigit**, **mbstowcs**, and **mbtowc**, which are unaffected)

LC_MONETARY Monetary-formatting information returned by the **localeconv** function

LC_NUMERIC Decimal-point character for the formatted output routines (such as **printf**), for the data-conversion routines, and for the nonmonetary-formatting information returned by **localeconv**

LC_TIME The **strftime** and **wcsftime** functions

The *locale* argument is a pointer to a string that specifies the name of the locale. If *locale* points to an empty string, the locale is the implementation-defined native environment. A value of "C" specifies the minimal ANSI conforming environment for C translation. The "C" locale assumes that all **char** data types are 1 byte and that their value is always less than 256. The "C" locale is the only locale supported in Microsoft Visual C++ version 1.0 and earlier versions of Microsoft C/C++. Microsoft Visual C++ version 4.0 supports all the locales listed in Appendix A, "Language and Country Strings." At program startup, the equivalent of the following statement is executed:

```
setlocale( LC_ALL, "C" );
```

The *locale* argument takes the following form:

```
locale :: "lang[_country[.code_page]]"
            | ".code_page"
            | ""
            | NULL
```

The set of available languages, countries, and code pages includes all those supported by the Win32 NLS API. The set of language and country codes supported by **setlocale** is listed in Appendix A, "Language and Country Strings."

If *locale* is a null pointer, **setlocale** queries, rather than sets, the international environment, and returns a pointer to the string associated with the specified *category*. The program's current locale setting is not changed. For example,

```
setlocale( LC_ALL, NULL );
```

returns the string associated with *category*.

The following examples pertain to the **LC_ALL** category. Either of the strings ".OCP" and ".ACP" can be used in place of a code page number to specify use of the system default OEM code page and system-default ANSI code page, respectively.

`setlocale( LC_ALL, "" );` Sets the locale to the default, which is the system-default ANSI code page obtained from the operating system.

`setlocale( LC_ALL, ".OCP" );` Explicitly sets the locale to the current OEM code page obtained from the operating system.

`setlocale( LC_ALL, ".ACP" );` Sets the locale to the ANSI code page obtained from the operating system.

`setlocale( LC_ALL, "[lang_ctry]" );` Sets the locale to the language and country indicated, using the default code page obtained from the host operating system.

`setlocale( LC_ALL, "[lang_ctry.cp]" );` Sets the locale to the language, country, and code page indicated in the [*lang_ctry.cp*] string. You can use various combinations of language, country, and code page. For example:

```
setlocale( LC_ALL, "French_Canada.1252" );
// Set code page to French Canada ANSI default
setlocale( LC_ALL, "French_Canada.ACP" );
// Set code page to French Canada OEM default
setlocale( LC_ALL, "French_Canada.OCP" );
```

`setlocale( LC_ALL, "[lang]" );` Sets the locale to the country indicated, using the default country for the language specified, and the system-default ANSI code page for that country as obtained from the host operating system. For example, the following two calls to **setlocale** are functionally equivalent:

```
setlocale( LC_ALL, "English" );
setlocale( LC_ALL, "English_United States.1252" );
```

`setlocale( LC_ALL, "[.code_page]" );` Sets the code page to the value indicated, using the default country and language (as defined by the host operating system) for the specified code page.

The category must be either **LC_ALL** or **LC_CTYPE** to effect a change of code page. For example, if the default country and language of the host operating system are "United States" and "English," the following two calls to **setlocale** are functionally equivalent:

```
setlocale( LC_ALL, ".1252" );
setlocale( LC_ALL, "English_United States.1252");
```

For more information see the **setlocale** pragma in *Preprocessor Reference*.

Example

```
/* LOCALE.C: Sets the current locale to "Germany" using the
 * setlocale function and demonstrates its effect on the strftime
 * function.
 */

#include <stdio.h>
#include <locale.h>
#include <time.h>

void main(void)
{
        time_t ltime;
        struct tm *thetime;
        unsigned char str[100];
```

```
        setlocale(LC_ALL, "German");
        time (&ltime);
        thetime = gmtime(&ltime);

        /* %#x is the long date representation, appropriate to
         * the current locale
         */
        if (!strftime((char *)str, 100, "%#x",
                      (const struct tm *)thetime))
                printf("strftime failed!\n");
        else
                printf("In German locale, strftime returns '%s'\n",
                       str);

        /* Set the locale back to the default environment */
        setlocale(LC_ALL, "C");
        time (&ltime);
        thetime = gmtime(&ltime);

        if (!strftime((char *)str, 100, "%#x",
                      (const struct tm *)thetime))
                printf("strftime failed!\n");
        else
                printf("In 'C' locale, strftime returns '%s'\n",
                       str);
}
```

Output

```
In German locale, strftime returns 'Donnerstag, 22. April 1993'
In 'C' locale, strftime returns 'Thursday, April 22, 1993'
```

See Also **localeconv**, **mblen**, **_mbstrlen**, **mbstowcs**, **mbtowc**, **strcoll** Functions, **strftime**, **strxfrm**, **wcstombs**, **wctomb**

_setmbcp

Sets a new multibyte code page.

int _setmbcp(int *codepage* **);**

Routine	Required Header	Optional Headers	Compatibility
_setmbcp	<mbctype.h>		Win 95, Win NT, Win32s, 68K, PMac

For additional compatibility information, see "Compatibility" on page ix in the Introduction.

Libraries

LIBC.LIB	Single thread static library, retail version
LIBCMT.LIB	Multithread static library, retail version
MSVCRT.LIB	Import library for MSVCRTx0.DLL, retail version
MSVCRTx0.DLL	Multithread DLL library, retail version

Return Value

_setmbcp returns 0 if the code page is set successfully. If an invalid code page value is supplied for *codepage*, the function returns –1 and the code page setting is unchanged.

Parameter

codepage New code page setting for locale-independent multibyte routines

Remarks

The **_setmbcp** function specifies a new multibyte code page. By default, the run-time system automatically sets the multibyte code page to the system-default ANSI code page. The multibyte code page setting affects all multibyte routines that are not locale-dependent. However, it is possible to instruct **_setmbcp** to use the code page defined for the current locale (see the following list of manifest constants and associated behavior results). For a list of the multibyte routines that are dependent on the locale code page rather than the multibyte code page, see "Interpretation of Multibyte-Character Sequences" on page 23.

The multibyte code page also affects multibyte-character processing by the following run-time library routines:

_exec functions	**_mktemp**	**_stat**
_fullpath	**_spawn functions**	**_tempnam**
_makepath	**_splitpath**	**tmpnam**

In addition, all run-time library routines that receive multibyte-character *argv* or *envp* program arguments as parameters (such as the **_exec** and **_spawn** families) process these strings according to the multibyte code page. Hence these routines are also affected by a call to **_setmbcp** that changes the multibyte code page.

The *codepage* argument can be set to any of the following values:

- **_MB_CP_ANSI** Use ANSI code page obtained from operating system at program startup
- **_MB_CP_LOCALE** Use the current locale's code page obtained from a previous call to **setlocale**
- **_MB_CP_OEM** Use OEM code page obtained from operating system at program startup
- **_MB_CP_SBCS** Use single-byte code page. When the code page is set to **_MB_CP_SBCS**, a routine such as **_ismbblead** always returns false.

- Any other valid code page value, regardless of whether the value is an ANSI, OEM, or other operating-sytem–supported code page.

See Also **_getmbcp**, **setlocale**

_setmode

Sets the file translation mode.

int _setmode (**int** *handle*, **int** *mode* **);**

Routine	Required Header	Optional Headers	Compatibility
_setmode	<io.h>	<fcntl.h>	Win 95, Win NT, Win32s, 68K, PMac

For additional compatibility information, see "Compatibility" on page ix in the Introduction.

Libraries	
LIBC.LIB	Single thread static library, retail version
LIBCMT.LIB	Multithread static library, retail version
MSVCRT.LIB	Import library for MSVCRTx0.DLL, retail version
MSVCRTx0.DLL	Multithread DLL library, retail version

Return Value

If successful, **_setmode** returns the previous translation mode. A return value of –1 indicates an error, in which case **errno** is set to either **EBADF**, indicating an invalid file handle, or **EINVAL**, indicating an invalid *mode* argument (neither **_O_TEXT** nor **_O_BINARY**).

Parameters

handle File handle

mode New translation mode

Remarks

The **_setmode** function sets to *mode* the translation mode of the file given by *handle*. The mode must be one of two manifest constants, **_O_TEXT** or **_O_BINARY**. **_O_TEXT** sets text (translated) mode. Carriage return–linefeed (CR-LF) combinations are translated into a single linefeed character on input. Linefeed characters are translated into CR-LF combinations on output. **_O_BINARY** sets binary (untranslated) mode, in which these translations are suppressed.

_setmode is typically used to modify the default translation mode of **stdin** and **stdout**, but you can use it on any file. If you apply **_setmode** to the file handle for a stream, call **_setmode** before performing any input or output operations on the stream.

Example

```
/* SETMODE.C: This program uses _setmode to change
 * stdin from text mode to binary mode.
 */

#include <stdio.h>
#include <fcntl.h>
#include <io.h>

void main( void )
{
   int result;

   /* Set "stdin" to have binary mode: */
   result = _setmode( _fileno( stdin ), _O_BINARY );
   if( result == -1 )
      perror( "Cannot set mode" );
   else
      printf( "'stdin' successfully changed to binary mode\n" );
}
```

Output

```
'stdin' successfully changed to binary mode
```

See Also **_creat, fopen, _open**

_set_new_handler

Transfer control to your error-handling mechanism if the **new** operator fails to allocate memory.

_PNH _set_new_handler(_PNH *pNewHandler* **);**

Routine	Required Header	Optional Headers	Compatibility
_set_new_handler	<new.h>		Win 95, Win NT, Win32s, 68K, PMac

For additional compatibility information, see "Compatibility" on page ix in the Introduction.

Libraries	
LIBC.LIB	Single thread static library, retail version
LIBCMT.LIB	Multithread static library, retail version
MSVCRT.LIB	Import library for MSVCRTx0.DLL, retail version
MSVCRTx0.DLL	Multithread DLL library, retail version

Return Value

_set_new_handler returns a pointer to the previous exception handling function registered by **_set_new_handler**, so that the previous function can be restored later. If no previous function has been set, the return value may be used to restore the default behavior; this value may be NULL.

Parameter

pNewHandler Pointer to the application-supplied memory handling function

Remarks

Call the C++ **_set_new_handler** function to specify an exception-handling function that is to gain control if the **new** operator fails to allocate memory. If **new** fails, the run-time system automatically calls the exception-handling function that was passed as an argument to **_set_new_handler**. **_PNH**, defined in NEW.H, is a pointer to a function that returns type **int** and takes an argument of type **size_t**. Use **size_t** to specify the amount of space to be allocated.

_set_new_handler is essentially a garbage-collection scheme. The run-time system retries allocation each time your function returns a nonzero value and fails if your function returns 0.

An occurrence of one of the **_set_new_handler** functions in a program registers the exception-handling function specified in the argument list with the run-time system:

```
#include <new.h>
int handle_program_memory_depletion( size_t )
{
   // Your code
}
void main( void )
{
   _set_new_handler( handle_program_memory_depletion );
   int *pi = new int[BIG_NUMBER];
}
```

You can save the function address that was last passed to the **_set_new_handler** function and reinstate it later:

```
_PNH old_handler = _set_new_handler( my_handler );
   // Code that requires my_handler
   _set_new_handler( old_handler )
   // Code that requires old_handler
```

In a multithreaded environment, handlers are maintained separately for each process and thread. Each new process lacks installed handlers. Each new thread gets a copy of the new handlers of the calling thread. Thus, each process and thread is in charge of its own free-store error handling.

The C++ **_set_new_mode** function sets the new handler mode for **malloc**. The new handler mode indicates whether, on failure, **malloc** is to call the new handler routine as set by **_set_new_handler**. By default, **malloc** does not call the new handler routine on failure to allocate memory. You can override this default behavior so that, when **malloc** fails to allocate memory, **malloc** calls the new handler routine in the same way that the **new** operator does when it fails for the same reason. To override the default, call

```
_set_new_mode(1)
```

early in your program, or link with NEWMODE.OBJ.

For more information, see the discussion of the **new** and **delete** operators in Chapter 4 of *C++ Language Reference*.

Example

```
/* HANDLER.CPP: This program uses _set_new_handler to
 * print an error message if the new operator fails.
 */

#include <stdio.h>
#include <new.h>

/* Allocate memory in chunks of size MemBlock. */
const size_t MemBlock = 1024;

/* Allocate a memory block for the printf function to use in case
 * of memory allocation failure; the printf function uses malloc.
 * The failsafe memory block must be visible globally because the
 * handle_program_memory_depletion function can take one
 * argument only.
 */
char * failsafe = new char[128];

/* Declare a customized function to handle memory-allocation failure.
 * Pass this function as an argument to _set_new_handler.
 */
int handle_program_memory_depletion( size_t );

void main( void )
{
   // Register existence of a new memory handler.
   _set_new_handler( handle_program_memory_depletion );
   size_t *pmemdump = new size_t[MemBlock];
   for( ; pmemdump != 0; pmemdump = new size_t[MemBlock] );
}

int handle_program_memory_depletion( size_t size )
{
   // Release character buffer memory.
   delete failsafe;
   printf( "Allocation failed, " );
   printf( "%u bytes not available.\n", size );
   // Tell new to stop allocation attempts.
   return 0;
}
```

Output

```
Allocation failed %0 bytes not available.
```

See Also **calloc**, **free**, **realloc**

_set_new_mode

Sets a new handler mode for **malloc**.

int _set_new_mode(int *newhandlermode* **);**

Routine	Required Header	Optional Headers	Compatibility
_set_new_mode	<new.h>		Win 95, Win NT, Win32s

For additional compatibility information, see "Compatibility" on page ix in the Introduction.

Libraries	
LIBC.LIB	Single thread static library, retail version
LIBCMT.LIB	Multithread static library, retail version
MSVCRT.LIB	Import library for MSVCRTx0.DLL, retail version
MSVCRTx0.DLL	Multithread DLL library, retail version

Return Value

_set_new_mode returns the previous handler mode set for **malloc**. A return value of 1 indicates that, on failure to allocate memory, **malloc** previously called the new handler routine; a return value of 0 indicates that it did not. If the *newhandlermode* argument does not equal 0 or 1, **_set_new_mode** returns –1.

Parameter

newhandlermode New handler mode for **malloc**; valid value is 0 or 1

Remarks

The C++ **_set_new_mode** function sets the new handler mode for **malloc**. The new handler mode indicates whether, on failure, **malloc** is to call the new handler routine as set by **_set_new_handler, set_new_handler**. By default, **malloc** does not call the new handler routine on failure to allocate memory. You can override this default behavior so that, when **malloc** fails to allocate memory, **malloc** calls the new handler routine in the same way that the **new** operator does when it fails for the same reason. For more information, see the **new** and **delete** operators in Chapter 4 of *C++ Language Reference*. To override the default, call

```
_set_new_mode(1)
```

early in your program, or link with NEWMODE.OBJ.

See Also **calloc**, **free**, **realloc**, **_query_new_handler**, **_query_new_mode**

_set_se_translator

Handles Win32 exceptions (C structured exceptions) as C++ typed exceptions.

typedef void (*_se_translator_function)(unsigned int, struct _EXCEPTION_POINTERS*);
_se_translator_function _set_se_translator(_se_translator_function *se_trans_func* **);**

Routine	Required Header	Optional Headers	Compatibility
_set_se_translator	<eh.h>		Win 95, Win NT, Win32s

For additional compatibility information, see "Compatibility" on page ix in the Introduction.

Libraries	
LIBC.LIB	Single thread static library, retail version
LIBCMT.LIB	Multithread static library, retail version
MSVCRT.LIB	Import library for MSVCRTx0.DLL, retail version
MSVCRTx0.DLL	Multithread DLL library, retail version

Return Value

_set_se_translator returns a pointer to the previous translator function registered by **_set_se_translator**, so that the previous function can be restored later. If no previous function has been set, the return value may be used to restore the default behavior; this value may be NULL.

Parameter

se_trans_func Pointer to a C structured exception translator function that you write

Remarks

The **_set_se_translator** function provides a way to handle Win32 exceptions (C structured exceptions) as C++ typed exceptions. To allow each C exception to be handled by a C++ **catch** handler, first define a C exception "wrapper" class that can be used, or derived from, in order to attribute a specific class type to a C exception. To use this class, install a custom C exception translator function that is called by the internal exception-handling mechanism each time a C exception is raised. Within your translator function, you can throw any typed exception that can be caught by a matching C++ **catch** handler.

To specify a custom translation function, call **_set_se_translator** with the name of your translation function as its argument. The translator function that you write is called once for each function invocation on the stack that has **try** blocks. There is no default translator function.

In a multithreaded environment, translator functions are maintained separately for each thread. Each new thread gets a copy of the new translator function of the calling thread. Thus, each thread is in charge of its own translation handling.

The *se_trans_func* function that you write must take an unsigned integer and a pointer to a Win32 **_EXCEPTION_POINTERS** structure as arguments. The arguments are the return values of calls to the Win32 API **GetExceptionCode** and **GetExceptionInformation** functions, respectively.

Example

```
/*  SETRANS.CPP
 */

#include <stdio.h>
#include <windows.h>
#include <eh.h>

void SEFunc();
void trans_func( unsigned int, EXCEPTION_POINTERS* );

class SE_Exception
{
private:
    unsigned int nSE;
public:
    SE_Exception() {}
    SE_Exception( unsigned int n ) : nSE( n ) {}
    ~SE_Exception() {}
    unsigned int getSeNumber() { return nSE; }
};
void main( void )
{
    try
    {
        _set_se_translator( trans_func );
        SEFunc();
    }
    catch( SE_Exception e )
    {
        printf( "Caught a __try exception with SE_Exception.\n" );
    }
}
void SEFunc()
{
    __try
    {
        int x, y=0;
        x = 5 / y;
    }
    __finally
```

```
    {
        printf( "In finally\n" );
    }
}
void trans_func( unsigned int u, EXCEPTION_POINTERS* pExp )
{
    printf( "In trans_func.\n" );
    throw SE_Exception();
}
```

Output

```
In finally.
In trans_func.
Caught a __try exception with SE_Exception.
```

See Also **set_terminate**, **set_unexpected**, **terminate**, **unexpected**

set_terminate

Installs your own termination routine to be called by **terminate**.

typedef void (*terminate_function)();
terminate_function set_terminate(terminate_function *term_func* **);**

Routine	Required Header	Optional Headers	Compatibility
set_terminate	<eh.h>		ANSI, Win 95, Win NT, Win32s, 68K, PMac

For additional compatibility information, see "Compatibility" on page ix in the Introduction.

Libraries	
LIBC.LIB	Single thread static library, retail version
LIBCMT.LIB	Multithread static library, retail version
MSVCRT.LIB	Import library for MSVCRTx0.DLL, retail version
MSVCRTx0.DLL	Multithread DLL library, retail version

Return Value

set_terminate returns a pointer to the previous function registered by **set_terminate**, so that the previous function can be restored later. If no previous function has been set, the return value may be used to restore the default behavior; this value may be NULL.

Parameter

term_func Pointer to a terminate function that you write

Remarks

The **set_terminate** function installs *term_func* as the function called by **terminate**. **set_terminate** is used with C++ exception handling and may be called at any point in your program before the exception is thrown. **terminate** calls **abort** by default. You can change this default by writing your own termination function and calling **set_terminate** with the name of your function as its argument. **terminate** calls the last function given as an argument to **set_terminate**. After performing any desired cleanup tasks, *term_func* should exit the program. If it does not exit (if it returns to its caller), **abort** is called.

In a multithreaded environment, termination functions are maintained separately for each thread. Each new thread gets a copy of the new termination function of the calling thread. Thus, each thread is in charge of its own termination handling.

The **terminate_function** type is defined in EH.H as a pointer to a user-defined termination function, *term_func*, that returns **void**. Your custom function *term_func* can take no arguments and should not return to its caller. If it does, **abort** is called. An exception may not be thrown from within *term_func*.

Example

See the example for **terminate**.

See Also **abort**, **set_unexpected**, **terminate**, **unexpected**

---

set_unexpected

Installs your own termination function to be called by **unexpected**.

typedef void (*unexpected_function)();
unexpected_function set_unexpected(unexpected_function *unexp_func* **);**

Routine	Required Header	Optional Headers	Compatibility
set_unexpected	<eh.h>		ANSI, Win 95, Win NT, Win32s, 68K, PMac

For additional compatibility information, see "Compatibility" on page ix in the Introduction.

Libraries

LIBC.LIB	Single thread static library, retail version
LIBCMT.LIB	Multithread static library, retail version
MSVCRT.LIB	Import library for MSVCRTx0.DLL, retail version
MSVCRTx0.DLL	Multithread DLL library, retail version

Return Value

_set_unexpected returns a pointer to the previous termination function registered by **_set_unexpected**, so that the previous function can be restored later. If no previous function has been set, the return value may be used to restore the default behavior; this value may be NULL.

Parameter

unexp_func Pointer to a function that you write to replace the **unexpected** function

Remarks

The **set_unexpected** function installs *unexp_func* as the function called by **unexpected**. **unexpected** is not used in the current C++ exception-handling implementation. The **unexpected_function** type is defined in EH.H as a pointer to a user-defined unexpected function, *unexp_func*, that returns **void**. Your custom *unexp_func* function should not return to its caller.

By default, **unexpected** calls **terminate**. You can change this default behavior by writing your own termination function and calling **set_unexpected** with the name of your function as its argument. **unexpected** calls the last function given as an argument to **set_unexpected**.

Unlike the custom termination function installed by a call to **set_terminate**, an exception can be thrown from within *unexp_func*.

In a multithreaded environment, termination functions are maintained separately for each thread. Each new thread gets a copy of the new termination function of the calling thread. Thus, each thread is in charge of its own unexpected termination handling.

In the current Microsoft implementation of C++ exception handling, **unexpected** calls **terminate** by default and is never called by the exception-handling run-time library. There is no particular advantage to calling **unexpected** rather than **terminate**.

See Also **abort**, **set_terminate**, **terminate**, **unexpected**

setvbuf

Controls stream buffering and buffer size.

int setvbuf(FILE ****stream*, **char ****buffer*, **int *mode*, **size_t** *size* **);**

Routine	Required Header	Optional Headers	Compatibility
setvbuf	<stdio.h>		ANSI, Win 95, Win NT, Win32s, 68K, PMac

For additional compatibility information, see "Compatibility" on page ix in the Introduction.

Libraries

LIBC.LIB	Single thread static library, retail version
LIBCMT.LIB	Multithread static library, retail version
MSVCRT.LIB	Import library for MSVCRTx0.DLL, retail version
MSVCRTx0.DLL	Multithread DLL library, retail version

Return Value

setvbuf returns 0 if successful, or a nonzero value if an illegal type or buffer size is specified.

Parameters

stream Pointer to **FILE** structure

buffer User-allocated buffer

mode Mode of buffering

size Buffer size in bytes. Allowable range: 2 < *size* < 32768. Internally, the value supplied for *size* is rounded down to the nearest multiple of 2.

Remarks

The **setvbuf** function allows the program to control both buffering and buffer size for *stream*. *stream* must refer to an open file that has not undergone an I/O operation since it was opened. The array pointed to by *buffer* is used as the buffer, unless it is **NULL**, in which case **setvbuf** uses an automatically allocated buffer of length *size*/2 * 2 bytes.

The mode must be **_IOFBF**, **_IOLBF**, or **_IONBF**. If *mode* is **_IOFBF** or **_IOLBF**, then *size* is used as the size of the buffer. If *mode* is **_IONBF**, the stream is unbuffered and *size* and *buffer* are ignored. Values for *mode* and their meanings are:

_IOFBF Full buffering; that is, *buffer* is used as the buffer and *size* is used as the size of the buffer. If *buffer* is **NULL**, an automatically allocated buffer *size* bytes long is used.

_IOLBF With MS-DOS, the same as **_IOFBF**.

_IONBF No buffer is used, regardless of *buffer* or *size*.

Example

```
/* SETVBUF.C: This program opens two streams: stream1
 * and stream2. It then uses setvbuf to give stream1 a
 * user-defined buffer of 1024 bytes and stream2 no buffer.
 */

#include <stdio.h>

void main( void )
{
   char buf[1024];
   FILE *stream1, *stream2;
```

```
   if( ((stream1 = fopen( "data1", "a" )) != NULL) &&
       ((stream2 = fopen( "data2", "w" )) != NULL) )
   {
      if( setvbuf( stream1, buf, _IOFBF, sizeof( buf ) ) != 0 )
         printf( "Incorrect type or size of buffer for stream1\n" );
      else
         printf( "'stream1' now has a buffer of 1024 bytes\n" );
      if( setvbuf( stream2, NULL, _IONBF, 0 ) != 0 )
         printf( "Incorrect type or size of buffer for stream2\n" );
      else
         printf( "'stream2' now has no buffer\n" );
      _fcloseall();
   }
}
```

Output

```
'stream1' now has a buffer of 1024 bytes
'stream2' now has no buffer
```

See Also **fclose**, **fflush**, **fopen**, **setbuf**

---

signal

Sets interrupt signal handling.

void (*signal(int *sig*, **void (__cdecl** ***func*) **(int** *sig* **[, int** *subcode* **]))) (int** *sig* **);**

Routine	Required Header	Optional Headers	Compatibility
signal	<signal.h>		ANSI, Win 95, Win NT, Win32s, 68K, PMac

For additional compatibility information, see "Compatibility" on page ix in the Introduction.

Libraries	
LIBC.LIB	Single thread static library, retail version
LIBCMT.LIB	Multithread static library, retail version
MSVCRT.LIB	Import library for MSVCRTx0.DLL, retail version
MSVCRTx0.DLL	Multithread DLL library, retail version

Return Value

signal returns the previous value of *func* associated with the given signal. For example, if the previous value of *func* was **SIG_IGN**, the return value is also **SIG_IGN**. A return value of **SIG_ERR** indicates an error, in which case **errno** is set to **EINVAL**.

Parameters

sig Signal value

func Function to be executed

subcode Optional subcode to the signal number

Remarks

The **signal** function allows a process to choose one of several ways to handle an interrupt signal from the operating system. The *sig* argument is the interrupt to which **signal** responds; it must be one of the following manifest constants, defined in SIGNAL.H.

sig Value	Description
SIGABRT	Abnormal termination
SIGFPE	Floating-point error
SIGILL	Illegal instruction
SIGINT	CTRL+C signal
SIGSEGV	Illegal storage access
SIGTERM	Termination request

By default, **signal** terminates the calling program with exit code 3, regardless of the value of *sig*.

Note **SIGINT** is not supported for any Win32 application including Windows NT and Windows 95. When a CTRL+C interrupt occurs, Win32 operating systems generate a new thread to specifically handle that interrupt. This can cause a single-thread application such as UNIX, to become multithreaded, resulting in unexpected behavior.

The *func* argument is an address to a signal handler that you write, or one of the manifest constants **SIG_DFL** or **SIG_IGN**, also defined in SIGNAL.H. If *func* is a function, it is installed as the signal handler for the given signal. The signal handler's prototype requires one formal argument, *sig*, of type **int**. The operating system provides the actual argument through *sig* when an interrupt occurs; the argument is the signal that generated the interrupt. Thus you can use the six manifest constants (listed in the preceding table) inside your signal handler to determine which interrupt occurred and take appropriate action. For example, you can call **signal** twice to assign the same handler to two different signals, then test the *sig* argument inside the handler to take different actions based on the signal received.

If you are testing for floating-point exceptions (**SIGFPE**), *func* points to a function that takes an optional second argument that is one of several manifest constants defined in FLOAT.H of the form **FPE_***xxx*. When a **SIGFPE** signal occurs, you can test the value of the second argument to determine the type of floating-point exception and then take appropriate action. This argument and its possible values are Microsoft extensions.

For floating-point exceptions, the value of *func* is not reset upon receiving the signal. To recover from floating-point exceptions, use **setjmp** with **longjmp**. If the function returns, the calling process resumes execution with the floating-point state of the process left undefined.

If the signal handler returns, the calling process resumes execution immediately following the point at which it received the interrupt signal. This is true regardless of the type of signal or operating mode.

Before the specified function is executed, the value of *func* is set to **SIG_DFL**. The next interrupt signal is treated as described for **SIG_DFL**, unless an intervening call to **signal** specifies otherwise. This feature lets you reset signals in the called function.

Because signal-handler routines are usually called asynchronously when an interrupt occurs, your signal-handler function may get control when a run-time operation is incomplete and in an unknown state. The list below summarizes restrictions that determine which functions you can use in your signal-handler routine.

- Do not issue low-level or STDIO.H I/O routines (such as **printf** and **fread**).
- Do not call heap routines or any routine that uses the heap routines (such as **malloc**, **_strdup**, and **_putenv**). See **malloc** for more information.
- Do not use any function that generates a system call (e.g., **_getcwd**, **time**).
- Do not use **longjmp** unless the interrupt is caused by a floating-point exception (i.e., *sig* is **SIGFPE**). In this case, first reinitialize the floating-point package with a call to **_fpreset**.
- Do not use any overlay routines.

A program must contain floating-point code if it is to trap the **SIGFPE** exception with the function. If your program does not have floating-point code and requires the run-time library's signal-handling code, simply declare a volatile double and initialize it to zero:

```
volatile double d = 0.0f;
```

The **SIGILL**, **SIGSEGV**, and **SIGTERM** signals are not generated under Windows NT. They are included for ANSI compatibility. Thus you can set signal handlers for these signals with **signal**, and you can also explicitly generate these signals by calling **raise**.

Signal settings are not preserved in spawned processes created by calls to **_exec** or **_spawn** functions. The signal settings are reset to the default in the new process.

See Also **abort**, **_exec** Functions, **exit**, **_fpreset**, **_spawn** Functions

sin, sinh

Calculate sines and hyperbolic sines.

double sin(double *x*);
double sinh(double *x*);

Routine	Required Header	Optional Headers	Compatibility
sin	<math.h>		ANSI, Win 95, Win NT, Win32s, 68K, PMac
sinh	<math.h>		ANSI, Win 95, Win NT, Win32s, 68K, PMac

For additional compatibility information, see "Compatibility" on page ix in the Introduction.

Libraries	
LIBC.LIB	Single thread static library, retail version
LIBCMT.LIB	Multithread static library, retail version
MSVCRT.LIB	Import library for MSVCRTx0.DLL, retail version
MSVCRTx0.DLL	Multithread DLL library, retail version

Return Value

sin returns the sine of *x*. If *x* is greater than or equal to 2^{63}, or less than or equal to -2^{63}, a loss of significance in the result occurs, in which case the function generates a **_TLOSS** error and returns an indefinite (same as a quiet NaN).

sinh returns the hyperbolic sine of *x*. If the result is too large, **sinh** sets **errno** to **ERANGE** and returns **±HUGE_VAL**. You can modify error handling with **_matherr**.

Parameter

x Angle in radians

Example

```
/* SINCOS.C: This program displays the sine, hyperbolic
 * sine, cosine, and hyperbolic cosine of pi / 2.
 */

#include <math.h>
#include <stdio.h>

void main( void )
{
   double pi = 3.1415926535;
   double x, y;
```

```
    x = pi / 2;
    y = sin( x );
    printf( "sin( %f ) = %f\n", x, y );
    y = sinh( x );
    printf( "sinh( %f ) = %f\n",x, y );
    y = cos( x );
    printf( "cos( %f ) = %f\n", x, y );
    y = cosh( x );
    printf( "cosh( %f ) = %f\n",x, y );
}
```

Output

```
sin( 1.570796 ) = 1.000000
sinh( 1.570796 ) = 2.301299
cos( 1.570796 ) = 0.000000
cosh( 1.570796 ) = 2.509178
```

See Also **acos**, **asin**, **atan**, **cos**, **tan**

_snprintf, _snwprintf

Write formatted data to a string.

int _snprintf(char ***buffer*, **size_t** *count*, **const char** ***format*** [, *argument*] ... **);**
int _snwprintf(wchar_t ***buffer*, **size_t** *count*, **const wchar_t** ***format*** [, *argument*] ... **);**

Routine	Required Header	Optional Headers	Compatibility
_snprintf	<stdio.h>		Win 95, Win NT, Win32s, 68K, PMac
_snwprintf	<stdio.h> or <wchar.h>		Win 95, Win NT, Win32s

For additional compatibility information, see "Compatibility" on page ix in the Introduction.

Libraries	
LIBC.LIB	Single thread static library, retail version
LIBCMT.LIB	Multithread static library, retail version
MSVCRT.LIB	Import library for MSVCRTx0.DLL, retail version
MSVCRTx0.DLL	Multithread DLL library, retail version

Return Value

_snprintf returns the number of bytes stored in *buffer*, not counting the terminating null character. If the number of bytes required to store the data exceeds *count*, then *count* bytes of data are stored in *buffer* and a negative value is returned. **_snwprintf** returns the number of wide characters stored in *buffer,* not counting the terminating null wide character. If the storage required to store the data exceeds *count* wide characters, then *count* wide characters are stored in *buffer* and a negative value is returned.

Parameters

buffer Storage location for output

count Maximum number of characters to store

format Format-control string

argument Optional arguments

Remarks

The **_snprintf** function formats and stores *count* or fewer characters and values (including a terminating null character, which is always appended unless *count* is zero) in *buffer*. Each *argument* (if any) is converted and output according to the corresponding format specification in *format*. The format consists of ordinary characters and has the same form and function as the *format* argument for **printf**. If copying occurs between strings that overlap, the behavior is undefined.

_snwprintf is a wide-character version of **_snprintf**; the pointer arguments to **_snwprintf** are wide-character strings. Detection of encoding errors in **_snwprintf** may differ from that in **_snprintf**. **_snwprintf**, like **swprintf**, writes output to a string rather than to a destination of type **FILE**.

Example

See the example for **sprintf**.

See Also **sprintf**, **fprintf**, **printf**, **scanf**, **sscanf**, **vprintf** Functions

---

_sopen, _wsopen

Open a file for sharing.

int _sopen(const char ****filename*, int** *oflag***, int** *shflag* [**, int** *pmode*] **);**
int _wsopen(const wchar_t ****filename*, int** *oflag***, int** *shflag* [**, int** *pmode*] **);**

Routine	Required Header	Optional Headers	Compatibility
_sopen	<io.h>	<fcntl.h>, <sys/types.h>, <sys/stat.h>, <share.h>	Win 95, Win NT, Win32s, 68K, PMac
_wsopen	<io.h> or <wchar.h>	<fcntl.h>, <sys/types.h>, <sys/stat.h>, <share.h>	Win NT

For additional compatibility information, see "Compatibility" on page ix in the Introduction.

Libraries

LIBC.LIB	Single thread static library, retail version
LIBCMT.LIB	Multithread static library, retail version
MSVCRT.LIB	Import library for MSVCRTx0.DLL, retail version
MSVCRTx0.DLL	Multithread DLL library, retail version

Return Value

Each of these functions returns a file handle for the opened file. A return value of –1 indicates an error, in which case **errno** is set to one of the following values:

EACCES Given path is a directory, or file is read-only, but an open-for-writing operation was attempted.

EEXIST **_O_CREAT** and **_O_EXCL** flags were specified, but *filename* already exists.

EINVAL Invalid *oflag* or *shflag* argument.

EMFILE No more file handles available.

ENOENT File or path not found.

Parameters

filename Filename

oflag Type of operations allowed

shflag Type of sharing allowed

pmode Permission setting

Remarks

The **_sopen** function opens the file specified by *filename* and prepares the file for shared reading or writing, as defined by *oflag* and *shflag*. **_wsopen** is a wide-character version of **_sopen**; the *filename* argument to **_wsopen** is a wide-character string. **_wsopen** and **_sopen** behave identically otherwise.

The integer expression *oflag* is formed by combining one or more of the following manifest constants, defined in the file FCNTL.H. When two or more constants form the argument *oflag*, they are combined with the bitwise-OR operator (|).

_O_APPEND Repositions file pointer to end of file before every write operation.

_O_BINARY Opens file in binary (untranslated) mode. (See **fopen** for a description of binary mode.)

_O_CREAT Creates and opens new file for writing. Has no effect if file specified by *filename* exists. The *pmode* argument is required when **_O_CREAT** is specified.

_O_CREAT | _O_SHORT_LIVED Create file as temporary and if possible do not flush to disk. The *pmode* argument is required when **_O_CREAT** is specified.

_O_CREAT | _O_TEMPORARY Create file as temporary; file is deleted when last file handle is closed. The *pmode* argument is required when **_O_CREAT** is specified.

_O_CREAT | _O_EXCL Returns error value if file specified by *filename* exists. Applies only when used with **_O_CREAT**.

_O_RANDOM Specifies primarily random access from disk

_O_RDONLY Opens file for reading only; cannot be specified with **_O_RDWR** or **_O_WRONLY**.

_O_RDWR Opens file for both reading and writing; cannot be specified with **_O_RDONLY** or **_O_WRONLY**.

_O_SEQUENTIAL Specifies primarily sequential access from disk

_O_TEXT Opens file in text (translated) mode. (For more information, see "Text and Binary Mode File I/O" on page 15 and **fopen**.)

_O_TRUNC Opens file and truncates it to zero length; the file must have write permission. You cannot specify this flag with **_O_RDONLY**. **_O_TRUNC** used with **_O_CREAT** opens an existing file or creates a new file.

Warning The **_O_TRUNC** flag destroys the contents of the specified file.

_O_WRONLY Opens file for writing only; cannot be specified with **_O_RDONLY** or **_O_RDWR**.

To specify the file access mode, you must specify either **_O_RDONLY**, **_O_RDWR**, or **_O_WRONLY**. There is no default value for the access mode.

The argument *shflag* is a constant expression consisting of one of the following manifest constants, defined in SHARE.H.

_SH_DENYRW Denies read and write access to file

_SH_DENYWR Denies write access to file

_SH_DENYRD Denies read access to file

_SH_DENYNO Permits read and write access

The *pmode* argument is required only when you specify **_O_CREAT**. If the file does not exist, *pmode* specifies the file's permission settings, which are set when the new file is closed the first time. Otherwise *pmode* is ignored. *pmode* is an integer expression that contains one or both of the manifest constants **_S_IWRITE** and **_S_IREAD**, defined in SYS\STAT.H. When both constants are given, they are combined with the bitwise-OR operator. The meaning of *pmode* is as follows:

_S_IWRITE Writing permitted

_S_IREAD Reading permitted

_S_IREAD | _S_IWRITE Reading and writing permitted

If write permission is not given, the file is read-only. Under Windows NT and Windows 95, all files are readable; it is not possible to give write-only permission. Thus the modes **_S_IWRITE** and **_S_IREAD | _S_IWRITE** are equivalent.

_sopen applies the current file-permission mask to *pmode* before setting the permissions (see **_umask**).

Example

See the example for **_locking**.

See Also **_close**, **_creat**, **fopen**, **_fsopen**, **_open**

_spawn, _wspawn Functions

Each of the **_spawn** functions creates and executes a new process.

_spawnl, _wspawnl	**_spawnv, _wspawnv**
_spawnle, _wspawnle	**_spawnve, _wspawnve**
_spawnlp, _wspawnlp	**_spawnvp, _wspawnvp**
_spawnlpe, _wspawnlpe	**_spawnvpe, _wspawnvpe**

The letter(s) at the end of the function name determine the variation.

_spawn Function Suffix	Description
e	*envp*, array of pointers to environment settings, is passed to new process.
l	Command-line arguments are passed individually to **_spawn** function. This suffix is typically used when number of parameters to new process is known in advance
p	**PATH** environment variable is used to find file to execute.
v	*argv,* array of pointers to command-line arguments, is passed to **_spawn** function. This suffix is typically used when number of parameters to new process is variable.

Remarks

The **_spawn** functions each create and execute a new process. They automatically handle multibyte-character string arguments as appropriate, recognizing multibyte-character sequences according to the multibyte code page currently in use. The **_wspawn** functions are wide-character versions of the **_spawn** functions; they do not handle multibyte-character strings. Otherwise, the **_wspawn** functions behave identically to their **_spawn** counterparts.

Enough memory must be available for loading and executing the new process. The *mode* argument determines the action taken by the calling process before and during **_spawn**. The following values for *mode* are defined in PROCESS.H:

_P_OVERLAY Overlays calling process with new process, destroying the calling process (same effect as **_exec** calls).

_P_WAIT Suspends calling process until execution of new process is complete (synchronous **_spawn**).

_P_NOWAIT or **_P_NOWAITO** Continues to execute calling process concurrently with new process (asynchronous **_spawn**).

_P_DETACH Continues to execute the calling process; new process is run in the background with no access to the console or keyboard. Calls to **_cwait** against the new process will fail (asynchronous **_spawn**).

The *cmdname* argument specifies the file that is executed as the new process and can specify a full path (from the root), a partial path (from the current working directory), or just a filename. If *cmdname* does not have a filename extension or does not end with a period (.), the **_spawn** function first tries the .COM extension, then the .EXE extension, the .BAT extension, and finally the .CMD extension.

If *cmdname* has an extension, only that extension is used. If *cmdname* ends with a period, the **_spawn** call searches for *cmdname* with no extension. The **_spawnlp**, **_spawnlpe**, **_spawnvp**, and **_spawnvpe** functions search for *cmdname* (using the same procedures) in the directories specified by the **PATH** environment variable.

If *cmdname* contains a drive specifier or any slashes (that is, if it is a relative path), the **_spawn** call searches only for the specified file; no path searching is done.

Note To ensure proper overlay initialization and termination, do not use the **setjmp** or **longjmp** function to enter or leave an overlay routine.

Arguments for the Spawned Process

To pass arguments to the new process, give one or more pointers to character strings as arguments in the **_spawn** call. These character strings form the argument list for the spawned process. The combined length of the strings forming the argument list for the new process must not exceed 1024 bytes. The terminating null character (`'\0'`) for each string is not included in the count, but space characters (automatically inserted to separate arguments) are included.

You can pass argument pointers as separate arguments (in **_spawnl**, **_spawnle**, **_spawnlp**, and **_spawnlpe**) or as an array of pointers (in **_spawnv**, **_spawnve**, **_spawnvp**, and **_spawnvpe**). You must pass at least one argument, *arg0* or *argv*[0], to the spawned process. By convention, this argument is the name of the program as you would type it on the command line. A different value does not produce an error.

The **_spawnl**, **_spawnle**, **_spawnlp**, and **_spawnlpe** calls are typically used in cases where the number of arguments is known in advance. The *arg0* argument is usually a pointer to *cmdname*. The arguments *arg1* through *argn* are pointers to the character strings forming the new argument list. Following *argn*, there must be a **NULL** pointer to mark the end of the argument list.

The **_spawnv**, **_spawnve**, **_spawnvp**, and **_spawnvpe** calls are useful when there is a variable number of arguments to the new process. Pointers to the arguments are passed as an array, *argv*. The argument *argv*[0] is usually a pointer to a path in real mode or to the program name in protected mode, and *argv*[1] through *argv*[*n*] are pointers to the character strings forming the new argument list. The argument *argv*[*n* +1] must be a **NULL** pointer to mark the end of the argument list.

Environment of the Spawned Process

Files that are open when a **_spawn** call is made remain open in the new process. In the **_spawnl**, **_spawnlp**, **_spawnv**, and **_spawnvp** calls, the new process inherits the environment of the calling process. You can use the **_spawnle**, **_spawnlpe**, **_spawnve**, and **_spawnvpe** calls to alter the environment for the new process by passing a list of environment settings through the *envp* argument. The argument *envp* is an array of character pointers, each element (except the final element) of which points to a null-terminated string defining an environment variable. Such a string usually has the form *NAME=value* where *NAME* is the name of an environment variable and *value* is the string value to which that variable is set. (Note that *value* is not enclosed in double quotation marks.) The final element of the *envp* array should be **NULL**. When *envp* itself is **NULL**, the spawned process inherits the environment settings of the parent process.

The **_spawn** functions can pass all information about open files, including the translation mode, to the new process. This information is passed in real mode through the **C_FILE_INFO** entry in the environment. The startup code normally processes this entry and then deletes it from the environment. However, if a **_spawn** function spawns a non-C process, this entry remains in the environment. Printing the environment shows graphics characters in the definition string for this entry because the environment information is passed in binary form in real mode. It should not have any other effect on normal operations. In protected mode, the environment information is passed in text form and therefore contains no graphics characters.

You must explicitly flush (using **fflush** or **_flushall**) or close any stream before calling a **_spawn** function.

You can control whether the open file information of a process is passed to its spawned processes. The external variable **_fileinfo** (declared in STDLIB.H) controls the passing of **C_FILE_INFO** information. If **_fileinfo** is 0 (the default), the **C_FILE_INFO** information is not passed to the new processes. If **_fileinfo** is not 0, **C_FILE_INFO** is passed to new processes. You can modify the default value of **_fileinfo** in one of two ways: link the supplied object file, FILEINFO.OBJ, into the program, or set the **_fileinfo** variable to a nonzero value directly in the C program.

New processes created by calls to **_spawn** routines do not preserve signal settings. Instead, the spawned process resets signal settings to the default.

Example

```
/* SPAWN.C: This program accepts a number in the range
 * 1-8 from the command line. Based on the number it receives,
 * it executes one of the eight different procedures that
 * spawn the process named child. For some of these procedures,
 * the CHILD.EXE file must be in the same directory; for
 * others, it only has to be in the same path.
 */

#include <stdio.h>
#include <process.h>

char *my_env[] =
{
   "THIS=environment will be",
   "PASSED=to child.exe by the",
   "_SPAWNLE=and",
   "_SPAWNLPE=and",
   "_SPAWNVE=and",
   "_SPAWNVPE=functions",
   NULL
};

void main( int argc, char *argv[] )
{
   char *args[4];

   /* Set up parameters to be sent: */
   args[0] = "child";
   args[1] = "spawn??";
   args[2] = "two";
   args[3] = NULL;

   if (argc <= 2)
   {
      printf( "SYNTAX: SPAWN <1-8> <childprogram>\n" );
      exit( 1 );
   }

   switch (argv[1][0])   /* Based on first letter of argument */
   {
   case '1':
      _spawnl( _P_WAIT, argv[2], argv[2], "_spawnl", "two", NULL );
      break;
   case '2':
      _spawnle( _P_WAIT, argv[2], argv[2], "_spawnle", "two",
               NULL, my_env );
      break;
```

```
   case '3':
      _spawnlp( _P_WAIT, argv[2], argv[2], "_spawnlp", "two", NULL );
      break;
   case '4':
      _spawnlpe( _P_WAIT, argv[2], argv[2], "_spawnlpe", "two",
                 NULL, my_env );
      break;
   case '5':
      _spawnv( _P_OVERLAY, argv[2], args );
      break;
   case '6':
      _spawnve( _P_OVERLAY, argv[2], args, my_env );
      break;
   case '7':
      _spawnvp( _P_OVERLAY, argv[2], args );
      break;
   case '8':
      _spawnvpe( _P_OVERLAY, argv[2], args, my_env );
      break;
   default:
      printf( "SYNTAX: SPAWN <1-8> <childprogram>\n" );
      exit( 1 );
   }
   printf( "from SPAWN!\n" );
}
```

Output

```
SYNTAX: SPAWN <1-8> <childprogram>
```

See Also **abort**, **atexit**, **_exec** Functions, **exit**, **_flushall**, **_getmbcp**, **_onexit**, **_setmbcp**, **system**

_spawnl, _wspawnl

Create and execute a new process.

int _spawnl(int *mode*, **const char** **cmdname*, **const char** **arg0*, **const char** **arg1*, ... **const char** **argn*, **NULL);**

int _wspawnl(int *mode*, **const wchar_t** **cmdname*, **const wchar_t** **arg0*, **const wchar_t** **arg1*, ... **const wchar_t** **argn*, **NULL);**

Routine	Required Header	Optional Headers	Compatibility
_spawnl	<process.h>		Win 95, Win NT, Win32s
_wspawnl	<stdio.h> or <wchar.h>		Win NT

For additional compatibility information, see "Compatibility" on page ix in the Introduction.

Libraries

LIBC.LIB	Single thread static library, retail version
LIBCMT.LIB	Multithread static library, retail version
MSVCRT.LIB	Import library for MSVCRTx0.DLL, retail version
MSVCRTx0.DLL	Multithread DLL library, retail version

Return Value

The return value from a synchronous **_spawnl** or **_wspawnl** (**_P_WAIT** specified for *mode*) is the exit status of the new process. The return value from an asynchronous **_spawnl** or **_wspawnl** (**_P_NOWAIT** or **_P_NOWAITO** specified for *mode*) is the process handle. The exit status is 0 if the process terminated normally. You can set the exit status to a nonzero value if the spawned process specifically calls the **exit** routine with a nonzero argument. If the new process did not explicitly set a positive exit status, a positive exit status indicates an abnormal exit with an abort or an interrupt. A return value of –1 indicates an error (the new process is not started). In this case, **errno** is set to one of the following values:

E2BIG Argument list exceeds 1024 bytes

EINVAL *mode* argument is invalid

ENOENT File or path is not found

ENOEXEC Specified file is not executable or has invalid executable-file format

ENOMEM Not enough memory is available to execute new process

Parameters

mode Execution mode for calling process

cmdname Path of file to be executed

arg0, ... *argn* List of pointers to arguments

Remarks

Each of these functions creates and executes a new process, passing each command-line argument as a separate parameter.

See Also **abort**, **atexit**, **_exec** Functions, **exit**, **_flushall**, **_getmbcp**, **_onexit**, **_setmbcp**, **system**

_spawnle, _wspawnle

Create and execute a new process.

int _spawnle(int *mode*, **const char** **cmdname*, **const char** **arg0*, **const char** **arg1*, ... **const char** **argn*, **NULL, const char *const** **envp* **);**

int _wspawnle(int *mode*, **const wchar_t** **cmdname*, **const wchar_t** **arg0*, **const wchar_t** **arg1*, ... **const wchar_t** **argn*, **NULL, const wchar_t *const** **envp* **);**

Routine	Required Header	Optional Headers	Compatibility
_spawnle	<process.h>		Win 95, Win NT, Win32s
_wspawnle	<stdio.h> or <wchar.h>		Win NT

For additional compatibility information, see "Compatibility" on page ix in the Introduction.

Libraries	
LIBC.LIB	Single thread static library, retail version
LIBCMT.LIB	Multithread static library, retail version
MSVCRT.LIB	Import library for MSVCRTx0.DLL, retail version
MSVCRTx0.DLL	Multithread DLL library, retail version

Return Value

The return value from a synchronous **_spawnle** or **_wspawnle** (**_P_WAIT** specified for *mode*) is the exit status of the new process. The return value from an asynchronous **_spawnle** or **_wspawnle** (**_P_NOWAIT** or **_P_NOWAITO** specified for *mode*) is the process handle. The exit status is 0 if the process terminated normally. You can set the exit status to a nonzero value if the spawned process specifically calls the **exit** routine with a nonzero argument. If the new process did not explicitly set a positive exit status, a positive exit status indicates an abnormal exit with an abort or an interrupt. A return value of –1 indicates an error (the new process is not started). In this case, **errno** is set to one of the following values:

E2BIG Argument list exceeds 1024 bytes

EINVAL *mode* argument is invalid

ENOENT File or path is not found

ENOEXEC Specified file is not executable or has invalid executable-file format

ENOMEM Not enough memory is available to execute new process

Parameters

mode Execution mode for calling process

cmdname Path of file to be executed

arg0, ... argn List of pointers to arguments

envp Array of pointers to environment settings

Remarks

Each of these functions creates and executes a new process, passing each command-line argument as a separate parameter and also passing an array of pointers to environment settings.

See Also **abort**, **atexit**, **_exec** Functions, **exit**, **_flushall**, **_getmbcp**, **_onexit**, **_setmbcp**, **system**

_spawnlp, _wspawnlp

Create and execute a new process.

int _spawnlp(int *mode*, **const char** **cmdname*, **const char** **arg0*, **const char** **arg1*, **... const char** **argn*, **NULL);**

int _wspawnlp(int *mode*, **const wchar_t** **cmdname*, **const wchar_t** **arg0*, **const wchar_t** **arg1*, **... const wchar_t** **argn*, **NULL);**

Routine	Required Header	Optional Headers	Compatibility
_spawnlp	<process.h>		Win 95, Win NT, Win32s
_wspawnlp	<stdio.h> or <wchar.h>		Win NT

For additional compatibility information, see "Compatibility" on page ix in the Introduction.

Libraries	
LIBC.LIB	Single thread static library, retail version
LIBCMT.LIB	Multithread static library, retail version
MSVCRT.LIB	Import library for MSVCRTx0.DLL, retail version
MSVCRTx0.DLL	Multithread DLL library, retail version

Return Value

The return value from a synchronous **_spawnlp** or **_wspawnlp** (**_P_WAIT** specified for *mode*) is the exit status of the new process. The return value from an asynchronous **_spawnlp** or **_wspawnlp** (**_P_NOWAIT** or **_P_NOWAITO** specified for *mode*) is the process handle. The exit status is 0 if the process terminated normally. You can set the exit status to a nonzero value if the spawned process specifically calls the **exit** routine with a nonzero argument. If the new process did not explicitly set a positive exit status, a positive exit status indicates an abnormal exit with an abort or an interrupt. A return value of –1 indicates an error (the new process is not started). In this case, **errno** is set to one of the following values:

E2BIG Argument list exceeds 1024 bytes

EINVAL *mode* argument is invalid

ENOENT File or path is not found

ENOEXEC Specified file is not executable or has invalid executable-file format

ENOMEM Not enough memory is available to execute new process

Parameters

mode Execution mode for calling process

cmdname Path of file to be executed

arg0, ... argn List of pointers to arguments

Remarks

Each of these functions creates and executes a new process, passing each command-line argument as a separate parameter and using the **PATH** environment variable to find the file to execute.

See Also **abort**, **atexit**, **_exec** Functions, **exit**, **_flushall**, **_getmbcp**, **_onexit**, **_setmbcp**, **system**

_spawnlpe, _wspawnlpe

Create and execute a new process.

int _spawnlpe(int *mode*, **const char** **cmdname*, **const char** **arg0*, **const char** **arg1*, **... const char** **argn*, **NULL, const char *const** **envp* **);**
int _wspawnlpe(int *mode*, **const wchar_t** **cmdname*, **const wchar_t** **arg0*, **const wchar_t** **arg1*, **... const wchar_t** **argn*, **NULL, const wchar_t *const** **envp* **);**

Routine	Required Header	Optional Headers	Compatibility
_spawnlpe	<process.h>		Win 95, Win NT, Win32s
_wspawnlpe	<stdio.h> or <wchar.h>		Win NT

For additional compatibility information, see "Compatibility" on page ix in the Introduction.

Libraries	
LIBC.LIB	Single thread static library, retail version
LIBCMT.LIB	Multithread static library, retail version
MSVCRT.LIB	Import library for MSVCRTx0.DLL, retail version
MSVCRTx0.DLL	Multithread DLL library, retail version

Return Value

The return value from a synchronous **_spawnlpe** or **_wspawnlpe** (**_P_WAIT** specified for *mode*) is the exit status of the new process. The return value from an asynchronous **_spawnlpe** or **_wspawnlpe** (**_P_NOWAIT** or **_P_NOWAITO** specified for *mode*) is the process handle. The exit status is 0 if the process terminated normally. You can set the exit status to a nonzero value if the spawned process specifically calls the **exit** routine with a nonzero argument. If the new process did not explicitly set a positive exit status, a positive exit status indicates an abnormal exit with an abort or an interrupt. A return value of –1 indicates an error (the new process is not started). In this case, **errno** is set to one of the following values:

E2BIG Argument list exceeds 1024 bytes

EINVAL *mode* argument is invalid

ENOENT File or path is not found

ENOEXEC Specified file is not executable or has invalid executable-file format

ENOMEM Not enough memory is available to execute new process

Parameters

mode Execution mode for calling process

cmdname Path of file to be executed

arg0, ... argn List of pointers to arguments

envp Array of pointers to environment settings

Remarks

Each of these functions creates and executes a new process, passing each command-line argument as a separate parameter and also passing an array of pointers to environment settings. These functions use the **PATH** environment variable to find the file to execute.

See Also **abort**, **atexit**, **_exec** Functions, **exit**, **_flushall**, **_getmbcp**, **_onexit**, **_setmbcp**, **system**

_spawnv, _wspawnv

Create and execute a new process.

int _spawnv(int *mode*, **const char** **cmdname*, **const char *const** **argv* **);**
int _wspawnv(int *mode*, **const wchar_t** **cmdname*, **const wchar_t *const** **argv* **);**

Routine	Required Header	Optional Headers	Compatibility
_spawnv	<stdio.h> or <process.h>		Win 95, Win NT, Win32s
_wspawnv	<stdio.h> or <wchar.h>		Win NT

For additional compatibility information, see "Compatibility" on page ix in the Introduction.

Libraries

LIBC.LIB	Single thread static library, retail version
LIBCMT.LIB	Multithread static library, retail version
MSVCRT.LIB	Import library for MSVCRTx0.DLL, retail version
MSVCRTx0.DLL	Multithread DLL library, retail version

Return Value

The return value from a synchronous **_spawnv** or **_wspawnv** (**_P_WAIT** specified for *mode*) is the exit status of the new process. The return value from an asynchronous **_spawnv** or **_wspawnv** (**_P_NOWAIT** or **_P_NOWAITO** specified for *mode*) is the process handle. The exit status is 0 if the process terminated normally. You can set the exit status to a nonzero value if the spawned process specifically calls the **exit** routine with a nonzero argument. If the new process did not explicitly set a positive exit status, a positive exit status indicates an abnormal exit with an abort or an interrupt. A return value of –1 indicates an error (the new process is not started). In this case, **errno** is set to one of the following values:

E2BIG Argument list exceeds 1024 bytes

EINVAL *mode* argument is invalid

ENOENT File or path is not found

ENOEXEC Specified file is not executable or has invalid executable-file format

ENOMEM Not enough memory is available to execute new process

Parameters

mode Execution mode for calling process

cmdname Path of file to be executed

argv Array of pointers to arguments

Remarks

Each of these functions creates and executes a new process, passing an array of pointers to command-line arguments.

See Also **abort**, **atexit**, **_exec** Functions, **exit**, **_flushall**, **_getmbcp**, **_onexit**, **_setmbcp**, **system**

_spawnve, _wspawnve

Create and execute a new process.

int _spawnve(int *mode*, **const char** ***cmdname*, **const char *const** ***argv*, **const char *const** ***envp* **);**
int _wspawnve(int *mode*, **const wchar_t** ***cmdname*, **const wchar_t *const** ***argv*, **const wchar_t *const** ***envp* **);**

Routine	Required Header	Optional Headers	Compatibility
_spawnve	<stdio.h> or <process.h>		Win 95, Win NT, Win32s
_wspawnve	<stdio.h> or <wchar.h>		Win NT

For additional compatibility information, see "Compatibility" on page ix in the Introduction.

Libraries	
LIBC.LIB	Single thread static library, retail version
LIBCMT.LIB	Multithread static library, retail version
MSVCRT.LIB	Import library for MSVCRTx0.DLL, retail version
MSVCRTx0.DLL	Multithread DLL library, retail version

Return Value

The return value from a synchronous **_spawnve** or **_wspawnve** (**_P_WAIT** specified for *mode*) is the exit status of the new process. The return value from an asynchronous **_spawnve** or **_wspawnve** (**_P_NOWAIT** or **_P_NOWAITO** specified for *mode*) is the process handle. The exit status is 0 if the process terminated normally. You can set the exit status to a nonzero value if the spawned process specifically calls the **exit** routine with a nonzero argument. If the new process did not explicitly set a positive exit status, a positive exit status indicates an abnormal exit with an abort or an interrupt. A return value of –1 indicates an error (the new process is not started). In this case, **errno** is set to one of the following values:

E2BIG Argument list exceeds 1024 bytes

EINVAL *mode* argument is invalid

ENOENT File or path is not found

ENOEXEC Specified file is not executable or has invalid executable-file format

ENOMEM Not enough memory is available to execute new process

Parameters

mode Execution mode for calling process

cmdname Path of file to be executed

argv Array of pointers to arguments

envp Array of pointers to environment settings

Remarks

Each of these functions creates and executes a new process, passing an array of pointers to command-line arguments and an array of pointers to environment settings.

See Also **abort**, **atexit**, **_exec** Functions, **exit**, **_flushall**, **_getmbcp**, **_onexit**, **_setmbcp**, **system**

_spawnvp, _wspawnvp

Create and execute a new process.

int _spawnvp(int *mode*, **const char** ****cmdname*, **const char *const** **argv* **);**
int _wspawnvp(int *mode*, **const wchar_t** **cmdname*, **const wchar_t *const** **argv* **);**

Routine	Required Header	Optional Headers	Compatibility
_spawnvp	<stdio.h> or <process.h>		Win 95, Win NT, Win32s
_wspawnvp	<stdio.h> or <wchar.h>		Win NT

For additional compatibility information, see "Compatibility" on page ix in the Introduction.

Libraries

LIBC.LIB	Single thread static library, retail version
LIBCMT.LIB	Multithread static library, retail version
MSVCRT.LIB	Import library for MSVCRTx0.DLL, retail version
MSVCRTx0.DLL	Multithread DLL library, retail version

Return Value

The return value from a synchronous **_spawnvp** or **_wspawnvp** (**_P_WAIT** specified for *mode*) is the exit status of the new process. The return value from an asynchronous **_spawnvp** or **_wspawnvp** (**_P_NOWAIT** or **_P_NOWAITO** specified for *mode*) is the process handle. The exit status is 0 if the process terminated normally. You can set the exit status to a nonzero value if the spawned process specifically calls the **exit** routine with a nonzero argument. If the new process did not explicitly set a positive exit status, a positive exit status indicates an abnormal exit with an abort or an interrupt. A return value of –1 indicates an error (the new process is not started). In this case, **errno** is set to one of the following values:

E2BIG Argument list exceeds 1024 bytes

EINVAL *mode* argument is invalid

ENOENT File or path is not found

ENOEXEC Specified file is not executable or has invalid executable-file format

ENOMEM Not enough memory is available to execute new process

Parameters

mode Execution mode for calling process

cmdname Path of file to be executed

argv Array of pointers to arguments

Remarks

Each of these functions creates and executes a new process, passing an array of pointers to command-line arguments and using the the **PATH** environment variable to find the file to execute.

See Also **abort**, **atexit**, **_exec** Functions, **exit**, **_flushall**, **_getmbcp**, **_onexit**, **_setmbcp**, **system**

_spawnvpe, _wspawnvpe

Create and execute a new process.

int _spawnvpe(int *mode*, **const char** **cmdname*, **const char *const** **argv*, **const char *const** **envp* **);**

int _wspawnvpe(int *mode*, **const wchar_t** **cmdname*, **const wchar_t *const** **argv*, **const wchar_t *const** **envp* **);**

Routine	Required Header	Optional Headers	Compatibility
_spawnvpe	<stdio.h> or <process.h>		Win 95, Win NT, Win32s
_wspawnvpe	<stdio.h> or <wchar.h>		Win NT

For additional compatibility information, see "Compatibility" on page ix in the Introduction.

Libraries	
LIBC.LIB	Single thread static library, retail version
LIBCMT.LIB	Multithread static library, retail version
MSVCRT.LIB	Import library for MSVCRTx0.DLL, retail version
MSVCRTx0.DLL	Multithread DLL library, retail version

Return Value

The return value from a synchronous **_spawnvpe** or **_wspawnvpe** (**_P_WAIT** specified for *mode*) is the exit status of the new process. The return value from an asynchronous **_spawnvpe** or **_wspawnvpe** (**_P_NOWAIT** or **_P_NOWAITO** specified for *mode*) is the process handle. The exit status is 0 if the process terminated normally. You can set the exit status to a nonzero value if the spawned process specifically calls the **exit** routine with a nonzero argument. If the new process did not explicitly set a positive exit status, a positive exit status indicates an abnormal exit with an abort or an interrupt. A return value of –1 indicates an error (the new process is not started). In this case, **errno** is set to one of the following values:

E2BIG Argument list exceeds 1024 bytes

EINVAL *mode* argument is invalid

ENOENT File or path is not found

ENOEXEC Specified file is not executable or has invalid executable-file format

ENOMEM Not enough memory is available to execute new process

Parameters

mode Execution mode for calling process

cmdname Path of file to be executed

argv Array of pointers to arguments

envp Array of pointers to environment settings

Remarks

Each of these functions creates and executes a new process, passing an array of pointers to command-line arguments and an array of pointers to environment settings. These functions use the **PATH** environment variable to find the file to execute.

See Also **abort**, **atexit**, **_exec** Functions, **exit**, **_flushall**, **_getmbcp**, **_onexit**, **_setmbcp**, **system**

_splitpath, _wsplitpath

Break a path name into components.

void _splitpath(const char **path*, **char** **drive*, **char** **dir*, **char** **fname*, **char** **ext* **);**
void _wsplitpath(const wchar_t **path*, **wchar_t** **drive*, **wchar_t** **dir*, **wchar_t** **fname*, **wchar_t** **ext* **);**

Routine	Required Header	Optional Headers	Compatibility
_splitpath	<stdlib.h>		Win 95, Win NT, Win32s
_wsplitpath	<stdlib.h> or <wchar.h>		Win 95, Win NT, Win32s

For additional compatibility information, see "Compatibility" on page ix in the Introduction.

Libraries	
LIBC.LIB	Single thread static library, retail version
LIBCMT.LIB	Multithread static library, retail version
MSVCRT.LIB	Import library for MSVCRTx0.DLL, retail version
MSVCRTx0.DLL	Multithread DLL library, retail version

Return Value

None

Parameters

path Full path

drive Optional drive letter, followed by a colon (**:**)

dir Optional directory path, including trailing slash. Forward slashes (**/**), backslashes (****), or both may be used.

fname Base filename (no extension)

ext Optional filename extension, including leading period (**.**)

Remarks

The **_splitpath** function breaks a path into its four components. **_splitpath** automatically handles multibyte-character string arguments as appropriate, recognizing multibyte-character sequences according to the multibyte code page currently in use. **_wsplitpath** is a wide-character version of **_splitpath**; the arguments to **_wsplitpath** are wide-character strings. These functions behave identically otherwise.

Each argument is stored in a buffer; the manifest constants **_MAX_DRIVE**, **_MAX_DIR**, **_MAX_FNAME**, and **_MAX_EXT** (defined in STDLIB.H) specify the maximum size necessary for each buffer. The other arguments point to buffers used to store the path elements. After a call to **_splitpath** is executed, these arguments contain empty strings for components not found in *path*. You can pass a **NULL** pointer to **_splitpath** for any component you don't need.

Example

See the example for **_makepath**.

See Also **_fullpath**, **_getmbcp**, **_makepath**, **_setmbcp**

---

sprintf, swprintf

Write formatted data to a string.

int sprintf(char ****buffer*, **const char** **format* [, *argument*] ... **);**
int swprintf(wchar_t **buffer*, **const wchar_t** **format* [, *argument*] ... **);**

Routine	Required Header	Optional Headers	Compatibility
sprintf	<stdio.h>		ANSI, Win 95, Win NT, Win32s, 68K, PMac
swprintf	<stdio.h> or <wchar.h>		ANSI, Win 95, Win NT, Win32s

For additional compatibility information, see "Compatibility" on page ix in the Introduction.

Libraries

LIBC.LIB	Single thread static library, retail version
LIBCMT.LIB	Multithread static library, retail version
MSVCRT.LIB	Import library for MSVCRTx0.DLL, retail version
MSVCRTx0.DLL	Multithread DLL library, retail version

Return Value

sprintf returns the number of bytes stored in *buffer,* not counting the terminating null character. **swprintf** returns the number of wide characters stored in *buffer,* not counting the terminating null wide character.

Parameters

buffer Storage location for output

format Format-control string

argument Optional arguments

For more information, see "printf Format Specification Fields" on page 485.

Remarks

The **sprintf** function formats and stores a series of characters and values in *buffer*. Each *argument* (if any) is converted and output according to the corresponding format specification in *format*. The format consists of ordinary characters and has the same form and function as the *format* argument for **printf**. A null character is appended after the last character written. If copying occurs between strings that overlap, the behavior is undefined.

swprintf is a wide-character version of **sprintf**; the pointer arguments to **swprintf** are wide-character strings. Detection of encoding errors in **swprintf** may differ from that in **sprintf**. **swprintf** and **fwprintf** behave identically except that **swprintf** writes output to a string rather than to a destination of type **FILE**.

Example

```
/* SPRINTF.C: This program uses sprintf to format various
 * data and place them in the string named buffer.
 */

#include <stdio.h>

void main( void )
{
   char  buffer[200], s[] = "computer", c = 'l';
   int   i = 35, j;
   float fp = 1.7320534f;
```

```
    /* Format and print various data: */
    j  = sprintf( buffer,     "\tString:    %s\n", s );
    j += sprintf( buffer + j, "\tCharacter: %c\n", c );
    j += sprintf( buffer + j, "\tInteger:   %d\n", i );
    j += sprintf( buffer + j, "\tReal:      %f\n", fp );

    printf( "Output:\n%s\ncharacter count = %d\n", buffer, j );
}
```

Output

```
Output:
   String:    computer
   Character: l
   Integer:   35
   Real:      1.732053

character count = 71
```

See Also **_snprintf**, **fprintf**, **printf**, **scanf**, **sscanf**, **vprintf** Functions

---

sqrt

Calculates the square root.

double sqrt(double *x* **);**

Routine	Required Header	Optional Headers	Compatibility
sqrt	<math.h>		ANSI, Win 95, Win NT, Win32s, 68K, PMac

For additional compatibility information, see “Compatibility” on page ix in the Introduction.

Libraries	
LIBC.LIB	Single thread static library, retail version
LIBCMT.LIB	Multithread static library, retail version
MSVCRT.LIB	Import library for MSVCRTx0.DLL, retail version
MSVCRTx0.DLL	Multithread DLL library, retail version

Return Value

The **sqrt** function returns the square-root of *x*. If *x* is negative, **sqrt** returns an indefinite (same as a quiet NaN). You can modify error handling with **_matherr**.

Parameter

x Nonnegative floating-point value

Example

```
/* SQRT.C: This program calculates a square root. */

#include <math.h>
#include <stdio.h>
#include <stdlib.h>

void main( void )
{
   double question = 45.35, answer;

   answer = sqrt( question );
   if( question < 0 )
      printf( "Error: sqrt returns %.2f\n, answer" );
   else
      printf( "The square root of %.2f is %.2f\n", question, answer );
}
```

Output

```
The square root of 45.35 is 6.73
```

See Also **exp**, **log**, **pow**

srand

Sets a random starting point.

void srand(unsigned int *seed*);

Routine	Required Header	Optional Headers	Compatibility
srand	<stdlib.h>		ANSI, Win 95, Win NT, Win32s, 68K, PMac

For additional compatibility information, see "Compatibility" on page ix in the Introduction.

Libraries	
LIBC.LIB	Single thread static library, retail version
LIBCMT.LIB	Multithread static library, retail version
MSVCRT.LIB	Import library for MSVCRTx0.DLL, retail version
MSVCRTx0.DLL	Multithread DLL library, retail version

Return Value

None

Parameter

seed Seed for random-number generation

Remarks

The **srand** function sets the starting point for generating a series of pseudorandom integers. To reinitialize the generator, use 1 as the *seed* argument. Any other value for *seed* sets the generator to a random starting point. **rand** retrieves the pseudorandom numbers that are generated. Calling **rand** before any call to **srand** generates the same sequence as calling **srand** with *seed* passed as 1.

Example

See the example for **rand**.

See Also **rand**

---

sscanf, swscanf

Read formatted data from a string.

int sscanf(const char ***buffer*****, const char** ***format*** **[,** ***argument*** **] ...);**
int swscanf(const wchar_t ***buffer*****, const wchar_t** ***format*** **[,** ***argument*** **] ...);**

Routine	Required Header	Optional Headers	Compatibility
sscanf	<stdio.h>		ANSI, Win 95, Win NT, Win32s, 68K, PMac
swscanf	<stdio.h> or <wchar.h>		ANSI, Win 95, Win NT, Win32s

For additional compatibility information, see "Compatibility" on page ix in the Introduction.

Libraries	
LIBC.LIB	Single thread static library, retail version
LIBCMT.LIB	Multithread static library, retail version
MSVCRT.LIB	Import library for MSVCRTx0.DLL, retail version
MSVCRTx0.DLL	Multithread DLL library, retail version

Return Value

Each of these functions returns the number of fields successfully converted and assigned; the return value does not include fields that were read but not assigned. A return value of 0 indicates that no fields were assigned. The return value is **EOF** for an error or if the end of the string is reached before the first conversion.

Parameters

buffer Stored data

format Format-control string

argument Optional arguments

For more information, see “scanf Format Specification Fields” on page 517.

Remarks

The **sscanf** function reads data from *buffer* into the location given by each *argument*. Every *argument* must be a pointer to a variable with a type that corresponds to a type specifier in *format*. The *format* argument controls the interpretation of the input fields and has the same form and function as the *format* argument for the **scanf** function; see **scanf** for a complete description of *format*. If copying takes place between strings that overlap, the behavior is undefined.

swscanf is a wide-character version of **sscanf**; the arguments to **swscanf** are wide-character strings. **sscanf** does not handle multibyte hexidecimal characters. **swscanf** does not handle Unicode fullwidth hexadecimal or “compatibility zone” characters. Otherwise, **swscanf** and **sscanf** behave identically.

Example

```
/* SSCANF.C: This program uses sscanf to read data items
 * from a string named tokenstring, then displays them.
 */

#include <stdio.h>

void main( void )
{
   char  tokenstring[] = "15 12 14...";
   char  s[81];
   char  c;
   int   i;
   float fp;

   /* Input various data from tokenstring: */
   sscanf( tokenstring, "%s", s );
   sscanf( tokenstring, "%c", &c );
   sscanf( tokenstring, "%d", &i );
   sscanf( tokenstring, "%f", &fp );

   /* Output the data read */
   printf( "String    = %s\n", s );
   printf( "Character = %c\n", c );
   printf( "Integer:  = %d\n", i );
   printf( "Real:     = %f\n", fp );
}
```

Output

```
String    = 15
Character = 1
Integer:  = 15
Real:     = 15.000000
```

See Also **fscanf**, **scanf**, **sprintf**, **_snprintf**

_stat, _wstat, _stati64, _wstati64

Get status information on a file.

int _stat(const char ***path*****, struct _stat** ***buffer* **);**
__int64 _stati64(const char ***path*****, struct _stat** ***buffer* **);**
int _wstat(const wchar_t ***path*****, struct _stat** ***buffer* **);**
__int64 _wstati64(const wchar_t ***path*****, struct _stat** ***buffer* **);**

Routine	Required Header	Optional Headers	Compatibility
_stat	<sys/types.h> followed by <sys/stat.h>	<errno.h>	Win 95, Win NT, Win32s, 68K, PMac
_wstat	<sys/types.h> followed by <sys/stat.h> or <wchar.h>	<errno.h>	Win NT
_stati64	<sys/types.h> followed by <sys/stat.h>	<errno.h>	Win 95, Win NT, Win32s
_wstati64	<sys/types.h> followed by <sys/stat.h> or <wchar.h>	<errno.h>	Win NT

For additional compatibility information, see "Compatibility" on page ix in the Introduction.

Libraries	
LIBC.LIB	Single thread static library, retail version
LIBCMT.LIB	Multithread static library, retail version
MSVCRT.LIB	Import library for MSVCRTx0.DLL, retail version
MSVCRTx0.DLL	Multithread DLL library, retail version

Return Value

Each of these functions returns 0 if the file-status information is obtained. A return value of –1 indicates an error, in which case **errno** is set to **ENOENT**, indicating that the filename or path could not be found.

Parameters

path Path of existing file

buffer Pointer to structure that stores results

Remarks

The **_stat** function obtains information about the file or directory specified by *path* and stores it in the structure pointed to by *buffer*. **_stat** automatically handles multibyte-character string arguments as appropriate, recognizing multibyte-character sequences according to the multibyte code page currently in use.

_wstat is a wide-character version of **_stat**; the *path* argument to **_wstat** is a wide-character string. **_wstat** and **_stat** behave identically except that **_wstat** does not handle multibyte-character strings.

The **_stat** structure, defined in SYS\STAT.H, includes the following fields.

gid Numeric identifier of group that owns file (UNIX-specific)

st_atime Time of last access of file.

st_ctime Time of creation of file.

st_dev Drive number of the disk containing the file (same as **st_rdev**).

st_ino Number of the information node (the *inode*) for the file (UNIX-specific). On UNIX file systems, the inode describes the file date and time stamps, permissions, and content. When files are soft-linked to one another, they share the same inode. The inode, and therefore **st_ino**, has no meaning in the FAT, HPFS, or NTFS file systems.

st_mode Bit mask for file-mode information. The **_S_IFDIR** bit is set if *path* specifies a directory; the **_S_IFREG** bit is set if *path* specifies an ordinary file or a device. User read/write bits are set according to the file's permission mode; user execute bits are set according to the filename extension.

st_mtime Time of last modification of file.

st_nlink Always 1 on non-NTFS file systems.

st_rdev Drive number of the disk containing the file (same as **st_dev**).

st_size Size of the file in bytes; a 64-bit integer for **_stati64** and **_wstati64**

uid Numeric identifier of user who owns file (UNIX-specific)

If *path* refers to a device, the size, time, **_dev**, and **_rdev** fields in the **_stat** structure are meaningless. Because STAT.H uses the **_dev_t** type that is defined in TYPES.H, you must include TYPES.H before STAT.H in your code.

Example

```
/* STAT.C: This program uses the _stat function to
 * report information about the file named STAT.C.
 */

#include <time.h>
#include <sys/types.h>
#include <sys/stat.h>
#include <stdio.h>

void main( void )
{
   struct _stat buf;
   int result;
   char buffer[] = "A line to output";
```

```
    /* Get data associated with "stat.c": */
    result = _stat( "stat.c", &buf );

    /* Check if statistics are valid: */
    if( result != 0 )
       perror( "Problem getting information" );
    else
    {
       /* Output some of the statistics: */
       printf( "File size     : %ld\n", buf.st_size );
       printf( "Drive         : %c:\n", buf.st_dev + 'A' );
       printf( "Time modified : %s", ctime( &buf.st_atime ) );
    }
}
```

Output

```
File size     : 745
Drive         : C:
Time modified : Tue May 03 00:00:00 1994
```

See Also **_access**, **_fstat**, **_getmbcp**, **_setmbcp**

_status87, _statusfp

Get the floating point status word.

unsigned int _status87(void);
unsigned int _statusfp(void);

Routine	Required Header	Optional Headers	Compatibility
_status87	<float.h>		Win 95, Win NT, Win32s
_statusfp	<float.h>		Win 95, Win NT, Win32s, 68K, PMac

For additional compatibility information, see "Compatibility" on page ix in the Introduction.

Libraries	
LIBC.LIB	Single thread static library, retail version
LIBCMT.LIB	Multithread static library, retail version
MSVCRT.LIB	Import library for MSVCRTx0.DLL, retail version
MSVCRTx0.DLL	Multithread DLL library, retail version

Return Value

The bits in the value returned indicate the floating-point status. See the FLOAT.H include file for a complete definition of the bits returned by **_status87**.

Many math library functions modify the 8087/80287 status word, with unpredictable results. Return values from **_clear87** and **_status87** are more reliable if fewer floating-point operations are performed between known states of the floating-point status word.

Remarks

The **_status87** function gets the floating-point status word. The status word is a combination of the 8087/80287/80387 status word and other conditions detected by the 8087/80287/80387 exception handler, such as floating-point stack overflow and underflow. Unmasked exceptions are checked for before returning the contents of the status word. This means that the caller is informed of pending exceptions.

_statusfp is a platform-independent, portable version of **_status87**. It is identical to **_status87** on Intel (x86) platforms and is also supported by the MIPS platform. To ensure that your floating-point code is portable to MIPS, use **_statusfp**. If you are only targeting x86 platforms, use either **_status87** or **_statusfp**.

Example

```
/* STATUS87.C: This program creates various floating-point errors and
 * then uses _status87 to display messages indicating these problems.
 * Compile this program with optimizations disabled (/Od). Otherwise,
 * the optimizer removes the code related to the unused floating-
 * point values.
 */

#include <stdio.h>
#include <float.h>

void main( void )
{
   double a = 1e-40, b;
   float  x, y;

   printf( "Status = %.4x - clear\n",_status87() );

   /* Assignment into y is inexact & underflows: */
   y = a;
   printf( "Status = %.4x - inexact, underflow\n", _status87() );

   /* y is denormal: */
   b = y;
   printf( "Status = %.4x - inexact underflow, denormal\n",
           _status87() );

   /* Clear user 8087: */
   _clear87();
}
```

Output

```
Status = 0000 - clear
Status = 0003 - inexact, underflow
Status = 80003 - inexact underflow, denormal
```

See Also **_clear87**, **_control87**

strcat, wcscat, _mbscat

Append a string.

char *strcat(char ***_string1_, const char ***_string2_ **);**
wchar_t *wcscat(wchar_t ***_string1_, const wchar_t ***_string2_ **);**
unsigned char *_mbscat(unsigned char ***_string1_, const unsigned char ***_string2_ **);**

Routine	Required Header	Optional Headers	Compatibility
strcat	<string.h>		ANSI, Win 95, Win NT, Win32s, 68K, PMac
wcscat	<string.h> or <wchar.h>		ANSI, Win 95, Win NT, Win32s
_mbscat	<mbstring.h>		Win 95, Win NT, Win32s, 68K, PMac

For additional compatibility information, see "Compatibility" on page ix in the Introduction.

Libraries	
LIBC.LIB	Single thread static library, retail version
LIBCMT.LIB	Multithread static library, retail version
MSVCRT.LIB	Import library for MSVCRTx0.DLL, retail version
MSVCRTx0.DLL	Multithread DLL library, retail version

Return Value

Each of these functions returns the destination string (*string1*). No return value is reserved to indicate an error.

Parameters

string1 Null-terminated destination string

string2 Null-terminated source string

Remarks

The **strcat** function appends *string2* to *string1* and terminates the resulting string with a null character. The initial character of *string2* overwrites the terminating null character of *string1*. No overflow checking is performed when strings are copied or appended. The behavior of **strcat** is undefined if the source and destination strings overlap.

wcscat and **_mbscat** are wide-character and multibyte-character versions of **strcat**. The arguments and return value of **wcscat** are wide-character strings; those of **_mbscat** are multibyte-character strings. These three functions behave identically otherwise.

Example

See the example for **strcpy**.

See Also **strncat**, **strncmp**, **strncpy**, **_strnicmp**, **strrchr**, **strspn**

strchr, wcschr, _mbschr

Find a character in a string.

char *strchr(const char ***string*, **int *c* **);**
wchar_t *wcschr(const wchar_t ***string*, **wint_t *c* **);**
unsigned char *_mbschr(const unsigned char ***string*, **unsigned int *c* **);**

Routine	Required Header	Optional Headers	Compatibility
strchr	<string.h>		ANSI, Win 95, Win NT, Win32s, 68K, PMac
wcschr	<string.h> or <wchar.h>		ANSI, Win 95, Win NT, Win32s
_mbschr	<mbstring.h>		Win 95, Win NT, Win32s, 68K, PMac

For additional compatibility information, see "Compatibility" on page ix in the Introduction.

Libraries	
LIBC.LIB	Single thread static library, retail version
LIBCMT.LIB	Multithread static library, retail version
MSVCRT.LIB	Import library for MSVCRTx0.DLL, retail version
MSVCRTx0.DLL	Multithread DLL library, retail version

Return Value

Each of these functions returns a pointer to the first occurrence of *c* in *string*, or **NULL** if *c* is not found.

Parameters

string Null-terminated source string

c Character to be located

Remarks

The **strchr** function finds the first occurrence of *c* in *string*, or it returns **NULL** if *c* is not found. The null-terminating character is included in the search.

wcschr and **_mbschr** are wide-character and multibyte-character versions of **strchr**. The arguments and return value of **wcschr** are wide-character strings; those of **_mbschr** are multibyte-character strings. **_mbschr** recognizes multibyte-character sequences according to the multibyte code page currently in use. These three functions behave identically otherwise.

Example

```
/* STRCHR.C: This program illustrates searching for a character
 * with strchr (search forward) or strrchr (search backward).
 */

#include <string.h>
#include <stdio.h>

int  ch = 'r';

char string[] = "The quick brown dog jumps over the lazy fox";
char fmt1[] =   "         1         2         3         4         5";
char fmt2[] =   "12345678901234567890123456789012345678901234567890";

void main( void )
{
   char *pdest;
   int result;

   printf( "String to be searched: \n\t\t%s\n", string );
   printf( "\t\t%s\n\t\t%s\n\n", fmt1, fmt2 );
   printf( "Search char:\t%c\n", ch );

   /* Search forward. */
   pdest = strchr( string, ch );
   result = pdest - string + 1;
   if( pdest != NULL )
      printf( "Result:\tfirst %c found at position %d\n\n",
              ch, result );
   else
      printf( "Result:\t%c not found\n" );

   /* Search backward. */
   pdest = strrchr( string, ch );
   result = pdest - string + 1;
   if( pdest != NULL )
      printf( "Result:\tlast %c found at position %d\n\n", ch, result );
   else
      printf( "Result:\t%c not found\n" );
}
```

Output

```
String to be searched:
      The quick brown dog jumps over the lazy fox
               1         2         3         4         5
      12345678901234567890123456789012345678901234567890

Search char:   r
Result:   first r found at position 12

Result:   last r found at position 30
```

See Also **strcspn**, **strncat**, **strncmp**, **strncpy**, **_strnicmp**, **strpbrk**, **strrchr**, **strstr**

---

strcmp, wcscmp, _mbscmp

Compare strings.

int strcmp(const char ****string1*, **const char** ****string2* **);**
int wcscmp(const wchar_t ****string1*, **const wchar_t** ****string2* **);**
int _mbscmp(const unsigned char ****string1*, **const unsigned char** ****string2* **);**

Routine	Required Header	Optional Headers	Compatibility
strcmp	<string.h>		ANSI, Win 95, Win NT, Win32s, 68K, PMac
wcscmp	<string.h> or <wchar.h>		ANSI, Win 95, Win NT, Win32s
_mbscmp	<mbstring.h>		Win 95, Win NT, Win32s, 68K, PMac

For additional compatibility information, see "Compatibility" on page ix in the Introduction.

Libraries	
LIBC.LIB	Single thread static library, retail version
LIBCMT.LIB	Multithread static library, retail version
MSVCRT.LIB	Import library for MSVCRTx0.DLL, retail version
MSVCRTx0.DLL	Multithread DLL library, retail version

Return Value

The return value for each of these functions indicates the lexicographic relation of *string1* to *string2*.

Value	Relationship of string1 to string2
< 0	*string1* less than *string2*
0	*string1* identical to *string2*
> 0	*string1* greater than *string2*

On an error, **_mbscmp** returns **_NLSCMPERROR**, which is defined in STRING.H and MBSTRING.H.

Parameters

string1, string2 Null-terminated strings to compare

Remarks

The **strcmp** function compares *string1* and *string2* lexicographically and returns a value indicating their relationship. **wcscmp** and **_mbscmp** are wide-character and multibyte-character versions of **strcmp**. The arguments and return value of **wcscmp** are wide-character strings; those of **_mbscmp** are multibyte-character strings. **_mbscmp** recognizes multibyte-character sequences according to the current multibyte code page and returns **_NLSCMPERROR** on an error. (For more information, see "Code Pages" on page 22.) These three functions behave identically otherwise.

The **strcmp** functions differ from the **strcoll** functions in that **strcmp** comparisons are not affected by locale, whereas the manner of **strcoll** comparisons is determined by the **LC_COLLATE** category of the current locale. For more information on the **LC_COLLATE** category, see **setlocale**.

In the "C" locale, the order of characters in the character set (ASCII character set) is the same as the lexicographic character order. However, in other locales, the order of characters in the character set may differ from the lexicographic order. For example, in certain European locales, the character 'a' (value 0x61) precedes the character 'ä' (value 0xE4) in the character set, but the character 'ä' precedes the character 'a' lexicographically.

In locales for which the character set and the lexicographic character order differ, use **strcoll** rather than **strcmp** for lexicographic comparison of strings according to the **LC_COLLATE** category setting of the current locale. Thus, to perform a lexicographic comparison of the locale in the above example, use **strcoll** rather than **strcmp**. Alternatively, you can use **strxfrm** on the original strings, then use **strcmp** on the resulting strings.

_stricmp, _wcsicmp, and **_mbsicmp** compare strings by first converting them to their lowercase forms.Two strings containing characters located between 'Z' and 'a' in the ASCII table ('[', '\', ']', '^', '_', and '`') compare differently, depending on their case. For example, the two strings `"ABCDE"` and `"ABCD^"` compare one way if the comparison is lowercase (`"abcde"` > `"abcd^"`) and the other way (`"ABCDE"` < `"ABCD^"`) if the comparison is uppercase.

Example

```
/* STRCMP.C */

#include <string.h>
#include <stdio.h>

char string1[] = "The quick brown dog jumps over the lazy fox";
char string2[] = "The QUICK brown dog jumps over the lazy fox";

void main( void )
{
   char tmp[20];
   int result;
   /* Case sensitive */
   printf( "Compare strings:\n\t%s\n\t%s\n\n", string1, string2 );
   result = strcmp( string1, string2 );
   if( result > 0 )
      strcpy( tmp, "greater than" );
   else if( result < 0 )
      strcpy( tmp, "less than" );
   else
      strcpy( tmp, "equal to" );
   printf( "\tstrcmp:   String 1 is %s string 2\n", tmp );
   /* Case insensitive (could use equivalent _stricmp) */
   result = _stricmp( string1, string2 );
   if( result > 0 )
      strcpy( tmp, "greater than" );
   else if( result < 0 )
      strcpy( tmp, "less than" );
   else
      strcpy( tmp, "equal to" );
   printf( "\t_stricmp:  String 1 is %s string 2\n", tmp );
}
```

Output

```
Compare strings:
    The quick brown dog jumps over the lazy fox
    The QUICK brown dog jumps over the lazy fox

    strcmp:   String 1 is greater than string 2
    _stricmp:  String 1 is equal to string 2
```

See Also **memcmp**, **_memicmp**, **strcoll** Functions, **_stricmp**, **strncmp**, **_strnicmp**, **strrchr**, **strspn**, **strxfrm**

strcoll Functions

Each of the **strcoll** and **wcscoll** functions compares two strings according to the **LC_COLLATE** category setting of the locale code page currently in use. Each of the **_mbscoll** functions compares two strings according to the multibyte code page currently in use. Use the **coll** functions for string comparisons when there is a difference between the character set order and the lexicographic character order in the current code page and this difference is of interest for the comparison. Use the corresponding **cmp** functions to test only for string equality.

strcoll Functions

SBCS	Unicode	MBCS	Description
strcoll	**wcscoll**	**_mbscoll**	Collate two strings
_stricoll	**_wcsicoll**	**_mbsicoll**	Collate two strings (case insensitive)
_strncoll	**_wcsncoll**	**_mbsncoll**	Collate first *count* characters of two strings
_strnicoll	**_wcsnicoll**	**_mbsnicoll**	Collate first *count* characters of two strings (case-insensitive)

Remarks

The single-byte character (SBCS) versions of these functions (**strcoll**, **stricoll**, **_strncoll**, and **_strnicoll**) compare *string1* and *string2* according to the **LC_COLLATE** category setting of the current locale. These functions differ from the corresponding **strcmp** functions in that the **strcoll** functions use locale code page information that provides collating sequences. For string comparisons in locales in which the character set order and the lexicographic character order differ, the **strcoll** functions should be used rather than the corresponding **strcmp** functions. For more information on **LC_COLLATE**, see **setlocale**.

For some code pages and corresponding character sets, the order of characters in the character set may differ from the lexicographic character order. In the "C" locale, this is not the case: the order of characters in the ASCII character set is the same as the lexicographic order of the characters. However, in certain European code pages, for example, the character 'a' (value 0x61) precedes the character 'ä' (value 0xE4) in the character set, but the character 'ä' precedes the character 'a' lexicographically. To perform a lexicographic comparison in such an instance, use **strcoll** rather than **strcmp**. Alternatively, you can use **strxfrm** on the original strings, then use **strcmp** on the resulting strings.

strcoll, **stricoll**, **_strncoll**, and **_strnicoll** automatically handle multibyte-character strings according to the locale code page currently in use, as do their wide-character (Unicode) counterparts. The multibyte-character (MBCS) versions of these functions, however, collate strings on a character basis according to the multibyte code page currently in use.

Because the **coll** functions collate strings lexicographically for comparison, whereas the **cmp** functions simply test for string equality, the **coll** functions are much slower than the corresponding **cmp** versions. Therefore, the **coll** functions should be used only when there is a difference between the character set order and the lexicographic character order in the current code page and this difference is of interest for the string comparison.

See Also **localeconv**, **_mbsnbcoll**, **setlocale**, **strcmp**, **strncmp**, **_strnicmp**, **strxfrm**

strcoll, wcscoll, _mbscoll

Compare strings using locale-specific information.

int strcoll(const char **string1*, **const char** **string2* **);**
int wcscoll(const wchar_t **string1*, **const wchar_t** **string2* **);**
int _mbscoll(const unsigned char **string1*, **const unsigned char** **string2* **);**

Routine	Required Header	Optional Headers	Compatibility
strcoll	<string.h>		ANSI, Win 95, Win NT, Win32s, 68K, PMac
wcscoll	<wchar.h>, <string.h>		ANSI, Win 95, Win NT, Win32s
_mbscoll	<mbstring.h>		Win 95, Win NT, Win32s, 68K, PMac

For additional compatibility information, see "Compatibility" on page ix in the Introduction.

Libraries	
LIBC.LIB	Single thread static library, retail version
LIBCMT.LIB	Multithread static library, retail version
MSVCRT.LIB	Import library for MSVCRTx0.DLL, retail version
MSVCRTx0.DLL	Multithread DLL library, retail version

Return Value

Each of these functions returns a value indicating the relationship of *string1* to *string2,* as follows.

Return Value	Relationship of string1 to string2
< 0	*string1* less than *string2*
0	*string1* identical to *string2*
> 0	*string1* greater than *string2*

Each of these functions returns **_NLSCMPERROR** on an error. To use **_NLSCMPERROR**, include either STRING.H or MBSTRING.H. **wcscoll** can fail if either *string1* or *string2* contains wide-character codes outside the domain of the collating sequence. When an error occurs, **wcscoll** may set **errno** to **EINVAL**. To check for an error on a call to **wcscoll**, set **errno** to 0 and then check **errno** after calling **wcscoll**.

Parameters

string1, string2 Null-terminated strings to compare

Remarks

Each of these functions performs a case-sensitive comparison of *string1* and *string2* according to the code page currently in use. These functions should be used only when there is a difference between the character set order and the lexicographic character order in the current code page and this difference is of interest for the string comparison.

See Also **localeconv**, **_mbsnbcoll**, **setlocale**, **strcmp**, **_stricmp**, **strncmp**, **_strnicmp**, **strxfrm**

_stricoll, _wcsicoll, _mbsicoll

Compare strings using locale-specific information.

int _stricoll(const char **string1*, **const char** **string2* **);**
int _wcsicoll(const wchar_t **string1*, **const wchar_t** **string2* **);**
int _mbsicoll(const unsigned char **string1*, **const unsigned char** **string2*);

Routine	Required Header	Optional Headers	Compatibility
_stricoll	<string.h>		Win 95, Win NT, Win32s, 68K, PMac
_wcsicoll	<wchar.h>, <string.h>		Win 95, Win NT, Win32s
_mbsicoll	<mbstring.h>		Win 95, Win NT, Win32s, 68K, PMac

For additional compatibility information, see "Compatibility" on page ix in the Introduction.

Libraries	
LIBC.LIB	Single thread static library, retail version
LIBCMT.LIB	Multithread static library, retail version
MSVCRT.LIB	Import library for MSVCRTx0.DLL, retail version
MSVCRTx0.DLL	Multithread DLL library, retail version

Return Value

Each of these functions returns a value indicating the relationship of *string1* to *string2,* as follows.

Return Value	Relationship of string1 to string2
< 0	*string1* less than *string2*
0	*string1* identical to *string2*
> 0	*string1* greater than *string2*

Each of these functions returns **_NLSCMPERROR**. To use **_NLSCMPERROR**, include either STRING.H or MBSTRING.H. **_wcsicoll** can fail if either *string1* or *string2* contains wide-character codes outside the domain of the collating sequence. When an error occurs, **_wcsicoll** may set **errno** to **EINVAL**. To check for an error on a call to **_wcsicoll**, set **errno** to 0 and then check **errno** after calling **_wcsicoll**.

Parameters

string1, string2 Null-terminated strings to compare

Remarks

Each of these functions performs a case-insensitive comparison of *string1* and *string2* according to the code page currently in use. These functions should be used only when there is a difference between the character set order and the lexicographic character order in the current code page and this difference is of interest for the string comparison.

See Also **localeconv**, **_mbsnbcoll**, **setlocale**, **strcmp**, **_stricmp**, **strncmp**, **_strnicmp**, **strxfrm**

_strncoll, _wcsncoll, _mbsncoll

Compare strings using locale-specific information.

int _strncoll(const char **string1*, **const char** **string2*, **size_t** *count* **);**
int _wcsncoll(const wchar_t **string1*, **const wchar_t** **string2*, **size_t** *count* **);**
int _mbsncoll(const unsigned char **string1*, **const unsigned char** **string2*, **size_t** *count* **);**

Routine	Required Header	Optional Headers	Compatibility
_strncoll	<string.h>		Win 95, Win NT, Win32s, 68K, PMac
_wcsncoll	<wchar.h> or <string.h>		Win 95, Win NT, Win32s
_mbsncoll	<mbstring.h>		Win 95, Win NT, Win32s, 68K, PMac

For additional compatibility information, see "Compatibility" on page ix in the Introduction.

Libraries

LIBC.LIB	Single thread static library, retail version
LIBCMT.LIB	Multithread static library, retail version
MSVCRT.LIB	Import library for MSVCRTx0.DLL, retail version
MSVCRTx0.DLL	Multithread DLL library, retail version

Return Value

Each of these functions returns a value indicating the relationship of the substrings of *string1* and *string2,* as follows.

Return Value	Relationship of string1 to string2
< 0	*string1* less than *string2*
0	*string1* identical to *string2*
> 0	*string1* greater than *string2*

Each of these functions returns **_NLSCMPERROR**. To use **_NLSCMPERROR**, include either STRING.H or MBSTRING.H. **_wcsncoll** can fail if either *string1* or *string2* contains wide-character codes outside the domain of the collating sequence. When an error occurs, **_wcsncoll** may set **errno** to **EINVAL**. To check for an error on a call to **_wcsncoll**, set **errno** to 0 and then check **errno** after calling **_wcsncoll.**

Parameters

string1, string2 Null-terminated strings to compare

count Number of characters to compare

Remarks

Each of these functions performs a case-sensitive comparison of the first *count* characters in *string1* and *string2* according to the code page currently in use. These functions should be used only when there is a difference between the character set order and the lexicographic character order in the current code page and this difference is of interest for the string comparison.

See Also **localeconv**, **_mbsnbcoll**, **setlocale**, **strcmp**, **_stricmp**, **strncmp**, **_strnicmp**, **strxfrm**

_strnicoll, _wcsnicoll, _mbsnicoll

Compare strings using locale-specific information.

int _strnicoll(const char **string1*, **const char** **string2*, **size_t** *count* **);**
int _wcsnicoll(const wchar_t **string1*, **const wchar_t** **string2* **, size_t** *count* **);**
int _mbsnicoll(const unsigned char **string1*, **const unsigned char** **string2*, **size_t** *count* **);**

Routine	Required Header	Optional Headers	Compatibility
_strnicoll	<string.h>		Win 95, Win NT, Win32s, 68K, PMac
_wcsnicoll	<wchar.h> or <string.h>		Win 95, Win NT, Win32s
_mbsnicoll	<mbstring.h>		Win 95, Win NT, Win32s, 68K, PMac

For additional compatibility information, see "Compatibility" on page ix in the Introduction.

Libraries	
LIBC.LIB	Single thread static library, retail version
LIBCMT.LIB	Multithread static library, retail version
MSVCRT.LIB	Import library for MSVCRTx0.DLL, retail version
MSVCRTx0.DLL	Multithread DLL library, retail version

Return Value

Each of these functions returns a value indicating the relationship of the substrings of *string1* and *string2*, as follows.

Return Value	Relationship of string1 to string2
< 0	*string1* less than *string2*
0	*string1* identical to *string2*
> 0	*string1* greater than *string2*

Each of these functions returns **_NLSCMPERROR**. To use **_NLSCMPERROR**, include either STRING.H or MBSTRING.H. **_wcsnicoll** can fail if either *string1* or *string2* contains wide-character codes outside the domain of the collating sequence. When an error occurs, **_wcsnicoll** may set **errno** to **EINVAL**. To check for an error on a call to **_wcsnicoll**, set **errno** to 0 and then check **errno** after calling **_wcsnicoll.**

Parameters

string1, string2 Null-terminated strings to compare

count Number of characters to compare

Remarks

Each of these functions performs a case-insensitive comparison of the first *count* characters in *string1* and *string2* according to the code page currently in use. These functions should be used only when there is a difference between the character set order and the lexicographic character order in the current code page and this difference is of interest for the string comparison.

See Also **localeconv**, **_mbsnbcoll**, **setlocale**, **strcmp**, **_stricmp**, **strncmp**, **_strnicmp**, **strxfrm**

strcpy, wcscpy, _mbscpy

Copy a string.

char *strcpy(char ***_string1_, const char ***_string2_ **);**
wchar_t *wcscpy(wchar_t ***_string1_, const wchar_t ***_string2_ **);**
unsigned char *_mbscpy(unsigned char ***_string1_, const unsigned char ***_string2_ **);**

Routine	Required Header	Optional Headers	Compatibility
strcpy	<string.h>		ANSI, Win 95, Win NT, Win32s, 68K, PMac
wcscpy	<string.h> or <wchar.h>		ANSI, Win 95, Win NT, Win32s
_mbscpy	<mbstring.h>		Win 95, Win NT, Win32s, 68K, PMac

For additional compatibility information, see "Compatibility" on page ix in the Introduction.

Libraries	
LIBC.LIB	Single thread static library, retail version
LIBCMT.LIB	Multithread static library, retail version
MSVCRT.LIB	Import library for MSVCRTx0.DLL, retail version
MSVCRTx0.DLL	Multithread DLL library, retail version

Return Value

Each of these functions returns the destination string. No return value is reserved to indicate an error.

Parameters

string1 Destination string

string2 Null-terminated source string

Remarks

The **strcpy** function copies *string2*, including the terminating null character, to the location specified by *string1*. No overflow checking is performed when strings are copied or appended. The behavior of **strcpy** is undefined if the source and destination strings overlap.

wcscpy and **_mbscpy** are wide-character and multibyte-character versions of **strcpy**. The arguments and return value of **wcscpy** are wide-character strings; those of **_mbscpy** are multibyte-character strings. These three functions behave identically otherwise.

Example

```
/* STRCPY.C: This program uses strcpy
 * and strcat to build a phrase.
 */

#include <string.h>
#include <stdio.h>

void main( void )
{
   char string[80];
   strcpy( string, "Hello world from " );
   strcat( string, "strcpy " );
   strcat( string, "and " );
   strcat( string, "strcat!" );
   printf( "String = %s\n", string );
}
```

Output

```
String = Hello world from strcpy and strcat!
```

See Also **strcat**, **strcmp**, **strncat**, **strncmp**, **strncpy**, **_strnicmp**, **strrchr**, **strspn**

strcspn, wcscspn, _mbscspn

Find a substring in a string.

size_t strcspn(const char ****string1*, **const char ****string2* **);
size_t wcscspn(const wchar_t ****string1*, **const wchar_t ****string2* **);
size_t _mbscspn(const unsigned char ****string1*, **const unsigned char ****string2* **);

Routine	Required Header	Optional Headers	Compatibility
strcspn	<string.h>		ANSI, Win 95, Win NT, Win32s, 68K, PMac
wcscspn	<string.h> or <wchar.h>		ANSI, Win 95, Win NT, Win32s
_mbscspn	<mbstring.h>		Win 95, Win NT, Win32s, 68K, PMac

For additional compatibility information, see "Compatibility" on page ix in the Introduction.

Libraries

LIBC.LIB	Single thread static library, retail version
LIBCMT.LIB	Multithread static library, retail version
MSVCRT.LIB	Import library for MSVCRTx0.DLL, retail version
MSVCRTx0.DLL	Multithread DLL library, retail version

Return Value

Each of these functions returns an integer value specifying the length of the initial segment of *string1* that consists entirely of characters not in *string2*. If *string1* begins with a character that is in *string2*, the function returns 0. No return value is reserved to indicate an error.

Parameters

string1 Null-terminated searched string

string2 Null-terminated character set

Remarks

The **strcspn** function returns the index of the first occurrence of a character in *string1* that belongs to the set of characters in *string2*. Terminating null characters are not included in the search.

wcscspn and **_mbscspn** are wide-character and multibyte-character versions of **strcspn.** The arguments of **wcscspn** are wide-character strings; those of **_mbscspn** are multibyte-character strings. These three functions behave identically otherwise.

Example

```
/* STRCSPN.C */

#include <string.h>
#include <stdio.h>

void main( void )
{
   char string[] = "xyzabc";
   int  pos;

   pos = strcspn( string, "abc" );
   printf( "First a, b or c in %s is at character %d\n",
           string, pos );
}
```

Output

```
First a, b or c in xyzabc is at character 3
```

See Also **strncat**, **strncmp**, **strncpy**, **_strnicmp**, **strrchr**, **strspn**

_strdate, _wstrdate

Copy a date to a buffer.

char *_strdate(char ***_datestr_ **);
wchar_t *_wstrdate(wchar_t ***_datestr_ **);

Routine	Required Header	Optional Headers	Compatibility
_strdate	<time.h>		Win 95, Win NT, Win32s, 68K, PMac
_wstrdate	<time.h> or <wchar.h>		Win 95, Win NT, Win32s

For additional compatibility information, see "Compatibility" on page ix in the Introduction.

Libraries	
LIBC.LIB	Single thread static library, retail version
LIBCMT.LIB	Multithread static library, retail version
MSVCRT.LIB	Import library for MSVCRTx0.DLL, retail version
MSVCRTx0.DLL	Multithread DLL library, retail version

Return Value

Each of these functions returns a pointer to the resulting character string *datestr*.

Parameter

datestr A pointer to a buffer containing the formatted date string

Remarks

The **_strdate** function copies a date to the buffer pointed to by *datestr,* formatted *mm*/*dd*/*yy*, where *mm* is two digits representing the month, *dd* is two digits representing the day, and *yy* is the last two digits of the year. For example, the string `12/05/99` represents December 5, 1999. The buffer must be at least 9 bytes long.

_wstrdate is a wide-character version of **_strdate**; the argument and return value of **_wstrdate** are wide-character strings. These functions behave identically otherwise.

Example

See the example for the **time** function.

See Also **asctime**, **ctime**, **gmtime**, **localtime**, **mktime**, **time**, **_tzset**

_strdup, _wcsdup, _mbsdup

Duplicate strings.

char *_strdup(const char ***string* **);
wchar_t *_wcsdup(const wchar_t ***string* **);
unsigned char *_mbsdup(const unsigned char ***string* **);

Routine	Required Header	Optional Headers	Compatibility
_strdup	<string.h>		Win 95, Win NT, Win32s, 68K, PMac
_wcsdup	<string.h> or <wchar.h>		Win 95, Win NT, Win32s
_mbsdup	<mbstring.h>		Win 95, Win NT, Win32s, 68K, PMac

For additional compatibility information, see "Compatibility" on page ix in the Introduction.

Libraries	
LIBC.LIB	Single thread static library, retail version
LIBCMT.LIB	Multithread static library, retail version
MSVCRT.LIB	Import library for MSVCRTx0.DLL, retail version
MSVCRTx0.DLL	Multithread DLL library, retail version

Return Value

Each of these functions returns a pointer to the storage location for the copied string or **NULL** if storage cannot be allocated.

Parameter

string Null-terminated source string

Remarks

The **_strdup** function calls **malloc** to allocate storage space for a copy of *string* and then copies *string* to the allocated space.

_wcsdup and **_mbsdup** are wide-character and multibyte-character versions of **_strdup**. The arguments and return value of **_wcsdup** are wide-character strings; those of **_mbsdup** are multibyte-character strings. These three functions behave identically otherwise.

Because **_strdup** calls **malloc** to allocate storage space for the copy of *string*, it is good practice always to release this memory by calling the **free** routine on the pointer returned by the call to **_strdup**.

Example

```
/* STRDUP.C */

#include <string.h>
#include <stdio.h>

void main( void )
{
   char buffer[] = "This is the buffer text";
   char *newstring;
   printf( "Original: %s\n", buffer );
   newstring = _strdup( buffer );
   printf( "Copy:     %s\n", newstring );
   free( newstring );
}
```

Output

```
Original: This is the buffer text
Copy:     This is the buffer text
```

See Also **memset**, **strcat**, **strcmp**, **strncat**, **strncmp**, **strncpy**, **_strnicmp**, **strrchr**, **strspn**

strerror, _strerror

Get a system error message (**strerror**) or prints a user supplied error message (**_strerror**).

char *strerror(int *errnum* **);**
char *_strerror(const char **string* **);**

Routine	Required Header	Optional Headers	Compatibility
strerror	<string.h>		ANSI, Win 95, Win NT, Win32s, 68K, PMac
_strerror	<string.h>		Win 95, Win NT, Win32s, 68K, PMac

For additional compatibility information, see "Compatibility" on page ix in the Introduction.

Libraries	
LIBC.LIB	Single thread static library, retail version
LIBCMT.LIB	Multithread static library, retail version
MSVCRT.LIB	Import library for MSVCRTx0.DLL, retail version
MSVCRTx0.DLL	Multithread DLL library, retail version

Return Value

strerror and **_strerror** return a pointer to the error-message string. Subsequent calls to **strerror** or **_strerror** can overwrite the string.

Parameters

errnum Error number

string User-supplied message

Remarks

The **strerror** function maps *errnum* to an error-message string, returning a pointer to the string. Neither **strerror** nor **_strerror** actually prints the message: For that, you need to call an output function such as **fprintf**:

```
if (( _access( "datafile",2 )) == -1 )
   fprintf( stderr, strerror(NULL) );
```

If *string* is passed as **NULL**, **_strerror** returns a pointer to a string containing the system error message for the last library call that produced an error. The error-message string is terminated by the newline character ('\n'). If *string* is not equal to **NULL**, then **_strerror** returns a pointer to a string containing (in order) your string message, a colon, a space, the system error message for the last library call producing an error, and a newline character. Your string message can be, at most, 94 bytes long.

The actual error number for **_strerror** is stored in the variable **errno**. The system error messages are accessed through the variable **_sys_errlist**, which is an array of messages ordered by error number. **_strerror** accesses the appropriate error message by using the **errno** value as an index to the variable **_sys_errlist**. The value of the variable **_sys_nerr** is defined as the maximum number of elements in the **_sys_errlist** array. To produce accurate results, call **_strerror** immediately after a library routine returns with an error. Otherwise, subsequent calls to **strerror** or **_strerror** can overwrite the **errno** value.

_strerror is not part of the ANSI definition but is instead a Microsoft extension to it. Do not use it where portability is desired; for ANSI compatibility, use **strerror** instead.

Example

See the example for **perror**.

See Also **clearerr**, **ferror**, **perror**

strftime, wcsftime

Format a time string.

size_t strftime(char **string*, **size_t** *maxsize*, **const char** **format*, **const struct tm** **timeptr* **);**
size_t wcsftime(wchar_t **string*, **size_t** *maxsize*, **const wchar_t** **format*, **const struct tm** **timeptr* **);**

Routine	Required Header	Optional Headers	Compatibility
strftime	<time.h>		ANSI, Win 95, Win NT, Win32s, 68K, PMac
wcsftime	<time.h> or <wchar.h>		ANSI, Win 95, Win NT, Win32s

For additional compatibility information, see "Compatibility" on page ix in the Introduction.

Libraries	
LIBC.LIB	Single thread static library, retail version
LIBCMT.LIB	Multithread static library, retail version
MSVCRT.LIB	Import library for MSVCRTx0.DLL, retail version
MSVCRTx0.DLL	Multithread DLL library, retail version

Return Value

strftime returns the number of characters placed in *string* if the total number of resulting characters, including the terminating null, is not more than *maxsize*. **wcsftime** returns the corresponding number of wide characters. Otherwise, the functions return 0, and the contents of *string* is indeterminate.

Parameters

string Output string

maxsize Maximum length of string

format Format-control string

timeptr **tm** data structure

Remarks

The **strftime** and **wcsftime** functions format the **tm** time value in *timeptr* according to the supplied *format* argument and store the result in the buffer *string*. At most, *maxsize* characters are placed in the string. For a description of the fields in the *timeptr* structure, see **asctime**. **wcsftime** is the wide-character equivalent of **strftime**; its string-pointer argument points to a wide-character string. These functions behave identically otherwise.

Note Prior to this version of Visual C++, the documentation described the *format* parameter of **wcsftime** as having the datatype **const wchar_t ***, but the actual implementation of the *format* datatype was **const char ***. In this version, the implementation of the *format* datatype has been updated to reflect the previous and current documentation, that is: **const wchar_t ***.

The *format* argument consists of one or more codes; as in **printf**, the formatting codes are preceded by a percent sign (%). Characters that do not begin with % are copied unchanged to *string*. The **LC_TIME** category of the current locale affects the output formatting of **strftime**. (For more information on **LC_TIME**, see **setlocale**.) The formatting codes for **strftime** are listed below:

%**a** Abbreviated weekday name

%**A** Full weekday name

%**b** Abbreviated month name

%**B** Full month name

%**c** Date and time representation appropriate for locale

%**d** Day of month as decimal number (01 – 31)

%**H** Hour in 24-hour format (00 – 23)

%**I** Hour in 12-hour format (01 – 12)

%**j** Day of year as decimal number (001 – 366)

%**m** Month as decimal number (01 – 12)

%**M** Minute as decimal number (00 – 59)

%**p** Current locale's A.M./P.M. indicator for 12-hour clock

%**S** Second as decimal number (00 – 59)

%**U** Week of year as decimal number, with Sunday as first day of week (00 – 51)

%**w** Weekday as decimal number (0 – 6; Sunday is 0)

%**W** Week of year as decimal number, with Monday as first day of week (00 – 51)

%**x** Date representation for current locale

%**X** Time representation for current locale

%**y** Year without century, as decimal number (00 – 99)

%**Y** Year with century, as decimal number

%**z**, %**Z** Time-zone name or abbreviation; no characters if time zone is unknown

%% Percent sign

As in the **printf** function, the **#** flag may prefix any formatting code. In that case, the meaning of the format code is changed as follows.

Format Code	Meaning
%#a, %#A, %#b, %#B, %#p, %#X, %#z, %#Z, %#%	# flag is ignored.
%#c	Long date and time representation, appropriate for current locale. For example: "Tuesday, March 14, 1995, 12:41:29".
%#x	Long date representation, appropriate to current locale. For example: "Tuesday, March 14, 1995".
%#d, %#H, %#I, %#j, %#m, %#M, %#S, %#U, %#w, %#W, %#y, %#Y	Remove leading zeros (if any).

Example

See the example for **time**.

See Also **localeconv**, **setlocale**, **strcoll**, **_stricoll**, **strxfrm**

_stricmp, _wcsicmp, _mbsicmp

Perform a lowercase comparison of strings.

int _stricmp(const char ***string1*****, const char** ***string2*** **);**
int _wcsicmp(const wchar_t ***string1*****, const wchar_t** ***string2*** **);**
int _mbsicmp(const unsigned char ***string1*****, const unsigned char_t** ***string2*** **);**

Routine	Required Header	Optional Headers	Compatibility
_stricmp	<string.h>		Win 95, Win NT, Win32s, 68K, PMac
_wcsicmp	<string.h> or <wchar.h>		Win 95, Win NT, Win32s
_mbsicmp	<mbstring.h>		Win 95, Win NT, Win32s, 68K, PMac

For additional compatibility information, see "Compatibility" on page ix in the Introduction.

Libraries	
LIBC.LIB	Single thread static library, retail version
LIBCMT.LIB	Multithread static library, retail version
MSVCRT.LIB	Import library for MSVCRTx0.DLL, retail version
MSVCRTx0.DLL	Multithread DLL library, retail version

Return Value

The return value indicates the relation of *string1* to *string2* as follows.

Return Value	Description
< 0	*string1* less than *string2*
0	*string1* identical to *string2*
> 0	*string1* greater than *string2*

On an error, **_mbsicmp** returns **_NLSCMPERROR**, which is defined in STRING.H and MBSTRING.H.

Parameters

string1, *string2* Null-terminated strings to compare

Remarks

The **_stricmp** function lexicographically compares lowercase versions of *string1* and *string2* and returns a value indicating their relationship. **_stricmp** differs from **_stricoll** in that the **_stricmp** comparison is not affected by locale, whereas the **_stricoll** comparison is according to the **LC_COLLATE** category of the current locale. For more information on the **LC_COLLATE** category, see **setlocale**.

The **_strcmpi** function is equivalent to **_stricmp** and is provided for backward compatibility only.

_wcsicmp and **_mbsicmp** are wide-character and multibyte-character versions of **_stricmp**. The arguments and return value of **_wcsicmp** are wide-character strings; those of **_mbsicmp** are multibyte-character strings. **_mbsicmp** recognizes multibyte-character sequences according to the current multibyte code page and returns **_NLSCMPERROR** on an error. (For more information, see "Code Pages" on page 22.) These three functions behave identically otherwise.

_wcsicmp and **wcscmp** behave identically except that **wcscmp** does not convert its arguments to lowercase before comparing them. **_mbsicmp** and **_mbscmp** behave identically except that **_mbscmp** does not convert its arguments to lowercase before comparing them.

Example

See the example for **strcmp**.

See Also **memcmp**, **_memicmp**, **strcmp**, **strcoll** Functions, **strncmp**, **_strnicmp**, **strrchr**, **_strset**, **strspn**

strlen, wcslen, _mbslen, _mbstrlen

Get the length of a string.

size_t strlen(const char **string* **);**
size_t wcslen(const wchar_t **string* **);**
size_t _mbslen(const unsigned char **string* **);**
size_t _mbstrlen(const char **string* **);**

Routine	Required Header	Optional Headers	Compatibility
strlen	<string.h>		ANSI, Win 95, Win NT, Win32s, 68K, PMac
wcslen	<string.h> or <wchar.h>		ANSI, Win 95, Win NT, Win32s
_mbslen	<stdlib.h>		Win 95, Win NT, Win32s, 68K, PMac
_mbstrlen	<stdlib.h>		Win 95, Win NT, Win32s, 68K, PMac

For additional compatibility information, see "Compatibility" on page ix in the Introduction.

Libraries	
LIBC.LIB	Single thread static library, retail version
LIBCMT.LIB	Multithread static library, retail version
MSVCRT.LIB	Import library for MSVCRTx0.DLL, retail version
MSVCRTx0.DLL	Multithread DLL library, retail version

Return Value

Each of these functions returns the number of characters in *string*, excluding the terminal **NULL**. No return value is reserved to indicate an error.

Parameter

string Null-terminated string

Remarks

Each of these functions returns the number of characters in *string*, not including the terminating null character. **wcslen** is a wide-character version of **strlen**; the argument of **wcslen** is a wide-character string. **wcslen** and **strlen** behave identically otherwise.

_mbslen and **_mbstrlen** return the number of multibyte characters in a multibyte-character string. **_mbslen** recognizes multibyte-character sequences according to the multibyte code page currently in use; it does not test for multibyte-character validity. **_mbstrlen** tests for multibyte-character validity and recognizes multibyte-character sequences according to the **LC_CTYPE** category setting of the current locale. For more information about the **LC_CTYPE** category, see **setlocale**.

Example

```
/*  STRLEN.C */

#include <string.h>
#include <stdio.h>
#include <conio.h>
#include <dos.h>

void main( void )
{
   char buffer[61] = "How long am I?";
   int  len;
   len = strlen( buffer );
   printf( "'%s' is %d characters long\n", buffer, len );
}
```

Output

```
'How long am I?' is 14 characters long
```

See Also **setlocale**, **strcat**, **strcmp**, **strcoll Functions**, **strcpy**, **strrchr**, **_strset**, **strspn**

_strlwr, _wcslwr, _mbslwr

Convert a string to lowercase.

char *_strlwr(char ***_string_ **);
wchar_t *_wcslwr(wchar_t ***_string_ **);
unsigned char *_mbslwr(unsigned char ***_string_ **);

Routine	Required Header	Optional Headers	Compatibility
_strlwr	<string.h>		Win 95, Win NT, Win32s, 68K, PMac
_wcslwr	<string.h> or <wchar.h>		Win 95, Win NT, Win32s
_mbslwr	<mbstring.h>		Win 95, Win NT, Win32s, 68K, PMac

For additional compatibility information, see "Compatibility" on page ix in the Introduction.

Libraries	
LIBC.LIB	Single thread static library, retail version
LIBCMT.LIB	Multithread static library, retail version
MSVCRT.LIB	Import library for MSVCRTx0.DLL, retail version
MSVCRTx0.DLL	Multithread DLL library, retail version

Return Value

Each of these functions returns a pointer to the converted string. Because the modification is done in place, the pointer returned is the same as the pointer passed as the input argument. No return value is reserved to indicate an error.

Parameter

string Null-terminated string to convert to lowercase

Remarks

The **_strlwr** function converts any uppercase letters in *string* to lowercase as determined by the **LC_CTYPE** category setting of the current locale. Other characters are not affected. For more information on **LC_CTYPE**, see **setlocale**.

The **_wcslwr** and **_mbslwr** functions are wide-character and multibyte-character versions of **_strlwr**. The argument and return value of **_wcslwr** are wide-character strings; those of **_mbslwr** are multibyte-character strings. These three functions behave identically otherwise.

Example

```
/* STRLWR.C: This program uses _strlwr and _strupr to create
 * uppercase and lowercase copies of a mixed-case string.
 */

#include <string.h>
#include <stdio.h>

void main( void )
{
   char string[100] = "The String to End All Strings!";
   char *copy1, *copy2;
   copy1 = _strlwr( _strdup( string ) );
   copy2 = _strupr( _strdup( string ) );
   printf( "Mixed: %s\n", string );
   printf( "Lower: %s\n", copy1 );
   printf( "Upper: %s\n", copy2 );
}
```

Output

```
Mixed: The String to End All Strings!
Lower: the string to end all strings!
Upper: THE STRING TO END ALL STRINGS!
```

See Also **_strupr**

strncat, wcsncat, _mbsncat

Append characters of a string.

char *strncat(char ***_string1_, const char ***_string2_**, size_t** _count_ **);**
wchar_t *wcsncat(wchar_t ***_string1_, const wchar_t ***_string2_**, size_t** _count_ **);**
unsigned char *_mbsncat(unsigned char ***_string1_, const unsigned char ***_string2_**, size_t** _count_**);**

Routine	Required Header	Optional Headers	Compatibility
strncat	<string.h>		ANSI, Win 95, Win NT, Win32s, 68K, PMac
wcsncat	<string.h> or <wchar.h>		ANSI, Win 95, Win NT, Win32s
_mbsncat	<mbstring.h>		Win 95, Win NT, Win32s, 68K, PMac

For additional compatibility information, see "Compatibility" on page ix in the Introduction.

Libraries	
LIBC.LIB	Single thread static library, retail version
LIBCMT.LIB	Multithread static library, retail version
MSVCRT.LIB	Import library for MSVCRTx0.DLL, retail version
MSVCRTx0.DLL	Multithread DLL library, retail version

Return Value

Each of these functions returns a pointer to the destination string. No return value is reserved to indicate an error.

Parameters

string1 Null-terminated destination string

string2 Null-terminated source string

count Number of characters to append

Remarks

The **strncat** function appends, at most, the first *count* characters of *string2* to *string1*. The initial character of *string2* overwrites the terminating null character of *string1*. If a null character appears in *string2* before *count* characters are appended, **strncat** appends all characters from *string2*, up to the null character. If *count* is greater than the length of *string2*, the length of *string2* is used in place of *count*. The resulting string is terminated with a null character. If copying takes place between strings that overlap, the behavior is undefined.

wcsncat and **_mbsncat** are wide-character and multibyte-character versions of **strncat**. The string arguments and return value of **wcsncat** are wide-character strings; those of **_mbsncat** are multibyte-character strings. These three functions behave identically otherwise.

Example

```
/* STRNCAT.C */

#include <string.h>
#include <stdio.h>

void main( void )
{
   char string[80] = "This is the initial string!";
   char suffix[] = " extra text to add to the string...";
   /* Combine strings with no more than 19 characters of suffix: */
   printf( "Before: %s\n", string );
   strncat( string, suffix, 19 );
   printf( "After:  %s\n", string );
}
```

Output

```
Before: This is the initial string!
After:  This is the initial string! extra text to add
```

See Also **_mbsnbcat**, **strcat**, **strcmp**, **strcpy**, **strncmp**, **strncpy**, **_strnicmp**, **strrchr**, **_strset**, **strspn**

strncmp, wcsncmp, _mbsncmp

Compare characters of two strings.

int strncmp(const char ****string1*****, const char** ****string2*****, size_t** *count* **);**
int wcsncmp(const wchar_t ****string1*****, const wchar_t** ****string2*****, size_t** *count* **);**
int _mbsncmp(const unsigned char ****string1*****, const unsigned char** *string2***, size_t** *count* **);**

Routine	Required Header	Optional Headers	Compatibility
strncmp	<string.h>		ANSI, Win 95, Win NT, Win32s, 68K, PMac
wcsncmp	<string.h> or <wchar.h>		ANSI, Win 95, Win NT, Win32s
_mbsncmp	<mbstring.h>		Win 95, Win NT, Win32s, 68K, PMac

For additional compatibility information, see "Compatibility" on page ix in the Introduction.

Libraries	
LIBC.LIB	Single thread static library, retail version
LIBCMT.LIB	Multithread static library, retail version
MSVCRT.LIB	Import library for MSVCRTx0.DLL, retail version
MSVCRTx0.DLL	Multithread DLL library, retail version

Return Value

The return value indicates the relation of the substrings of *string1* and *string2* as follows.

Return Value	Description
< 0	*string1* substring less than *string2* substring
0	*string1* substring identical to *string2* substring
> 0	*string1* substring greater than *string2* substring

On an error, **_mbsncmp** returns **_NLSCMPERROR**, which is defined in STRING.H and MBSTRING.H.

Parameters

string1, *string2* Strings to compare

count Number of characters to compare

Remarks

The **strncmp** function lexicographically compares, at most, the first *count* characters in *string1* and *string2* and returns a value indicating the relationship between the substrings. **strncmp** is a case-sensitive version of **_strnicmp**. Unlike **strcoll**, **strncmp** is not affected by locale. For more information on the **LC_COLLATE** category, see **setlocale**.

wcsncmp and **_mbsncmp** are wide-character and multibyte-character versions of **strncmp**. The arguments and return value of **wcsncmp** are wide-character strings; those of **_mbsncmp** are multibyte-character strings. **_mbsncmp** recognizes multibyte-character sequences according to the current multibyte code page and returns **_NLSCMPERROR** on an error. For more information, see "Code Pages" on page 22. These three functions behave identically otherwise. **wcsncmp** and **_mbsncmp** are case-sensitive versions of **_wcsnicmp** and **_mbsnicmp**.

Example

```
/* STRNCMP.C */
#include <string.h>
#include <stdio.h>

char string1[] = "The quick brown dog jumps over the lazy fox";
char string2[] = "The QUICK brown fox jumps over the lazy dog";
```

```
void main( void )
{
   char tmp[20];
   int result;
   printf( "Compare strings:\n\t\t%s\n\t\t%s\n\n", string1, string2 );
   printf( "Function:\tstrncmp (first 10 characters only)\n" );
   result = strncmp( string1, string2 , 10 );
   if( result > 0 )
      strcpy( tmp, "greater than" );
   else if( result < 0 )
      strcpy( tmp, "less than" );
   else
      strcpy( tmp, "equal to" );
   printf( "Result:\t\tString 1 is %s string 2\n\n", tmp );
   printf( "Function:\tstrnicmp _strnicmp (first 10 characters only)\n" );
   result = _strnicmp( string1, string2, 10 );
   if( result > 0 )
      strcpy( tmp, "greater than" );
   else if( result < 0 )
      strcpy( tmp, "less than" );
   else
      strcpy( tmp, "equal to" );
   printf( "Result:\t\tString 1 is %s string 2\n\n", tmp );
}
```

Output

```
Compare strings:
      The quick brown dog jumps over the lazy fox
      The QUICK brown fox jumps over the lazy dog

Function:   strncmp (first 10 characters only)
Result:      String 1 is greater than string 2

Function:   _strnicmp (first 10 characters only)
Result:      String 1 is equal to string 2
```

See Also **_mbsnbcmp**, **_mbsnbicmp**, **strcmp**, **strcoll** Functions, **_strnicmp**, **strrchr**, **_strset**, **strspn**

---

strncpy, wcsncpy, _mbsncpy

Copy characters of one string to another.

char *strncpy(char ***_string1_, const char ***_string2_**, size_t** _count_ **);**
wchar_t *wcsncpy(wchar_t ***_string1_, const wchar_t ***_string2_**, size_t** _count_ **);**
unsigned char *_mbsncpy(unsigned char ***_string1_, const unsigned char ***_string2_**, size_t** _count_ **);**

Routine	Required Header	Optional Headers	Compatibility
strncpy	<string.h>		ANSI, Win 95, Win NT, Win32s, 68K, PMac
wcsncpy	<string.h> or <wchar.h>		ANSI, Win 95, Win NT, Win32s
_mbsncpy	<mbstring.h>		Win 95, Win NT, Win32s, 68K, PMac

For additional compatibility information, see "Compatibility" on page ix in the Introduction.

Libraries	
LIBC.LIB	Single thread static library, retail version
LIBCMT.LIB	Multithread static library, retail version
MSVCRT.LIB	Import library for MSVCRTx0.DLL, retail version
MSVCRTx0.DLL	Multithread DLL library, retail version

Return Value

Each of these functions returns *string1*. No return value is reserved to indicate an error.

Parameters

string1 Destination string

string2 Source string

count Number of characters to be copied

Remarks

The **strncpy** function copies the initial *count* characters of *string2* to *string1* and returns *string1*. If *count* is less than or equal to the length of *string2*, a null character is not appended automatically to the copied string. If *count* is greater than the length of *string2*, the destination string is padded with null characters up to length *count*. The behavior of **strncpy** is undefined if the source and destination strings overlap.

wcsncpy and **_mbsncpy** are wide-character and multibyte-character versions of **strncpy**. The arguments and return value of **wcsncpy** and **_mbsncpy** vary accordingly. These three functions behave identically otherwise.

Example

```
/* STRNCPY.C */

#include <string.h>
#include <stdio.h>

void main( void )
```

```
{
   char string[100] = "Cats are nice usually";
   printf ( "Before: %s\n", string );
   strncpy( string, "Dogs", 4 );
   strncpy( string + 9, "mean", 4 );
   printf ( "After:  %s\n", string );
}
```

Output

```
Before: Cats are nice usually
After:  Dogs are mean usually
```

See Also **_mbsnbcpy**, **strcat**, **strcmp**, **strcpy**, **strncat**, **strncmp**, **_strnicmp**, **strrchr**, **_strset**, **strspn**

_strnicmp, _wcsnicmp, _mbsnicmp

Compare characters of two strings without regard to case.

int _strnicmp(const char ****string1*****, const char** ****string2*****, size_t** *count* **);**
int _wcsnicmp(const wchar_t ****string1*****, const wchar_t** ****string2*****, size_t** *count* **);**
int _mbsnicmp(const unsigned char ****string1*****, const unsigned char** ****string2*****, size_t** *count* **);**

Routine	Required Header	Optional Headers	Compatibility
_strnicmp	<string.h>		Win 95, Win NT, Win32s, 68K, PMac
_wcsnicmp	<string.h> or <wchar.h>		Win 95, Win NT, Win32s
_mbsnicmp	<mbstring.h>		Win 95, Win NT, Win32s, 68K, PMac

For additional compatibility information, see "Compatibility" on page ix in the Introduction.

Libraries	
LIBC.LIB	Single thread static library, retail version
LIBCMT.LIB	Multithread static library, retail version
MSVCRT.LIB	Import library for MSVCRTx0.DLL, retail version
MSVCRTx0.DLL	Multithread DLL library, retail version

Return Value

The return value indicates the relationship between the substrings as follows.

Return Value	Description
< 0	*string1* substring less than *string2* substring
0	*string1* substring identical to *string2* substring
> 0	*string1* substring greater than *string2* substring

On an error, **_mbsnicmp** returns **_NLSCMPERROR**, which is defined in STRING.H and MBSTRING.H.

Parameters

string1, *string2* Null-terminated strings to compare

count Number of characters to compare

Remarks

The **_strnicmp** function lexicographically compares, at most, the first *count* characters of *string1* and *string2*. The comparison is performed without regard to case; **_strnicmp** is a case-insensitive version of **strncmp**. The comparison ends if a terminating null character is reached in either string before *count* characters are compared. If the strings are equal when a terminating null character is reached in either string before *count* characters are compared, the shorter string is lesser.

Two strings containing characters located between `'Z'` and `'a'` in the ASCII table (`'['`, `'\'`, `']'`, `'^'`, `'_'`, and `'`'`) compare differently, depending on their case. For example, the two strings `"ABCDE"` and `"ABCD^"` compare one way if the comparison is lowercase (`"abcde"` > `"abcd^"`) and the other way (`"ABCDE"` < `"ABCD^"`) if it is uppercase.

_wcsnicmp and **_mbsnicmp** are wide-character and multibyte-character versions of **_strnicmp**. The arguments and return value of **_wcsnicmp** are wide-character strings; those of **_mbsnicmp** are multibyte-character strings. **_mbsnicmp** recognizes multibyte-character sequences according to the current multibyte code page and returns **_NLSCMPERROR** on an error. For more information, see "Code Pages" on page 22. These three functions behave identically otherwise. These functions are not affected by the current locale setting.

Example

See the example for **strncmp**.

See Also **strcat**, **strcmp**, **strcpy**, **strncat**, **strncmp**, **strncpy**, **strrchr**, **_strset**, **strspn**

_strnset, _wcsnset, _mbsnset

Initialize characters of a string to a given format.

char *_strnset(char *_string_, int _c_, size_t _count_);
wchar_t *_wcsnset(wchar_t *_string_, wchar_t _c_, size_t _count_);
unsigned char *_mbsnset(unsigned char *_string_, unsigned int _c_, size_t _count_);

Routine	Required Header	Optional Headers	Compatibility
_strnset	<string.h>		Win 95, Win NT, Win32s, 68K, PMac
_wcsnset	<string.h> or <wchar.h>		Win 95, Win NT, Win32s
_mbsnset	<mbstring.h>		Win 95, Win NT, Win32s, 68K, PMac

For additional compatibility information, see "Compatibility" on page ix in the Introduction.

Libraries	
LIBC.LIB	Single thread static library, retail version
LIBCMT.LIB	Multithread static library, retail version
MSVCRT.LIB	Import library for MSVCRTx0.DLL, retail version
MSVCRTx0.DLL	Multithread DLL library, retail version

Return Value

Each of these functions returns a pointer to the altered string.

Parameters

string String to be altered

c Character setting

count Number of characters to be set

Remarks

The **_strnset** function sets, at most, the first *count* characters of *string* to *c* (converted to **char**). If *count* is greater than the length of *string*, the length of *string* is used instead of *count*.

_wcsnset and **_mbsnset** are wide-character and multibyte-character versions of **_strnset**. The string arguments and return value of **_wcsnset** are wide-character strings; those of **_mbsnset** are multibyte-character strings. These three functions behave identically otherwise.

Example

```
/* STRNSET.C */

#include <string.h>
#include <stdio.h>

void main( void )
{
   char string[15] = "This is a test";
   /* Set not more than 4 characters of string to be *'s */
   printf( "Before: %s\n", string );
   _strnset( string, '*', 4 );
   printf( "After:  %s\n", string );
}
```

Output

```
Before: This is a test
After:  **** is a test
```

See Also **strcat**, **strcmp**, **strcpy**, **_strset**

strpbrk, wcspbrk, _mbspbrk

Scan strings for characters in specified character sets.

char *strpbrk(const char ***_string1_, const char ***_string2_ **);**
wchar_t *wcspbrk(const wchar_t ***_string1_, const wchar_t ***_string2_ **);**
unsigned char *_mbspbrk(const unsigned char*_string1_**, const unsigned char ***_string2_ **);**

Routine	Required Header	Optional Headers	Compatibility
strpbrk	<string.h>		ANSI, Win 95, Win NT, Win32s, 68K, PMac
wcspbrk	<string.h> or <wchar.h>		ANSI, Win 95, Win NT, Win32s
_mbspbrk	<mbstring.h>		Win 95, Win NT, Win32s, 68K, PMac

For additional compatibility information, see “Compatibility” on page ix in the Introduction.

Libraries	
LIBC.LIB	Single thread static library, retail version
LIBCMT.LIB	Multithread static library, retail version
MSVCRT.LIB	Import library for MSVCRTx0.DLL, retail version
MSVCRTx0.DLL	Multithread DLL library, retail version

Return Value

Each of these functions returns a pointer to the first occurrence of any character from *string2* in *string1*, or a **NULL** pointer if the two string arguments have no characters in common.

Parameters

string1 Null-terminated, searched string

string2 Null-terminated character set

Remarks

The **strpbrk** function returns a pointer to the first occurrence of a character in *string1* that belongs to the set of characters in *string2*. The search does not include the terminating null character.

wcspbrk and **_mbspbrk** are wide-character and multibyte-character versions of **strpbrk**. The arguments and return value of **wcspbrk** are wide-character strings; those of **_mbspbrk** are multibyte-character strings. These three functions behave identically otherwise. **_mbspbrk** is similar to **_mbscspn** except that **_mbspbrk** returns a pointer rather than a value of type **size_t**.

Example

```
/* STRPBRK.C */

#include <string.h>
#include <stdio.h>

void main( void )
{
   char string[100] = "The 3 men and 2 boys ate 5 pigs\n";
   char *result;
   /* Return pointer to first 'a' or 'b' in "string" */
   printf( "1: %s\n", string );
   result = strpbrk( string, "0123456789" );
   printf( "2: %s\n", result++ );
   result = strpbrk( result, "0123456789" );
   printf( "3: %s\n", result++ );
   result = strpbrk( result, "0123456789" );
   printf( "4: %s\n", result );
}
```

Output

```
1: The 3 men and 2 boys ate 5 pigs

2: 3 men and 2 boys ate 5 pigs

3: 2 boys ate 5 pigs

4: 5 pigs
```

See Also **strcspn**, **strchr**, **strrchr**

strrchr, wcsrchr, _mbsrchr

Scan a string for the last occurrence of a character.

char *strrchr(const char ***_string_, int** _c_ **);**
char *wcsrchr(const wchar_t ***_string_, int** _c_ **);**
int _mbsrchr(const unsigned char ***_string_, unsigned int** _c_ **);**

Routine	Required Header	Optional Headers	Compatibility
strrchr	<string.h>		ANSI, Win 95, Win NT, Win32s, 68K, PMac
wcsrchr	<string.h> or <wchar.h>		ANSI, Win 95, Win NT, Win32s
_mbsrchr	<mbstring.h>		Win 95, Win NT, Win32s, 68K, PMac

For additional compatibility information, see "Compatibility" on page ix in the Introduction.

Libraries	
LIBC.LIB	Single thread static library, retail version
LIBCMT.LIB	Multithread static library, retail version
MSVCRT.LIB	Import library for MSVCRTx0.DLL, retail version
MSVCRTx0.DLL	Multithread DLL library, retail version

Return Value

Each of these functions returns a pointer to the last occurrence of *c* in *string*, or **NULL** if *c* is not found.

Parameters

string Null-terminated string to search

c Character to be located

Remarks

The **strrchr** function finds the last occurrence of *c* (converted to **char**) in *string*. The search includes the terminating null character.

wcsrchr and **_mbsrchr** are wide-character and multibyte-character versions of **strrchr**. The arguments and return value of **wcsrchr** are wide-character strings; those of **_mbsrchr** are multibyte-character strings. These three functions behave identically otherwise.

Example

See the example for **strchr**.

See Also **strchr**, **strcspn**, **_strnicmp**, **strpbrk**, **strspn**

_strrev, _wcsrev, _mbsrev

Reverse characters of a string.

char *_strrev(char ***_string_ **);
wchar_t *_wcsrev(wchar_t ***_string_ **);
unsigned char *_mbsrev(unsigned char ***_string_ **);

Routine	Required Header	Optional Headers	Compatibility
_strrev	<string.h>		Win 95, Win NT, Win32s, 68K, PMac
_wcsrev	<string.h> or <wchar.h>		Win 95, Win NT, Win32s
_mbsrev	<mbstring.h>		Win 95, Win NT, Win32s, 68K, PMac

For additional compatibility information, see "Compatibility" on page ix in the Introduction.

Libraries	
LIBC.LIB	Single thread static library, retail version
LIBCMT.LIB	Multithread static library, retail version
MSVCRT.LIB	Import library for MSVCRTx0.DLL, retail version
MSVCRTx0.DLL	Multithread DLL library, retail version

Return Value

Each of these functions returns a pointer to the altered string. No return value is reserved to indicate an error.

Parameter

string Null-terminated string to reverse

Remarks

The **_strrev** function reverses the order of the characters in *string*. The terminating null character remains in place. **_wcsrev** and **_mbsrev** are wide-character and multibyte-character versions of **_strrev**. The arguments and return value of **_wcsrev** are wide-character strings; those of **_mbsrev** are multibyte-character strings. For **_mbsrev**, the order of bytes in each multibyte character in *string* is not changed. These three functions behave identically otherwise.

Example

```
/* STRREV.C: This program checks an input string to
 * see whether it is a palindrome: that is, whether
 * it reads the same forward and backward.
 */
```

```
#include <string.h>
#include <stdio.h>

void main( void )
{
   char string[100];
   int result;

   printf( "Input a string and I will tell you if it is a palindrome:\n" );
   gets( string );

   /* Reverse string and compare (ignore case): */
   result = _stricmp( string, _strrev( _strdup( string ) ) );
   if( result == 0 )
      printf( "The string \"%s\" is a palindrome\n\n", string );
   else
      printf( "The string \"%s\" is not a palindrome\n\n", string );
}
```

Output

```
Input a string and I will tell you if it is a palindrome:
Able was I ere I saw Elba
The string "Able was I ere I saw Elba" is a palindrome
```

See Also **strcpy**, **_strset**

_strset, _wcsset, _mbsset

Set characters of a string to a character.

char *_strset(char ***_string_, int** _c_ **);**
wchar_t *_wcsset(wchar_t ***_string_, wchar_t** _c_ **);**
unsigned char *_mbsset(unsigned char ***_string_, unsigned int** _c_ **);**

Routine	Required Header	Optional Headers	Compatibility
_strset	<string.h>		Win 95, Win NT, Win32s, 68K, PMac
_wcsset	<string.h> or <wchar.h>		Win 95, Win NT, Win32s
_mbsset	<mbstring.h>		Win 95, Win NT, Win32s, 68K, PMac

For additional compatibility information, see "Compatibility" on page ix in the Introduction.

Libraries

LIBC.LIB	Single thread static library, retail version
LIBCMT.LIB	Multithread static library, retail version
MSVCRT.LIB	Import library for MSVCRTx0.DLL, retail version
MSVCRTx0.DLL	Multithread DLL library, retail version

Return Value

Each of these functions returns a pointer to the altered string. No return value is reserved to indicate an error.

Parameters

string Null-terminated string to be set

c Character setting

Remarks

The **_strset** function sets all the characters of *string* to *c* (converted to **char**), except the terminating null character. **_wcsset** and **_mbsset** are wide-character and multibyte-character versions of **_strset**. The data types of the arguments and return values vary accordingly. These three functions behave identically otherwise.

Example

```
/* STRSET.C */

#include <string.h>
#include <stdio.h>

void main( void )
{
   char string[] = "Fill the string with something";
   printf( "Before: %s\n", string );
   _strset( string, '*' );
   printf( "After:  %s\n", string );
}
```

Output

```
Before: Fill the string with something
After:  ******************************
```

See Also **_mbsnbset**, **memset**, **strcat**, **strcmp**, **strcpy**, **_strnset**

strspn, wcsspn, _mbsspn

Find the first substring.

size_t strspn(const char ****string1*, **const char** ****string2* **);**
size_t wcsspn(const wchar_t ****string1*, **const wchar_t** ****string2* **);**
size_t _mbsspn(const unsigned char ****string1*, **const unsigned char** ****string2* **);**

Routine	Required Header	Optional Headers	Compatibility
strspn	<string.h>		ANSI, Win 95, Win NT, Win32s, 68K, PMac
wcsspn	<string.h> or <wchar.h>		ANSI, Win 95, Win NT, Win32s
_mbsspn	<mbstring.h>		Win 95, Win NT, Win32s, 68K, PMac

For additional compatibility information, see "Compatibility" on page ix in the Introduction.

Libraries	
LIBC.LIB	Single thread static library, retail version
LIBCMT.LIB	Multithread static library, retail version
MSVCRT.LIB	Import library for MSVCRTx0.DLL, retail version
MSVCRTx0.DLL	Multithread DLL library, retail version

Return Value

strspn, **wcsspn**, and **_mbsspn** return an integer value specifying the length of the substring in *string1* that consists entirely of characters in *string2*. If *string1* begins with a character not in *string2,* the function returns 0. No return value is reserved to indicate an error. For each of these routines, no return value is reserved to indicate an error.

Parameters

string1 Null-terminated string to search

string2 Null-terminated character set

Remarks

The **strspn** function returns the index of the first character in *string1* that does not belong to the set of characters in *string2*. The search does not include terminating null characters.

wcsspn and **_mbsspn** are wide-character and multibyte-character versions of **strspn.** The arguments of **wcsspn** are wide-character strings; those of **_mbsspn** are multibyte-character strings. These three functions behave identically otherwise.

Example

```
/* STRSPN.C: This program uses strspn to determine
 * the length of the segment in the string "cabbage"
 * consisting of a's, b's, and c's. In other words,
 * it finds the first non-abc letter.
 */

#include <string.h>
#include <stdio.h>

void main( void )
{
   char string[] = "cabbage";
   int  result;
   result = strspn( string, "abc" );
   printf( "The portion of '%s' containing only a, b, or c "
           "is %d bytes long\n", string, result );
}
```

Output

```
The portion of 'cabbage' containing only a, b, or c is 5 bytes long
```

See Also **_mbsspnp**, **strcspn**, **strncat**, **strncmp**, **strncpy**, **_strnicmp**, **strrchr**

---

strstr, wcsstr, _mbsstr

Find a substring.

char *strstr(const char ****string1*, const char ****string2***);**
wchar_t *wcsstr(const wchar_t ****string1*, const wchar_t ****string2***);**
unsigned char *_mbsstr(const unsigned char ****string1*, const unsigned char ****string2***);**

Routine	Required Header	Optional Headers	Compatibility
strstr	<string.h>		ANSI, Win 95, Win NT, Win32s, 68K, PMac
wcsstr	<string.h> or <wchar.h>		ANSI, Win 95, Win NT, Win32s
_mbsstr	<mbstring.h>		Win 95, Win NT, Win32s, 68K, PMac

For additional compatibility information, see "Compatibility" on page ix in the Introduction.

Libraries

LIBC.LIB	Single thread static library, retail version
LIBCMT.LIB	Multithread static library, retail version
MSVCRT.LIB	Import library for MSVCRTx0.DLL, retail version
MSVCRTx0.DLL	Multithread DLL library, retail version

Return Value

Each of these functions returns a pointer to the first occurrence of *string2* in *string1*, or **NULL** if *string2* does not appear in *string1*. If *string2* points to a string of zero length, the function returns *string1*.

Parameters

string1 Null-terminated string to search

string2 Null-terminated string to search for

Remarks

The **strstr** function returns a pointer to the first occurrence of *string2* in *string1*. The search does not include terminating null characters. **wcsstr** and **_mbsstr** are wide-character and multibyte-character versions of **strstr**. The arguments and return value of **wcsstr** are wide-character strings; those of **_mbsstr** are multibyte-character strings. These three functions behave identically otherwise.

Example

```
/* STRSTR.C */

#include <string.h>
#include <stdio.h>

char str[] =    "lazy";
char string[] = "The quick brown dog jumps over the lazy fox";
char fmt1[] =   "         1         2         3         4         5";
char fmt2[] =   "12345678901234567890123456789012345678901234567890";

void main( void )
{
   char *pdest;
   int  result;
   printf( "String to be searched:\n\t%s\n", string );
   printf( "\t%s\n\t%s\n\n", fmt1, fmt2 );
   pdest = strstr( string, str );
   result = pdest - string + 1;
   if( pdest != NULL )
      printf( "%s found at position %d\n\n", str, result );
   else
      printf( "%s not found\n", str );
}
```

Output

```
String to be searched:
   The quick brown dog jumps over the lazy fox
            1         2         3         4         5
   12345678901234567890123456789012345678901234567890

lazy found at position 36
```

See Also **strcspn**, **strcmp**, **strpbrk**, **strrchr**, **strspn**

_strtime, _wstrtime

Copy the time to a buffer.

char *_strtime(char ***timestr* **);
wchar_t *_wstrtime(wchar_t ***timestr* **);

Routine	Required Header	Optional Headers	Compatibility
_strtime	<time.h>		Win 95, Win NT, Win32s, 68K, PMac
_wstrtime	<time.h> or <wchar.h>		Win 95, Win NT, Win32s

For additional compatibility information, see "Compatibility" on page ix in the Introduction.

Libraries	
LIBC.LIB	Single thread static library, retail version
LIBCMT.LIB	Multithread static library, retail version
MSVCRT.LIB	Import library for MSVCRTx0.DLL, retail version
MSVCRTx0.DLL	Multithread DLL library, retail version

Return Value

Each of these functions returns a pointer to the resulting character string *timestr*.

Parameter

timestr Time string

Remarks

The **_strtime** function copies the current local time into the buffer pointed to by *timestr*. The time is formatted as *hh:mm:ss* where *hh* is two digits representing the hour in 24-hour notation, *mm* is two digits representing the minutes past the hour, and *ss* is two digits representing seconds. For example, the string `18:23:44` represents 23 minutes and 44 seconds past 6 P.M. The buffer must be at least 9 bytes long.

_wstrtime is a wide-character version of **_strtime**; the argument and return value of **_wstrtime** are wide-character strings. These functions behave identically otherwise.

Example

```
/* STRTIME.C */

#include <time.h>
#include <stdio.h>

void main( void )
{
   char dbuffer [9];
   char tbuffer [9];
   _strdate( dbuffer );
   printf( "The current date is %s \n", dbuffer );
   _strtime( tbuffer );
   printf( "The current time is %s \n", tbuffer );
}
```

Output

```
The current date is 03/23/93
The current time is 13:40:40
```

See Also **asctime**, **ctime**, **gmtime**, **localtime**, **mktime**, **time**, **_tzset**

strtod, strtol, strtoul Functions

Convert a string to a double precision value (**strtod**, **wcstod**), a long-integer value (**strtol**, **wcstol**), or an unsigned long-integer value (**strtoul**, **wcstoul**).

strtod, **wcstod**

strtol, **wcstol**

strtoul, **wcstoul**

Return Value

strtod returns the value of the floating-point number, except when the representation would cause an overflow, in which case the function returns **+/–HUGE_VAL**. The sign of **HUGE_VAL** matches the sign of the value that cannot be represented. **strtod** returns 0 if no conversion can be performed or an underflow occurs.

strtol returns the value represented in the string *nptr*, except when the representation would cause an overflow, in which case it returns **LONG_MAX** or **LONG_MIN**. **strtoul** returns the converted value, if any, or **ULONG_MAX** on overflow. Each of these functions returns 0 if no conversion can be performed.

wcstod, **wcstol**, and **wcstoul** return values analogously to **strtod**, **strtol**, and **strtoul,** respectively.

For all six functions in this group, **errno** is set to **ERANGE** if overflow or underflow occurs.

Parameters

nptr Null-terminated string to convert

endptr Pointer to character that stops scan

base Number base to use

Remarks

The **strtod**, **strtol**, and **strtoul** functions convert *nptr* to a double-precision value, a long-integer value, or an unsigned long-integer value, respectively.

The input string *nptr* is a sequence of characters that can be interpreted as a numerical value of the specified type. Each function stops reading the string *nptr* at the first character it cannot recognize as part of a number. This may be the terminating null character. For **strtol** or **strtoul**, this terminating character can also be the first numeric character greater than or equal to *base*.

For all six functions in the **strtod** group, the current locale's **LC_NUMERIC** category setting determines recognition of the radix character in *nptr;* for more information, see **setlocale**. If *endptr* is not **NULL**, a pointer to the character that stopped the scan is stored at the location pointed to by *endptr*. If no conversion can be performed (no valid digits were found or an invalid base was specified), the value of *nptr* is stored at the location pointed to by *endptr*.

strtod expects *nptr* to point to a string of the following form:

[*whitespace*] [*sign*] [*digits*] [**.***digits*] [{**d** | **D** | **e** | **E**}[*sign*]*digits*]

A *whitespace* may consist of space or tab characters, which are ignored; *sign* is either plus (**+**) or minus (**–**); and *digits* are one or more decimal digits. If no digits appear before the radix character, at least one must appear after the radix character. The decimal digits can be followed by an exponent, which consists of an introductory letter (**d**, **D**, **e**, or **E**) and an optionally signed integer. If neither an exponent part nor a radix character appears, a radix character is assumed to follow the last digit in the string. The first character that does not fit this form stops the scan.

The **strtol** and **strtoul** functions expect *nptr* to point to a string of the following form:

[*whitespace*] [{**+** | **–**}] [**0** [{ **x** | **X** }]] [*digits*]

If *base* is between 2 and 36, then it is used as the base of the number. If *base* is 0, the initial characters of the string pointed to by *nptr* are used to determine the base. If the first character is 0 and the second character is not `'x'` or `'X'`, the string is interpreted as an octal integer; otherwise, it is interpreted as a decimal number. If the first character is `'0'` and the second character is `'x'` or `'X'`, the string is interpreted as a hexadecimal integer. If the first character is `'1'` through `'9'`, the string is interpreted as a decimal integer. The letters `'a'` through `'z'` (or `'A'` through `'Z'`) are assigned the values 10 through 35; only letters whose assigned values are less than *base* are permitted. **strtoul** allows a plus (+) or minus (–) sign prefix; a leading minus sign indicates that the return value is negated.

wcstod, **wcstol**, and **wcstoul** are wide-character versions of **strtod**, **strtol**, and **strtoul,** respectively; the *nptr* argument to each of these wide-character functions is a wide-character string. Otherwise, each of these wide-character functions behaves identically to its single-byte–character counterpart.

Example

```
/* STRTOD.C: This program uses strtod to convert a
 * string to a double-precision value; strtol to
 * convert a string to long integer values; and strtoul
 * to convert a string to unsigned long-integer values.
 */

#include <stdlib.h>
#include <stdio.h>

void main( void )
{
   char   *string, *stopstring;
   double x;
   long   l;
   int    base;
   unsigned long ul;
   string = "3.1415926This stopped it";
   x = strtod( string, &stopstring );
   printf( "string = %s\n", string );
   printf("   strtod = %f\n", x );
   printf("   Stopped scan at: %s\n\n", stopstring );
   string = "-10110134932This stopped it";
   l = strtol( string, &stopstring, 10 );
   printf( "string = %s", string );
   printf("   strtol = %ld", l );
   printf("   Stopped scan at: %s", stopstring );
   string = "10110134932";
   printf( "string = %s\n", string );
   /* Convert string using base 2, 4, and 8: */
   for( base = 2; base <= 8; base *= 2 )
   {
      /* Convert the string: */
      ul = strtoul( string, &stopstring, base );
      printf( "   strtol = %ld (base %d)\n", ul, base );
      printf( "   Stopped scan at: %s\n", stopstring );
   }
}
```

Output

```
string = 3.1415926This stopped it
   strtod = 3.141593
   Stopped scan at: This stopped it
```

```
string = -10110134932This stopped it   strtol = -2147483647   Stopped scan at: This
stopped itstring = 10110134932
   strtol = 45 (base 2)
   Stopped scan at: 34932
   strtol = 4423 (base 4)
   Stopped scan at: 4932
   strtol = 2134108 (base 8)
   Stopped scan at: 932
```

See Also **atof**, **localeconv**, **setlocale**

strtod, wcstod

Convert strings to a double-precision value.

double strtod(const char ***nptr*, **char** ****endptr* **);**
double wcstod(const wchar_t ***nptr*, **wchar_t** ****endptr* **);**

Each of these functions converts the input string *nptr* to a **double**.

Routine	Required Header	Optional Headers	Compatibility
strtod	<stdlib.h>		ANSI, Win 95, Win NT, Win32s, 68K, PMac
wcstod	<stdlib.h> or <wchar.h>		ANSI, Win 95, Win NT, Win32s, 68K, PMac

For additional compatibility information, see "Compatibility" on page ix in the Introduction.

Libraries	
LIBC.LIB	Single thread static library, retail version
LIBCMT.LIB	Multithread static library, retail version
MSVCRT.LIB	Import library for MSVCRTx0.DLL, retail version
MSVCRTx0.DLL	Multithread DLL library, retail version

Return Value

strtod returns the value of the floating-point number, except when the representation would cause an overflow, in which case the function returns +/–**HUGE_VAL**. The sign of **HUGE_VAL** matches the sign of the value that cannot be represented. **strtod** returns 0 if no conversion can be performed or an underflow occurs.

wcstod returns values analogously to **strtod.** For both functions, **errno** is set to **ERANGE** if overflow or underflow occurs.

Parameters

nptr Null-terminated string to convert

endptr Pointer to character that stops scan

Remarks

The **strtod** function converts *nptr* to a double-precision value. **strtod** stops reading the string *nptr* at the first character it cannot recognize as part of a number. This may be the terminating null character. **wcstod** is a wide-character version of **strtod**; its *nptr* argument is a wide-character string. Otherwise these functions behave identically.

The **LC_NUMERIC** category setting of the current locale determines recognition of the radix character in *nptr;* for more information, see **setlocale**. If *endptr* is not **NULL**, a pointer to the character that stopped the scan is stored at the location pointed to by *endptr*. If no conversion can be performed (no valid digits were found or an invalid base was specified), the value of *nptr* is stored at the location pointed to by *endptr*.

strtod expects *nptr* to point to a string of the following form:

[*whitespace*] [*sign*] [*digits*] [*.digits*] [{**d** | **D** | **e** | **E**}[*sign*]*digits*]

A *whitespace* may consist of space and tab characters, which are ignored; *sign* is either plus (+) or minus (–); and *digits* are one or more decimal digits. If no digits appear before the radix character, at least one must appear after the radix character. The decimal digits can be followed by an exponent, which consists of an introductory letter (**d**, **D**, **e**, or **E**) and an optionally signed integer. If neither an exponent part nor a radix character appears, a radix character is assumed to follow the last digit in the string. The first character that does not fit this form stops the scan.

Example

See the example for **strtod** on page 622.

Output

```
string = 3.1415926This stopped it
   strtod = 3.141593
   Stopped scan at: This stopped it

string = -10110134932This stopped it   strtol = -2147483647   Stopped scan at: This
stopped itstring = 10110134932
   strtol = 45 (base 2)
   Stopped scan at: 34932
   strtol = 4423 (base 4)
   Stopped scan at: 4932
   strtol = 2134108 (base 8)
   Stopped scan at: 932
```

See Also **strtol, strtoul, atof, localeconv, setlocale**

strtol, wcstol

Convert strings to a long-integer value.

long strtol(const char **nptr*, **char** ***endptr*, **int** *base* **);**
long wcstol(const wchar_t **nptr*, **wchar_t** ***endptr*, **int** *base* **);**

Routine	Required Header	Optional Headers	Compatibility
strtol	<stdlib.h>		ANSI, Win 95, Win NT, Win32s, 68K, PMac
wcstol	<stdlib.h> or <wchar.h>		ANSI, Win 95, Win NT, Win32s, 68K, PMac

For additional compatibility information, see "Compatibility" on page ix in the Introduction.

Libraries	
LIBC.LIB	Single thread static library, retail version
LIBCMT.LIB	Multithread static library, retail version
MSVCRT.LIB	Import library for MSVCRTx0.DLL, retail version
MSVCRTx0.DLL	Multithread DLL library, retail version

Return Value

strtol returns the value represented in the string *nptr*, except when the representation would cause an overflow, in which case it returns **LONG_MAX** or **LONG_MIN**. **strtol** returns 0 if no conversion can be performed. **wcstol** returns values analogously to **strtol**. For both functions, **errno** is set to **ERANGE** if overflow or underflow occurs.

Parameters

nptr Null-terminated string to convert

endptr Pointer to character that stops scan

base Number base to use

Remarks

The **strtol** function converts *nptr* to a **long**. **strtol** stops reading the string *nptr* at the first character it cannot recognize as part of a number. This may be the terminating null character, or it may be the first numeric character greater than or equal to *base*.

wcstol is a wide-character version of **strtol**; its *nptr* argument is a wide-character string. Otherwise these functions behave identically.

The current locale's **LC_NUMERIC** category setting determines recognition of the radix character in *nptr;* for more information, see **setlocale**. If *endptr* is not **NULL**, a pointer to the character that stopped the scan is stored at the location pointed to by *endptr*. If no conversion can be performed (no valid digits were found or an invalid base was specified), the value of *nptr* is stored at the location pointed to by *endptr*.

strtol expects *nptr* to point to a string of the following form:

[*whitespace*] [{+ | –}] [**0** [{ **x** | **X** }]] [*digits*]

A *whitespace* may consist of space and tab characters, which are ignored; *digits* are one or more decimal digits. The first character that does not fit this form stops the scan. If *base* is between 2 and 36, then it is used as the base of the number. If *base* is 0, the initial characters of the string pointed to by *nptr* are used to determine the base. If the first character is 0 and the second character is not 'x' or 'X', the string is interpreted as an octal integer; otherwise, it is interpreted as a decimal number. If the first character is '0' and the second character is 'x' or 'X', the string is interpreted as a hexadecimal integer. If the first character is '1' through '9', the string is interpreted as a decimal integer. The letters 'a' through 'z' (or 'A' through 'Z') are assigned the values 10 through 35; only letters whose assigned values are less than *base* are permitted.

Example

See the example for **strtod** on page 622.

See Also **strtod**, **strtoul**, **atof**, **localeconv**, **setlocale**

strtoul, wcstoul

Convert strings to an unsigned long-integer value.

unsigned long strtoul(const char **nptr*, **char** ***endptr*, **int** *base* **);**
unsigned long wcstoul(const wchar_t **nptr*, **wchar_t** ***endptr*, **int** *base* **);**

Routine	Required Header	Optional Headers	Compatibility
strtoul	<stdlib.h>		ANSI, Win 95, Win NT, Win32s, 68K, PMac
wcstoul	<stdlib.h> or <wchar.h>		ANSI, Win 95, Win NT, Win32s, 68K, PMac

For additional compatibility information, see "Compatibility" on page ix in the Introduction.

Libraries

LIBC.LIB	Single thread static library, retail version
LIBCMT.LIB	Multithread static library, retail version
MSVCRT.LIB	Import library for MSVCRTx0.DLL, retail version
MSVCRTx0.DLL	Multithread DLL library, retail version

Return Value

strtoul returns the converted value, if any, or **ULONG_MAX** on overflow. **strtoul** returns 0 if no conversion can be performed. **wcstoul** returns values analogously to **strtoul.** For both functions, **errno** is set to **ERANGE** if overflow or underflow occurs.

Parameters

nptr Null-terminated string to convert

endptr Pointer to character that stops scan

base Number base to use

Remarks

Each of these functions converts the input string *nptr* to an **unsigned long**.

strtoul stops reading the string *nptr* at the first character it cannot recognize as part of a number. This may be the terminating null character, or it may be the first numeric character greater than or equal to *base*. The **LC_NUMERIC** category setting of the current locale determines recognition of the radix character in *nptr;* for more information, see **setlocale**. If *endptr* is not **NULL**, a pointer to the character that stopped the scan is stored at the location pointed to by *endptr*. If no conversion can be performed (no valid digits were found or an invalid base was specified), the value of *nptr* is stored at the location pointed to by *endptr*.

wcstoul is a wide-character version of **strtoul**; its *nptr* argument is a wide-character string. Otherwise these functions behave identically.

strtoul expects *nptr* to point to a string of the following form:

[*whitespace*] [{+ | –}] [**0** [{ **x** | **X** }]] [*digits*]

A *whitespace* may consist of space and tab characters, which are ignored; *digits* are one or more decimal digits. The first character that does not fit this form stops the scan. If *base* is between 2 and 36, then it is used as the base of the number. If *base* is 0, the initial characters of the string pointed to by *nptr* are used to determine the base. If the first character is 0 and the second character is not 'x' or 'X', the string is interpreted as an octal integer; otherwise, it is interpreted as a decimal number. If the first character is '0' and the second character is 'x' or 'X', the string is interpreted as a hexadecimal integer. If the first character is '1' through '9', the string is interpreted as a decimal integer. The letters 'a' through 'z' (or 'A' through 'Z') are assigned the values 10 through 35; only letters whose assigned values are less than *base* are permitted. **strtoul** allows a plus (+) or minus (–) sign prefix; a leading minus sign indicates that the return value is negated.

Example

See the example for **strtod** on page 622.

See Also **strtod**, **strtol**, **atof**, **localeconv**, **setlocale**

strtok, wcstok, _mbstok

Find the next token in a string.

char *strtok(char ***string1, const char ***string2**);**
wchar_t *wcstok(wchar_t ***string1, const wchar_t ***string2**);**
unsigned char *_mbstok(unsigned char**string1**, const unsigned char ***string2**);**

Routine	Required Header	Optional Headers	Compatibility
strtok	<string.h>		ANSI, Win 95, Win NT, Win32s, 68K, PMac
wcstok	<string.h> or <wchar.h>		ANSI, Win 95, Win NT, Win32s
_mbstok	<mbstring.h>		Win 95, Win NT, Win32s, 68K, PMac

For additional compatibility information, see "Compatibility" on page ix in the Introduction.

Libraries	
LIBC.LIB	Single thread static library, retail version
LIBCMT.LIB	Multithread static library, retail version
MSVCRT.LIB	Import library for MSVCRTx0.DLL, retail version
MSVCRTx0.DLL	Multithread DLL library, retail version

Return Value

All of these functions return a pointer to the next token found in *string1*. They return **NULL** when no more tokens are found. Each call modifies *string1* by substituting a NULL character for each delimiter that is encountered.

Parameters

string1 String containing token(s)

string2 Set of delimiter characters

Remarks

The **strtok** function finds the next token in *string1*. The set of characters in *string2* specifies possible delimiters of the token to be found in *string1* on the current call. **wcstok** and **_mbstok** are wide-character and multibyte-character versions of **strtok**. The arguments and return value of **wcstok** are wide-character strings; those of **_mbstok** are multibyte-character strings. These three functions behave identically otherwise.

On the first call to **strtok**, the function skips leading delimiters and returns a pointer to the first token in *string1*, terminating the token with a null character. More tokens can be broken out of the remainder of *string1* by a series of calls to **strtok**. Each call to **strtok** modifies *string1* by inserting a null character after the token returned by that call. To read the next token from *string1*, call **strtok** with a **NULL** value for the *string1* argument. The **NULL** *string1* argument causes **strtok** to search for the next token in the modified *string1*. The *string2* argument can take any value from one call to the next so that the set of delimiters may vary.

Warning Each of these functions use a static variable for parsing the string into tokens. If multiple or simultaneous calls are made to the same function, a high potential for data corruption and inaccurate results exists. Therefore, do not attempt to call the same function simultaneously for different strings and be aware of calling one of these functions from within a loop where another routine may be called that uses the same function.

Example

```
/* STRTOK.C: In this program, a loop uses strtok
 * to print all the tokens (separated by commas
 * or blanks) in the string named "string".
 */

#include <string.h>
#include <stdio.h>

char string[] = "A string\tof ,,tokens\nand some  more tokens";
char seps[]   = " ,\t\n";
char *token;

void main( void )
{
   printf( "%s\n\nTokens:\n", string );
   /* Establish string and get the first token: */
   token = strtok( string, seps );
   while( token != NULL )
   {
      /* While there are tokens in "string" */
      printf( " %s\n", token );
      /* Get next token: */
      token = strtok( NULL, seps );
   }
}
```

Output

```
A string   of ,,tokens
and some  more tokens

Tokens:
 A
 string
 of
 tokens
```

```
and
some
more
tokens
```

See Also **strcspn**, **strspn**, **setlocale**

_strupr, _wcsupr, _mbsupr

Convert a string to uppercase.

char *_strupr(char ***_string_ **);
wchar_t *_wcsupr(wchar_t ***_string_ **);
unsigned char *_mbsupr(unsigned char ***_string_ **);

Routine	Required Header	Optional Headers	Compatibility
_strupr	<string.h>		Win 95, Win NT, Win32s, 68K, PMac
_wcsupr	<string.h> or <wchar.h>		Win 95, Win NT, Win32s
_mbsupr	<mbstring.h>		Win 95, Win NT, Win32s, 68K, PMac

For additional compatibility information, see "Compatibility" on page ix in the Introduction.

Libraries	
LIBC.LIB	Single thread static library, retail version
LIBCMT.LIB	Multithread static library, retail version
MSVCRT.LIB	Import library for MSVCRTx0.DLL, retail version
MSVCRTx0.DLL	Multithread DLL library, retail version

Return Value

These functions return a pointer to the altered string. Because the modification is done in place, the pointer returned is the same as the pointer passed as the input argument. No return value is reserved to indicate an error.

Parameter

string String to capitalize

Remarks

The **_strupr** function converts, in place, each lowercase letter in *string* to uppercase. The conversion is determined by the **LC_CTYPE** category setting of the current locale. Other characters are not affected. For more information on **LC_CTYPE**, see **setlocale**.

_wcsupr and **_mbsupr** are wide-character and multibyte-character versions of **_strupr**. The argument and return value of **_wcsupr** are wide-character strings; those of **_mbsupr** are multibyte-character strings. These three functions behave identically otherwise.

Example

See the example for **_strlwr**.

See Also **_strlwr**

---

strxfrm, wcsxfrm

Transform a string based on locale-specific information.

size_t strxfrm(char ***string1*****, const char** ***string2*****, size_t** *count* **);**
size_t wcsxfrm(wchar_t ***string1*****, const wchar_t** ***string2*****, size_t** *count* **);**

Routine	Required Header	Optional Headers	Compatibility
strxfrm	<string.h>		ANSI, Win 95, Win NT, Win32s, 68K, PMac
wcsxfrm	<string.h> or <wchar.h>		ANSI, Win 95, Win NT, Win32s

For additional compatibility information, see "Compatibility" on page ix in the Introduction.

Libraries	
LIBC.LIB	Single thread static library, retail version
LIBCMT.LIB	Multithread static library, retail version
MSVCRT.LIB	Import library for MSVCRTx0.DLL, retail version
MSVCRTx0.DLL	Multithread DLL library, retail version

Return Value

Each of these functions returns the length of the transformed string, not counting the terminating null character. If the return value is greater than or equal to *count*, the content of *string1* is unpredictable. On an error, each of the functions sets **errno** and returns **(size_t)** –1.

Parameters

string1 Destination string

string2 Source string

count Maximum number of characters to place in *string1*

Remarks

The **strxfrm** function transforms the string pointed to by *string2* into a new collated form that is stored in *string1*. No more than *count* characters, including the null character, are transformed and placed into the resulting string. The transformation is made using the current locale's **LC_COLLATE** category setting. For more information on **LC_COLLATE**, see **setlocale**.

After the transformation, a call to **strcmp** with the two transformed strings yields results identical to those of a call to **strcoll** applied to the original two strings. As with **strcoll** and **stricoll**, **strxfrm** automatically handles multibyte-character strings as appropriate.

wcsxfrm is a wide-character version of **strxfrm**; the string arguments of **wcsxfrm** are wide-character pointers. For **wcsxfrm**, after the string transformation, a call to **wcscmp** with the two transformed strings yields results identical to those of a call to **wcscoll** applied to the original two strings. **wcsxfrm** and **strxfrm** behave identically otherwise.

In the "C" locale, the order of the characters in the character set (ASCII character set) is the same as the lexicographic order of the characters. However, in other locales, the order of characters in the character set may differ from the lexicographic character order. For example, in certain European locales, the character `'a'` (value 0x61) precedes the character 'ä' (value 0xE4) in the character set, but the character 'ä' precedes the character 'a' lexicographically.

In locales for which the character set and the lexicographic character order differ, use **strxfrm** on the original strings and then **strcmp** on the resulting strings to produce a lexicographic string comparison according to the current locale's **LC_COLLATE** category setting. Thus, to compare two strings lexicographically in the above locale, use **strxfrm** on the original strings, then **strcmp** on the resulting strings. Alternatively, you can use **strcoll** rather than **strcmp** on the original strings.

The value of the following expression is the size of the array needed to hold the **strxfrm** transformation of the source string:

```
1 + strxfrm( NULL, string, 0 )
```

In the "C" locale only, **strxfrm** is equivalent to the following:

```
strncpy( _string1, _string2, _count );
return( strlen( _string1 ) );
```

See Also **localeconv**, **setlocale**, **strcmp**, **strncmp**, **strcoll** Functions

_swab

Swaps bytes.

void _swab(char ****src*, **char** ****dest*, **int** *n* **);**

Routine	Required Header	Optional Headers	Compatibility
_swab	<stdlib.h>		Win 95, Win NT, Win32s, 68K, PMac

For additional compatibility information, see "Compatibility" on page ix in the Introduction.

Libraries	
LIBC.LIB	Single thread static library, retail version
LIBCMT.LIB	Multithread static library, retail version
MSVCRT.LIB	Import library for MSVCRTx0.DLL, retail version
MSVCRTx0.DLL	Multithread DLL library, retail version

Return Value

None

Parameters

src Data to be copied and swapped

dest Storage location for swapped data

n Number of bytes to be copied and swapped

Remarks

The **_swab** function copies *n* bytes from *src*, swaps each pair of adjacent bytes, and stores the result at *dest*. The integer *n* should be an even number to allow for swapping. **_swab** is typically used to prepare binary data for transfer to a machine that uses a different byte order.

Example

```
/* SWAB.C illustrates:
 *      _swab
 */

#include <stdlib.h>
#include <stdio.h>

char from[] = "BADCFEHGJILKNMPORQTSVUXWZY";
char to[] =   "..........................";

void main()
```

```
{
    printf( "Before:\t%s\n\t%s\n\n", from, to );
    _swab( from, to, sizeof( from ) );
    printf( "After:\t%s\n\t%s\n\n", from, to );
}
```

Output

```
Before:   BADCFEHGJILKNMPORQTSVUXWZY
   ..........................

After:   BADCFEHGJILKNMPORQTSVUXWZY
   ABCDEFGHIJKLMNOPQRSTUVWXYZ
```

system, _wsystem

Execute a command.

int system(const char ****command* **);**
int _wsystem(const wchar_t ****command* **);**

Routine	Required Header	Optional Headers	Compatibility
system	<process.h> or <stdlib.h>		ANSI, Win 95, Win NT, Win32s
_wsystem	<process.h> or <stdlib.h> or <wchar.h>		Win NT

For additional compatibility information, see “Compatibility” on page ix in the Introduction.

Libraries	
LIBC.LIB	Single thread static library, retail version
LIBCMT.LIB	Multithread static library, retail version
MSVCRT.LIB	Import library for MSVCRTx0.DLL, retail version
MSVCRTx0.DLL	Multithread DLL library, retail version

Return Value

If *command* is **NULL** and the command interpreter is found, the function returns a nonzero value. If the command interpreter is not found, it returns 0 and sets **errno** to **ENOENT**. If *command* is not **NULL**, **system** returns the value that is returned by the command interpreter. It returns the value 0 only if the command interpreter returns the value 0. A return value of –1 indicates an error, and **errno** is set to one of the following values:

E2BIG Argument list (which is system-dependent) is too big.

ENOENT Command interpreter cannot be found.

ENOEXEC Command-interpreter file has invalid format and is not executable.

ENOMEM Not enough memory is available to execute command; or available memory has been corrupted; or invalid block exists, indicating that process making call was not allocated properly.

Parameter

command Command to be executed

Remarks

The **system** function passes *command* to the command interpreter, which executes the string as an operating-system command. **system** refers to the **COMSPEC** and **PATH** environment variables that locate the command-interpreter file (the file named CMD.EXE in Windows NT). If *command* is NULL, the function simply checks to see whether the command interpreter exists.

You must explicitly flush (using **fflush** or **_flushall**) or close any stream before calling **system**.

_wsystem is a wide-character version of **_system**; the *command* argument to **_wsystem** is a wide-character string. These functions behave identically otherwise.

Example

```
/* SYSTEM.C: This program uses
 * system to TYPE its source file.
 */

#include <process.h>

void main( void )
{
   system( "type system.c" );
}
```

Output

```
/* SYSTEM.C: This program uses
 * system to TYPE its source file.
 */
#include <process.h>
void main( void )
{
   system( "type system.c" );
}
```

See Also **_exec** Functions, **exit**, **_flushall**, **_spawn** Functions

tan, tanh

Calculate the tangent (**tan**) or hyperbolic tangent (**tanh**).

double tan(double *x* **);**
double tanh(double *x* **);**

Routine	Required Header	Optional Headers	Compatibility
tan	<math.h>		ANSI, Win 95, Win NT, Win32s, 68K, PMac
tanh	<math.h>		ANSI, Win 95, Win NT, Win32s, 68K, PMac

For additional compatibility information, see "Compatibility" on page ix in the Introduction.

Libraries	
LIBC.LIB	Single thread static library, retail version
LIBCMT.LIB	Multithread static library, retail version
MSVCRT.LIB	Import library for MSVCRTx0.DLL, retail version
MSVCRTx0.DLL	Multithread DLL library, retail version

Return Value

tan returns the tangent of *x*. If *x* is greater than or equal to 2^{63}, or less than or equal to -2^{63}, a loss of significance in the result occurs, in which case the function generates a **_TLOSS** error and returns an indefinite (same as a quiet NaN). You can modify error handling with **_matherr**.

tanh returns the hyperbolic tangent of *x*. There is no error return.

Parameter

x Angle in radians

Example

```
/* TAN.C:  This program displays the tangent of pi / 4
 * and the hyperbolic tangent of the result.
 */

#include <math.h>
#include <stdio.h>

void main( void )
{
   double pi = 3.1415926535;
   double x, y;
```

```
    x = tan( pi / 4 );
    y = tanh( x );
    printf( "tan( %f ) = %f\n", x, y );
    printf( "tanh( %f ) = %f\n", y, x );
}
```

Output

```
tan( 1.000000 ) = 0.761594
tanh( 0.761594 ) = 1.000000
```

See Also **acos, asin, atan, cos, sin**

_tell, _telli64

Get the position of the file pointer.

long _tell(int *handle* **);**
__int64 _telli64(int *handle* **);**

Routine	Required Header	Optional Headers	Compatibility
_tell	<io.h>		Win 95, Win NT, Win32s, 68K, PMac
_telli64	<io.h>		Win 95, Win NT, Win32s

For additional compatibility information, see “Compatibility” on page ix in the Introduction.

Libraries	
LIBC.LIB	Single thread static library, retail version
LIBCMT.LIB	Multithread static library, retail version
MSVCRT.LIB	Import library for MSVCRTx0.DLL, retail version
MSVCRTx0.DLL	Multithread DLL library, retail version

Return Value

A return value of –1L indicates an error, and **errno** is set to **EBADF** to indicate an invalid file-handle argument. On devices incapable of seeking, the return value is undefined.

Parameter

handle Handle referring to open file

Remarks

The **_tell** function gets the current position of the file pointer (if any) associated with the *handle* argument. The position is expressed as the number of bytes from the beginning of the file. For the **_telli64** function, this value is expressed as a 64-bit integer.

Example

```
/* TELL.C:  This program uses _tell to tell the
 * file pointer position after a file read.
 */

#include <io.h>
#include <stdio.h>
#include <fcntl.h>

void main( void )
{
   int  fh;
   char buffer[500];

   if( (fh = _open( "tell.c", _O_RDONLY )) != -1 )
   {
      if( _read( fh, buffer, 500 ) > 0 )
         printf( "Current file position is: %d\n", _tell( fh ) );
      _close( fh );
   }
}
```

Output

```
Current file position is: 434
```

See Also **ftell**, **_lseek**

_tempnam, _wtempnam, tmpnam, _wtmpnam

Create temporary filenames.

char *_tempnam(char ****dir*, char ****prefix*** **);**
wchar_t *_wtempnam(wchar_t ****dir*, wchar_t ****prefix*** **);**
char *tmpnam(char ****string* **);**
wchar_t *_wtmpnam(wchar_t ****string* **);**

Routine	Required Header	Optional Headers	Compatibility
_tempnam	<stdio.h>		Win 95, Win NT, Win32s, 68K, PMac
_wtempnam	<stdio.h> or <wchar.h>		Win 95, Win NT, Win32s

Routine	Required Header	Optional Headers	Compatibility
tmpnam	<stdio.h>		ANSI, Win 95, Win NT, Win32s, 68K, PMac
_wtmpnam	<stdio.h> or <wchar.h>		Win 95, Win NT, Win32s

For additional compatibility information, see "Compatibility" on page ix in the Introduction.

Libraries	
LIBC.LIB	Single thread static library, retail version
LIBCMT.LIB	Multithread static library, retail version
MSVCRT.LIB	Import library for MSVCRTx0.DLL, retail version
MSVCRTx0.DLL	Multithread DLL library, retail version

Return Value

Each of these functions returns a pointer to the name generated, unless it is impossible to create this name or the name is not unique. If the name cannot be created or if a file with that name already exists, **tmpnam** and **_tempnam** return **NULL**. **_tempnam** and **_wtempnam** also return **NULL** if the file search fails.

Note The pointer returned by **tmpnam** points to an internal static buffer. **free** does not need to be called to deallocate this pointer.

Parameters

prefix Filename prefix

dir Target directory to be used if TMP not defined

string Pointer to temporary name

Remarks

The **tmpnam** function generates a temporary filename that can be used to open a temporary file without overwriting an existing file.

This name is stored in *string*. If *string* is **NULL**, then **tmpnam** leaves the result in an internal static buffer. Thus any subsequent calls destroy this value. If *string* is not **NULL**, it is assumed to point to an array of at least **L_tmpnam** bytes (the value of **L_tmpnam** is defined in STDIO.H). The function generates unique filenames for up to **TMP_MAX** calls.

The character string that **tmpnam** creates consists of the path prefix, defined by the entry **P_tmpdir** in the file STDIO.H, followed by a sequence consisting of the digit characters '0' through '9'; the numerical value of this string is in the range 1–65,535. Changing the definitions of **L_tmpnam** or **P_tmpdir** in STDIO.H does not change the operation of **tmpnam**.

_tempnam creates a temporary filename for use in another directory. This filename is different from that of any existing file. The *prefix* argument is the prefix to the filename. **_tempnam** uses **malloc** to allocate space for the filename; the program is responsible for freeing this space when it is no longer needed. **_tempnam** looks for the file with the given name in the following directories, listed in order of precedence.

Directory Used	Conditions
Directory specified by **TMP**	**TMP** environment variable is set, and directory specified by **TMP** exists.
dir argument to **_tempnam**	**TMP** environment variable is not set, or directory specified by **TMP** does not exist.
P_tmpdir in STDIO.H	*dir* argument is **NULL**, or *dir* is name of nonexistent directory.
Current working directory	**P_tmpdir** does not exist.

_tempnam and **tmpnam** automatically handle multibyte-character string arguments as appropriate, recognizing multibyte-character sequences according to the OEM code page obtained from the operating system. **_wtempnam** is a wide-character version of **_tempnam**; the arguments and return value of **_wtempnam** are wide-character strings. **_wtempnam** and **_tempnam** behave identically except that **_wtempnam** does not handle multibyte-character strings. **_wtmpnam** is a wide-character version of **tmpnam**; the argument and return value of **_wtmpnam** are wide-character strings. **_wtmpnam** and **tmpnam** behave identically except that **_wtmpnam** does not handle multibyte-character strings.

Example

```
/* TEMPNAM.C: This program uses tmpnam to create a unique
 * filename in the current working directory, then uses
 * _tempnam to create a unique filename with a prefix of stq.
 */

#include <stdio.h>

void main( void )
{
   char *name1, *name2;

   /* Create a temporary filename for the current working directory: */
   if( ( name1 = tmpnam( NULL ) ) != NULL )
      printf( "%s is safe to use as a temporary file.\n", name1 );
   else
      printf( "Cannot create a unique filename\n" );

   /* Create a temporary filename in temporary directory with the
    * prefix "stq". The actual destination directory may vary
    * depending on the state of the TMP environment variable and
    * the global variable P_tmpdir.
    */
```

```
   if( ( name2 = _tempnam( "c:\\tmp", "stq" ) ) != NULL )
      printf( "%s is safe to use as a temporary file.\n", name2 );
   else
      printf( "Cannot create a unique filename\n" );
}
```

Output

```
\s5d. is safe to use as a temporary file.
C:\temp\stq2 is safe to use as a temporary file.
```

See Also **_getmbcp**, **malloc**, **_setmbcp**, **tmpfile**

---

terminate

Calls **abort** or a function you specify using **set_terminate**.

void terminate(void);

Routine	Required Header	Optional Headers	Compatibility
terminate	<eh.h>		ANSI, Win 95, Win NT, Win32s, 68K, PMac

For additional compatibility information, see "Compatibility" on page ix in the Introduction.

Libraries	
LIBC.LIB	Single thread static library, retail version
LIBCMT.LIB	Multithread static library, retail version
MSVCRT.LIB	Import library for MSVCRTx0.DLL, retail version
MSVCRTx0.DLL	Multithread DLL library, retail version

Return Value

None

Remarks

The **terminate** function is used with C++ exception handling and is called in the following cases:

- A matching catch handler cannot be found for a thrown C++ exception.
- An exception is thrown by a destructor function during stack unwind.
- The stack is corrupted after throwing an exception.

terminate calls **abort** by default. You can change this default by writing your own termination function and calling **set_terminate** with the name of your function as its argument. **terminate** calls the last function given as an argument to **set_terminate**.

Example

```
/* TERMINAT.CPP:
 */
#include <eh.h>
#include <process.h>
#include <iostream.h>

void term_func();

void main()
{

    int i = 10, j = 0, result;
    set_terminate( term_func );
    try
    {
        if( j == 0 )
            throw "Divide by zero!";
        else
            result = i/j;

    }
    catch( int )
    {
        cout << "Caught some integer exception.\n";
    }
    cout << "This should never print.\n";

}
void term_func()
{
    cout << "term_func() was called by terminate().\n";

    // ... cleanup tasks performed here

    // If this function does not exit, abort is called.

    exit(-1);
}
```

Output

```
term_func() was called by terminate().
```

See Also **abort**, **_set_se_translator**, **set_terminate**, **set_unexpected**, **unexpected**

time

Gets the system time.

time_t time(time_t **timer*);

Routine	Required Header	Optional Headers	Compatibility
time	<time.h>		ANSI, Win 95, Win NT, Win32s, 68K, PMac

For additional compatibility information, see "Compatibility" on page ix in the Introduction.

Libraries	
LIBC.LIB	Single thread static library, retail version
LIBCMT.LIB	Multithread static library, retail version
MSVCRT.LIB	Import library for MSVCRTx0.DLL, retail version
MSVCRTx0.DLL	Multithread DLL library, retail version

Return Value

time returns the time in elapsed seconds. There is no error return.

Parameter

timer Storage location for time

Remarks

The **time** function returns the number of seconds elapsed since midnight (00:00:00), January 1, 1970, coordinated universal time, according to the system clock. The return value is stored in the location given by *timer*. This parameter may be **NULL**, in which case the return value is not stored.

Example

```
/* TIMES.C illustrates various time and date functions including:
 *      time            _ftime          ctime       asctime
 *      localtime       gmtime          mktime      _tzset
 *      _strtime        _strdate        strftime
 *
 * Also the global variable:
 *      _tzname
 */

#include <time.h>
#include <stdio.h>
#include <sys/types.h>
#include <sys/timeb.h>
#include <string.h>
```

```
void main()
{
    char tmpbuf[128], ampm[] = "AM";
    time_t ltime;
    struct _timeb tstruct;
    struct tm *today, *gmt, xmas = { 0, 0, 12, 25, 11, 93 };

    /* Set time zone from TZ environment variable. If TZ is not set,
     * operating system default is used, otherwise PST8PDT is used
     * (Pacific standard time, daylight savings).
     */
    _tzset();

    /* Display operating system-style date and time. */
    _strtime( tmpbuf );
    printf( "OS time:\t\t\t\t%s\n", tmpbuf );
    _strdate( tmpbuf );
    printf( "OS date:\t\t\t\t%s\n", tmpbuf );

    /* Get UNIX-style time and display as number and string. */
    time( &ltime );
    printf( "Time in seconds since UTC 1/1/70:\t%ld\n", ltime );
    printf( "UNIX time and date:\t\t\t%s", ctime( &ltime ) );

    /* Display UTC. */
    gmt = gmtime( &ltime );
    printf( "Coordinated universal time:\t\t%s", asctime( gmt ) );

    /* Convert to time structure and adjust for PM if necessary. */
    today = localtime( &ltime );
    if( today->tm_hour > 12 )
    {
   strcpy( ampm, "PM" );
   today->tm_hour -= 12;
    }
    if( today->tm_hour == 0 )  /* Adjust if midnight hour. */
   today->tm_hour = 12;

    /* Note how pointer addition is used to skip the first 11
     * characters and printf is used to trim off terminating
     * characters.
     */
    printf( "12-hour time:\t\t\t\t%.8s %s\n",
       asctime( today ) + 11, ampm );

    /* Print additional time information. */
    _ftime( &tstruct );
    printf( "Plus milliseconds:\t\t\t%u\n", tstruct.millitm );
    printf( "Zone difference in seconds from UTC:\t%u\n",
             tstruct.timezone );
    printf( "Time zone name:\t\t\t\t%s\n", _tzname[0] );
    printf( "Daylight savings:\t\t\t%s\n",
             tstruct.dstflag ? "YES" : "NO" );
```

```
    /* Make time for noon on Christmas, 1993. */
    if( mktime( &xmas ) != (time_t)-1 )
   printf( "Christmas\t\t\t\t%s\n", asctime( &xmas ) );

    /* Use time structure to build a customized time string. */
    today = localtime( &ltime );

    /* Use strftime to build a customized time string. */
    strftime( tmpbuf, 128,
         "Today is %A, day %d of %B in the year %Y.\n", today );
    printf( tmpbuf );
}
```

Output

```
OS time:                                21:51:03
OS date:                                05/03/94
Time in seconds since UTC 1/1/70:       768027063
UNIX time and date:                     Tue May 03 21:51:03 1994
Coordinated universal time:             Wed May 04 04:51:03 1994
12-hour time:                           09:51:03 PM
Plus milliseconds:                      279
Zone difference in seconds from UTC:    480
Time zone name:
Daylight savings:                       YES
Christmas                               Sat Dec 25 12:00:00 1993

Today is Tuesday, day 03 of May in the year 1994.
```

See Also **asctime**, **_ftime**, **gmtime**, **localtime**, **_utime**

tmpfile

Creates a temporary file.

FILE *tmpfile(void);

Routine	Required Header	Optional Headers	Compatibility
tmpfile	<stdio.h>		ANSI, Win 95, Win NT, Win32s, 68K, PMac

For additional compatibility information, see "Compatibility" on page ix in the Introduction.

Libraries

LIBC.LIB	Single thread static library, retail version
LIBCMT.LIB	Multithread static library, retail version
MSVCRT.LIB	Import library for MSVCRTx0.DLL, retail version
MSVCRTx0.DLL	Multithread DLL library, retail version

Return Value

If successful, **tmpfile** returns a stream pointer. Otherwise, it returns a **NULL** pointer.

Remarks

The **tmpfile** function creates a temporary file and returns a pointer to that stream. If the file cannot be opened, **tmpfile** returns a **NULL** pointer. This temporary file is automatically deleted when the file is closed, when the program terminates normally, or when **_rmtmp** is called, assuming that the current working directory does not change. The temporary file is opened in **w+b** (binary read/write) mode.

Example

```
/* TMPFILE.C: This program uses tmpfile to create a
 * temporary file, then deletes this file with _rmtmp.
 */

#include <stdio.h>

void main( void )
{
   FILE *stream;
   char tempstring[] = "String to be written";
   int  i;

   /* Create temporary files. */
   for( i = 1; i <= 3; i++ )
   {
      if( (stream = tmpfile()) == NULL )
         perror( "Could not open new temporary file\n" );
      else
         printf( "Temporary file %d was created\n", i );
   }

   /* Remove temporary files. */
   printf( "%d temporary files deleted\n", _rmtmp() );
}
```

Output

```
Temporary file 1 was created
Temporary file 2 was created
Temporary file 3 was created
3 temporary files deleted
```

See Also **_rmtmp**, **_tempnam**

to Functions

Each of the **to** functions and its associated macro, if any, converts a single character to another character.

__toascii | **toupper, _toupper, towupper**

tolower, _tolower, towlower

Remarks

The **to** functions and macro conversions are as follows.

Routine	Macro	Description
__toascii	**__toascii**	Converts *c* to ASCII character
tolower	**tolower**	Converts *c* to lowercase if appropriate
_tolower	**_tolower**	Converts *c* to lowercase
towlower	None	Converts *c* to corresponding wide-character lowercase letter
toupper	**toupper**	Converts *c* to uppercase if appropriate
_toupper	**_toupper**	Converts *c* to uppercase
towupper	None	Converts c to corresponding wide-character uppercase letter

To use the function versions of the **to** routines that are also defined as macros, either remove the macro definitions with **#undef** directives or do not include CTYPE.H. If you use the /Za compiler option, the compiler uses the function version of **toupper** or **tolower**. Declarations of the **toupper** and **tolower** functions are in STDLIB.H.

The **__toascii** routine sets all but the low-order 7 bits of *c* to 0, so that the converted value represents a character in the ASCII character set. If *c* already represents an ASCII character, *c* is unchanged.

The **tolower** and **toupper** routines:

- Are dependent on the **LC_CTYPE** category of the current locale (**tolower** calls **isupper** and **toupper** calls **islower**).
- Convert *c* if *c* represents a convertible letter of the appropriate case in the current locale and the opposite case exists for that locale. Otherwise, *c* is unchanged.

The **_tolower** and **_toupper** routines:

- Are locale-independent, much faster versions of **tolower** and **toupper.**
- Can be used only when **isascii(***c***)** and either **isupper(***c***)** or **islower(***c***)**, respectively, are true.
- Have undefined results if *c* is not an ASCII letter of the appropriate case for converting.

The **towlower** and **towupper** functions return a converted copy of *c* if and only if both of the following conditions are true. Otherwise, *c* is unchanged.

- *c* is a wide character of the appropriate case (that is, for which **iswupper** or **iswlower,** respectively, is true).
- There is a corresponding wide character of the target case (that is, for which **iswlower** or **iswupper,** respectively, is true).

Example

```
/* TOUPPER.C: This program uses toupper and tolower to
 * analyze all characters between 0x0 and 0x7F. It also
 * applies _toupper and _tolower to any code in this
 * range for which these functions make sense.
 */

#include <conio.h>
#include <ctype.h>
#include <string.h>

char msg[] = "Some of THESE letters are Capitals\r\n";
char *p;

void main( void )
{
   _cputs( msg );

   /* Reverse case of message. */
   for( p = msg; p < msg + strlen( msg ); p++ )
   {
      if( islower( *p ) )
         _putch( _toupper( *p ) );
      else if( isupper( *p ) )
         _putch( _tolower( *p ) );
      else
         _putch( *p );
   }
}
```

Output

```
Some of THESE letters are Capitals
sOME OF these LETTERS ARE cAPITALS
```

See Also is Routines

_ _toascii

Converts characters.

int _ _toascii(int *c* **);**

Routine	Required Header	Optional Headers	Compatibility
__toascii	<ctype.h>		Win 95, Win NT, Win32s, 68K, PMac

For additional compatibility information, see "Compatibility" on page ix in the Introduction.

Libraries	
LIBC.LIB	Single thread static library, retail version
LIBCMT.LIB	Multithread static library, retail version
MSVCRT.LIB	Import library for MSVCRTx0.DLL, retail version
MSVCRTx0.DLL	Multithread DLL library, retail version

Return Value

__toascii converts a copy of *c* if possible, and returns the result. There is no return value reserved to indicate an error.

Parameter

c Character to convert

Remarks

The _ _**toascii** routine converts the given character to an ASCII character.

See Also **is** Routines, **to** Functions

tolower, _tolower, towlower

Convert character to lowercase.

int tolower(int *c* **);**
int _tolower(int *c* **);**
int towlower(wint_t *c* **);**

Routine	Required Header	Optional Headers	Compatibility
tolower	<stdlib.h> and <ctype.h>		ANSI, Win 95, Win NT, Win32s, 68K, PMac
_tolower	<ctype.h>		Win 95, Win NT, Win32s, 68K, PMac
towlower	<ctype.h> or <wchar.h>		ANSI, Win 95, Win NT, Win32s

For additional compatibility information, see "Compatibility" on page ix in the Introduction.

Libraries	
LIBC.LIB	Single thread static library, retail version
LIBCMT.LIB	Multithread static library, retail version
MSVCRT.LIB	Import library for MSVCRTx0.DLL, retail version
MSVCRTx0.DLL	Multithread DLL library, retail version

Return Value

Each of these routines converts a copy of *c,* if possible, and returns the result. There is no return value reserved to indicate an error.

Parameter

c Character to convert

Remarks

Each of these routines converts a given uppercase letter to a lowercase letter if possible and appropriate.

See Also **is** Routines, **to** Functions

toupper _toupper, towupper

Convert character to uppercase.

int toupper(**int** *c* **);**
int _toupper(**int** *c* **);**
int towupper(**wint_t** *c* **);**

Routine	Required Header	Optional Headers	Compatibility
toupper	<stdlib.h> and <ctype.h>		ANSI, Win 95, Win NT, Win32s, 68K, PMac
_toupper	<ctype.h>		Win 95, Win NT, Win32s, 68K, PMac
towupper	<ctype.h> or <wchar.h>		ANSI, Win 95, Win NT, Win32s

For additional compatibility information, see "Compatibility" on page ix in the Introduction.

Libraries

LIBC.LIB	Single thread static library, retail version
LIBCMT.LIB	Multithread static library, retail version
MSVCRT.LIB	Import library for MSVCRTx0.DLL, retail version
MSVCRTx0.DLL	Multithread DLL library, retail version

Return Value

Each of these routines converts a copy of *c*, if possible, and returns the result.

If *c* is a wide character for which **iswlower** is true and there is a corresponding wide character for which **iswupper** is true, **towupper** returns the corresponding wide character; otherwise, **towupper** returns *c* unchanged.

There is no return value reserved to indicate an error.

Parameter

c Character to convert

Remarks

Each of these routines converts a given lowercase letter to an uppercase letter if possible and appropriate.

See Also **is** Routines, **to** Functions

_tzset

Sets time environment variables.

void _tzset(void);

Routine	Required Header	Optional Headers	Compatibility
_tzset	<time.h>		Win 95, Win NT, Win32s, 68K, PMac

For additional compatibility information, see "Compatibility" on page ix in the Introduction.

Libraries

LIBC.LIB	Single thread static library, retail version
LIBCMT.LIB	Multithread static library, retail version
MSVCRT.LIB	Import library for MSVCRTx0.DLL, retail version
MSVCRTx0.DLL	Multithread DLL library, retail version

Return Value

None

Remarks

The **_tzset** function uses the current setting of the environment variable **TZ** to assign values to three global variables: **_daylight**, **_timezone**, and **_tzname**. These variables are used by the **_ftime** and **localtime** functions to make corrections from coordinated universal time (UTC) to local time, and by the **time** function to compute UTC from system time. Use the following syntax to set the **TZ** environment variable:

set TZ=*tzn*[+ | –]*hh*[**:***mm*[**:***ss*]][*dzn*]

tzn Three-letter time-zone name, such as PST. You must specify the correct offset from UTC.

hh Difference in hours between UTC and local time. Optionally signed.

mm Minutes. Separated from *hh* by a colon (**:**).

ss Seconds. Separated from *mm* by a colon (**:**).

dzn Three-letter daylight-saving-time zone such as PDT. If daylight saving time is never in effect in the locality, set **TZ** without a value for *dzn*.

For example, to set the **TZ** environment variable to correspond to the current time zone in Germany, you can use one of the following statements:

```
set TZ=GST1GDT
set TZ=GST+1GDT
```

These strings use GST to indicate German standard time, assume that Germany is one hour ahead of UTC, and assume that daylight saving time is in effect.

If the **TZ** value is not set, **_tzset** attempts to use the time zone information specified by the operating system. Under Windows NT and Windows 95, this information is specified in the Control Panel's Date/Time application. If **_tzset** cannot obtain this information, it uses PST8PDT by default, which signifies the Pacific time zone.

Based on the **TZ** environment variable value, the following values are assigned to the global variables **_daylight**, **_timezone**, and **_tzname** when **_tzset** is called:

Global Variable	Description	Default Value
_daylight	Nonzero value if a daylight-saving-time zone is specified in **TZ** setting; otherwise, 0	1
_timezone	Difference in seconds between UTC and local time.	28800 (28800 seconds equals 8 hours)
_tzname[0]	String value of time-zone name from **TZ** environmental variable; empty if **TZ** has not been set	PST
_tzname[1]	String value of daylight-saving-time zone; empty if daylight-saving-time zone is omitted from **TZ** environmental variable	PDT

The default values shown in the preceding table for **_daylight** and the **_tzname** array correspond to "PST8PDT." If the DST zone is omitted from the **TZ** environmental variable, the value of **_daylight** is 0 and the **_ftime**, **gmtime**, and **localtime** functions return 0 for their DST flags. For more information, see "**_daylight**, **_timezone**, and **_tzname**" on page 40.

Example

```
/* TZSET.C: This program first sets up the time zone by
 * placing the variable named TZ=EST5 in the environment
 * table. It then uses _tzset to set the global variables
 * named _daylight, _timezone, and _tzname.
 */

#include <time.h>
#include <stdlib.h>
#include <stdio.h>

void main( void )
{
   if( _putenv( "TZ=EST5EDT" ) == -1 )
   {
      printf( "Unable to set TZ\n" );
      exit( 1 );
   }
   else
   {
      _tzset();
      printf( "_daylight = %d\n", _daylight );
      printf( "_timezone = %ld\n", _timezone );
      printf( "_tzname[0] = %s\n", _tzname[0] );
   }
   exit( 0 );
}
```

Output

```
_daylight = 1
_timezone = 18000
_tzname[0] = EST
```

See Also **asctime**, **_ftime**, **gmtime**, **localtime**, **time**, **_utime**

_ultoa, _ultow

Convert an unsigned long integer to a string.

char *_ultoa(unsigned long *value*, **char** **string*, **int** *radix* **);**
wchar_t *_ultow(unsigned long *value*, **wchar_t** **string*, **int** *radix* **);**

Routine	Required Header	Optional Headers	Compatibility
_ultoa	<stdlib.h>		Win 95, Win NT, Win32s, 68K, PMac
_ultow	<stdlib.h> or <wchar.h>		Win 95, Win NT, Win32s

For additional compatibility information, see "Compatibility" on page ix in the Introduction.

Libraries	
LIBC.LIB	Single thread static library, retail version
LIBCMT.LIB	Multithread static library, retail version
MSVCRT.LIB	Import library for MSVCRTx0.DLL, retail version
MSVCRTx0.DLL	Multithread DLL library, retail version

Return Value

Each of these functions returns a pointer to *string*. There is no error return.

Parameters

value Number to be converted

string String result

radix Base of *value*

Remarks

The **_ultoa** function converts *value* to a null-terminated character string and stores the result (up to 33 bytes) in *string*. No overflow checking is performed. *radix* specifies the base of *value*; *radix* must be in the range 2–36. **_ultow** is a wide-character version of **_ultoa**.

Example

See the example for **_itoa**.

See Also **_itoa**, **_ltoa**

_umask

Sets the default file-permission mask.

int _umask(int *pmode* **);**

Routine	Required Header	Optional Headers	Compatibility
_umask	<io.h> and <sys/stat.h> and <sys/types.h>		Win 95, Win NT, Win32s, 68K, PMac

For additional compatibility information, see "Compatibility" on page ix in the Introduction.

Libraries	
LIBC.LIB	Single thread static library, retail version
LIBCMT.LIB	Multithread static library, retail version
MSVCRT.LIB	Import library for MSVCRTx0.DLL, retail version
MSVCRTx0.DLL	Multithread DLL library, retail version

Return Value

_umask returns the previous value of *pmode*. There is no error return.

Parameter

pmode Default permission setting

Remarks

The **_umask** function sets the file-permission mask of the current process to the mode specified by *pmode*. The file-permission mask modifies the permission setting of new files created by **_creat**, **_open**, or **_sopen**. If a bit in the mask is 1, the corresponding bit in the file's requested permission value is set to 0 (disallowed). If a bit in the mask is 0, the corresponding bit is left unchanged. The permission setting for a new file is not set until the file is closed for the first time.

The argument *pmode* is a constant expression containing one or both of the manifest constants **_S_IREAD** and **_S_IWRITE**, defined in SYS\STAT.H. When both constants are given, they are joined with the bitwise-OR operator (|). If the *pmode* argument is **_S_IREAD**, reading is not allowed (the file is write-only). If the *pmode* argument is **_S_IWRITE**, writing is not allowed (the file is read-only). For example, if the write bit is set in the mask, any new files will be read-only. Note that with MS-DOS, Windows NT, and Windows 95, all files are readable; it is not possible to give write-only permission. Therefore, setting the read bit with **_umask** has no effect on the file's modes.

Example

```
/* UMASK.C: This program uses _umask to set
 * the file-permission mask so that all future
 * files will be created as read-only files.
 * It also displays the old mask.
 */

#include <sys/stat.h>
#include <sys/types.h>
#include <io.h>
#include <stdio.h>

void main( void )
{
   int oldmask;

   /* Create read-only files: */
   oldmask = _umask( _S_IWRITE );
   printf( "Oldmask = 0x%.4x\n", oldmask );
}
```

Output

```
Oldmask = 0x0000
```

See Also **_chmod**, **_creat**, **_mkdir**, **_open**

---

unexpected

Calls **terminate** or function you specify using **set_unexpected**.

void unexpected(void);

Routine	Required Header	Optional Headers	Compatibility
unexpected	<eh.h>		ANSI, Win 95, Win NT, Win32s, 68K, PMac

For additional compatibility information, see "Compatibility" on page ix in the Introduction.

Libraries	
LIBC.LIB	Single thread static library, retail version
LIBCMT.LIB	Multithread static library, retail version
MSVCRT.LIB	Import library for MSVCRTx0.DLL, retail version
MSVCRTx0.DLL	Multithread DLL library, retail version

Return Value

None

Remarks

The **unexpected** routine is not used with the current implemenation of C++ exception handling. **unexpected** calls **terminate** by default. You can change this default behavior by writing a custom termination function and calling **set_unexpected** with the name of your function as its argument. **unexpected** calls the last function given as an argument to **set_unexpected**.

See Also **abort**, **_set_se_translator**, **set_terminate**, **set_unexpected**, **terminate**

ungetc, ungetwc

Pushes a character back onto the stream.

int ungetc(int *c*, **FILE** **stream* **);**
wint_t ungetwc(wint_t *c*, **FILE** **stream* **);**

Routine	Required Header	Optional Headers	Compatibility
ungetc	<stdio.h>		ANSI, Win 95, Win NT, Win32s, 68K, PMac
ungetwc	<stdio.h> or <wchar.h>		ANSI, Win 95, Win NT, Win32s

For additional compatibility information, see "Compatibility" on page ix in the Introduction.

Libraries	
LIBC.LIB	Single thread static library, retail version
LIBCMT.LIB	Multithread static library, retail version
MSVCRT.LIB	Import library for MSVCRTx0.DLL, retail version
MSVCRTx0.DLL	Multithread DLL library, retail version

Return Value

If successful, each of these functions returns the character argument *c*. If *c* cannot be pushed back or if no character has been read, the input stream is unchanged and **ungetc** returns **EOF**; **ungetwc** returns **WEOF**.

Parameters

c Character to be pushed

stream Pointer to **FILE** structure

Remarks

The **ungetc** function pushes the character *c* back onto *stream* and clears the end-of-file indicator. The stream must be open for reading. A subsequent read operation on *stream* starts with *c*. An attempt to push **EOF** onto the stream using **ungetc** is ignored.

Characters placed on the stream by **ungetc** may be erased if **fflush**, **fseek**, **fsetpos**, or **rewind** is called before the character is read from the stream. The file-position indicator will have the value it had before the characters were pushed back. The external storage corresponding to the stream is unchanged. On a successful **ungetc** call against a text stream, the file-position indicator is unspecified until all the pushed-back characters are read or discarded. On each successful **ungetc** call against a binary stream, the file-position indicator is decremented; if its value was 0 before a call, the value is undefined after the call.

Results are unpredictable if **ungetc** is called twice without a read or file-positioning operation between the two calls. After a call to **fscanf**, a call to **ungetc** may fail unless another read operation (such as **getc**) has been performed. This is because **fscanf** itself calls **ungetc**.

ungetwc is a wide-character version of **ungetc**. However, on each successful **ungetwc** call against a text or binary stream, the value of the file-position indicator is unspecified until all pushed-back characters are read or discarded.

Example

```
/* UNGETC.C: This program first converts a character
 * representation of an unsigned integer to an integer. If
 * the program encounters a character that is not a digit,
 * the program uses ungetc to replace it in the  stream.
 */

#include <stdio.h>
#include <ctype.h>

void main( void )
{
   int ch;
   int result = 0;

   printf( "Enter an integer: " );

   /* Read in and convert number: */
   while( ((ch = getchar()) != EOF) && isdigit( ch ) )
      result = result * 10 + ch - '0';    /* Use digit. */
   if( ch != EOF )
      ungetc( ch, stdin );                /* Put nondigit back. */
   printf( "Number = %d\nNextcharacter in stream = '%c'",
            result, getchar() );
}
```

Output

```
Enter an integer: 521a
Number = 521
Nextcharacter in stream = 'a'
```

See Also **getc**, **putc**

_ungetch

Pushes back the last charcter read from the console.

int _ungetch(int *c* **);**

Routine	Required Header	Optional Headers	Compatibility
_ungetch	<conio.h>		Win 95, Win NT, Win32s

For additional compatibility information, see "Compatibility" on page ix in the Introduction.

Libraries	
LIBC.LIB	Single thread static library, retail version
LIBCMT.LIB	Multithread static library, retail version
MSVCRT.LIB	Import library for MSVCRTx0.DLL, retail version
MSVCRTx0.DLL	Multithread DLL library, retail version

Return Value

_ungetch returns the character *c* if it is successful. A return value of **EOF** indicates an error.

Parameter

c Character to be pushed

Remarks

The **_ungetch** function pushes the character *c* back to the console, causing *c* to be the next character read by **_getch** or **_getche**. **_ungetch** fails if it is called more than once before the next read. Thc *c* argument may not be **EOF**.

Example

```
/* UNGETCH.C: In this program, a white-space delimited
 * token is read from the keyboard. When the program
 * encounters a delimiter, it uses _ungetch to replace
 * the character in the keyboard buffer.
 */

#include <conio.h>
#include <ctype.h>
#include <stdio.h>

void main( void )
```

```
{
   char buffer[100];
   int count = 0;
   int ch;
   ch = _getche();
   while( isspace( ch ) )      /* Skip preceding white space. */
      ch = _getche();
   while( count < 99 )         /* Gather token. */
   {
      if( isspace( ch ) )      /* End of token. */
         break;
      buffer[count++] = (char)ch;
      ch = _getche();
   }
   _ungetch( ch );            /* Put back delimiter. */
   buffer[count] = '\0';      /* Null terminate the token. */
   printf( "\ntoken = %s\n", buffer );
}
```

Output

```
White
token = White
```

See Also **_cscanf**, **_getch**

_unlink, _wunlink

Delete a file.

int _unlink(const char ***filename*** **);**
int _wunlink(const wchar_t ***filename*** **);**

Routine	Required Header	Optional Headers	Compatibility
_unlink	<io.h> and <stdio.h>		Win 95, Win NT, Win32s, 68K, PMac
_wunlink	<io.h> or <wchar.h>		Win NT

For additional compatibility information, see "Compatibility" on page ix in the Introduction.

Libraries

LIBC.LIB	Single thread static library, retail version
LIBCMT.LIB	Multithread static library, retail version
MSVCRT.LIB	Import library for MSVCRTx0.DLL, retail version
MSVCRTx0.DLL	Multithread DLL library, retail version

Return Value

Each of these functions returns 0 if successful. Otherwise, the function returns –1 and sets **errno** to **EACCES**, which means the path specifies a read-only file, or to **ENOENT**, which means the file or path is not found or the path specified a directory.

Parameter

filename Name of file to remove

Remarks

The **_unlink** function deletes the file specified by *filename*. **_wunlink** is a wide-character version of **_unlink**; the *filename* argument to **_wunlink** is a wide-character string. These functions behave identically otherwise.

Example

```
/* UNLINK.C: This program uses _unlink to delete UNLINK.OBJ. */

#include <stdio.h>

void main( void )
{
   if( _unlink( "unlink.obj" ) == -1 )
      perror( "Could not delete 'UNLINK.OBJ'" );
   else
      printf( "Deleted 'UNLINK.OBJ'\n" );
}
```

Output

```
Deleted 'UNLINK.OBJ'
```

See Also **_close**, **remove**

_utime, _wutime

Set the file modification time.

int _utime(unsigned char ****filename*, struct _utimbuf ****times* **);**
int _wutime(wchar_t ****filename*, struct _utimbuf ****times* **);**

Routine	Required Headers	Optional Headers	Compatibility
_utime	<sys/utime.h>	<errno.h>	Win 95, Win NT, Win32s, 68K, PMac
_wutime	<utime.h> or <wchar.h>	<errno.h>	Win 95, Win NT, Win32s

For additional compatibility information, see “Compatibility” on page ix in the Introduction.

Libraries	
LIBC.LIB	Single thread static library, retail version
LIBCMT.LIB	Multithread static library, retail version
MSVCRT.LIB	Import library for MSVCRTx0.DLL, retail version
MSVCRTx0.DLL	Multithread DLL library, retail version

Return Value

Each of these functions returns 0 if the file-modification time was changed. A return value of –1 indicates an error, in which case **errno** is set to one of the following values:

EACCES Path specifies directory or read-only file

EINVAL Invalid *times* argument

EMFILE Too many open files (the file must be opened to change its modification time)

ENOENT Path or filename not found

Parameters

filename Path or filename

times Pointer to stored time values

Remarks

The **_utime** function sets the modification time for the file specified by *filename*. The process must have write access to the file in order to change the time. Under Windows NT and Windows 95, you can change the access time and the modication time in the **_utimbuf** structure. If *times* is a **NULL** pointer, the modification time is set to the current local time. Otherwise, *times* must point to a structure of type **_utimbuf**, defined in SYS\UTIME.H.

The **_utimbuf** structure stores file access and modification times used by **_utime** to change file-modification dates. The structure has the following fields, which are both of type **time_t**:

actime Time of file access

modtime Time of file modification

_utime is identical to **_futime** except that the *filename* argument of **_utime** is a filename or a path to a file, rather than a handle to an open file.

_wutime is a wide-character version of **_utime**; the *filename* argument to **_wutime** is a wide-character string. These functions behave identically otherwise.

Example

```
/* UTIME.C: This program uses _utime to set the
 * file-modification time to the current time.
 */

#include <stdio.h>
#include <stdlib.h>
#include <sys/types.h>
#include <sys/utime.h>

void main( void )
{
   /* Show file time before and after. */
   system( "dir utime.c" );
   if( _utime( "utime.c", NULL ) == -1 )
      perror( "_utime failed\n" );
   else
      printf( "File time modified\n" );
   system( "dir utime.c" );
}
```

Output

```
 Volume in drive C is ALDONS
 Volume Serial Number is 0E17-1702

 Directory of C:\dolphin\crt\code

05/03/94  10:00p                    451 utime.c
               1 File(s)            451 bytes
                              83,320,832 bytes free
 Volume in drive C is ALDONS
 Volume Serial Number is 0E17-1702

 Directory of C:\dolphin\crt\code

05/03/94  10:00p                    451 utime.c
               1 File(s)            451 bytes
                              83,320,832 bytes free
File time modified
```

See Also **asctime**, **ctime**, **_fstat**, **_ftime**, **_futime**, **gmtime**, **localtime**, **_stat**, **time**

va_arg, va_end, va_start

Access variable-argument lists.

type **va_arg(va_list** *arg_ptr*, *type* **);**
void va_end(va_list *arg_ptr* **);**
void va_start(va_list *arg_ptr* **);** (UNIX version)
void va_start(va_list *arg_ptr*, *prev_param* **);** (ANSI version)

Routine	Required Header	Optional Headers	Compatibility
va_arg	<stdio.h> and <stdarg.h>	<varargs.h>[1]	ANSI, Win 95, Win NT, Win32s, 68K, PMac
va_end	<stdio.h> and <stdarg.h>	<varargs.h>[1]	ANSI, Win 95, Win NT, Win32s, 68K, PMac
va_start	<stdio.h> and <stdarg.h>	<varargs.h>[1]	ANSI, Win 95, Win NT, Win32s, 68K, PMac

1 Required for UNIX V compatibility.

For additional compatibility information, see "Compatibility" on page ix in the Introduction.

Libraries	
LIBC.LIB	Single thread static library, retail version
LIBCMT.LIB	Multithread static library, retail version
MSVCRT.LIB	Import library for MSVCRTx0.DLL, retail version
MSVCRTx0.DLL	Multithread DLL library, retail version

Return Value

va_arg returns the current argument; **va_start** and **va_end** do not return values.

Parameters

type Type of argument to be retrieved

arg_ptr Pointer to list of arguments

prev_param Parameter preceding first optional argument (ANSI only)

Remarks

The **va_arg**, **va_end**, and **va_start** macros provide a portable way to access the arguments to a function when the function takes a variable number of arguments. Two versions of the macros are available: The macros defined in STDARG.H conform to the ANSI C standard, and the macros defined in VARARGS.H are compatible with the UNIX System V definition. The macros are:

va_alist Name of parameter to called function (UNIX version only)

va_arg Macro to retrieve current argument

va_dcl Declaration of **va_alist** (UNIX version only)

va_end Macro to reset *arg_ptr*

va_list **typedef** for pointer to list of arguments defined in STDIO.H

va_start Macro to set *arg_ptr* to beginning of list of optional arguments (UNIX version only)

Both versions of the macros assume that the function takes a fixed number of required arguments, followed by a variable number of optional arguments. The required arguments are declared as ordinary parameters to the function and can be accessed through the parameter names. The optional arguments are accessed through the macros in STDARG.H or VARARGS.H, which set a pointer to the first optional argument in the argument list, retrieve arguments from the list, and reset the pointer when argument processing is completed.

The ANSI C standard macros, defined in STDARG.H, are used as follows:

- All required arguments to the function are declared as parameters in the usual way. **va_dcl** is not used with the STDARG.H macros.
- **va_start** sets *arg_ptr* to the first optional argument in the list of arguments passed to the function. The argument *arg_ptr* must have **va_list** type. The argument *prev_param* is the name of the required parameter immediately preceding the first optional argument in the argument list. If *prev_param* is declared with the register storage class, the macro's behavior is undefined. **va_start** must be used before **va_arg** is used for the first time.
- **va_arg** retrieves a value of *type* from the location given by *arg_ptr* and increments *arg_ptr* to point to the next argument in the list, using the size of *type* to determine where the next argument starts. **va_arg** can be used any number of times within the function to retrieve arguments from the list.
- After all arguments have been retrieved, **va_end** resets the pointer to **NULL**.

The UNIX System V macros, defined in VARARGS.H, operate somewhat differently:

- Any required arguments to the function can be declared as parameters in the usual way.
- The last (or only) parameter to the function represents the list of optional arguments. This parameter must be named **va_alist** (not to be confused with **va_list**, which is defined as the type of **va_alist**).
- **va_dcl** appears after the function definition and before the opening left brace of the function. This macro is defined as a complete declaration of the **va_alist** parameter, including the terminating semicolon; therefore, no semicolon should follow **va_dcl**.

- Within the function, **va_start** sets *arg_ptr* to the beginning of the list of optional arguments passed to the function. **va_start** must be used before **va_arg** is used for the first time. The argument *arg_ptr* must have **va_list** type.
- **va_arg** retrieves a value of *type* from the location given by *arg_ptr* and increments *arg_ptr* to point to the next argument in the list, using the size of *type* to determine where the next argument starts. **va_arg** can be used any number of times within the function to retrieve the arguments from the list.
- After all arguments have been retrieved, **va_end** resets the pointer to **NULL**.

Example

```
/* VA.C: The program below illustrates passing a variable
 * number of arguments using the following macros:
 *      va_start            va_arg              va_end
 *      va_list             va_dcl (UNIX only)
 */

#include <stdio.h>
#define ANSI              /* Comment out for UNIX version     */
#ifdef ANSI               /* ANSI compatible version          */
#include <stdarg.h>
int average( int first, ... );
#else                     /* UNIX compatible version          */
#include <varargs.h>
int average( va_list );
#endif

void main( void )
{
   /* Call with 3 integers (-1 is used as terminator). */
   printf( "Average is: %d\n", average( 2, 3, 4, -1 ) );

   /* Call with 4 integers. */
   printf( "Average is: %d\n", average( 5, 7, 9, 11, -1 ) );

   /* Call with just -1 terminator. */
   printf( "Average is: %d\n", average( -1 ) );
}

/* Returns the average of a variable list of integers. */
#ifdef ANSI               /* ANSI compatible version    */
int average( int first, ... )
{
   int count = 0, sum = 0, i = first;
   va_list marker;

   va_start( marker, first );     /* Initialize variable arguments. */
   while( i != -1 )
```

```
   {
      sum += i;
      count++;
      i = va_arg( marker, int);
   }
   va_end( marker );              /* Reset variable arguments.      */
   return( sum ? (sum / count) : 0 );
}
#else       /* UNIX compatible version must use old-style definition.  */
int average( va_alist )
va_dcl
{
   int i, count, sum;
   va_list marker;

   va_start( marker );            /* Initialize variable arguments. */
   for( sum = count = 0; (i = va_arg( marker, int)) != -1; count++ )
      sum += i;
   va_end( marker );              /* Reset variable arguments.      */
   return( sum ? (sum / count) : 0 );
}
#endif
```

Output

```
Average is: 3
Average is: 8
Average is: 0
```

See Also **vfprintf**

vprintf Functions

Each of the **vprintf** functions takes a pointer to an argument list, then formats and writes the given data to a particular destination.

vfprintf, vfwprintf	**_vsnprintf, _vsnwprintf**
vprintf, vwprintf	**vsprintf, vswprintf**

Remarks

The **vprintf** functions are similar to their counterpart functions as listed in the following table. However, each **vprintf** function accepts a pointer to an argument list, whereas each of the counterpart functions accepts an argument list.

These functions format data for output to destinations as follows.

Function	Counterpart Function	Output Destination
vfprintf	**fprintf**	*stream*
vfwprintf	**fwprintf**	*stream*
vprintf	**printf**	**stdout**
vwprintf	**wprintf**	**stdout**
vsprintf	**sprintf**	memory pointed to by *buffer*
vswprintf	**swprintf**	memory pointed to by *buffer*
_vsnprintf	**_snprintf**	memory pointed to by *buffer*
_vsnwprintf	**_snwprintf**	memory pointed to by *buffer*

The *argptr* argument has type **va_list**, which is defined in VARARGS.H and STDARG.H. The *argptr* variable must be initialized by **va_start,** and may be reinitialized by subsequent **va_arg** calls; *argptr* then points to the beginning of a list of arguments that are converted and transmitted for output according to the corresponding specifications in the *format* argument. *format* has the same form and function as the *format* argument for **printf**. None of these functions invokes **va_end**. For a more complete description of each **vprintf** function, see the description of its counterpart function as listed in the preceding table.

_vsnprintf differs from **vsprintf** in that it writes no more than *count* bytes to *buffer*.

vfwprintf, **_vsnwprintf**, **vswprintf**, and **vwprintf** are wide-character versions of **vfprintf**, **_vsnprintf**, **vsprintf,** and **vprintf**, respectively; in each of these wide-character functions, *buffer* and *format* are wide-character strings. Otherwise, each wide-character function behaves identically to its SBCS counterpart function.

For **vsprintf**, **vswprintf**, **_vsnprintf** and **_vsnwprintf**, if copying occurs between strings that overlap, the behavior is undefined.

See Also **fprintf**, **printf**, **sprintf**, **va_arg**

vfprintf, vfwprintf

Write formatted output using a pointer to a list of arguments.

int vfprintf(FILE ****stream*, const char ****format***, va_list** *argptr* **);**
int vfwprintf(FILE ****stream*, const wchar_t ****format***, va_list** *argptr* **);**

Routine	Required Header	Optional Headers	Compatibility
vfprintf	<stdio.h> and <stdarg.h>	<varargs.h>[1]	ANSI, Win 95, Win NT, 68K, PMac
vfwprintf	<stdio.h> or <wchar.h>, and <stdarg.h>	<varargs.h>[1]	ANSI, Win 95, Win NT

1 Required for UNIX V compatibility.

For additional compatibility information, see “Compatibility” on page ix in the Introduction.

Libraries

LIBC.LIB	Single thread static library, retail version
LIBCMT.LIB	Multithread static library, retail version
MSVCRT.LIB	Import library for MSVCRTx0.DLL, retail version
MSVCRTx0.DLL	Multithread DLL library, retail version

Return Value

vfprintf and **vfwprintf** return the number of characters written, not including the terminating null character, or a negative value if an output error occurs.

Parameters

stream Pointer to **FILE** structure

format Format specification

argptr Pointer to list of arguments

For more information, see “printf Format Specification Fields” on page 485.

Remarks

Each of these functions takes a pointer to an argument list, then formats and writes the given data to *stream*.

See Also **fprintf**, **printf**, **sprintf**, **va_arg**

vprintf, vwprintf

Write formatted output using a pointer to a list of arguments.

int vprintf(const char ***format*, **va_list *argptr* **);**
int vwprintf(const wchar_t ***format*, **va_list *argptr* **);**

Routine	Required Header	Optional Headers	Compatibility
vprintf	<stdio.h> and <stdarg.h>	<varargs.h>[1]	ANSI, Win 95, Win NT, 68K, PMac
vwprintf	<stdio.h> or <wchar.h>, and <stdarg.h>	<varargs.h>[1]	ANSI, Win 95, Win NT

[1] Required for UNIX V compatibility.

For additional compatibility information, see “Compatibility” on page ix in the Introduction.

Libraries

LIBC.LIB	Single thread static library, retail version
LIBCMT.LIB	Multithread static library, retail version
MSVCRT.LIB	Import library for MSVCRTx0.DLL, retail version
MSVCRTx0.DLL	Multithread DLL library, retail version

Return Value

vprintf and **vwprintf** return the number of characters written, not including the terminating null character, or a negative value if an output error occurs.

Parameters

format Format specification

argptr Pointer to list of arguments

Remarks

Each of these functions takes a pointer to an argument list, then formats and writes the given data to **stdout**.

See Also **fprintf**, **printf**, **sprintf**, **va_arg**

_vsnprintf, _vsnwprintf

Write formatted output using a pointer to a list of arguments.

int _vsnprintf(char ***buffer*, size_t** *count*, **const char** ***format*, va_list** *argptr* **);**
int _vsnwprintf(wchar_t ***buffer*, size_t** *count*, **const wchar_t** ***format*, va_list** *argptr* **);**

Routine	Required Header	Optional Headers	Compatibility
_vsnprintf	<stdio.h> and <stdarg.h>	<varargs.h>[1]	Win 95, Win NT, Win32s, 68K, PMac
_vsnwprintf	<stdio.h> or <wchar.h>, and <stdarg.h>	<varargs.h>[1]	Win 95, Win NT, Win32s

1 Required for UNIX V compatibility.

For additional compatibility information, see "Compatibility" on page ix in the Introduction.

Libraries

LIBC.LIB	Single thread static library, retail version
LIBCMT.LIB	Multithread static library, retail version
MSVCRT.LIB	Import library for MSVCRTx0.DLL, retail version
MSVCRTx0.DLL	Multithread DLL library, retail version

Return Value

_vsnprintf and **_vsnwprintf** return the number of characters written, not including the terminating null character, or a negative value if an output error occurs. For **_vsnprintf**, if the number of bytes to write exceeds *buffer,* then *count* bytes are written and –1 is returned.

Parameters

buffer Storage location for output

count Maximum number of bytes to write

format Format specification

argptr Pointer to list of arguments

Remarks

Each of these functions takes a pointer to an argument list, then formats and writes the given data to the memory pointed to by *buffer*.

See Also **fprintf**, **printf**, **sprintf**, **va_arg**

---

vsprintf, vswprintf

Write formatted output using a pointer to a list of arguments.

int vsprintf(char ***buffer**, **const char** **format*, **va_list** *argptr* **);**
int vswprintf(wchar_t **buffer*, **size_t** *count*, **const wchar_t** **format*, **va_list** *argptr* **);**

Routine	Required Header	Optional Headers	Compatibility
vsprintf	<stdio.h> and <stdarg.h>	<varargs.h>[1]	ANSI, Win 95, Win NT, Win32s, 68K, PMac
vswprintf	<stdio.h> or <wchar.h>, and <stdarg.h>	<varargs.h>[1]	ANSI, Win 95, Win NT, Win32s

[1] Required for UNIX V compatibility.

For additional compatibility information, see "Compatibility" on page ix in the Introduction.

Libraries	
LIBC.LIB	Single thread static library, retail version
LIBCMT.LIB	Multithread static library, retail version
MSVCRT.LIB	Import library for MSVCRTx0.DLL, retail version
MSVCRTx0.DLL	Multithread DLL library, retail version

Return Value

vsprintf and **vswprintf** return the number of characters written, not including the terminating null character, or a negative value if an output error occurs. For **vswprintf**, a negative value is also returned if *count* or more wide characters are requested to be written.

Parameters

buffer Storage location for output

format Format specification

argptr Pointer to list of arguments

count Maximum number of bytes to write

Remarks

Each of these functions takes a pointer to an argument list, then formats and writes the given data to the memory pointed to by *buffer*.

See Also **fprintf**, **printf**, **sprintf**, **va_arg**

---

wcstombs

Converts a sequence of wide characters to a corresponding sequence of multibyte characters.

size_t wcstombs(char ***mbstr*****, const wchar_t** ***wcstr*****, size_t** *count* **);**

Routine	Required Header	Optional Headers	Compatibility
wcstombs	<stdlib.h>		ANSI, Win 95, Win NT, Win32s, 68K, PMac

For additional compatibility information, see "Compatibility" on page ix in the Introduction.

Libraries	
LIBC.LIB	Single thread static library, retail version
LIBCMT.LIB	Multithread static library, retail version
MSVCRT.LIB	Import library for MSVCRTx0.DLL, retail version
MSVCRTx0.DLL	Multithread DLL library, retail version

Return Value

If **wcstombs** successfully converts the multibyte string, it returns the number of bytes written into the multibyte output string, excluding the terminating **NULL** (if any). If the *mbstr* argument is **NULL**, **wcstombs** returns the required size of the destination string. If **wcstombs** encounters a wide character it cannot be convert to a multibyte character, it returns –1 cast to type **size_t**.

Parameters

mbstr The address of a sequence of multibyte characters

wcstr The address of a sequence of wide characters

count The maximum number of bytes that can be stored in the multibyte output string

Remarks

The **wcstombs** function converts the wide-character string pointed to by *wcstr* to the corresponding multibyte characters and stores the results in the *mbstr* array. The *count* parameter indicates the maximum number of bytes that can be stored in the multibyte output string (that is, the size of *mbstr*). In general, it is not known how many bytes will be required when converting a wide-character string. Some wide characters will require only one byte in the output string; others require two. If there are two bytes in the multibyte output string for every wide character in the input string (including the wide character **NULL**), the result is guaranteed to fit.

If **wcstombs** encounters the wide-character null character (L'\0') either before or when *count* occurs, it converts it to an 8-bit 0 and stops. Thus, the multibyte character string at *mbstr* is null-terminated only if **wcstombs** encounters a wide-character null character during conversion. If the sequences pointed to by *wcstr* and *mbstr* overlap, the behavior of **wcstombs** is undefined.

If the *mbstr* argument is **NULL**, **wcstombs** returns the required size of the destination string.

Example

```
/* WCSTOMBS.C illustrates the behavior of the wcstombs function. */

#include <stdio.h>
#include <stdlib.h>

void main( void )
{
   int      i;
   char    *pmbbuf   = (char *)malloc( MB_CUR_MAX );
   wchar_t *pwchello = L"Hello, world.";

   printf( "Convert wide-character string:\n" );
   i = wcstombs( pmbbuf, pwchello, MB_CUR_MAX );
   printf( "\tCharacters converted: %u\n", i );
   printf( "\tMultibyte character: %s\n\n", pmbbuf );
}
```

Output

```
Convert wide-character string:
    Characters converted: 1
    Multibyte character: H
```

See Also **mblen, mbstowcs, mbtowc, wctomb**

wctomb

Converts a wide character to the corresponding multibyte character.

int wctomb(char ****mbchar*, wchar_t** *wchar* **);**

Routine	Required Header	Optional Headers	Compatibility
wctomb	<stdlib.h>		ANSI, Win 95, Win NT, Win32s, 68K, PMac

For additional compatibility information, see "Compatibility" on page ix in the Introduction.

Libraries	
LIBC.LIB	Single thread static library, retail version
LIBCMT.LIB	Multithread static library, retail version
MSVCRT.LIB	Import library for MSVCRTx0.DLL, retail version
MSVCRTx0.DLL	Multithread DLL library, retail version

Return Value

If **wctomb** converts the wide character to a multibyte character, it returns the number of bytes (which is never greater than **MB_CUR_MAX**) in the wide character. If *wchar* is the wide-character null character (L'\0'), **wctomb** returns 1. If the conversion is not possible in the current locale, **wctomb** returns –1.

Parameters

mbchar The address of a multibyte character

wchar A wide character

Remarks

The **wctomb** function converts its *wchar* argument to the corresponding multibyte character and stores the result at *mbchar*. You can call the function from any point in any program.

Example

```
/* WCTOMB.CPP illustrates the behavior of the wctomb function */

#include <stdio.h>
#include <stdlib.h>

void main( void )
{
   int i;
   wchar_t wc = L'a';
   char *pmbnull = NULL;
   char *pmb = (char *)malloc( sizeof( char ) );

   printf( "Convert a wide character:\n" );
   i = wctomb( pmb, wc );
   printf( "\tCharacters converted: %u\n", i );
   printf( "\tMultibyte character: %.1s\n\n", pmb );

   printf( "Attempt to convert when target is NULL:\n" );
   i = wctomb( pmbnull, wc );
   printf( "\tCharacters converted: %u\n", i );
   printf( "\tMultibyte character: %.1s\n", pmbnull );
}
```

Output

```
Convert a wide character:
   Characters converted: 1
   Multibyte character: a

Attempt to convert when target is NULL:
   Characters converted: 0
   Multibyte character: (
```

See Also **mblen**, **mbstowcs**, **mbtowc**, **wcstombs**

_write

Writes data to a file.

int _write(int *handle*, **const void** **buffer*, **unsigned int** *count* **);**

Routine	Required Header	Optional Headers	Compatibility
_write	<io.h>		Win 95, Win NT, Win32s, 68K, PMac

For additional compatibility information, see "Compatibility" on page ix in the Introduction.

Libraries

LIBC.LIB	Single thread static library, retail version
LIBCMT.LIB	Multithread static library, retail version
MSVCRT.LIB	Import library for MSVCRTx0.DLL, retail version
MSVCRTx0.DLL	Multithread DLL library, retail version

Return Value

If successful, **_write** returns the number of bytes actually written. If the actual space remaining on the disk is less than the size of the buffer the function is trying to write to the disk, **_write** fails and does not flush any of the buffer's contents to the disk. A return value of –1 indicates an error. In this case, **errno** is set to one of two values: **EBADF**, which means the file handle is invalid or the file is not opened for writing, or **ENOSPC**, which means there is not enough space left on the device for the operation.

If the file is opened in text mode, each linefeed character is replaced with a carriage return–linefeed pair in the output. The replacement does not affect the return value.

Parameters

handle Handle of file into which data is written

buffer Data to be written

count Number of bytes

Remarks

The **_write** function writes *count* bytes from *buffer* into the file associated with *handle*. The write operation begins at the current position of the file pointer (if any) associated with the given file. If the file is open for appending, the operation begins at the current end of the file. After the write operation, the file pointer is increased by the number of bytes actually written.

When writing to files opened in text mode, **_write** treats a CTRL+Z character as the logical end-of-file. When writing to a device, **_write** treats a CTRL+Z character in the buffer as an output terminator.

Example

```
/* WRITE.C: This program opens a file for output
 * and uses _write to write some bytes to the file.
 */

#include <io.h>
#include <stdio.h>
#include <stdlib.h>
#include <fcntl.h>
#include <sys/types.h>
#include <sys/stat.h>

char buffer[] = "This is a test of '_write' function";
```

```
void main( void )
{
   int fh;
   unsigned byteswritten;

   if( (fh = _open( "write.o", _O_RDWR | _O_CREAT,
                              _S_IREAD | _S_IWRITE )) != -1 )
   {
      if(( byteswritten = _write( fh, buffer, sizeof( buffer ))) == -1 )
         perror( "Write failed" );
      else
         printf( "Wrote %u bytes to file\n", byteswritten );

      _close( fh );
   }
}
```

Output

```
Wrote 36 bytes to file
```

See Also **fwrite**, **_open**, **_read**

_wtoi, _wtol

Converts a wide-character string to an integer (**_wtoi**) or to a long integer (**_wtol**).

int _wtoi(const wchar_t ***_string_ **);
long _wtol(const wchar_t ***_string_ **);

Routine	Required Header	Optional Headers	Compatibility
_wtoi	<stdlib.h> or <wchar.h>		Win 95, Win NT, Win32s
_wtol	<stdlib.h> or <wchar.h>		Win 95, Win NT, Win32s

For additional compatibility information, see "Compatibility" on page ix in the Introduction.

Libraries	
LIBC.LIB	Single thread static library, retail version
LIBCMT.LIB	Multithread static library, retail version
MSVCRT.LIB	Import library for MSVCRTx0.DLL, retail version
MSVCRTx0.DLL	Multithread DLL library, retail version

Return Value

Each function returns the **int** or **long** value produced by interpreting the input characters as a number. If the input cannot be converted to a value of the appropriate type, **_wtoi** returns 0 and **_wtol** returns 0L. The return value is undefined in case of overflow.

Parameter

string String to be converted

Remarks

The **_wtoi** function converts a wide-character string to an integer value. **_wtol** converts a wide-character string to a long integer value. The input string is a sequence of characters that can be interpreted as a numerical value of the specified type. The output value is affected by the setting of the **LC_NUMERIC** category of the current locale. (For more information on the **LC_NUMERIC** category, see **setlocale**.The function stops reading the input string at the first character that it cannot recognize as part of a number. This character may be the null character (L'\0') terminating the string.

The *string* argument for these functions has the form

[*whitespace*] [*sign*]*digits*

A *whitespace* consists of space and/or tab characters, which are ignored. *sign* is either plus (+) or minus (–). *digits* is one or more decimal digits. **_wtoi** and **_wtol** do not recognize decimal points or exponents.

Example

See the example for **atoi**.

See Also **atoi**, **_ecvt**, **_fcvt**, **_gcvt**

APPENDIX A

Language and Country Strings

Language and Country Strings

The *locale* argument to the **setlocale** function takes the following form:

```
locale  "lang[_country[.code_page]]"
         | ".code_page"
         | ""
         | NULL
```

This appendix lists the language strings and country strings available to **setlocale**. All country and language codes currently supported by the Win32 NLS API are supported by **setlocale**. For information on code pages, see "Code Pages" on page 23 in Chapter 1.

Language Strings

The following language strings are recognized by **setlocale**. Any language not supported by the operating system is not accepted by **setlocale**. The three-letter language-string codes are only valid in Windows NT and Windows 95.

Primary Language	Sublanguage	Language String
Chinese	Chinese	"chinese"
Chinese	Chinese (simplified)	"chinese-simplified" or "chs"
Chinese	Chinese (traditional)	"chinese-traditional" or "cht"
Czech	Czech	"csy" or "czech"
Danish	Danish	"dan"or "danish"
Dutch	Dutch (Belgian)	"belgian", "dutch-belgian", or "nlb"
Dutch	Dutch (default)	"dutch" or "nld"
English	English (Australian)	"australian", "ena", or "english-aus"

Primary Language	Sublanguage	Language String
English	English (Canadian)	"canadian", "enc", or "english-can"
English	English (default)	"english"
English	English (New Zealand)	"english-nz" or "enz"
English	English (UK)	"eng", "english-uk", or "uk"
English	English (USA)	"american", "american english", "american-english", "english-american", "english-us", "english-usa", "enu", "us", or "usa"
Finnish	Finnish	"fin" or "finnish"
French	French (Belgian)	"frb" or "french-belgian"
French	French (Canadian)	"frc" or "french-canadian"
French	French (default)	"fra" or "french"
French	French (Swiss)	"french-swiss" or "frs"
German	German (Austrian)	"dea" or "german-austrian"
German	German (default)	"deu" or "german"
German	German (Swiss)	"des", "german-swiss", or "swiss"
Greek	Greek	"ell" or "greek"
Hungarian	Hungarian	"hun" or "hungarian"
Icelandic	Icelandic	"icelandic" or "isl"
Italian	Italian (default)	"ita" or "italian"
Italian	Italian (Swiss)	"italian-swiss" or "its"
Japanese	Japanese	"japanese" or "jpn"
Korean	Korean	"kor" or "korean"
Norwegian	Norwegian (Bokmal)	"nor" or "norwegian-bokmal"
Norwegian	Norwegian (default)	"norwegian"
Norwegian	Norwegian (Nynorsk)	"non" or "norwegian-nynorsk"
Polish	Polish	"plk" or "polish"
Portuguese	Portuguese (Brazilian)	"portuguese-brazilian" or "ptb"
Portuguese	Portuguese (default)	"portuguese" or "ptg"
Russian	Russian (default)	"rus" or "russian"
Slovak	Slovak	"sky" or "slovak"
Spanish	Spanish (default)	"esp" or "spanish"
Spanish	Spanish (Mexican)	"esm" or "spanish-mexican"
Spanish	Spanish (Modern)	"esn" or "spanish-modern"
Swedish	Swedish	"sve" or "swedish"
Turkish	Turkish	"trk" or "turkish"

Country Strings

The following is a list of country strings recognized by **setlocale**. Strings for countries that are not supported by the operating system are not accepted by **setlocale**. Three-letter country-name codes are from ISO/IEC (International Organization for Standardization, International Electrotechnical Commission) specification 3166.

Country	Country String
Australia	"aus" or "australia"
Austria	"austria" or "aut"
Belgium	"bel" or "belgium"
Brazil	"bra" or "brazil"
Canada	"can" or "canada"
Czech Republic	"cze" or "czech"
Denmark	"denmark" or "dnk"
Finland	"fin" or "finland"
France	"fra" or "france"
Germany	"deu" or "germany"
Greece	"grc" or "greece"
Hong Kong	"hkg", "hong kong", or "hong-kong"
Hungary	"hun" or "hungary"
Iceland	"iceland" or "isl"
Ireland	"ireland" or "irl"
Italy	"ita" or "italy"
Japan	"japan" or "jpn"
Mexico	"mex" or "mexico"
Netherlands	"nld", "holland", or "netherlands"
New Zealand	"new zealand", "new-zealand", "nz", or "nzl"
Norway	"nor" or "norway"
People's Republic of China	"china", "chn", "pr china", or "pr-china"
Poland	"pol" or "poland"
Portugal	"prt" or "portugal"
Russia	"rus" or "russia"
Singapore	"sgp" or "singapore"
Slovak Repubic	"svk" or "slovak"
South Korea	"kor", "korea", "south korea", or "south-korea"
Spain	"esp" or "spain"
Sweden	"swe" or "sweden"

Country	Country String
Switzerland	"che" or "switzerland"
Taiwan	"taiwan" or "twn"
Turkey	"tur" or "turkey"
United Kingdom	"britain", "england", "gbr", "great britain", "uk", "united kingdom", or "united-kingdom"
United States of America	"america", "united states", "united-states", "us", or "usa"

APPENDIX B

Generic-Text Mappings

To simplify writing code for international markets, generic-text mappings are defined in TCHAR.H for:

- Data types
- Constants and global variables
- Routine mappings

For more information, see "Using Generic-Text Mappings" on page 25 in Chapter 1. Generic-text mappings are Microsoft extensions that are not ANSI-compatible.

Data Type Mappings

These data-type mappings are defined in TCHAR.H and depend on whether the constant **_UNICODE** or **_MBCS** has been defined in your program.

Generic-Text Data Type Mappings

Generic-Text Data Type Name	SBCS (_UNICODE, _MBCS Not Defined)	_MBCS Defined	_UNICODE Defined
_TCHAR	**char**	**char**	**wchar_t**
_TINT	**int**	**int**	**wint_t**
_TSCHAR	**signed char**	**signed char**	**wchar_t**
_TUCHAR	**unsigned char**	**unsigned char**	**wchar_t**
_TXCHAR	**char**	**unsigned char**	**wchar_t**
_T or **_TEXT**	No effect (removed by preprocessor)	No effect (removed by preprocessor)	**L** (converts following character or string to its Unicode counterpart)

Constant and Global Variable Mappings

These generic-text constant, global variable, and standard-type mappings are defined in TCHAR.H and depend on whether the constant **_UNICODE** or **_MBCS** has been defined in your program.

Generic-Text Constant and Global Variable Mappings

Generic-Text – Object Name	SBCS (_UNICODE, _MBCS Not Defined)	_MBCS Defined	_UNICODE Defined
_TEOF	**EOF**	**EOF**	**WEOF**
_tenviron	**_environ**	**_environ**	**_wenviron**
_tfinddata_t	**_finddata_t**	**_finddata_t**	**_wfinddata_t**

Routine Mappings

The following generic-text routine mappings are defined in TCHAR.H. **_tccpy** and **_tclen** map to functions in the MBCS model; they are mapped to macros or inline functions in the SBCS and Unicode models for completeness.

Generic-Text Routine Mappings

Generic-Text Routine Name	SBCS (_UNICODE, _MBCS Not Defined)	_MBCS Defined	_UNICODE Defined
_fgettc	**fgetc**	**fgetc**	**fgetwc**
_fgettchar	**fgetchar**	**fgetchar**	**_fgetwchar**
_fgetts	**fgets**	**fgets**	**fgetws**
_fputtc	**fputc**	**fputc**	**fputwc**
_fputtchar	**fputchar**	**fputchar**	**_fputwchar**
_fputts	**fputs**	**fputs**	**fputws**
_ftprintf	**fprintf**	**fprintf**	**fwprintf**
_ftscanf	**fscanf**	**fscanf**	**fwscanf**
_gettc	**getc**	**getc**	**getwc**
_gettchar	**getchar**	**getchar**	**getwchar**
_getts	**gets**	**gets**	**getws**
_istalnum	**isalnum**	**_ismbcalnum**	**iswalnum**
_istalpha	**isalpha**	**_ismbcalpha**	**iswalpha**
_istascii	**__isascii**	**__isascii**	**iswascii**
_istcntrl	**iscntrl**	**iscntrl**	**iswcntrl**
_istdigit	**isdigit**	**_ismbcdigit**	**iswdigit**

Generic-Text Routine Mappings *(continued)*

Generic-Text Routine Name	SBCS (_UNICODE, _MBCS Not Defined)	_MBCS Defined	_UNICODE Defined
_istgraph	**isgraph**	**_ismbcgraph**	**iswgraph**
_istlead	Always returns false	**_ismbblead**	Always returns false
_istleadbyte	Always returns false	**isleadbyte**	Always returns false
_istlegal	Always returns true	**_ismbclegal**	Always returns true
_istlower	**islower**	**_ismbclower**	**iswlower**
_istprint	**isprint**	**_ismbcprint**	**iswprint**
_istpunct	**ispunct**	**_ismbcpunct**	**iswpunct**
_istspace	**isspace**	**_ismbcspace**	**iswspace**
_istupper	**isupper**	**_ismbcupper**	**iswupper**
_istxdigit	**isxdigit**	**isxdigit**	**iswxdigit**
_itot	**_itoa**	**_itoa**	**_itow**
_ltot	**_ltoa**	**_ltoa**	**_ltow**
_puttc	**putc**	**putc**	**putwc**
_puttchar	**putchar**	**putchar**	**putwchar**
_putts	**puts**	**puts**	**putws**
_tmain	**main**	**main**	**wmain**
_sntprintf	**_snprintf**	**_snprintf**	**_snwprintf**
_stprintf	**sprintf**	**sprintf**	**swprintf**
_stscanf	**sscanf**	**sscanf**	**swscanf**
_taccess	**_access**	**_access**	**_waccess**
_tasctime	**asctime**	**asctime**	**_wasctime**
_tccpy	Maps to macro or inline function	**_mbccpy**	Maps to macro or inline function
_tchdir	**_chdir**	**_chdir**	**_wchdir**
_tclen	Maps to macro or inline function	**_mbclen**	Maps to macro or inline function
_tchmod	**_chmod**	**_chmod**	**_wchmod**
_tcreat	**_creat**	**_creat**	**_wcreat**
_tcscat	**strcat**	**_mbscat**	**wcscat**
_tcschr	**strchr**	**_mbschr**	**wcschr**
_tcsclen	**strlen**	**_mbslen**	**wcslen**
_tcscmp	**strcmp**	**_mbscmp**	**wcscmp**
_tcscoll	**strcoll**	**_mbscoll**	**wcscoll**
_tcscpy	**strcpy**	**_mbscpy**	**wcscpy**
_tcscspn	**strcspn**	**_mbscspn**	**wcscspn**

Generic-Text Routine Mappings *(continued)*

Generic-Text Routine Name	SBCS (_UNICODE, _MBCS Not Defined)	_MBCS Defined	_UNICODE Defined
_tcsdec	_strdec	_mbsdec	_wcsdec
_tcsdup	_strdup	_mbsdup	_wcsdup
_tcsftime	strftime	strftime	wcsftime
_tcsicmp	_stricmp	_mbsicmp	_wcsicmp
_tcsicoll	_stricoll	_stricoll	_wcsicoll
_tcsinc	_strinc	_mbsinc	_wcsinc
_tcslen	strlen	_mbslen	wcslen
_tcslwr	_strlwr	_mbslwr	_wcslwr
_tcsnbcnt	_strncnt	_mbsnbcnt	_wcnscnt
_tcsncat	strncat	_mbsnbcat	wcsncat
_tcsnccat	strncat	_mbsncat	wcsncat
_tcsncmp	strncmp	_mbsnbcmp	wcsncmp
_tcsnccmp	strncmp	_mbsncmp	wcsncmp
_tcsnccnt	_strncnt	_mbsnccnt	_wcsncnt
_tcsnccpy	strncpy	_mbsncpy	wcsncpy
_tcsncicmp	_strnicmp	_mbsnicmp	_wcsnicmp
_tcsncpy	strncpy	_mbsnbcpy	wcsncpy
_tcsncset	_strnset	_mbsnset	_wcsnset
_tcsnextc	_strnextc	_mbsnextc	_wcsnextc
_tcsnicmp	_strnicmp	_mbsnicmp	_wcsnicmp
_tcsnicoll	_strnicoll	_strnicoll	_wcsnicoll
_tcsninc	_strninc	_mbsninc	_wcsninc
_tcsnccnt	_strncnt	_mbsnccnt	_wcsncnt
_tcsnset	_strnset	_mbsnbset	_wcsnset
_tcspbrk	strpbrk	_mbspbrk	wcspbrk
_tcsspnp	_strspnp	_mbsspnp	_wcsspnp
_tcsrchr	strrchr	_mbsrchr	wcsrchr
_tcsrev	_strrev	_mbsrev	_wcsrev
_tcsset	_strset	_mbsset	_wcsset
_tcsspn	strspn	_mbsspn	wcsspn
_tcsstr	strstr	_mbsstr	wcsstr
_tcstod	strtod	strtod	wcstod
_tcstok	strtok	_mbstok	wcstok
_tcstol	strtol	strtol	wcstol
_tcstoul	strtoul	strtoul	wcstoul

Generic-Text Routine Mappings *(continued)*

Generic-Text Routine Name	SBCS (_UNICODE, _MBCS Not Defined)	_MBCS Defined	_UNICODE Defined
_tcsupr	_strupr	_mbsupr	_wcsupr
_tcsxfrm	strxfrm	strxfrm	wcsxfrm
_tctime	ctime	ctime	_wctime
_texecl	_execl	_execl	_wexecl
_texecle	_execle	_execle	_wexecle
_texeclp	_execlp	_execlp	_wexeclp
_texeclpe	_execlpe	_execlpe	_wexeclpe
_texecv	_execv	_execv	_wexecv
_texecve	_execve	_execve	_wexecve
_texecvp	_execvp	_execvp	_wexecvp
_texecvpe	_execvpe	_execvpe	_wexecvpe
_tfdopen	_fdopen	_fdopen	_wfdopen
_tfindfirst	_findfirst	_findfirst	_wfindfirst
_tfindnext	_findnext	_findnext	_wfindnext
_tfopen	fopen	fopen	_wfopen
_tfreopen	freopen	freopen	_wfreopen
_tfsopen	_fsopen	_fsopen	_wfsopen
_tfullpath	_fullpath	_fullpath	_wfullpath
_tgetcwd	_getcwd	_getcwd	_wgetcwd
_tgetenv	getenv	getenv	_wgetenv
_tmain	main	main	wmain
_tmakepath	_makepath	_makepath	_wmakepath
_tmkdir	_mkdir	_mkdir	_wmkdir
_tmktemp	_mktemp	_mktemp	_wmktemp
_tperror	perror	perror	_wperror
_topen	_open	_open	_wopen
_totlower	tolower	_mbctolower	towlower
_totupper	toupper	_mbctoupper	towupper
_tpopen	_popen	_popen	_wpopen
_tprintf	printf	printf	wprintf
_tremove	remove	remove	_wremove
_trename	rename	rename	_wrename
_trmdir	_rmdir	_rmdir	_wrmdir
_tsearchenv	_searchenv	_searchenv	_wsearchenv
_tscanf	scanf	scanf	wscanf

Generic-Text Routine Mappings *(continued)*

Generic-Text Routine Name	SBCS (_UNICODE, _MBCS Not Defined)	_MBCS Defined	_UNICODE Defined
_tsetlocale	**setlocale**	**setlocale**	**_wsetlocale**
_tsopen	**_sopen**	**_sopen**	**_wsopen**
_tspawnl	**_spawnl**	**_spawnl**	**_wspawnl**
_tspawnle	**_spawnle**	**_spawnle**	**_wspawnle**
_tspawnlp	**_spawnlp**	**_spawnlp**	**_wspawnlp**
_tspawnlpe	**_spawnlpe**	**_spawnlpe**	**_wspawnlpe**
_tspawnv	**_spawnv**	**_spawnv**	**_wspawnv**
_tspawnve	**_spawnve**	**_spawnve**	**_wspawnve**
_tspawnvp	**_spawnvp**	**_spawnvp**	**_tspawnvp**
_tspawnvpe	**_spawnvpe**	**_spawnvpe**	**_tspawnvpe**
_tsplitpath	**_splitpath**	**_splitpath**	**_wsplitpath**
_tstat	**_stat**	**_stat**	**_wstat**
_tstrdate	**_strdate**	**_strdate**	**_wstrdate**
_tstrtime	**_strtime**	**_strtime**	**_wstrtime**
_tsystem	**system**	**system**	**_wsystem**
_ttempnam	**_tempnam**	**_tempnam**	**_wtempnam**
_ttmpnam	**tmpnam**	**tmpnam**	**_wtmpnam**
_ttoi	**atoi**	**atoi**	**_wtoi**
_ttol	**atol**	**atol**	**_wtol**
_tutime	**_utime**	**_utime**	**_wutime**
_tWinMain	**WinMain**	**WinMain**	**wWinMain**
_ultot	**_ultoa**	**_ultoa**	**_ultow**
_ungettc	**ungetc**	**ungetc**	**ungetwc**
_vftprintf	**vfprintf**	**vfprintf**	**vfwprintf**
_vsntprintf	**_vsnprintf**	**_vsnprintf**	**_vsnwprintf**
_vstprintf	**vsprintf**	**vsprintf**	**vswprintf**
_vtprintf	**vprintf**	**vprintf**	**vwprintf**

Index

C

D

E

F

G

L

M

N

O

S

T

U

V

W

X

Contributors to *Run-Time Library Reference*

Samuel Dawson, Index Editor

Linda Robinson, Production

Kerry Lehto, Editor

Marilyn Johnstone, Writer

Seth Manheim, Writer

Beth-Anne Harvey, Writer

David Adam Edelstein, Art Director

"I strongly recommend David Kruglinski's *Inside Visual C++*....a superb primer on MFC.... I can't recommend it highly enough."

Compute

ISBN 1-55615-661-8
512 pages, with one CD-ROM
$39.95 ($53.95 Canada)

The Microsoft® Visual C++™ development system offers an exciting new way to create Windows™-based applications. Now you can combine the power of object-oriented programming with the efficiency of the C language. The application framework approach in Visual C++ version 1.5—centering on the Microsoft Foundation Class Library version 2.5—enables programmers to simplify and streamline the process of creating robust, professional applications for Windows.

INSIDE VISUAL C++ takes you one step at a time through the process of creating real-world applications for Windows—the Visual C++ way. Using ample source code examples, this book explores MFC 2.5, App Studio, and the product's nifty "wizards"—AppWizard and ClassWizard—in action. The book also provides a good explanation of application framework theory, along with tips for exploiting hidden features of the MFC library.

Third Edition Available November 1995!
ISBN 1-55615-891-2

Microsoft Press® books are available wherever quality books are sold and through CompuServe's Electronic Mall—**GO MSP**.
Call **1-800-MSPRESS** for more information or to place a credit card order.* Please refer to **BBK** when placing your order. Prices subject to change.
*In Canada, contact Macmillan Canada, Attn: Microsoft Press Dept., 164 Commander Blvd., Agincourt, Ontario, Canada M1S 3C7, or call 1-800-667-1115.
Outside the U.S. and Canada, write to International Coordinator, Microsoft Press, One Microsoft Way, Redmond, WA 98052-6399, or fax +1-206-936-7329.

Microsoft Press